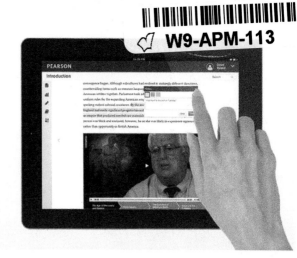

REVEL enables students to read and interact with course material on the devices they use, **anywhere** and **anytime**. Responsive design allows students to access REVEL on their tablet devices, with content displayed clearly in both portrait and landscape view.

Highlighting, **note taking**, and a **glossary** personalize the learning experience. Educators can add **notes** for students, too, including reminders or study tips

REVEL's variety of **writing** activities and assignments develop and assess concept **mastery** and **critical thinking**.

Superior assignability and tracking

REVEL's assignability and tracking tools help educators make sure students are completing their reading and understanding core concepts.

REVEL allows educators to indicate precisely which readings must be completed on which dates. This clear, detailed schedule helps students stay on task and keeps them motivated throughout the course.

REVEL lets educators monitor class assignment completion and individual student achievement. It offers actionable information that helps educators intersect with their students in meaningful ways, such as points earned on quizzes and time on task.

The Journey of Adulthood

UPDATED EIGHTH EDITION

Barbara R. Bjorklund
Wilkes Honors College of Florida Atlantic University

Boston Columbus Hoboken Indianapolis New York San Francisco Amsterdam
Cape Town Dubai London Madrid Milan Munich Paris Montréal Toronto
Delhi Mexico City São Paulo Sydney Hong Kong Seoul Singapore Taipei Tokyo

Editor-in-Chief: Ashley Dodge
Managing Editor: Amber Mackey
Program Manager: Carly Czech
Editorial Assistant (Program Support): Casseia Lewis
Editorial Assistant (Customer Support): Pauline Kitele
Senior Marketing Coordinator: Susan Osterlitz
Editorial Project Manager: David Ploskonka, iEnergizer Aptara®, Ltd.
Development Editor: David Ploskonka, iEnergizer Aptara®, Ltd.
Asset Development Project Management: LearningMate Solutions, Ltd.
Senior Operations Supervisor: Mary Fischer
Operations Specialist: Diane Peirano
Associate Director of Design: Blair Brown
Interior Design: Kathryn Foot
Cover Director: Maria Lange
Cover Project Manager: Heather Marshall, Lumina Datamatics, Inc.
Cover Image: Pavlovic A/Shutterstock
Director of Digital Studio: Sacha Laustsen
Digital Studio Project Manager: Liz Roden Hall
Full-Service Project Management and Composition: Jogender Taneja, iEnergizer Aptara®, Lt
Printer/Binder: Manufactured in the United States by RR Donnelley
Cover Printer: Manufactured in the United States by RR Donnelley

Credits and acknowledgments borrowed from other sources and reproduced, with permissio
in this textbook appear on appropriate page within.

Library of Congress Cataloging-in-Publication Data
Bjorklund, Barbara R.
   The journey of adulthood/Barbara R. Bjorklund, Wilkes Honors College of Florida Atlantic
University. —Updated eighth edition.
      pages cm
   ISBN 978-0-13-397379-2—ISBN 0-13-397379-4
   1. Adulthood—Psychological aspects.   2. Aging—Psychological aspects.   3. Adulthood.
4. Aging.   I. Title.
   BF724.5.B44 2016
   155.6—dc23

                                                                    2015011647

10 9 8 7 6 5 4 3 2 1

ISBN-10:   0-134-12780-3
ISBN-13: 978-0-134-12780-4

Brief Contents

1 Introduction to Adult Development   1

2 Physical Changes   31

3 Health and Health Disorders   67

4 Cognitive Abilities   97

5 Social Roles   129

6 Social Relationships   163

7 Work and Retirement   198

8 Personality   233

9 The Quest for Meaning   262

10 Stress, Coping, and Resilience   291

11 Death and Bereavement   319

12 The Successful Journey   343

Contents

Preface   ix

1 Introduction to Adult Development   1

1.1: Basic Concepts in Adult Development   3
     1.1.1: Stages   4
1.2: Sources of Change   5
     1.2.1: Normative Age-Graded Influences   5
     1.2.2: Normative History-Graded Influences   6
     1.2.3: Nonnormative Life Events   9
1.3: Sources of Stability   9
     1.3.1: Genetics   10
     1.3.2: Environment   10
     1.3.3: Interactionist View   11
1.4: A Word About "Age"   11
     1.4.1: Social Age   12
1.5: Setting the Course   13
     1.5.1: Life-Span Developmental Psychology Approach   13
     1.5.2: Bioecological Model of Development   14
1.6: Developmental Research   15
     1.6.1: Methods   16
     1.6.2: Measures   22
     1.6.3: Analyses   23
     1.6.4: Designs   26
1.7: A Final Word about Adulthood Development   29
     Summary: Introduction to Adult Development   29

2 Physical Changes   31

2.1: Theories of Primary Aging   32
     2.1.1: Oxidative Damage   33
     2.1.2: Genetic Limits   33
     2.1.3: Caloric Restriction   34
     2.1.4: A Word on Theories of Primary Aging   35
2.2: Physical Changes During Adulthood   36
     2.2.1: Outward Appearance   36
     2.2.2: The Senses   41
     2.2.3: Bones and Muscles   45
     2.2.4: Cardiovascular and Respiratory Systems   48
     2.2.5: Brain and Nervous System   49
     2.2.6: Immune System   50
     2.2.7: Hormonal System   50
2.3: Changes in Physical Behavior   53
     2.3.1: Athletic Abilities   53
     2.3.2: Stamina, Dexterity, and Balance   54
     2.3.3: Sleep   55
     2.3.4: Sexual Activity   56

2.4: Individual Differences in Primary Aging   60
     2.4.1: Genetics   61
     2.4.2: Lifestyle   61
     2.4.3: Race, Ethnicity, and Socioeconomic Group   62
2.5: Can We "Turn Back the Clock" of Primary Aging?   63
2.6: An Overview of the Physical Changes in Adulthood   63
     Summary: Physical Changes   65

3 Health and Health Disorders   67

3.1: Mortality Rates and Causes of Death   68
3.2: Morbidity Rates, Disease, and Disability   69
     3.2.1: Common Health Conditions   69
     3.2.2: Disability   69
     3.2.3: Self-Ratings of Health   71
3.3: Specific Diseases   71
     3.3.1: Cardiovascular Disease   71
     3.3.2: Cancer   73
     3.3.3: Diabetes   75
     3.3.4: Alzheimer's Disease   76
     3.3.5: People Living with Age-Related Diseases and Disability   78
3.4: Mental Disorders   79
     3.4.1: Anxiety Disorders   80
     3.4.2: Mood Disorders   81
     3.4.3: Impulse Control Disorders   82
     3.4.4: Substance Abuse Disorders   83
     3.4.5: Treatment of Mental Health Disorders   83
3.5: Nonmedical Solutions   84
     3.5.1: Assistive Technology   84
     3.5.2: Assistance Animals   84
3.6: Individual Differences in Health   85
     3.6.1: Lifestyle   85
     3.6.2: Gender   86
     3.6.3: Socioeconomics, Race, and Ethnicity   87
     3.6.4: Personality and Behavior Patterns   90
     3.6.5: Genetics   92
     3.6.6: Developmental Origins   92
     3.6.7: The Road to Good Health   94
     Summary: Health and Health Disorders   95

4 Cognitive Abilities   97

4.1: Intelligence   98
     4.1.1: Age Changes in Overall Intelligence   99
     4.1.2: Components of Intelligence   101
     4.1.3: Reversing Declines in Intellectual Abilities   102

4.2: Memory 103
  4.2.1: Short-Term and Working Memory 104
  4.2.2: Declarative and Nondeclarative (Procedural) Memory 106
  4.2.3: Prospective Memory 109
  4.2.4: Slowing Declines in Memory Abilities 109
  4.2.5: Memory in Context 110
4.3: Decision Making and Problem Solving 112
4.4: Individual Differences in Cognitive Change 116
  4.4.1: Health 116
  4.4.2: Genetics 117
  4.4.3: Demographics and Sociobiographical History 118
  4.4.4: Schooling 119
  4.4.5: Intellectual Activity 119
  4.4.6: Physical Exercise 120
  4.4.7: Subjective Evaluation of Decline 121
4.5: Cognitive Assistance 122
  4.5.1: Medication Adherence 122
  4.5.2: Social Networking 122
  4.5.3: E-Readers and Electronic Games 123
  4.5.4: Safe Driving 124
4.6: Review of Cognitive Changes over the Adult Years and a Search for Balance 126
  Summary: Cognitive Abilities 127

5 Social Roles 129

5.1: Social Roles and Transitions 130
5.2: Gender Roles and Gender Stereotypes 131
5.3: Social Roles in Young Adulthood 134
  5.3.1: Leaving (and Returning) Home 135
  5.3.2: Becoming a Spouse or Partner 137
  5.3.3: Becoming a Parent 142
5.4: Social Roles in Middle Adulthood 145
  5.4.1: The Departure of the Children: The Empty Nest 146
  5.4.2: Gender Roles at Midlife 147
  5.4.3: Becoming a Grandparent 147
  5.4.4: Caring for an Aging Parent 149
5.5: Social Roles in Late Adulthood 151
  5.5.1: Living Alone 152
  5.5.2: Becoming a Care Receiver 153
5.6: Social Roles in Atypical Families 154
  5.6.1: Lifelong Singles 154
  5.6.2: The Childless 155
  5.6.3: Divorced (and Remarried) Adults 156
5.7: The Effect of Variations in Timing 158
  Summary: Social Roles 161

6 Social Relationships 163

6.1: Theories of Social Relationships 164
  6.1.1: Attachment Theory 165
  6.1.2: The Convoy Model 166
  6.1.3: Socioemotional Selectivity Theory 167
  6.1.4: Evolutionary Psychology 167
6.2: Intimate Partnerships 169
  6.2.1: Establishing an Intimate Relationship 169
  6.2.2: Successful Marriages 174
  6.2.3: Cohabitation and Marriage 176
  6.2.4: Same-Sex Partnerships 178
6.3: Relationships with Other Family Members 180
  6.3.1: General Patterns of Family Interaction 181
  6.3.2: Parent–Child Relationships in Adulthood 182
  6.3.3: Grandparent–Grandchild Relationships 186
  6.3.4: Relationships with Brothers and Sisters 190
6.4: Friendships in Adulthood 192
  6.4.1: Friendship Networks 192
  6.4.2: Pets as Friends 193
  6.4.3: Facebook Friends 193
  Summary: Social Relationships 196

7 Work and Retirement 198

7.1: The Importance of Work in Adulthood 199
  7.1.1: Super's Theory of Career Development 200
  7.1.2: Gender Differences in Career Patterns 201
7.2: Selecting a Career 202
  7.2.1: Theories of Career Selection 202
  7.2.2: The Effects of Gender 204
  7.2.3: Family Influences 206
  7.2.4: The Role of Genetics 208
7.3: Age Trends in Work Experience 209
  7.3.1: Job Performance 209
  7.3.2: Job Training and Retraining 210
  7.3.3: Job Satisfaction 211
7.4: Work and Personal Life 211
  7.4.1: Work and the Individual 212
  7.4.2: Work and Marriage 214
  7.4.3: Work and Parenthood 215
  7.4.4: Work and Caregiving for Adult Family Members 217
  7.4.5: Household Labor 218
7.5: Retirement 219
  7.5.1: Preparation for Retirement 220
  7.5.2: Timing of Retirement 220
  7.5.3: Reasons for Retirement 222
  7.5.4: Effects of Retirement 224
  7.5.5: Alternatives to Full Retirement 227
7.6: A Concluding Note on Work and Retirement 229
  Summary: Work and Retirement 231

8 Personality 233

8.1: Personality Structures 234
  8.1.1: Personality Traits and Factors 234
  8.1.2: Differential Continuity 237
  8.1.3: Mean-Level Change 238
  8.1.4: Intra-Individual Variability 239

8.1.5: Continuity, Change, and Variability Coexist 240

8.1.6: What Do Personality Traits Do? 240

8.2: Explanations of Continuity and Change 243

8.2.1: Genetics 243

8.2.2: Environmental Influences 244

8.2.3: Evolutionary Psychology Explanations 245

8.2.4: Cultural Differences 246

8.2.5: Summing Up Personality Structure 246

8.3: Theories of Personality Development 247

8.3.1: Psychosocial Development 247

8.3.2: Ego Development 252

8.3.3: Mature Adaptation 254

8.3.4: Gender Crossover 256

8.3.5: Positive Well-Being 257

Summary: Personality 260

9 The Quest for Meaning 262

9.1: Why a Chapter on the Quest for Meaning? 264

9.2: The Study of Age-Related Changes in Meaning Systems 265

9.2.1: Changes in the Quest for Meaning 266

9.2.2: Religion, Spirituality, and Health 269

9.3: Theories of Spiritual Development 271

9.3.1: Development of Moral Reasoning 272

9.3.2: Development of Faith 278

9.3.3: Some Basic Points about Fowler's Stages 281

9.4: Integrating Meaning and Personality: A Preliminary Theoretical Synthesis 282

9.4.1: A Synthesizing Model 283

9.4.2: Stages of Mystical Experience 284

9.5: The Process of Transition 285

9.6: Commentary and Conclusions 287

Summary: The Quest for Meaning 289

10 Stress, Coping, and Resilience 291

10.1: Stress, Stressors, and Stress Reactions 292

10.2: Types of Stress 294

10.3: Effects of Stress 296

10.3.1: Physical Disease 297

10.3.2: Mental Health Disorders 298

10.3.3: Individual Differences in Stress-Related Disorders 300

10.3.4: Stress-Related Growth 305

10.4: Coping with Stress 306

10.4.1: Types of Coping Behaviors 306

10.4.2: Social Support 310

10.4.3: Personality Traits and Coping 312

10.5: Resilience 312

10.5.1: Reactions to Trauma 313

10.5.2: Individual Differences in Resilience 314

10.5.3: Resilience in Military Combat and Deployment 315

10.5.4: A Final Word on Stress and Resilience 316

Summary: Stress, Coping, and Resilience 317

11 Death and Bereavement 319

11.1: Achieving an Understanding of Death 320

11.1.1: Meanings of Death 321

11.1.2: Death Anxiety 321

11.1.3: Accepting the Reality of One's Eventual Death 323

11.2: The Process of Death 324

11.2.1: Stages of Reactions to Death 324

11.2.2: The Importance of Farewells 326

11.2.3: Individual Adaptations to Dying 326

11.2.4: Choosing Where to Die 329

11.2.5: Choosing When to Die 332

11.3: After Death Occurs: Rituals and Grieving 333

11.3.1: Ritual Mourning: Funerals and Ceremonies 333

11.3.2: The Process of Grieving 338

11.4: Living and Dying: A Final Word 341

Summary: Death and Bereavement 341

12 The Successful Journey 343

12.1: Themes of Adulthood Development 344

12.1.1: Emerging Adulthood (Ages 18 to 24) 346

12.1.2: Young Adulthood (Ages 25 to 39) 348

12.1.3: Middle Adulthood (Ages 40 to 64) 350

12.1.4: Older Adulthood (Ages 65 to 74) 353

12.1.5: Late Adulthood (Age 75 and Older) 354

12.2: Variations in Successful Development 357

12.2.1: Individual Differences in Quality of Life 358

12.2.2: Other Measure of Life Success 360

12.2.3: A Model of Adult Growth and Development: Trajectories and Pathways 363

12.2.4: The Relationship of Stable Periods and Age 365

Summary: The Successful Journey 370

Glossary 371

Bibliography 377

References 384

Credits 411

Author Index 415

Subject Index 428

Preface

The Journey of Adulthood continues to capture the dynamic process of adult development from early adulthood to the end of life. Its core is made up of research findings from large-scale projects and major theories of adult development, but it also reflects smaller studies of diverse groups, showing the influences of gender, culture, ethnicity, race, and socioeconomic background on this journey. I have balanced new research with classic studies from pioneers in the field of adult development. And I have sweetened this sometimes medicinal taste with a spoonful of honey—a little personal warmth and humor. After all, I am now officially an older adult who is on this journey along with my husband, looking ahead at the examples our parents' journeys gave us, and back toward our children, who are blazing their own trails. As of this edition, we have nine grandchildren—six of whom are beginning their own journeys of adulthood either as college students or starting their careers.

New in This Edition

- New information on electronics use: the proportion of people of different ages using the Internet, cell phones, e-readers, and e-games; the sleep-related problems related to using electronic "blue screen" devices before bedtime or during the night; the popularity of online dating services and some words of caution about their claims; and the relationship between early hearing loss and the use of MP3 players at top volume with earbuds.

- Increased importance of animals in our lives: the use of dogs and monkeys as assistance animals for people with disabilities; the use of comfort animals for people in stressful situations or with mental health problems; and the social support people of all ages report receiving from their pets.

- New research on veterans: the association between head injuries and PTSD; the association between head injuries and dementia; the collaboration between researchers in positive psychology and the U.S. Army to boost resilience in combat troops.

- More studies of the effects of discrimination and inequality: older people reminded of the "poor memory" stereotype score lower on memory tests; young girls of mothers who believe the "girls are not good at math" stereotype score lower on math tests; people in minority groups who perceive they are discriminated against have lower levels of health; African-American adults experience middle age differently than other groups; same-sex couples experience more violence and aggression, less family support, less openness about their relationships; the increase in neighborhoods designated "food deserts" because of scarcity of grocery stores and abundance of fast-food restaurants.

- More research on a wider range of younger and older adults. More older people are in the workforce in the United States and some European countries; longitudinal studies of attachment between infancy and age 18; long-time married couples report being "very intensely in love"; social convoys of people from emerging adulthood to age 90; increase in sex without commitment, or "hookups" for young adults; survey results of sexuality from age 70 to 94.

- New information on top age-related diseases, including heart disease, cancer, diabetes, and Alzheimer's disease. Updated risk factors for common age-related conditions, including cataracts, glaucoma, macular degeneration, osteoporosis, and osteoarthritis. All the tables of risk factors contain information about what younger adults can do for prevention. New findings on genetic contributions to age-related diseases.

The first chapter of the book contains the basics for the course—definitions, methods, and guiding perspectives for the study of adult development. The next seven chapters cover traditional developmental topics, featuring recent research, classic studies, current theories, new directions, and practical applications. The next three chapters cover topics not traditionally found in adult development texts, but which I feel are important to round out a student's experience in this course—the quest for meaning; the inevitability of stress, coping, and resilience in adult life; and the way we face our own deaths and that of our loved ones. The final chapter takes a chronological look at adult development, in contrast to the topical themes in the earlier chapters, and also suggests a model of adult development that will pull the threads together and tie up loose ends.

REVEL™

Educational technology designed for the way today's students read, think, and learn.

When students are engaged deeply, they learn more effectively and perform better in their courses. This simple fact inspired the creation of REVEL: an immersive learning experience designed for the way today's students read, think, and learn. Built in collaboration with educators and students nationwide, REVEL is the newest, fully digital way to deliver respected Pearson content.

REVEL enlivens course content with media interactives and assessments—integrated directly within the authors' narrative—that provide opportunities for students to read about and practice course material in tandem. This immersive educational technology boosts student engagement, which leads to better understanding of concepts and improved performance throughout the course.

Learn more about REVEL

Changes in the Field of Adult Development

The study of adult development is a fairly new field, and it expands exponentially from year to year. It began as a field of psychology, but more and more disciplines have shown interest in the changes that take place over the adult years. This book includes information from researchers who identify themselves as psychologists, sociologists, anthropologists, neuroscientists, epidemiologists, behavior geneticists, cellular biologists, biogerontologists, and many other types of scientists. The terminology and methods in these fields have become more and more similar, and many researchers publish in the journals of a variety of fields. This edition of *The Journey of Adulthood* reflects the wonderful collaboration going on and the richness of a number of multidisciplinary projects. It is an exciting time in developmental science, and this book reflects that energy.

Some of the projects that have been tapped for this textbook are the Midlife in the United States Study (MIDUS), the Berlin Study of Aging, the Grant Study of Harvard Men, the National Comorbidity Study, the Nun Study of the School Sisters of Notre Dame, the Victoria Longitudinal Study, the Swedish Twin Study, the National Survey of Sexual and Health Behavior, The Women's Health Study, and the National Longitudinal Mortality Study.

To emphasize these collaborations, I have identified each major researcher or theorist with his or her field of study. Two editions ago I was struck with the diversity of scientific fields contributing to the adult development literature. I want this book to reflect that diversity. When I discuss some particular work in detail, I give the full names of the researchers and how they identify their field of study. I hope that the students who are interested in adult development will take note and consider these areas when they declare their majors or make plans for graduate school. As professors, we need to remember that we not only teach the content of the courses, but also guide our students in career decisions.

Another change in the field of adult development is that increasingly more research projects reported in major journals are done by international groups of researchers in settings all over the developed world. We no longer are limited to information on adults in the United States; we also have research being done by Swedish, Japanese, and Egyptian scientists using Swedish, Japanese, and Egyptian participants. When the findings are similar to studies done in the United States, we can be more confident that the developmental phenomenon being studied is an integral part of the human experience and not something particular to people in the United States. When the findings are different from studies done in the United States, we can investigate these differences and find their roots. I have identified these international research teams and the nationalities of their participants. I hope this accentuates the global aspects of our academic community, and as a seasoned traveler myself, I hope it inspires students to consider "study abroad" programs.

I include full names of major researchers and theorists when I discuss their work in detail. Seeing the first and last names makes the researchers more real to the students than conventional citations of "last names, comma, date." Full names also reflect the diversity of scientists—often their gender and their national or ethnic backgrounds. Our students represent a wide range of races and ethnicities, and the time of science being the sole domain of an elite group most of us cannot identify with is gone.

One of the most exciting changes in the field of adult development has been its expansion to emphasize a wider and wider range of age groups. When I first began writing in this area, the focus of interest was older adults. The last two editions of this book have featured more and more studies of young adults, middle-aged adults, and emerging adults. This edition has added more research on the opposite end of the age spectrum—those who are 75, 80, 90 years of age and older. Although having people in this age group is nothing new, the growing numbers of them have made it important (and relatively easy) to include them in studies of adult development. Clearly the study of adult development is no longer the study of certain specific age groups; it is now truly a study of every aspect of adulthood. I have tried to capture this inclusion by choosing topics, examples, opening stories, photos, suggested reading, and critical thinking questions that represent the entire adult life span.

Changes in the World Around Us

Since the last edition of this book, there have been many changes in the world around us. As I write this preface, we seem to be recovering from the financial setbacks that began in 2008. Unemployment and underemployment are still a problem for many, and almost every family has been touched by financial setbacks of one sort or another. Troops are coming back from Iraq, but many have war-related disabilities that include posttraumatic stress disorder (PTSD) and traumatic brain injury (TBI). Single-parent families and dual-earner families in the United States (and in many other developed countries) are having a rough time; they receive little cooperation from the government, the workplace, or the community to assist them in caring for both job and family. Many older women, especially those who live alone, are living below the poverty line. The United States has the highest rates of mental disorders of any developed country, and most of the people experiencing these symptoms do not get adequate treatment. Unhealthy lifestyles are resulting in increased health problems for many adults in the developing world, and the ages of those affected are extending to both the younger and older end of the spectrum. Although I try to maintain a positive tone in this book, these aspects of adult life are realities, and I have included them in the topics discussed in *The Journey of Adulthood*.

Other changes in the world around us are more positive. Health awareness is increasing at all ages, advances are being made in many areas of disease prevention, detection, and treatment, and a greater percentage of people in developed countries are living into old age. The rate of cancer deaths continues to decline as advances are made in early detection and treatment. Although there is still no treatment for aging and no sign of a way to increase the existing maximum life span, people are increasing the number of healthy years in their lives. Programs such as hospice are making it possible for a growing number of people to choose to have "a good death" when that time comes. Women are making great strides in professional careers and in their positive adjustment to children leaving home and widowhood. Communication technology has made it easier for families to stay in touch and for older adults to live independently. The average age of people using social media, cell phones, and e-games is increasing. These are also among the topics selected for this book.

Changes in the Classroom

Courses in adult development are offered in all major colleges and universities in the United States and are becoming popular around the world. It is safe to say that graduates in almost all majors will be working in fields that deal with the changes that occur during adulthood. It is also safe to say that students in all majors will be dealing with the topic on a personal level, both their own progress through adulthood and that of their parents. My students at Florida Atlantic University this semester are majoring in psychology, counseling, nursing, criminal justice, premedical sciences, prelaw, social work, occupational therapy,

sociology, and education. About one half are bilingual, and about one third speak English as a second language. The majority will be the first in their families to graduate from college. I no longer assume that they have the same academic backgrounds as students a decade ago. For these reasons, I include basic definitions of key terms in the text of each chapter, clear explanations of relevant statistical methods, and basic details of major theories. I meet the readers knowing that the "typical student" is an outdated stereotype, but I meet them with respect for their intelligence and motivation. I firmly believe that it is possible to explain complex ideas clearly and connect with students from a variety of backgrounds and experiences. I do it every week in my lectures, and I do it in this book.

Highlights of Chapters in This Edition

Chapter 1 serves as an introduction to the study of adult development, beginning with the concept of development being both stable and changing. I use my own journey of adulthood as an example of these concepts and invite students to think of their own lives in these terms. Two guiding perspectives are introduced, Baltes's life-span developmental approach and Bronfenbrenner's bioecological model. Hopefully students will feel comfortable with those straightforward theories and move smoothly into the next section on developmental research. I don't assume that all students have taken a research methods class, so I limit the methods, measures, analyses, and designs to those that are used in later chapters. In fact, I use some of these later studies as examples, hoping that students will feel comfortable with them when they encounter them later in the book.

New in this chapter:

- Current events added to table of normative history-graded influences.
- The role of *methylation* in epigenetic inheritance.

The theme of Chapter 2 is *primary aging*, the physical changes that take place predictably in most of us when we reach certain milestones in our journeys of adulthood. Again, I begin with some basic theories, including Harmon's theory of oxidative damage, Hayflick's theory of genetic limits, and the theory of caloric restriction. Then I cover age-related physical changes, including outward appearance, the senses, the bones and muscles, the cardiovascular and respiratory systems, the brain and nervous system, the immune system, and the hormonal system. Most of the age-related changes in these systems are gradual, but much can be done to avoid premature aging (and much of that can be done in early adulthood, such as avoiding excessive exposure to sunlight and tobacco use). Next I cover four areas of more complex functioning—(a) athletic abilities; (b) stamina, dexterity, and balance; (c) sleep; and (d) sexual activity, all of which decline gradually with age. I cover some of the ways these declines can be slowed, but end the chapter with the caution that so far, we have no proven way to "turn back the clock" of time.

New in this chapter:

• Research on noise exposure levels for MP3 players.

• Evidence that high levels of sports participation in adolescents is a risk factor for osteoarthritis in young and middle adulthood.

• Studies of master athletes (up to age 90) and their oxygen uptake abilities.

• The connection between *blue screens* (smart phones, tablets, e-games) and insomnia.

• The prevalence of *hookups*—casual sex without commitment—among emerging adults.

• The concept of *food deserts*—neighborhoods with a high number of fast-food restaurants and a low number of stores selling healthy food.

• Results of a new national survey on sexual activities for adults aged 70 to 94.

• The question of *resveratrol* as an anti-aging supplement.

Chapter 3 is about age-related disease, or *secondary aging*. I try to keep this separate from the normal changes discussed in the previous chapter. Not everyone suffers from these diseases no matter how long they live, and many age-related conditions can be prevented or cured. I start with data of mortality rates by age because I think it helps students put the risk of death and disease into perspective. For most of our students, the risk of premature death is very low, and the top cause of death is accidents. I then discuss four of the top age-related diseases and explain their causes, their risk factors, and some preventative measures. These are heart disease, cancer, diabetes, and Alzheimer's disease. I try to balance good news (lower rates of cancer deaths due to early detection and treatment, lower disability rates in the United States) with the bad (rising rates of diabetes at all ages, still no cure for Alzheimer's disease). The second part of the chapter is about mental health disorders. I try to impress on the students that most of these disorders begin early in adulthood (or even in adolescence) and that most can be treated. However, the individuals suffering from these disorders (or their families) need to seek help and seek competent help. I end the chapter by telling that these physical and mental health disorders are not distributed randomly. Some groups are more apt to suffer than others, depending on their genes, socioeconomic background, gender, lifestyle, personality patterns, and events that happened to them in very early childhood or even before birth.

New in this chapter:

• New findings on genes that are associated with Alzheimer's disease.

• The relationship between sports-related head injury and Alzheimer's disease.

• The prevalence of head injury in combat veterans and the increased risk of PTSD and Alzheimer's disease.

• The health risk of perceived racial discrimination.

• The rising use of *assistance animals* and *comfort animals* to foster independence in people with disability.

• The increased number of people living with chronic disease in our communities and how we are learning to put the emphasis on the *people* part of the label.

Cognitive aging is covered in Chapter 4. I had discussed a little about primary aging of the brain in Chapter 2 and Alzheimer's disease in Chapter 3, but this chapter is about age-related changes in intelligence, as measured by IQ tests, and changes in specific components of memory, in terms of information processing theory. I explain how flaws in early research led to the conclusions that intelligence declines sharply with age, starting about age 40. Newer longitudinal studies with improved methodology show an increase in IQ scores until about 65, then a gradual decline, growing steeper around age 80. For components of intelligence, the fluid abilities that are controlled by biological processes show more of a decline than the crystallized abilities, which depend on formal schooling. Various memory components follow the same pattern—some decline more sharply than others. It is possible to train older people to show limited improvement in some memory processes. Decision making and problem solving are more real-world tasks, and older people are able to do them well while using less time and less examination of facts than younger people.

New in this chapter:

• New research on executive function and working memory.

• Evidence of stereotype threat affecting memory abilities of older people.

• Assistance with medication adherence provided by electronic devices and pharmacy packaging.

• Increased use of social networking by older adults, along with cell phone use and e-games; e-readers have not gained as much in popularity.

• New research on effective driver's training for older adults.

Chapter 5 is about social roles and the changes that takes place during adulthood. Social roles refer to the attitudes and behaviors we adopt when we make a transition into a particular role, such as worker, husband, or grandmother. This chapter covers changes within a person due to these life transitions. Gender is a major part of social roles, and several theories suggest how we learn what attitudes and behaviors fit the gender roles we fill. Bem's learning schema theory, Eagly's social role theory, and Buss's evolutionary psychology theory are presented. Various social roles, arranged chronologically, are discussed that include the transition from living in one's parents' home to living independently to living with a romantic partner in a cohabitation relationship or a marriage. Being part of a committed couple is related to good mental and physical health. Another role transition is from being part of a couple to being a parent. Social role transitions in middle adulthood involve going from having children living in your home to having children who are independently living adults to becoming a grandparent. Another role in middle adulthood is often as caregiver for one's own parents. In late adulthood, many move into the role of living alone and becoming a care receiver. Not everyone fits these role transitions. Some adults never marry, and some never have children but still have happy and productive lives. Lots of new social roles appear when there is a divorce in a family and then a remarriage, as most students know firsthand.

New in this chapter:

- Research on emerging adults and young adults who return to their parents' home due to the poor economy in the last decade. Findings show that it fosters intergenerational solidarity.

- Increased cohabitation rates in the United States and other countries that have more progressive attitudes toward women and lower religious involvement.

- New studies about the toll of long-term unhappy marriages on self-esteem and health.

- Lower birthrates for teens and higher birthrates for women over 40 in the United States.

- More gender equality in housework and child-care tasks for dual-career parents.

- Research on how same-sex parents divide up housework and child-care tasks.

- Racial inequality in how roles in middle adulthood are experienced.

- The concept of *grandfamilies*, children being raised by grandparents when parents are not present in the household.

- Increase in one-person households.

Social relationships are covered in Chapter 6 and differ from social roles because they involve two-way interactions between individuals, not just the behavior a person performs in a certain role. This is a difficult distinction, but there is just too much material on social-related topics for one chapter, so this seems like a good division. It also roughly fits the division between sociology studies (roles) and psychology studies (relationships). I begin this chapter with Bowlby's attachment theory, Ainsworth's model of attachment behaviors, Anotnucci's convoy model, Carstensen's socioemotional selectivity theory, and Buss's evolutionary psychology approach. Then I start with various relationships adults participate in, beginning with intimate partnerships, which includes opposite sex cohabitation, marriage, and same-sex partnerships. Next is parent–child relationships in adulthood, grandparent–grandchild relationships, and sibling relationships in adulthood. The chapter ends up with a section on friendship. Students of all ages relate to this chapter personally and it works well in the middle of the book.

New in this chapter:

- Several studies investigating online dating services along with some advice about how best to use them.

- Comparison of social convoys for age groups up to 90 years.

- Longitudinal study of attachment from birth to 18 years.

- Five key components that predict very accurately a couple's relationship quality 5 years into the future.

- Long-term married couples—almost half report being "very intensely in love."

- Long-term unhappily married couples—lower mental and physical health than those who divorced and remarried or divorced and did not remarry.

- New research on gay, lesbian, and bisexual couples.

- Increase in late-life divorces and their effect on adult children.

- The effect adult children's problems have on older parents.

- Increase in contributions from grandparents in time, gifts, and money.

- The effect involved grandparents have on young families.

- Adult siblings raising younger siblings.

- The role of pets as part of one's social network.

- The role of Facebook friends as part of one's social network.

The topics of work and retirement are covered in Chapter 7. When I started writing this textbook, students applied the information in this chapter to their futures or to their parents lives, but recently many apply it to themselves because they are part of the labor force, and some are retraining for a second career. A few are even retired and attending college as a pastime. I start the chapter with Super's theory of career development and Holland's theory of career selection. Students are usually familiar with vocational preference tests and interested in finding out what type of work they would enjoy most. Gender differences are an important part of career selection, and I question the reasons that even though women are found in almost every line of work and attend college in greater numbers than men, they still make less money and are not equally represented in top-paying, high-prestige jobs. The next section deals with age differences in job performance and job satisfaction. The section on work and personal life includes how jobs can affect individuals, intimate relationships, and responsibilities for other family members, including how household chores are divided up. The section on retirement includes reasons a person decides to retire or not, the effects of retirement, and some middle ground between full-time work and full-time retirement. I try to impress on the young student that much of one's quality of life in retirement depends on early planning ahead, and I hope they take that more seriously than I would have at their age.

New in this chapter:

- New research on gender differences in the workplace, including children's reactions to parents' sexism.
- Recent data on workforce participation at different ages.
- Discussion of how the recent recession affected people in the workplace, including an increase in suicides that match the downturn in the economy.
- Increase in "nontraditional" students in college (38%).
- The concept of *work engagement*, as opposed to *work burnout*.
- Increase in number of dual-employed parents and increase in fathers' participation in child care and household chores.
- Increase in older adults in the U.S. workforce and in some European countries.
- New studies of the benefits of doing volunteer work after retirement.

The topic of Chapter 8 is personality. I divide the chapter into two parts—first the research on personality structures, featuring Costa and McCrae's Five-Factor Model, and then I discuss some of the grand theories of personality, including Erikson's theory of psychosocial development, Loevinger's theory of ego development, Vaillant's theory of mature adaptation, Gutmann's theory of gender crossover, and Maslow's theory of positive well-being. I selected these from the many because they have continued to inform research into age-related personality stability and change.

New in this chapter:

- A new study of cohort effects in the way personality factors are expressed.
- New cross-cultural research that yields different personality factors for people in collectivist cultures.
- Erikson's stage of identity versus role confusion applied to age of self-identification by gay, lesbian, and bisexual youths.

Chapter 9 presents information on the quest for meaning and how it is manifested at different stages of adult life. This continues to be the most controversial chapter in the book, with some adopters rating it as the best chapter in the book and others questioning why it is included. My belief is that it fills an important place in the journey of adulthood as we question how this journey started and where, exactly, we are going. It's a chance to look a little further up the road and a little further back than the other chapters give us. I start by showing how the topic of religion and spirituality has ballooned in empirical journals over the last four decades and the importance of having a sense of the sacred in our lives. Then I cover some diverse theories, including Kohlberg's theory of moral reasoning and Fowler's theory of faith development, showing the similarities in those and two of the theories from the personality chapter we just covered, Loevinger's theory of ego development and Maslow's theory of positive well-being. I illustrate this complex comparison in a table that lays them out side-by-side to make it easier to understand. I conclude the chapter with material about mystical experiences and transitions, which William James, one of the founding fathers of psychology, wrote about in 1902.

New in this chapter:

- Increase in the percent of people in the United States who report belief in God.
- Argument that spirituality is an evolved trait in humans.
- Research on the relationship of religious beliefs and sound mental health, even when SES, health behaviors, and specific religious practices are considered.

The related topics of stress and resilience comprise the subject matter for Chapter 10. This type of research is usually done by health psychologists and medical researchers but has recently been of interest to social psychologists, sociologists, forensic psychologists, and military leaders. This is another chapter that students take very personally because most are dealing with more than their fair share of stressors. I begin with Selye's concept of the general adaptation syndrome and then present Holmes and Rahe's measurement of life-change events. Research is cited to show that high levels of stress are related to physical and mental disorders. The timely topic of PTSD is covered, and individual differences, such as gender and age, are included. I cover racial discrimination as a source of chronic stress and talk about stress-related growth—the idea that what doesn't kill you makes you stronger. Types of coping mechanisms are presented, followed by the topic of *resilience*. Recent studies have shown that the most frequent reaction to trauma is resilience and that some people are more apt to be resilient than others.

New in this chapter:

- Research using the life-change events scale predicts heart disease and diabetes 5 years later.

- A new study showing that people with long-lasting reactions to stress are more susceptible to mood disorders.

- Evidence showing that 10% of people who experience trauma will have PTSD a year later.

- Studies done with 2,000 people who survived the September 11 terrorist attack show that the older group (75 to 102 years of age) had higher stress symptoms immediately after the event, but declined rapidly to the level of younger adults after 12 months.

- All age groups of survivors of the September 11 terrorist attack showed a return of stress symptoms on anniversaries of 9/11.

- The concept of *human social genomics*—stressful life events can change our genomes.

- *General Assessment Tool*—an assessment tool the U.S. Army has worked on with the American Psychological Association to evaluate soldiers in terms of emotional, social, family, and spiritual fitness. Those who are low in any aspect can get counseling. It predicts PTSD risk and may be put into use in the near future.

Chapter 11 covers death—how we think about it at different ages, how we cope with the death of loved ones, and how we face the reality of our own deaths. There are mixed opinions about where this chapter belongs in this book. Some reviewers suggest that it be placed earlier in the book because it leaves a depressed feeling at the end of the course. I don't disagree with that, but I can't find any agreement about what would be a better placement. I begin the chapter with a discussion of how we acquire an understanding of death, both the deaths of others and the eventual death of ourselves. This includes abstract methods like overcoming the fear of death as well as practical methods, like making a living will and becoming an organ donor. The place of one's death is important to many people, and most want to die at home with their families. That is becoming more feasible because of the hospice approach, and I explain that in detail. Others who are terminally ill would like to choose the time of their deaths, and that has become possible in several states that have

legalized physician-assisted suicide, and I explain how that is arranged and what types of people make that decision. For the next section, I have compiled numerous mourning rituals that take place in different cultures in the United States. It is not an exhaustive list, and there may be many exceptions, but it is a good way to start a discussion about our multicultural society and about respecting and understanding others at these most personal times. The chapter ends on a hopeful note with a study of bereavement that shows that the most common response to the loss of a spouse in older adulthood is resilience.

New in this chapter:

- Cross-cultural studies show that the attitudes toward death are similar in many countries (United States, Egypt, Kuwait, Syria, Malaysia, Turkey).

- Increase in number of people who have living wills at all ages.

- Information that Facebook lets you announce your status as an organ donor on your wall.

In Chapter 12, the final chapter, I wrap up everything in the previous 11 chapters and do so in a chronological order rather than the topical arrangement these chapters feature. I add in the relevant new material and present my own model of adult development complete with a flowchart of how we move from disequilibrium to equilibrium in several areas of our lives. I also include a master table of age-related changes throughout adulthood.

Available Instructor Resources

The following resources are available for instructors. These can be downloaded at http://www.pearsonhighered. com/irc. Login required.

- **PowerPoint**—provides a core template of the content covered throughout the text. Can easily be added to customize for your classroom.

- **Instructor's Manual**—includes a description, in-class discussion questions, a research assignment for each chapter.

- **Test Bank**—includes additional questions beyond the REVEL in multiple choice and open-ended—short and essay response—formats.

- **MyTest**—an electronic format of the Test Bank to customize in-class tests or quizzes. Visit: http://www. pearsonhighered.com/mytest.

Acknowledgments

I am deeply grateful to Helen Bee, who authored the first three editions of this book. In turning over *The Journey of Adulthood* to me 16 years ago, she presented an opportunity that provided a sharp turn in my own "journey of adulthood," and I have enjoyed the new scenery and new people I have met along the way. Some of them are Erin Mitchell, Acquisitions Editor; Sherry Lewis, Project Manager; and Annemarie Franklin, Program Manager. Thanks also to the many reviewers who offered valuable suggestions for this revision and previous editions: Doug Abbott, University of Nebraska–Lincoln; Karola Alford, St. Mary of the Woods College; Jeffrey M. Arciola, University of Florida; Charles Bagley, Granite State College; Karen Lynne Barnes, University of Central Oklahoma; Ralph Brockett, University of Tennessee; Gary Creasey, Illinois State University; Heidi Dobish, Shepherd University; Jane E. Dwyer, Rivier College; Diane Edwards, Saddleback College; Nancy K. Elwell, Concordia University; Diane K. Feibel, Raymond Walters College–University of Cincinnati; Oney D. Fitzpatrick, Lamar University; Katiapaz Goldfarb, The University of New Mexico; M. James Hannush, Rosemont College; Sara Holland, Texas State University; George Lough, California State University, Northridge; LeeAnn Miner, Mount Vernon Nazarene University; Fereshteh Oboudiat, St. Joseph's University; Mary Ogles, Metro State College of Denver; Lloyd Pickering, University of Southern Mississippi; Sudha Shreeniwas, University of North Carolina at Greensboro; Donna J. Tyler Thompson, Midland College; Marcia L. Weinstein, Salem State College; and Joan Zook, SUNY Geneseo.

I greatly appreciate the interest and patience of my family and friends over the long course of updating this edition of *The Journey of Adulthood,* especially my husband, David Bjorklund.

Barbara R. Bjorklund
Jupiter Farms, Florida

Chapter 1
Introduction to Adult Development

Learning Objectives

1.1 Explain adult development in terms of "stability and change" and "stages and continuity"

1.2 Explain sources of change that influence adult development as per gradations of age and history and life events

1.3 Explain sources of stability that influence adult development as per genetic and environment

1.4 Illustrate adult development in terms of biological, social, psychological, and chronological ages

1.5 Identify adult development as life long and the adult is exposed to multiple environments

1.6 Analyze research methods, behavioral measures and analyses methods, and experimental design

1.7 Express the quest to know the universal rules and processes that influence aging

MY JOURNEY OF adulthood began early, as did that of many women of my generation, when I married shortly after high school and began a family. But unlike many women in my peer group, I spent more time reading than I did having morning coffee with the other moms. I always took a book along to read while the kids had music lessons, baseball practice, and orthodontist appointments. The library was a weekly stop along with the grocery store and was as important to me. By the time my youngest child began kindergarten, I enrolled in college as a freshman—at the age of 29, which was much older than the average at that time. For the next 7 years, my children and I did our homework together at the kitchen table, counted the days to the next holiday break, and posted our grade reports on the refrigerator. Today, as adults, they tell me that they can't remember a time in their childhood when I wasn't in school. Just before I received my master's degree in developmental psychology, the marriage ended, and I spent some time as a single mother. I abandoned plans for a PhD and took a job at the university, teaching psychology courses and doing research on children's memory development. And just as my children began to leave the nest, I married a man whose own journey of adulthood had brought him to fatherhood rather late, making me stepmother of a 5-year-old, who quickly became an important part of my life. Not too much later, the grandchildren began to arrive, and life settled into a nice routine. It seemed I had done it all—marriage, parenthood, career, single parenthood, stepparenthood, and grandparenthood; my life was full.

Suddenly, my 50th birthday loomed, and it seemed to represent so much more to me than turning "just another year older." The half-century mark was quite a shock and caused me to reevaluate my life. I realized that I wasn't ready to ride slowly into the sunset for the next several decades; I needed to get back on track and move forward with my education. The next fall I entered a PhD program in life-span developmental psychology at the University of Georgia. It was an invigorating experience and also very humbling. Instead of being the teacher, I was the student. Instead of supervising the research project, I was the newbie. Instead of being the one giving advice, I was the one who had to ask where the bookstore was, where to park, and how to use the copy machine. But 3 years later I was awarded a red-and-black hood in a formal graduation ceremony with my children and grandchildren, parents, and siblings cheering for me from the audience.

Now I teach part time at the local university and write college textbooks. Twelve years ago my husband and I moved from our city home to a country home in southeastern Florida, complete with a cypress stand in the front yard and a small pine forest in the back. Our neighbors have horses, and we wake to roosters crowing in the morning. Two of our younger grandchildren live nearby, and my typical day consists of teaching a university class in the morning and then picking up my 15-year-old grandson at high school so he can drive me around town on whatever errands I might have. He just got his learner's permit, and I am enjoying that magical year when he seemingly wants to go everywhere with me. Last week I helped my 10-year-old grandson with his fifth-grade science project—growing flowers with and without magnesium sulfate to see which have the brightest blooms. It was fun, but I was a little irked when "we" only got a B+.

Three years ago, with three adult children and eight grandchildren ranging in age from 7 to 25, my husband and I felt that our lives were settling down a little. But then my older son, who had been divorced for many years (and had four children in college), remarried and surprised us with Miss Lily Pearl—Grandchild #9! She just had her first birthday last week, and we can't imagine how we ever thought our family was complete without her. So if there is a message to take from this book it is this:

development doesn't stop at 21—or 40 or 65. Your life will never stop surprising you until you breathe your last breath. My wish for you is that the surprises are mostly happy ones.

1.1: Basic Concepts in Adult Development

1.1 **Explain adult development in terms of "stability and change" and "stages and continuity"**

Some of you reading this are just beginning the journey of your own adult life; some of you are partway along the road, having traveled through your 20s, 30s, and perhaps 40s, 50s, and beyond. Whatever your age, you are traveling, moving through the years and through the transformations that come along the way. We do not all follow the same itinerary on this journey; you may spend a long time in a location that I do not visit at all; I may make an unscheduled side trip. Or we may visit the same places but experience them very differently. Every journey has **individual differences**, aspects that are unique to the individual. You may not have experienced the trials of single parenthood as I have or the joys of grandparenthood, and I cannot relate to the independence you must feel when living alone or the confusion you experience when your parents divorce. Likewise, there also have to be some **commonalities**, typical aspects of adult life that most of us can relate to (either now or in the future). Most of us have moved out of our parents' homes (or plan to soon), experienced romantic relationships, entered college with some plans for the future, and either started a family or given some serious thought to parenthood. Without these common hopes and experiences, there would be no reason for a book on adult development. My goal for this book is to explore with you both the uniqueness and the common grounds of our adult lives.

Two of the concepts featured in this book are stability and change during the developmental process. **Stability** describes the important parts of ourselves that make up a consistent core. It is the constant set of attributes that makes each of us the individuals that we are throughout our lifetimes. In other words, your 40-year-old self will be similar to your 20-year-old self in some ways, as will your 60-year-old self. For example, one of the stable themes of my adult life is a love for books. In fact, it goes back to my childhood. Some of my most prized possessions are the books in my library. I always have several books sitting around the house that I am in the process of reading. And 10 years ago I started a book club in my neighborhood that has become a big source of joy for me. Another theme that keeps popping up in my life is children, beginning early on with three younger sisters, then my own children, then my stepdaughter, nieces and nephews, then grandchildren. I have always had a toy box in my living room and sippy cups in the kitchen cabinet. In fact, the two themes of books and children often mix. I send books on birthdays for the children on my gift list, and when visiting children spend the night, I have a shelf of children's books in the guestroom, some of them that belonged to their own parents so many years ago. Perhaps you find stability in your life in terms of playing a musical instrument or participating in sports. The genre of books I read may change over the years, and your choice of musical selections or sporting events may be different from time to time, but the core essence of these stable themes remains an integral part of our lives.

Change is the opposite force to stability. It is what happens to us over time that makes us different from our younger (and older) selves. An example from my life that illustrates this is travel. As a child I never traveled too far out of my home state of Florida. Almost all my relatives lived nearby, and those who didn't were more than happy to visit us in the warm climate during the winter. In fact, at the age of 35, I had

Middle adulthood can bring large-scale changes in lifestyle and interests, as illustrated by this photo of author Barbara Bjorklund along the city wall of Siena, Italy.

never been on an airplane. But when I married my current husband (and no longer had children living at home), I had the opportunity to travel with him to national conferences and accompany him on international trips as he collaborated with colleagues and worked as a visiting professor around the world. In the last 20 years, we have spent extended periods of time in Germany, Spain, and New Zealand. We have made shorter trips to Japan, China, Italy, Sweden, Norway, Denmark, England, Scotland, Wales, Austria, Switzerland, and Egypt. Last year we made it to Paris! I am an expert packer, and my office is filled with framed photos I have taken in many exotic locations. To compare myself at 30 and 50, my travel habits would constitute a dramatic change. Other examples of change in the adult developmental process occur when one becomes a parent, switches careers, or decides to move to another part of the country (or to an entirely different country). One way to view the journey of adulthood is to consider both the stability and the change that define our lives.

1.1.1: Stages

Still another way of looking at this journey is gauging how straight the road is. Some stretches of our lives are **continuous**—slow and gradual, taking us in a predictable direction. My gardening certainly fits this definition. In my earliest apartments I had potted plants, and when we rented our first house, I persuaded the landlord to let me put in a small flower garden. As our yards have grown bigger, so have my garden projects. I enjoy plant fairs, trade plant cuttings with friends, and of course, read books about gardening. I find it relaxing to spend time "digging in the dirt." I have increased my knowledge and skill over the years. Now that our yard is measured in acres instead of square feet, I'm in heaven. So far I have a butterfly garden in the front yard, and I'm working on a vegetable garden in the back. Hopefully I will continue to "develop" as a gardener for many years.

In contrast, our lives also have **stages**, parts of the journey where there seems to be no progress for some time, followed by an abrupt change. Stages are much like driving on a quiet country road for a long time and then getting onto a busy interstate highway (or vice versa). In my adult life I view the years of being home with my young children as a stage that was followed by the abrupt change of the youngest entering school and me starting college. I suddenly went from having minute-to-minute, hands-on parenting duties to the type that involve preparations the night before and then dropping the children off at school in the morning. And I also went from having mostly tasks that involved physical work and concrete thinking skills (how to get crayon marks off the walls) to those that required abstract thinking (Psychology 101). This mother/student stage continued for many years until I reached the single-mother/researcher stage. An interesting question in the study of adulthood is exploring how **typical** these stages of adult life are: Do most adults go through them along their journeys, and if so, do they go through them in the same order and at the same age? Or are they **atypical**, unique to the individual? I think that sending one's youngest child off to school is probably a universal event in a mother's life, signaling the end of one stage and the beginning of another, but I don't think that the transition from full-time mother to full-time student is typical, though it is more common today than it was a generation ago.

A final theme of this book has to do with inner versus outer changes. As we proceed along the journey of adulthood, many **outer changes** are visible and apparent to those we encounter. We enter early adulthood and become more confident in our step and our carriage; we fill out and mature; some of us become pregnant; some begin to lose their hair. In middle age many of us lose and gain weight, increase and decrease in fitness. **Inner changes** are not as apparent to the casual observer. We fall in and out of love, hold our children close and then learn to give them space. We look to our parents for guidance at the beginning of our journeys and then assist them at the end of theirs. And we grow in wisdom and grace. Of course the inner and outer changes are not independent of one another. Outer changes can affect the way we feel about ourselves, and vice versa. They also affect the way others perceive us, and this, in turn, affects our self-perceptions. Untangling this conceptual ball of yarn is another goal of this book.

1.2: Sources of Change

1.2 **Explain sources of change that influence adult development as per gradations of age and history and life events**

Multiple explanations about what influences adult development are quite common, much to the dismay of students (and textbook authors). In fact, the types of influences that result in change have been classified as (a) normative age-graded influences, (b) normative history-graded influences, and (c) nonnormative life events. In the following section I will describe these various influences and give you some examples so you can see them at work in your own lives.

1.2.1: Normative Age-Graded Influences

When you hear the phrase "sources of change," your first thought is probably of what we call **normative age-graded influences**, those influences that are linked to age and experienced by most adults of every generation as they grow older. At least three types of age-graded influences impinge on the typical adult.

BIOLOGY Some of the changes we see in adults are shared by all of us because we are all members of our species undergoing natural aging processes. This is often represented by the idea of a **biological clock**, ticking away to mark the common changes that occur with time. Many such changes are easy to see, such as hair gradually turning gray or skin becoming wrinklier. Others are not visible directly from the outside but occur inwardly, such as the loss of muscle tissue, which results in a gradual loss of physical strength. The rate at which such physical changes occur varies quite a lot from one person to another.

SHARED EXPERIENCES Another normative influence that is dictated for most of us by our ages can be envisioned by a **social clock** defining the normal sequence of adult life experiences, such as the timing of marriage, college graduation, and retirement. Even though our society has expanded the choices we have in the timing of these experiences, we still are aware of the "normative" timing of these events. Where we stand in relation to the social clock can affect our own sense of self-worth. The middle-aged man still living at home, the "perpetual student," the older working woman whose friends have retired—all may be doing well in important aspects of their lives, but if those lives are out of sync with what society expects in the way of timing, it may lead to some personal doubts. In contrast, the young adult who is CEO of his own high-tech company, the middle-aged woman who completes law school, and the octogenarian who finishes the Boston Marathon may have reason to celebrate over and above the face value of their accomplishments.

Another effect the social clock can have is **ageism**, a type of discrimination in which opinions are formed and decisions are made about others based solely on the fact that they are in a particular age group. Older adults are sometimes perceived to be cranky, sexless, forgetful, and less valuable than younger people. These stereotypes are perpetuated by television sitcoms, commercials, birthday cards, and jokes on Facebook. Emerging adults can also be targets of ageism, when they are perceived as being less capable than their older coworkers or when they are stereotyped as delinquents because of their style of clothes and speech. One of my goals for this book is to give a realistic and respectful look at adults of every age.

Another manifestation of the influence of the social clock in virtually all cultures is the pattern of experiences associated with family life. For example, the vast majority of adults experience parenthood, and once their first child is born, they begin a fixed pattern of shared social experiences with other parents that move along with their children's stages of life—infancy, toddlerhood, the school years, adolescence, and preparation to leave home. Each of these periods in a child's life makes a different set of demands on parents—attending childbirth classes, setting preschool playdates, hosting scout meetings, coaching Little League baseball, visiting potential colleges—and this sequence shapes 20 or 30 years of most adults' lives, regardless of their own biological ages.

Obviously, shared developmental changes based on the social clock are much less likely to be universal than those based on the biological clock. But within any given culture, shared age-graded experiences can explain some of the common threads of adult development.

INTERNAL CHANGE PROCESSES At a deeper level, there may be shared inner changes resulting from the way we respond to the pressures of the biological and social clocks. For example, several theorists have observed that in early adulthood, particularly after the birth of children, parents tend to exaggerate traditional masculine or feminine traits. Then at midlife, after the children are grown and no longer living in the home, many men and women seek to balance their feminine and masculine qualities. Men tend to become more emotionally expressive and warmer than they were during the parenting years, whereas women become more assertive and independent. In fact, there is some evidence that such an expansion of gender qualities occurs in many cultures. For now my point is simply that this is an example of an internal change that may be linked to the biological and social clocks, but is not caused entirely by one or the other. It is determined by the way we respond to the changes they entail.

1.2.2: Normative History-Graded Influences

Experiences that result from historical events or conditions, known as **normative history-graded influences**, also shape adult development. These influences are helpful for explaining both the similarities found among people within certain groups and also the dissimilarities between people in those same groups. Both are important parts of a course on adult development.

The large social environments in which development takes place are known as **cultures**, and they can vary enormously in the ways they influence the adult life pattern: the expected age of marriage or childbearing, the typical number of children (and wives), the roles of men and women, class structures, religious practices, and laws. I was reminded of this on a trip several years ago, when a young Chinese mother in Beijing struck up a conversation with me, and we began talking about our families. She had a toddler daughter with her who was 2 1/2, just the age of my youngest grandson, I told her. "*Youngest* grandson?" she asked, "How many grandchildren do you have?" I told her I had eight, then realized from her expression of surprise that this was very unusual in China. She explained to me that since 1979 there has been a one-child policy in China. Almost all Chinese parents in urban areas limit their families to one child. She was an only child; her daughter was an only child (and the only grandchild of both sets of grandparents). The typical person in her culture has no siblings, no aunts or uncles, and no cousins. She asked to see pictures of my grandchildren and wanted to know their ages and details about them.

We had a very friendly visit, but I could not help but wonder how different my life would be in that culture, and what her life will be like when she is my age.

A **cohort** is a more finely grained concept than a culture because it refers to a group of people who share a common historical experience at the same stage of life. The term is roughly synonymous with generation, but narrower—a generation refers to about 20 years, whereas a cohort can be a much shorter period. And a generation can refer to a much larger geographic area, whereas a cohort can be just one country or one region of one country. For example, Cuban Americans who came to the United States in the 1960s to flee Fidel Castro make up an important cohort in south Florida.

THE GREAT DEPRESSION COHORT   One of the most studied cohorts in the social sciences is the group of people who grew up during the Great Depression of the 1930s. This was a time in the United States (and in most of the world) that crops failed, factories closed, the stock market crashed, unemployment skyrocketed, and without unemployment benefits and government social programs, the only help available was from family, neighbors, or churches (none of whom had much to share). Almost no one escaped the effects of this disaster. But what were its effects, and were people affected differently depending on what age they were when the Great Depression hit? That was the thrust of the research on growing up in the Great Depression done by sociologist Glen H. Elder, Jr. (1979). He found that the cohort of people who were teenagers in the depths of the Great Depression showed fewer long-term effects than those who had been in early elementary school at the same time. The younger cohort spent a greater portion of their childhood under conditions of economic hardship. The hardship altered family interaction patterns, educational opportunities, and even the personalities of the children, so that the negative effects could still be detected in adulthood. Those who were teenagers during the Great Depression did not show negative effects in adult life; on the contrary, some of them seemed to have grown from the experience of hardship and showed more independence and initiative in adulthood as a result. Thus two cohorts, rather close in actual age, experienced the same historical event differently because of their ages. The timing of events interacts with tasks, issues, and age norms, producing unique patterns of influence for each cohort and helping to create common adult-life trajectories for those in the same cohort.

Although the era of the Great Depression is past, this research should remind us that every one of us, as an adult, bears the marks of the events we have lived through and the age-specific ways we reacted to those events. Do you remember the death of Princess Diana? Hurricane Katrina? Certainly all adults today remember the terrorist attacks of September 11. They all had effects on us, and a different effect depending on our ages. Less-dramatic happenings also have an influence on different cohorts, such as the economic conditions of the times, the political and religious climate, the educational system, and the popular culture. As many of these influences as possible need to be considered when researchers are comparing people of different ages to find age effects in some characteristic or ability. Table 1.1 shows some of the salient events that occurred in the recent past and the ages of seven different cohorts when these events happened.

The terrorist attack of September 11, 2001, is surely a defining event for the cohorts who experienced it.

Table 1.1 Selected Events from 1980 to 2013 and the Ages at Which They Were Experienced by Seven Cohorts

Year	Event	1940 Cohort	1950 Cohort	1960 Cohort	1970 Cohort	1980 Cohort	1990 Cohort	2000 Cohort
1980		Age: 40s	Age: 30s	Age: 20s	Age: Teens	Age: Children	Age: Not born yet	Age: Not born yet
1981	Ronald Reagan becomes president of the U.S.							
1981	Prince Charles and Diana (Princess of Wales) marry							
1981	AIDS identified							
1983	Sally Ride becomes first woman in space							
1989	Berlin Wall falls							
1989	Students massacred in China's Tiananmen Square							
1989	George H. W. Bush becomes president of the U.S.							
1990		Age: 50s	Age: 40s	Age: 30s	Age: 20s	Age: Teens	Age: Children	Age: Not born yet
1991	Collapse of USSR							
1991	Operation Desert Storm begins							
1993	Bill Clinton becomes president of the U.S.							
1994	O. J. Simpson arrested for murder							
1994	Kurt Cobain commits suicide							
1995	Oklahoma City bombing							
1997	Death of Princess Diana							
1999	Columbine High School massacre							
2000		Age: 60s	Age: 50s	Age: 40s	Age: 30s	Age: 20s	Age: Teens	Age: Children
2001	George W. Bush becomes president of the U.S.							
2001	World Trade Center/Pentagon attacked by terrorists							
2003	Iraqi War begins							
2003	Saddam Hussein captured by U.S. forces in Tikrit							
2004	Tsunami kills 230,000 in Indonesia area							
2005	Hurricane Katrina hits New Orleans							
2009	Barack Obama becomes president of the U.S.							
2009	Michael Jackson dies							
2010		Age: 70s	Age: 60s	Age: 50s	Age: 40s	Age: 30s	Age: 20s	Age: Teens
2010	Earthquake devastates Haiti							
2011	Sen. Gabrielle Giffords is shot in Arizona							
2011	President Mubarak of Egypt resigns after Arab Spring protests							
2011	Tsunami devastates Japan							
2011	Prince William marries Kate (Duchess of Cambridge)							
2011	Osama bin Laden is killed by Navy SEALS							
2012	Sandy Hook elementary school massacre							
2012	Jerry Sandusky convicted of 45 counts of child molestation							
2012	Superstorm Sandy hits northeast U.S.							
2013	Lance Armstrong admits using illegal drugs and doping							

Table 1.1 Activity

Find the decade of your birth in the row of dates across the top of the table and then review what age you were when various events happened. If you compare your own cohort with that of your parents (or your children), you will see that the sequence of history may have had different effects on members of the same family.

Critical Thinking

Take a look at Table 1.1. Which event is the most salient to you? Ask this of people who are younger or older than you. Determine if there is a pattern. Write a brief response that will be ready by your classmates explaining you findings. Be sure to provide specific examples.

1.2.3: Nonnormative Life Events

Along with the aspects of yourself that you share with most other adults your age and in your culture, there are **nonnormative life events**, aspects that influence your life that are unique to you, not shared with many others. These can have an important effect on the pathway of your life. Examples of nonnormative life events are having one's spouse die in early adulthood, inheriting enough money to retire at age 40, taking over parental responsibility for one's grandchildren, and starting one's own business at 65.

Some of these events are nonnormative for anyone at any age, such as inheriting a large amount of money, but others are nonnormative because of the timing. The death of a spouse is, unfortunately, a normative event in older adulthood, but not so in the earlier years. And starting one's own business may be remarkable in early adulthood, but it is highly nonnormative at the age of 65. As pioneering developmental psychologist Bernice Neugarten advised us back in 1976, we have to pay attention not only to the event itself, but also to the timing. Events that are on time are much easier to cope with (even the death of a spouse) than those that are off time.

I can speak from experience as one who was off time in several aspects of my life—becoming a parent early, going to college late, becoming a grandparent early, going to graduate school late. It makes for a good opening chapter of a textbook, but it was not always easy. One problem is the lack of peers—I was always "the older one" or "the younger one," never just one of the group. You don't fit in with your age-mates because you are doing something different, but you don't fit in with your fellow students or soccer moms either because you are not their age. And if this situation is easy to deal with yourself, sometimes others have problems, such as administrators who don't want to hire beginning professors who are older than they are. So in the best of all possible worlds, it is probably easier to do things "on time" than march to your own drummer—I've just never lived in the best of all possible worlds.

1.3: Sources of Stability

1.3 **Explain sources of stability that influence adult development as per genetic and environment**

In my discussion so far, I have focused on explanations of change. However, some traits and behaviors show patterns of stability, having little or no change for significant periods of time. To understand adult development, we must also explore and understand different types of stability. I have divided them according to the classic nature—nurture dichotomy, the biology we are born with and the environment we experience around us.

1.3.1: Genetics

Each of us inherits, at conception, a unique combination of genes. A very large percentage of these genes is identical from one member of the species to the next, which is why our developmental patterns are so much alike—why children all over the world walk at about 12 months, why we go through puberty in our early teens and menopause around 51. But our genetic inheritance is individual as well as collective. The study of **behavior genetics**, or the contributions genes make to individual behavior, has been a particularly active research topic in recent decades. We now know that specific heredity affects a remarkably broad range of behaviors, including cognitive abilities such as IQ, physical characteristics, such as height or body shape or a tendency to fatness or leanness, personality characteristics, and even pathological behavior, such as a tendency toward alcoholism, schizophrenia, or depression (Plomin, DeFries, Kropnick, et al., 2012). The extent to which these traits and tendencies remain in place throughout our lives shows the influence of heredity on stability in development.

In searching for genetic influences on variations in adult behavior, behavior geneticists rely primarily on **twin studies**. These are studies that compare monozygotic twins with dizygotic twins on some behavior. Such studies are based on the fact that *monozygotic twins* develop from the same sperm and ovum and thus share exactly the same genetic patterning at conception, whereas *dizygotic twins* each develop from a separate sperm and ovum and are therefore no more alike, genetically, than any other pair of siblings. In typical twin studies, measurements of some trait or ability are taken on each twin, and then the pairs are compared to see how similar their scores are. If the monozygotic twin pairs are more similar for that trait or ability than the dizygotic twin pairs, then it is taken as evidence that the trait or ability is more influenced by genetics than by environmental factors.

Twin studies are difficult to do because the statistics involved require large numbers of participants, and it is difficult for a researcher to recruit hundreds of pairs of twins. For this reason, several countries that have central databanks of their citizens' birth records and health records have taken the lead in this type of research. The largest databank of twins is in Sweden at the Karolinska Institute in Stockholm. It maintains a database of information on over 85,000 twin pairs. Several studies in this book were based on data from the Swedish Twin Study database, as you will soon find out.

1.3.2: Environment

If our genetic makeup contributes to the parts of ourselves that remain relatively stable over time, so does our environment. Although neither our biology nor our upbringing dictates our destiny, both have long-term effects. The lifelong effect of early family experience has been clearly demonstrated by the Grant Study of Harvard Men. Psychiatrist George Vaillant (2002), the study's current director, has concluded that those who lived in the warmest, most trusting homes as children are more apt to be living well-adjusted lives in adulthood than those who spent their childhoods in the bleakest homes. Men from the warmest homes are more able, as adults, to express emotions appropriately and openly, to see the world and the people in it as trustworthy, and to have friends with whom they enjoy leisure-time activities. Vaillant's interpretation is that parents who provide basic trust to their children (in this case, their sons), instill a sense of self-worth, good coping skills, the ability to form meaningful relationships, and in general construct a solid foundation for the core values the child will take with him or her throughout adulthood. And what's more, subsequent studies show that these data could predict which men at age 75 would most likely be aging successfully (i.e., are healthy and happy) and which would be aging unsuccessfully (i.e., are sick and sad). Taken together,

Vaillant's studies show that at least for extreme situations, early childhood environment can set the course for a lifetime of either emotional openness, trust, and good health or loneliness, mistrust, and illness. This research led Vaillant to propose a major theory of personality development.

1.3.3: Interactionist View

Of course there are no simple partitions between genes and environment, and we can't separate their contributions to the stability we experience throughout adulthood. Most developmentalists now subscribe to an **interactionist view** in which one's genetic traits determine how one interacts with the environment and even the environment itself (Greenberg, Halpern, Hood, et al., 2010). For example, a boy with a genetic makeup that promotes avoiding risks will grow up with a certain pattern of interactions with his parents and siblings and will seek out friends and activities that do not involve high risk. Teachers may view this as stable and sensible and steer him to a career such as accounting. The result is a young adult with risk-avoiding genes working in a low-risk career environment and enjoying low-risk activities with his friends. He will no doubt marry someone who shares these interests, giving him even more support for this lifestyle. You can imagine the life course of this person, perhaps having one child, living in the same home and working in the same job until retirement. Quiet evenings would be spent at home or at the neighborhood tavern. He would have good health because of regular checkups, exercise, and sensible eating habits. He (and his wife) would use their seatbelts and drive defensively. Vacations would be carefully planned tours of scenic places, and retirement would bring regular golf games with the same friends each week and volunteer work with the foster grandparent program at the local elementary school. Risk avoidance is the theme of this person's life, but can we really say it was caused by his genetic makeup? Or was it the environment? It's the interactionist's chicken-and-egg dilemma.

Recently, a biological mechanism has been identified for this interaction between genes and environment. **Epigenetic inheritance** is a process in which the genes one receives at conception are modified by subsequent environmental events that occur during the prenatal period and throughout the life span (Kreman & Lyons, 2011). This process by which genes are modified is known as **DNA methylation** because it involves the chemical modification of DNA through the addition of a methyl group, resulting in reduced gene expression. This type of inheritance explains how the environment can cause permanent, lifelong characteristics that were not part of the original genetic endowment at conception. For example, autopsies of adults who committed suicide show that those who had a history of childhood abuse are more apt to have modified glucocorticoid receptor genes in their brains than both adults who committed suicide but had no history of childhood abuse and a control group of adults who died of other causes (McGowan, Sasaki, D'Alessio, et al., 2009). Glucocorticoid receptors determine how an individual responds to stress and this case, it seems that early childhood experiences bring forth changes in the children's genetic expression that have lifelong consequences.

1.4: A Word About "Age"

1.4 **Illustrate adult development in terms of biological, social, psychological, and chronological ages**

Most people know that age is just a number. Perhaps ages in childhood give valid information about what to expect in the way of appearance or behavior, but once a child reaches adolescence, many more factors take over. In fact, the further we venture on the journey of adulthood, the more variability there is among people our "own" age. Several types of age have been identified, and they illustrate the many dimensions of adult development.

The number of years that have passed since your birth or the number of candles on your last birthday cake is your **chronological age**. As I mentioned before, this may be important in childhood, when all 7-year-olds look similar and have similar interests and abilities, but in adulthood, this number is seldom relevant, except for young adulthood when driving, purchasing alcohol, and voting are determined by chronological age and in older adulthood when eligibility for Social Security and Medicare are determined by chronological age. However, your development in adulthood does not occur because the clocks have struck a certain number of times any more than because the heat from your birthday candles reaches a certain temperature. It may be related, but chronological age does not *cause* developmental changes.

Biological age is a measure of how an adult's physical condition compares with others. "He has the memory of a 50-year-old" and "She runs like a 30-year-old" are examples of informal measures of biological age. Of course, it depends on the person's chronological age. Having the memory of a 50-year-old means one thing if the person is 70, a much different thing if 30! Biological age is used to evaluate aging of the physical systems, such as with bone density scans, in which patients' bones are compared to those of a healthy 20-year-old. Biological age can often be affected by lifestyle changes.

Another type of age is **psychological age**, which is a measure of how an adult's ability to deal effectively with the environment compares to others. A 30-year-old woman who can't pay her electric bill because she couldn't resist buying designer jeans and is often late for work because she oversleeps is functioning like a teenager. Her psychological age is much below her chronological age.

1.4.1: Social Age

Social age is based on the expected roles a person takes on at a specific point in his or her life. A woman who has her first child at 40 is taking on a role that has a social age at least a decade younger. A 23-year-old who works full time, goes to school full time, and sends money home to help support her grandmother has a social age much greater than her years. Sometimes biological age, psychological age, and social age are considered in a package as **functional age**, or how well a person is functioning as an adult compared to others. But it seems clear that the question, "How old are you?" has a number of answers.

As developmental psychologists, we try not to depend solely on chronological age when investigating some aspect of adult behavior. As you will see in the following chapters, many studies use age groups (young adults compared to middle-aged groups) or roles (couples without children compared to couples with children). Often they avoid the chronological age question by comparing the same people before and after they take on a role, such as parenthood or retirement. It is important to keep in mind that development and chronological age do not travel hand in hand, and this becomes more and more apparent the older we get.

WRITING PROMPT

How old are you? What would you estimate your biological age to be? Your social and psychological age? How do they match with your chronological age?

The response entered here will appear in the performance dashboard and can be viewed by your instructor.

Submit

1.5: Setting the Course

1.5 **Identify adult development as life long and the adult is exposed to multiple environments**

Before any questions about adult development can be asked, we need to determine what platform to stand on—the base from which we set the course of this journey. The next 10 chapters in this book cover specific areas of development and include specific theories to guide that research, but two broad approaches are used for all the chapters, and they define the tone of the book.

Critical Thinking

Before you read on, do you think it is possible for people in their 70s to make developmental gains? What about the 80s? Do people in their 20s experience developmental losses?

1.5.1: Life-Span Developmental Psychology Approach

Development encompasses both gains and losses. Sometimes a health crisis (loss) can result in a healthy new lifestyle (gain).

One major approach of this text is the **life-span developmental psychology approach**, which states that development is lifelong, multidimensional, plastic, contextual, and has multiple causes (Baltes, Reese, & Lipsitt, 1980). Psychologist Paul Baltes and his colleagues introduced these ideas in 1980, and although this approach sounds very ordinary today, it defined a turning point in developmental psychology, which before that time was focused almost exclusively on child development. The major points of the life-span developmental approach are illustrated in Table 1.2, along with some examples of each, and as you read them over, you will see that this approach opened the door for the study of development at all ages—not just your 12-year-old brother, but also you, your fellow students, your parents, your professor, and even your grandparents.

Table 1.2 Life-Span Developmental Psychology: Concepts, Propositions, and Examples

Concept	Proposition	Example
Life-span development	Human development is a lifelong process. No single age is more important than another. At every age, various developmental processes are at work. Not all developmental processes are present at birth.	A 38-year-old single woman makes plans to adopt a child; a 52-year-old bookkeeper becomes less satisfied with her job now that her kids are grown and she has more attention to give to her work; a 75-year-old Civil War buff becomes uninterested in attending re-enactments and begins taking a class in memoir writing. They are all experiencing development.
Multidirectionality	We develop in different directions and at different rates. Developmental processes increase and decrease. At one time of life, we can change in some areas and remain stable in others.	Some intellectual abilities increase with age, and some decline. Young adults show independence when they complete college and start a career, but show dependence at the same time when they remain in their parents' home.
Development as gain and loss	Development is a combination of gains and losses at every age, and we need to learn how to anticipate and adapt to both.	Middle-aged adults may lose their parents, but gain a new feeling of maturity. Young adults add a baby to their family, but may lose some equality in their marriage. Workers start losing speed and precision as they age, but they gain expertise.
Plasticity	Many aspects of development can be modified. Not much is set in stone, but there are limits.	Young people who enter adulthood with behavior problems or substance-abuse problems can overcome them and become responsible, successful adults. Couples with a lot of conflict in their marriages during the child-rearing years can be happy once the children are grown. Fathers can stay home with kids and be nurturing and attentive while mothers work outside the home. Older parents can change their values as a result of their young adult children's lifestyles.
Historical embeddedness	Development is influenced by historical and cultural conditions.	People who grew up in the 1970s have more open attitudes toward legalizing drugs than earlier or later cohorts. Those who lived through the Great Depression have different attitudes toward work than members of other cohorts.
Contextualism	Development depends on the interaction of normative age-graded, normative history-graded, and nonnormative influences.	Each of us is an individual because of the interaction of influences we share with other adults in general, those we share because of the times we live in, and those that are unique to us.
Multidisciplinary	The study of human development across the life span does not belong to psychology alone. It is the territory of many other disciplines, and we can benefit from the contributions of all.	Contributions to the study of development come from the field of psychology, but also from sociology, anthropology, economics, public health, social work, nursing, epidemiology, education, and other disciplines. Each brings a different and valuable point of view.

SOURCE: Adapted from Baltes (1987).

1.5.2: Bioecological Model of Development

A second major approach this text takes is based on the **bioecological model**, which points out that we must consider the developing person within the context of multiple environments. This idea is that development must take place within biological, psychological, and, especially, social contexts that change over time, and that these various influences are in constant interaction (Lerner, 2006; Sameroff, 2009). These ideas were introduced by psychologist Urie Bronfenbrenner in 1979 and have been modified over the last three decades (Bronfenbrenner & Morris, 2006). Bronfenbrenner proposed five systems: the *microsystem,* the *exosystem,* and the *macrosystem,* as shown in Figure 1.1 with the *mesosystem* being the interaction between elements in the microsystem. In addition, there is the *chronosystem,* which reflects the fact that the other three systems are dynamic—constantly changing over time. This change can be as individual as physical maturation or as encompassing as a large-scale earthquake or an economic recession in one's country.

WRITING PROMPT

In Bronfenbrenner's system, what are the specific influences on your development at each level? Does one level have more influence than the others? Do you think this is true of others or unique to you? Write a response that will be read by your instructor. Be sure to include concrete examples in your response.

   The response entered here will appear in the performance dashboard and can be viewed by your instructor.

Submit

The major point of Bronfenbrenner's theory, and other developmental contextual approaches in general, is that individuals and their development cannot be studied "out of context." Rather, we must consider the social environment, from family and friends through community and the broader culture—all in interaction—when trying to explain the factors that influence the course of a person's journey to and through adulthood.

Figure 1.1 Bronfenbrenner's model of the ecological-systems approach to studying development. He suggested that researchers look beyond behavior in laboratory settings and consider how development takes place within multiple environments and through time.

SOURCE: Based on Bronfenbrenner (1979).

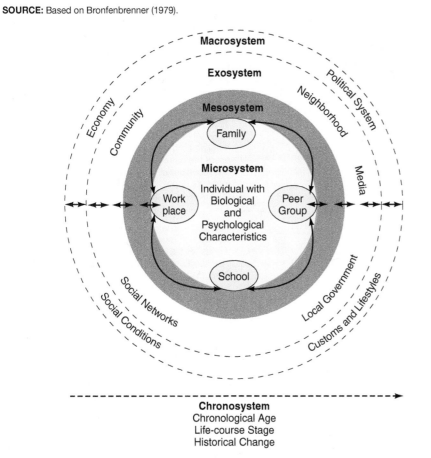

As you will see throughout this text, recent research in most areas of the social sciences has reflected this model, investigating the development of adults in the context of their lives as individuals, as partners in relationships, as parents in families, as workers on job sites, and as members of particular cultural groups and cohorts.

1.6: Developmental Research

1.6 **Analyze research methods, behavioral measures and analyses methods, and experimental design**

To understand adult development, it is important to know a little about the research process because information today in the social sciences is, for the most part, science based. I won't attempt to present a whole course on research methods and statistics, but I will cover some of the methods that are used in the studies I describe in the upcoming chapters of this text.

All research begins with questions. Suppose, for example, that I want to know something about change or stability in personal relationships over the adult years—relationships with a spouse, with other family members, or with friends. Or suppose that I wanted to study memory over adulthood. Older adults frequently complain that they can't remember things as well as when they were younger. Is this a valid perception? Is there really a loss in memory ability in old age, or earlier? How would I go about designing research to answer such questions? In every instance, there is a set of decisions:

Table 1.3 Designing Research

Question Type	Question
Research methods	Should I study groups of people of different ages, or should I study the same group of people over time, or some combination of the two?
Research measures	How will I measure the behavior, thought, or emotion I am studying? How can I best inquire about the quality of marriage—with a questionnaire or in an interview? How do I measure depression—is there a set of questions I can use?
Research analysis	What will I do with the data? Is it enough merely to compare the average number of friends, or the average relationship satisfaction described by subjects in each age group? What else would I want to do to tease out some of the possible explanations?
Research design	What do the results mean? Depending on the research method, measures, and analysis, what is the overall conclusion? What is the answer to the research question I began with?

| Hide All Cells | Show All Cells |

1.6.1: Methods

Choosing a research method is perhaps the most crucial decision the researcher makes. This is true in any area of science, but there are special considerations when the topic of study is development. There are essentially three choices: (a) You can choose different groups of subjects at each of a series of ages and compare their responses—in other words, the cross-sectional method; (b) you can study the same subjects over a period of time, observing whether their responses remain the same or change in systematic ways—the longitudinal method; or (c) you can combine the two in any of several ways, collectively called sequential methods.

A **cross-sectional study** in developmental psychology describes a study that is based on data gathered at one time from groups of participants who represent different age groups. Each subject is measured or tested only once, and the results give us information about differences between the groups.

Here is an example of a study using the cross-sectional method. Public health researcher Paul Cleary and his colleagues were interested in knowing whether there were any differences in personal health practices for adults of different ages (Cleary,

Zaborski, & Ayanian, 2004). The researchers were part of a large-scale project known as the Midlife in the United States (MIDUS) National Survey, so they included questions pertaining to personal health in the surveys sent out to 7,000 participants between the ages of 25 and 74. One of the questions was, "How much effort do you devote to your personal health?" Answers were given as scores on a 10-point scale, with 1 being "very little effort" and 10 being "very much effort." When the results were compiled, the researchers divided them into five groups according to the age of the participants and then by gender, resulting in 10 data points, each giving the average score for one gender at one age group. Figure 1.2 shows the results displayed on a graph. As you can see, the average responses to the question, "How much time do you devote to your personal health?" were between 6.8 and 7.8 points. The most obvious result (to me) was that women in every age group responded that they devoted more effort to their health than men, with the biggest difference being in the two groups of people 35 to 44 and 45 to 54 years of age. Men and women were the most similar in the older years of 65 to 74. Women's health efforts increased steadily across the adult years, whereas men's actually declined slightly at 35 to 44 years and then began a sharp increase. Just considering age in general, the figure shows us that the older we get, the more effort we spend on our health. Of course, there are many more findings in the MIDUS study, and I will be discussing them in more detail in later chapters, but for now, this gives you a good example of a cross-sectional research study.

Figure 1.2 Cross-sectional data showing that the amount of effort spent on personal health care increases with age and is greater for women than for men at every age.

SOURCE: Cleary, Zaborski, & Ayanian (2004).

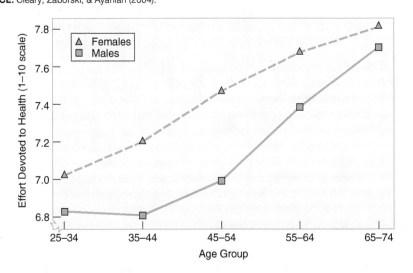

Some cross-sectional studies do not use age groups. Instead they use stages in life, such as comparing young couples without children to couples who have already had their first child to see the effects of parenthood on a marriage. Or comparing young people entering college with those who are graduating to see the effects of education on political views. But all cross-sectional studies are designed to test different people at the same point in time—kind of a shortcut for following those people throughout that time period and charting individual changes. The benefit is that it is quicker, easier, and less expensive than following the same people around the whole time. The downside is that it only shows *age differences*, not change. When cross-sectional studies are done with older adults, it is possible that the people in the older groups do not represent the general population as well as those in the younger groups, due to transportation problems, chronic health concerns, and difficulty in recruiting older participants. It is also the case that older participants are those who have survived into old age and may be healthier and wealthier (and perhaps wiser). But again, the minimal time and effort it takes to conduct cross-sectional studies makes them attractive to most researchers, and many of these problems can be predicted and controlled for.

LONGITUDINAL METHOD A **longitudinal study**, by contrast, is one in which a researcher follows the same group of people over a period of time, taking measurements of some behavior of interest at regular intervals. In comparison to the cross-sectional study discussed earlier, a longitudinal study might start with a group of people who are 35 to 44, asking how much effort they devote to their health. Then, 10 years later, the researchers could find the same people, now at the ages of 45 to 54, and ask them the same question again. Finally, another 10 years later, the last data could be gathered when the participants are 55 to 64 years of age. Then comparisons could be made, telling the story of these individuals, at least in regard to *age-related changes* in the time they devoted to their health over their middle years (not just *age-related differences* as are revealed by correlational studies).

An example of a study using the longitudinal method is one done by psychologist Nancy Galambos and her colleagues, who were interested in the development of self-esteem in young adults (Galambos, Barker, & Krahn, 2006). They began the study at the end of the school year in 1984 by giving out questionnaires to 983 high school seniors in a large western Canadian city. Among other things, the questionnaire contained six items from a self-esteem inventory in which participants read such statements as, "On the whole I am satisfied with myself" and "I feel that I have a number of good qualities." They rated each item on a scale of 1 (strongly disagree) to 5 (strongly agree). As Figure 1.3 shows, a year later, when the participants were 19, they received a second questionnaire containing the same questions (and others). Of the 983 original participants, 665 returned the second questionnaire. The third year the process was repeated, and 547 participants, who were now 20 years of age, returned the third questionnaire. Two years later, the researchers sent out a fourth questionnaire and received 503 in return. Finally, in 1992, when the participants were 25 years of age, the final questionnaire was sent out, and the return was 404. Although this return was only 45% of the original sample size, the response rate is typical of longitudinal studies.

Figure 1.3 Model of a longitudinal study in which 983 students were surveyed in 1984 and then again in 1985, 1986, 1988, and 1992. Note their ages and also the number of students who returned the questionnaires (*n*).

SOURCE: Data from Galambos, Barker, & Krahn (2006).

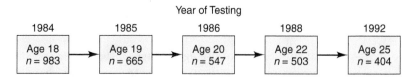

Galambos and her colleagues compiled the data on self-esteem by finding average scores for the group of participants at each age they were surveyed. They also divided the group into male and female subgroups. The results are shown in Figure 1.4. As the graph shows, the average scores for these young adults range between 3.75 and 4.05, and self-esteem for both groups increased between the ages of 18 and 25. There is also a different rate of increase for the males and the females. The males had higher self-esteem at 18, but by 25, their rate was not much higher than that of the females. The females had lower scores at 18, but their rate of increase was greater than that of the males.

Figure 1.4 Young adults increase in self-esteem between the ages of 18 and 25, according to this longitudinal study.

SOURCE: Galambos, Barker, & Krahn (2006).

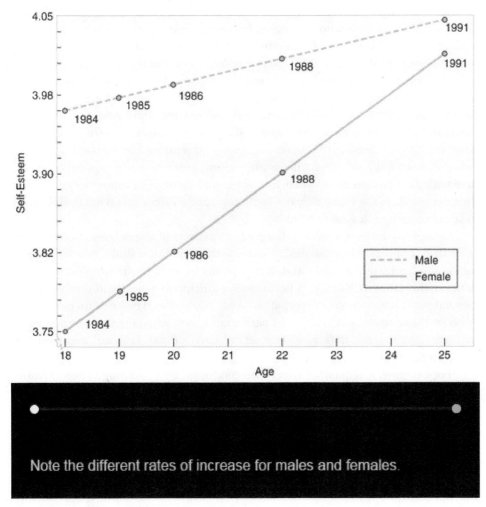

Note the different rates of increase for males and females.

The longitudinal method used by Galambos and her colleagues truly demonstrates *change* because the same participants were tested at each age. There were only 404 participants (compared to over 7,000 in the cross-sectional study described earlier), but the data points on the graph show increases in self-esteem for the same participants over the course of 7 years. Another plus for longitudinal studies is that the participants are from the same cohort, which increases the probability that the changes in self-esteem are age related and not the result of some normative history-graded influence on that cohort. However, the minuses of longitudinal studies should be apparent. From the first wave of testing to the published article, the study took 22 years! This method is time consuming and expensive. In a profession that bases promotion and tenure on annual publication lists, researchers need to balance longitudinal studies with shorter-term work to not "perish" due to lack of publications. The most ambitious longitudinal studies I am aware of are done in large European research institutes. For example, in the Berlin Study of Aging, there are 40 researchers on the staff and hundreds of students and paid researchers. The study began in 1990 by assessing 516 people between 70 and 100 years of age, and it took 14 sessions for each person to receive the initial assessment—a project that took the research staff 3 years (Baltes & Mayer, 1999). In the next three decades, surviving participants were assessed eight more times. Some of the participants outlived the principle investigator, psychologist Paul Baltes, who died at the age of 67 in 2006. The findings from the Berlin

Study of Aging and similar research efforts will be discussed in the upcoming chapters of this book.

LONGITUDINAL STUDIES AND ATTRITION Another drawback to longitudinal studies is **attrition**, or participant dropout. The Galambos study began with a fairly general sample of high school students, but as the years went by, each wave of data collection yielded fewer and fewer returns. More than half of the original participants were absent from the last wave of the study. When attrition is present, we need to ask whether those who dropped out might have made a difference in the results. The researchers mentioned this in the discussion section of their journal article. They said that the self-esteem scores of those who dropped out and those who remained in the study did not differ in the earlier parts of the survey in which all participated. However, there were some other differences. Those who remained in the study were more apt to be from families with higher socioeconomic levels and more apt to continue to live with their parents in the years following graduation. The researchers caution us that the results of the study may not apply to young adults who do not fit this profile (Galambos, Barker, & Krahn, 2006).

One of the ways to combine the positive aspects of the cross-sectional design with those of the longitudinal design is to use the **sequential study**, which is a series of longitudinal studies begun at different points in time. In the simplest form, one longitudinal study (Cohort 1) is begun with participants who are in one age group. Several years later, a second longitudinal study (Cohort 2) is begun with participants who are the same age as the Cohort 1 participants were when the study began. As the two studies progress, they yield two sets of longitudinal data, but they also give cross-sectional data.

For example, a sequential study was conducted by psychologist Susan Krauss Whitbourne and her colleagues (Whitbourne, Zuschlag, Elliot, et al., 1992) to answer the question of whether young adults' personalities change or remain stable as they moved into middle age. The study began in 1966 with a group of 347 undergraduate students at the University of Rochester whose average age was 20. They were given a personality inventory questionnaire asking them, among other things, to rate statements about their industry (or work ethic) according to how well each described them. In Figure 1.5, this group is shown in the top left box labeled Cohort 1, 1966. In 1977, this group was on average 31 years old, and the researchers sent out questionnaires again, receiving 155 in return, as shown in the box labeled Cohort 1, 1977. Also in 1977 a new group of 20-year-old students from the University of Rochester were given the personality inventory questionnaire (Cohort 2, 1977). In 1988 the process was repeated for the participants in Cohort 1, who were now 42 years of age, and Cohort 2, who were now 31 years of age. As you can see, 99 of the original 347 in Cohort 1 returned questionnaires, and 83 of the original 296 in Cohort 2 returned questionnaires.

Figure 1.5 Model of a sequential study in which two cohorts were followed beginning at age 20. One cohort was followed for 22 years; one for 11 years. Note ages and number of participants (*n*).

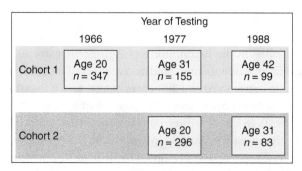

At this point, there are two longitudinal studies going on, Cohort 1 with data available for the ages of 20, 31, and 42, and Cohort 2 with data available for the ages of 20 and 31. There is also a cross-sectional study going on, with a group of 20-year-olds, a group of 31-year-olds, and a group of 42-year-olds. Figure 1.6 shows how Whitbourne and her colleagues analyzed the results.

Figure 1.6 Results from a sequential study of two cohorts tested at three ages and at three different points in time. Comparing longitudinal results, Cohort 1 shows a sharper increase in industry scores between 20 and 31 years than does Cohort 2, though both have similar scores at age 31. Cross-sectional results suggest that the normative history-graded influences (Vietnam War, civil rights issues) lowered the young adults' scores in 1966.

SOURCE: Adapted from Whitbourne, Zuschlag, Elliot, et al. (1992).

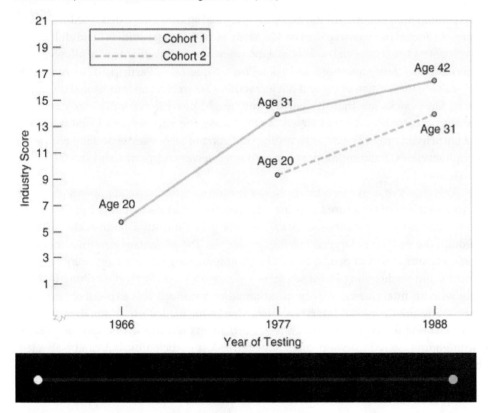

The top line shows the industry scores for Cohort 1 at ages 20, 31, and 42. The scores increase sharply between 20 and 31, and the increase becomes more gradual from 31 to 42. This definitely shows change in personality traits during adulthood, but does the same hold for other cohorts? The lower line in the figure shows the pattern for Cohort 2, tested at 20 years and 31 years of age. The pattern is different than for Cohort 1. First, the industry scores are much higher at age 20 for Cohort 2 (6.54 for Cohort 1 and 9.19 for Cohort 2), and second, the rate of increase is much slower for Cohort 2. Still, both groups had similar industry scores at the age of 31 (13.58 for Cohort 1 and 14.32 for Cohort 2). The researchers suggest that the 20-year-olds in Cohort 1 were in college during the 1960s, when the work ethic of the establishment was being questioned and rejected, and their low scores on industry were reflections of that era. Once out of school and in the workplace, this group had some catching up to do. Their catching up is represented by the sharp increase in industry scores, which at 31 are very close to the scores of Cohort 2, who were not part of the protest era. Clearly there are nonnormative history-graded influences going on here. Perhaps the normative age-graded pattern of change in the personality trait of industry is more like that of Cohort 2, but when history (the Vietnam War, civil rights issues) brings about a large student protest movement, it causes a detour in the journey of adulthood for many in that cohort, although in the case of the personality trait of industry, these college students were able to catch up to speed and be back on track by the time they were age 31. This study serves as a good example of using the sequential method to study development.

1.6.2: Measures

Once the research design is determined, the next major set of decisions has to do with how to measure the behavior of interest. Each method has its own set of advantages and disadvantages, and I will discuss them here briefly.

One of the most common instruments used to gather data is a **personal interview**, that is, having the experimenter ask the participant questions, one-on-one. Personal interviews can be *structured,* like a multiple-choice test, or *open ended,* like an essay test, or a combination of both. All the major longitudinal studies I have described so far, for example, included extensive interviews. Many cross-sectional studies of adult life also involve structured interviews. Personal interviews have the advantage of allowing the interviewer to clarify questions and ask follow-up questions. Participants feel comfortable talking to a human being and not just writing answers on an impersonal questionnaire. Drawbacks are that the participants might provide responses they feel are socially acceptable to the interviewer, and similarly, the interviewer's feelings toward the participant might cloud the recording or coding of responses, especially with very long interviews. Building rapport between interviewer and participant can be a plus or a minus.

This problem is avoided by using the **survey questionnaire**, a paper-and-pencil form consisting of structured and focused questions that participants can fill out on their own. Survey questionnaires are usually given out on a large scale, such as through the mail or at large gatherings of people. The advantages are that they can reach a large number of people in a wide geographic range. Participants may be more truthful and forthcoming about sensitive topics with a survey than if talking face-to-face with an interviewer. Survey questionnaires are much less expensive and time consuming than personal interviews. Drawbacks for mailed questionnaires are that there is a low return rate (about 30% of participants return the first questionnaire). Group-administered questionnaires have fewer lost participants, but can be affected by peer influence (especially if given out in the social environment of high school auditoriums or retirement condominium recreation rooms). Survey questionnaires are also incredibly difficult to construct.

WRITING PROMPT

How would you design a questionnaire for your class to find out other students' opinions on the classroom design (the light, seating, room temperature, and so forth)? Consider this question and write a brief response, which will be read by your teacher.

▶ The response entered here will appear in the performance dashboard and can be viewed by your instructor.

Submit

Some of the problems of survey questionnaire construction can be avoided by using **standardized tests**. These are instruments that measure some trait or behavior and have already been established in your field of interest. Drawbacks are that many of these tests are owned by publishing companies, and you have to purchase the right to use them in your research. An example is measuring IQ using the Wechsler Scales or personality using the MMPI or the Myers-Briggs Type Indicator. However, a number of tests are also available at no charge that have been standardized and published in research articles, along with instructions for administering and scoring them. For example, researchers in a number of studies in this text measure depression in their participants with an instrument known as the CES-D-10, or the Center for Epidemiological Studies Short Depressive Symptoms Scale (Radloff, 1977). This test is easily retrieved from the Internet after a quick search. It is a good example of a standardized test that is easily scored and has a good record of **validity** (it measures what it claims to measure) and **reliability** (it does so consistently). How to select a standardized test for your own research? There are reference books that review tests periodically, such as the *Mental Measurements Yearbook* (Spies, Carlson, & Geisinger, 2010), but the advice I give students is to read similar studies published by other researchers and use what they use. Selecting a research measure is probably not the best time to be creative.

These are by no means the only research measures available. As you will see throughout this text, there are many ways to measure human behavior, from complex brain imaging techniques to one-item questionnaires ("How would you rate your health? Circle one of the following: Very Good, Good, Average, Poor, Very Poor"). Depending on the research question, it's important to find the most appropriate way to measure the behavior of interest.

1.6.3: Analyses

Once the research method has been chosen and the behavior has been measured, researchers must make another set of decisions about how to analyze the resulting data. Some of the statistical methods now being used are extremely sophisticated and complex. I'll be describing a few of these in later chapters when I discuss specific studies that include them. At this early point, all I want to do is talk about the two most common ways of looking at adult development.

The most common and the simplest way to describe age-related differences is to collect the data (scores, measurement results) for each group, find the means (averages), and determine whether the differences in the means are large enough to be significant, a process known as **comparison of means**. With cross-sectional studies, the means of the age groups are compared. With longitudinal studies, the means of the scores for the same people at different ages are compared. With sequential studies, both comparisons are possible. However, the similarity remains—we are looking for an age-related pattern of change.

If the group of participants is large enough, it is often possible to divide it into smaller groups and look for age differences or continuities in the subgroups, such as women versus men, working class versus middle class, those with young children versus those without young children. If the same pattern appears in all subgroups, we'd be more likely to conclude that this is a significant age-related pattern. However, if the change is different for the subgroups (as is often the case), it opens the door for follow-up questions. For example, in the cross-sectional study described earlier (Cleary, Zaborski, & Ayanian, 2004), researchers divided the age groups into gender groups also, and they found that different patterns emerged for men and women in the amount of time spent on health-related activities. Not only did the researchers find answers to their questions about age-related change (yes, it increases with age), but they also found that it increased more for men, and men started out at a disadvantage. That gave the researchers the opportunity to speculate on why men seem to have so little concern about their health at 25 and do not change in this respect until about 45. In contrast, women have more concern at 24, and they increase in concern their whole lives. Perhaps at 25, women are concerned with childbearing and visit their doctors more often. Perhaps the cultural emphasis on women's appearance causes them to notice subtle signs of aging sooner, whereas men "coast" for awhile until the signs are more evident. These questions make for good discussion and inspire new research to find answers.

CORRECTIONAL ANALYSIS Comparisons of means for different age groups, either cross-sectionally or longitudinally, can give us some insights into possible age changes or developmental patterns, but they cannot tell us whether there has been stability or change within individuals. For this information, a different type of analysis is required: a **correlational analysis**. A correlation is simply a statistic that tells us the extent to which two sets of scores on the same people tend to vary together. Correlations (r) can range from +1.00 to −1.00. A positive correlation shows that high scores on the two dimensions occur together. A negative correlation tells us that high scores on one dimension occur with low scores on the other. The closer the correlation is to 1.00 (positive or negative), the stronger the relationship. A correlation of 0.00 indicates no relationship.

Critical Thinking

What would you predict the correlation direction would be for the number of hours students study for an exam and their grades? What about the average speed they drive and the number of infraction points on their driver's licenses?

For example, height and weight are positively correlated: taller people generally weigh more, shorter people less. But the correlation is not perfect (not +1.00) because there are some short, heavy people, and some tall, light people. If you are on a diet, the number of pounds you lose is negatively correlated with the number of calories you eat: high calories go with low weight loss. But this correlation, too, is not a perfect −1.00 (as any of you who have dieted know full well!).

Correlations are also used to reveal patterns of stability or change. For example, researchers interested in personality traits might give personality assessments to participants over a number of years and then correlate the early scores with the later scores for each person. A high positive correlation would show stability for that trait.

Ultimately, however, correlations can tell us only about relationships; they cannot tell us about causality, even though it is often very tempting to make the conceptual leap from a correlation to a cause. Some cases are easy. If I told you that there was a negative correlation between the per capita incidence of television sets in the countries of the world and the infant mortality rates in those countries, you would not be tempted to conclude that the presence of TV *causes* lower infant mortality. You'd look for other kinds of societal characteristics that might explain the link between the two facts such as income level. But if I tell you there is a correlation between the amount of time adults spend with friends and family and the overall life satisfaction those adults report, you would be much more tempted to jump to the conclusion that greater happiness is *caused* by contact with friends and family. And it may be. But the correlation, by itself, doesn't tell us that; it only tells us that there is a relationship. It remains for further research and theorizing to uncover the causal links, if any. Perhaps the greater life satisfaction people have, the more time their friends and family want to spend with them.

One unique way correlational analyses are used in developmental research is to determine the genetic contributions to various behaviors and abilities. I introduced twin studies in an earlier section and will just explain them in a little more detail here. The typical twin study involves comparing two types of twins, monozygotic and dizygotic, on the behavior you are interested in. For a simple example, let's use height (and twins of the same sex to rule out sex differences). Each twin would be measured and the height recorded. Then two correlations would be computed comparing the twins—one for monozygotic twins and one for dizygotic twins. Which do you think would be more similar in height? Of course the monozygotic twins because they have the same genes, and height is something that is determined by inheritance to a great extent. But what about other characteristics, like IQ, the tendency toward alcoholism, how religious one is? Those are all characteristics that have been shown to be influenced by heredity to a significant extent. And the research that revealed this involved correlational analyses.

WRITING PROMPT

If adopted children are more similar to their adoptive parents on some measure than to their biological parents, what conclusions could you make from that?

▶ The response entered here will appear in the performance dashboard and can be viewed by your instructor.

Submit

For example, in a study using data from the Swedish Twin Registry, epidemiologist Erica Spotts and her colleagues (Spotts, Neiderhiser, Towers, et al., 2004) investigated whether marital happiness is influenced by heredity. They gave a test of marital happiness to over 300 pairs of twins (all women) and their husbands. About half of the women were monozygotic twins and half were dizygotic twins. When the scores were analyzed, the monozygotic twin pairs were more alike than the dizygotic twin pairs. As you can see in Figure 1.7, if one monozygotic twin wife was happy in her marriage, the other twin tended to be happy too—and if one was unhappy, there was a good chance that the other was too. Their marital happiness scores were positively correlated. This was not the case for the dizygotic twin wives, whose correlations were about half what the monozygotic twins' correlations were. Comparing the two types of twins' correlations shows the extent of the genetic contribution to marital happiness because the monozygotic twins share the same genes, whereas the dizygotic twins share only half, and as in the case of height, we would not expect them to be as similar.

Figure 1.7 Wives who are monozygotic twin pairs are more similar in their marital happiness than wives who are dizygotic twin pairs. Interestingly, this genetic effect carried over to their husbands who were not related (compare striped columns).

SOURCE: Data from Spotts, Neiderhiser, Towers, et al. (2004).

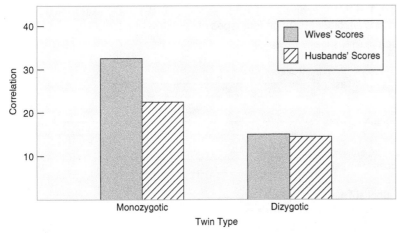

In a surprise twist, the researchers also gave the marital happiness questionnaires to the husbands of the twins, who were not related to each other or to anyone else in the study. As you can see in the figure, the husbands of the monozygotic twins also were more similar in their marital happiness scores than the husbands of the dizygotic twins. It seems that the genetic endowment of the monozygotic twins not only gave the women similar outlooks on marriage, but that the women, in turn, influenced the marital happiness of their husbands.

Critical Thinking

What are some specific ways women can pass on their level of marital happiness to their husbands? What about marital unhappiness?

META-ANALYSIS   Another way of analyzing data is the **meta-analysis**. This approach combines data from a large number of studies that deal with the same research question. A researcher conducting a meta-analysis selects a research question, such as whether or not aerobic exercise affects cognitive functioning in older adults. This has been a topic of interest for several decades and is a prominent topic in Chapter 4 of this text. A number of studies have shown that older adults (and laboratory animals) who participate in vigorous physical activity have better cognitive abilities than their age-mates who are sedentary. However, the studies have used different age groups, different types of physical activity, and different measures of cognitive ability (not to mention different species). Psychologists Stanley Colcombe and Arthur Kramer (2003) reviewed this research and conducted a meta-analysis to evaluate the combined results. The first step was an online search to find all the studies of human cognition published in a certain time frame (2000—2001) that had any mention of age, fitness, exercise, and a number of other key words. They narrowed down the 167 articles to 18 (totaling 101 participants) that were longitudinal, supervised (not surveys), dealt with aerobic exercise, had participants assigned randomly to exercise and nonexercise groups, and had participants over the age of 55. They regrouped the data in the studies to fit one overall scheme. Participants' data were divided into three groups: 55–65, 66–70, and 71+. The cognitive tasks that were measured were divided into four types: planning, speed, control, and visuospatial. As you can see in Figure 1.8, the researchers found that the participants in the exercise groups performed significantly better on all four types of cognitive tasks than those who were in the nonexercise groups, no matter what age or gender and no matter what type of aerobic exercise was done. These are very impressive results. This meta-analysis tells us that the smaller, individual studies were all tapping into the same big pot—the idea that aerobic exercise is good for the cognitive functioning of people over 55.

Figure 1.8 Meta-analysis of 18 studies shows that aerobic exercise causes better performance in older adults on four types of cognitive tasks.

SOURCE: Colcombe & Kramer (2003).

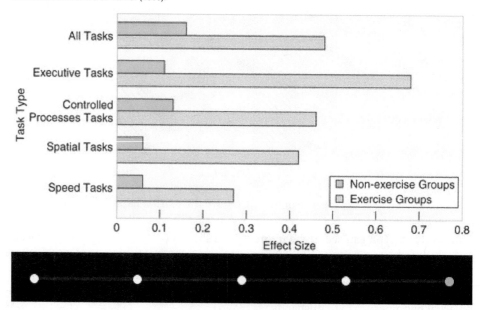

1.6.4: Designs

The closing statement researchers are allowed to make depends on what kind of research design has been used, experimental or nonexperimental. If it is experimental, researchers are able to say their findings show that their factor of interest *caused* the change observed in their subjects. If it is not experimental research, they must limit themselves to saying that their results show a relationship or an association with the change.

The distinctions between experimental and nonexperimental designs could fill a whole book (and there are a number of good ones available), but for now, let me just say that the feature that distinguishes experimental designs from nonexperimental designs is how much control the experimenter has over the way the study is conducted. In the strictest sense of the word, an **experimental design** has a control group, the participants are selected randomly from the population of interest, they are assigned randomly to groups, there is random assignment of groups to treatment and control conditions, and there is a high degree of control over any outside factors that might affect the outcome. The more of these features that are present, the stronger the case the researcher can make for causality. Table 1.4 shows three types of experimental designs and the presence or absence of these controls.

Table 1.4 Experimental Designs and Their Comparative Features

	Pre-Experimental Design	True Experimental Design	Quasi-Experimental Design
Presence of a control group?	In some cases, but usually not	Always	Often
Random selection of subjects from a population?	No	Yes	No
Random assignment of subjects to groups?	No	Yes	No
Random assignment of treatment to groups?	No	Yes	No
Degree of control over extraneous variables	None	Yes	Some

Hide All Cells	Show All Cells

SOURCE: Salkind (2011).

Experimental designs include true experiments, pre-experiments, and quasi-experiments, depending on which of the controls listed in the table are present. These experiments are difficult to conduct and are not very useful in answering developmental research questions. One reason is that when comparisons are made between age groups (or between groups of people at different stages of life, such as preretirement versus postretirement), the participants cannot be assigned to groups; they are already in one group or the other. That automatically takes a large amount of control out of the hands of the researcher and opens the door for a number of problems.

OTHER DESIGNS   Other designs include descriptive research and qualitative research. **Descriptive research** tells the current state of the participants on some measure of interest. The number of people of different ages who die of suicide each year is descriptive research. The rate of births to unmarried women over the past 50 years is descriptive research. And the cross-sectional, longitudinal, and sequential studies discussed earlier are descriptive research. What they have in common is the lack of a high level of experimenter control. They are still valuable sources of information on development.

Qualitative research is, quite simply, research without the numbers. It is a very old tradition that has only recently been included in developmental sciences. Although research without numbers may sound very enticing to students who have just completed a statistics course, it is not really a replacement for **quantitative research** (research with the numbers), but a different approach that is used to supplement quantitative research. Qualitative research includes case studies, interviews, participant observations, direct observations, and exploring documents, artifacts, and archival records. If you have ever done genealogy research to find your family history in old records and documents, you have done a form of qualitative research.

WRITING PROMPT

If you had access to your hometown newspaper's archives from 100 years ago, what kind of qualitative research could you do that would shed some light on adult development then versus now?

> The response entered here will appear in the performance dashboard and can be viewed by your instructor.

Submit

An example of qualitative research is a study by sociologists Amy Hequembourg and Sara Brallier (2005). They were interested in the role transitions that go on among adult siblings when their elderly parents need care. We have long been aware that daughters are most likely to be the major caregiver of an aging parent, but these researchers found eight brother–sister pairs and interviewed them at length about their roles and feelings about their caregiving responsibilities. They recorded the answers in detail and then spent many months analyzing them. The finished product was a very interesting view of these families. Yes, the sisters did more, but sometimes they were pleased to be in that role. And other times the brothers stepped in and took over. There was evidence of adult sisters and brothers growing closer to each other as they shared the care for their parents. Although it was a study of only 16 participants, it gave more depth than a questionnaire sent out to 5,000. Clearly there is a place in developmental psychology for this type of research, and I am pleased to see it being discussed in research methods books.

Qualitative research is not easy. It needs to be carefully planned, the sources need to be wisely chosen, and questions need to be designed to focus on the topic at hand. If the research involves spending a lot of time with the people being interviewed, the experimenter needs to be able to remain as objective as possible. Data must be recorded precisely and completely. And then the findings need to be organized and written up to share with others.

Qualitative research is an excellent way to begin a new line of research. Epidemiologist David Snowden, former director of the Nun Study of the School Sisters of Notre Dame, started his research by visiting with the elderly nuns in a convent in Minnesota. As a beginning professor, he had no idea what he wanted to do for a research program, but one day he stumbled onto a room that contained the archives of the convent. Each sister had a file going back to her first days as a nun, often 50 or 60 years before. They had all written essays about their childhoods and why they wanted to be nuns. Snowdon (2001) wrote that "for an epidemiologist, this sort of find is equivalent to an archaeologist's discovering an undisturbed tomb or a paleontologist's unearthing a perfectly preserved skeleton" (p. 24). From this beginning, he began the research that became his career. For example, he and his colleagues (Riley, Snowdon, Derosiers, et al., 2005) found that the more complex the language in the essays the nuns had written as young women, the less likely they were to have Alzheimer's disease in late adulthood. Some of his other research findings are discussed later in this text, but for now, this serves as a good example of qualitative research based on archival records.

1.7: A Final Word about Adulthood Development

1.7 **Express the quest to know the universal rules and processes that influence aging**

On a personal note, I approach the topic of this book both as a developmental psychologist and on a more personal level. Like many people, I am on this journey of adulthood with my sisters, my husband, my friends, my adult children, and now my college-aged grandchildren who are in emerging adulthood, so my interest is both scientific and personal. I want to understand how it all works and why, both because that is what I have chosen for my career and also because it is what I think about a good deal of the time that I am not at work. My journey through adulthood is no doubt similar to yours, but it is also different in other ways. What I am searching for in this text are the basic rules or processes that account for both the similarities and the differences. I hope you can share with me the sense of adventure in the scientific search as well as in the personal journey.

Summary: Introduction to Adult Development

LISTEN TO THE AUDIO:

`06:18`

1. Developmental psychology includes the study of change and stability over time during childhood, adolescence, and adulthood. The study of adult development covers the time from emerging adulthood to the end of life and is based on empirical research.

2. This text covers individual differences between people and also the commonalities they share. It looks at stability and change, continuity and stages, typical development and atypical development, and the outer and inner changes that occur over the years of adulthood.

3. Sources of change in adulthood are classified into three types: (a) Normative age-graded influences are linked to age and happen to most people as they grow older. They come from both biological and environmental causes, and also from interactions between the two. (b) Normative history-graded influences are factors that affect only some people or groups. These changes include cultural conditions

and cohort experiences. One of the best-studied cohorts is the group of people who lived through the Great Depression. (c) Nonnormative life events are unique to the individual and cause developmental changes that are not shared by many.

4. Sources of stability in adulthood include genetics and environmental influences and also the interactions between the two.

5. The word age has many more meanings than how many years one has been alive (chronological age). In various usages it also designates estimates of a person's physical condition compared to others (physical age), the abilities one displays in dealing effectively with the environment (psychological age), and the roles one has taken on (social age). The last three make up a person's functional age. Developmental psychologists seldom depend on chronological age alone in their studies because of these factors. Instead, most use age groups or stages in life.

6. This text will approach the topic of adult development using the tenets of life-span developmental psychology, a set of ideas introduced by Baltes in 1980 that

encouraged psychologists to study development at many ages and to view development in a broader scope than they had before.

7. A second approach this text will take is based on the ecological systems view introduced by Bronfenbrenner in 1979. This set of ideas inspired psychologists to consider the whole person, not just the isolated behavior of a participant in a laboratory experiment.

8. The first step in doing developmental research is to select a research method. There are three possibilities: (a) cross-sectional studies gather data on a group of people representing different age groups, (b) longitudinal studies follow the same people over a longer period of time, gathering data at several points along the way, and (c) sequential studies combine the preceding methods by conducting two longitudinal studies during different time periods, thereby making it possible to do both longitudinal and cross-sectional comparisons. There are pros and cons to each method.

9. After a method is chosen, a researcher needs to choose an appropriate measure. Some of the most common ones in developmental research are personal interviews, survey questionnaires, and standardized tests.

10. The next step in developmental research is selecting analyses. Most research uses either comparison of means, which involves computing the means of the measurement scores for each group and testing them statistically to see if they are significantly different, or correlational analysis, in which the researcher compares scores on several measurements for the participants to see if there is a relationship between the characteristics being measured. Correlations are used to show both change and stability. They are also used to demonstrate heritability by comparing scores of monozygotic twin pairs with scores of dizygotic twin pairs.

11. The meta-analysis is another way to analyze research data. It combines data from a number of previously published studies that focus on the same research question. This is done by combining the data and reanalyzing it as a larger, more powerful study.

12. The final step in developmental research involves stating conclusions, and this depends on whether the research design was experimental or not. If the design was experimental, it is possible to conclude that the results of the study were caused by the factor of interest. Experimental designs include true experiments, preexperiments, and quasi-experiments, and they differ in the amount of control the experimenter has over the conditions of the study and the outside factors that might also cause similar results. Experimental designs are not often used in developmental research.

13. Research designs that are not experimental provide valuable knowledge about development even though researchers cannot conclude that their factor of interest caused the results. These designs include descriptive research and qualitative research.

SHARED WRITING: STABLE THEMES

Consider this chapter's discussion of stable "themes" over the course of adult development. Why do you think this is? Write a short response that your classmates will read. Be sure to discuss specific examples from your own life regarding stable themes and themes that have changed over time.

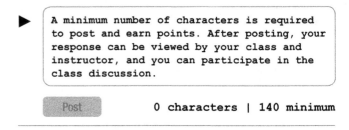

▶ A minimum number of characters is required to post and earn points. After posting, your response can be viewed by your class and instructor, and you can participate in the class discussion.

Post   0 characters | 140 minimum

Chapter 1 Quiz: Introduction to Adult Development

Chapter 2
Physical Changes

∨ Learning Objectives

2.1 Analyze theories of primary aging arguing in favor and against each

2.2 Assess physical changes during adult development including outward appearance, faculties, bodily systems, and individual differences

2.3 Discuss changes in physical behavior like decline of stamina, dexterity, and balance; changes in sleep habits and sexual functioning

2.4 Identify the proportionate relationship between aging and individual differences based on genetics, lifestyle, race, and socio-economic factors

2.5 Discuss becoming young once again

2.6 Relate age to physical changes

LISTEN TO THE AUDIO:

03:37

WHEN MY GRANDSON, Nicholas, was 5, I was writing a book on child development. I wanted to open each chapter with a warm and personal story that would introduce the topic (much as I am doing now). Nicholas was a rich source of material. I was writing about children's cognitive processes, and I knew that at 5, they tend to judge everything at face value. They are convinced that the glass with the highest level of lemonade holds the most, regardless of how narrow the diameter is. The longest line of M&Ms has the most candy, regardless of how far apart they are spaced. And people who are taller are older, period.

So I asked Nicholas who was older, Grandma or Dad. He quickly answered that Dad (who is 5' 11") is certainly older than Grandma (who is 5' 7"), although he also knew that Dad was Grandma's son. He knew that Dad was 30 and Grandma was 54, and that 54 is more than 30, but logic is not important at 5. I was pleased—so far, he was perfectly illustrating the important concepts in my textbook chapter.

Then I asked, "How do you tell how old a person is?" I expected him to comment on the height or the color of their hair. But I was surprised when he replied, "You look at their hands." Hands? Well, I thought, I guess that's true. The hands of older people have dark spots and larger knuckles. Adolescents have larger hands in proportion to their other body parts. And infants have hands that are closed in reflexive fists. I thought he may be onto something interesting. So I asked, "What do you look for when you look at their hands?"

"Their fingers," he said patiently. He held up one hand with outstretched fingers and said, "You ask someone how old they are and when they hold up their fingers, you count them. See, I'm five."

Nicholas's hypothesis of determining age by looking at hands may hold up with kids up to the age of 10, but it's not much use in adulthood. In fact, the further we get from "holding up fingers" to tell our ages, the more difficult it is to determine age just by looking at someone. One of the reasons is that we have two processes of aging going on. **Primary aging**, which is the topic of this chapter, consists of the gradual, inevitable changes that will happen to most of us as we go through adulthood. Research over the last few decades has given us two major facts about primary aging: first, that it can be differentiated from disease, and second, that there are many different "normal" time lines for primary aging (National Institutes of Health, 2008). **Secondary aging**, which will be the topic of the following chapter, refers to the changes that happen more suddenly and that are usually the result of disease, injury, or some environmental event.

I will begin this chapter with some of the theories of primary aging and then describe the changes in the major systems of the body most adults experience as they age. Then I will discuss the effects of primary aging on complex behaviors like sleep and sexual activity. Finally, I will cover some of the individual differences that are found in primary aging patterns and answer the age-old question, "Can we turn back the clock?"

2.1: Theories of Primary Aging

2.1 Analyze theories of primary aging arguing in favor and against each

Why do we age? This has been the subject of speculation for centuries, but the technology necessary to evaluate it is fairly new. As a result, the biology of aging is a relatively young field with a plethora of data but no grand theories on which a significant number of scientists agree (Finch & Austad, 2001). Instead, a hundred or more fledgling theories have been offered by various biologists. As behavior geneticists Gerald

McClearn and Debra Heller (2000) suggested, "The scientific pessimist might lament the absence of a compelling unified theory; the scientific optimist will revel in the richness of the empirical data and the diversity of the current theoretical propositions" (p. 1). I have selected a few of the more recent theories to describe here, along with support and criticism for each.

2.1.1: Oxidative Damage

One theory of primary aging is based on random damage that takes place on the cellular level. This process, first identified by biogerontologist Denham Harmon in 1956, involves the release of **free radicals**, molecules, or atoms that possess an unpaired electron and are by-products of normal body metabolism as well as a response to diet, sunlight, X-rays, and air pollution. These molecules enter into many potentially damaging chemical reactions, most of which the healthy body can resist or repair. But, according to this theory, our resistance and repair functions decline as we age, the oxidative damage increases, and the result is primary aging. We now have over 60 years of research showing that oxidative damage *accompanies* aging, but we still are not able to state that it *causes* aging (Bengston, Gans, Putney, et al., 2009). The most researchers are willing to say is that oxidative damage is one of several factors involved in primary aging (Lustgarten, Muller, & Van Remmen, 2011).

A number of vitamins and vitamin-like substances have been identified as **antioxidants**, substances with properties that protect against oxidative damage. Some of these are vitamins E and C, coenzyme Q10, beta-carotene, and creatine. Many nutritional supplements on the market contain large doses of these substances and advertise themselves as having antioxidant properties. However, there is no evidence that they can delay primary aging in humans or extend the life span. Most people in developed countries have adequate supplies of these nutrients in their diets, and no benefit has been shown for higher-than-recommended doses.

2.1.2: Genetic Limits

The theory of genetic limits centers on the observation that every species has a characteristic maximum life span. Something between 110 and 120 years appears to be the effective maximum life span for humans, whereas for turtles it is far longer, and for chickens (or dogs, or cats, or cows, or most other mammals) it is far shorter. Such observations led cellular biologist Leonard Hayflick (1977, 1994) to propose that there is a genetic program setting the upper age limit of each species. Hayflick showed that when human embryo cells are placed in nutrient solutions and observed over a period of time, the cells divide only about 50 times, after which they stop dividing and enter a state known as **replicative senescence** (Hornsby, 2001). Furthermore, cells from the embryos of longer-lived creatures such as the Galápagos tortoise double perhaps 100 times, whereas chicken embryo cells double only about 25 times. The number of divisions a species will undergo before reaching replicative senescence is known as its **Hayflick limit**, and there is a positive correlation between that number and the species' longevity. According to the genetic limits theory, primary aging results when we approach the Hayflick limit for the human species, exhausting our cells' ability to replicate themselves.

The suggested mechanism behind the genetic limits theory of aging comes from the discovery that chromosomes in many human body cells (and those of some other species, too) have, at their tips, lengths of repeating DNA called **telomeres**. Telomeres are necessary for DNA replication and appear to serve as timekeepers for the cells. On average, the telomeres in the cells of a middle-aged adult are shorter than those of a young adult; the telomeres of an older adult are shorter still. And once the telomeres are used up, the cell stops dividing. In addition, telomere lengths for males and females are the same at birth, but by adulthood, they are longer in females than in males, leading some to ask whether this is related to the fact that women live about 6 years longer than men in developed countries (Aviv, 2011).

Telomere length has been related to both primary and secondary aging. People who are at high risk for heart disease or type 2 diabetes have shorter telomere lengths than healthy individuals the same age. Telomere length has also been related to chronic stress conditions. In one study, a group of mothers who were caregivers for children with chronic illnesses were found to have telomere lengths equivalent to women 10 years older who were caregivers for healthy children (Epel, Blackburn, Lin, et al., 2004). Seemingly, the stress that comes with caring for a child with chronic illness adds 10 years to one's biological age.

Is it possible to slow down the loss of telomere length in one's cells? This was the focus of a study by medical researcher Tim D. Spector and his colleagues (Cherkas, Hunkin, Kato, et al., 2008), who interviewed over 2,400 individuals between 18 and 81 years of age about their leisure time exercise. Following the interview, a sample of blood was drawn from each participant, and the telomeres from their white blood cells were examined. The researchers found that those in the light, moderate, and heavy exercise groups had cells with significantly longer telomeres than those in the inactive group. Participants in the heavy exercise group had telomere lengths similar to the people in the inactive group who were 10 years younger. The heavy exercise group averaged about 30 minutes of exercise a day; the inactive group averaged just over 2 minutes a day. It was interesting that the exercise described in this study was "leisure time exercise." When researchers examined the amount of work-related exercise the participants got (such as stocking shelves in a grocery store), the results were not significant. This suggests that the "leisure" mode is a key feature of beneficial exercise.

It seems that shorter telomere lengths are good predictors of premature aging and age-related diseases. It also seems that shorter telomere lengths go hand in hand with poor health habits such as obesity, cigarette smoking, and a sedentary lifestyle. None of this research shows that telomere length *determines* the rate of aging, but the relationships are very strong (Aviv, 2011). Again, the advice to take away from this research is to eat healthy, find ways to reduce or cope with chronic stressors, and enjoy leisure time exercise regularly.

2.1.3: Caloric Restriction

One of the most promising explanations of why we age is that aging is connected with our diets—not so much what we eat, but how many calories we metabolize per day. This idea was first suggested 60 years ago when researchers studied the effects of **caloric restriction** (CR) on lab animals by feeding them diets drastically reduced in calories (60% to 70% of normal diets), but containing all the necessary nutrients. Early researchers found that animals put on these diets shortly after weaning stayed youthful longer, suffered fewer late-life diseases, and lived significantly longer than their normally fed counterparts (McCay, Crowell, & Maynard, 1935). More recent studies have supported these findings. For example, studies with rhesus monkeys show that animals on caloric restriction show a lower incidence of age-related disease, including type 2 diabetes, cancer, heart disease, and brain atrophy (Colman, Anderson, Johnson, et al., 2009).

Would caloric restriction increase human longevity? One problem is that to receive maximum benefits, we would have to reduce our caloric intake by 30%. People eating a 2,000-calorie diet would need to cut back to 1,400 calories—difficult enough for a few months, but close to impossible as a lifetime regimen. Limited studies using human subjects on CR have shown some positive health benefits such as protection against type 2 diabetes and heart disease and a reduction in cancer incidence and cancer deaths (Fontana, Colman, Holloszy, et al., 2011); however, a number of adverse effects have also been documented. These include cold intolerance, increases in stress hormones, decreases in sex hormones, and the psychological effects of extreme hunger—obsessive thoughts about food, social withdrawal, irritability, and loss of interest in sex. If the goals of caloric restriction are longevity and freedom from disease, this practice seems successful. But if the goals are quality of life, severely restricting calories does not seem to be the answer, especially in the developed countries of the world, where food cues are abundant and attractive (Polivy, Herman, & Coelho, 2008).

WRITING PROMPT

What would a daily meal plan be for someone on a diet of 1,400 calories per day?

▶ The response entered here will appear in the performance dashboard and can be viewed by your instructor.

Submit

Scientists have now turned to finding a substance that provides the same health and longevity as caloric restriction without reducing normal food intake. Several candidates have been found, such as *resveratrol*, a substance found in red wine that extended the life spans of yeast, worms, and flies. However, the results on mammals were disappointing. Another substance, *rapamycin*, has been more promising (Kapahi & Kockel, 2011). Originally found in soil collected on Easter Island, rapamycin inhibits cell growth and was first used as an antirejection medication for organ transplant patients. Studies of the effects of rapamycin on mice extended maximum life span by some 12% (Miller, Harrison, Astle, et al., 2011), including some mice that were the human equivalent of 60 years of age (Harrison, Strong, Sharp, et al., 2009). Rapamycin works to block the effects of a protein called *TOR*, which scientists believe is implicated in many age-related diseases and perhaps primary aging itself. TOR has the effect of sensing the availability of food in the organism, and in times of plenty, it becomes active and directs cell metabolism and division. When food is scarce (as in caloric restriction), TOR reduces cell metabolism and division, and one of the results seems to be increased longevity (Sharp, 2011). Unfortunately, rapamycin itself has side effects that rule it out for human consumption, but it is the most compelling evidence I have seen that aging in mammals (maybe eventually humans) can someday be slowed by a pharmaceutical product.

2.1.4: A Word on Theories of Primary Aging

I should caution you again not to expect that any single theory will be proven to be the one and only correct answer to the question of why we age. In fact, the "separate" theories presented here are beginning to cross boundaries and merge. For example, researchers who suggest that caloric restriction may reduce the neuronal damage of Alzheimer's disease and Parkinson's disease explain that the mechanism for this is that it protects against oxidative stress in the DNA of neurons, an explanation that blends the dietary intake theory and the oxidative stress theory. And the study of high-stressed women with prematurely shortened telomeres also reports that these women had more free radical damage to their cells than women in the control group—a finding that combines genetic limits and oxidative stress.

What can I say? This is clearly a good example of the process of scientific investigation. It is not so much a competition over which theory is right, but different researchers approaching the same question, "Why do we age?" with their own methods and theories, converging on similar answers that bring us closer to the truth.

2.2: Physical Changes During Adulthood

2.2   Assess physical changes during adult development including outward appearance, faculties, bodily systems, and individual differences

Later chapters in this book cover changes in thinking abilities, personality, spirituality, and disease patterns during adulthood. This one deals with the physical aspect of adult development, beginning with outward appearance and working through the senses, various systems of the body, and ending with a discussion of individual differences in primary aging.

2.2.1 Outward Appearance

Most of us are concerned about our outward appearance and how it will change as we navigate the years of adulthood. Many of the most obvious signs of aging belong in this category, and we see them in our parents and grandparents, in our friends, and sometimes in our mirrors. I have selected two categories for this section—weight and body composition, skin and hair. These are concerns for adults of all ages, including textbook authors.

Studies of adults in the United States show that changes in total body weight follow a pattern over adulthood, as you can see in Figure 2.1, first rising from the 20s to the 40s, staying level into the 50s and 60s, then declining in the 70s, following the shape on a graph of an inverted U (Rossi, 2004). The upswing in weight that takes place during young adulthood and middle age can be attributed to our tendency to become more and more sedentary during that time without changing our eating habits to compensate (Masoro, 2011). The downturn in total body weight that takes place in later adulthood is due to loss of bone density and muscle tissue (Florido, Tchkonia, & Kirkland, 2011).

Figure 2.1 Appearance of Men and Women

Both men and women gain weight in young adulthood and middle adulthood, losing in the late 50s, but in slightly different patterns.

SOURCE: Adapted from Rossi (2004).

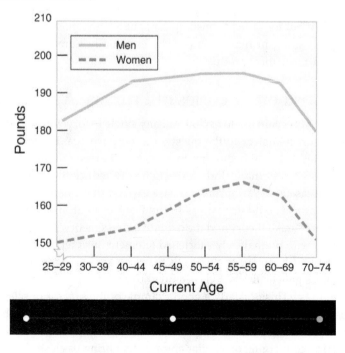

WEIGHT   Along with changes in total body weight, there are also changes in where the weight is distributed; starting in middle age, fat slowly leaves the face and extremities and begins to accumulate around the abdomen, resulting in a loss of plump cheeks and lips, a loss of protective padding on the soles of the feet, and a gain in waistline circumference.

When a person's body weight is higher than what is considered to be optimally healthy for their height, they are classified as overweight. This is a concern for adults of all ages, and rightly so—almost two thirds of us in the United States are above optimal weight. Being overweight can impair movement and flexibility, and it can alter appearance. Our society does not generally view overweight individuals as healthy and attractive, and this can result in social and economic discrimination (Lillis, Levin, & Hayes, 2011).

When the weight-to-height ratio increases to the point that it has an adverse effect on the person's health, it is a medical condition known as **obesity**. Over one third of adults in the United States have this condition—or half of the overweight people in this country have total body weight that puts them at risk for numerous health disorders.

BODY   How do you stand in the body composition evaluation? Table 2.1 shows how to find your **body mass index (BMI)** by finding your height (in inches) in the far left column and moving across that row to find your weight. The number at the top of the column is your BMI. According to the Centers for Disease Control and Prevention (CDC, 2011b), BMIs less than 19 are considered underweight, 19 to 24 are considered normal weight, 25 to 29 are overweight, and 30 and above are obese. This is not a perfect system because some healthy, very muscular people would be assigned the "overweight" label based on their height and weight, but the BMI is used by most health organizations and medical researchers around the world to evaluate body composition.

WRITING PROMPT

Where do some of the people on the "Ten Most Beautiful" lists rank on the BMI scale? What are the implications of this and why does it matter? Write a short response that will be read by your instructor.

▶ The response entered here will appear in the performance dashboard and can be viewed by your instructor.

Submit

Adults who are 60 and over are slightly more likely to be obese, but as you can see in Figure 2.2, the proportion of obese adults in other age groups is not much lower (Ogden, Carroll, Kit, et al., 2012). Still, the fact remains that over one third of all adults (and 17% of children) have total body weight that is considered a serious medical condition (CDC, 2011b).

What can be done about age-related changes in body composition? An active lifestyle in young adulthood and middle adulthood will help minimize age-related weight gain and the amount of fat that accumulates in the abdomen at middle age. Strength training and flexibility exercises throughout adulthood will help maintain bone density and muscle. Healthy eating habits can reduce excess fat. However, nothing has been found that will totally *prevent* these changes. Even people who are top athletes throughout the adult years decrease in bone mass and muscle to some extent, just not as much as those who are sedentary (Masaro, 2011).

Table 2.1 Body Mass Index (BMI) Table

To use this table, find the appropriate height in the left-hand column. Move across row to a given weight. The number at the top of the column is the BMI at that height and weight.

BMI	Normal Weight						Overweight					Obese											Weight (Pounds)
Height (Inches)	19	20	21	22	23	24	25	26	27	28	29	30	31	32	33	34	35	36	37	38	39	40	
58	91	96	100	105	110	115	119	124	129	134	138	143	148	153	158	162	167	172	177	181	186	191	
59	94	99	104	109	114	119	124	128	133	138	143	148	153	158	163	168	173	178	183	188	193	198	
60	97	102	107	112	118	123	128	133	138	143	148	153	158	163	168	174	179	184	189	194	199	204	
61	100	106	111	116	122	127	132	137	143	148	153	158	164	169	174	180	185	190	195	201	206	211	
62	104	109	115	120	126	131	136	142	147	153	158	164	169	175	180	186	191	196	202	207	213	218	
63	107	113	118	124	130	135	141	146	152	158	163	169	175	180	186	191	197	203	208	214	220	225	
64	110	116	122	128	134	140	145	151	157	163	169	174	180	186	192	197	204	209	215	221	227	232	
65	114	120	126	132	138	144	150	156	162	168	174	180	186	192	198	204	210	216	222	228	234	240	
66	118	124	130	136	142	148	155	161	167	173	179	186	192	198	204	210	216	223	229	235	241	247	
67	121	127	134	140	146	153	159	166	172	178	185	191	198	204	211	217	223	230	236	242	249	255	
68	125	131	138	144	151	158	164	171	177	184	190	197	203	210	216	223	230	236	243	249	256	262	
69	128	135	142	149	155	162	169	176	182	189	196	203	209	216	223	230	236	243	250	257	263	270	
70	132	139	146	153	160	167	174	181	188	195	202	209	216	222	229	236	243	250	257	264	271	278	
71	136	143	150	157	165	172	179	186	193	200	208	215	222	229	236	243	250	257	265	272	279	286	
72	140	147	154	162	169	177	184	191	199	206	213	221	228	235	242	250	258	265	272	279	287	294	
73	144	151	159	166	174	182	189	197	204	212	219	227	235	242	250	257	265	272	280	288	295	302	
74	148	155	163	171	179	186	194	202	210	218	225	233	241	249	256	264	272	280	287	295	303	311	
75	152	160	168	176	184	192	200	208	216	224	232	240	248	256	264	272	279	287	295	303	311	319	
76	156	164	172	180	189	197	205	213	221	230	238	246	254	263	271	279	287	295	304	312	320	328	

SOURCE: Centers for Disease Control and Prevention (2011b).

Figure 2.2 About one-third of adults in the U.S. are obese. The greatest proportion is found in those 60 years of age and older.

SOURCE: Ogden, Carroll, Kit, et al. (2012).

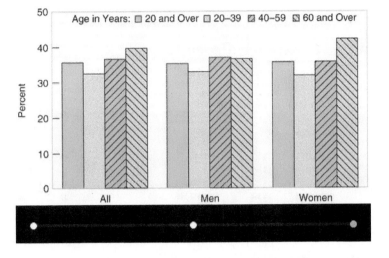

SKIN Youth is signaled by smooth skin, but beginning about age 45, wrinkles of the skin become evident, resulting in part from the redistribution of body fat discussed in the previous section. It also occurs because of a loss of elasticity in the skin, part of a pervasive loss of elasticity that affects muscles, tendons, blood vessels, and internal organs as well as skin. The loss of elasticity is especially noticeable in skin that has been continually exposed to the sun, such as the skin of the face and hands.

From a quick trip down the beauty aisle of a drugstore or a look at the annual earnings of a cosmetic company, you would get the impression that many miracle cures are available for aging skin. However, the only effective products available over the counter are those that will cover up the wrinkles and age spots. One product available by prescription seems to be effective in reversing skin damage due to exposure to the sun. Several well-designed lab studies have shown that applying Retin-A (tretinoin) to the skin for several months not only changed the appearance of damaged skin but also reversed some of the underlying changes that had occurred (Rosenfeld, 2005). It is much easier to prevent sun damage by limiting strong, direct sun exposure. When that is not possible, it helps to use sunblock and protective clothing (Porter, 2009).

WRITING PROMPT

What are your thoughts on products that claim to restore age or hide the signs of aging? Are these products helpful emotionally? Why or why not? Write a brief response that will be read by your teacher. Be sure to include specific details.

▶ The response entered here will appear in the performance dashboard and can be viewed by your instructor.

Submit

Skin damage that is too severe to be remedied by prescription creams can be treated by medical procedures, such as chemical peels or microdermabrasion, in which the outer layers of the skin are removed. As you might expect, these minimally invasive procedures are more expensive than skin creams and carry more risks. Nevertheless, many people have been pleased with the results and find that when they look younger, they feel younger. Table 2.2 shows the top procedures performed by plastic surgeons in the United States, along with the average surgeon's fee and the percentage of patients having these procedures in each of five age groups. As you can see, the 40- to 54-year-old age group makes up the largest segment (48%) for these procedures (American Society of Plastic Surgeons, 2012).

Table 2.2 Top Plastic Surgery Procedures in the U.S., Prices, Number, and Age of Patients for 2011

⊗ Minimally Invasive Procedures

Procedure	Average Surgeon's Fee	Number of Procedures Performed in 2011	Percent of Patients in Each Age Group				
			13–19 Years	20–29 Years	30–39 Years	40–54 Years	55+ Years
Minimally Invasive Procedures							
Botox	$365	5,670,788	0	2	19	57	23
Soft-tissue filler	$529	1,891,158	0	3	11	50	36
Chemical peel	$653	1,110,464	1	1	12	43	43
Laser hair removal	$358	1,078,612	6	22	30	36	6
Microdermabrasion	$141	900,439	1	8	24	43	24

Source: American Society of Plastic Surgeons (2012).

⊗ Cosmetic Surgery Procedures

Procedure	Average Surgeon's Fee	Number of Procedures Performed in 2011	Percent of Patients in Each Age Group				
			13–19 Years	20–29 Years	30–39 Years	40–54 Years	55+ Years
Cosmetic Surgery Procedures							
Breast augmentation	$3,388	307,180	3	29	36	29	2
Nose reshaping	$4,422	243,772	14	30	24	21	10
Liposuction	$2,859	204,702	2	15	33	40	10
Eyelid surgery	$2,741	196,286	1	2	7	42	48
Face-lift	$6,426	119,026	0	0	1	33	65

Source: American Society of Plastic Surgeons (2012).

Men make up about 10% of plastic surgery patients. Surgical procedures that are popular with both genders are nose reshaping, liposuction, and eyelid surgery. Women have breast augmentation and tummy tucks; men have breast reduction and face-lifts. There has been a recent increase in two other surgical procedures for men—chin augmentation and lip augmentation (American Society of Plastic Surgeons, 2012).

Several minimally invasive procedures have increased in popularity recently for both men and women. One is injections of Botox, a diluted preparation of a neurotoxin that paralyzes the muscles under the skin and eliminates creases and frown lines. This is now the most frequent procedure done by plastic surgeons for both men and women. Another popular procedure is injections of Restylane (hyaluronic acid). This is a natural substance found in connective tissues throughout the body, and it cushions, lubricates, and keeps the skin plump. When injected into soft tissue, it fills the area and adds volume, temporarily reducing wrinkles and sagging of the skin. Botox has to be reinjected every few months; Restylane lasts somewhat longer—typically 6 months. Both procedures need to be administered by qualified medical professionals, and they carry slight risks. And needless to say, all are expensive—with Botox at an average of $365 a treatment and hyaluronic acid being $529—which is not covered by most health-care insurance plans (American Society of Plastic Surgeons, 2012).

Table 2.2 also shows the proportion of patients having these procedures in each age group. For example, the younger group (13 to 19 years) favors nose reshaping, whereas the older group (55 and older) tends to have eyelid surgery

Primary aging means changes in hair color and skin texture for almost everyone.

and face-lifts. It's an interesting picture of what procedures are favored at different ages. It is also interesting to see that almost half of all procedures are undertaken by people from 40 to 54 years of age, probably reflecting the intersection of declining youth and increasing incomes.

HAIR   Hair loss is a common characteristic of aging for both men and women, although it is more noticeable in men. About 67% of men in the United States show some hair loss by the age of 35, and 85% show significantly thinning hair by 50 (American Hair Loss Association, 2010). Graying of hair differs widely among ethnic groups and among individuals within any one group. Asians, collectively, gray much later than Caucasians, for example.

Men and women have used chemical and natural dyes to conceal gray hair throughout history, and it is still a widespread practice today. Other old solutions in new boxes are wigs, hairpieces, and hair replacement "systems." In addition, drugs are available that slow down or reverse hair loss, some over the counter for men and women, such as Rogaine (monoxidil), and others by prescription for men only, such as Propecia (finasteride). The most extreme solution to hair loss is hair transplant, a surgical procedure in which small plugs of hair and skin are transplanted from a high-hair-growth area of the body to the hairless part of the scalp. Over 15,000 people in the United States underwent this procedure in 2011, about 70% of them men and most of them over the age of 55 (American Society of Plastic Surgeons, 2012). Again, none of these antiaging measures actually turns back the clock, but when they are done by experienced professionals and patients have realistic expectations, they can give a good morale boost for those who need one.

2.2.2: The Senses

A second series of body changes noted by many adults as they age affects the senses of vision, hearing, taste, and smell. Vision is by far the most researched, followed by hearing, with taste and smell trailing far behind.

VISION   This is the last sense to develop in infants and the first to show signs of decline in middle age. It is also the sensory system that has the most complex structure and function and, as you might guess, has the most to go wrong. A diagram of the parts of the eye is shown in Figure 2.3. During normal aging, the **lens** of the eye gradually thickens and yellows, and the **pupils** lose their ability to open efficiently in response to reduced light. The result is that the older we get, the less light gets to our **retinas**, the site of visual receptor cells. In fact by age 60, our retinas are getting only one third of the light they did in our 20s (Porter, 2009). One of the changes we experience as a result is a gradual loss of **visual acuity**, the ability to perceive detail in a visual

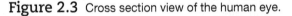

Figure 2.3   Cross section view of the human eye.

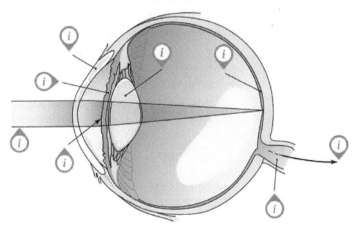

pattern. To test this yourself, try reading a small-print book both indoors where you usually study and outdoors in the full sunlight. If you are like most adults, you will notice that the clarity of the print is better in the bright sunlight.

Around the age of 45, the lens of the eye, which has been accumulating layers of cells since childhood and gradually losing elasticity, shows a sharp decrease in its ability to **accommodate**, or change shape to focus on near objects or small print. This loss further reduces overall visual acuity in middle-aged and older adults. Most people with reduced visual acuity or loss of near vision, a condition known as **presbyopia**, can function quite well with prescription glasses or contact lenses (Porter, 2009).

Another visual change that takes place throughout adulthood is a gradual loss of **dark adaptation**, the ability of the pupil to adjust to changes in the amount of available light. This begins around 30, but most people experience a marked decline after the age of 60. This causes minor inconveniences, such as difficulty reading menus in dimly lit restaurants or finding seats in darkened movie theaters. It also causes more dangerous situations, such as problems seeing road signs at night or recovering from the sudden glare of oncoming headlights (Porter, 2009). This is one of the reasons older people prefer attending matinee performances, making "early-bird" dinner reservations, and taking daytime classes at the university instead of participating in nighttime activities.

Three more age-related conditions in the visual system may or may not be part of normal aging, but they are so common that I will include them here. The first is **cataracts**, gradual clouding of the lens of the eye, so that images are no longer transmitted sharply and in accurate color to the retina. Cataracts are the most common eye disorder found in adulthood. More than half of adults over 80 either have cataracts or have had them surgically removed. This outpatient procedure is done quickly and safely under local anesthesia (National Eye Institute, 2012a). It involves removing the cloudy part of the lens and implanting an artificial lens that can even be designed to correct for visual acuity. Cataract surgery has become the most common surgical procedure in the United States; over 1.5 million are done each year. Despite the ease and success of surgery, and the fact that the procedure is covered under Medicare, cataracts remain a major cause of vision loss in the United States (Gohdes, Balamurugan, Larsen, et al., 2005) and the leading cause of blindness in the world (Hildreth, Burke, & Glass, 2009). Risk factors for cataracts are shown in Table 2.3.

A second common age-related condition of the visual system is **glaucoma**, a buildup of pressure inside the eye that ultimately can destroy the optic nerve and lead to blindness. Glaucoma is the second leading cause of blindness for all people in the United States and the first leading cause of blindness for people with African ancestry. Glaucoma can be treated with eye drops, laser treatment, or surgery, but first it has to be detected. What are the warning signs of glaucoma? Like other hypertension problems, there are not many. It is estimated that 2 million people in the United States currently have glaucoma, but only half are aware that they have it. Glaucoma can be detected as part of a routine eye examination, and it is recommended that people in high-risk groups be screened at age 40. Everyone should be screened at 60 (National Eye Institute, 2012b). Risk factors for glaucoma are also shown in Table 2.3.

Table 2.3 Risk Factors for Age-Related Visual Conditions

Cataracts	Glaucoma	Age-Related Macular Degeneration
• Increased age • Family history • Female gender • Diabetes • Sunlight exposure* • Smoking*	• Increased age • Family history • African or Mexican ancestry	• Increased age • Family history • European ancestry • Smoking*

*Can be controlled or prevented.

SOURCE: National Eye Institute (2012a, 2012b); Hildreth, Burke, & Glass (2009).

A third common condition of the visual system is age-related **macular degeneration**, a disorder that affects the retina, causing central vision loss. The cause of this disorder is not clear, but the prevalence is; symptoms of macular degeneration appear in about 10% of people 66 to 74 years of age and 30% of people 75 to 85 years of age (Klein, Chou, Klein, et al., 2011). Vitamin therapy and laser treatment have shown hopeful results for some types of this disorder, and rehabilitative interventions have helped people with low vision to function independently and increase their quality of life (Gohdes, Balamurugan, Larsen, et al., 2005). Risk factors for age-related macular degeneration are also included in Table 2.3.

The overall result of declining visual ability over middle and late adulthood can be limiting in many ways. Often older adults give up driving, which means they are no longer able to do their shopping and banking and no longer as able to visit friends, participate in leisure activities, attend religious services, or go to doctors' offices on their own. There is also a loss of status for some older adults when they must stop driving. Decreased vision is associated with many other problems in older adults, such as falls, hip fractures, family stress, and depression.

The World Health Organization (2011) estimates that over 80% of visual impairments worldwide can be prevented or cured. Problems involve lack of information about diagnosis and treatment, such as the mistaken belief many adults have that the eye exam given to renew drivers' licenses will screen for these visual conditions. Another problem is that many people in the United States and around the world live in areas without access to eye-care specialists. And still another problem arises when older adults and their family members believe that failing eyesight is an unavoidable part of aging (Gohdes, Balamurugan, Larsen, et al., 2005).

HEARING   Most adults begin to experience some hearing loss in their 30s, mainly of higher tones. There is also shortening of the *loudness scale*—that is, there is confusion between loud tones that are not being heard as well as before and softer tones that are still being heard accurately. Without the loud–soft discrimination, it is difficult to perceive which sounds are coming from nearby and which are from across a noisy room—which words are coming from your dinner partner and which from the server taking an order two tables over. This condition is known as **sensorineural hearing loss**, and it is caused by damage to the tiny hairs inside the **cochlea**, a small shell-shaped structure in the inner ear. This mechanism is responsible for picking up sound vibrations and turning them into nerve impulses that will be transmitted to the hearing centers of the brain.

WRITING PROMPT

What are some specific ways that severe hearing loss might cause problems in close relationships? Explain how these problems could be overcome. Write a short response that will be read by your teacher.

▶ | The response entered here will appear in the performance dashboard and can be viewed by your instructor.

Submit

By age 65, about a third of adults have some significant hearing impairment, and the numbers rise sharply thereafter. The best prevention of hearing loss is for people of all ages to limit exposure to loud noise, both on the job and in leisure activities. The louder the noise, the shorter the safe exposure time (National Institutes of Health, 2012). Workplace noise in the United States is regulated by the Department of Labor, and those standards are shown in Table 2.4, but many of our after-hours and weekend activities involve noise that exceeds those levels. For example, motorcycles produce 95 decibels of noise, snowmobiles 100 decibels, and rock concerts 110 decibels (American Speech-Language-Hearing Association, 2012).

Table 2.4 Permissible Noise Exposure

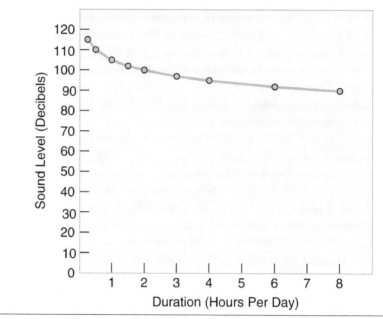

SOURCE: U.S. Department of Labor (2012).

An area of recent concern involves iPods and other MP3 players, which can produce 120 decibels of noise when turned to full volume. If you will look at Table 2.4, you will see that the highest noise considered is 115 decibels, and the safe exposure time is ¼ hour or less. Yet many adolescents and emerging adults play their iPods or other MP3 players at high volume for many hours of the day. We don't know how prevalent this is, but as of 2011, 400 million iPods and MP3 players had been sold worldwide (Albanesius, 2011). Recently, several European countries have enacted laws that limited the manufacture of MP3 players to 100 decibels, but soon afterward, websites appeared giving information about how to reprogram the MP3 player to override that limit (Valeo, 2012). At the same time, medical specialists reported a 20% increase during the last decade in the prevalence of hearing loss among 18- and 19-year-olds (Shargorodsky, Curhan, Curhan, et al., 2010). The solution here is education and self-monitoring, though many emerging adults consider themselves invulnerable to hearing loss and have confidence that the scientific community will find a cure by the time they are affected. (This should sound familiar to their middle-aged parents, professors, and textbook authors, who are currently experiencing mild hearing loss, probably due to rock concerts and motorcycle trips when they were that age.)

If hearing loss becomes a problem, hearing aids are available that feature digital technology, directional microphones, feedback control devices, and even specific programs for listening to music or listening to conversation. These devices amplify and direct sound to better its chance of being picked up by the impaired hearing system. When sensorineural hearing loss is severe, doctors may recommend *cochlear implants*, a surgical procedure that allows sound waves to bypass the hair cells and go directly to the acoustic nerve.

TASTE AND SMELL   Taste and smell depend on three mechanisms that interact to enable us to enjoy the food we eat and the fragrances in our environment. They also provide survival information that keeps us from eating food that is spoiled and warns us of dangerous substances such as smoke or gas leaks. These mechanisms consist of smell, taste, and common chemical sense. Smell takes place in the **olfactory membrane**, a specialized part of the nasal membrane. It consists of millions of receptors and thousands of different kinds of cells. This variety lets us experience subtle and complex flavors. In addition, we experience more basic flavors through the **taste buds**, which are receptor cells found on the tongue, mouth, and throat. Saliva dissolves food, and the molecules that are released stimulate the receptors. Taste buds specialize; they respond to either sweet or salty tastes (at the front of the tongue), sour tastes (on the sides of the tongue), or bitter tastes (at the back of the tongue). Irritating properties of food and odors are sensed by receptors on the moist surfaces of the mouth, nose, throat, and eyes. These convey the spiciness of chili peppers and the coolness of mint. All three types of receptors take information to different parts of the brain, where the total experience is integrated and translated into messages, such as knowing you are having a pleasurable dining experience or that the milk in your refrigerator has out-lived its expiration date (Fukunaga, Uematsu, & Sugimoto, 2005).

The ability to taste and smell declines over the adult years, beginning about 30 years of age and becoming more noticeable around 65 or 70. Over 2 million people in the United States have disorders of taste or smell, and most of them are older adults. This happens for several reasons. First, less saliva is produced in older people, reduc-ing the release of molecules in food to be sensed by the taste buds. Second, there are fewer taste buds—about half as many at 70 years of age as at 20; those that detect sweet and salty flavors decline more rapidly, making us salt our food and sweeten our coffee or tea to a greater extent than in earlier years. There is also a decrease in the number of odor receptors in the nose as we age (Rosenfeld, 2005).

The risk factors for loss of taste and smell are older age, belonging to the male gender, smoking, living in urban areas, and working in industries such as paper and chemical manufacturing.

Critical Thinking

What are some of the health and safety implications of older adults' decline in ability to detect tastes and smells?

2.2.3: Bones and Muscles

The major change involved in primary aging of the bones is calcium loss, which causes bones to become less dense. Peak bone mass is reached around the age of 30, followed by a gradual decline for both men and women, but the overall effect of this bone loss is greater for women for several reasons. First, women's bones are smaller and contain less calcium—in other words, even if the decline is equal, women have started out at a disadvantage. Second, the decline is not equal; women's bone loss rate shows a marked acceleration between the ages of 50 and 65, whereas men's decline is more gradual. Severe loss of bone mass, or **osteoporosis**, makes the bones more likely to break than those of a younger person. There is controversy over whether osteopo-rosis is a disease or not because the process is not distinguishable from normal aging of the bones, except in degree of severity. I have chosen to include it in this chapter, but it's a judgment call.

Osteoporosis is based on a measure of **bone mass density (BMD)**, which is easily determined with a test called a DXA scan (dual-energy X-ray absorptiometry scan) of the hips and spine. The results are compared to those of a young healthy person. BMD measures at either hip or spine that are more than 2.5 standard deviations below nor-mal are considered osteoporosis.

Osteoporosis affects 16% of women and 4% of men over 50. Figure 2.4 shows the prevalence of osteoporosis for men and women in four different age groups. As you can see, women are more apt to develop osteoporosis and to develop it at an earlier age than men (Looker, Borrud, Dawson-Hughes, et al., 2012).

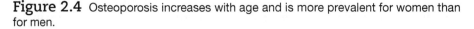

Figure 2.4 Osteoporosis increases with age and is more prevalent for women than for men.

SOURCE: Looker, Borrud, Dawson-Hughes, et al. (2012)

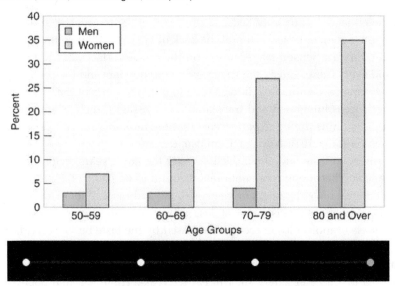

The biggest problem caused by osteoporosis is the increased risk of injury after a fall. Diminished eyesight and a decreased sense of balance result in a greater number of falls as we get older. When brittle bones are entered into the equation, falls can result in serious injury, disability, loss of independent living, and even death. The typical sites of breaks are wrist, spine, and hip.

New strategies to prevent osteoporosis focus on promoting bone health throughout life, starting with childhood, through proper diet containing required amounts of calcium and vitamin D. Healthy bones also require a regimen of exercise of the weight-bearing muscles, including high-impact exercise such as running and jumping (Kuehn, 2005).

Measuring bone mass density is becoming more and more a part of routine examinations by gynecologists, internists, and family physicians. Treatment of bone loss consists of vitamin D, estrogen, and drugs that increase the effect of estrogen and restore lost bone integrity, such as Fosomax (bisophonates). Recently more emphasis is being placed on *patient adherence* to treatment for bone loss. Patients are being urged to refill their prescriptions before they run out of medication and to follow the instructions carefully to ensure that the drug is being absorbed well into the system and to avoid unpleasant side effects. New medication-delivery systems are available that allow patients to take only one pill a month or one IV treatment a year. The major risk factors for osteoporosis are given in Table 2.5.

Table 2.5 Risk Factors for Osteoporosis and Osteoarthritis

Osteoporosis	Osteoarthritis
• Increased age	• Increased age
• Family history	• Female gender (after 50)
• Female gender	• Family history
• European, Asian, or Latin ancestry	• History of joint injury
• History of earlier bone fracture	• History of repeated joint stress*
• Sedentary lifestyle*	• Overweight or obese BMI*
• Smoking*	
• Excessive alcohol consumption*	
• Underweight BMI*	

* Can be controlled or prevented.

SOURCE: Adapted from National Institute on Aging (2013); CDC (2013).

Over the adult years, bones also change at the joints. **Osteoarthritis** is a condition that occurs when the soft cartilage that covers the ends of the bones wears away with use and age. This allows the bones to rub together and causes pain, swelling, and loss of motion at the joint. According to the CDC (2011a), over 27 million people in the United States have osteoarthritis, most of them over the age of 65. In older adults this condition is more prevalent in females; in younger adults it is more apt to appear in males and be the result of work and sports injuries.

Researchers are investigating the long-term effects of middle-school and high-school sports injuries. For example, professor of orthopedic surgery Klaus Siebenrock and his colleagues (Siebenrock, Ferner, Noble, et al., 2011) examined young male athletes who had played in an elite Swiss basketball club since the age of 8. They found that these young men were 10 times more likely to have hip deformities that put them at risk for osteoarthritis than a group of young men the same age who did not play high-level sports. In addition, 19% of the athletes reported at least one episode of hip pain in the previous 6 months, compared to 1.5% of a nonathlete group. Other studies have shown that adult athletes are significantly more likely to have osteoarthritis than nonathletes, and the prevalence depends on the sport. The most likely culprits are soccer, handball, basketball, baseball, and track and field events that involve running and jumping.

What can be done? Coaches and sports therapists recommend that young athletes and their parents should be aware of the consequences of extreme training and also take all injuries seriously, report them, allow adequate healing time, and not "play through pain." Hopefully there is a happy medium that can let young athletes excel at their sports and still have many years of pain-free mobility ahead of them.

Osteoarthritis, no matter the age or cause, can lead to depression, anxiety, feelings of helplessness, lifestyle limitations, job limitations, and loss of independence. However, most people with this condition find that the pain and stiffness of osteoarthritis can be relieved with anti-inflammatory and pain-relief medication and also an appropriate balance of rest and exercise to preserve range of motion. Weight management is also helpful for many.

Some people with osteoarthritis report that they have found help through alternative and complementary medical treatment, such as acupuncture, massage therapy, vitamins, and nutritional supplements. Others have injections of *hyaluranic acid,* which is a natural component of cartilage and joint fluid. Studies are currently being done on all these treatments. For example, researchers recently conducted a meta-analysis of 29 randomized control trials of over 17,000 patients who either had needles inserted at traditional acupuncture sites or at sham sites, chosen randomly. When researchers asked patients about the effectiveness of the treatment in alleviating osteoarthritis pain, there was a modest but significant difference in the two treatments, showing that the results patients experience from traditional acupuncture sites is more than a placebo effect (Vickers, Cronin, Maschino, et al., 2012).

When people with osteoarthritis cannot find relief with these treatments, there is the surgical option of joint replacement. In recent years, over 285,000 hip joints and over 600,000 knee joints have been replaced annually in the United States with high success rates. The vast majority of these surgeries are due to osteoarthritis (American Academy of Orthopaedic Surgeons, 2011a; 2011b). Risk factors for osteoarthritis are also shown in Table 2.5.

MUSCLE With age, most adults experience a gradual decrease in muscle mass and strength. The reason for this is that the number of muscle fibers decreases, probably as a result of reduced levels of growth hormones and testosterone. Another normal, age-related change is that muscles slowly lose their ability to contract as quickly as they did at younger ages. In addition, older people do not regain muscle mass as quickly as younger people after periods of inactivity, such as when recovering from illness or injury. All this being said, most older people have adequate muscle strength to attend to the tasks they need to do, and many stay at high levels of functioning as master athletes. However, even the best will notice some decline as they age.

Two types of exercise help rebuild muscle mass and strength: *resistance training*, which involves contracting muscles by lifting or pushing and holding the contraction for up to 6 seconds, and *stretching*, which lengthens muscles and increases flexibility. Stretches should be held for 5 seconds when beginning, but up to 30 seconds with increased practice. One good way to combine these two types of exercise is water aerobics, and I have used that as part of my exercise plan for many years. Stretching is much easier when the water is supporting much of your weight, and the water also provides more resistance than doing the same exercises on land. I'm lucky enough to live in south Florida and can attend the outdoor classes year-round. (But to be honest, they do heat the pool in the winter, and I stay home when the air temperature is below 60.)

2.2.4: Cardiovascular and Respiratory Systems

The cardiovascular system includes the heart and its blood vessels, and you may be glad to hear that the heart of an older person functions about as well as a younger person on a day-to-day basis unless there is some disease present. The difference arises when the cardiovascular system is challenged, as happens during heavy exercise. Then the older heart is slow to respond to the challenge and cannot increase its function as well as a younger heart.

Another age-related change is that the walls of the arteries become thicker and less supple, so they do not adjust to changes in blood flow as well as younger arteries. This loss of elasticity can cause hypertension, or high blood pressure, which is more prevalent in older people than in younger ones. Figure 2.5 shows the proportion of men and women of different ages in the United States who have been diagnosed with high blood pressure. As you can see, the proportion increases with age for both men and women, with the proportion of women being lower than men until 45 or so, equal to men from 45 to 64, and then higher than men after 64.

Figure 2.5 The proportion of men and women who have been diagnosed with high blood pressure increases with age. Men are more likely to have this condition in earlier adulthood; women in later adulthood.

SOURCE: American Heart Association (2012)

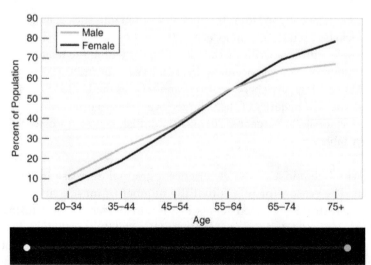

The respiratory system is made up of the lungs and the muscles involved in breathing. This system weakens slightly with age, but in healthy people who don't smoke, the respiratory function is good enough to support daily activities. As with the cardiovascular system, the difference is noticed when the system is challenged, as it is with vigorous exercise or at high altitudes (Beers, 2004).

One good piece of news is that regular exercise can reduce some of these effects of aging. Exercise can make the heart stronger and lower blood pressure; well-toned muscles can aid in circulation and breathing. Aerobic exercise, which includes brisk walking, running, and bicycling, is recommended for the cardiovascular and respiratory systems.

2.2.5: Brain and Nervous System

Many people believe that aging means deterioration of the brain, and research in the past seemed to support this, but recent studies using new technology have shown that loss of **neurons**, or brain cells, in primary aging is much less severe than once thought. Evidence now shows that the nervous system is characterized by lifelong **plasticity**, meaning that neurons are capable of making changes with age. For example, neurons form new connections with other neurons, change thresholds and response rates, and take over the functions of nearby neurons that have been damaged (Beers, 2004).

Another example of plasticity in the brain is **pruning**, the ability to shut down neurons that are not needed in order to "fine-tune" the system and improve functioning of the remaining neurons. Most pruning takes place in early infancy, but there is also evidence that some neuron loss in old age may reflect this process (Woodruff-Pak, 1997). So, although there is a loss in the total number of neurons with age, not all the loss translates into functional decline.

Along with neuronal loss and plasticity, the role of **neurogenesis**, or growth of new neurons, has been investigated in adult brains. Contrary to long-held beliefs that mature neurons do not divide and replicate, researchers have found that neurogenesis takes place throughout the adult years, primarily in the dentate gyrus, a small area of the hippocampus, which is crucial for forming memories (Eriksson, Perfilieva, Bjork-Eriksson, et al., 1998). The process involves the production of **stem cells**, immature undifferentiated cells that can multiply easily and mature into many different kinds of cells. Although neurogenesis continues well into older adulthood, the rate at which neurons are produced slows down as we age, presumably leading to age-related cognitive loss. Researchers are trying to find ways to boost the rate of neurogenesis in the later years either by increasing stem cell production or by identifying factors that lead to the slowdown and finding ways to reduce their effects. Studies have shown that a combination of physical exercise and cognitive stimulation promotes neurogenesis in aging animals (Klempin & Kempermann, 2007).

Neuron bodies comprise the *gray matter* of the brain; **myelin**, which is a fatty substance that insulates and protects the neuronal axons, is a major component of the *white matter* of the brain. It was once thought that white matter was simply insulation, but recently researchers have found that the white matter of the brain may be as important to development as the gray matter. Myelin aids in the processing speed of information along the neuron, and its formation begins shortly before birth (Sherin & Bartzokis, 2011). The developmental timing of white matter more closely fits the changes we experience in our cognitive, behavioral, and emotional abilities over the life span than the developmental timing of gray matter. Furthermore, it is white matter that makes the major difference between human brains and those of other primates (Schoenemann, Sheehan, & Glotzer, 2005), leading scientists to suggest that myelin underlies our human thinking processes, such as consciousness, language, memory, and inhibitory control (Salthouse, 2000).

Using imaging techniques, researchers have demonstrated that myelin increases with age through childhood and early adulthood, peaks in middle age, and then rapidly decreases in old age. When compared to reaction time measures such as finger tapping, both follow the same inverted U pattern, leading to the speculation that the slowdown of cognitive speed found in old age may be caused more by the breakdown of myelin—the white matter of the brain, than the loss of neurons—the gray matter (Sherin & Bartzokis, 2011). The gradual breakdown of myelin seems to be a part of primary aging, but it can also be exacerbated by brain trauma, hypertension, diabetes, high cholesterol, and substance abuse.

In summary, the aging process is not as destructive to the brain and nervous system as was once thought. There is gain in many areas throughout adulthood, and not all the changes are related to decline. Researchers are investigating ways to increase neurogenesis or at least slow down its decline. They are also working on ways to boost the myelin production and repair processes in older adulthood. However, the overall result of primary aging is that the brain and nervous system may function less well with age. Older people take somewhat longer to react to stimuli than younger people and may show a reduction in certain mental abilities, such as short-term memory and the ability to recall words. Many of these changes of primary aging are apparent only in laboratory tests and may not be noticeable to healthy people in their day-to-day lives.

2.2.6: Immune System

The immune system protects the body in two ways: The **B cells**, produced in the bone marrow, make proteins called **antibodies**, which react to foreign organisms (such as viruses and other infectious agents), and the **T cells**, produced in the thymus gland, reject and consume harmful or foreign cells, such as bacteria and transplanted organs. B cells show abnormalities with age, and these have been implicated in the increase of autoimmune disorders in older adults. With age, T cells show reduced ability to fight new infection. It is difficult to establish that the aging body's decreasing ability to defend itself from disease is a process of primary aging. It is possible, instead, that the immune system becomes weakened in older adulthood as chronic diseases become more prevalent and exercise and nutrition decline.

Taking nutritional supplements to boost immune function is a topic of controversy. On one side are warnings from the U.S. Food and Drug Administration that supplements are not intended to treat, prevent, or cure disease. On the other side are research findings that various antioxidant supplements (vitamins C, E, and others) increase immune function in lab animals (Catoni, Peters, & Schaefer, 2008) and the nutritional supplement manufacturers, who claim that their products will prevent (and reverse) many aspects of primary aging. My personal conclusion is that unless your physician tells you otherwise, middle-aged adults (and younger) with relatively healthy diets and lifestyles don't need to take vitamin supplements. For older adults, especially those with appetite loss or who don't get outdoors much, a daily multiple vitamin may help and can't hurt—except for the cost (Porter, 2009).

2.2.7: Hormonal System

Both men and women experience changes in their hormonal systems over the course of adult life, beginning about age 30. Growth hormone decreases with age, reducing muscle mass, as discussed earlier in this chapter. *Aldosterone* production decreases, leaving some older adults prone to dehydration and heatstroke when summer temperatures soar. However, as with many other aspects of primary aging, most of these changes are not noticeable until late adulthood (Halter, 2011). One change in the neuroendocrine system that is more obvious is the reduction of hormones that results in loss of reproductive ability, a time of life known as the **climacteric**. The climacteric takes place gradually for men over middle and late adulthood and more abruptly for women around the late 40s and early 50s.

THE CLIMACTERIC IN MEN   Research on healthy adults suggests that the quantity of viable sperm produced begins to decline in a man's 40s, but the decline is not rapid, and there are documented cases of men in their 80s fathering children. The testes shrink gradually, and after about age 60, the volume of seminal fluid begins to decline. These changes are associated in part with testicular failure and the resulting gradual decline in **testosterone**, the major male hormone, beginning in early adulthood and extending into old age (Rhoden & Morgentaler, 2004). Declining hormone levels in men are also associated with decreases in muscle mass, bone density, sexual desire, and cognitive functions and with increases in body fat and depressive symptoms (Almeida, Waterreus, Spry, et al., 2004).

THE CLIMACTERIC IN WOMEN   During middle adulthood, women's menstrual periods become irregular, then further apart, and then stop altogether. **Menopause** is defined as occurring 12 months after a woman's final menstrual period. *Premenopause* is the time when a woman is having regular periods, but hormone levels have begun to change. *Perimenopause* is the time a woman begins having irregular periods but has had a period in the last 12 months. *Postmenopause* is the time after a woman has not had a period for 12 months, and it extends until the end of her life (Bromberger, Schott, Kravitz, et al., 2010). The main cause of menopause is ovarian failure, leading to a drop in **estrogen** and complex changes in **progesterone**, both important hormones in women's reproductive health.

WRITING PROMPT

Before you read on, what have you heard about menopause? Do you think men undergo a similar period of change in midlife? If so, why? What picture do the media give us of this part of adulthood? Write a short response that will be read by your instructor.

▶ The response entered here will appear in the performance dashboard and can be viewed by your instructor.

Submit

Women's health in general, and menopause specifically, have not been topics of vast research until the last few decades (Oertelt-Prigione, Parol, Krohn, et al., 2010). Common knowledge came from old wives' tales or advice passed down from mother to daughter. Fortunately, several large-scale longitudinal studies have contributed accurate, scientific-based information on the timing of menopause and the changes that most women experience during this process. One of the best-known and largest of these studies is the Women's Health Study (WHS), which has gathered data from almost 40,000 women health professionals over the age of 45. Although the initial study lasted only 10 years, researchers continue to gather data annually from the participants, and this has been the basis for valuable findings about women's health from middle age to the end of life (Buring & Lee, 2013). From studies such as this, we know that the average age of menopause for women in the United States is 51.3 years, ranging from 47 to 55 years of age. Considering that women today can expect to live well into their 70s, most will spend about one third of their lives in the postmenopause years.

As with men, this series of hormone changes is accompanied by changes in more than reproductive ability. There is some loss of tissue in the genitals and the breasts, and breast tissue becomes less dense and firm. The ovaries and uterus become smaller, the vagina becomes shorter and smaller in diameter with thinner and less elastic walls, and there is less lubrication produced in response to sexual stimulation.

The most frequently reported and most distressing physical symptom that comes with the menopausal transition is the *hot flash,* a sudden sensation of heat spreading over the body, especially the chest, face, and head. It is usually accompanied by flushing, sweating, chills, and often palpitations and anxiety. The duration of a hot flash averages about 4 minutes. About a third of women in the Women's Health Study reported that they had consulted their doctors for treatment because the hot flashes were frequent and severe.

What about women's psychological functioning around the time of menopause? It has long been believed by some that menopause can bring irrational behavior and volatile mood changes. However, recent studies that divided women into pre-, peri-, and postmenopausal status have shown that women in the perimenopausal and postmenopausal stages are more apt to have depressive symptoms, especially those women who also report upsetting life events, lack of social support, lower education, and hot flashes (Bromberger, Schott, Kravitz, et al., 2010).

However, I must remind you that even though these studies show that depressive symptoms are more likely to occur in women who are perimenopausal and postmenopausal, the absolute number of women who experience them is very small, and unlike major depression, depressive symptoms are not severe and often do not last for long.

HORMONE REPLACEMENT   *If primary aging is due to a decline in hormone production in men and women, why not replace the lost hormones and reverse the process?* This is not a new suggestion; it has been the impetus behind many failed "fountain-of-youth" therapies throughout history, including the injection of pulverized sheep and guinea pig testicles into patients in the 1890s and chimpanzee testicle and ovary implants into elderly men and women in the 1920s (Epelbaum, 2008). Needless to say, none of these measures restored youth, but more recent attempts to replace diminished hormone supplies in aging adults have met with some success. Although none reverse the aging process, they may slow it down somewhat.

The most-used hormone replacement regimen is a combination of estrogen and progesterone prescribed for women at menopause. This **hormone replacement therapy** provides perimenopausal and postmenopausal women with the hormones once produced by their ovaries and can reduce some of the adverse symptoms of the climacteric. Hormone replacement therapy can alleviate hot flashes, vaginal dryness, and bone fractures; however, it has also been related to an increased risk for breast cancer, heart attacks, stroke, and blood clots in women in certain high-risk groups. Women are advised to talk to their physicians about their menopausal symptoms to decide on the best course of action for them.

Although controversial, testosterone replacement therapy is popular among middle-aged and older men in the form of injections, skin patches, and gels applied to the underarms. Although only about 20% of men over 60 have lower-than-normal testosterone levels, prescriptions for testosterone replacement in the United States increased from 692,000 in 2000 to 2,660,000 in 2008. Despite this increase in use, the benefits and risks of long-term testosterone replacement therapy (over 3 years) is unknown at this time. For the 20% of men who have lower-than-normal testosterone levels, 3 years of treatment has brought increased bone mineral density and improved sexual function without adverse effects (Gruntmanis, 2012).

Age-related declines in both sexes have been documented for two other hormones, **DHEA** (dehydroepiandrosterone) and **GH** (growth hormone). Not only do these hormones decline naturally with age, but animal studies suggest that replacing these hormones reverses aging and provides protection against disease. What about humans? Results have been mixed. An early study using DHEA with a small group of older men and women showed promise, but large clinical trials using placebo controls have failed to demonstrate that it has any effect on body composition, physical performance, or quality of life (Nair, Rizza, O'Brien, et al., 2006). A meta-analysis of 31 randomized, controlled studies of GH's effects on healthy adults over 50 showed that there were small decreases in body fat and small increases in lean body mass, but increased rates of adverse effects (Liu, Bravata, Olkin, et al., 2007). A similar study showed that GH has little effect on athletic performance in young, active adults (Liu, Bravata, Okin, et al., 2008).

All that being said, DHEA is widely used by adults of all ages in the United States, where it is considered a nutritional supplement and sold in health food stores and over the Internet. GH is also widely available in the United States, despite the fact that it must be prescribed by a doctor and the FDA has not approved it as an antiaging drug. Products claiming to contain GH account for millions of dollars of Internet sales each year (Perls, Reisman, & Olshansky, 2005). Clearly, the age-old quest for restored youth continues.

WRITING PROMPT

If the GH replacement sold on the Internet is worthless, why do you think are there so many websites selling it and so many repeat customers? What need is it fulfilling? Write a short response that will be read by your teacher. Be sure to provide specific details in your response.

> The response entered here will appear in the performance dashboard and can be viewed by your instructor.

Submit

2.3: Changes in Physical Behavior

2.3   Discuss changes in physical behavior like decline of stamina, dexterity, and balance; changes in sleep habits and sexual functioning

The changes in various body systems discussed so far form the foundation for age-related changes in more complex behaviors and day-to-day activities. These changes include a gradual slowing of peak athletic performance; the decline of stamina, dexterity, and balance; changes in sleep habits; and the changes that occur in sexual functioning for both men and women.

2.3.1: Athletic Abilities

In any sport, the top performers are in their teens or 20s, especially any sport involving speed. Gymnasts peak in their teens, short-distance runners in their early 20s, and baseball players at about 27. As endurance becomes more involved in performance, such as for longer-distance running, the peak performance age rises, but the top performers are still in their 20s. Few of us have reached the heights of athletic superstars, but most of us notice some downturn in athletic ability shortly after the high school years.

WRITING PROMPT

Based on what you have learned so far, what would you guess the peak ages would be for soccer players, golfers, and discus throwers? Write a brief response that will be read by your teacher. Explain why you guessed these ages and what assumptions you are working from.

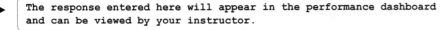
> The response entered here will appear in the performance dashboard and can be viewed by your instructor.

Submit

Cross-sectional comparisons of athletes of different ages show this dramatically. Figure 2.6 shows the oxygen uptake for three groups of men ranging in age from 20 to 90 years of age (Kusy, Król-Zielinska, Dormaszewska, et al., 2012). The group represented by the set of bars on the left are professional athletes and masters athletes in Poland who trained for endurance sports (cyclists, triathletes, and long-distance runners). The group represented by the bars in the center is their countrymen who have trained for speed-power sports (sprinters, jumpers, and throwers). The set of bars on the right are for untrained men, defined as those who do not have more than 150 minutes of vigorous activity per week. As you can see, the athletes trained for endurance sports have significantly higher levels of oxygen uptake than those trained for speed-power sports. And both types of athletes have significantly higher oxygen uptake levels than the nonathletes at all age levels. Furthermore, although all the men decline with age in oxygen uptake, the differences in the three groups continue, with some trained athletes in their late 80s still testing higher than some nonathletes in their 20s. The lesson is clear; we slow down as we get older, but when we start out in better shape and keep exercising, we are still ahead of those who never trained at all.

Figure 2.6 Athletes who train in endurance sports have greater oxygen uptake at all ages than those who train in speed-power sports. Both groups of athletes have greater oxygen uptake across the adult years than nonathletes.

SOURCE: Kusy, Król-Zieliska, Domaszewska, et al. (2012)

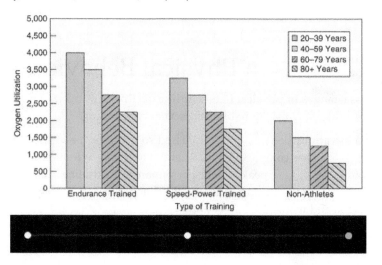

A slowdown in athletic ability begins in the 20s, although it is only noticeable for those who are top performers.

2.3.2: Stamina, Dexterity, and Balance

In addition to loss of speed, all the physical changes associated with aging combine to produce a reduction in stamina, dexterity, and balance. The loss of **stamina**, which is the ability to sustain moderate or strenuous activity over a period of time, clearly arises in large part from the changes in the cardiovascular and respiratory systems, as well as from changes in muscles. **Dexterity**, the ability to use the hands or body in a skillful way, is lost primarily as a result of arthritic changes in the joints.

Another significant change, one with clear practical ramifications, is a gradual loss of **balance**, the ability to adapt body position to change. Older adults are likely to have greater difficulty handling uneven sidewalks or snowy streets or adapting the body to a swaying bus. All these situations require flexibility and muscle strength, both of which decline in old age. One result of less steady balance is a greater incidence of falls among the elderly. As mentioned before, declining eyesight and brittle bones combine with the decline in balance to produce a hazardous situation for older adults.

The seriousness of this problem and the increasing number of older adults has led to exercise programs being instituted around the world, in community centers, veteran's halls, and private homes, offering strength and flexibility training, aerobic endurance training, and other activities, such as Tai Chi, a gentle form of martial arts that emphasizes fluid movements and balance. These programs also include visits from social workers to give advice on "fall-proofing" the home (for example, have well-lit stairs and no throw rugs, avoid loose-fitting shoes, and mark the edges of steps). The results have been very positive, and the CDC has endorsed a number of community programs (Stevens, 2010).

2.3.3: Sleep

Most of us think of sleep as simply the absence of conscious thought and purposeful activity, and this is true to some extent. It is a period of time set aside for cellular restoration, energy conservation, and consolidation of newly formed memories and learning. But sleep also has an active component. There are important processes going on while we sleep. We find new answers to problems we have mulled over during the day, our creativity is fired up after a good night's sleep, and mental roadblocks have been circumvented during the night ranging from how to end the opera we are writing to how to solve a family relationship problem that seemed hopeless the night before (Lockley & Foster, 2012). So it stands to reason that it is important for us to get a healthy dose of sleep on a regular basis.

Younger adults typically need 8.5 hours of sleep each night, and older adults need 7.5 hours. Yet the average adult gets only 7 hours of sleep each night. Almost half of all adults report having sleep problems every night, and 70% of emerging adults report not getting the recommended amount of sleep on school nights (National Institutes of Health, 2011). This chronic sleep deprivation can lead to increases in accidents, heart disease, obesity, diabetes, cancer, and mental disorders and a decrease in immune function.

Sleep problems differ by age in adulthood. Emerging adults have sleep/wake cycles that are about 2 or 3 hours behind that of other adults, making them "night owls" who don't get sleepy until late at night and then don't feel wakeful until mid-morning. This has been interpreted by generations of parents as laziness, lack of discipline, and general belligerence, but recently sleep researchers have come down on the side of the younger generation, stating that this is a normal developmental phenomenon and that parents (and educators) should be more understanding and let them sleep in (Carskadon, 2009). Several states have acted on these findings and delayed the start of high school classes, with a subsequent reduction of absences, tardiness, behavior problems, breakfast-skipping, and auto accidents involving teenage drivers (National Sleep Foundation, 2011). Not all school districts have done this, including mine. As I am writing this, my 14-year-old grandson, Brendan, is starting his second week of high school, going from a middle-school start time of 9:20 in the morning to a high school start time of 7:30. His bus picks him up four blocks from his house at 6:30. His laments remind me of how unfair adolescence can seem when both biology and bureaucracy conspire against you!

Young adults continue to have sleep/wake cycles that are slightly behind their older counterparts, but most of their sleep problems are related to work schedules, family obligations, and stress. In middle age, lack of sleep due to health problems becomes a factor, especially if weight has increased and activity level has decreased. Stress also contributes to sleep problems at this age, when children are entering adulthood and careers are demanding (or uncertain). Menopause affects sleep with hot flashes and also an increase in **sleep apnea**, which is a pause in breathing during sleep due to a constriction of the airway (Lockley & Foster, 2012).

Older adults sleep about an hour less at night than younger adults, waking about an hour earlier on average, but also being more apt to take naps during the day. Sleep problems in older adults can be the effect of physical and mental disorders and also medication. Sleep researchers believe that although sleep patterns change in old age, it does not mean that insomnia is part of aging—it's just that health problems and medication increase with age (Lockley & Foster, 2012) and time spent exercising decreases (Buman, Hekler, Bliwise, et al., 2011).

Insomnia—the inability to sleep—increases with age and affects women more than men. There are three major causes. First, some people seem to be inherently predisposed to insomnia. Second are outside factors such as disease, medication, depression and anxiety, and stress. Third are lifestyle factors such as alcohol use, overuse of caffeine, lack of exercise, daily napping, and the use of blue-screen electronic devices before bedtime (and during the night). Besides not allowing us to clear our minds and relax, the light from tablets and phones mimics daylight and confuses the circadian rhythms much like jet lag does. Some people, especially adolescents and emerging adults, are extremely sensitive to this, and it results in insomnia.

Remedies for insomnia include increased physical exercise and time spent outdoors.

As you can see, some of these factors can be changed easily and others not at all. It is relatively easy to monitor caffeine intake and get regular exercise, but dealing with health problems and medication requires working with your physician (Punnoose, 2012). However, this is the best place to start before moving on to medication, which has not proven to be as safe and effective as it would seem on TV commercials.

2.3.4: Sexual Activity

As a result of normal changes in various systems of the body, sexual behavior shows the effects of primary aging. The key indicator used in research is the average number of times per month people of different ages have intercourse. A number of early studies showed that among people in their 20s with regular partners, the number is high—as much as 10 times or more per month, dropping to about 3 times per month for people in their 60s and 70s, and this is found in both cross-sectional and longitudinal studies.

How would you design a study to determine whether the drop in sexual activity with age is a function of age or of length of partnership? Write a brief response that will be read by your instructor. Be sure to provide concrete details in your response.

▶ The response entered here will appear in the performance dashboard and can be viewed by your instructor.

Submit

However, one problem with this research question is that it reduces a very complex human interaction into a simple frequency count. Few studies tell us about the quality of the sexual relations people have at different ages or about types of sexual expression that don't involve intercourse. An exception was a study by social psychologists John DeLamater and Sara Moorman (2007) using data collected by the AARP in their Modern Maturity Sexuality Survey. In this survey, over 1,300 men and women from the ages of 45 to 94 were asked about sexual activities such as kissing and hugging, sexual touching, oral sex, and masturbation, as well as sexual intercourse. Although participation in all these sexual activities was related to age, other factors were important, too, such as physical ability, sexual desire, social surroundings, and environmental aspects of life at different points in adulthood. Let's look at some of these factors in more detail.

PHYSICAL ABILITY   Studies of the physiological components of the sexual responses of younger men and women (aged 20 to 40) compared to older men and women (aged 50 to 78) show that there are differences in all four stages of sexual response (Medina, 1996; Shifren & Hanfling, 2010). These changes, which are described in Table 2.6, show that sexual responses of younger men and women are a little faster and a little more intense than the older group. Although many changes may result in less sexual activity with age, some can have the opposite result, such as lack of concerns about pregnancy, more privacy in the home, greater experience, fewer inhibitions, and a deeper understanding of one's personal needs and those of one's partner (Fraser, Maticka-Tyndale, & Smylie, 2004; Shifren & Hanfling, 2010).

Table 2.6 Sexual Response in Older Adults (50–78 Years of Age) Compared to Younger Adults (20–40 Years of Age)

SOURCE: Medina (1996); Shifren & Hanfling (2010).

Phase	Women	Men
Physical changes	Decreased blood flow to genitals. Lower levels of estrogen and testosterone. Thinning of vaginal lining. Loss of vaginal elasticity and muscle tone.	Decreased blood flow to the genitals. Lower levels of testosterone. Less sensitivity in the penis.
Desire	Decreased libido. Fewer sexual thoughts and fantasies.	Decreased libido. Fewer sexual thoughts and fantasies.
Excitement	Slower arousal. Vaginal lubrication takes 1–5 minutes (compared to 15–30 seconds in younger women).	Greater difficulty achieving an erection. Erection after stimulation takes 10 seconds to several minutes (compared to 3–5 seconds in younger men). Erections not as rigid.

Plateau	Vagina does not expand as much. Less blood congestion in the clitoris and lower vagina. Diminished clitoral sensitivity (compared to the response of younger women).	Pressure for ejaculation is not felt as quickly (compared to younger men).
Orgasm	Less intense orgasms. Vagina contracts and expands in 4 to 5 smooth, rhythmic waves occurring at 0.8-second intervals (compared to 8 to 10 waves occurring at 0.8-second intervals in younger women). Uterus contracts and is sometimes more painful (compared to younger women).	Less intense orgasms. Urethra contracts in 1 to 2 waves at 0.8-second intervals (compared to 3 to 4 waves at 0.8-second intervals for younger men), and the semen can travel 3 to 5 inches after expulsion (compared to 12 to 24 inches in younger men). Smaller volume of semen.
Resolution	Return to prearousal stage is more rapid (compared to younger women).	Return to prearousal stages takes only a few seconds (compared to return in younger men, which take from minutes to hours). More time between erections.

Hide All Cells   Show All Cells

One of the most common sexual problems is **erectile dysfunction (ED)**, which is defined as the inability for a man to have an erection adequate for satisfactory sexual performance. This problem occurs in an estimated 30 million men in the United States, half of them over 65. Thus, erectile dysfunction is associated with age, occurring in 5% of men between 40 and 65, and in 25% of men over 65 (Schover, Fouladi, Warneke, et al., 2004). Although erectile dysfunction occurs for many reasons (heart disease, diabetes, excessive alcohol consumption, medication, smoking), the underlying mechanism seems to be similar in most cases—a shortage of **cyclic GMP**, a substance that is released by the brain during sexual arousal. Part of the job of cyclic GMP is to close down the veins of the penis that normally drain away blood so that the blood supply increases and the tissues become engorged and erect. When cyclic GMP is in short supply, regardless of the reason, the result is erectile dysfunction. In the last decade, drugs have been developed that magnify the effects of cyclic GMP, making erections possible if even a small amount of the substance is present. The first of these drugs, Viagra (sildenafil citrate), was approved in 1997. In the last few years, new drugs have become available for ED, such as Levitra (vardenafil) and Cialis (tadalafil) that are time released to give men a wider window of opportunity in the timing of their sexual activity (Shifren & Hanfling, 2010). In 2010, $2 billion was spent on ED medication, and another $100 million was spent by drug companies to advertise them (Cohen, 2012).

As mentioned before, one of the effects of menopause for some women is vaginal dryness and the reduced ability to lubricate when sexually aroused. This is often alleviated by estrogen treatment, either pills, patches, or creams, or the use of an artificial lubricant. However, as will be discussed later in this section, sexual behavior involves more than erectile functioning and vaginal lubrication; there is also general health and well-being, relationship quality, conducive surroundings, and the perception of oneself as a sexual being, regardless of age. So far there is no "little blue pill" that will correct problems in all these areas.

SEXUAL DESIRE   The desire to participate in sexual activity waxes and wanes throughout adulthood. For example, young adults report loss of desire when career pressures and parental responsibilities are at a peak. Middle-aged adults report increased sexual desire when the day-to-day responsibilities of parenthood end. Older adults report loss of desire because they believe that sex is only for the young or those with youthful bodies. But all in all, the desire to have sex is highest in emerging adulthood and declines with age as part of primary aging. Although lack of physical ability is the major sex-related complaint of men, clinicians report that lack of desire is by far the most common complaint of women (Tomic, Gallicchio, Whiteman, et al., 2006).

Sexual desire is driven by testosterone in women as well as in men. By menopause, women have about half of the amount of testosterone as they did in their 20s, and that decline can contribute to reduced desire for sex and briefer, less pleasurable orgasms for some women. Testosterone replacement therapy for women is fairly recent and controversial. Several studies have shown that daily testosterone, delivered via a skin patch, can boost sexual desire and increase orgasms for postmenopausal women, but questions remain about the side effects, which can include excess hair growth, acne, liver problems, and lower levels of HDL (the "good" cholesterol). The FDA will not give approval for the use of testosterone replacement for women with low sexual desire until further long-term studies are completed (Shifren & Hanfling, 2010), though it is widely prescribed "off label."

It should be noted that there are safe and proven remedies for female sexual dysfunction that have been helpful to many couples, such as reducing alcohol consumption and stress, increasing exercise and quality time together as a couple, and consulting a professional sex therapist.

SEXUAL PARTNER.   Regardless of age, the main reason most people do not have sexual relations is that they don't have a partner. Emerging adults may be new to the dating scene or busy with studies, not to mention living in their parents' homes. Young adults may be between partners or recovering from a bad breakup and just not ready to put themselves "out there" again. Middle-aged adults could be divorced after a long-term marriage and uncomfortable with the changes in the dating culture (and changes in themselves) since they were last single. And older adults, divorced or widowed, may have problems finding suitable sexual partners, especially women, who are more plentiful than men at this age. Some feel content to be alone, feeling that no one can live up to their former spouses. Still others face criticism from their adult children, who see Mom or Dad's sexuality as a threat to the memory of their deceased parents (or a threat to their inheritances). Regardless of the reason, being without a suitable partner is a bigger factor in people's sex lives than their lack of physical abilities and desire.

Age-related differences exist in the nature of the relationship one has with his or her sexual partners, too. Emerging adults' sexual encounters increasingly take the form of **hookups**, or casual sex without commitment (Garcia, Reiber, Massey, et al., 2012). We don't know if this is age-specific or if it will continue for this cohort through their adult years. Middle-aged and older adults today want more commitment with their sex and, furthermore, want a warm and loving relationship. In a study of 60- to 90-year-old couples in Greece, researchers found that those who married out of love, as opposed to being in arranged marriages, reported stronger sexual desire for each other and more frequent sexual relations. The same was true of those who reported that they were "still in love with each other" (Papaharitou, Nakopoulou, Kirana, et al., 2008). Other studies have shown that for adults of all ages, having a happier marriage is related to more frequent sexual intercourse (DeLamater, 2012).

SEXUAL PRIVACY AND OTHER MATTERS   For the 5% of older adults who are in nursing homes and for those who live with their adult children, privacy is a major stumbling block to sexual relations, even if they have the desire, the ability, and a willing partner. Nursing homes and other residential facilities for older adults can be problematic for sexually active residents, married or single. Courses in gerontology for nursing home directors and staff often include information on sexuality in older adults and how to structure the environment to be conducive to their activities (Mahieu & Gastmans, 2012). Homophobic attitudes make it very difficult for older gay and lesbian adults to establish or maintain relationships in nursing homes or the homes of their adult children. For many the answer has been gay and lesbian retirement homes and assisted-living centers (Clunis, Fredriksen-Goldsen, Freeman, et al., 2005).

OTHER FORMS OF SENSUAL ACTIVITY. Not all types of sensual pleasure entail all these requirements. Erotic dreams and sexual fantasies can be sources of arousal and pleasure for older adults who lack partners or the physical capability to have intercourse. The National Survey of Sexual Health and Behavior found that almost half of men and almost a third of women 70 to 94 years of age reported engaging in masturbation in the past year (Laumann, Das, & Waite, 2008). A substantial number of men and women over 50 report having oral sex in the past year, including about 25% of men and 8% of women over 70 (DeLamater, 2012). We don't know if this was in place of vaginal intercourse or along with vaginal intercourse, and we don't know the statistics for same-sex couples. However, it seems clear that sexual interest and activity remain a significant part of life and relationships throughout the adult years.

TREATMENT FOR SEXUAL PROBLEMS. We previously discussed several treatments for sexual problems, such as medication for erectile dysfunction and various hormone replacement therapies. Studies have shown that somewhere between 10% and 40% of middle-aged and older adults have sought treatment from a professional for a problem related to sexual functioning. Although that is a pretty wide range, one thing is common among all the studies—over half of those who sought help did so from their primary care physician. This points out the need for these medical personnel (family practice physicians, nurse-practitioners, and physician assistants) to possess an understanding of the treatment of sexual problems for patients of all ages. They also need to feel comfortable discussing the topic with even their oldest patients. Interestingly, the participants in this study who did seek treatment for sexual problems reported no increased frequency of intercourse after the treatment, but the majority of them did experience an increase in sexual satisfaction (DeLamater, 2012).

2.4: Individual Differences in Primary Aging

2.4 Identify the proportionate relationship between aging and individual differences based on genetics, lifestyle, race, and socio-economic factors

There is often a big difference between group means and individual measurements in research findings. The accounts of primary aging in this chapter so far have followed the practice, for example, of reporting the *average* scores for 40-year-old men or the *mean* scores for 75-year-old women. But we can look around us and see that there is a lot of diversity among people of the same ages. In fact, the older we get, the more differences there are between us and our own agemates. If you have had the opportunity to attend a high school reunion, you will know what I mean. Seniors in high school are very similar, and they look and behave in much the same manner, but at your 10-year reunion—at the age of 28 or so—differences are already apparent. Some have not changed much from their 18-year-old appearances, but others have begun to show changes in body shape and thinning of hair. By the time you reach your 30-year reunion—at the age of 48 or so—the differences will be even more dramatic. What factors are involved in this diversity? And, more specifically, you may ask, "What factors might affect the aging process for *me*?"

2.4.1: Genetics

Twin studies and other family studies show that the number of years a person lives is moderately heritable (McClearn, Vogler, & Hofer, 2001), but this may be due more to the absence of genetic predispositions for certain diseases, as you will see in the next chapter. Still, living a long life doesn't tell us much about the rate of primary aging. Do genes influence the rate at which we age? Would a pair of identical twins start showing wrinkles at the same age and have their hair start turning gray together? In one study, researchers gathered data about the aging of skin at the Annual Twins Festival days in Twinsburg, Ohio, and compared identical twins' faces and those of fraternal twins. For 130 pairs of twins ranging up to 77 years of age, they found that the identical twin pairs were more alike in their facial skin aging patterns than the fraternal twin pairs and that the genetic contribution to facial skin aging is about 60%. This means that 40% of our facial skin aging is due to other causes, such as smoking and UV radiation exposure from the sun (Martires, Fu, Polster, et al., 2009), as well as the use of tanning beds (Robinson & Bigby, 2011). In addition, about 60% of the variation in total body weight is influenced by genetics, as well as the pattern of age-related weight change (Ortega-Alonso, Sipilä, Kujala, et al., 2009), though physical exercise can modify the genetic influence of both total body weight and waist circumference (Mustelin, Silventoinen, Pietiläinen, et al., 2009).

In a study of overall perception of aging, epidemiologist Kaare Christensen and her colleagues (Christensen, Iachina, Rexbye, et al., 2004) took head-shot photos of 387 same-sex twin pairs who were at least 70 years of age. About half the pairs were identical twins and half were fraternal twins, and the pairs were about evenly split between males and females. Twenty female nurses viewed the photos and estimated the age of each person pictured. On one day, they were questioned about one twin of each pair; on another day they were questioned about the other twin. The perceived ages of the identical twins were significantly more alike than the perceived ages of the fraternal twins. Results showed that 60% of perceived age is genetic and 40% is due to other factors. Furthermore, the judgments turned out to be more than perceptions of age when, two years later, researchers found that twins who were judged as looking older than their twin siblings were more apt to have died during that period. "Looking old" and "looking young" are traits that run in families, and these traits are more than appearances—they are related to mortality.

2.4.2: Lifestyle

Another broad category of factors that affect the rate of primary aging involves the lifestyle choices we make. This involves exercise, diet, and use of alcohol, tobacco products, and other substances. All through this chapter we have seen risk factors for various age-related conditions, and one of the most frequently mentioned risk factors is sedentary lifestyle. All experts on healthy aging emphasize the importance of an active lifestyle. I try to follow my own advice and get a balance of aerobic exercise, strength and flexibility training, and yoga. I attend early morning classes almost every weekday before settling down at my desk to write. It does wonders for my back and gives me an energy boost. The social aspects of visiting with others in my classes are important to my mood, too.

Although I have never been a competitive athlete, I do take inspiration from the master athletes discussed previously in this chapter. These people 35 to 90 years of age (and older) who train for athletic events have better aerobic fitness, higher levels of "good" cholesterol, fewer risk factors for diabetes, and better bone density than their peers who are not master athletes. They also are able to consume more calories while weighing less than people of comparable ages who have more sedentary lifestyles (Rosenbloom & Bahns, 2006). This doesn't make them immune from primary aging, but their appearances and physical abilities are much "younger" than their chronological agemates.

For those who dread the idea of starting an exercise program, there is some encouraging news. Researchers have found that people typically think negatively about *starting* a physical workout regimen, but feel more positive about it once they get started. In other words, even if it seems difficult and unpleasant ahead of time, just do it. You will be happier once you get involved in it (Ruby, Dunn, Perrino, et al., 2011).

Another important factor in primary aging is diet. I recently bit the bullet (and a lot of celery sticks) and lost 20 pounds that had crept up on me slowly over the last few years. Losing that 20 pounds increased my energy level and made me a little happier about exercising. I noticed when traveling that my knees didn't hurt after a long day of sightseeing, and I was not out of breath when I climbed stairs or hills (both a rarity in south Florida). Better yet, it lowered my cholesterol level and blood pressure so I no longer take medication for them.

Adopting a healthy diet has multilevel benefits. There is the weight and appearance benefit and also the health benefit. When we eat healthy food, there is no need to spend money on questionable nutritional supplements and antiaging potions. Recently researchers uncovered a hidden problem with dependence on nutritional supplements by demonstrating their "ironic effects." Puzzled by the increase in nutritional supplements on the world market but a decline in healthy lifestyles, social psychologist Wen-Bin Chiou and colleagues (Chiou, Yang, & Wan, 2011) thought there might be a connection. They gave Taiwanese participants placebo nutritional supplements and found that they were more apt to express favorable opinions about hedonic activities (casual sex, excessive drinking, and wild parties) over healthier activities (yoga, swimming, and bicycling). They also scored higher on a test of perceived invulnerability (agreeing with statements such as "Nothing can harm me") and, when given their choice of a free meal in exchange for their cooperation in the study, those who thought they were taking a nutritional supplement pill were less likely to choose a healthy organic meal over an all-you-can-eat buffet of less healthy food. The researchers concluded that the use of nutritional supplements can have the ironic effect of making people feel they can indulge in unhealthy behaviors because they are protected by taking the supplements.

Another lifestyle factor that contributes to accelerated primary aging is exposure to UV radiation from the sun. This is a major cause of aging of the skin, specifically coarse texture, dark and white "age spots," and spider veins—those red webs that appear on the face and legs near the knees and ankles. Although aging of the skin is unavoidable in the long run, we can avoid premature aging by limiting the time we spend outdoors during peak sun exposure, wearing protective clothing, and using sunscreen.

2.4.3: Race, Ethnicity, and Socioeconomic Group

Race and ethnicity are risk factors for many conditions involved with primary aging such as obesity, glaucoma, macular degeneration, and osteoporosis, as we have seen earlier in this chapter. But when socioeconomic factors are added to race and ethnicity, more differences emerge. Many factors that determine the rate of primary aging depend on education and income levels. Healthy eating requires information about nutrition, exercise takes time, and early screening and treatment for conditions such as glaucoma and osteoporosis are difficult unless families can afford medical care.

Some low-income neighborhoods are *food deserts*, meaning that residents have limited access to fresh fruits and vegetables, food is relatively expensive, and residents have little access to transportation so they can shop elsewhere. The American Nutrition Association (2011) points out that food deserts not only lack healthy food, but they are also usually areas that have a high density of fast-food restaurants and quickie marts offering processed food that is high in sugar and fat.

The CDC (2009) has found that people who have lower levels of education and lower incomes are more apt to have limited access to medical care, dental care, and prescription drugs. Add to that findings that black Americans are more likely to be shut out of these forms of health care than Hispanic Americans, who are more likely to be shut out than white Americans, and you have a perfect storm that explains why primary aging is more rapid for some racial and ethnic groups than others (Olshansky, Antonucci, Berkman, et al., 2012). I will discuss this further in the next chapter.

2.5: Can We "Turn Back the Clock" of Primary Aging?

2.5   Discuss becoming young once again

Is there a Fountain of Youth? Is it possible to be young again? Despite many claims to the contrary throughout human history, the answer at this time is, "No." We can't turn back the clock and be young again. The best we can do is to prevent premature aging, cover up the signs of aging we choose to cover, and enjoy life.

WRITING PROMPT

What are some of the differences between slowing down aging and increasing longevity? What are the implications of each? If you had to choose one as an option, which would you choose and why? Write a brief response that will be read by your instructor.

▶ | The response entered here will appear in the performance dashboard and can be viewed by your instructor.

Submit

Although we can't reverse primary aging, some researchers are working on ways to slow it down. Biodemographer S. Jay Olshansky (2012) proposes that we start with the molecular causes of primary aging, such as the genes that slow growth in early life and hormonal signals related to insulin that help cells buffer the damaging effects of antioxidants, radiation, and environmental toxins. Other researchers are studying healthy centenarians, people who have lived to their 100th birthday and beyond free from disease, disability, and fragility. This research is identifying genetic markers in these individuals that are related to their longevity (Sebastiani, Solovieff, DeWan, et al., 2012), and Olshansky suggests that such people may be aging at a slower rate than others because they have genes that make their cells resistant to oxidative damage (Harmon, 2012).

Each time I revise this textbook I am amazed at the progress being made to extend the years of healthy life through delayed aging. These lines of research are much more appealing to me than simply increasing longevity and much more probable than "turning back the clock."

2.6: An Overview of the Physical Changes in Adulthood

2.6   Relate age to physical changes

I have reviewed the myriad details of primary aging in Table 2.7, showing the physical characteristics of adults at different ages. When you look at the information this way, you can see that adults are clearly at their physical peak in the years from 18 to 39. In the years of midlife, from 40 to 64, the rate of physical change varies widely from one person to the next, with some experiencing a loss of physical function quite early, and others much later. From age 65 to 74, the loss of some abilities continues, along with significant increases in chronic diseases—both trends that accelerate in late adulthood. But here, too, there are wide individual differences in the rate of change and effective compensations. Many adults maintain perfectly adequate (or even excellent) physical functioning well past 75 and into their 80s. In the oldest group, however, all these changes accelerate, and compensations become more and more difficult to maintain.

Table 2.7 Review Table of Physical Changes in Adulthood

18–24 Years	25–39 Years	40–64 Years	65–74 Years	75+ Years
Weight and body mass are optimal for most. About 17% are obese.	Weight and girth begin to increase around 30. About 1/3 are obese.	Weight continues to increase until 50s, remains stable until 60; girth continues to increase and fat moves from extremities to abdomen. Over 1/3 are obese.	Weight and girth begin to decrease in 70s. Over 1/3 are obese.	Weight and girth remain stable. About 15% are obese.
Facial features and skin tone are youthful; hair is full.	Facial features remain youthful for most; some men begin hair loss.	Skin begins to wrinkle and lose elasticity. Thinning of hair for men and women, more extreme for men. Largest group for cosmetic surgery.	Wrinkles and loss of skin elasticity increase.	Wrinkles and loss of skin elasticity increase.
Vision is at peak acuity; hearing may start to decline for some due to loud sports and leisure-time activities.	Beginning of vision and hearing losses, declines in taste and smell, but not generally noticeable.	Near vision loss in 40s; dark adaptation becomes apparent in 60s; cataracts begin in 40s. Slight losses in taste and smell. Hearing loss is more noticeable.	Vision loss continues. Cataracts common. Loss of taste and smell becomes noticeable, especially sweet and salty tastes.	Visual and hearing losses continue.
Bone mass is still building.	Peak bone mass reached at 30.	Bone mass begins to decline gradually for men and more sharply for women, especially after menopause.	Bone mass continues to decline. Risk for fractures increases, especially for women.	Bone mass continues to decline. Risk for fractures increases sharply, especially for women.
Neuronal development is completed.	Some neuronal loss, but not noticeable.	Neuronal loss continues, especially in brain centers related to memory. Myelination and reaction time are at peak.	Neuronal loss continues. Some decrease of myelin, slowing of reaction time, and decline in some cognitive processes apparent.	Neuronal loss continues. Myelin decreases and cognitive processes show definite decline.
Hormones are fully functioning; fertility is at optimal level.	Production of major hormones begins to decline, but not noticeable.	Hormones continue to decline, fertility declines gradually for men; sharply for women after menopause.	Hormones continue to decline.	Continued low levels of major hormones.
Sexual response is at optimal level.	Sexual responses begin slow decline.	Sexual responses become slower, less intense.	Sexual responses continue to decline, though lack of partner is top reason for not having sexual relations.	Sexual responses continue to decline, though many continue to enjoy sexual relations throughout adulthood.

Summary: Physical Changes

LISTEN TO THE AUDIO:

► ━━━━━━ 01:49 ◄)) ━━━

1. The oxidative damage theory of primary aging says that we age as a result of damage from free radicals that are released during normal cell metabolism. The genetic limits theory says that we age because our cells are programmed to stop dividing once we have reached a certain age. The caloric restriction theory says that our longevity is controlled by the number of calories we metabolize in our lifetime. Each theory has research supporting it, and many of the findings seem to support more than one theory.

2. Weight increases gradually, starting toward the end of young adulthood, remains stable in middle adulthood, and then begins to decline in later adulthood. This is accompanied by a gradual increase in hip and waist measurements for both men and women, leveling off in later adulthood.

3. Obesity rates are high and increasing steadily for adults of all ages in the United States and other developed countries. This condition is linked to a number of diseases, and it also affects self-perceptions of health, ability to exercise, and social interactions. The main causes are eating an unhealthy diet and leading a sedentary lifestyle.

4. Skin begins to wrinkle toward the end of young adulthood and becomes more noticeable in the middle years. "Remedies" sold over the counter for aging skin only cover the signs of aging. An increasing number of men and women are having cosmetic surgery and other medical procedures to change their appearances, and it is most common for those from 40 to 54 years of age.

5. Vision begins to decline in early adulthood, but is not noticeable until middle age. Around 45, near vision is lost more suddenly, but can be corrected with reading glasses or contact lenses. The incidence of cataracts, glaucoma, and macular degeneration increases beginning in middle age. Hearing loss begins in the 30s, but is not noticeable until middle age, when adults have problems hearing higher and softer tones. Taste and smell begin to decline in the 30s, and this becomes more noticeable in the late years of middle age.

6. Bone mass density peaks around 30 and then begins to decline for both men and women. The decline is gradual for men and sharp for women at menopause. Women are at greater risk for osteoporosis and fractures. Osteoarthritis is a common condition in older adults and can lead to decreased activity and depressive symptoms.

7. Muscle mass and strength decline slowly and do not affect the daily activities of most adults. Resistance training and stretching exercises can help slow down the decline. Changes in the heart and respiratory system are gradual and do not affect the daily activities of most adults, but heavy exercise brings slower responses in the later years. Aerobic exercise can help.

8. The brain loses neurons with age, but not at the high rate once believed. However, the nervous system is capable of making adjustments to the losses, and there is evidence that new neurons can be created in parts of the adult brain. Myelination peaks in middle age and starts a slow decline, following the same curve as reaction time and cognitive speed.

9. The immune system does not function as well in later adulthood as it did in earlier years, possibly due to the greater prevalence of chronic diseases and susceptibility to stress. Vitamin supplements may help in later adulthood.

10. There is a gradual decline in hormone production and reproductive ability in both men and women from early adulthood into middle age, with a sharp decrease for women at menopause. Hormone replacement is possible, but should be approached with caution and in consultation with a medical professional.

11. Sleep becomes lighter as we age, and insomnia is more common. Sleep patterns change to earlier bedtimes and earlier awakenings. Lifestyle changes can help and should be tried before medication.

12. Sexual activity is a complex set of behaviors determined by physical ability, desire, availability of a partner, and privacy. New medication is available to help with physical ability in men, but other factors can cause sexual activity to decline with age. Many people remain sexually active throughout their lives.

13. Primary aging is affected by many individual differences. Genes spare some people from predispositions to certain conditions, such as glaucoma and

osteoporosis. Genes also account for about 60% of the timing of skin wrinkling, age-related weight gain, and perceived age. Lifestyle factors, such as exercise and healthy diet, promote slower decline. Race, ethnicity, and socioeconomic factors affect access to health care and living in neighborhoods where exercise and good nutrition are easily obtained.

14. Most experts agree that there is as yet no way to "turn back the clock" of primary aging. We should avoid products and therapies that make this claim and support responsible research that slows the aging process and extends years of healthy life.

SHARED WRITING: PHYSICAL CHANGES

Consider this chapter's discussion of the physical changes that occur as people age. What are some changes that you have noticed (good or bad) about yourself or your parents as you have progressed into adulthood? How can you use awareness of these changes to better prepare for your own changes later in life? Write a short response that your classmates will read. Be sure to discuss specific examples.

▶ A minimum number of characters is required to post and earn points. After posting, your response can be viewed by your class and instructor, and you can participate in the class discussion.

Post   0 characters | 140 minimum

Chapter 2 Quiz: Physical Changes

Chapter 3
Health and Health Disorders

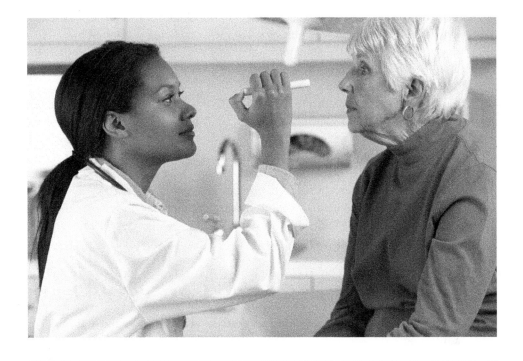

Learning Objectives

3.1 Discuss changes in mortality rates and causes of death as we move through adulthood

3.2a Relate secondary aging to morbidity rates, disease, and disability

3.2b Explain major causes of death and disability for adults at different ages

3.3 Identify the effect of health on daily life due a specific diseases across the adult years

3.4 Identify the various mental disorders and their treatment for adults of different ages

3.5 Describe the growing use of nonmedical solutions by the older population

3.6 Describe the individual health differences within an age group caused by lifestyle, gender, socioeconomic class, and race

EVERY YEAR a race is run in our town, and probably in yours too, called the "Race for the Cure," and it is intended to raise awareness (and money) for breast cancer prevention, detection, treatment, and research. The term *race* is fairly loose—ours is in January, and many women go in groups to enjoy a brisk walk in the Florida sun along the waterway, talking with each other and greeting friends they see along the route. A good number of men participate too, and lots of kids on skateboards, rollerblades, and in strollers. But the theme of the day is on everyone's minds—this form of cancer will strike (or has struck) one of every nine women in the United States. Almost everyone in the crowd has been touched by breast cancer, either by being diagnosed themselves or having a loved one counted among its statistics. Despite the festive atmosphere, the unescapable theme of the day is clear: *A whole lot of women (and many men) have had breast cancer and survived to walk in the sun.*

This chapter is about health and disease. I wish it were more about health and less about disease, but in truth, disease is part of adult life, and the longer we live the greater the chance we will have one disease or another. Many diseases, like breast cancer, have greater detection rates and survival rates all the time. Some, like lung cancer, can be prevented to a great extent through lifestyle decisions. And others, like Alzheimer's disease, are more difficult to prevent or to treat at present. I will start this chapter with some general statistics about disease patterns and then cover the most prevalent physical and mental health disorders. Finally, I will review the research on individual differences in health and disease.

3.1: Mortality Rates and Causes of Death

3.1 **Discuss changes in mortality rates and causes of death as we move through adulthood**

Figure 3.1 shows the **mortality rate**, or the probability of dying in any one year, for American men and women in various age groups. You can see that fewer than one tenth of 1% of emerging adults 15 to 24 die in any given year, whereas about 13% of adults over 85 die each year (Centers for Disease Control and Prevention [CDC], 2012e). The fact that older people are more likely to die is surely no great surprise (although you may be comforted to see how small the increases are into the 60s).

Figure 3.1 The mortality rate for adults in the United States increases slowly with age into the 60s, then rises more sharply.

SOURCE: CDC (2012e).

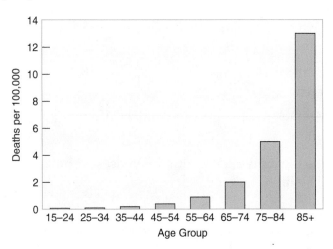

There are also different causes of death for people at different ages. Table 3.1 gives the major causes of death for people in the United States by age. Three of the top five causes of death for emerging adults (aged 15 to 24) aren't even diseases; they are accidents, homicides, and suicides. By young adulthood (25 to 44) accidents are still in first place, but cancer and heart disease are second and third. Middle-aged adults (aged 45 to 64) have cancer and heart disease in first and second place, and for older adults (aged 65 and over) these two diseases are reversed in first and second place, and Alzheimer's disease makes its first appearance in the top five causes of death (CDC, 2012e).

Table 3.1 Major Causes of Death in the United States by Age Group

Rank	15–24 Years	25–44 Years	45–64 Years	65+ Years
1	Accidents	Accidents	Cancer	Heart disease
2	Homicide	Cancer	Heart disease	Cancer
3	Suicide	Heart disease	Accidents	Lower respiratory disease
4	Cancer	Suicide	Lower respiratory disorders	Stroke
5	Heart disease	Homicide	Diabetes	Alzheimer's disease

SOURCE: Data from National Center for Health Statistics (2012).

3.2: Morbidity Rates, Disease, and Disability

3.2a Relate secondary aging to morbidity rates, disease, and disability

3.2b Explain major causes of death and disability for adults at different ages

Secondary aging, the topic of this chapter, involves changes that happen to some people as they move through adulthood and that are caused by external factors, such as infection, or internal factors, such as disease of particular organs or systems. They can also be caused by accidents. Not all diseases lead to disability, and not all disability is caused by disease. But the truth is that the further one journeys into adulthood, the higher the chance that he or she will find impediments in their lives due to one or more of these conditions.

3.2.1: Common Health Conditions

Before you read on, which age group would you predict has the highest rate of acute short-term health problems such as colds and flu, college students or their grandparents? You might assume that an age-related pattern would emerge for the **morbidity rate**, or illness rate, with older adults suffering from more of all types of health conditions. But that is not the case. Younger adults are actually about twice as likely as are those over 65 to suffer from short-term health problems, which physicians call **acute conditions**, including colds, flu, infections, or short-term intestinal upsets. It is only the rates of **chronic conditions**, longer-lasting disorders, such as heart disease, arthritis, or high blood pressure, that show an age-related increase. Older adults are two to three times more likely to suffer from such disorders than adults in their 20s and 30s.

3.2.2: Disability

Psychologists, epidemiologists, gerontologists, and even lawyers who deal with guardianship cases all define disability as the extent to which an individual is unable to perform two groups of activities: (a) basic self-care activities, such as bathing, dressing, getting around inside the home, shifting from a bed to a chair, using the toilet, and eating, collectively called **ADLs (activities of daily living)**, and (b) more complex everyday tasks, such as preparing meals, shopping for personal items, doing light housework, doing laundry, using transportation, handling finances, using the telephone, and taking medications, referred to as **IADLs (instrumental activities of daily living)**.

Although disabilities occur in all age groups, the incidence increases with age. As you can see in Figure 3.2, the U.S. Census Bureau reports that up until the age of 44, about 1 in 10 adults report having any disability at all, and a little more than half of those report that their disability is severe. By the age of 75, over half of adults report having a disability and a larger number of those consider it to be severe (Brault, 2012). As you can imagine, older adults spend more time on ADLs and IADLs than younger adults, and their ability to perform them is a key indicator of their quality of life.

Figure 3.2 The percent of adults with any disability increases with age, and so does the percent of those whose disability is severe.

SOURCE: Data from Brault (2012).

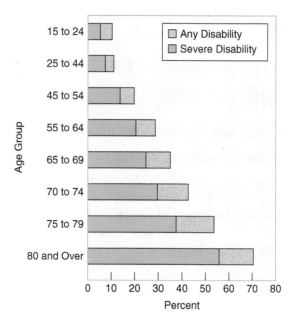

Having a chronic illness or health condition does not directly translate into being disabled. It is quite possible to have one or more chronic conditions without experiencing significant impairment. One person may have high blood pressure that is controlled with medication and exercise; another may have arthritis that responds well to medication and places no limitation on major activities. For most adults, the crucial issue is not whether they have a chronic condition but whether that condition has an impact on their daily lives, requiring restriction in daily activities or reducing their ability to care for themselves or participate in a full life without assistance.

In the past 20 years, the disability rates among older adults in the United States have declined substantially. There are a number of reasons for this. Population epidemiologist Vicki A. Freedman (2011) reviewed the evidence for this phenomenon and concluded that this decline is likely due to advances in medical care and changes in attitudes toward health. People are healthier today in all age groups, and this translates to less disability in old age. New surgical procedures and medications help manage diseases such as cardiovascular disease, cataracts, and arthritic knees and hips. Another factor is assistive technology, which has increased over the last two decades. People who would have been considered disabled in the past are able to function well because of items such as personal computers, cell phones, motorized wheelchairs, and portable oxygen tanks. Older people today have higher incomes and more education, which often results in healthier diets, less stress, and better medical care.

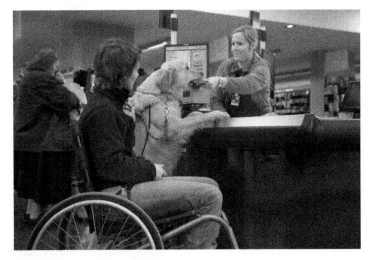

Having a chronic illness or health condition does not necessarily mean losing one's autonomy. With the help of assistance technology and assistance animals, many adults retain much of their independent lifestyles.

Increases in income and education have indirect effects, too (Schoeni, Freedman, & Martin, 2008). For example, people with higher educations are less apt to have jobs that are strenuous and can lead to disabilities in later years. Young adults and middle-aged adults who have higher incomes are more able to afford preventive medical care and healthy lifestyles, which in turn affect their health when they reach older adulthood.

As a result of these various factors, only about 3% of people over 65 live in nursing homes or skilled care facilities. About 81% of women and 90% of men over 65 are **community dwelling**, living in their own homes either with their spouses or alone. The remaining people this age live in senior residences or assisted-living facilities that provide limited help or live in the homes of family members (National Institute on Aging, 2011). Even at the age of 90 years and older, almost three fourths are living in their own homes or in the homes of family members (He & Muenchrath, 2011).

3.2.3: Self-Ratings of Health

Another way of measuring health, instead of evaluating activities of daily living, is to ask adults of different ages to rate their own health on a simple scale such as (1) excellent/very good, (2) good, or (3) fair/poor. These types of rating scales have compared well to more objective measures of physical and mental health (Pinquart & Sorensen, 2001). One such study was included in the U.S. National Health Interview Survey, and not surprisingly, young adults rated their health better than older adults. However, 40% of adults over the age of 75 rated themselves as being in excellent or very good health (Schiller, Lucas, Ward, et al., 2012). This does not mean, of course, that an 85-year-old who describes himself or herself as being in "excellent or very good" health has the same physical functioning as a 25-year-old who chooses the same description.

3.3: Specific Diseases

3.3 Identify the effect of health on daily life due a specific diseases across the adult years

In the previous section I discussed the major causes of death and disability for adults. This section covers four diseases in detail—cardiovascular disease, cancer, diabetes, and Alzheimer's disease. I certainly don't intend to turn you into medical experts; my aim is to offer a picture of how health affects our daily lives (and also how our daily lives affect our health).

3.3.1: Cardiovascular Disease

Disease of the heart and blood vessels, or **cardiovascular disease**, covers a number of physical deteriorations; the key change is in the coronary arteries, which slowly develop a dangerous accumulation of **plaques,** or fat-laden deposits. This process is known as **atherosclerosis,** and it is caused by inflammation, which normally is a protective process of the immune system. But chronic inflammation causes plaques to form in the artery walls, which can rupture and form blood clots that block the arteries, leading to heart attack or stroke (Smith, Lightfoot, Lerner, et al., 2009).

The death rate from cardiovascular disease has been dropping rapidly in the past two decades in the United States and most other industrialized countries. Yet it remains the leading cause of death and disability among both men and women in the United States (Hoyert & Xu, 2012) and throughout the developed world (World Health Organization, 2012). Some people are at greater risk for cardiovascular disease than others. Risk factors are listed in Table 3.2. As you will notice, some of these factors are under our control, such as sedentary lifestyle, and others are not, such as being older than 50.

Table 3.2 Risk Factors for Cardiovascular Disease

Factors that Cannot be Modified or Prevented	Factors that Can be Modified or Prevented
Being older than 50	Tobacco use and environmental exposure to tobacco smoke
Family history of cardiovascular disease	Obesity
	Sedentary lifestyle
	Diabetes
	High cholesterol
	High blood pressure

| Hide All Cells | Show All Cells |

SOURCE: From CDC (2012f).

Critical Thinking

What are some of the reasons that the rate of cardiovascular disease is declining in the United States?

I feel I should emphasize something here: *Cardiovascular disease is the number-one killer of women throughout the developed world.* The numbers can be misleading because the average age that men have heart attacks and die from cardiovascular disease is younger than the average age for women. Comparing cardiovascular disease rates by age can give the impression that it is a men's health problem; however, it can be just as dangerous for women.

In some ways, cardiovascular disease is even more dangerous for women because the early symptoms can be different. When we think of a heart attack, we think of crushing pain on the right side of the chest, but for women, it is more likely to be nausea, fatigue, dizziness, cold sweats, shortness of breath, and sharp pain in the upper body, neck, or jaw. When these warning signs are not heeded or are misinterpreted, cardiovascular disease can advance to the point that the first time medical assistance is sought, the disease has progressed much further than would be the case for men (CDC, 2012g). In addition, women's cardiovascular disease often involves smaller arteries of the heart instead of the large coronary arteries that are typically affected in men. In these cases, routine tests on the larger arteries show low risk of cardiovascular disease when, in fact, the women can be in advanced stages of microvascular disease (MVD), which has few symptoms (National Heart Lung and Blood Institute, 2011). For this reason, almost two thirds of women who die suddenly from cardiovascular disease have had no previous symptoms (CDC, 2012f).

3.3.2: Cancer

The second leading cause of death for men and women in the United States is **cancer**, a disease in which abnormal cells undergo rapidly accelerated, uncontrolled division and often move into adjacent normal tissues. Cancer can then spread through the bloodstream or lymph vessels to more distant tissues in the body, including the brain and other parts of the body.

The incidence of cancer increases with age. According to the National Cancer Registry, there are 22 times as many cancer cases in 70-year-olds than there are in 20-year-olds (CDC, 2012c). Another change with age is in the type of cancer one is likely to have. Breast cancer is the most frequent cause of cancer deaths for women under 55, whereas leukemia is most frequent for young adult men, and lung cancer is most frequent for middle-aged men. Once men and women reach 55, lung cancer remains the top cancer killer and stays there through the rest of the life span (Gibbs, 2004).

The search for a cause of cancer has made dramatic progress recently. It has been long believed that cancer begins with a series of random mutations that make the tumor-suppressing genes in a cell turn off and the tumor-stimulating genes turn on. Once this occurs, the mutated cell divides and replicates itself excessively, resulting in cancer. Recently, this explanation has been expanded. Although genetic mutations do occur, a major cause of cancer is now thought to be **epigenetic inheritance**, which involves environmental events that cause changes in gene expression (Berdasco & Esteller, 2010). Epigenetic inheritance is thought to go hand in hand with random mutations in causing a number of diseases, including cancer. Genetic characteristics that are caused by epigenetic inheritance are not those that are encoded in the genome at conception, like gender or Down syndrome. Rather, they are the result of environmental influences during the prenatal period or during the life span that affect how existing genes are expressed. In its normal function, epigenetic inheritance works to *downregulate* (or silence) one gene so that the other gene at that location is expressed. When the mechanism reacts abnormally, it switches off tumor-suppressing genes or turns on tumor-stimulating genes. The difference between this explanation and the traditional "random mutations" explanation is that it is possible to discover which environmental factors tend to create harmful epigenetic inheritance and to work toward preventions. There will be more discussion of this topic in later chapters.

Table 3.3 Risk Factors for Cancer

Factors that Cannot be Modified or Prevented	Factors that Can be Modified or Prevented
Being older than 50	Tobacco use (cigarettes, cigars, chewing tobacco, snuff)
Family history of cancer	Unhealthy diet (low in fruits and vegetables)
	Chemical and radiation exposure in the workplace
	Sexually transmitted diseases
	Sedentary lifestyle
	Obesity
	Excessive alcohol use
	Unprotected exposure to strong sunlight

Hide All Cells   Show All Cells

SOURCE: From Torpy (2004); CDC (2011d).

Beginning in 1990, the incidence and death rate from cancer began to decline significantly in the United States for the first time since national recordkeeping began, and this has continued to decrease at about 0.6% per year (Eheman, Henley, Ballard-Barbash, et al., 2012). The decline in cancer deaths in the last two decades is due to advances in prevention, early detection, and treatment. Recent prevention measures include the human papillomavirus (HPV) vaccine, which reduces chances of cervical cancer, and the hepatitis B vaccine, which helps prevent liver cancer (CDC, 2011d). Early detection has decreased the number of deaths from cervical, colorectal, and breast cancers. A growing number of people have made lifestyle changes to reduce their risks of cancer. The risk factors are shown in Table 3.3.

Advances have been made recently in the treatment of cancer, which has evolved from surgery to radiation to chemotherapy. Now the DNA of a tumor can be examined to determine which type of treatment would be most successful. In one study of breast cancer tumors, 18 genes were found that were frequently mutated. Interestingly, five of the genes had been previously linked to leukemia (Ellis, Ding, Shen, et al., 2012). These findings have led to tumors being classified by genes rather than by the tumor's location in the body. The implication is that drugs can be selected based on the mutation and not the body location. Researchers have found that one person's breast cancer may be similar in DNA to another person's leukemia and should be treated with similar drugs. This method has opened up the possibility that drugs that have been successful against cancer at one location of the body can be used on genetically similar tumors at other locations.

3.3.3: Diabetes

Diabetes is a disease in which the body is not able to metabolize insulin. Because insulin is required for the utilization of glucose, diabetes results in high levels of glucose in the blood and a reduction of nourishment to the body. Diabetes is related to increased risk of heart disease and stroke and is a major cause of blindness, kidney disease, amputations of feet and legs, complications during pregnancy leading to birth defects, and premature death. Although some diabetes (type 1) appears in childhood or young adulthood, over 90% of diabetes (type 2) is associated with older age, obesity, and physical inactivity.

The incidence of type 2 diabetes has increased dramatically in recent years and has become one of the major causes of disability and death for middle-aged adults in the United States (Table 3.1). Over 25 million adults and children in the United States have diabetes, but only 18 million are being treated for it; the other 7 million are not aware that they have it. When these data are examined by age, over 11% of all adults in the United States have diabetes. For the age group of 65 years and over, the proportion goes up to over 27% (American Diabetes Association, 2011). The mortality rate for a 65-year-old person with diabetes is twice the rate of someone the same age who does not have diabetes (Halter, 2011). Worldwide, it is the ninth leading cause of death, affecting about 10% of the adult population (World Health Organization, 2011).

Because type 2 diabetes is related to obesity and lack of exercise, the rates of this disease have increased along with the increase in BMI and sedentary lifestyle in the United States and many developing countries. The hopeful news is that the vast majority of cases of type 2 diabetes are preventable when individuals adopt a healthy diet and lifestyle, especially those in high-risk categories, which are shown in Table 3.4. Other hopeful news is that people diagnosed with prediabetes can slow down the progression to diabetes by weight loss and increased exercise, even when they are over the age of 60 (Halter, 2011). And a good number of obese people who have severe diabetes benefit dramatically from gastric bypass surgery, once considered a treatment of last resort (Arterburn, Bogart, Sherwood, et al., 2013).

Table 3.4 Risk Factors for Diabetes

Factors that Cannot be Modified or Prevented	Factors that Can be Modified or Prevented
Being older than 45	Obesity
Family history of diabetes	High blood pressure
	High cholesterol
	Sedentary lifestyle
	Hide All Cells Show All Cells

SOURCE: From American Diabetes Association (2012).

3.3.4: Alzheimer's Disease

The fifth leading cause of death for people 65 and over is **Alzheimer's disease**, a progressive, irreversible deterioration of key areas of the brain involved in various cognitive functions. The hallmark loss with Alzheimer's disease is short-term memory, which is important for remembering newly learned information such as recent events or earlier conversations. These deficits increase to affect social, cognitive, and movement abilities and end in death approximately 8 to 10 years after diagnosis (although most patients die of other causes such as pneumonia or complications after a fall). Unlike cardiovascular disease and cancer, which can occur throughout adulthood, Alzheimer's disease is truly a disease of old age, with 90% of the cases developing after the age of 65. Once considered a rare disorder, Alzheimer's disease has become a major public health problem in the United States and throughout the world, primarily because of the increasing proportion of older people in our population. Alzheimer's disease afflicts one out of eight people in the United States over 65—almost 5.5 million people—and almost half of people 85 and older (Alzheimer's Association, 2013). If you are like 25 million other people in the United States, you are acutely aware of this disease because you have a family member with Alzheimer's disease and are experiencing its effects firsthand.

Alzheimer's disease is the most prevalent type of **dementia**, a category of conditions that involve global deterioration in intellectual abilities and physical function. Other types of dementia can be caused by multiple small strokes, Parkinson's disease, multiple blows to the head (as among boxers), a single head trauma, advanced stages of AIDS, depression, drug intoxication, hypothyroidism, some kinds of tumors, vitamin B_{12} deficiency, anemia, and alcohol abuse. I don't expect you to memorize this list, but I do want you to realize that a decline in cognitive functioning is not necessarily Alzheimer's disease; sometimes it is a condition that can be treated and has a more favorable outcome. The cause of Alzheimer's disease is not clear, but we have known since the early part of the 20th century that autopsies of people who die of dementia often reveal specific abnormalities in the brain tissue. One of these abnormalities, first identified by neuropathologist Alois Alzheimer in 1907, is called *senile plaque*. These are small, circular deposits of a dense protein, beta-amyloid; another abnormality is *neurofibrillary tangles,* or webs of degenerating neurons.

According to the Alzheimer's Association (2012), several genes have been found that contribute to Alzheimer's disease. One gene, APOE E4, increases one's risk for Alzheimer's disease. If you inherit one copy of this gene you are at higher risk for Alzheimer's disease than someone who does not have this form of the gene. If you inherit two copies of this gene, you are at even greater risk, though it is not certain you will have the disease. Three other genes, APP, PSEN1, and PSEN2, determine with certainty that a person will have Alzheimer's disease.

The type of Alzheimer's disease caused by all these genes is the early-onset type, occurring in middle age (sometimes as early as 30 or 40), and affecting many family members in each generation. However, this type of Alzheimer's disease accounts for only 5% of the total cases. Scientists have identified a few hundred families in the world with these genes, and they study them in hopes of learning something about the more common forms of the disease. For example, possible vaccines against Alzheimer's disease are tested on these families instead of individuals in the general population because of the higher probability that they will develop the disease in a shorter amount of time.

WRITING PROMPT

What are the pros and cons of being tested for the Alzheimer's gene? Explain your answer in a brief response that will be read by your instructor.

 The response entered here will appear in the performance dashboard and can be viewed by your instructor.

Submit

Advances are being made in the diagnosis of Alzheimer's disease also. Until the 1990s, it could only be diagnosed with certainty after death with an autopsy. It is now possible to identify areas of senile plaque and neurofibrillary tangles in living patients using imaging techniques such as PET scans (Clark, Schneider, Bedell, et al., 2011). Cognitive and behavioral tests are also used with good accuracy.

A pre-Alzheimer's stage is called **mild cognitive impairment (MCI)**, in which patients show some cognitive symptoms, but not all those necessary for a diagnosis of Alzheimer's disease. About half the individuals with mild cognitive impairment will progress to Alzheimer's disease within the next 3 to 4 years. Interestingly, memory deficits are not early symptoms for about one third of the people with MCI. Instead, they exhibit visuospatial deficits, as tested by mental manipulations of three-dimensional figures, and executive function deficits, as tested by digit span tests (Storandt, 2008).

As mentioned earlier, the greatest risk factor for Alzheimer's disease is age. Other risk factors are shown in Table 3.5. Some of the risk factors should seem familiar to you by now because they are the same factors that put us at risk for cardiovascular disease. In fact, people with cardiovascular disease are more apt to get Alzheimer's disease than people with healthy hearts, probably because of the inflammation that underlies both diseases.

Table 3.5 Risk Factors for Alzheimer's Disease

Factors that Cannot be Modified or Prevented	Factors that Can be Modified or Prevented
Being over 50	High cholesterol levels
Head injury	High blood pressure
Family history of Alzheimer's disease	Sedentary lifestyle
	Tobacco use
	Obesity

| Hide All Cells | Show All Cells |

SOURCE: Alzheimer's Association (2013)

ADDITIONAL RISK FACTORS FOR ALZHEIMER'S DISEASE   Another risk factor for Alzheimer's disease and other types of dementia is **traumatic brain injury (TBI)**. Studies have shown that individuals who sustain head injuries severe enough to lose consciousness are two to four times more likely to develop dementia in later life than those who do not have this injury, especially a type of dementia known as **chronic traumatic encephalopathy (CTE)**. This line of research began in England in the 1960s when the Royal College of Physicians asked medical researcher A. H. Roberts to examine a randomly selected sample of retired boxers. He found that 17% of them fit the diagnosis for CTE (Roberts, 1969). Since that time, autopsies on football, soccer, and ice hockey players have confirmed the presence of CTE, the symptoms of which can include explosive rages, depression, substance abuse, memory impairment, and suicide (Shively, Scher, Perl, et al., 2012).

Of particular concern are military personnel who experience TBI as a result of improvised explosive devices (IEDs), the weapon of choice by our enemies in Iraq and Afghanistan (Hope, McGurk, Thomas, et al., 2008). TBI has been strongly associated with posttraumatic stress syndrome (PTSD), leading to the hypothesis that many of the combat veterans with PTSD have CTE (Omalu, Hammers, Bailes, et al., 2011). Both the professional sports organizations and the Veterans Administration are working on better protection for the young men and women involved and ways to avoid the long-term damage done by these injuries.

I will end this section with a few words about Alzheimer's disease and normal aging of the brain. The memory of an older adult is not as sharp or as quick as it once was, and it becomes somewhat more difficult for them to learn new information. This might lead you to believe that Alzheimer's disease is just an extreme form of normal aging, but this is not true. Alzheimer's disease is a different creature entirely. With normal aging, we may forget for a minute what day it is, have trouble retrieving a specific name, or misplace our car keys. Cognitive symptoms of Alzheimer's disease include losing track of the season, being unable to carry on a conversation, and being lost in a familiar neighborhood (Alzheimer's Association, 2013).

It is important to attend to personality and cognitive changes in older adults. Although there is currently no cure for Alzheimer's disease, there is treatment available for other conditions with similar symptoms. Medications are now available that slow down the progression of Alzheimer's disease in its early stages. There is counseling and community assistance for patients with Alzheimer's disease and their caregivers.

3.3.5: People Living with Age-Related Diseases and Disability

The number of people with age-related diseases and disabilities is increasing for two reasons: first, there are more older adults in our population today, and second, some of the diseases, such as diabetes, are on the increase. Chances are that you have people living with age-related diseases or disabilities in your family or among your friends and neighbors. I do. Living in south Florida, where the proportion of older adults is higher than most places in the country, people with age-related diseases and disabilities have become increasingly common. There are several examples demonstrating this fact.

- In my yoga class are two women with Alzheimer's disease. One comes with a professional caregiver (who does yoga alongside her), and the other comes with a long-time friend, who drives her to class and then takes her out to lunch afterwards, giving her caregiver husband a break twice a week.
- On our highways are digital signs for posting messages about accidents or other public service announcements. Now, along with Amber Alerts for missing children, we frequently have Silver Alerts, for older adults with dementia who are missing from their homes.
- The golf club where some of my friends play has a golf pro who takes people living with disabilities out to play golf on Thursday afternoons. Most have cardiovascular disease and can't play all 18 holes, some have Alzheimer's disease but are able to play with some assistance, but all enjoy being out on the course in the golf cart and being with fellow golfers.
- My water aerobics class of about 50 women almost always has one or two with colorful headscarves covering bald heads—the temporary side effect of cancer treatment. After class there is conversation among the current patients and the survivors, talking about wigs, tattooed eyebrows, and care for damaged skin.

The message in this is not "get used to it," but that we need to learn to look beyond the symptoms and statistics to see the *people* living with age-related diseases. Being diagnosed with Alzheimer's disease or cancer or heart disease is not the end of a person's personhood. There are often many years between the diagnosis and the end of life, and family members, friends, professional caregivers, and even golf pros can help make those years pleasurable and meaningful. If it takes a village to raise a child, it takes the same village to care for its elders.

3.4: Mental Disorders

3.4   Identify the various mental disorders and their treatment for adults of different ages

The diagnosis and treatment of mental disorders is a fairly new topic of scientific investigation. Before Freud's time, mental disorders were more the realm of religion or philosophy, and once they became accepted as treatable health conditions, each school of therapy had its own classification system and treatment plan. It was not until 1980 that a standardized system of symptoms and diagnoses was agreed on by mental health professionals in the United States in the form of the *Diagnostic and Statistical Manual,* 3rd edition, or *DSM-III* (American Psychiatric Association, 1980). This advance was important for therapists and their patients, but it also made it possible for epidemiologists to compile data and answer questions about our country's mental health. Since that time several large-scale surveys have been conducted, giving us answers about the state of the nation's mental health. The DSM is now in its fifth edition, reflecting the ongoing changes in our knowledge about mental health disorders and their treatments (American Psychiatric Association, 2013).

The largest and most comprehensive study of this type, the National Comorbidity Survey, conducted by sociologist Ronald Kessler and his colleagues (Kessler, Berglund, Demler, et al., 2005), consists of data from face-to-face interviews with over 9,000 randomly selected adults in the United States. This study replicates a similar study done 10 years earlier, and the results have been compared to see what changes have occurred during that time. They have also been compared to related studies done in other countries. General findings from this survey tell us that about 46% of people in the United States experience some sort of mental illness during their lifetimes—disorders either of mood, anxiety, substance abuse, or impulse control. Furthermore, within a 12-month period, 26% experience some sort of mental health disorder. The good news is that these numbers are the same as those from a similar study conducted 10 years earlier, showing that mental illness has not increased in the United States. The bad news is that these numbers are the highest in any developed country. The four categories included in this study are shown in Table 3.6, along with the disorders included in each category

Table 3.6 Mental Health in the United States: Survey Results

DSM Classification	Examples	Lifetime Prevalence[a]	12-month Prevalence[b]	Median Age of Onset[c]	% Male/ % Female
Anxiety Disorders	Phobias, posttraumatic stress disorder, obsessive-compulsive disorder	28.8%	18.1%	11 years	38% male/ 62% female
Mood Disorders	Depression, bipolar disorder	20.8%	9.5%	30 years	40% male/ 60% female
Impulse Control Disorders	Conduct disorder, intermittent explosive disorder, ADHD	24.8%	8.9%	11 years	59% male/ 41% female
Substance Abuse Disorders	Alcohol and drug abuse or dependence	14.6%	3.8%	20 years	71% male/ 29% female
Any Disorder Above		46.4%	26.2%	14 years	48% male/ 52% female

[a]Percent who have had this type of disorder at least once in their lifetime.
[b]Percent who have had this type of disorder in the last 12 months.
[c]Age at which 50% of the cases had appeared.

SOURCE: Data from Kessler, Berglund, Demler, et al. (2005), Table 2, p. 595 & Table 3, p. 596; Kessler, Chiu, Demler, et al. (2005), Table 1, p. 619; Wang, Berglund, Olfson, et al. (2005), p. 605.

and findings from the study. (Less common disorders, such as schizophrenia and autism, were not included because they are not amenable to a household survey.)

Table 3.6 shows the median age of onset for each of the four groups of disorders. **Onset** refers to first occurrence, and as you can see, unlike most physical disorders, mental disorders generally have their onsets in adolescence and early adulthood. Thus, they result in more years of chronic illness and disability and cause more premature deaths than chronic physical disorders. Further complicating the duration of these disorders is the recent finding that the median time it takes for a person with a mental disorder to seek treatment can range from 8 years for some types of mood disorders to 23 years for some types of anxiety disorders. Even more problematic is the finding that a significant proportion of people never seek treatment (Wang, Berglund, Olfson, et al., 2005).

The National Comorbidity Survey also provides data on the **prevalence** of mental disorders, which is the percentage of people experiencing a certain disorder for a given period, such as in their lifetimes or during the last 12 months. As you can see in Table 3.6, the lifetime prevalence for various types of mental health disorders ranges from 14.6% (substance abuse disorders) to 28.8% (anxiety disorders). Forty-eight percent of people reporting a mental health disorder in this study were men; 52% were women, mirroring the gender distribution in the United States. Across the adult years, the 12-month prevalence of most mental disorders increases from young adulthood to middle adulthood and then declines, with the lowest rates being for adults who are 60 years of age and older (Kessler, Berglund, Demler, et al., 2005).

Participants in this study were rated as to the severity of their symptoms. The results showed that 22% were serious, 37% were moderate, and 40% were mild. More than 40% of the respondents classified as having one of the four types of mental disorders listed earlier were **comorbid**, meaning that they had more than one disorder, and not surprisingly the more disorders they reported, the greater the severity of their symptoms (Kessler, Chiu, Demler, et al., 2005).

Following is a discussion of the four types of disorders included in this study and some information about the treatment that adults in the United States seek for their mental health disorders.

3.4.1: Anxiety Disorders

Anxiety disorders involve feelings of fear, threat, and dread when no obvious danger is present. They are the most common type of mental health disorder for adults in the United States. During a 12-month period, approximately 18% of American adults report experiencing an anxiety disorder (Kessler, Chiu, Demler, et al., 2005).

The most common anxiety disorders are as follows:

- **Phobias**: This includes fears and avoidance out of proportion to the danger presented.
- **Posttraumatic Stress Disorder (PTSD)**: This is an emotional reaction experienced repeatedly to a traumatic event that happened in the past.
- **Obsessive-Compulsive Disorder**: This involves guilt and anxiety over certain thoughts or impulses.

Although many adults experience anxiety disorders, these usually begin in childhood. Half the people who have anxiety disorders experience the first one before the age of 11; three quarters of the people who have anxiety disorders have already experienced one before the age of 21. More women than men experience anxiety disorders (Kessler, Berglund, Demler, et al., 2005).

In the past year, about one in five adults in the United States reported symptoms of anxiety disorder that took them out of the flow of everyday life.

3.4.2: Mood Disorders

Mood disorders involve a loss in the sense of control over emotions, resulting in feelings of distress. They are the second most common type of mental health disorder for adults in the United States and include major depression and bipolar disorder. A fifth of us will experience some sort of mood disorder over the course of our lifetimes. More women than men experience mood disorders. **Major depression** is typified by a long-term, pervasive sense of sadness and hopelessness. In the National Comorbidity Survey, major depression was the most prevalent disorder for adults in the United States, affecting over 16% of respondents during their lifetimes. Current depression was assessed by the researchers using a survey that asked people in the United States if they had experienced certain symptoms in the last 2 weeks (CDC, 2012a). About 4% met the criteria for major depression. The rates of major depression are high all over the world and increasing; it was the fourth leading cause of disease-related disability in the world in 1990 and will become the second leading cause by 2020 (Bloom, 2005). The World Health Organization reports that for women, major depression is the leading cause of disease-related disability in the developed nations of the world (World Health Organization, 2013).

The question of whether more older adults than younger adults suffer from depression seems like an easy one, but it is not. First, we need to define what we mean by "depression."

⊗ Definition:

The National Comorbidity Survey discussed earlier and other studies often use the guidelines set out by the *DSM-IV* to define major depression. These guidelines state that for a 12-week period, the patient must be in a depressed mood most of the day and show a loss of interest or pleasure in almost all activities. They may in addition show a change in weight or sleep patterns, fatigue, feelings of worthlessness, problems with decision making, or thoughts of suicide (**American Psychiatric Association, 2000**).

When this strict definition is used, the onset is most often in early adulthood, around the age of 30, with three quarters of people who will ever have major depression already experiencing it by the age of 43. When age groups are compared, rates of major depression are significantly lower for older adults than young and middle-aged adults. In fact, when major depression occurs for the first time in an older person, it is often related to Alzheimer's disease (van Reekum, Binns, Clarke, et al., 2005) or cardiovascular disease (Bjerkeset, Nordahl, Mykletun, et al., 2005).

In comparison, when it comes to **depressive symptoms**, the results are quite different. Studies in this area are done using symptoms checklists, such as the Center for Epidemiologic Studies Short Depression Scale (CES-D 10), shown in Table 3.7 (Radloff, 1977; Andresen, Malmgren, Carter, et al., 1994). As you can see, the symptoms are not as severe or as long-lasting as with major depression. When this criteria is used in research, older adults exhibit higher rates of depression than those in the middle years (Kessler, Mickelson, Walters, et al., 2004). Depressive symptoms include more indicators related to chronic health problems or the deaths of a spouse, friends, or relatives, all of which are more common in older adults than middle-aged adults.

Table 3.7 Test for Depressive Symptoms: Center for Epidemiologic Studies Short Depression Scale (CES-D 10)

Instructions: Following is a list of some of the ways you may have felt or behaved. Please indicate how often you have felt this way during the past week by checking the appropriate box for each question.

Item	Rarely or none of the time (less than 1 day)	Some or a little of the time (1–2 days)	Occasionally or a moderate amount of the time (3–4 days)	All of the time (5–7 days)
1. I was bothered by things that usually don't bother me.	❏	❏	❏	❏
2. I had trouble keeping my mind on what I was doing.	❏	❏	❏	❏
3. I felt depressed.	❏	❏	❏	❏
4. I felt that everything I did was an effort.	❏	❏	❏	❏
5. I felt hopeful about the future.*	❏	❏	❏	❏
6. I felt fearful.	❏	❏	❏	❏
7. My sleep was restless.	❏	❏	❏	❏
8. I was happy.*	❏	❏	❏	❏
9. I felt lonely.	❏	❏	❏	❏
10. I could not "get going."	❏	❏	❏	❏
Score for each check in column	0	1	2	3
*Reverse scoring for items 5 & 8	*3	*2	*1	*0

A score of 10 or more is considered depressed.

SOURCE: Radloff (1977); Andresen, Malmgren, Carter, et al. (1994).

In summary, major depression and other mood disorders are generally mental health problems of young adults. Older adults may exhibit a number of depressive symptoms, but these may be the result of the health problems, bereavement, and loss of social contacts that occur more often at that stage of life. Chronic depression that begins in older adulthood is often related to disease.

WRITING PROMPT

Not everyone with a mental health disorder seeks treatment. Is there one type of disorder for which you think people would be more likely to seek treatment than others? Why? Write a short response that will be read by your instructor.

> The response entered here will appear in the performance dashboard and can be viewed by your instructor.

Submit

3.4.3: Impulse Control Disorders

The category of **impulse control disorders** is defined as those disorders that affect a person's judgment or ability to control strong and often harmful impulses. It includes disorders of conduct, oppositional-defiant behavior, intermittent explosive disorder, and attention-deficit/hyperactivity disorder (ADHD). More men experience impulse control disorders than women. All these disorders, with the exception of intermittent explosive disorder, are usually considered childhood disorders, but recent studies have shown that over 4% of adults report experiencing symptoms of attention-deficit/hyperactivity disorder in the past 12 months, just half the rate that is reported in childhood. This suggests that about half the children with this disorder will continue to experience it in adulthood (Kessler, Chiu, Demler, et al., 2005).

3.4.4: Substance Abuse Disorders

The category of **substance abuse disorders** involves abuse or dependence on drugs or alcohol about 15% of adults in the United States experience one of these disorders during their lives, with half reporting onset before age 20 and half after age 20.

Three quarters of the people who will ever experience one of these disorders will do so by the age of 27. Substance abuse disorders are more common in men than in women. The most common disorder in this category is alcohol abuse, which is experienced by about 13% of people in the United States, the second most common disorder after major depression (about 17%).

Besides taking large personal tolls on the individual and family, the CDC estimates that alcohol abuse contributes to 79,000 deaths in the United States each year and over $224 billion in lost productivity, health-care costs, and criminal justice costs, or about $746 for each person in the country—most attributed to binge drinking, which is defined as having five or more drinks on a single occasion (Bouchery, Harwood, Sacks, et al., 2011). And of course this does not even touch on intangibles such as pain, suffering, and bereavement brought by substance abuse disorder. I speak of this both from reading the research and from a personal perspective. Our family has been seriously affected by abuse of prescription pain medication, and I have yet to meet a family who does not have a similar story to tell.

3.4.5: Treatment of Mental Health Disorders

Only about 40% of adults with mental health disorders seek some sort of treatment. Considering all the recent advances in psychopharmacology and psychotherapy, this shows that the optimistic picture of "curing" mental illness is not a reality for the majority of people who suffer from these disorders. To make matters worse, only about a third of those who seek help actually get treatment that is judged adequate by professional guidelines (Wang, Lane, Olfson, et al., 2005).

Another third of the people who seek treatment for mental health disorders go to **complementary and alternative medicine providers**, such as chiropractors, acupuncturists, herbalists, or spiritualists, none of whose methods for treating mental health disorders have been supported by scientific data. Still, patients report that these complementary and alternative medicine providers listen to them and include them in treatment decisions. It is important for mainstream mental health professionals to adopt some of this "bedside manner" and use it to make their conventional treatment more attractive (Wang, Lane, Olfson, et al., 2005). Other studies have shown that a brief screening for mental health problems during visits with primary care physicians can be very effective in diagnosing patients at risk for depression and substance abuse disorders and providing counseling or further treatment (Maciosek, Coffield, Flottemesch, et al., 2010).

One group that has become the target of concern among educators and mental health professionals is emerging adults. Twenty-one-year-olds who report symptoms of depression are less likely to receive treatment than 16-year-olds. Some of the other reasons they give are that they can't afford treatment, they think the symptoms will go away on their own, and they are too busy (Yu, Adams, Burns, et al., 2008). Another reason is that until recently, young adults were not eligible for insurance coverage under their parents' health-care policies, and few have jobs that provide health-care benefits.

Most mental health disorders first appear in adolescence and emerging adult-hood, and if diagnosed and treated early, they are less likely to cause lifelong prob-lems. Research has revealed that mental health disorders are responsible for over 10% of high school dropouts and almost 3% of college dropouts (Breslau, Lane, Sampson, et al., 2008). Yet parents, pediatricians, and school officials are not trained to identify early symptoms or high-risk variables. Hopefully some of the results of the recent mass killings in Aurora, Colorado, and Newtown, Connecticut, will be an emphasis on early intervention in mental health diagnosis and treatment.

In summary, it seems that the advances in pharmaceuticals and therapy for mental health disorders are not interfacing well with the actual needs of adults of all ages. We need more education about what is a mental disorder and what is not, more information about proven treatment and where to find it, better treatment for people who do seek it, and more people-friendly professionals providing proven, conventional therapies. Let's hope that future waves of studies show some progress in this area.

3.5: Nonmedical Solutions

3.5 Describe the growing use of nonmedical solutions by the older population

Not all the answers to disease and disability involve medication and surgery; some involve assistive technology and assistance animals, and as our population grows older, these "devices" are becoming more and more common.

3.5.1: Assistive Technology

When life-span developmental psychology meets technology, the result can be products that improve the quality of life and independence for adults with age-related conditions or disabilities. These devices can range in complexity from sim-ple reach extenders to complex electronics. For example, wireless personal emergency response systems are widely available that transmit information about falls, inactivity, room temperature, fire, and carbon monoxide to remote caregivers or family members, allowing older adults or adults with disabilities to have more independence in their own homes. Personal computers run software that translates text to speech or magnifies text for people with vision limitations. Household robots may seem like science fiction to some adults, but they are already present in many homes. (I have one that cleans my pool and another that vacuums my floors.) Other robots can be operated by distant caregivers to communicate with elderly or disabled people via camera, microphone, and speaker. On the horizon are more humanlike robots that cook simple meals, declutter the living area, and give reminders about medication schedules. Smartphone apps now perform basic med-ical tests like measuring heart rate, blood pressure, and blood sugar, keeping a record of the results for the user to monitor or sending the information to a car-egiver or physician.

3.5.2: Assistance Animals

Much lower-tech help comes from assistance animals. Their roles include guiding the visually impaired, signaling the hearing impaired, or performing services such as flip-ping on light switches, picking up dropped objects, and alerting their human to alarms, telephone rings, and doorbells. Most of these assistance animals are dogs, but capuchin monkeys can be trained to perform tasks that require fine motor skills like turning the pages of a book and pushing buttons on a microwave oven.

Another type of assistance animal is a comfort animal, again usually a dog, that is used to calm people in stressful situations, such as psychotherapy sessions. In fact, Sigmund Freud used his chow, Jofi, during psychoanalysis sessions to help patients relax (Coren, 2010). Comfort animals are also used to calm people who are institutionalized in nursing homes, mental hospitals, and prisons (Baun & Johnson, 2010). At my university, volunteers bring comfort animals to campus during midterm and final exam weeks, and they receive a very warm reception from students who are often missing their own "comfort animals" back home.

3.6: Individual Differences in Health

3.6 **Describe the individual health differences within an age group caused by lifestyle, gender, socioeconomic class, and race**

So far in this chapter I have covered age-linked patterns for various physical diseases and mental health conditions. However, as you no doubt realize, this is not a matter of "one rule fits all." Within these age patterns are a variety of individual differences caused by factors we are born with, such as gender, and factors we acquire along the way, such as exercise habits. The following is a discussion of some of these factors.

3.6.1: Lifestyle

At the risk of repeating myself, I must point out that two of the biggest factors in age-related disease are sedentary lifestyle and obesity. They appear on every table of risk factors in this chapter and are also implicated as risk factors for mental health disorders (Gómez-Pinilla, 2008; Walsh, 2011; Lindwall, Larsman, & Hagger, 2011). However, it may surprise you to know that fewer than 20% of adults in the United States get the recommended aerobic and muscle-strengthening exercise each week (CDC, 2012d). Over one third of U.S. adults are obese due to lack of exercise and diets high in calories from sugar and fat. Primary care physicians are increasingly recommending physical exercise for their patients of all ages, as you can see in Figure 3.3. The largest increase has been for patients 85 years of age and older, almost doubling in the past decade (Barnes & Schoenborn, 2012).

Figure 3.3 The percent of adults advised by their physicians to exercise has increased steadily since 2000 for all age groups.

SOURCE: CDC (2012d).

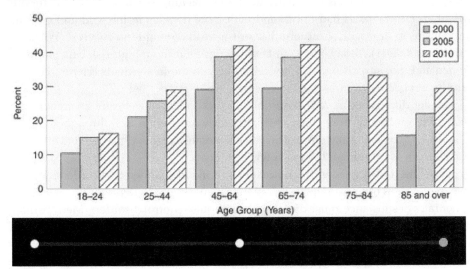

Other lifestyle factors that contribute to poor health are tobacco and other substance abuse. Tobacco is a risk factor for almost every form of cancer as well as heart disease and Alzheimer's disease, yet 20% of people in the United States smoke cigarettes, and more use other tobacco products. The good news in this is that the rate of tobacco use is down in the last two decades, and the rate of exercise is up. The bad news is that the obesity rate is up, too.

3.6.2: Gender

Another fact apparent in this chapter is that men and women have different patterns of health problems. Men have shorter life expectancies than women and higher rates of heart disease, hypertension, death by accident, and overall cancer rates. Women live longer than men, but when they die, they do so from basically the same diseases that men do; they just develop them later in life.

Women have more chronic health conditions than men, including arthritis, asthma, migraine headaches, thyroid disease, gallbladder problems, and urinary and bladder problems, among others (Cleary, Zaborski, & Ayanian, 2004). Women have more visits to doctors, take more medication, and spend more time in hospitals than men do (Austad, 2011).

WRITING PROMPT

Men have higher rates of impulse control disorders. Could you make an argument that it was an adaptive mechanism for our ancestral fathers? Why or why not? Write a short response that will be read by your instructor.

▶ The response entered here will appear in the performance dashboard and can be viewed by your instructor.

Submit

Where might such gender differences come from? The explanations are partly biological, partly environmental. Most investigators agree that the differences in longevity and in later onset of major disease are primarily biological: Women have a genetic endowment that gives them protection in early adulthood against many fatal diseases, such as cardiovascular disease. Why this discrepancy? Many theorists believe that it is because women's overall health during the childbearing and early parenting years has been more important to the survival of the species than men's (Allman, Rosin, Kumar, et al., 1998).

A related hypothesis is that males do not live as long as females because, for our ancient ancestors, males had to contend with more dangers in the wild and evolved mechanisms to deal with short-term hazards instead of long-term survival (Williams, 1957; Austad, 2011). Today, men still tend to engage in more high-risk behavior than women and, not surprisingly, are twice as likely to die in accidents (Heron, Hoyert, Murphy, et al., 2009).

Gender differences include behavioral factors too, such as health awareness and effort spent on health care, which are higher for women than men throughout adulthood. Perhaps one reason women live longer is because of this vigilance (and also why men with wives live longer than men without them).

There are robust gender differences for specific mental health disorders; women have higher rates of major depression and most anxiety disorders, whereas men have higher rates of substance abuse disorders and impulse control disorders. Men are more likely to commit suicide. Women's heightened vulnerability to disorders that affect emotional functioning is thought to be due, in part, to estrogen levels—the same hormones that provide protection from some physical diseases. Testosterone, on the other hand, tends to protect men against depression by blunting the effect of stress and negative emotions (Holden, 2005).

3.6.3: Socioeconomics, Race, and Ethnicity

The United States is one of the wealthiest countries in the world, and we spend more on health care than any other country, yet we have one of the lowest life expectancies of any developed country. The largest discrepancy is found in the groups of people with lower incomes and less education. Because people in minority racial and ethnic groups are more prevalent in the lower socioeconomic levels, it is difficult to separate the effects of income, education, and minority status on health, but I will attempt to do that in the following section.

SOCIOECONOMIC STATUS   The combined rating of income and education makes up one's **socioeconomic status (SES)**. A report on socioeconomic status and health in the United States commissioned by the MacArthur Foundation reached two general conclusions:

1.   the health of people in lower SES groups in the United States is notably worse than that of people in higher SES groups and

2.   people in lower SES groups use health services less and have less adequate health-related behaviors than those in higher SES groups (Adler, Stewart, Cohen, et al., 2007).

Figure 3.4 shows how many more years of expected life remains for 25-year-old men and women with different education levels. As you can see, each step on the education ladder brings more expected years of life for both young men and young women (CDC, 2012b).

Figure 3.4 Young adults with more education can expect to live longer than those with less education.

SOURCE: CDC (2012b).

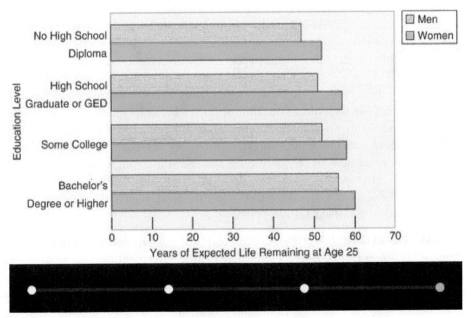

Socioeconomic status also has a large effect on mental health. In the National Health and Nutrition Examination Survey, adults were asked about their depressive symptoms. When responses were examined by income level, respondents at every age who had lower income levels reported more symptoms of depression (CDC, 2012b). Figure 3.5 shows the results.

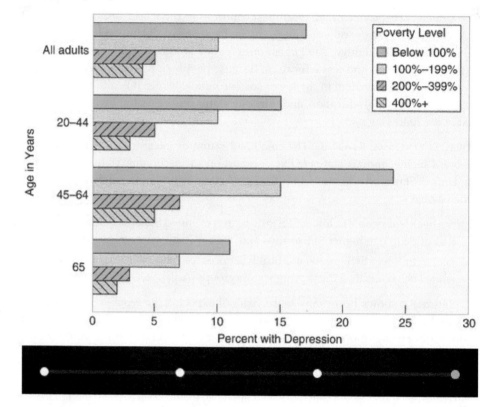

Figure 3.5 Adults of all ages whose incomes are below the poverty level are more apt to experience depression than those with higher incomes, and the lower the income is, the higher the risk for depression.

SOURCE: CDC (2012b).

When age is factored into the equation, the detrimental effects of low socioeconomic level are multiplied. Older adults with low incomes and little education have more physical and mental health problems, more disabilities, and shorter lifetimes than older adults with higher incomes and more education (Herd, Robert, & House, 2011).

Income and education contribute independently to poor health. That is, within an income group, those with more education will have better health than those with less education. And within an education group, those with higher incomes will have better health than those with lower incomes (Herd, Goesling, & House, 2007).

Economic conditions in neighborhoods also contribute to the health of the people who live there. High poverty areas are related to poor health outcomes because of factors such as stress, isolation, and the lack of healthy food, exercise facilities, and medical care providers (Sheffield & Peek, 2009).

RACIAL AND ETHNIC GROUPS Before I start this section I need to caution you that this topic is not as simple as it seems. There is little agreement on how to categorize people in the United States into racial and ethnic groups, how to define those groups, and what to do with those who don't quite fit into a group (or those who fit into more than one group). The following information is based on the groups identified by the most recent U.S. census, but I acknowledge that there are other widely used classification systems and terminology.

The ethnic group within the U.S. population that seems to have the best health picture is Asian Americans and Pacific Islanders. They have the lowest rates of cardiovascular disease, hypertension, arthritis, cancer, and serious psychological distress (Miller, Chu, Hankey, et al., 2007). They are, understandably, the most likely to rate their health as "excellent." Why the good health? The traditional diets of these groups are healthier than the typical diet in the United States, and the smoking rate is low (Edwards, Brown, & Wingo, 2005). However, as with other immigrant groups, the longer they live in the United States, the higher the risk of disease due to their adopted lifestyle (Reed & Yano, 1997).

Non-Hispanic white adults have the longest overall life expectancy of any group in the United States. They have the highest rates of anxiety disorders, mood disorders, and substance abuse disorders (Kessler, Berglund, Demler, et al., 2005), but they are more apt to seek treatment for mental disorders, especially if they are under 60 and have good incomes (Wang, Lane, Olfson, et al., 2005).

Hispanic Americans are, in general, at higher risk for early death than their non-Hispanic white counterparts, but have lower rates of anxiety disorders and mood disorders (Kessler, Berglund, Demler, et al., 2005). Similar to the Asian Pacific Islanders, the length of time Hispanic Americans have been in the United States is a health factor. The longer they have lived here, the more apt they are to have adopted an unhealthy diet and a sedentary lifestyle, leading to higher rates of obesity and related chronic diseases than those who only recently arrived in the United States (Goel, McCarthy, Phillips, et al., 2004). Country of origin is also a factor; for example, Cuban Americans have substantially better health than other Hispanic American groups (Herd, Robert, & House, 2011).

Adults classified as non-Hispanic blacks in the United States have shorter life expectancies than white adults, especially black males. They have the highest rates of death from heart disease, cancer, stroke, diabetes, HIV, and homicide than any other racial or ethnic group in the United States (CDC, 2012b). Non-Hispanic blacks have lower rates of osteoporosis than other groups and a resulting lower rate of disability from bone fractures. Women in this group are less likely to commit suicide than any other subgroup, but are more likely to be obese. Non-Hispanic black men and women have lower risks of mood disorders, anxiety disorders, and substance abuse disorders than non-Hispanic white adults (Kessler, Berglund, Demler, et al., 2005).

The group consisting of American Indians and Alaskan Natives have the worst health and lowest life expectancy of any group in the United States (Harrington Myer & Herd, 2007). They have the highest rates of diabetes, hypertension, tuberculosis, arthritis, alcoholism and substance abuse, smoking, and serious psychological distress, all potentially disabling. Of all racial/ethnic groups in the United States, members of this one are the least likely to rate their health as "excellent." The two leading causes of death for this group are similar to other groups (heart disease and cancer), but the third most common cause of death is accidents (CDC, 2012b). These high rates of disease and premature death are due in large part to economic conditions, cultural barriers, and geographic isolation, but sociohistorical factors are at work too. The only hopeful thing I can offer is that some progress is being made. For example, the incidence of breast cancer for women in this group is now the lowest of all racial/ethnic groups (CDC, 2011c), but reviewing the overall health data for this group of U.S. citizens, descendants of the original inhabitants of this continent, is disturbing.

RACIAL DISCRIMINATION IN HEALTH CARE   It seems clear that some racial and ethnic minorities have a greater prevalence of early death, physical health problems, and mental health disorders than others. There is also evidence that some groups also receive lower levels of health care, especially African Americans and Hispanic Americans. One study compared mental health care for African American patients and non-Hispanic white patients, finding that the gap between the two groups had increased during the past decade, with fewer African Americans getting adequate treatment for mental health disorders compared to white patients (Ault-Brutus, 2012). Much of this can be explained by socioeconomic factors—the high price of visits to mental health-care providers and the cost of medication. It is also more difficult for people with lower levels of income and education to take time off from work and to travel to medical centers if they are not located in their neighborhoods. It is difficult to know when mental health care is needed or what type of provider is appropriate. But many individuals in these groups also report to researchers that they perceive they are discriminated against in the health-care arena because of their race or ethnicity. A decade of research has shown that inequalities in medical treatment are a reality, but overt racial or ethnic discrimination may not be as large a factor as others, such as English proficiency, health literacy, neighborhood social cohesion, and cultural distrust of the medical system (Lyles, Karter, Young, et al., 2011).

Whether the perception of discrimination is accurate or not, it has an effect on health (Brondolo, Hausmann, Jhalani, et al., 2011). For example, African Americans who perceive that they are discriminated against in medical settings as well as in everyday life are more apt to seek treatment from complementary and alternative medical providers (Shippee, Schafer, & Ferraro, 2012), who may not be as effective as conventional medical providers.

Another way racial discrimination affects health is through stress. Racial and ethnic minorities (as well as women and people living in poverty) are exposed to different experiences than mainstream society members. These different experiences lead to higher levels of stress, which in turn lead to higher levels of physical and mental health disorders. One of these experiences is discrimination, and it adds its own stress load, which further contributes to health problems. Stress burdens increase over the life course and result in an increasing health gap between the "haves" and "have-nots." So even if systematic discrimination in health care is not apparent, 40 years of research shows that belonging to a racial or ethnic minority can contribute to early death, more physical and mental health disorders, less treatment (or less-effective treatment), and a lower quality of life than those in the mainstream (Thoits, 2010).

3.6.4: Personality and Behavior Patterns

The idea that one's personality contributes to one's physical health dates back at least to the time of Hippocrates in ancient Greece. The first empirical demonstration of this relationship was provided by cardiologists Meyer Friedman and Ray Rosenman (1959), when they identified a behavior pattern that predicted risk for coronary heart disease. Since then, this area of research has become well accepted. Specific stable patterns of thinking, feeling, and behaving are indeed associated with increased risk of illness and premature death (Smith & Gallo, 2001).

Individuals classified as having a **type A behavior pattern** are achievement-striving, competitive, and involved in their jobs to excess; they feel extreme urgency with time-related matters and are easily provoked to hostility. People who do not fit this description are referred to as type B. Although the issue has been debated actively for over 50 years, it seems clear that when careful measures are made, people who fit the type A behavior pattern are at greater risk of coronary heart disease than those with type B behavior (Smith & Gallo, 2001).

A great deal of research has been done to determine how this effect takes place, and generally researchers have found both a direct link (type A behavior affects physical health through such mechanisms as increasing stress reactions and lowering immune function) and an indirect link (type A behavior causes the person to create and seek out stressful situations that, in turn, elicit more type A behavior, which leads to physical responses). In other words, people who have this personality style are apt to create other situations that call for similar responses. People who are always racing against the clock to get to important appointments will place themselves in traffic situations that bring forth additional type A responses, thus further increasing the risk for physical problems.

Another personality component, **hostility**, which is defined as a negative cognitive set against others, is related to increased heart rate and blood pressure, direct pathways to cardiovascular disease and premature death (Chida & Hamer, 2008). In addition, there are indirect pathways.

ⓧ Example:

People who are high in hostility no doubt have hostile relationships with others, such as in their marriages, and these hostile interactions add more health risk (and subtract the protective effect of social support). Hostile people are also known to engage in more high-risk behavior, such as smoking and excessive alcohol use, which could increase the chance of negative health outcomes (**Siegler, 1994**).

HOSTILITY AND OPTIMISM   In contrast, people who are high in **optimism**, that is, who have a positive outlook on life, believe that good things are going to happen to them, and cope with life's problems by taking steps to find direct solutions (instead of hoping that someone will rescue them or placing blame on others), are less apt to suffer from serious physical illness and less likely to die prematurely (Seligman, 1991). Since the initial research, the trait of optimism has been linked with positive health outcomes all around the world (Gallagher, Lopez, & Pressman, 2013). For example, optimism was related to longevity in a group of older African-American women (average age of 77 years) who have Caribbean roots (Unson, Trella, Chowdhury, et al., 2008), to better health-care outcomes in a group of Native American elders (Ruthig & Allery, 2008), to successful aging in a group of white and Hispanic women over the age of 60 (Lamond, Depp, Allison, et al., 2008), and to better health during the year following diagnosis in a group of heart disease patients in Ireland (Hevey, McGee, & Horgan, 2012). I would be remiss not to add one study that shows the dark side of optimism— college students whose optimism is too high (unrealistic optimism) are more apt to ignore the use of sunscreen protection, even though they are aware of the dangers of ultraviolet radiation exposure, believing that "it won't happen to me" (Calder & Aitken, 2008).

WRITING PROMPT

If negative behavior patterns such as hostility have both direct and indirect effects on health, how about positive behavior patterns such as optimism? What would the direct and indirect effects be?

▶ The response entered here will appear in the performance dashboard and can be viewed by your instructor.

Submit

If you are like me, you may be wondering whether anything can be done to change people who are type A, hostile, or pessimistic because personality is considered an enduring component of the individual. Many of the researchers cited in this section are cautious about using the term *personality* for this very reason; instead, they use other terms, such as *behavior patterns.* But whatever terms are used, the question remains: Is it possible to recognize these unhealthy traits in oneself and make some modifications? Preliminary studies show that this is possible to some extent. For example, one group of researchers managed to reduce hostility in men with heart disease and show some short-term improvement (Gidron, Davidson, & Bata, 1999). Another study produced positive effect in a group of college students by asking them to write a short essay about a happy event each week for 4 weeks and also keep a diary of happy events. At the end of the study, they reported better overall health status than a control group of students who had written on neutral topics (Yamasaki, Uchida, & Katsuma, 2009).

3.6.5: Genetics

One's **genotype**, the personal complement of genes that each of us possesses, has a big influence on our health. Most of us are aware of diseases that "run in families," such as breast cancer, heart disease, and substance abuse. Few diseases are determined by a single gene. (One example is early-onset Alzheimer's disease caused by the APP, PS-1, or PS-2 genes discussed earlier in this chapter.) Other diseases, such as depression and cancer, are transmitted by a combination of genes. In these cases, the gene combinations don't cause the disease as much as they predispose the individual to the disease by making him or her more susceptible than others to environmental factors, such as tobacco smoke leading to lung cancer, head injury leading to Alzheimer's disease, or fatty diets leading to cardiovascular disease. In other words, genes seldom determine our destinies.

Other genes have been found that have a protective effect. For example, a mutation of the APP gene, which causes Alzheimer's in its nonmutated form, has been found in a small number of Icelanders and seems to serve as protection against Alzheimer's disease. People who carry this mutation also live longer and are less likely to suffer from other types of cognitive decline (Jonsson, Atwal, Steinberg, et al., 2012).

Genetic information also can affect our individual responses to different treatments for diseases. For example, a number of genes have been identified that determine which of several drugs would be most successful in treating leukemia patients. Progress is also being made in identifying genes relating to drug responses for cancer, asthma, and cardiovascular disease treatment (Couzin, 2005). These findings have led to the practice of personalized medicine, in which your own DNA sequence becomes part of your medical record and is used in making decisions about which screening tests you should have for early diagnosis of diseases and, if treatment in necessary, what type is best suited for you.

3.6.6: Developmental Origins

Several researchers have presented evidence suggesting that some diseases of adulthood are determined partly by environmental events earlier in life. Epidemiologist David Barker and his colleagues (Barker, Winter, Osmond, et al., 1989) introduced this idea almost three decades ago when they examined birth and death records for over 5,000 men born within a 20-year period in the same area of England. They found that the men with the lowest weights at birth had the highest likelihood of dying from strokes. Since that time, research with humans and other species has given rise to the **developmental origins hypothesis**, which states that growth during the fetal period, infancy, and the early years of childhood is a significant factor in adult health (Barker, 2004).

Environmental factors present in early development that have been studied include maternal nutrition, season of birth, and maternal smoking. The resulting adult health outcomes include hypertension, diabetes, osteoporosis, and mood disorders (Gluckman & Hanson, 2004). Figure 3.6 shows data from more than 22,000 men indicating that those with lower birth weights were at higher risk for hypertension and diabetes in adulthood.

Figure 3.6 Data from more than 22,000 men over the age of 40 shows the relationship between birth weight and the risk for two diseases in adulthood—hypertension and diabetes. The lower the birthweight the greater the risk.

SOURCE: Gluckman and Hanson (2004).

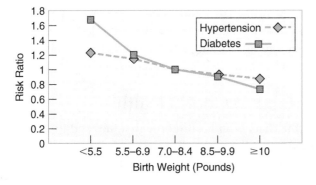

A similar study linked family income during very early childhood with adult obesity (Ziol-Guest, Duncan, & Kalil, 2009). Individuals whose parents made less than $25,000 a year during the child's prenatal period and the first year of life were more apt to be obese in adulthood than those whose families had higher incomes. Interestingly, family income during subsequent years of childhood (from the age of 1 to 15) had no impact on adult obesity.

Furthermore, evidence has been found that if a woman suffers malnutrition during pregnancy, her child is likely to be born at a low birth weight. And if that child is a daughter, *her* children's birth weight and subsequent health could be affected by the malnutrition experienced during the grandmother's pregnancy, even if the daughter did not experience malnutrition herself (Gluckman & Hanson, 2004). The explanation for this is that ova are formed during the prenatal period. Malnutrition of the pregnant woman affects her developing fetus, and if the fetus is female, the malnutrition would affect the development of her ova. Not only can we trace our health status back to our childhood and prenatal experiences, but we can also go back to our *mothers'* prenatal months when half our genetic material was being formed, influences referred to as **intergenerational effects**.

One more connection between early environment and adult health is the relationship between childhood infectious disease and cardiovascular disease, cancer, and diabetes. One study demonstrating this connection was done by economic historians Tommy Bengtsson and Martin Lindström (2003), who examined 18th-century medical records in four parishes in Sweden for a period of 128 years. They found that the people who had the fewest infectious diseases in infancy were the ones who had the greatest longevity. Even when periods of food shortage were considered, infant infections remained the strongest factor in determining adult longevity. It is suggested that the link between early childhood infections and early death in adulthood is inflammation (Finch & Crimmins, 2004), which, as mentioned earlier in this chapter, is implicated in a number of major diseases in adulthood, such as heart disease, cancer, and Alzheimer's disease.

In a study using lab animals, neuroscientist Francesca Mastorci and her colleagues (Mastorci, Vicentini, Viltart, et al., 2009) employed different types of stressors to pregnant rats and then investigated the outcomes of the offspring once they reached adulthood. Interestingly, there was no change for any biological structure or function as a result of the prenatal stress alone, but once these adult animals were exposed to environmental stressors themselves, they were less able to regulate their cardiovascular systems and were rendered more susceptible to heart disease than rats that had not experienced the prenatal stress. It seems that the prenatal stress did not produce heart disease itself, but produced a predisposition for heart disease once the animals encountered their own environmental stress.

For those of us in developed countries, the incidence of childhood infectious disease is low, and some researchers suggest that the increase in our life spans during the 20th century was due to this fact. However, in developing countries, diseases like tuberculosis, diarrheal illnesses, and malaria are still prevalent. Epidemiologists believe that once these childhood diseases are controlled, there will be a corresponding drop in the rates of life-limiting adult diseases that involve inflammation and a resulting increase in longevity (Finch & Crimmins, 2004).

3.6.7: The Road to Good Health

I have reviewed the changes in health through adulthood in Table 3.8, but I want to end with a reminder that the health disorders and diseases discussed in this chapter don't happen to everyone and don't happen at random.

Table 3.8 Review of Health and Illness over the Adult Years

18–24 Years	25–39 Years	40–64 Years	65–74 Years	75+ Years
Very low death rate (0.08%); top causes of death are accidents, homicide, and suicide.	Low death rate (0.1%): top causes of death are accidents and cancer.	Low death rate (0.6%); top causes of death are cancer and heart disease.	Death rate begins to increase (2%); top causes of death are heart disease and cancer. Diabetes deaths are fifth.	Higher death rate (8%); top causes of death are heart disease and cancer. Alzheimer's disease deaths are fifth.
Acute illnesses most common. Lowest levels of disability.	Acute illnesses most common. Low levels of disability.	Some acute illnesses; moderate risk for chronic illnesses. Early-onset Alzheimer's can begin, but accounts for only 5% of all cases. Moderate levels of disability.	Chronic conditions present, but most report having none. Almost all are aging in place. Alzheimer's present in 5–10%; other dementias present but some can be treated. Disability levels increase.	Chronic conditions and disability more common. Most are community dwelling; 40% report their health as "excellent or very good." Increased levels of disability. About 50% over 85 have Alzheimer's disease.
Most mental disorders have their onset before age 14. High rates of treatment before 21, low rates afterward.	Most mood disorders have their onset before age 30. Moderate rates of depressive symptoms. Higher rates of seeking treatment for mental health problems.	Lower rates of onset for major depression. Lower rates of depressive symptoms. Higher rates of seeking treatment for mental health problems.	Very low rates of onset for major depression. Higher rates of depressive symptoms. Low rates of seeking treatment for mental health disorders.	Major depression is rare and often related to disease. Higher rates of depressive symptoms, probably due to chronic health problems and bereavement. Low rates of seeking treatment for mental health disorders.

Many can be prevented; others can be detected early and treated successfully, or at least controlled. The best advice is still to eat healthy foods, exercise, get regular checkups, know your family health history, and seek scientifically proven treatment early for whatever disorders occur. Live a balanced life with time for supportive relationships and activities that reduce stress. Don't smoke; if you do smoke, quit. Practice safe sex. Wear your seatbelts and safety helmets. With all the medical advances I have read about in preparation for this chapter, I have seen no evidence for magic potions or pills that provide a shortcut to good health and long life.

WRITING PROMPT

Do you know your family's health history? Does it contain health conditions that may be inherited? What could you do to reduce your risk for these conditions? Write a brief response that will be read by your instructor.

▶ The response entered here will appear in the performance dashboard and can be viewed by your instructor.

Summary: Health and Health Disorders

1. Mortality rates increase with age, especially after 60. Causes of death are different for different ages, with accidents, homicides, and suicides leading the list for emerging adults, heart disease and cancer for older adults.

2. Younger adults have a greater incidence of acute illnesses; older adults have a greater incidence of chronic conditions such as arthritis, high blood pressure, and cardiovascular disease.

3. Rates of disability also increase with age, although more than 29% of adults aged 80 years or more report having no disability.

4. About 81% of women aged 65 and older and 90% of men this age are community dwelling. Only 3% are in nursing homes, and most of those are in their 80s or older.

5. Cardiovascular disease is the top cause of death among adults throughout the world. It involves the blocking of coronary arteries by plaques in the artery walls and can lead to heart attack. Some risk factors are under our control, such as smoking and leading a sedentary lifestyle. Others are not under our control, such as family history and age. Women get cardiovascular disease at the same rate as men, only later in life and with different symptoms.

6. The second leading cause of death for adults in the United States is cancer, which involves rapid division of abnormal cells invading nearby tissue or spreading to other parts of the body. The incidence of cancer increases with age. Risk factors for cancer that are under our control are smoking, obesity, and unprotected exposure to bright sunlight. Factors that are not under our control are age and family history.

7. Type 2 diabetes is increasing in prevalence as a major cause of death and disability for middle-aged adults and older. Diabetes is a hormonal condition in which the body does not produce enough insulin to utilize the glucose produced by the digestive system. Type 2 diabetes is often the result of a sedentary lifestyle and unhealthy eating habits, and can be controlled by making changes in these areas of one's life and sometimes by gastric bypass surgery.

8. The fifth leading cause of death among older adults is Alzheimer's disease, caused by progressive deterioration of certain parts of the brain. The result is loss of cognitive ability and physical function. Alzheimer's disease is seldom seen before 50, and 90% of the cases occur after 65. Many of the risk factors for Alzheimer's disease are the same as for cardiovascular disease, and both may be linked to inflammation earlier in life. Some of the risk factors that can be modified are smoking, sedentary lifestyles, and obesity. Factors that can't are age and genetic predisposition. Traumatic brain injuries (TBI) from contact sports and combat can cause a type of dementia in later life called chronic traumatic encephalopathy (CTE).

9. The rate of mental health disorders in U.S. adults has remained stable in the past decade but is higher than in any other developed country. The most common types are anxiety disorders (phobias, PTSD, and obsessive-compulsive disorder) and mood disorders (major depression and bipolar disorder). The onset of most mental health disorders is in adolescence and early adulthood. Major depression is more apt to affect young adults than older adults, who are more apt to report depressive symptoms.

10. The majority of people who experience symptoms of mental health disorders do not seek treatment, and a third who do receive treatment that is inadequate or inappropriate. Those who do not seek treatment are more likely to be older adults than younger or middle-aged adults.

11. Many physical and mental health disorders can be prevented through healthy lifestyles. Others can be detected early and treated successfully. There are no shortcuts to good health and no magic pills.

12. Men and women have different patterns of both physical and mental health problems. Men have shorter life expectancies, higher rates of life-threatening physical diseases, more mental disorders involving alcohol and substance abuse, and more impulse control disorders. Women have more chronic diseases and higher rates of major depression and anxiety disorders. This difference is partly biological and partly sociocultural.

13. People in lower socioeconomic groups have lower levels of physical and mental health than higher socioeconomic groups and decline in physical health more quickly. This difference is due to health-care availability, health habits, and the effects of stress.

14. Asian Americans and Pacific Islanders have the best health picture of any group in the United States, due

in part to their traditional lifestyles, which include healthy diets and low smoking rates. The lowest level of health in the United States is found in Native American and Alaskan Native groups.

15. Another factor that can affect health is behavior patterns (type A, hostility, pessimism) that lead to cardiovascular disease and early death.

16. The genetic contribution to disease ranges from actually determining that an individual will have a certain disease (some types of Alzheimer's disease) to providing a predisposition that environmental factors will cause a disease (tobacco and lung cancer). One's genotype may even provide protection against certain diseases. Some medical treatments are now being designed for individuals based on their genotypes.

17. Low birth weight, early childhood infections, and low family income during the first year of life have been linked to adult health problems such as diabetes, mood disorders, and obesity.

SHARED WRITING: INDIVIDUAL DIFFERENCES IN HEALTH

Consider this chapter's discussion of individual differences in health as they relate to a variety of factors (genetics, socioeconomics, race, gender). What are some specific factors that have influenced your health (for better or for worse)? How have they impacted you? Can you make changes? How can you adapt to them? Write a short response that your classmates will read. Be sure to discuss specific examples.

▶
> A minimum number of characters is required to post and earn points. After posting, your response can be viewed by your class and instructor, and you can participate in the class discussion.

Post   0 characters | 140 minimum

Chapter 3 Quiz: Health and Health Disorders

Chapter 4
Cognitive Abilities

 ## Learning Objectives

4.1 Describe intelligence, its relation to age, its components, and reversing its decline

4.2 Define memory, its type and reversing its decline

4.3 Analyze whether cognitive process is age-related

4.4 Assess factors that affect age-related differences in cognitive change

4.5 Identify solutions to cognitive limitations

4.6 Argue that cognitive ability does not entirely decline with age; an element exists, if balanced

LISTEN TO THE AUDIO:

▶ ⬤━━━━━━━━━━ 01:45   🔇 ⬤

MY PARENTS TOOK me out to a steakhouse for my 53rd birthday, and when I had trouble getting catsup to pour out of a new bottle onto my fries, Dad showed me a trick he had learned from a catsup salesman—you tap the neck of the bottle sharply against your outstretched index finger and the catsup comes out easily. Then he and Mom reminisced about their friend Don Iverson, the catsup salesman. He lived in Savannah, Georgia, and they had last visited him on the way home from their honeymoon. Don's wife had made a standing rib roast for dinner with peach cobbler for dessert. What a great time they had, eating and playing cards and talking until early morning. What was Don's wife's name? Neither could remember. They talked back and forth a little, trying to come up with the name of the catsup salesman's wife they had not seen in 55 years but finally agreed in desperation: "We just can't remember anything anymore!"

It's true that my parents were growing old—they were 77 and 80 at the time of that birthday dinner—but remembering the catsup salesman's name, the city he lived in, and even what his wife had served for dinner that evening over 50 years before is impressive at any age. Yet one of the most popular stereotypes of aging is cognitive loss, and it is a stereotype that even older adults hold about themselves. The same lost car keys or forgotten phone number that at the age of 30 or 40 is a normal slipup is viewed as a symptom of early senility at 70 or 80. But what is typical of cognitive aging, and what is myth? One of the busiest fields of aging research has some surprising answers.

A common view of cognitive aging is that people become passive victims of the deterioration of their brains, with a corresponding decline in competent thought and behavior. It seems without question that basic cognitive abilities such as memory, attention, and the speed with which we process information *do* take a turn for the worse as we age. But the picture is not so bleak. Although cognitive decline with advancing age is real, in many cases older adults maintain, and sometimes even increase, their mental skills, and studies using functional brain imaging—which examines not just the structure of the brain but also looks at how the brain functions when performing cognitive tasks—shows that the aging brain is a dynamic organ, adapting to cognitive challenges and neural deterioration (Park & McDonough, 2013).

4.1: Intelligence

4.1   Describe intelligence, its relation to age, its components, and reversing its decline

When we think of evaluating age changes in cognitive processes, most of us think immediately of IQ scores. Does IQ change as we get older? If so, is there a sudden drop at a certain age, or is the change gradual? Are some types of intelligence affected more than others? These types of questions have long been the basis of cognitive aging studies, but before I review their findings, let me say a few words about the concept of intelligence and about IQ tests, the tools we use to measure that concept.

Defining **intelligence** is one of the slipperier tasks in psychology. The typical definition goes something like this: "the aggregate or global capacity of the individual to act purposefully, to think rationally and to deal effectively with his environment" (Wechsler, 1939, p. 3). In other words, intelligence is a visible indicator of the efficiency of various cognitive processes that work together behind the scenes to process information in various ways (Nisbett, Aronson, Blair, et al., 2012). The field of psychology that studies the measurement of human abilities such as intelligence is **psychometrics**.

Many psychologists assume that there is a central, general intellectual capacity, often called **g**, which influences the way we approach a great number of different tasks (Jensen, 1998; Spearman, 1904). The score on an intelligence test is intended to describe this general capacity, known as the **IQ (intelligence quotient)**. As you may know from previous courses, the average IQ score is normally set at 100, with scores above 100 reflecting above-average performance and scores below 100 reflecting below-average performance.

In addition to g, some psychologists who study intelligence are interested in the specific components of intellectual capacity. On standard IQ tests, these capacities are measured by the various subtests that make up the total IQ score. For example, the latest version of the Wechsler Adult Intelligence Scale (WAIS-IV; Pearson Education, 2008) provides a Full Scale IQ based on four separate indexes: Verbal Comprehension, Perceptual Reasoning, Working Memory, and Processing Speed, each of which consists of a number of different subtests (for example, vocabulary in Verbal Comprehension; block design in Perceptual Reasoning; digit span in Working Memory; and symbol search, assessing visual perception, and speed in Processing Speed).

4.1.1: Age Changes in Overall Intelligence

Now let's get to some of the research findings on age changes in intelligence. Do IQ scores decline with age or stay constant? Most of the early information on consistency or change in adult intelligence came from cross-sectional studies (1920s to 1950s), which seemed to show that declines in IQ began in early adulthood and continued steadily thereafter. However, in the decades since then, we have learned a lot more about adult intelligence. Researchers of cognitive aging have developed new designs that do away with some of the confounds of traditional methods and have extended longitudinal studies to include healthy, community-dwelling people in their 60s, 70s, 80s, and beyond. Although results continue to show some cognitive decline with age, the news is much more optimistic. Some aspects of adult thought processes function at very high levels into very old age. When decline occurs, it is often much less extreme than once thought, and we often compensate so that it is not noticeable. Moreover, there are precautions we can take that will increase our chances of staying bright and high functioning throughout our lives.

Figure 4.1 shows the contrast between longitudinal and cross-sectional analyses of IQ scores in the Seattle Longitudinal Study. This study used a sequential design that allowed for both longitudinal and cross-sectional comparisons. The numbers are not traditional IQ scores with a mean of 100. Instead they have been calculated to show the change in scores for each participant over the course of the study, with the beginning score set at 50 and a standard deviation of 10. Thus two thirds of all adults should fall between scores of 40 and 60 (one standard deviation on either side of the mean), and about 95% should fall between 30 and 70 (Schaie, 1994; Schaie & Zanjani, 2006).

When you compare the longitudinal and cross-sectional data, you can see that they yield very different answers to the question, "What happens to IQ over the course of adulthood?" The cross-sectional evidence, of which the lower curve is very typical, shows a decline in IQ starting somewhere between ages 32 and 39. In contrast, the longitudinal information actually suggests a slight rise in IQ through middle adulthood. Only in the period from 67 to 74 do the total IQ scores begin to drop, although, even here, the decline is not substantial. In fact, according to developmental psychologist, K. Warner Schaie, codirector of the Seattle Longitudinal Project, "The average magnitude of intellectual decline … is quite small during the 60s and 70s and is probably of little significance for competent behavior of the young old" (2006, p. 601). Average declines become more substantial, however, in the 80s (Schaie, 1996).

Figure 4.1 Age changes in total IQ based on cross-sectional data (lower line) and longitudinal data (upper line) can show very different trajectories. Depending on cross-sectional data in the past led to erroneous conclusions that cognitive performance begins to decline around 40 and that the decline is very fast.

SOURCE: Data from Schaie (1983).

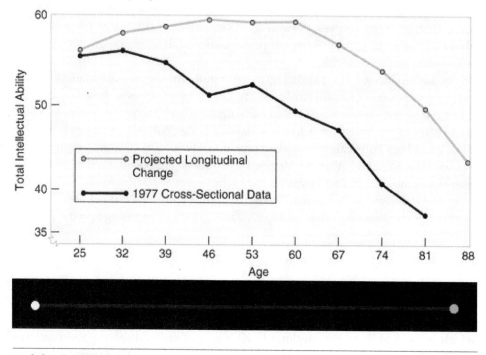

Critical Thinking

If these cross-sectional studies measured the height of participants who were 20, 40, 60, and 80 years of age, what would you predict the results would show? How might you explain the results?

The obvious explanation for the difference between the cross-sectional and longitudinal comparisons is that there are cohort effects at work here. As years of education, good health, and the cognitive complexities of life have increased over the past century, the average scores for each successive cohort have gone up. In fact, researchers have found that average verbal IQ scores for groups of older adults are increasing by over four and a half points each decade (Uttl & Van Alstine, 2003). This is related to the **Flynn effect**, named after psychologist James Flynn (1987, 2012), who documented that average IQ had increased steadily over the 20th century. Flynn argues that the increase is due mainly to changes in modern life. Advances in education, greater use of technology, and more people being engaged in intellectually demanding work has led to a greater proportion of people with experience manipulating abstract concepts than was the case in decades past, and this, in turn, is responsible for elevated IQ scores for people of all ages. As a result, cross-sectional studies comparing people born decades apart may show lower IQ scores for older people, but they are not accurate predictors of what the future holds in store for young people today.

Although IQ tends to decline with advancing age (and more for some types of abilities than others), overall, intelligence as measured by IQ is highly stable over one's lifetime. By stable, I'm referring to differences among people being similar over time. For example, will the bright 10- or 20-year-old also be the bright 70- or 80-year-old, relative to other people measured in the sample? The answer seems to be "yes." Based on data from a 76-year longitudinal study, psychologist Alan Gow and his colleagues (Gow, Johnson, Pattie, et al., 2011) reported that at least 50% of IQ differences among people in late adulthood could be accounted for by their test performance as children. There's still 50% of the differences to be accounted for by other factors, so change is as much a part of the picture as stability. But IQ, from childhood into older adulthood, is one of the most stable psychological traits behavioral scientists have studied.

To summarize, there is good support for the optimistic view that general intellectual ability remains fairly stable through most of adulthood. But now let's dissect intelligence a little and see what happens with age to some of the specific intellectual abilities that are components of IQ.

4.1.2: Components of Intelligence

As I mentioned earlier, standardized IQ tests yield more than a single score. They also provide subtest scores, representing different types of cognitive abilities associated with intelligence. One distinction that is widely used by researchers is between crystallized and fluid abilities, initially proposed and developed by psychologists Raymond Cattell and John Horn (Cattell, 1963; Horn & Cattell, 1966). **Crystallized intelligence** is heavily dependent on education and experience. It consists of the set of skills and bits of knowledge that we each learn as part of growing up in a given culture, such as the ability to reason about real-life problems and technical skills learned for a job and other aspects of life (balancing a checkbook, counting change, finding the salad dressing in the grocery store). On standardized tests, crystallized abilities are measured by vocabulary and by verbal comprehension, such as reading a paragraph and then answering questions about it (Blair, 2006).

In contrast, **fluid intelligence** is a more basic set of abilities believed to be more under the influence of biological processes, "requiring adaptation to new situations and for which prior education or learning provide relatively little advantage" (Berg & Sternberg, 2003, p. 105). A common measure of this is a letter-series test. You may be given a series of letters like F, G, I, L, P and have to figure out what letter should go next (U). This demands abstract reasoning rather than reasoning about familiar or everyday events. Most tests of memory measure fluid intelligence, as do many tests measuring response speed or reproducing designs with blocks.

Whatever labels we apply to these two broad categories of intellectual ability, the results are similar. Nonverbal, fluid tasks decline earlier than verbal, crystallized tasks (Lindenberger & Baltes, 1997; Salthouse, 2003). In fact, aspects of crystallized abilities, such as world knowledge, continue to grow into the 60s and show only gradual declines into the 70s (Ackerman, 2008; Ornstein & Light, 2010). In contrast, specific aspects of fluid abilities, such as speed of processing and working memory (how many items one can keep in mind at one time while doing something to those items) show initial declines around 35 to 40 years of age (Dykiert, Der, Starr, et al., 2012; Horn & Hofer, 1992).

This pattern of change in crystallized and fluid abilities were demonstrated in research by psychologist Shu-Chen Li and her colleagues (Li, Lindenberger, Hommel, et al., 2004). People from 6 to 89 years of age were given a battery of both crystallized and fluid tasks. Performance on the fluid tasks peaked for people in their mid-20s, with declines being obvious by the mid-30s. In comparison, crystallized abilities did not peak until the 40s and remained stable until about age 70, when a decline was seen.

Older adults who "exercise" their crystallized abilities often continue to display improvements on specific cognitive tasks well into their 70s. Consider people who do crossword puzzles regularly. Figure 4.2 shows the combined results of several studies in which participants of different ages were given *New York Times* crossword puzzles to solve (Salthouse, 2004). As shown in the figure, the number of words participants completed correctly increased with age; the most words were solved by those in their 60s, whereas those in their 20s and 30s solved fewer than those in their 70s. Doing crossword puzzles, as well as identifying synonyms and other verbal tasks, represent components of intelligence that depend more on accrued knowledge than on speed of processing or learning new skills, and they fit hand-in-glove with the cognitive abilities of healthy older adults.

Figure 4.2 The number of words correctly completed in the *New York Times* crossword puzzle increases with age, showing the effect of mental "exercise" on crystallized abilities. **SOURCE:** Salthouse (2004).

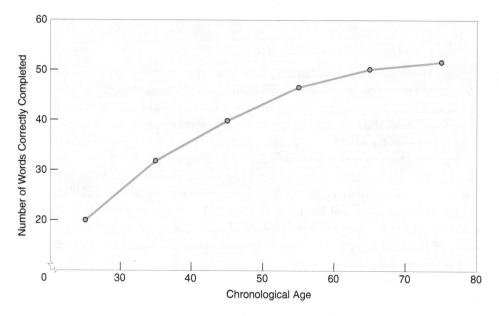

Not only does intelligence decline more slowly than the experts once thought, but we are also finding out that few rules apply to everyone when it comes to cognitive aging. In other words, even when the mean scores are higher for younger people than for older people, there are still a lot of people in the old group who do better than a lot of the people in the young group, and vice versa. Schaie (1996) measured this variability and found that even at 80 years and older, 53% of the people were performing comparably to the young people on tests of both fluid and crystallized intelligence.

One interesting finding is that intelligence predicts health and longevity. This is true when intelligence is measured by IQ-type tests (Gottfredson & Deary, 2004; Deary, Batty, Pattie, et al., 2008) or by tests assessing everyday cognitive abilities, such as those associated with medication use, financial management, food preparation, and nutrition (Weatherbee & Allaire, 2008). The reason for this connection is not clear, although one possibility is that people with better reasoning and problem-solving skills make better decisions with respect to health care and avoiding accidental injuries (Gottfredson & Deary, 2004).

4.1.3: Reversing Declines in Intellectual Abilities

Beginning in the 1970s, when it became apparent that intelligence did not drop off drastically with age, researchers began asking if anything could be done to reverse the moderate decline in IQ shown in longitudinal studies. The answer was yes (Kramer & Willis, 2002). Different studies showed that physical exercise brought about significant improvement in intellectual performance (Colcombe & Kramer, 2003), as did training in the components specific to the task being tested (Labouvie-Vief & Gonda, 1976; Willis, Tennstedt, Marsiske, et al., 2006) and training in nonspecific aspects of the test, such as willingness to guess when one is not sure of the correct answer (Birkhill & Schaie, 1975).

Schaie and his colleague (Schaie & Willis, 1986) included a training study in one wave of their ongoing longitudinal project to determine whether training was effective for people who were already showing a decline or just for those who had not yet begun to decline. Participants, aged 64 to 94, received 5 hours of training. About half of the participants had shown a decline over the last 14 years, and about half had not. Some received training on spatial orientation and some on inductive reasoning, both abilities that tend to decline with age and are considered more resistant to intervention. When the results of the training were examined for those who had declined, it was found that about half had gained significantly, and 40% had returned to their former levels of performance. Of those who had not yet shown declines, one third had increased their abilities above their previous levels.

WRITING PROMPT

What games can you think of that might be beneficial to older adults' spatial orientation? What games might boost inductive reasoning? Write a brief response that will be read by your instructor. Be sure to explain the reasoning behind your answers.

▶ The response entered here will appear in the performance dashboard and can be viewed by your instructor.

Submit

Seven years later, the same researchers retested about half of these participants and compared them to others in the study who were the same age and had not received training. The scores of the group that received training had declined from their previous levels, but they still performed better than the controls, even though it had been 7 years since their training. These participants were then given an additional 5 hours of training, which again raised their test scores significantly, but not to the level of 7 years earlier (Willis & Schaie, 1994). Similar results have been found for memory training in a visuomotor task over a 2-year period (Smith, Walton, Loveland, et al., 2005), a perceptual-motor task over a 5-year period (Rodrigue, Kennedy, & Raz, 2005), and a strategic memory task over a 5-year period (Gross & Rebok, 2011).

4.2: Memory

4.2 Define memory, its type and reversing its decline

Memory is defined as the ability to retain or store information and retrieve it when needed. Although IQ is the most familiar concept in cognition for most adults, memory is clearly the topic that causes the most concern. As illustrated in my story about the catsup salesman at the beginning of this chapter, older adults often incorrectly interpret minor memory lapses as signs of serious mental failure, and at the same time they do not give themselves credit for the many accurate and important memory tasks they perform each day. Most adults over the age of 65 report that they have noticed a recent decline in their memory abilities, and most express concern over it, associating it with illness, loss of independence, and their own mortality (Lane & Zelinski, 2003; Wilson, Bennett, & Swartzendruber, 1997). For some older people, the effect goes beyond normal concern. Clinical psychologists have reported an increase in the number of patients who show pathological levels of anxiety that their failing memory is symptomatic of Alzheimer's disease (Centofanti, 1998). So this is an important topic on several levels—for professionals who work with older clients, for young and middle-aged adults who have older parents, and for older adults themselves. It is important to know the real facts about age-related change in memory ability, its causes, and what, if anything, can be done to prevent, reverse, or compensate for it.

Memory, however, is not a single ability, and psychologists have studied various types of memory and how they change with age. For example, the information-processing perspective makes a distinction between different *memory stores*. The **sensory store** refers to the initial step as information is picked up by the senses and processed briefly by the perceptual system; the **short-term store** is the second step, as information is held for several seconds or so and either discarded or encoded for storage in the **long-term store**, where it can remain for years. Psychologists also make a distinction about the *type* of memories that are stored in the long-term memory, with declarative memory referring to memories for facts and events that can be consciously evaluated and nondeclarative memory referring to memories for procedures that are generally not available to conscious awareness. I will discuss age-related changes in these and other types of memory in this section, as well as looking at ways that older adults can improve their memory functioning.

4.2.1: Short-Term and Working Memory

One type of memory that is important for performing nearly all other cognitive tasks is *short-term memory*, the ability to hold information in mind for a brief period of time. Short-term memory, often referred to as **primary memory**, reflects the passive maintenance of information in the short-term store and is assessed by tests such as the **digit-span task**. In the digit-span task, an examiner reads a series of randomly arranged digits at a rate of about one per second, and at the end of the list the person must repeat them back in exact order. In contrast to primary memory is **working memory** (Baddeley, 1986). Working memory refers to the amount of information we can hold in mind while performing some type of operation on it. Researchers have found that primary memory, as measured by tests of digit span, shows relatively small declines with age through the 70s and 80s (Gregoire & Van der Linden, 1997) and remains relatively stable through the mid-90s (Bäckman, Small, Wahlin, et al., 2000). In contrast, tests of working memory show more substantial decline with age (Berg & Sternberg, 2003; Hale, Rose, Myerson, et al., 2011).

This split between primary memory and working memory was demonstrated by psychologist Denise Park and her colleagues (Park, Lautenschlager, Hedden, et al., 2002). They gave a variety of memory tasks to participants in seven groups, ranging in age from the 20s to the 80s. The results of some of these tests are shown in Figure 4.3. Short-term memory tasks included watching the experimenter point to a sequence of colored blocks and then repeating the sequence and listening to the experimenter give a sequence of numbers and repeating them back. As you can see, performance declined with age for short-term memory, long-term memory, and speed of processing. Declines were sharper, however, for tests of working memory. These tests involved storing information in memory while performing some computation on it. For example, in the reading-span test, participants listened to a sentence ("After dinner the chef prepared dessert"). They were then asked to answer a multiple-choice question about the sentence ("What did the chef prepare? a. fish, b. dessert, c. salad"). Participants were presented a number of different sentences and questions, then asked to remember the last word in each sentence in exact order. The trajectory for these tasks, as you can see, shows a much steeper decline with age than for the primary memory tasks. But the rate of decline also depends on what people are remembering. For example, age-related declines in working memory are greater for spatial information (for example, remembering the location of a series of Xs on a grid) than for verbal information (for example, remembering the last word in each of several sentences; Hale, Rose, Myerson, et al., 2011).

Figure 4.3 Age-related cross-sectional changes are demonstrated on a variety of cognitive tasks. Note that although both short-term (primary) and working memory decline with advancing age, the decline is steeper for working memory.

SOURCE: Park, Lautenschlager, Hedden, et al. (2002).

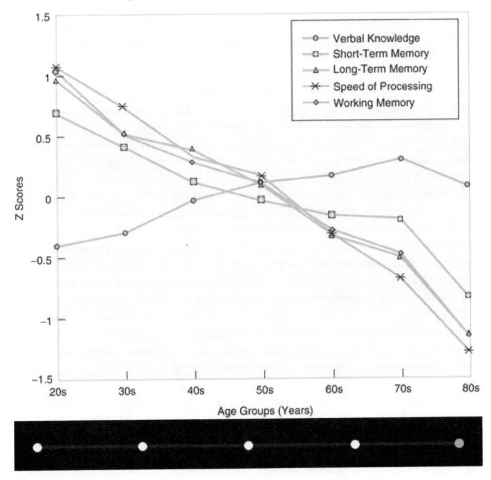

We also have some longitudinal data to consider on the subject of age-related change in working-memory abilities. Psychologist David Hultsch and his colleagues (Hultsch, Hertzog, Dixon, et al., 1998) gave various memory tests to a group of 297 older Canadian adults who were participants in the Victoria Longitudinal Study. The average age of one group of participants was 65 when they were first tested, and the average age of the other group was 75. Three years later, both the younger group (now 68) and the older group (now 78) showed significant declines in verbal working memory, and the older group had a significantly greater decline than the younger group.

DECLINE OF WORKING MEMORY AND ITS IMPORTANCE   What is the reason for this decline in working memory? One theory is that older people don't have the mental energy, or attentional resources, that younger people do (Craik & Byrd, 1982). A related idea is that older people are not as able to use the strategies required by working-memory tasks (Brébion, Smith, & Ehrlich, 1997). Another explanation offered is a decline in processing speed (Salthouse, 1996). Recent research has contrasted the "strategy-use" versus "speed" hypotheses and found that although strategy use can account for some individual differences in working memory, it cannot account for age differences. In contrast, differences in processing speed account for a substantial amount of the age differences in working memory performance among older adults (Bailey, Dunlosky, & Hertzog, 2009). A fourth hypothesis is that older adults are less able to inhibit irrelevant and confusing information (Hasher & Zacks, 1988;

Schlaghecken, Birak, & Maylor, 2011). And a fifth idea is that older adults are not as able to engage in the reflective processes required for successful working-memory functioning (Johnson, Reeder, Raye, et al., 2002). All these ideas are represented in current memory research, so it will be interesting to see what unfolds.

It is also interesting to know that when younger and older adults perform comparably on working-memory tasks, such as when the memory load is small (for example, only two to four items have to be remembered), brain imaging studies reveal that they use different parts of their brains (Reuter-Lorenz, 2013). For example, for small memory loads older adults show more activation in the frontal regions of the brain, an area associated with higher-order cognition. As the task becomes more demanding, younger adults also show increased activation in these areas (Cappell, Gmeindl, & Reuter-Lorenz, 2010; Schneider-Garces, Gordon, Brumback-Peltz, et al., 2010). This pattern of neural activation suggests that older adults are not the passive victims of a deteriorating brain, but rather are developing alternate neural strategies to maintain their levels of cognitive performance.

Why is working memory, in particular, so important? The primary reason is that working memory is associated with performing almost all other cognitive tasks. The ability to keep information active in one's mind and do something with that information (that is, "think" about it) is central to almost every problem people set out to solve, from the mundane act of preparing one's coffee in the morning to making decisions on buying a new flat-screen TV. Working memory is a central component of what psychologists call **executive function**, which refers to the processes involved in regulating attention and in determining what to do with information just gathered or retrieved from long-term memory (Jones, Rothbart, & Posner, 2003; Miyake & Friedman, 2012). In addition to working memory, executive function includes the ability to inhibit responding and resist interference, the ability to selectively attend to information, and cognitive flexibility, as reflected by how easily individuals can switch between different sets of rules or different tasks. Each of these skills declines in efficiency in older adults (Goh, An, & Resnick, 2012; Madden, 2007; Passow, Westerhausen, Wartenburger, et al., 2012; Wasylyshyn, Verhaeghen, & Sliwinski, 2011).

4.2.2: Declarative and Nondeclarative (Procedural) Memory

As I mentioned earlier in the chapter, memory is not a single process. In fact, *memories* themselves are not a single thing—a specific event that is retrieved from the long-term store and brought to consciousness. Rather, psychologists have proposed that information is represented in the long-term store in one of two general ways: declarative memory and nondeclarative memory (Tulving, 1985, 2005). **Declarative memory**, sometimes called *explicit memory*, refers to knowledge that is available to conscious awareness and can be directly (explicitly) assessed by tests of recall or recognition memory. Declarative memory comes in two types: **semantic memory**, our knowledge of language, rules, and concepts, and **episodic memory**, the ability to recall events. When you appear on the TV program *Jeopardy* and come up with the correct name of the 15th president of the United States, you are using your semantic memory. When you come home and tell your friends and family about your trip to Los Angeles and the whole game-show experience, you are using your episodic memory. (And when I write here that the 15th U.S. president was James Buchanan, I am using Google, an external memory device, which is on my computer.)

When older people say, "My memory isn't as sharp as it used to be," they are talking about their episodic memory. In information-processing terms, it would be expressed this way: "My storage and retrieval processes don't seem to be working as efficiently as they once did." Episodic memory is typically studied by presenting people of different ages with lists of words or stories for memorization. Later (anywhere between a few seconds and several days) they are instructed to recall as many of the words or as much of the story as they can. The typical findings are that older adults do not recall as many of the words as younger adults, and that this decline, though relatively slow, is continuous over the adult years; it begins early, perhaps as early as the late teens and early 20s, and is continuous into at least the mid-90s (Hoyer & Verhaeghen, 2006; Ornstein & Light, 2010).

Critical Thinking

If your memory was like a refrigerator, encoding would be like putting the groceries away in the right drawers and compartments. What analogies could you make about storage and retrieval? How would you explain forgetting the name of an old friend in "refrigerator terms?"

In other studies, researchers have looked at older adults' abilities to remember events and the people who were involved in them (Earles, Kersten, Curtayne, et al., 2008; Kersten, Earles, Curtayne, et al., 2008; Old & Naveh-Benjamin, 2008). For instance, younger and older adults may be shown a series of video clips of people performing simple actions (a young woman peeling an apple, for example), and later shown another series of video clips, some of which are the same clips they saw before and others are different. Among the different clips are the same people witnessed earlier performing different actions and different people performing the same actions they had seen earlier. When asked to identify only the clips that are of the same people performing the same actions they had seen earlier, older adults (65 years and older) do poorer than younger adults (typically college students). One hypothesis about this age difference is that older adults have difficulty forming associations among single units of episodic memory and retrieving them from long-term memory. This interpretation is also consistent with the finding that older adults have more difficulty than younger adults learning the names of new acquaintance (Old & Naveh-Benjamin, 2012).

What about semantic memory? We know that IQ subtests that deal with vocabulary and general knowledge show very little, if any, decline with age (Salthouse, 1991), so it seems that semantic memory is fairly stable before the age of 75. In addition, studies of middle-aged adults (aged 35 to 50) show no age changes on semantic memory tasks (Bäckman & Nilsson, 1996; Burke & Shafto, 2008). Studies of participants in the Berlin Aging Study between the ages of 70 and 103 showed a gradual but systematic decline in the performance of tasks that tap this store of facts and word meanings (Lindenberger & Baltes, 1994). Figure 4.4 presents estimates for changes in semantic and episodic memory from 35 to 85 years of age (Rönnlund, Nyberg, Bäckman, et al., 2005). As you can see, semantic memory abilities actually show increases into the 70s before experiencing a moderate decline, whereas episodic memory abilities show a sharp decline beginning in the mid-60s.

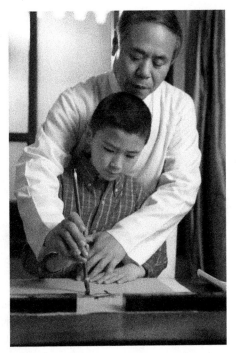

Procedural memory includes skills that are handed down in a culture from generation to generation.

The one exception to the rule of semantic memory remaining stable over the years is the case of **word-finding failures**—that feeling many middle-aged and older adults get when they know the word they want to use but just can't locate it at the moment, often referred to as the *tip-of-the-tongue phenomenon*. This would certainly be a task that taps semantic memory (Shafto, Burke, Stamatakis, et al., 2007). The related semantic memory phenomenon of **name-retrieval failures**, for example, the failure to come up with "the name of that actor who used to be on *Star Trek* and now does hotel commercials," also begins to increase in middle age (Maylor, 1990). Psychologist Fergus Craik (2000) explained these exceptions by suggesting that specificity is the key to whether a long-term memory system component is stable or declines with age—tasks that require

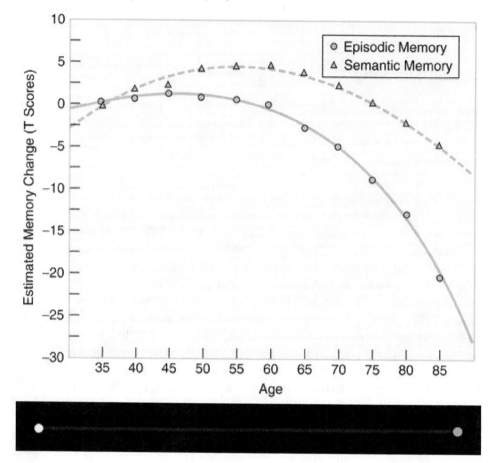

Figure 4.4 Estimated age-related changes in semantic and episodic memory abilities. Semantic memory abilities show increases over middle adulthood and a slow decline in older age, whereas episodic abilities display a sharper decline in the mid-60s.

SOURCE: Rönnlund, Nyberg, Bäckman, et al. (2005).

a specific word or name as an answer are more difficult and show a decline with age, whereas other tasks that require a more general answer are easier and remain stable up to late adulthood. In the example given earlier of the *Jeopardy* game experience, "James Buchanan" is a very specific item of information, and failure to recall it could not be compensated for by the use of other words. However, the story about the trip to L.A. consists of more general information, and even if some specific items could not be recalled (for example, the name of the host of *Jeopardy*), the story could still be told using "the game-show host" or "the star of the show" instead of "Alex Trebek." Using Craik's explanation, the reason semantic memory is so stable with age is that it is usually general rather than specific. And the reason there are age-related changes in episodic memory is due to the specificity required.

NONDECLARATIVE MEMORY In contrast to declarative memory, **nondeclarative (or procedural) memory** is the memory system responsible for skill learning and retention (Tulving, 1985). The skills that depend on this system include many motor systems such as driving a car, tying one's shoes, or riding a bike. Once learned, these skills involve well-learned, automatic mental processes that are not available to conscious awareness. We don't have to remind ourselves how to use a can opener or how to ride a bike, and the fact that these skills are independent of conscious memory seems to protect them from the effects of aging and brain damage. Relatively few direct studies of age-related changes in procedural memory have been conducted, but general findings are that there is little change with age over adulthood, except for tasks that require speeded performance (Dixon, de Frias, & Maitland, 2001). Further evidence on the durability of procedural memory is found in studies of individuals suffering from various types of amnesia. Although this condition is defined by loss of memory ability in many areas, procedural memory abilities often remain at normal levels (Schacter, 1997).

WRITING PROMPT

What's in your procedural memory? What contents would you have in common with other students in your class, and what contents would be unique? Write a short response that will be read by your teacher. Be sure to include specifics in your answer.

▶ | The response entered here will appear in the performance dashboard and can be viewed by your instructor. |

Submit

4.2.3: Prospective Memory

One other type of memory that is of importance to older adults is **prospective memory**, remembering to do something later on or in the future (Einstein & McDaniel, 2005). This can involve remembering to perform a specific one-time task (remembering to call the golf course for a tee time on Saturday) or performing some habitual routine (remembering to take your medication every day after lunch). Prospective memory requires not only that a person remember to do something in the future, but also to remember what it is that needs to be done. Perhaps some of you can recall staring at your calendar knowing that there was something you were supposed to do on Tuesday at 2:30, but not recalling what that "something" was. Research has consistently reported that older adults perform more poorly on prospective memory tasks than younger adults, but the magnitude of the difference is usually smaller than for episodic memory (Henry, MacLeod, Phillips, et al., 2004). The exception seems to be when there is interfering material or activities involved. For example, when participants must quickly switch from performing one task to performing another, so that the second task interferes with the first, older adults (and first-grade children) perform more poorly than young adults, although the differences among the younger and older adults are much smaller or nonexistent when there is no interference (Kliegel, Mackinlay, & Jäger, 2008). One explanation for this finding is that aspects of prospective memory are dependent on executive function, which shows declines in older adults (Cepeda, Kramer, & Gonzalez de Sather, 2001).

4.2.4: Slowing Declines in Memory Abilities

If some types of memory abilities decline with age, is it possible for older adults to be taught special strategies to compensate for their processing problems? This is the idea behind a good many memory-training studies. For example, older adults have been successfully trained to remember names of people they have just met by using internal memory aids such as mental imagery to form associations between the people's faces and their names (Yesavage, Lapp, & Sheikh, 1989). In other studies, older adults have been given training on encoding, attention, and relaxation strategies to improve word recall (Gross & Rebok, 2011; Stigsdotter & Bäckman, 1989, 1993) or in consciously controlled recollection, in which older participants are taught to continuously discriminate between old and new items on a recognition test (Bissig & Lustig, 2007; Jennings, Webster, Kleykamp, et al., 2005). And participants in the Berlin Aging Study learned to use the method of loci to improve their recall performances by associating words on the recall list with landmark buildings along a familiar route in their city (Kliegel, Smith, & Baltes, 1990).

To answer the question about the efficacy of training, yes, training improves declining memory function, but no, it doesn't do away with the decline completely. In none of these studies did the performance of older adults reach the level of young adults, but all brought significant improvement over the participants' earlier performance or over a control group of older adults who received no training. Moreover, children and younger adults typically benefit more from training than older adults. For example, 9- to 12-year-old children and 65- to 78-year-old adults were trained to use an imagery-based memory strategy to help them encode and retrieve words by using location cues (Brehmer, Li, Müller, et al., 2007). The researchers reported that although the children and adults had similar performance at the beginning of the study and that each showed improvement as a result of the training, the children displayed greater benefits than the older adults.

Other memory researchers have focused on training older adults to use external memory aids, such as making lists, writing notes, placing items-to-be-remembered in obvious places, and using voice mail, timers, and handheld audio recorders. In one such study, psychologists Orah Burack and Margie Lachman (1996) randomly assigned young and old adults to two groups—list-making and non–list-making—and gave them word recall and recognition tests. As expected, in the standard recall condition (non–list makers), the older adults performed less well than the younger adults, but for the list makers, there were no significant differences between the old and young groups. In addition, the older list makers performed better than the older non–list makers.

Critical Thinking

How many external memory aids do you use in a typical day? (You might start with class notes.)

In an interesting twist, the authors of this study added a condition in which some of the list-making participants were told ahead of time that they would be able to refer to their lists during the recall test but then were not allowed to use them. These participants benefited as much from making the lists and not using them as the participants who made the lists and did use them, suggesting that the activity of list making improves memory, even when the list is not available at recall. (If you have ever made a grocery list and left it at home, you will realize that the act of making the list is almost as good as having it with you.)

Studies such as these show that training on both internal and external memory aids can benefit older adults whose memories are not as sharp as they were in younger years. They may not bring back 100% of earlier abilities, but intervention and improvement are possible.

4.2.5: Memory in Context

Laboratory studies of age changes in memory have yielded valuable insights into this aspect of adult development. However, their dependence on out-of-context tasks may not tell the complete story of how thinking changes with age. Typical tasks in memory experiments "are relatively stripped down in terms of familiarity or meaningfulness," and little attention is paid to individual characteristics of the participants (Hess, 2005, p. 383).

A number of researchers have adopted an approach to adult cognition known as the **contextual perspective**. Its proponents believe that traditional laboratory studies fail to consider that cognitive processes across adulthood take place in everyday life and appear in a different light when age-related contexts are considered. The contextual perspective considers the **adaptive nature of cognition**, the idea that as we age our lives change, and that successful aging depends on how we adapt our cognitive styles to fit those changes.

For example, younger adults tend to be involved in education or job training and thus are more apt to focus their cognitive abilities on acquisition of specific facts and skills, often for the approval of authority figures. In contrast, older adults are often involved in transmitting their knowledge to the younger generation and thus may focus their cognitive abilities on extracting the emotional meaning from information and integrating it with their existing knowledge. Traditional lab tasks that investigate age differences are more similar to the typical cognitive activities of young people (Hess, 2005).

This difference was demonstrated in a study by psychologist Cynthia Adams and her colleagues (Adams, Smith, Pasupathi, et al., 2002) in which women in two age groups were given a story to remember and retell either to the experimenter or to a young child. The younger group's average age was 20; the older group's was 68. Those who had been instructed to retell the story to an experimenter resembled a typical laboratory experiment, and the results were not surprising; younger women recalled more of the story than older women. However, for those who were instructed to retell the story to a young child, older women recalled as much of the story as younger women. In addition, the older women were more apt to adjust the complexity of the story to fit the young listener. Adams and her colleagues concluded that older people can recall stories as well as younger people when the goals are adjusted to fit the context of their lives—when they are given a task appropriate for a grandmother's goals rather than those of a young student.

MEMORY AND NEGATIVE STEREOTYPES   Another factor that is not considered in traditional lab studies is the role of negative stereotypes of aging and memory ability. When members of a group are aware of a negative stereotype that is widely held about their group, they can experience anxiety when they are put in a position that might confirm the stereotype. This contextual factor is known as **stereotype threat**, and one example is the negative stereotype of older adults as forgetful. As I mentioned in the beginning of this section, age-related memory loss is a very touchy topic for many adults, and some researchers argue that older adults' cognitive abilities can be compromised just by the knowledge that they are in a memory study (Desrichard & Köpetz, 2005; Levy & Leifheit-Limson, 2009). In fact, when the "memory" part of the study is de-emphasized, older adults perform better (Hess, Hinson, & Statham, 2004). In a study of older adults who were around the age of 78, researchers found that their memory abilities declined as more words describing negative stereotypes were added to the test materials. When asked if they had concerns about their own memory abilities, those who expressed more concerns were the ones whose recall was affected the most by the stereotypes (Hess, Auman, Colcombe, et al., 2003). Negative stereotypes affect memory performance for older adults, and the size of the effect is related to the amount of concern they express about their own memories.

But why should being reminded of negative age stereotypes cause older adults to remember less? Psychologist Marie Mazerolle and her colleagues (Mazerolle, Régner, Morisset, et al., 2012) hypothesized that stereotype threat may consume more working-memory resources in older than in younger adults, accounting for the greater decline in memory performance. To test this, younger (average age of 21 years) and older (average age of 69 years) adults were given a working-memory task, in which participants read short sentences and were asked to recall the last word in each sentence in the order they were presented. They were also given a cued-recall task in which they read 40 words displayed one at a time on a computer screen and later were shown the first three letters of those words and asked to recall the entire word. Participants were told that these tasks were "fully validated and diagnostic of memory capacity." Both the younger and older participants were then assigned to one of two conditions. In the stereotype-threat condition, participants were simply told that both younger and older adults would be performing these tasks, which is usually enough to remind older adults that memory is typically worse in older than younger adults. In the reduced-threat condition, participants were also told that both younger and older adults would be taking the test but further told these were "age-fair" tests in which performance does not vary with age.

As expected, the younger adults performed better than the older adults on the cued-recall task, with the difference being greatest in the stereotype condition. This finding is not new, but simply confirms that older adults perform worse on declarative memory tasks when they are reminded of the negative age stereotype. What is interesting in this study is that this effect was associated with performance on the working-memory measure. Figure 4.5 shows younger and older adults' scores on the working-memory task in both the stereotype-threat and reduced-threat conditions. As you can see, although the younger adults performed the same in the two conditions, the older adults' working-memory scores were significantly reduced in the stereotype-threat condition. The authors interpreted these results as indicating that one reason for older adults' reduced performance on declarative memory tasks when they are reminded of the negative age stereotype is that such reminders consume working-memory capacity, which in turn affects how well they can remember the task information.

Figure 4.5 Working memory scores for older adults decreased sharply when they were reminded of the negative age stereotype. When this reminder was reduced, their scores were more similar to the younger group.

SOURCE: Mazerolle, Régner, Morisset, et al. (2012).

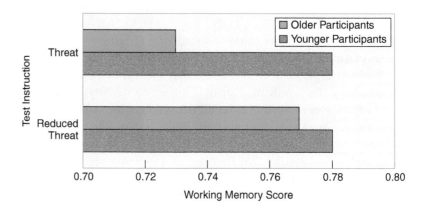

4.3: Decision Making and Problem Solving

4.3 Analyze whether cognitive process is age-related

Solving problems and making decisions are complex cognitive skills that require the coordinated interplay of various types and levels of thinking. These abilities were important for the survival of the earliest humans and are also important today. Although the study of decision making and problem solving is an established area of cognitive psychology, it has only recently been applied to adulthood and aging. We are all aware that the types of judgments and decisions people are required to make change with age, but the question asked in the following section is whether the quality of the judgments and decisions they make changes—that is, whether there are age-related changes in the underlying cognitive processes (Sanfey & Hastie, 2000).

One type of decision that adults are frequently required to make across the life span is *choice*, or choosing among a set of alternatives that have multiple attributes. Which university should you attend when you have been accepted by three, all having different tuition costs, distances from home, levels of prestige, and amounts offered in scholarships? Or which of two treatments to choose for your illness, when each has different risks, side effects, costs, and probabilities of success?

Many studies of this skill are done in labs using a matrix of attributes known as a *choice board*. Figure 4.6 shows a car-buying dilemma. Key factors in a decision include comparing total price, number of passengers each car will hold, fuel efficiency, and manufacturers' rebates offered for each car. At the beginning, the categories are visible, but the attributes are on cards, placed facedown on the matrix. (Some labs use computer screens.) Participants are told to look at whatever information they need and take the time necessary to make the decision. The cards that the participant turns over, the pattern in which they are turned, and the time each card is studied are all recorded. When the choice-making processes of younger and older adults are compared, we learn something about age differences in this type of judgment and decision making.

Figure 4.6 Example of a choice board used in studies of decision making. This one includes four factors for each of four car choices.

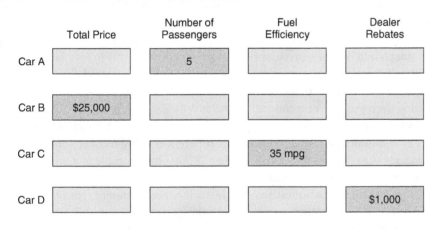

Using a choice-board technique, researchers investigated how young adults (mean age 23) and older adults (mean age 68) chose which of six cars to buy after having an opportunity to compare them on nine features. A later study compared the apartment-rental choices of the two groups when five apartments were shown on the choice board with 12 features available for each apartment (Johnson, 1993). Another research group examined decision-making processes of 20-year-olds versus people in their 60s and 70s as they made complex financial decisions (Hershey & Wilson, 1997). In a study of medical-treatment choice, young women, middle-aged women, and older women were compared on their decision-making processes in a simulated situation involving breast cancer treatment (Meyer, Russo, & Talbot, 1995). Although these studies ran the gamut on decision topics, they all had similar results. Basically, older people used less information and took less time than younger people to make their choices. Regardless, there was essentially no difference between the choices made by the two groups.

One possible explanation for these findings is that older people recognize their cognitive limitations and make decisions based on less complex thought processes. However, the fact that their decisions are the same as those of younger people in these studies suggests an alternative explanation. This hypothesis is that older people are experts on making choices such as which apartment to rent, which car to buy, or which medical treatment to undergo. By the time most adults reach the older stage of life, they have gone through these thought processes many times, and they approach them much like a chess master approaching a chess board, using deductive reasoning and tapping their long-term store of experiences. This explanation is supported by the accounts given by some of the participants when asked to "think aloud" while making choices (Johnson, 1993).

These studies affirm that when adults of any age are evaluated in the context of their current lifestyles, interests, and areas of expertise, they show much better cognitive capabilities than on traditional, "one-size-fits-all" laboratory tests.

EMOTIONS AND MEMORY   One interesting finding about problem solving in older adults is that, despite cognitive declines in executive function as I discussed earlier, their ability to regulate their emotions, particularly in the context of problem solving, is often as good as those younger adults (Blanchard-Fields, 2007). In fact, older adults often show better decision-making skills than younger adults, especially when interpersonal problems are confronted. For example, researchers gave younger and older adults problems dealing with interpersonal issues (for instance, "Your parent or child criticizes you for some habit you have that annoys him or her") or nonpersonal issues (for instance, "A complicated form you completed was returned because you misinterpreted the instructions on how to fill it out"). Older adults were more apt to solve the nonpersonal problems using what has been described as a *problem-focused approach* (for example, "Obtain more information on how to complete the form correctly"), but were more likely to use an *avoidant-denial strategy* (for example, "Try to evaluate realistically whether the criticism is valid") for interpersonal problems (Blanchard-Fields, Mienaltowski, & Seay, 2007). When participants' problem solving was evaluated in terms of effectiveness, the older adults were rated as more effective than the younger adults, especially for the interpersonal problems. Moreover, the older adults' use of an avoidant-denial strategy was not due to their lack of energy to actively solve problems or the fact that they are too emotional. Instead, "they may effectively recognize that not all problems can be fixed immediately or can be solved without considering the regulation of emotions" (Blanchard-Fields, 2007, p. 27).

In fact, older adults in general show better cognitive performance for emotional than for nonemotional information, with age differences being most apparent for positive emotions (Carstensen, Mikels, & Mather, 2006). One example is a study by psychologists Helene Fung and Laura Carstensen (2003) in which people ranging in age from 20 to 83, were shown advertisements featuring three different types of appeals—emotional, knowledge-related, or neutral. As illustrated in Figure 4.7, the older participants remembered more information from the emotional advertisements than the other two types, and the younger participants remembered more information from the knowledge-related and neutral advertisements.

Figure 4.7 Older participants remember more information than younger participants when material has emotional appeal; younger participants remember more when material has knowledge or neutral appeal.

SOURCE: Fung & Carstensen (2003).

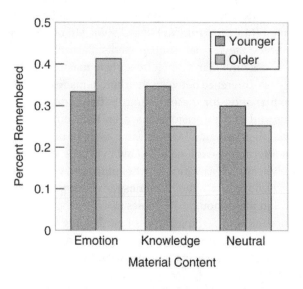

Carstensen and her colleagues suggest that younger people are interested in processing information to acquire knowledge; in contrast, older people are interested in processing information to enhance positive emotions. Unfortunately, most laboratory studies of memory are devoid of emotional content, thus favoring younger participants.

In related research, young (19 to 29 years), middle-aged (41 to 53 years), and older (65 to 85 years) adults were shown a series of positive, negative, and neutral images to examine and remember for later on (Charles, Mather, & Carstensen, 2003). Although the young and middle-aged adults recalled more images overall than the older adults, there was a significant difference in the pattern of performance, which is shown in Figure 4.8.

Figure 4.8 The number of positive, negative, and neutral images recalled is a function of age, with older adults showing a distinct positivity bias.

SOURCE: From Charles, Mather, & Carstensen (2003).

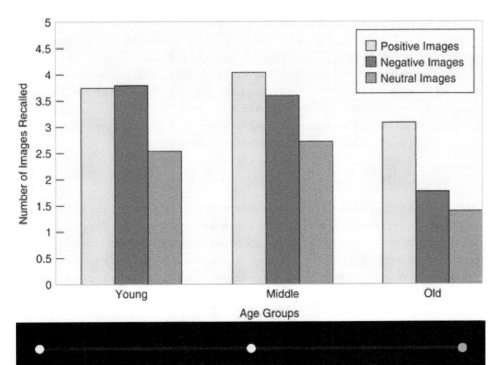

As you can see, the older adults displayed higher levels of performance for the positive images compared to the neutral and negative images. Differences in recall between the positive and negative images were smaller or nonexistent for the young and middle-aged adults.

This **positivity bias** is not limited to memory, but has been found in a number of situations (Carstensen & Mikels, 2005). For example, older adults are more apt than younger adults to direct their attention away from negative stimuli (Mather & Carstensen, 2003), have greater working memory for positive than for negative emotional images (Mikels, Larkin, Reuter-Lorenz, et al., 2005), evaluate events in their own lives (positive, negative, and neutral ones) more positively than younger adults (Schryer & Ross, 2012), and are generally more satisfied with the decisions they make than younger adults (Kim, Healey, Goldstein, et al., 2008). In general, older adults are more emotionally positive than younger adults.

One explanation for older peoples' positivity bias is provided by **socioemotional selectivity theory** proposed by Laura Carstensen and her colleagues (Carstensen,

Isaacowitz, & Charles, 1999; Carstensen & Mikels, 2005). According to this theory, younger people view time as expansive and tend to focus on the future. As such, they invest their time in new activities with an eye to expanding their horizons. Older people, in contrast, view time as more limited and as a result "direct attention to emotionally meaningful aspects of life, such as the desire to lead a meaningful life, to have emotionally intimate social relationships, and to feel socially interconnected" (Carstensen & Mikels, 2005, p. 118). As a result, they tend to emphasize the positive aspects of experiences and devote more cognitive (and social) effort to them.

4.4: Individual Differences in Cognitive Change

4.4 Assess factors that affect age-related differences in cognitive change

If cognitive decline with age were the rule, we would all fade away together in a predictable pattern, showing little variation in change from our age-mates. As you have surely observed in your family or your community, this is not the case; chronological age is only part of the story. Your grandmother and her best friend, Lillian, may be only a few years apart and may have had similar cognitive abilities in early and middle adulthood, but now, in their early 70s, Grandma may be an honor student at the community college and know the names of all 56 people in her water aerobics class, whereas Lillian needs help balancing her checkbook and making a grocery list. What factors might predict this difference in cognitive change?

4.4.1: Health

As is well known, poor health can affect cognition, but it is important to keep in mind that this is true for people of any age. The reason health is a topic for discussion here is that older adults are more apt to experience health problems that interfere with cognition. Another word of caution is necessary; most of these factors are known only to be predictive of or associated with cognitive change—whether they are causes has not been well established.

VISION AND HEARING   My first candidate for markers of cognitive change would be vision and hearing difficulties (Lindenberger & Baltes, 1994; Wingfield, Tun, & McCoy, 2005). Over a third of people over 65 have hearing impairment, and most have some visual disability. The prevalence of decline in these two sensory systems is further illustrated by psychologists Ulman Lindenberger and Paul Baltes (1994; Baltes & Lindenberger, 1997), who tested the vision and hearing abilities of 156 participants, aged 70 to 103, from the Berlin Study of Aging. Tests of cognitive abilities showed the expected decline with age, but when the vision and auditory evaluations for the participants were added to the equation, the researchers found that these deficits explained 93% of the variance in IQ measures. In a more recent cross-sectional study, older adults' (60 to 82 years of age) auditory working-memory span was more influenced by reductions in the intensity of the spoken stimuli than that of younger adults (18 to 30 years of age; Baldwin & Ash, 2011). The results of this study show age differences in listening memory span as a function of the decibel level of the stimuli. The authors interpreted these findings as pointing to *auditory acuity* as an important factor in older adults' working-memory performance.

Does this mean that vision and hearing loss are responsible for declines in cognitive ability? Not really; it only shows a relationship between sensory abilities and cognitive abilities. The explanation suggested is a *common-cause hypothesis,* meaning that the declines in intellectual abilities and the corresponding declines in sensory abilities are most likely caused by some other factor that underlies them all (Lindenberger & Baltes, 1994; Salthouse, Hancock, Meinz, et al., 1996). The general term for this common factor is "brain aging," and we do not know with certainty what specific mechanisms are involved. The best guess at the moment is age-related changes in the white matter of the brain, which was discussed in more detail in Chapter 2 (Bäckman, Small, & Wahlin, 2001). However, although there seems no doubt that changes in brain structure and function are responsible for corresponding changes in cognition, the relationships are not always straightforward, the effects are often small, and much more research needs to be done to be able to specify how the aging brain is related to cognitive aging (Li, 2012; Salthouse, 2011).

CHRONIC DISEASE   The major diseases contributing to cognitive decline are Alzheimer's disease and other dementias, but others have been implicated also, such as obesity combined with high blood pressure (Waldstein & Katzel, 2006), deficiencies of vitamin B_{12} and folic acid, thyroid disease (Bäckman, Small, & Wahlin, 2001), clinical depression (Kinderman & Brown, 1997), and subclinical depression (Bielak, Gerstorf, Kiely, et al., 2011). Cardiovascular disease accounts for a large proportion of cognitive decline, and it predicts performance on tests of episodic memory and visuospatial skills even when age, education, gender, medication, and mood are controlled for (Emery, Finkel, & Pedersen, 2012; Fahlander, Wahlin, Fastbom, et al., 2000).

MEDICATION   Related to health is another cause of cognitive decline in later adulthood—the medication people take for their chronic conditions. Many drugs have side effects that affect cognitive processes in people of all ages, and some drugs affect older people more strongly because metabolism slows with age. Often these side effects are mistaken for signs of normal aging, such as bodily aches and pains, sleep disturbances, and feelings of sadness and loss. Other drug-related problems that can contribute to cognitive decline in older people are overmedication and drug interactions. Many older people see a number of different doctors, and it is important for each to know what drugs are being prescribed by the others.

4.4.2: Genetics

A factor that undoubtedly underlies many of the health-related differences in cognitive aging is genetics. The strength of genetic influence on a behavior is measured by *heritability scores*. Studies comparing the traits and abilities of pairs of individuals with varying degrees of family relationship have demonstrated that cognitive abilities are among the most heritable of behavioral traits. Meta-analyses of studies involving over 10,000 pairs of twins show that about 50% of the variance in individual IQ scores can be explained by genetic differences among individuals (Plomin, DeFries, McClearn, et al., 2008). Furthermore, researchers report that for general cognitive ability, heritability increases with age, starting as low as 20% in infancy and increasing to 40% in childhood, 50% in adolescence, and 60% in adulthood (McGue, Bouchard, Iacono, et al., 1993).

To find out about the heritability of cognitive abilities in older adulthood, behavioral geneticist Gerald McClearn and his colleagues (McClearn, Johansson, Berg, et al., 1997) conducted a study of Swedish twin pairs who were 80 years of age or older. In this study, 110 identical twin pairs and 130 same-sex fraternal twin pairs were given tests of overall cognitive ability as well as tests of specific components of cognition. As the graph in Figure 4.9 shows, identical twin pairs, who have the same genes, had scores on the tests that were significantly more similar to each other than did fraternal twin pairs, who share only about half their genes. Because we know that genes are implicated in many diseases and chronic conditions, these findings of a genetic contribution to cognitive decline should come as no surprise.

Figure 4.9 Correlations on tests for a number of cognitive abilities are higher for monozygotic twin pairs (who share the same genes) than for dizygotic twin pairs (who share about 50% of their genes), demonstrating significant and separate genetic contributions for those abilities.

SOURCE: McClearn, Johansson, Berg, et al. (1997).

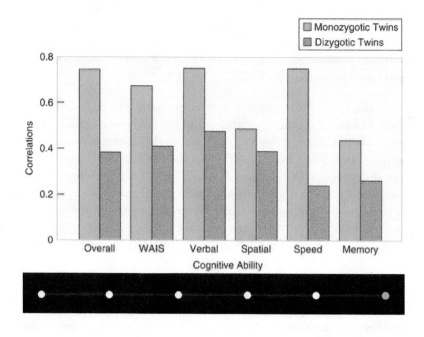

Another interesting result of this study is the variation in heritability for the different cognitive abilities, ranging from 32% to 62%. Taken together, these findings show not only that cognitive ability is influenced by genetics, but also that different types of cognition are influenced to different extents.

As a final word on this subject, I must point out that even if approximately 60% of the individual differences in general cognitive ability in older adults can be explained by genetics, 40% must be considered environmental in origin. In Figure 4.9, you should note that none of the bars reaches the 100% level. This means that even identical twins with identical genes are not identical in cognitive abilities.

4.4.3: Demographics and Sociobiographical History

Women have a slight advantage over men in several cognitive areas (episodic memory, verbal tasks, and maintaining brain weight), and these gender differences continue into very old age (Bäckman, Small, & Wahlin, 2001). Military service is another factor that predicts levels of cognitive ability in later adulthood. Researchers followed a group of 208 veterans for over 11 years and found that their cognitive abilities declined less than those of a civilian control group, even after education was taken into account, suggesting that military training or service might have some long-term effect on cognitive well-being (McLay & Lyketsos, 2000).

WRITING PROMPT

Can you think of an alternative explanation for the findings that veterans show less decline in cognitive abilities than the civilian population? What would the alternative be and why? Write a brief response that will be read by your instructor.

▶ The response entered here will appear in the performance dashboard and can be viewed by your instructor.

Submit

Another set of factors is what Paul Baltes calls **sociobiographical history**, the level of professional prestige, social position, and income experienced throughout one's life. It was once thought that people who had led privileged lives in these respects would be less likely to decline in cognitive abilities as they grew older, but most of the research evidence shows otherwise; the *rate* of decline is the same, regardless of what blessings people have received or earned in their lifetime (Lindenberger & Baltes, 1997; Salthouse, Babcock, Skovronek, et al., 1990). The only difference is that the more privileged individuals usually attain higher levels of cognitive ability, so that even if the rate of decline is equal, their cognitive scores are still higher at every age (Smith & Baltes, 1999).

4.4.4: Schooling

Formal education predicts the rate of cognitive decline with age. All other things being equal, people with fewer years of formal schooling will show more cognitive decline as years go by than will their same-aged peers with more years of formal education. This evidence comes from the repeated finding that better-educated adults not only perform some intellectual tasks at higher levels but also maintain their intellectual skill longer in old age, a pattern found in studies in both the United States (Compton, Bachman, Brand, et al., 2000; Schaie, 1996) and in Europe (Cullum, Huppert, McGee, et al., 2000; Laursen, 1997).

There are several possible explanations of the correlation between schooling and maintenance of intellectual skill. One possibility is that better-educated people remain more intellectually active throughout their adult years. It may thus be the intellectual activity ("exercise" in the sense in which I have been using the term) that helps to maintain the mental skills. Another possibility is that it may not be education per se that is involved here, but underlying intellectual ability, leading both to more years of education and to better maintenance of intellectual skills in old age. A related explanation is that some tests used to measure cognitive ability may actually be measuring education level instead (Ardila, Ostrosky-Solis, Rosselli, et al., 2000). Studies with illiterate, nonschooled adults (Manly, Jacobs, Sano, et al., 1999) have shown that some types of cognitive tests reflect lack of literacy and schooling (comprehension and verbal abstraction), whereas others reflect true cognitive decline (delayed recall and nonverbal abstraction).

4.4.5: Intellectual Activity

Adults who read books, take classes, travel, attend cultural events, and participate in clubs or other group activities seem to fare better intellectually over time (Schaie, 1994; Wilson, Bennett, Beckett, et al., 1999). It is the more isolated and inactive adults (whatever their level of education) who show the most decline in IQ. Longitudinal studies have shown that demanding job environments (Schooler, Caplan, & Oates, 1998) and life with spouses who have high levels of cognitive functioning (Gruber-Baldini, Schaie, & Willis, 1995) help to ward off cognitive decline. In contrast, widows who had not worked outside the home showed the greatest risk of cognitive decline in the Seattle Longitudinal Study (Schaie, 1996).

A number of studies have shown that cognitive processes are preserved in later adulthood for people who exercise those processes regularly through such activities as playing chess (Charness, 1981) or bridge (Clarkson-Smith & Hartley, 1990), doing crossword puzzles (Salthouse, 2004), or playing the game of Go (Masunaga & Horn, 2001). The sets of highly exercised skills required for such activities are known as *expertise,* and studies have shown that older people who have expertise in specific areas retain their cognitive abilities in those areas to a greater extent than age-mates who do not share this expertise.

However, before you rush out to join a chess club, I must warn you that most of these studies are correlational, which means that other factors may be contributing to the retention of cognitive ability. These individuals might be in better health to begin with or receive more social stimulation and support at the gym or bridge club.

Older people who exercise cognitive skills, like these chess players, retain those skills well into late adulthood.

4.4.6: Physical Exercise

Overall, the case for a causal link between physical exercise and intellectual skill is a bit stronger than the link for cognitive exercise, although still not robust. The fundamental argument, of course, is that exercise helps to maintain cardiovascular (and possibly neural) fitness, which we know is linked to mental maintenance. And researchers who compare mental performance scores for physically active and sedentary older adults consistently find that the more active people have higher scores.

Aerobic exercise has been targeted specifically because of its role in promoting cell growth in the hippocampus and other brain structures involved in memory. Most of these studies are correlational, so we face the problem of determining whether the memory changes are caused by the aerobic exercise or by other factors, such as higher education level, better health, or more social support. Nonetheless, a meta-analysis of studies that randomly assigned participants to exercise and nonexercise conditions found that exercise has positive effects on cognitive functioning. In fact, the greatest effects were on tasks such as inhibition and working memory, which are directly relevant to normative age differences in memory performance (Colcombe & Kramer, 2003).

In a follow-up study, the researchers used MRIs to compare the brain structures of older people who exercise with those who do not. They found that the biggest difference was in the cortical areas most affected by aging. Although the participants in this study had not been randomly assigned to exercise and nonexercise groups, the combination of studies provides reasonable support for exercise having an impact on age-related memory performance. Clearly the extent to which an individual exercises (or doesn't) should be considered when assessing memory abilities in later adulthood (Colcombe, Erikson, Raz, et al., 2003).

A longitudinal study by psychologist Robert Rogers and his colleagues points us in the same direction (Rogers, Meyer, & Mortel, 1990). They followed a group of

85 men from age 65 to 69. All were in good health at the beginning of the study, and all were highly educated. During the 4 years of the study, some of these men chose to continue working, some retired but remained physically active, and some retired and adopted a sedentary lifestyle. When these three groups were compared at the end of the study on a battery of cognitive tests, the inactive group performed significantly worse than the two active groups.

Of course (as many of you will have figured out yourselves), there is a difficulty built into these studies and many others like them, despite the researchers' care in matching the active and inactive groups for education and health. These groups are self-selected rather than randomly assigned. The active group chose to be active, and it remains possible that adults who are already functioning at higher intellectual levels are simply more likely to choose to maintain their physical fitness. A better test would be an experiment in which healthy, sedentary adults are randomly assigned to exercise or nonexercise groups and then tested over a period of time. Such studies have been done, and results are mixed. Some find that the exercise group improves or maintains mental test scores better than the nonexercise control group (Hawkins, Kramer, & Capaldi, 1992; Hill, Storandt, & Malley, 1993), whereas others do not (Buchner, Beresford, Larson, et al., 1992; Emery & Gatz, 1990). There is some indication that physical exercise is more likely to have positive effects on mental performance when the exercise program lasts for a longer period of time, such as a year or more, although there are not many data to rely on here.

This is by no means an exhaustive review of the research in this very active field. I simply wanted to give some examples of work that supports the argument of those who take the contextual perspective of cognitive aging. Sure, no one argues with the evidence that cognitive abilities decline with age, but there is active debate about how much the decline is and in which areas of cognition. There are also some lessons in the research on individual differences about steps that might be taken to delay or slow down the inevitable decline. Certainly it seems that we would increase the probability of maintaining our cognitive abilities as we grow older if we engage in physical and cognitively challenging activities throughout adulthood.

4.4.7: Subjective Evaluation of Decline

One factor that is not implicated in cognitive decline is our own opinion of our cognitive abilities. There is a very strong relationship between age and subjective reports of cognitive decline—the older the group is, the more reports there are of intellectual failure. However, when reports of cognitive decline are compared with actual tests of intellectual functioning, there is virtually no relationship. In a very thorough investigation of this phenomenon, researchers questioned almost 2,000 people in the Netherlands ranging in age from 24 to 86. They asked about various components of cognitive functioning (such as memory, mental speed, decision making) and how they rated themselves compared to their age-mates, compared to themselves 5 to 10 years earlier, and compared to themselves at 25 years of age. Results showed that participants' perceptions of cognitive decline began about age 50 and increased with age, covering all the cognitive domains included in the questionnaire. However, when participants' actual cognitive abilities were measured, there was no relationship between their abilities and their subjective assessments (Ponds, van Boxtel, & Jolles, 2000). This suggests that adults believe that cognitive decline begins around 50 and begin to interpret their cognitive failures and mistakes as being due to aging, whereas the same lapses at earlier ages would have been attributed to other causes, such as having too much on their mind or not getting enough sleep the night before. (This should bring you back to the beginning of the chapter and the story of my parents and the catsup salesman.)

4.5: Cognitive Assistance

4.5 **Identify solutions to cognitive limitations**

If you take notes on your laptop while your professor lectures or make a list of things to do before your weekend trip, you are using cognitive assistance.

We are all familiar with nonmedical solutions to various health disorders and disabilities, such as personal wireless response systems for emergencies, household robots, and assistance animals that enable people to live in their own homes and remain independent. Here are some solutions to cognitive limitations that serve the same purposes.

4.5.1: Medication Adherence

One of our biggest preventable healthcare problems is **medication adherence**, or the ability of patients to follow their physicians' instructions about taking their prescribed medication in the right dosages, at the right time, and for the right length of time. It is estimated that about half the people in the United States who suffer from chronic conditions such as high blood pressure and diabetes do not adhere to their physicians' instructions (Sabaté, 2003), leading to poor outcomes, higher death rates, and reduced quality of life. Many reasons have been found for this nonadherence, such as economic circumstances, side effects of the medication, and the doctor—patient relationship quality, but one that has been of interest to cognitive psychologists is memory ability, specifically *prospective memory,* or the ability to remember to do something at a later time, as was discussed earlier in this chapter. Studies have shown prospective memory problems are linked to medication adherence in adults of various ages suffering from a variety of diseases and chronic conditions, such as HIV, diabetes, and rheumatoid arthritis, independent of economic factors, side effects, and patient–doctor relationships (Zogg, Woods, Sauceda, et al., 2012). Electronic devices are available that can be set to signal people that it is time to take their medication, what the proper dosage is, and any other instructions necessary. Pharmacies are able to package multiple pills in blister packs, clearly labeled with the date and time they should be taken. Once the medication is taken, the empty place on the card serves as feedback. Automated phone calls can remind people when it is time to take medication, and there are smart phone apps that keep track of medication and also give reminders. Although this doesn't solve all the problems of nonadherence, it can help with those cases that are caused by age-related cognitive problems.

4.5.2 Social Networking

Almost every chapter of this book mentions the importance of social support in adulthood, but in the later years, social groups get smaller as friends and relatives move away or die. It probably seems to younger adults that the use of personal computers for social networking would be the perfect solution for staying in touch, but it has taken a long time for older adults to get on the grid. Now that is finally changing. In 2012, over half the people in the United States 65 and older used the Internet, and of those who used it, most used it almost daily, mainly for e-mail. Furthermore, one in three older adults use Facebook, LinkedIn, or other social networking sites (Zickuhr & Madden, 2012). Figure 4.10 shows the proportion of adults in four age groups who own various electronic devices. As you can see, the ownership of devices used for social networking—cell phones, desktop computers, laptop computers, and tablets—is lower for older adults than younger adults, but it has increased almost fourfold since 2000.

Figure 4.10 Ownership of electronic devices is higher among young adults than older adults, but almost 70% of people in the United States over 65 own cell phones.

SOURCE: Zickuhr & Madden (2012).

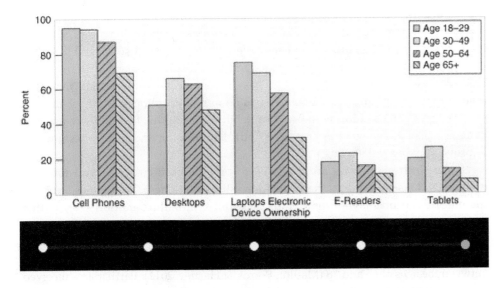

Almost all of today's adults are long-time telephone users, and most have made the switch to cell phones. Even among people 76 and older, most own a cell phone. Adults 65 and older make an average of 100 calls a month, according to Neilson Communications, which sounds like a lot until you compare that group with emerging adults, who average about 275 calls a month (Zickuhr & Madden, 2012). Texting has not caught on as much with older adults, perhaps due to the dexterity required and the small screen on the phone. However, because many older adults report that their motivation to use e-mail is to keep in touch with grandchildren, I predict that their texting will increase in the near future because it is already the preferred mode of communication with emerging adults. Perhaps cell phones with larger texting keys and larger screens will be available soon for this market.

4.5.3: E-Readers and Electronic Games

Intellectual activity is important for cognitive function, but for older adults, there are more barriers to keeping up with newspapers, magazines, and books than with younger adults. Visual problems are more prevalent as we get older, it may be difficult to travel to a bookstore or library, and the cost of reading material may be too high. Many middle-aged and older adults have started using e-books and find this a solution to some of these problems. E-books allow the reader to increase the font size and adjust the back lighting. Some have text-to-speech features so can be used as an audiobook. It is possible to order a book, newspaper, or magazine at any time or place that wifi is available, and the cost is usually lower than the cost of a conventional book. For avid readers, it is much lighter to carry an e-reader than to weigh oneself down with conventional books. I recently started reading our local newspaper on my tablet because I could increase the size of the font for some of the small print, such as movie theater timetables. Before that realization, I had been one of those people who claimed they would never give up the smell of the newsprint and the rustle of the pages as they turn. Plus the "paper" arrives much earlier on my tablet than in the front yard.

Despite all the advantages of e-readers, they are not as popular with older people as computers and cell phones, as you can see in Figure 4.10. In fact, some research has shown that even though older adults read faster and comprehend just as much when reading an e-reader than a book with paper pages, they overwhelmingly prefer to read traditional books (Kretzschmr, Pleimling, Hosemann, et al., 2013).

Research also shows that cognitive abilities are sustained by playing games, preferably in a social setting. When one's ability and motivation to go out with friends decline, so do the bridge parties and poker nights. But many people now play the same games using handheld electronic devices such as Nintendo DS, allowing them to play chess, bridge, and scrabble with friends (and strangers) who live around the world. I am currently engaged in a Scrabble tournament with my sister, Rose. We live about 250 miles apart and have very busy lives, but we are "in touch" several times a day through the game apps on our smart phones. My husband has several chess games going with our grandchildren using his tablet. There are also games to play alone, such as crossword puzzles, sudoku, and games designed to improve thinking skills.

Some electronic games are designed to provide both cognitive and physical exercise, and research shows that they accomplish both. These "exergames," such as the ones found on PlayStation3, Xbox 360, and Wii, feature motion sensors that incorporate the gamers' movements within the game. Some of the activities available are bowling, tennis, and dancing. The potential benefits of exergames on physical and cognitive performance was assessed in a recent study with French adults between the ages of 65 and 78 (Maillot, Perrot, & Hartley, 2012). Participants received pre- and posttest assessments of their physical fitness (for example, heart-rate measures, ratings of perceived effort in doing everyday tasks, BMI) as well as their cognitive performances on a series of tasks measuring executive control, speed of processing, and visuospatial abilities. One group then received 12 weeks of training playing Nintendo Wii games, whereas the control group received no special training. The researchers reported that participants in the exergame training group demonstrated significant gains on most measures of both physical fitness and cognitive abilities, a clear indication that playing videogames can be beneficial for older adults' physical and cognitive health.

4.5.4: Safe Driving

The topic of older adults and driving brings forth a variety of opinions, most very emotional. In many parts of the United States, the ability to drive a car is synonymous with being an adult. Emerging adults count the days until they can drive, and older adults dread the day they must give it up. One of the biggest problems between middle-aged adults and their elderly parents is "the driving issue," when and how to convince Mom or Dad to give up the car keys. Yet an automobile is a dangerous piece of machinery, and auto accidents are the leading cause of death for people in the United States between the ages of 8 to 34 and the ninth highest cause of death for all ages (National Highway Traffic Safety Administration, 2012). The question of whether age-related cognitive changes are detriments to driving safety is an important one, and research has been done trying to pinpoint just what is involved in unsafe driving and if anything can be done to retrain older drivers to make them safer.

About 7% of all drivers in the United States are over the age of 74 and account for 28% of all auto accident fatalities (U.S. Census Bureau, 2012a). However, these numbers don't give us an accurate picture of older adults' driving records because older adults don't drive as much as younger adults. When the accident rates for different age groups are adjusted for the number of miles driven per year, the results gave a clearer picture of the situation. As you can see in Figure 4.11, drivers under 20 and over 70 are more apt to be involved in fatal two-car crashes, and the rate increases dramatically after the age of 80 (National Highway Traffic Safety Administration, 2009).

Figure 4.11 Drivers under 20 years of age and those in their 70s have similarly high rates of two-vehicle fatal crashes, but the highest rated group is 80 years and older.

SOURCE: National Highway Traffic Safety Administration (2009).

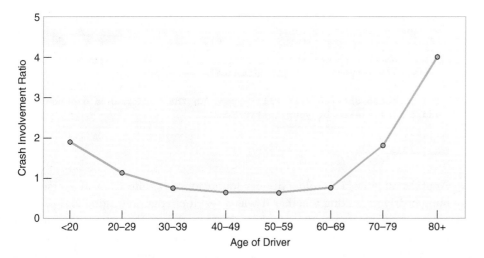

Older drivers have problems navigating intersections with flashing signals or yield signs and making left turns at stop signs or traffic signals, among other things. It has been suggested by some that although older adult drivers have the visual acuity to pass the vision tests, they are limited in their **useful field of view**, the area of the visual field that can be processed in one glance. Older drivers who had a reduction in their useful field view of 40% or more were twice as likely to be involved in an auto crash as those with normal visual fields (Sims, McGwin, Allman, et al., 2000).

Research has shown that the useful field of view is not a constant perceptual ability; it decreases in lab studies when the individual is attending to other activities. In one study of young, healthy college students, the time it took to detect visual stimuli in the periphery of their visual fields was significantly reduced when a spoken word-selection task was added to the test (Atchley & Dressel, 2004). Although this was a test done in the lab and not on the road, it has serious implications for drivers of all ages who multitask behind the wheel. Driving is a very demanding and complex cognitive activity and should not be combined with competing tasks, such as talking or texting, especially for older drivers who may have reduced functional visual fields.

TRAINING FOR SAFE DRIVING After this somber message, there is some bright news; it is possible to train people to have larger useful fields of view. For example, in one study older drivers (average age of 72 years) who had reduced useful fields of view were given either speed-of-processing training or driver simulator training (Roenker, Cissell, Ball, et al., 2003). The speed-of-processing training involved a touchscreen computer on which targets appeared for various durations in the periphery of the visual field. Participants were required to respond to the targets as soon as they were detected until they reached proficiency (about 4.5 hours of training). Two weeks later in a driving simulation test, the speed-of-processing group made fewer dangerous maneuvers than they had at baseline, such as ignoring traffic signals at intersections and misgauging the space between cars when making turns across an intersection, two behaviors that contribute substantially to car crashes. They also had increased their reaction time an average of 277 milliseconds. (In real-life terms, this translates into being able to stop 22 feet sooner when going 55 miles an hour—not a trivial improvement.) The driving simulator group did not improve on reaction time, but did improve on the specific skills on which they were trained. Eighteen months later, improvements for the speed of processing group were, for the most part, still present.

The researchers suggest that the training in speed of processing serves to increase the useful field of view for older drivers, and that this increase translates to improvement in driving ability, specifically the speed with which drivers process and act on complex visual information.

WRITING PROMPT

What is the law in your area pertaining to cell phone use and driving? What about texting? Do you agree or disagree? Why? Write a brief response that will be read by your instructor.

> ► The response entered here will appear in the performance dashboard and can be viewed by your instructor.

Submit

Another study looked at older drivers' failure to scan as effectively at intersections as younger drivers, asking whether it was a result of cognitive aging and physical decline or unsafe driving habits, which could be modified. The latter was concluded when a training group who received feedback on videos of their everyday driving and who spent time in a driving simulator learning to scan more thoroughly at intersections performed better than a control group who only received coaching about the importance of scanning, but no video feedback or simulator training. In fact, the training group performed as well as a control group of younger drivers (Pollatsek, Romoser, & Fisher, 2012). The authors concluded that a major problem with older drivers is the failure to scan adequately for upcoming hazards at intersections. They feel that this is more of a bad habit than a result of cognitive or physical deterioration because a short training session involving feedback and practice in a driving simulator led to significant improvement.

4.6: Review of Cognitive Changes over the Adult Years and a Search for Balance

4.6 Argue that cognitive ability does not entirely decline with age; an element exists, if balanced

The changes in cognitive abilities due to age are reviewed in Table 4.1. There is no doubt that people become slower and less accurate with age on many types of cognitive tasks, and this is the case even for the healthiest among us. But what is the best way to view these overall changes? Psychologist Roger Dixon takes the position that we should look at cognitive change in terms of both losses and gains (Dixon, 2000).

Dixon pointed out that there are gains in terms of abilities that continue to grow throughout adulthood, such as new stages of understanding (Sinnott, 1996) and increases in wisdom (Baltes & Staudinger, 1993; Worthy, Gorlik, Pacheco, et al., 2011). There are also gains in terms of doing better than expected. For example, although Schaie (1994) found a general trend of decline in cognitive abilities with advanced age, not all abilities follow that trend. In fact, 90% of all the participants in his study maintained at least two intellectual abilities over the 7-year time period they were studied. Dixon (2000) also pointed to compensation as a gain in the later years, when we find new ways of performing old tasks, find improvements in one skill as the result of losses in another, and learn to use our partners or others around us as collaborators. This viewpoint may be overly rosy, but there is a good deal of truth in it. The process of cognitive aging is not entirely a story of losses, and this gives us a nice balance with which to end the chapter.

Table 4.1 Review of Cognitive Changes over the Adult Years

18–24 Years	25–39 Years	40–64 Years	65–74 Years	75+ Years
Peak performance on Full Scale IQ tests.	Full Scale IQ remains high and stable.	Full Scale IQ scores remain stable until around 60, then begin gradual decline.	Full Scale IQ scores continue gradual decline.	Full Scale IQ scores begin to decline more rapidly around 80.
Crystallized and fluid intelligence scores are high.	Crystallized scores remain high; fluid scores begin slight decline.	Crystallized scores peak; fluid scores continue to decline.	Crystallized scores remain stable; fluid scores continue to decline.	Crystallized scores begin to show some decline in the 80s; fluid scores continue to decline.
Primary and working memory are both high. Episodic and semantic memory are both high. Procedural memory performance is high.	Primary memory declines slightly; working memory declines more. Episodic and semantic memory both increase. Procedural memory performance is high.	Primary memory remains fairly stable; working memory begins to decline. Episodic memory begins gradual decline around 60; semantic memory increases. Procedural memory performance is high.	Primary memory begins to decline around 70; working memory continues gradual decline; episodic memory continues decline; semantic memory shows slight decline. Procedural memory performance is high (unless it involves speeded tasks).	Primary memory and working memory both decline; episodic memory continues decline; semantic memory shows gradual decline. Procedural memory performance is high (unless it involves speeded tasks).
Memory in context of gathering knowledge is high, but emerging adults lack the experience on which to base decisions. They examine the facts longer than older adults.	Memory in context of gathering knowledge is high. Good practical judgments are made by examining all the information available.	Memory in context of gathering knowledge begins to decline, and emotion becomes more important.	Memory in context of emotion increases, as well as passing down information to the next generation.	Emotional content and generativity continue to be major contexts for memory.
Real-life cognition is good, but many emerging adults depend on parents for assistance with many aspects of independent living. Driving safety is at a low level. Internet use and all electronics are integral parts of life.	Real-life cognition is good, but increases through these years. Cognitive systems are equal to the activities of daily living for most adults. Driving safety improves around 30. Internet use and most electronics are integral part of life.	Real-life cognition remains high. Good decisions are made more quickly than in younger years due to expertise. Cognitive systems are still able to support daily life activities. Driving ability is safe. Most use the Internet and own computers and cell phones.	Increase in number of prescriptions plus declines in memory cause problems with medication adherence. Driving ability begins to decline, calling for many to avoid night driving and have vision tests. Driver retraining may be valuable. About two-thirds use cell phones, and half use the Internet. One third uses social networking sites.	Declining health and memory abilities bring need for clear instructions for medication adherence. Driving ability declines sharply, calling for many to restrict driving to familiar areas and undergo tests of vision, hearing, and reaction time. Driver training is valuable. Most have cell phones, and about one third use the Internet. About one fifth use social networking sites.

Summary: Cognitive Abilities

LISTEN TO THE AUDIO:

05:45

1. Early studies of IQ scores for people of different ages showed that intelligence began to decline in the early 30s and continued sharply downward. Later, longitudinal studies showed that the decline didn't start until people reached their 60s, and the decline was moderate. The difference is primarily due to cohort effects.

2. Scores of fluid intelligence abilities decline starting in the 60s. Crystallized intelligence abilities remain stable well into the 70s or 80s.

3. Declines in intellectual abilities can be reversed using specific training for various abilities, physical exercise, and general test-taking training. This training has long-term effects.

4. Memory is most often studied using an information-processing perspective that divides the memory function into three storage areas, sensory store, short-term store, and long-term store, and makes the distinction between declarative (explicit) memory (memory with awareness) and nondeclarative, or procedural memory (memory without awareness).

5. Age-related declines are less for short-term, or primary memory (holding information "in mind") than for working memory (performing operations on information held "in mind"). The long-term store includes episodic memory—information about recent events,

and semantic memory—general factual information. Episodic memory declines with age, whereas semantic memory is stable until the 70s except for the recall of specific words or names. Another component, procedural memory—how to perform familiar tasks—is relatively unaffected by age or injury. Older adults also perform more poorly than younger adults on prospective memory tasks—remembering to do something in the future—but the magnitude of the difference is usually smaller than for episodic memory.

6. Memory loss can be partially compensated for by external aids (lists, calendars) and training (mental imagery, method of loci).

7. Some researchers, using the contextual perspective, show that older people do better on memory tests if the tasks better fit the cognitive styles they have adapted to fit their lifestyles, such as using information with emotional content, proposing a task that involves transmitting knowledge to the next generation, or avoiding stereotype threat.

8. In real-world cognition, older people are able to make good decisions and judgments in less time and using less information than younger people, probably drawing on their greater store of experience. In fact, older adults often show better decision-making skills than younger adults, especially when interpersonal problems are confronted. Older adults tend to show a positivity bias, being more attentive to positive than negative events and emotions and performing better on tasks involving positive images or emotions.

9. Not everyone ages in cognitive abilities at the same rate. Some of the individual differences are in the area of health, including vision and hearing, chronic disease, and medication. Genes play a role, as does one's education and income history. Mental and physical exercise can lead to better cognitive abilities in later years.

10. Older people's subjective evaluations of their cognitive abilities are based more on their stereotypes of aging than on any actual decline.

11. Cognitive assistance involves practical solutions to the age-related cognitive decline. Examples are electronic timers and phone apps to help people take their medication as prescribed and new pharmacy packaging that bundles multiple pills onto cards with time- and date-labeled windows.

12. Social relationships are assisted by the use of the Internet for e-mail and participating in social networking sites. The majority of people over 65 are regular Internet users and a third are on Facebook or other such sites. Over two-thirds of older adults use cell phones. E-readers and electronic games keep many older adults' minds engaged and active.

13. The number of older drivers on the road is increasing, and they are very safe drivers up until the age of 70, when their involvement in accidents increases dramatically. Because driving is essential to daily life in many areas, researchers have identified the useful field of view as a critical factor in safe driving. It is possible to retrain older adults to increase this visual ability. It is also possible to reduce distractions (such as cell phone use) that decrease the useful field of view. Other studies point out poor driving habits that can be remedied by instruction with feedback for older drivers.

SHARED WRITING: INDIVIDUAL DIFFERENCES IN COGNITIVE ABILITIES

Consider this chapter's discussion of individual differences in cognitive abilities as they relate to a variety of factors (health, schooling, physical exercise, etc.). What are some specific factors that have influenced people you have known (family, friends, relatives)? How have these factors impacted these people? How much of an impact do you think these factors have? Write a short response that your classmates will read. Be sure to discuss specific examples.

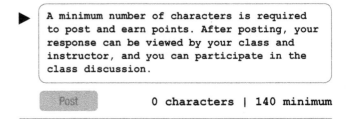

▶ A minimum number of characters is required to post and earn points. After posting, your response can be viewed by your class and instructor, and you can participate in the class discussion.

Post   0 characters | 140 minimum

Chapter 4 Quiz: Cognitive Abilities

Chapter 5
Social Roles

Learning Objectives

5.1 Indicate that roles are neither gained or lost but change with circumstances of the individual

5.2 Discuss that gender roles are affected by situations we meet and are reflected in the gender stereotypes

5.3a Describe the transition to adulthood and its effects on the individual

5.3b List features that distinguish young adulthood from adolescence or emerging adulthood

5.4 Describe the transition to adulthood and its effects on the individual socially, biologically, and career-wise

5.5 Describe the transition to late adulthood and its effects on the individual socially

5.6 Discuss social roles of individuals in non-confirming families

5.7 Discuss the timing of social roles in adulthood

LISTEN TO THE AUDIO:

```
▶ ━━●━━━━━━━━ 03:23   🔇●
```

I TEACH DEVELOPMENTAL psychology courses at a university in south Florida, and I enjoy the role of professor. I am fortunate to be at a satellite campus of a larger school, so I am able to get to know the students. Many of them recognize me around campus and stop to talk to me about the courses they are planning to take, the graduate schools they are applying to, or some point we covered in class. It is especially enjoyable for me because the other part of my career, writing this textbook, is very isolated. For that job I have an office at home where I have little social interaction on the days I do not teach. Together, the two professional roles provide a pleasing balance.

Interestingly, my husband is a professor on the main campus of the same university, and I find myself on "his" campus from time to time. The difference in my social roles from one campus to the other is striking. On "my" campus, colleagues ask me about my classes, my book, or some bit of academic intrigue; on my husband's campus, I'm asked about the family or our latest vacation. Clearly, I have the role of professor on one campus and the role of professor's wife on the other.

However, being viewed as a professor is not my most prestigious role. The first Friday of the month is Lunch with Family Day at the elementary school my youngest grandson attends, and after 6 years I know the drill. I pack lunches and wait on the patio outside the cafeteria. When the fifth-grade classes arrive, he scans the group of waiting family members, looking for a familiar face. Then I hear, "Grandma, Grandma!" and he comes running to give me kisses and hugs (and to see what I brought for lunch). We eat together under the trees, and he proudly tells passing friends and teachers, "This is my grandmother! She came to have lunch with me!" Although I am aware that he may not be as pleased to have me hanging around his middle school next year, I am enjoying the fame while I can. I don't think the president of our university gets such accolades—at least not on such a regular basis.

In addition to these roles, I am a wife, a mother, a sister, an aunt, and a stepmother. Many of these roles, such as textbook author and grandmother, are fairly new, and many of the old ones, such as sister and mother, have the same titles but have changed in content over the years. Reflecting on the changing roles in my life gives me a good measure of my progress on the journey of adulthood.

This chapter is about the roles we occupy in adulthood, with an emphasis on the adjustments we make as they change over time. I will begin with a short discussion of social roles and transitions, and then will go on to the roles that are typical in young adulthood, middle adulthood, and older adulthood. Sprinkled among these is a discussion of gender roles and how they change within our other roles. Finally I will talk about those who don't fit the broad categories—the lifelong singles, the childless, and the divorced and remarried. And I want to emphasize, as you may know already, that the transitions from one role to another are often as challenging as the roles themselves.

5.1: Social Roles and Transitions

5.1   **Indicate that roles are neither gained or lost but change with circumstances of the individual**

The term **social roles** refers to the expected behaviors and attitudes that come with one's position in society. One way adult development is studied is by examining the succession of social roles that adults typically occupy over the years. In the early days of social role theory, adulthood was described in terms of the *number* of roles an individual occupied at different stages of life. The theory was that people acquired a large number of roles in the early years of adulthood and then began shedding them in the later years. In fact, "successful aging" was once measured by how many roles an older person had relinquished and how willingly they had been relinquished (Cumming & Henry, 1961). In the last few decades, this viewpoint has changed to one of **role transitions**. This new emphasis acknowledges that, with few exceptions, roles are neither gained nor lost; they change as the life circumstances of the individual change (Ferraro, 2001). The emerging adult moves from the constraints of being a high-school student to the relative freedom of a college student's role; the young adult makes the transition from being a spouse to being a new parent; the middle-aged adult moves from being the parent of a dependent teenager to the parent of an independent adult; and the older adult may lose some roles as friends and family members die, but the remaining roles increase in richness and the satisfaction they provide (Neugarten, 1996). Studying role transitions involves finding out how people adjust when they change from one role to another and how the transition affects their other roles.

In the past chapters, I have talked about patterns of change over adulthood in health and physical functioning—changes that are analogous to the hours on a **biological clock**. In this chapter, I will talk about patterns of change over adulthood in social roles—comparable to the hours of a **social clock**. To understand the social role structure of adult life, we need to look at the age-linked social clock and at the varying gender roles within each period of adult life. Here I will begin with a brief look at what we know about gender roles and stereotypes before looking at age changes in social roles.

5.2: Gender Roles and Gender Stereotypes

5.2 **Discuss that gender roles are affected by situations we meet and are reflected in the gender stereotypes**

It is useful to distinguish between gender roles and gender stereotypes. **Gender roles** describe what men and women actually do in a given culture during a given historical era; **gender stereotypes** refer to sets of shared beliefs or generalizations about what men and women in a society have in common, often extending to what members of each gender *ought* to do and how they *should* behave. Although gender stereotypes can be useful, they also can be inaccurate, and they are particularly harmful when they are used to judge how well an individual man or woman is measuring up to some standard of behavior.

Gender stereotypes are surprisingly consistent across cultures. In an early, comprehensive study, psychologists John Williams and Deborah Best (1990) investigated gender stereotypes in 25 countries. In each country, college students were given a list of 300 adjectives (translated into the local language where necessary), and asked whether the word was more frequently associated with men, with women, or neither. The results showed a striking degree of agreement across cultures. In 23 countries, a vast majority of the people agreed that the male stereotype is centered around a set of qualities often labeled **instrumental qualities**, such as being competitive, adventurous, and physically strong, whereas the female stereotype centered around qualities of affiliation and expressiveness, often referred to as **communal qualities**, such as being sympathetic, nurturing, and intuitive.

WRITING PROMPT

Is the concept of expecting communal behavior from females and instrumental behavior from men becoming outdated? Why or why not?

> The response entered here will appear in the performance dashboard and can be viewed by your instructor.

Submit

If gender roles are what men and women actually do in a particular culture, what are the origins of these roles? How do boys and girls learn to be men and women? The classic answer comes from **learning-schema theory**, which states that children are taught to view the world and themselves through gender-polarized lenses that make artificial or exaggerated distinctions between what is masculine and what is feminine. As adults, they direct their own behavior to fit these distinctions (Bem 1981, 1993). A similar explanation comes from **social role theory**, stating that gender roles are the result of young children observing the division of labor within their culture, thus learning what society expects of them as men and women, and then following these expectations (Eagly, 1987, 1995).

Both of these theories of origins of gender roles deal with **proximal causes**, factors that are present in the immediate environment. Other theories explain the origins of gender roles using **distal causes**, factors that were present in the past. For example, **evolutionary psychology** traces the origins of gender roles to solutions our primitive ancestors evolved in response to problems they faced millions of years ago. It explains that females and males are genetically predisposed to behave in different ways. The genes for these behaviors are present in us today because throughout human history they have allowed men and women in our species to survive and to select mates who help them produce and protect children who, in turn, pass the genes along to the next generation (Geary, 2005).

The debate between proponents of these theories has been going on for several years (Eagly & Wood, 1999; Ellis & Ketelaar, 2000; Friedman, Bleske, & Sheyd, 2000; Kleyman, 2000), and all sides seem to have broadened their ideas and drawn closer, adopting a viewpoint that considers both proximal and distal causes. This **biosocial perspective** considers that a bias for masculine roles and feminine roles evolved over the course of human evolution, based on biological differences (distal causes), and interacts with current social and cultural influences (proximal causes) to produce gender roles that reflect the individual's biology, developmental experiences, and social position (Wood & Eagly, 2002). Recently there has been a call for a wider range of research methods with a more diverse population to investigate the cultural contributions to gender differences and similarities (Eagly & Wood, 2011).

CHANGING GENDER ROLES   An interesting demonstration of this perspective on gender roles was based on the question: What happens when social and economic situations change suddenly within a culture? If gender roles are based on interactions between biological and social influences, a change in the social environment should bring changes in gender roles and gender stereotypes. This was the question psychologist Alice Eagly and her colleagues investigated (Diekman, Eagly, Mladinic, et al., 2005) by comparing the prevailing gender stereotypes held by young adults in the United States with those in Chile and Brazil to determine whether actual changes in the roles of men and women influence gender stereotypes. The United States was chosen for this study because the roles of men and women have changed asymmetrically—women have moved into the workplace in large numbers and taken on traditionally masculine roles, but men have not taken on feminine roles to the same extent. Chile and Brazil were chosen because their political history involved a transfer from authoritarian military rule to democracy in the late 1980s, giving both men and women more self-determination and independence. Although women in these countries lag behind women in the United States in filling jobs that were traditionally held by males, the changes for both men and women in the past 20 years have been more drastic in Chile and Brazil than in the United States. The authors predicted that this symmetrical change, essentially the same for men and women, would produce a different pattern in gender role stereotypes.

WRITING PROMPT

What would you predict would be the results of a similar study using retired adults in Chile, Brazil, and the United States as participants instead of young adults? Explain your answer and your reasoning in a brief response that will be read by your instructor.

 The response entered here will appear in the performance dashboard and can be viewed by your instructor.

Submit

In this study, Eagly and her colleagues gave young adults in the three countries a list of characteristics and asked them to rate how well each would apply to the average person in their country. The attributes (from Cejka & Eagly, 1999) are listed in Table 5.1. To add another dimension to the mix, the participants each reported on three "average persons" in their culture—one who was an adult in 1950, one who is currently an adult, and one who would be an adult in 2050.

Table 5.1 Examples of Gender-Role Stereotypes

⊗ Communal (Feminine Stereotype)	⊗ Instrumental (Masculine Stereotype)
• Affectionate	• Competitive
• Sympathetic	• Daring
• Gentle	• Adventurous
• Sensitive	• Aggressive
• Supportive	• Courageous
• Kind	• Dominant
• Nurturing	• Unexcitable
• Warm	• Stands up under pressure
• Imaginative	• Good with numbers
• Intuitive	• Analytical
• Artistic	• Good at problem solving
• Creative	• Quantitatively skilled
• Expressive	• Good at reasoning
• Tasteful	• Mathematical
• Cute	• Rugged
• Gorgeous	• Muscular
• Beautiful	• Physically strong
• Pretty	• Burly
• Petite	• Physically vigorous
• Sexy	• Brawny

SOURCE: Adapted from Cejka & Eagly (1999).

Results showed, as expected, that both men and women in the South American countries were viewed as increasing in instrumental, stereotypical male attributes from 1950 to 2050, reflecting the societal changes that these young adults had been witness to in their lifetimes. However, for the U.S. sample, only the women were viewed as increasing in these instrumental attributes, reflecting the fact that women have made big gains in expanding their roles in the United States, whereas men's roles have remained near the same high level of determination and independence.

My conclusion from this is that although gender roles are part of our evolutionary legacy, they are moderated by conditions we experience during our lifetimes, and these changes are reflected in the gender stereotypes of our contemporary culture. It also shows me that gender roles (and stereotypes) are dynamic; they change as our culture changes. Our job is to examine the stereotypes we hold in our minds (and hearts) to make sure they reflect current conditions for men and women, not try to make men and women reflect stereotypes that may be out of date.

5.3: Social Roles in Young Adulthood

5.3a Describe the transition to adulthood and its effects on the individual

5.3b List features that distinguish young adulthood from adolescence or emerging adulthood

Anyone who has been through the years of young adulthood and anyone who is currently in this time of life would surely agree that there are more changes in social roles at this time than in any other period of life. Emerging adults are searching for the right paths in life, but their roles are still slight modifications of their adolescent roles (Shanahan, 2000). Young adulthood, by definition, involves leaving the role of student and beginning the role of worker. It also can involve becoming independent of one's parents, becoming a spouse or committed partner, and becoming a parent. The **transition to adulthood**, or the process by which young people move into their adult roles, varies enormously. Some people complete high school, go to college or enter some type of career training, establish themselves economically, and move out of the parental home. Others complete high school, move out of their parents' homes, take a series of entry-level jobs around the country for a few years, and then move back with their parents, ready to begin college. A few marry immediately after high school, but many leave the parental home to enter cohabiting relationships as they make this transition. So there are clearly a variety of options open to young people as they navigate their way into the roles of adulthood.

WRITING PROMPT

What role transition made you feel that you were finally an adult? Why? If you haven't reached this point, what role transition do you anticipate will do this in the future? Explain why. Write a brief response that will be read by your instructor.

▶ The response entered here will appear in the performance dashboard and can be viewed by your instructor.

Submit

The lack of ironclad rules and expectations has benefits; young people are not necessarily pushed into roles that may not be right for them, such as spending 4 years studying for a career for which they are ill-fitted or rushing into an early marriage with someone who is not a good match. Research suggests that this long period of transition also serves to correct problem trajectories begun in childhood and provides a discontinuity or turning point toward successful adulthood (Schulenberg, Sameroff, & Cicchetti, 2004). Studies have shown that a number of young people entering adulthood with less-than-optimal mental health outlooks, including antisocial behavior and substance abuse, are able to turn their lives around during the extended transition to adulthood, often after assuming the role of member of the military (Elder, 2001) or spouse (Craig & Foster, 2013).

This time of transition between late adolescence and full-fledged adulthood has become so common in developed countries that it is now considered to be a new stage of adulthood. Developmental psychologist Jeffrey Arnett (2000) proposed the term **emerging adulthood** for this time of life, roughly between the ages of 18 and 25. He described it as a time in which young people try out different experiences and gradually make their way toward commitments in love and work. He later described five features that make emerging adulthood different from either adolescence or adulthood: It is (a) the age of identity explorations, (b) the age of instability, (c) the self-focused age, (d) the age of feeling in-between, and (e) the age of possibilities (Arnett, 2007).

Although emerging adulthood does not occur in all cultures, it has been noted, with some variations, among American Indian youths (Van Alstine Makomenaw, 2012) and in China (Nelson & Chen, 2007), Argentina (Facio, Resett, Micocci, et al., 2007), Japan (Rosenberger, 2007), Latin America (Galambos & Martínez, 2007; Manago, 2012), and some European countries (Douglass, 2007; Tynkkynen, Tolvanen, & Salmela-Aro, 2012). Most of these studies have been conducted with university students in urban settings and suggest that the focus on self and the exploration of individual identity may not be present to the same extent with young people in rural areas and less-privileged families. Adolescents in those areas who move immediately into full-time work and family responsibilities show the traditional role transitions found in the United States up until the 1950s.

5.3.1: Leaving (and Returning) Home

The leaving-home process for emerging adults has a lot of variability today, both in the timing and the destination, and this is demonstrated well in my own family. One of my children moved out immediately after high school into a cohabiting relationship. Another went away to college and came home each summer through graduate school. And my husband's daughter, who never lived with us on a permanent basis during childhood, has moved in and out of our "empty nest" several times during her emerging adult years as she attended college or was "between apartments."

What is the most accurate picture of the moving-out process for young people? As seen in Figure 5.1, the most recent U.S. census shows that almost 59% of young men and 50% of young women in the United States aged 18 to 24 were living in their parents' homes at the time of the interview. In addition, 19% of men aged 25 to 34 were living with their parents as well as 10% of women that age (U.S. Census Bureau, 2011b). As you can see, these numbers have increased significantly in the past few years. Although this gives us an account of where people lived on one particular day, it also raises a lot of questions: Why were they living at home? Did they always live there, or did they move out and then come back? Why are males more likely to live with their parents than females? How do the young people feel about living at home, and how do their parents feel about it? These questions are a little harder to answer.

Figure 5.1 The proportion of young adults living in their parents' homes has increased from 2005 to 2011. Younger adults are more likely to live at home, and men are more likely to live at home than women.

SOURCE: Data from U.S. Census Bureau (2011b).

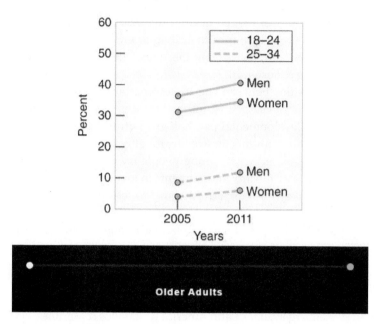

Many households today include young adults who have not moved out of their parents' homes (or who have moved out and returned).

The average age young people leave their family home is currently around 20. The reasons for staying in the parental home until later are many: Young people have a high unemployment rate due to the recent recession, today's jobs require more years of education, more young people borrow money to go to college, the high cost of housing makes it difficult for entry-level workers to have their own place, more young people attend community colleges or satellite campuses of larger universities near their parental home, parents are more affluent and better able to support their adult children, parents have larger homes and fewer children to support, young adults are not drafted into military service as in generations past, couples are marrying later, and adult children of recent immigrants from certain countries are traditionally expected to remain in the family home until marriage.

There are more men in these age groups living at home than women because when couples marry or move in together, the male is usually older than the female; in other words, he has remained in the family home until a later age than she has. Another reason (according to many of my students) is that some parents are less restrictive of sons who live at home than of daughters and also expect less from their sons in terms of doing their own laundry and cleaning up after themselves. This makes it more attractive for the daughters to move out earlier and the sons to stay.

RETURNING HOME   Many young adults leave their parents' homes and then return. In a number of countries surveyed, the incidence of these "boomerang kids" has doubled in the last few decades. In the United States, it is estimated that about half of all young people who move out of their parents' homes for at least 4 months will return again. The younger they are when they move out, the more likely they are to return. The reasons young people return to the family home are similar to the reasons for not leaving in the first place and often are precipitated by some misfortune, such as losing a job, filing for bankruptcy, or a relationship breakup. (Sometimes it is the parents' misfortunes, such as poor health or financial reversals, that cause the adult child to return home.)

What is the result of young people remaining in their parents' homes after the "normal" time to leave? First, we need to remember that the timing of most life transitions are socially created within the specific cultural and historical setting (Hagestad & Neugarten, 1985). When the majority of young adults in the United States between the ages of 18 and 24 are still living with their parents, the "normal" time to move out has a different meaning.

Sociologist Thomas Leopold (2012) examined this phenomenon in Europe to determine the effects of young adults living with their parents. He used data from over 6,000 families who represented 14 countries in Europe and identified a group of young adults as being late leavers relative to others in their country and birth cohort. The ages ranged from just under 20 years in Denmark to just over 26 in Italy. When Leopold investigated the subsequent relationships between the late leavers and their aging parents, he found that these adults shared a higher level of solidarity with their parents than siblings who moved out at a younger age. They lived closer to their parents, maintained more frequent contact, and provided more help to their parents than their siblings. The solidarity went both ways—these late-leaving adult children also were more apt to have received support from their parents after they moved out. He concluded that the practice of remaining in the home of one's parents later than others in that culture and at that time serves to promote generational solidarity for both the adult child and their parents as they grow older.

For some young people, making the transition to adult roles means entering a different culture. Examples of this would be American Indian youths who have attended schools on their reservations and then entered a state university where they are a minority (Van Alstine Makomenaw, 2012), or young people in developing countries who move out of their parents' rural homes to a larger city with changed values, wide choices, and new norms for behavior and gender equality (Manago, 2012). For some emerging adults in developing countries, the drive to be independent is a key factor in their decisions to emigrate to countries with greater opportunities (Azaola, 2012).

5.3.2: Becoming a Spouse or Partner

Marriage remains the traditional form of intimate partnerships in the United States and around the world, but the proportion of people who marry is decreasing, and the age at which they marry is increasing. According to the most recent figures from the

U.S. Census Bureau, the age at which most women marry is 26, and the age at which most men marry is 28. The average age has increased by about 3 years over the last three decades (Copen, Daniels, Vespa, et al., 2012). When couples marry later, the result is an overall decline in number of marriages each year and fewer married people in the adult population. Why do young people today delay marriage? Some of the answers are that couples want to enjoy a higher standard of living in their marriages than couples in the past, and there is not as much pressure as in the past for a couple to marry to have a sexual relationship (or even children).

Another reason young adults are marrying at later ages is the increased rate of **cohabitation**, or living together without marriage, which has increased dramatically in United States in the last few decades. Figure 5.2 shows both the decline in marriage and the increase in cohabitation for different-sex partners over this time period. In fact, if the age of entry into a marriage *or* a cohabitation relationship is computed, it would be close to the age of marriage 30 years ago. Today a young adult's first living arrangement with a romantic partner is more apt to be a cohabiting relationship than a marriage. Currently about 11% of all young, opposite-sex couples are currently living in a cohabiting relationship (U.S. Census Bureau, 2012c). Most couples who marry today have been living together before the wedding.

Figure 5.2 More U.S. women between the ages of 15 and 44 are currently living in marriages than in cohabiting relationships. The proportion who are married has decreased since 1982 and the proportion who are cohabiting has increased.

SOURCE: Copen, Daniels, Vespa, et al. (2012).

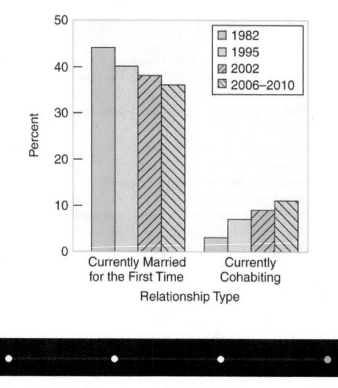

Worldwide, different-sex cohabitation rates vary from country to country. Figure 5.3 shows the percent of women between 18 and 75 years of age in 20 countries who reported that they were currently living in a cohabitation relationship, ranging from a high of over 25% in Sweden to a low of 1% in the Philippines (Lee & Ono, 2012). These numbers reflect differences in the economy, religion, partnership laws and benefits, and availability of affordable housing in each country, among other factors. (The difference in numbers for U.S. women in Figure 5.2 [11%] and Figure 5.3 [7%] is

Figure 5.3 International data show that the proportion of women between 18 and 75 years of age living in cohabitation relationships ranges from 25% in Sweden to less than 1% in the Philippines.

SOURCE: Data from Lee & Ono (2012).

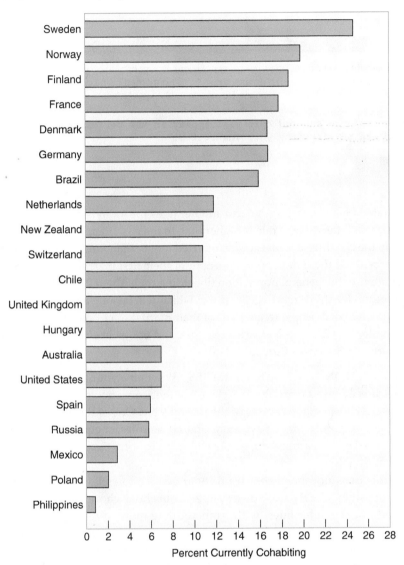

probably a result of the former, which shows results from a younger group of women who are more apt to cohabit.)

Comparing the percentages of people who cohabit in each country doesn't tell the whole story; there are different types of cohabitation. One group of couples cohabit as an *alternative to marriage*. They live together for an extended period of time with no plans to marry. This group includes couples in countries such as Sweden, France, and Denmark, where traditional religious practices do not hold much importance among young people and where the state provides health care and other benefits directly to the individuals (Heuveline & Timberlake, 2004). This type of cohabitation is also common in the United States among older adults whose long-term marriages have ended with the death of one spouse or divorce, and who wish to have a long-term, intimate relationship but not merge finances or displease adult children by remarrying (Gold, 2012). In addition, it should be mentioned that cohabitation is still the only option for many committed same-sex couples and that same-sex cohabiting partners (as well as same-sex married partners) are not included in the research cited in this section unless specifically identified as such.

Another group cohabits as a *prelude to marriage,* with couples living together for a period of time and then marrying. This pattern is found in countries such as Switzerland and Finland. A third group cohabits as an *alternative to being single.* These relationships do not last very long and do not result in marriage. The countries that fit this pattern are New Zealand and the United States.

WRITING PROMPT

Do you agree with Heuveline & Timberlake's conclusions that cohabitation in the United States is an alternative to being single instead of an alternative to being married? Why or why not? Write a brief response that will be read by your teacher. Be sure to explain your reasoning.

> ► `The response entered here will appear in the performance dashboard and can be viewed by your instructor.`

Submit

As stated before, marriages occur at later ages for today's generation of young adults. Although the divorce rate is higher than in the past, there is a trend for couples married in the last three decades to stay married longer than their earlier counterparts. Of course most of these data refer to people in their first marriages and may not be representative of the general population (including me). About 21% of married people are in a second (or third) marriage, many of which will be long and happy unions. Of all currently married people (regardless of their marital track records), over one third will celebrate their 25th anniversaries together, and 6% will be together on their 50th anniversaries (U.S. Census Bureau, 2011a).

GENDER ROLES IN EARLY PARTNERSHIPS   Whether a young person cohabits first or moves directly into a marriage, it is clear that the acquisition of this new role brings profound changes to many aspects of the person's life. One of the major changes is in gender roles. Men and women have more **egalitarian roles**, or equal roles, at the beginning of a marriage or partnership, before children are born, than at any time until late adulthood.

But this does not mean that traditional gender roles have no impact at this time of life—they clearly do. For example, household chores tend to be divided along traditional gender lines, with women doing more of the cooking and cleaning, and men more of the yard work, household repairs, and auto maintenance. And even in this relatively egalitarian period of early marriage, wives still perform more total hours of household work than their husbands, even when both are employed. Single women do an average of 13 hours of housework a week compared to single men's 9 hours. But marriage brings an increase for both, with married women doing 17 hours a week and married men doing 14 hours a week. So marriage brings more chores to be done, but married women do the lion's share—or the lioness's share in this case (University of Michigan Institute for Social Research, 2009).

MARITAL STATUS AND HEALTH   One of the cornerstones of the field of health psychology is that social relationships enhance health. Because marriage is the most important relationship for most people, researchers have compared the health and longevity of married people and unmarried people. They have found that for a wide variety of mental and physical conditions, the health of married people, both male and female, is reliably and significantly better than the health of unmarried people (Hughes & Waite, 2009), and this is true to some extent for men and women in all racial-ethnic groups in the United States (Carr & Springer, 2010). These results are consistent with studies done in a large number of cultures across the world (Diener,

Gohm, Suh, et al., 2000). Furthermore, in the National Longitudinal Mortality Study (Johnson, Backlund, Sorlie, et al., 2000), married people lived longer than single people in any category (divorced, separated, widowed, never married). More recently, studies have combined married and cohabiting individuals in a "coupled" category and have shown that both relationships provide similar measures of physical and psychological health and well-being (Musick & Bumpass, 2012). Recent research has shown that same-sex cohabiting couples report health statuses similar to different-sex cohabiting couples, but poorer health than different-sex married couples (Liu, Reczek, & Brown, 2013). Plans are underway to gather enough same-sex married couples to make a valid comparison between them and different-sex married couples, investigating whether the "marriage benefit" extends to married couples of all gender combinations (Cherlin, 2013).

Why would one's marital status affect their mental and physical health? One quick thought is that one's health actually affects one's marital status—people in poor mental and physical health are not as likely to marry as those who are better off. This is known as the **marital selection effect**, and it does account for some of the differences in health ratings among the various groups. But when that is taken into account, there is still a difference in health ratings between the married and the unmarried. This is also true when family income is considered (Liu & Umberson, 2008).

A second explanation offered is the **marital resources effect**—being married gives people more advantages in terms of financial resources, social support, and healthier lifestyles (Robles & Kiecolt-Glaser, 2003). This explanation may predict some of the health differences between married and unmarried people, but it still does not give a full explanation, especially when we consider that lifelong single people report being in excellent or good health almost as frequently as those who are in long-term marriages (Liu & Umberson, 2008).

A more recent explanation for the health benefits of marriage is the **marital crisis effect**—married people are healthier because they have not endured the crisis of being divorced or widowed. In other words, it's not that marriage provides good health per se, but that the trauma of being divorced or widowed brings poor health. This possibility was explored by sociologists Kristi Williams and Debra Umberson (2004), using longitudinal data that followed over 3,600 people of different ages for 8 years. Their results generally supported the marital crisis theory. First, people who remained unmarried throughout the years covered in the study, whether they had always been single or had been divorced or widowed before the study began, were as healthy as those who remained married throughout the study. It was those who became divorced or widowed during the years of the study who suffered declines in mental and physical health, especially in later adulthood.

One caution relevant to this topic is that *marital stability* (staying married) is not necessarily the same as *marital happiness*. You have, no doubt, known couples who have long but unhappy marriages, and it will not surprise you to know that when researchers divide married people into "happy" and "unhappy" groups, those who are unhappily married report more health problems than the happily married group. For example, researchers followed unhappily married couples from 15 countries in a 12-year longitudinal study and found that those who remained in their unhappy marriages were more apt to experience low levels of physical and psychological health than those who either divorced and entered happier marriages or divorced and remained unmarried (Hawkins & Booth, 2005). Another study showed that middle-aged men and women who felt excessive demands and worries from significant others were more apt to develop symptoms of heart disease than those who had more carefree relationships (Lund, Rod, & Christensen, 2012).

How would you design a study to determine whether people celebrating their 50th anniversaries in your community had high levels of marital happiness or just high levels of marital stability?

> ▶ The response entered here will appear in the performance dashboard and can be viewed by your instructor.

Submit

Taken together, these studies provide compelling evidence for a significant link between marital happiness and health, both mental and physical. Health psychologists Janice Kiecolt-Glaser and Tamara Newton (2001) reviewed a number of these studies and identified some key components of marital discord, particularly verbal conflict, that are implicated in differential health outcomes. Couples whose discussions included conflict, especially conflict with hostility expressed, showed higher heart rates, blood pressure, muscular reactivity, and changes in endocrine and immune functions than did those who had discussions without conflict. Not only do we know that unhappy marriages and poor health go hand in hand, but we also have some firm evidence now of the physical–emotional mechanisms involved. Unhappy relationships can be hazardous to your health!

5.3.3: Becoming a Parent

One of the major transitions that most adults experience in the years of early adulthood is becoming a parent. Roughly 85% of adults in the United States will eventually become parents, most often in their 20s or 30s. For most, the arrival of the first child brings deep satisfaction, an enhanced feeling of self-worth, and perhaps (as in my case) a sense of being an adult for the first time. It also involves a profound role transition, often accompanied by considerable changes in many aspects of one's former life.

Just as young adults are leaving their parents' homes and marrying at later ages, they are also delaying the transition to parenthood. For teenagers and emerging adults, the childbirth rate is currently at a historic low. This is accompanied by declines in teen pregnancy, abortions, and fetal loss rates, and is probably due to the strong pregnancy prevention messages directed at young people and the increased use of contraception. On the other hand, births to women over 40 have increased, partly the result of delayed childbirth at earlier ages, advances in fertility technology, and growing acceptance of single motherhood. (These numbers include over 500 births to women over 50; Martin, Hamilton, & Ventura, 2012.)

The average age at which U.S. women give birth for the first time is now 25.4 years and has increased almost 4 years over the past three decades. The trend toward later childbearing is evident in most developed countries, as you can see in Figure 5.4, which shows the average age women give birth to their first children in 30 developed countries. The average is almost 28 years, and the range is from just over 21 years in Mexico to almost 30 in Germany and the United Kingdom, with the United States having one of the lowest average ages (Organisation for Economic Cooperation and Development, 2013).

Another trend is that when adults in the United States (and in many countries around the world) do become parents, they often do it without being married first. The old adage of "first comes love, then comes marriage" has been replaced, for many, by "first comes love, then comes the baby carriage." According to the most recent reports, about 41% of all births were to unmarried parents. However, this trend seems to have slowed down since 2008, when over half of all births were to unmarried parents. This downward trend holds true for couples of all ages and all racial-ethnic groups.

Figure 5.4 The average age at which women first give birth ranges from just over 21 in Mexico to almost 30 in the United Kingdom and Germany. The worldwide average is almost 28 and the United States is relatively low at 25.

SOURCE: Organisation for Economic Cooperation and Development (2013).

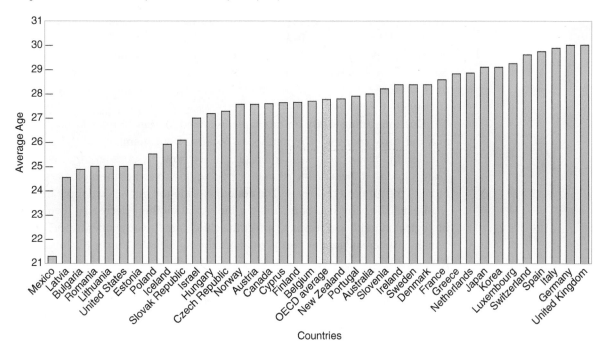

The other important part of this situation is that an increasing number of these "nonmarital" births (58%) are actually to couples who are in cohabiting relationships (Martin, Hamilton, Ventura, et al., 2012). The stereotype of "unwed mothers" being young and alone does not fit the reality of the situation any more.

GENDER ROLES AMONG COUPLES WITH CHILDREN   The transition from being single to being part of a couple brings a slight shift in gender roles toward the more traditional or stereotypical male and female roles. The effect of the birth of the first child continues this shift (Katz-Wise, Priess, & Hyde, 2010). Anthropologist David Guttmann (1987) referred to this process as the **parental imperative** and argues that the pattern is wired in, or genetically programmed. He suggests that because human children are so vulnerable, parents must meet both the emotional and the physical needs of the child, and doing this is very difficult for one person. The woman bears the child and nurses it, so it is natural, Guttmann suggests, for the division of role responsibility to fall along the traditional lines.

Related to Guttmann's ideas are those found in **parental investment theory**, which holds that women and men evolved different gender role behaviors and interests because they differ in how much time and resources they invest in each child. Women, who invest 9 months of pregnancy and several years of hands-on care for each child, devote more to the role of caregiver for each child than men, who invest only their sperm at the time of conception and could produce a large number of offspring in the same time it takes women to produce one (Trivers, 1972).

A third explanation for gender role differences among new parents is the **economic exchange theory**, which says that men and women function as a couple to exchange goods and services. Women bring to the relationship the ability to bear children and in exchange, men take over the financial responsibility of paid work (Becker, 1981).

Research backs up these ideas somewhat. When men become fathers, they spend more time at their jobs; when women become mothers, they spend less (Sanchez & Thomson, 1997), but these gender differences are getting smaller and smaller. In fact, the majority of women with children under 18 are now working full time, and the

Bureau of Labor Statistics estimates that these women spend about 12 hours a week on child-related activities, whereas their husbands spend 8.4 hours a week. Mothers who work full time outside the home also spend more time than fathers on housework, reporting 24 hours a week on tasks such as cleaning, food preparation, and laundry, whereas fathers report 20 hours a week. But when home maintenance and repair is considered, the numbers tip toward the fathers, who report 14 hours versus 8 hours the mother spend per week on this activity (Foster & Kreisler, 2012). Of course when one of the spouses works part time, they naturally spend fewer hours on the job than their full-time spouse and more hours on housework and child care, and these spouses are usually the wives.

One interesting study on this topic followed lesbian couples through pregnancy and the early months of parenthood. Because both members of the couples were females, the researchers were interested to see how the parental roles were divided. They found that the housework was shared equally, but that the biological mother did more of the primary child care. The nonbiological mothers worked more hours of paid work after the baby was born, and the biological mothers decreased their workloads. Biological parenthood seems to affect the child-care/breadwinner aspects of the relationship, whereas gender seems to affect the household chores (Goldberg & Perry-Jenkins, 2007).

A more recent study bypassed the biological roles by examining adoptive parents who were gay, lesbian, and heterosexual couples adopting their first child. Results showed that even among adoptive parents with no biological tasks (pregnancy, childbirth, breastfeeding), housework is not shared equally. Instead, regardless of gender, the parent who worked the most hours outside the home did less child care (feeding, changing diapers, getting up at night, bathing the child). The parent who contributed the most income to the family did less housework (cooking, cleaning, kitchen cleanup, laundry). Same-sex couples (both male and female) shared household tasks more equally than heterosexual couples (Goldberg, Smith, & Perry-Jenkins, 2012).

As this textbook has developed over the years, I have seen this "housework" gender gap grow smaller and smaller. I think this is partly because we have had a large number of mothers in the workforce for several generations now. We know that boys who grow up in families with working mothers are more apt to share the household chores when they marry or cohabit. My guess is that girls who grow up with working mothers have egalitarian expectations when establishing a partnership. With more women working, and working at such a variety of careers, they have more power in their relationships, which translates into better cooperation from their husbands and partners with child-care and household chores.

PARENTHOOD AND MARITAL HAPPINESS   Unlike the transition to marriage, which seems to be accompanied by an increase in happiness and marital satisfaction for a couple, the new role of parent seems to bring a decrease. This decrease is small, but it is reliably found in various age groups, SES groups, and other countries. The general finding is of a curvilinear relationship between marital satisfaction and family stage, with the highest satisfaction being before the birth of the first child and after all the children have left home.

The decline in new parents' marital happiness is not new. Almost 50 years ago social scientists identified this transition as one of the most difficult adjustments in the family cycle (Lemasters, 1957). A good number of studies over the years have traced this phenomenon for many couples (Belsky & Kelly, 1994; Belsky, Spanier, & Rovine, 1983; Cowan & Cowan, 1995; Crawford & Huston, 1993; Feldman, 1971). However, not all new parents show this decline, and certainly not all new parents end up unhappy and divorced. What makes the difference, and is there a way to predict which newlywed couples will make it through the transition to parenthood and which will falter along the way?

One study that has identified some important factors in the transition to parenthood was done by psychologist John Gottman and his colleagues (Shapiro, Gottman, & Carrére, 2000). The study was unique in that it began with newlyweds and then followed them for the next 6 to 7 years. The researchers found that the wives who became mothers during the course of the study had higher marital happiness scores as newlyweds than the wives who remained childless. They also had steeper rates of decline in marital happiness, sometimes continuing for several years after the birth of their child. Husbands who became fathers showed no difference from husbands who remained childless.

Gottman then divided the couples who had become parents into two groups—those in which the wife had declined in marital happiness and those in which the wife had stayed the same or increased in marital happiness. Looking back over the initial interview these couples had participated in as newlyweds, several differences were found that could predict whether the wives would decline in happiness or not. First, if the husband expressed fondness for and admiration of his wife during the interview, and awareness of his wife and their relationship, the wife would show stability or even increase in marital happiness as they made the transition to parenthood. However, if the husband had expressed negativity toward his wife or disappointment in the marriage, the wife's marital happiness would decline as they became parents. The wife had a hand in this also—her happiness was predicted by the awareness she expressed of her husband and their relationship. Gottman explains these predictors as components of the *marital friendship* that makes difficult times, such as the transition to parenthood, easier to get through. It seems that the fondness and admiration the spouses express for each other serves as the glue that holds the marriage together and a buffer that protects the relationship. If new parents are aware of the state of their relationship and the difficult time their respective spouses are having during this role transition, they will feel more satisfaction and happiness in their marriage.

Parents who grew up in dual-earner families are more apt to share household tasks equally than those who grew up in single-earner families.

To wrap up this section, let me reiterate that young adulthood is the time that the greatest number of social role transitions take place and also a time of extremely complex and demanding adjustments. Adapting to these changes is not simple, even when they are done gradually through extended periods of emerging adulthood, such as living in the parental home longer, moving into a cohabiting relationship instead of marrying, and delaying parenthood. All I can say is that it is a good thing that this time of life usually coincides with peaks in mental and physical well-being. My message for young adults is that it gets easier, and it gets better. And my message to those who are past this time of life is to think back and offer a little help (or at least a few words of encouragement) to the young adults in their lives who are navigating these important role transitions.

5.4: Social Roles in Middle Adulthood

5.4 Describe the transition to adulthood and its effects on the individual socially, biologically, and career-wise

During the middle years, existing roles are redefined and renegotiated. This time of life brings stable levels of physical health and increases in self-reported quality of life (Fleeson, 2004). Between the ages of 40 and 65, the parenting role becomes less demanding as children become more self-sufficient. Women's childbearing years end during this time, and most men and women become grandparents, a role that is, for most, less demanding than parenthood and more pleasurable. Marriages and partnerships become happier (or people end troublesome ones and either find more agreeable partners or opt to live alone). Relationships with one's parents slowly change as they grow older and begin to need assistance in their daily lives. The work role is still demanding early in middle adulthood, but most adults have settled into their careers and are usually competent in their jobs. Many experience a role transition from junior worker to senior worker and mentor, taking the time to help younger colleagues learn the ropes of the workplace. This is not to say that the biological and social clocks have stopped, just that they are ticking less loudly than in early adulthood.

5.4.1: The Departure of the Children: The Empty Nest

Middle age is sometimes called "postparental," as if the role of parent stopped when the last child walked out the door, suitcase in hand. Clearly, it does not. Adults who have reared children go on being parents the rest of their lives. They often continue to give advice, provide financial assistance and instrumental help, baby-sit with grandchildren, and provide a center for the extended family. But on a day-to-day basis, the role of parent clearly changes, becoming far less demanding and less time consuming.

When children are "launched" into independence, their parents often find new interests together and renew their preparenting closeness.

Folklore would have it that this empty-nest stage is a particularly sad and stressful period, especially for women. Research shows, to the contrary, that the results of this role transition are more positive than negative for most (Hareven, 2001). Marriages are happier than they have been since before the children were born, and many couples report experiencing this phase of their marriage as a second honeymoon (Rossi, 2004). Women who have fewer day-to-day family responsibilities often take the opportunity to restructure their lives, moving to a new career, seeking out new interests, or returning to college for the degree they postponed when the children came along. Journalist Gail Sheehy (2006) traveled around the United States interviewing women in this age group and found them to be assured, alluring, and open to sex, love, new dreams, and spirituality. Surely these findings are not consistent with the pessimistic view of this time of life that many hold.

What is your opinion on the empty-nest syndrome? Have you observed this in your parents or perhaps in yourself? Did this time of life bring an increase in life satisfaction? A decrease?

▶ | The response entered here will appear in the performance dashboard and can be viewed by your instructor. |

Submit

Although middle age is a positive time for most in the United States, it needs to be mentioned that these years can be negative ones for racial and ethnic minorities, whose life expectancies are lower than the white majority and whose health is worse. In contrast, the psychological health of these groups tends to be better than the white majority. In the MIDUS study, minorities had better feelings of well-being, personal growth, contentment, and accomplishment than the white majority (Newman, 2003).

5.4.2: Gender Roles at Midlife

A big topic of interest in the study of midlife is that of changes in gender roles. Anthropologist David Gutmann (1975), who believes that men and women become more traditionally gendered as they enter the transition to parenthood, suggests that a **crossover of gender roles** occurs at midlife. According to this theory, women take on more and more of the traditionally masculine qualities or role responsibilities, becoming more assertive, whereas men become more passive (Guttmann, 1987). Even earlier, psychoanalyst Carl Jung wrote that a major task of midlife is integrating or merging the feminine and masculine parts of the self (Jung, 1971).

There appears to be some truth in Guttmann's and Jung's views of these changes, but more systematic studies suggest that it is more accurate to describe the changes as an **expansion of gender roles** rather than a crossing-over or merging. There are signs of agentic qualities emerging in middle-age women and communal qualities emerging in middle-age men (Lachman, 2004). Perhaps because the children are gone from home, there is less pressure toward traditional role divisions, and both men and women at midlife can begin to express previously unexpressed parts of themselves.

5.4.3: Becoming a Grandparent

For today's adults, one of the central roles of middle adulthood is that of grandparent. There are more grandparents in the world today than at any time before. In 2004, there were over 60 million grandparents in the United States, and it is predicted that by 2020, one third of the people in the United States will be grandparents. This increase began back in 1990 when the baby boomers reached grandparenting age. And even though people are having children at later ages, with longevity increasing, men and women can expect to spend over half their lives in the roles of grandparents (Silverstein & Marenco, 2001).

Grandparents today in the United States are healthy *and* wealthy. Today the majority of grandparents are under 65, though that age will increase in the future as the baby boomers get older. By 2020, the majority will be 65 and older. As they head for retirement, today's grandparents have help from Medicare for medical costs and have better pensions and retirement savings than generations before. And they have fewer children (and presumably grandchildren) to spend all that time, energy, and money on.

A survey conducted by the AARP revealed that most grandparents live within 10 miles of at least one grandchild and see them weekly. They watch TV or videos together, go shopping, play sports and exercise together, cook or bake, and go to outings like movies, museums, and amusement parks. Even when they do not live nearby, most grandparents reported that they communicate with their grandchildren weekly, mostly by telephone, and they discuss morals, safety, college plans, current events, problems the grandchildren are dealing with, health, bullying, smoking, drugs, and alcohol use. Over one third of grandparents report talking with their grandchildren about dating and sex (Lampkin, 2012).

About one fourth of grandparents report spending more than $1,000 on their grandchildren in the last year—mostly for gifts and fun activities, but also for educational and medical expenses. Over one third of the grandparents reported helping out with their grandchildren's everyday living expenses. Most grandparents report feeling as close to their son's children as they do to their daughter's children. If they are closer to some grandchildren than others, it is because they live nearby. Most grandparents believe that they play an important role in their grandchildren's lives and that they are doing an excellent or above average job as a grandparent (Lampkin, 2012).

My house has a "grandchild" room with books, games, a folding crib, and about a dozen swimsuits in various sizes. The garage contains skateboards, bicycles, a pogo stick, snorkel gear, and a basketball hoop overlooking the driveway. There is a swing in the tree by the front door and a horseshoe pit in the back yard. The pantry and refrigerator contain the grandchildren's favorite foods, and I often find their requests written on my grocery list, such as "dubble choklot ise creem." I buy their school supplies at the beginning of the year, and part of my husband's paycheck each month goes to the Florida Prepaid College Fund. It is kind of comforting to know that we are not outliers in this focus on grandchildren.

Clearly this is not the role that our grandparents had or even our parents. We don't have role models for being today's type of grandparents, and most of us are learning as we go. The role of grandparent depends so much on the age of the grandparents and the grandchildren, the distance between their homes, the relationship between the grandparents and parents, the health and income of everyone concerned, and many other factors.

However, there are some broad generalizations I can talk about. There are gender differences; grandmothers, especially maternal grandmothers, have broader and more intimate roles than grandfathers, especially with granddaughters.

To be fair, I should include evidence of the less-than-fun side of the grandparent role. There can be problems, and the most frequent stem from disagreements over child rearing between the grandparents and their adult children—the parents of the grandchildren. Some grandparents have trouble making the transition from full-time parent of dependent children to the more egalitarian role of parent to an adult child who has children of his or her own. (And some adult children have had problems in their role transitions, too.)

GRANDPARENTS RAISING GRANDCHILDREN   A substantial number of grandparents have taken their grandchildren into their homes and assumed parental responsibility for them, forming a family referred to sometimes as **grandfamilies**. Usually this takes place when the children's parents are unable (or unwilling) to fulfill their roles as parents due to immaturity, drug use, imprisonment, mental illness, or death. According to the U.S. Census Bureau, 7% of children live in grandparent-headed homes, and about one fifth of those have neither parent present in the home, amounting to 900,000 children, or 1.3% of all U.S. children. This number has gone down in the last decade, mostly because the economic decline has caused the absent parents to move back into the grandparents' home, often stretching the household budget even further. This grandparenting role does not entail simply living with the grandchild's parents and helping out, but consists of reassuming the parenting role for the grandchildren in one's own home when the parents are either absent or not able to fulfill their roles as parents. Although this situation is not unusual in

African-American families, it has become increasingly common among white and Hispanic families as well (Goyer, 2010).

One study that examined the role of grandparents as surrogate parents was done by social work researchers Roberta Sands and Robin Goldberg-Glen (2000). They interviewed 129 grandparents who were in the role of surrogate parent for at least one grandchild, asking about the sources of stress in their lives. Results showed that regardless of the grandparents' age, race, or number of grandchildren living in the home, the major sources of stress came from problems with the grandchildren's parents (they weren't involved in supporting their children either with attention and emotional support or with financial support, and they added to the grandparents' stress with their own financial and personal problems) and problems with the grandchildren's learning (they had attention-deficit/hyperactivity disorder or were discipline problems at school).

Although most research involves grandmothers, social work researchers Stacey Kolomer and Philip McCallion (2005) interviewed 33 grandfathers who were caregivers for their grandchildren and compared them to a group of grandmothers. They found that the grandfathers were more apt to be raising the grandchildren with the help of their spouse, more likely to be working full time outside the home, more apt to be white, and had lower depression levels than the grandmothers. Their big concerns were the loss of freedom that their family situation brought and also concerns for their own health, worrying about what would happen to the family if their health failed.

Grandparents who take on the role of surrogate parent have difficulty getting financial help. In most states, if unrelated people take in children whose parents cannot take care of them, they are eligible for foster-parent funds, but grandparents and other relatives are not. It is also difficult for grandparents to collect child support from their grandchildren's fathers (or mothers), even when the court has ordered it as part of a custody agreement. They are in a legal limbo unless the parents agree to relinquish their parental rights, and without legal guardianship, grandparents have difficulty getting medical treatment for their grandchildren and information from the schools. With more and more middle-aged people taking on the role of surrogate parents to their grandchildren (and more and more people being grandparents in general), one hopes that this situation will soon change.

5.4.4: Caring for an Aging Parent

For most of today's middle-aged adults, an important role is that of being the adult child of an aging parent. Over a fourth of middle-aged adults report that their mothers and fathers are living, and only 10% of middle-aged adults report that both parents are in good health (Marks, Bumpass, & Jun, 2004). Figure 5.5 illustrates these data along with the proportion of middle-aged men and women who report having various combinations of parents in various states of health.

As you can see, over a third of middle-aged adults in this survey report having at least one parent who is not in good health. Although the major caregiver of an older adult is most commonly his or her spouse, the task is usually taken on by the adult children when the spouse is not available due to divorce, poor health, or death.

GENDER AND CAREGIVING Daughters and daughters-in-law have traditionally been the adult children who take on the care of a parent in poor health, but that is changing, perhaps because more and more women are working outside the home and not as available for caregiving responsibilities as they were in the past. In a national survey, over one fourth of the respondents reported that they had served as unpaid caregivers for an elderly person during the past year. Two thirds were women and one third were men, and the average age was 48 years. The ages of both caregivers and care receivers have increased in the past 5 years. About one fourth responded that the reason their loved one needs care is "old age" or "dementia."

Figure 5.5 About 78% of middle-aged adults (aged 40–59) have at least one living parent, and for over a third of those, one or more of their parents is not in good health.

SOURCE: Data from Marks, Bumpass, & Jun (2004).

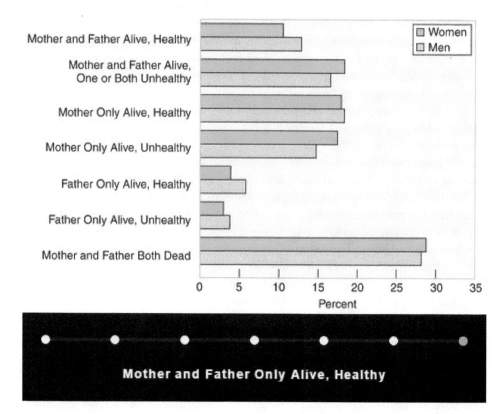

Mother and Father Only Alive, Healthy

The question, "Who provides the care?" seldom has a one-word answer. Most situations require several paragraphs. In my own family, my three sisters provided most of the care for our elderly parents because they lived nearby, and I'm four hours away. My parents also had a home healthcare worker who visited on a daily basis. I pitched in when I was in town. Our husbands had their roles too—one managed a rental property my parents owned, and another made sure my father went out several times a week to have lunch "in town" or walk around the hardware store. And then there was the staff at the senior residence where my parents lived, who provided meals and laundry service. My parents were also able to help each other out; my father joked that he was able to push my mother's wheelchair, and she was able to remember where they were going.

With baby boomers entering their 60s, researchers predict a change in caregiving roles for elderly parents. First, the baby boomers have a record number of siblings available to share the caregiving tasks. Second, for a variety of reasons discussed previously, many baby boomers have adult children of their own still living at home. Psychologist Karen L. Fingerman and her colleagues (Fingerman, Pillemer, Silverstein, et al., 2012) interviewed 300 aging parents and over 700 of their middle-aged children. They found that when there were several adult children, parents (especially mothers) had a specific adult child in mind as the most likely to care for them if they became disabled or ill. This was not necessarily the child who was the most available to help, but the child (usually a daughter) who shared their values, lived nearby, had provided help in the past, and with whom they felt the most emotional closeness. They also found that the baby boomers differentiated between their parents when they were called on to offer caregiving, especially divorced fathers with whom they had experienced detachment.

THE IMPACT OF CAREGIVING   In the past 20 years, a great number of studies have explored the effect of parent care on the lives of the caregivers. In most of these studies, the recipient of care had been diagnosed with some form of dementia, most often Alzheimer's disease. Because such patients gradually lose their ability to perform the simplest of daily functions, they require a steadily increasing amount of care, and the demands on the caregiver can be very large indeed, up to and including constant supervision. When the middle-aged caregiver is also holding down a job, sharing the life of a spouse, and assisting grown children and grandchildren, the impact can be substantial.

The cumulative evidence indicates that caregivers of elderly parents report having more depressive symptoms, take more antidepressant and antianxiety medication, and report lower marital satisfaction than is true for matched comparison groups of similar age and social class (Martire & Schulz, 2001; Bookwala, 2009; Sherwood, Given, Given, et al., 2005). They are less likely to exercise or follow a nutritious diet, get adequate sleep, take time to rest when ill, or remember to take their medication than similar people who are not caregivers. The results are lower levels of overall physical health (Pinquart & Sörensen, 2007). Collectively, these effects on mental and physical health go by the name of **caregiver burden**. African-American family members who provide care for elderly relatives are less apt to experience caregiver burden and depression than white caregivers (Pinquart & Sörensen, 2005), though they report lower levels of physical health than white caregivers (Kim, Knight, & Longmire, 2007).

A study of middle-aged baby boomers concluded that the area of life that was the most satisfying and important for this group was family. Even for those who reported having caregiving responsibilities for both children and aging parents, most felt that this was not a source of stress. The impact of multiple social roles in the lives of middle-aged adults depends on many factors other than simply the number of roles, such as having adequate social support, a satisfying marriage or partnership, a rewarding job, and a good relationship with aging parents (Marks, Bumpass, & Jun, 2003). It also helps to have good mental health and confidence in one's role as caregiver (Campbell, Wright, Oyebode, et al., 2008). Clearly, the effect of multiple roles isn't a simple one of just having too many items on one's list of things to do. It also depends on what the roles are, what social support is forthcoming, and whether or not one perceives them as rewarding.

5.5: Social Roles in Late Adulthood

5.5   **Describe the transition to late adulthood and its effects on the individual socially**

In late adulthood, we make transitions into simplified forms of former roles—we move into smaller homes or retirement communities; we leave our full-time jobs and spend our time on part-time work, volunteer work, or caregiving for spouse, relatives, or friends; we take pride in the development of our grandchildren and great-grandchildren; we watch our children mature; and we enjoy their success and happiness. Some roles are not of our choosing, such as the role of living alone, usually as widow or widower, and the role of care receiver, but they are also part of the journey of adulthood for many older adults.

At one time, late adulthood was considered a time of role loss. Even when the concept of role transition became popular, the normative results of these transitions for older adults were often considered to be stress, grief, and a sense of loss. More recently, studies have shown that there are no typical ways that adults react to role transitions in late adulthood. Different people experience these transitions in different ways, and even the same person may experience extreme disruption in his or her life during these transitions, only to recover and takes on new roles with gusto (Ferraro, 2001). So instead of viewing late adulthood as a time of loss, researchers are busily investigating the wide range of outcomes possible and the personal factors that might predict the outcomes for different individuals.

5.5.1: Living Alone

One of the new challenges that comes to many adults in their later years, most frequently to women, is that of learning to live alone, a change brought about by losing the role of spouse due to widowhood or sometimes divorce. I will talk about the experience and adjustment to the death of a spouse elsewhere, but here I want to take up the topic of living alone in late adulthood for whatever reason. Figure 5.6 shows the living arrangements for people 65 years of age and older in the United States. As you can see, almost 20% of men and 37% of women fall into this group. Such a choice is less common among people of Hispanic and Asian origins than among non-Hispanic white and black adults. Hispanic Americans and Asian Americans have higher proportions of older adults living with relatives other than spouses (Federal Interagency Forum on Aging, 2012).

Living arrangements for older adults depend on a number of factors. Gender is important because of the age difference between married partners. Men are typically older than their wives, so women are more apt to be widowed at younger ages than men. For example, a 70-year-old woman is likely to be married to a man who is 73 or so, whereas a 70-year-old man is likely to be married to a woman who is 67 or 68. This is apparent in Figure 5.6, where men in every group are significantly more likely to be living with a spouse than women are. Other factors are the number of children the older adult has, the location of the children, and the relationship they have with the children (and their spouses). For most older people in the United States, the wish to live independently is very strong, and if they can afford it and are able to take care of themselves, most without a spouse prefer to live alone. Still, it is not an easy transition.

Figure 5.6 Over 70% of men 65 years of age or older live with their spouses and almost 20% live alone. For women this age, only 42% live with their spouses and almost that many live alone (37%). The proportion living with relatives depends on the racial/ethnic group and gender.

SOURCE: Federal Interagency Forum on Aging Related Statistics (2012).

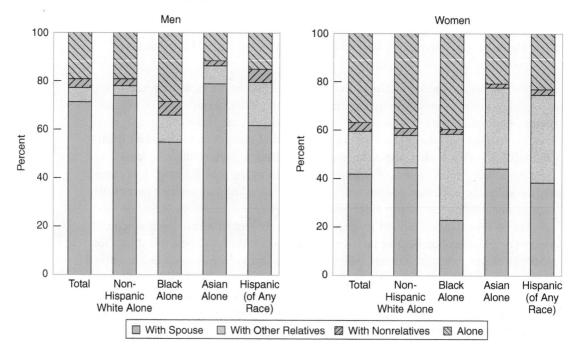

Our family experienced this situation a few years ago when my father-in-law died and left his wife of 64 years living alone in the house they had shared in New England. Although she would technically be classified as "living alone," that was hardly the case. Three adult children lived nearby with their spouses, and there were seven adult grandchildren within easy driving distance. One daughter-in-law called her every morning on her way to work, one son stopped by on his way home from work each afternoon, another son and his wife took her out to dinner every Wednesday and for breakfast every Sunday. A daughter had the whole family over for dinner on Sunday nights. Each day a community volunteer stopped by to visit and bring her lunch, and women from her church picked her up for activities there. My mother-in-law had not driven for years, so she gave her car to a granddaughter who needed one. In exchange, the granddaughter was happy to drive her grandmother on her errands and appointments. Another son and daughter-in-law (my husband and I), who live in Florida, visited often and would have loved for her to come and spend the winter, but she always declined. I think this may be the case with many older men and women who are listed as "living alone."

5.5.2: Becoming a Care Receiver

One role that few older adults plan to fill is that of care receiver. After spending many years of one's life as an independent adult and caregiver to their children, their own parents, and sometimes their grandchildren, many adults find themselves on the other end of the caregiving process, either moving into a residential facility or being cared for by family members. Although it sounds like a long-overdue reward, most older adults feel otherwise. In a dissertation study of almost 2,000 adults who were 65 years of age or older, the quality of "remaining independent" was named as important by over 93% of the respondents, second only to "having good health" (Phelan, 2005).

In an innovative qualitative study, public health researchers, Lee Chin and Susan Quine (2012) interviewed women over 65 years of age about their concepts of "home." Some of the women lived in their own homes, and some lived in residential care facilities. Women who lived at home expressed fears of moving into residential care because of anticipated loss of privacy, loss of freedom to do things on their own schedule, and loss of personal space. They spoke of how much they valued their independence and the contact they have with special friends. They told about special places in their homes and gardens that gave them comfort and a sense of self. Not surprisingly, the women in the residential care facilities mourned the loss of the same things that the women living in their own homes valued and feared losing, showing that these fears were not unfounded.

The women in residential care who had adapted to their new surroundings talked about the importance of acceptance and of strategies they had found to deal with the losses they experienced. For example, one woman who had lived on a farm started waking up early in the morning and going out in the garden before anyone else was out. She filled the bird feeders and walked around the grounds by herself, feeling that this was her own personal space for a while. Other women in the residential care homes wished that they could choose their own seats at dinner instead of being assigned a seat. They did not like sharing a bedroom or bathroom. They would like to have meals on their own schedule instead of as a group. They enjoyed small benches in the garden or private nooks indoors where they could be alone or take their visitors instead of using the large community room. The authors suggest that their findings be translated into the design and management of residential facilities to make life more pleasant for the people living there and to reduce the fears of those who may need to move there in the future (Chin & Quine, 2012).

Receiving care from family members has a number of advantages, the most obvious being that it allows one to remain in their own home and decreases the amount of paid help that is necessary. Less-obvious benefits are that it gives the opportunity to become closer to family members in the time remaining, time for mending fences and deepening feelings for each other. Regardless of the source of care, it is important for the recipient to feel in control of as much of their day-to-day decisions as possible (Martire & Schulz, 2001).

Being the recipient of care also has its negative effects. We are familiar with cases of elder abuse or incidents of intentional criticism or hostility directed at older adults by family caregivers and paid caregivers, but even well-intentioned caregiving can have negative effects on the recipient. Studies show that older adults who are recipients of excessive caregiving may lose confidence in their own ability to function and as a result become even more disabled (Seeman, Bruce, & McAvay, 1996). In one study, many of the people who were caregivers for their spouses with arthritis tended to overestimate the pain of their spouse. Those who did this were more apt to have spouses who reported lower satisfaction with the care and support they were receiving. Interestingly, these spouses who overestimated their partner's arthritis pain were also more apt to experience more stress in their roles as caregivers (Martire, Keefe, Shulz, et al., 2006). New studies are being done to investigate this issue more thoroughly, and the results will hopefully show the way to fit caregiving behavior more closely to the needs of those who are receiving it so it can have its intended benefits.

5.6: Social Roles in Atypical Families

5.6 **Discuss social roles of individuals in non-confirming families**

Except for a few paragraphs on unmarried or widowed individuals, everything I have said so far in this chapter describes the life patterns of adults who move through the social roles of single young adult, spouse (or cohabiting partner), parent, and grandparent. But of course a great many adults do not follow such a pattern. Some remain single, others have no children, and many start out on the typical path and decide on an alternative journey. In the most recent census, we learned that for the first time since data collection began in 1940, the majority of households (52%) do *not* contain a married couple. Who lives in U.S. households? About 10% are single mothers or fathers with children. About 34% are men and women living alone. Six percent are opposite-sex partners, and 1% are same-sex partners. And 7% are people living in non-romantic relationships with other adult roommates (Lofquist, Lugaila, O'Connell, et al., 2012). Clearly our stereotypical family of a husband and wife, several children, and no divorce (the pattern on which much of family sociology was based on until quite recently) is not a valid representation of today's families. So in fairness to families like mine (and probably yours), I cannot leave this chapter without talking about those whose social role experience in adulthood differs from this mythical "norm."

5.6.1: Lifelong Singles

Over one third of households in the United States consist of just one person—no partner, no children, no roommate. This category covers a lot of situations—young people who have not found a partner yet, older people who are divorced or widowed and whose children are grown, or individuals who have chosen living alone as their preferred lifestyle. It is estimated that about 4% of the U.S. population over 65 has never married, more of them being men than women and more of them being black and Hispanic than white and Asian (Kreider & Ellis, 2012).

Reasons for being a lifelong single person range from being focused on a career to being very shy. Women who have never married tend to be more educated and have higher incomes than men who have never married, making it difficult for them to match up with each other. Lifelong single people often worry (or are warned by well-meaning friends) that when they get older and need help, there will be no one to care for them because they lack both a partner and, usually, children. However, research shows that most older people who have never married have formed a network of friends and more distant relatives who offer the instrumental and social support they need (Wolf & Kasper, 2006).

Developmental psychologist Martin Pinquart (2003) studied loneliness in different groups of people and found that those who had never been married reported being less lonely when they had close relationships with siblings and friends. Interestingly, widowed and divorced people the same age did not report that their ties with sibling and friends were as important in alleviating loneliness. Their loneliness depended on whether their adult children were close to them or not. Piquart concluded that people who have been married depend on the social support of their spouses and children, whereas those who have always been single have cultivated close relationships with siblings and friends.

The health of the older lifelong single adult has been the topic of a number of studies. Although married people report higher levels of well-being than widowed, divorced, separated, and lifelong single people, the lifelong single group is a close second and gaining each decade (Marks, 1996). Of the large group of older single adults (divorced, separated, widowed, and lifelong single), the lifelong singles have the best health and fewest disabilities. Furthermore, they report the most satisfaction with being single (Newtson & Keith, 1997). This certainly dispels the myth of fading spinsters and frail elderly bachelors!

5.6.2: The Childless

Despite all the current news about advances in infertility treatment, late-life pregnancies, and women choosing to have children without the benefit of marriage (or even a partner in their lives), the rate of childlessness is increasing for U.S. women. (And we assume the same is true for men, although most statistics report only women's fertility rates.) According to the most recent census figures, about 20% of U.S. women end their childbearing years with no children (Livingston & Cohn, 2010). This is almost double the proportion of childless women in the 1970s. These data are shown in Figure 5.7.

Figure 5.7 The percent of U.S. women aged 40 to 44 who have had no children has increased over the last three decades, declining slightly since 2000.

SOURCE: Data from U.S. Census Bureau (2013).

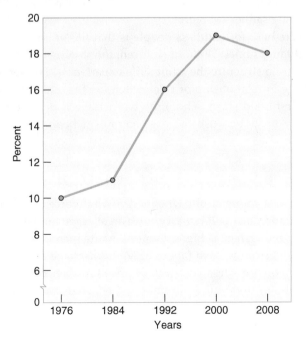

The increase in childlessness has also occurred in other developed countries, with the United Kingdom and Spain having similar rates as the United States, and eastern European countries, Mexico, and Portugal reporting about half the rate as the United States (Organisation for Economic Cooperation and Development, 2011).

In a recent survey of women from 40 to 44 years of age, about 6% report that they are not able to have children, and about 6% report having chosen to remain childless. About 2% of this group still plans to have children. The higher a woman's education, the greater chance she will be childless. White women were more apt to be childless than those of other races or ethnic groups (Livingston & Cohn, 2010).

Critical Thinking

What do you think are some of the reasons for the increase in voluntary childlessness in the United States and around the world?

For women without children, another major difference is in the role of worker. Without children to care for, there is far less barrier to a woman's pursuit of a full-time career. Whether women who have made a commitment to a career choose not to have children or whether those who do not have children subsequently make a stronger career commitment is not completely clear. Some of both may well occur. What is clear is that childless women are more likely to work throughout their adult lives, to have somewhat higher-level jobs, and to earn more money.

One concern of childless people is that they will have no one to take care of them when they are old. Research has shown that this is not a valid concern. Studies of older adults who need assistance show that those who are parents have no more assistance from social networks than those who are not parents (Chang, Wilbur, & Silverstein, 2010). Childless adults seem to have a strong social network of siblings, cousins, nieces, and nephews and may also receive support from children of neighbors and close friends. Many have raised stepchildren. It seems clear that childlessness is not an age-related status; older adults who are childless were also middle-aged childless adults. Most invested in deep friendships and nurtured ties with their siblings and other relatives. The social networks they have in older adulthood are not much different in size and function from older adults who are parents (Zhang & Hayward, 2001). I think it is safe to say that the picture of adults without children is not one of persisting sadness or regret.

One real decrement for childless people is that life in our society seems to be shaped by family milestones. Without children, the rhythm of the family timetable is simply not there to structure the adult's life experiences. For better or for worse, there is no change in relationship or roles when the first child is born, no celebration when the first child starts school, no bar mitzvahs or first dates or leaving home—no empty nests because the nest has never been full (or, perhaps, has always been full).

5.6.3: Divorced (and Remarried) Adults

About 30% of today's young adults who marry will divorce before they reach their 10th anniversary, and most will remarry, with an average unmarried interval of 3.5 years. The rate of remarriage is highest among white men (about 75%) and lowest among African-American women (about 32%). Remarriage rates are also linked to age: the younger you are when you divorce and the fewer children you have, the greater the likelihood that you will remarry. And among all who remarry, more than half will divorce a second time. About a third of these will remarry once again (Kreider, 2005).

Nonetheless, it is clear that divorce brings with it a larger and more complex set of roles to fill. The single parent must often fill a larger share of the adult family roles: breadwinner, emotional supporter, housekeeper, child caregiver, activities director, chauffeur, and the rest. With remarriage, more new roles emerge. One becomes a spouse again and frequently a stepparent. About 90% of men and women in a second marriage have at least one child from a previous relationship. If the new spouse's children are young, one might easily go from being a childless adult to having children in the home on a daily basis. This is especially true for men because children most often have their primary residence with their mothers.

Although women who marry men with children may seem to have an easier role because the children often don't have their primary residence with their father (and her), in many ways, being a stepmother can be more difficult than being a stepfather. The role of a stepmother starts out with one of the most threatening false stereotypes found in legends and classic children's literature—the evil stepmother. I doubt if there is a stepmother alive who has not said, "I don't want to seem like a wicked stepmother!" I know I have. Another complication is that our cultural stereotypes allow for only one mother per child, so a stepmother must be careful not to intrude in the special relationship the child has with his or her "real" mother. At the same time, the traditional division of household tasks often means that the stepmother does the extra cooking, laundry, and nurturing when the stepchildren visit. This ambiguity in role content is no doubt also present in the stepchild's reaction to the stepmother. I doubt if there is a stepchild alive who has not said to his or her stepmother, "But you aren't my *real* mother."

Although the role of stepmother is hardly new, researchers have only recently begun to study its dynamics. In one of the few studies I am aware of, researchers surveyed 265 stepmothers about the contents of their roles. They found that most of these women defined their roles as being either motherlike or a supportive adult (Orchard & Solberg, 1999). More recently, family studies researchers Shannon Weaver and Marilyn Coleman (2005) interviewed 11 stepmothers in depth and found that the women described one of three distinct roles. The first role is "mothering, but not mother," in which women describe serving as a responsible and caring adult, a friend, a provider of emotional support, or a mentor. The second is an "other-focused" role in which the women described serving as a liaison or buffer between the biological parents. The third role is that of "outsider," in which the stepmother has no direct role with the stepchildren.

Weaver and Coleman concluded their study by calling for more research into the role of stepmother and how it relates to women's well-being. It is surely one area where the feelings involved in caring for a child who belongs to one's spouse are often in conflict with the expectations of the spouse, the child's biological mother, the stepchildren themselves, the extended family, and the culture. For a role that is so prevalent in today's families and shows no sign of decreasing in the near future, it seems like a much-needed line of inquiry.

And before we end this section on divorce and remarriage, let's not forget the economics of it all. Divorce means that a one-family income needs to be stretched to support two families, a fact that lowers the standard of living for all family members. Many of the detrimental effects of divorce for both parents and children can be traced to the economic loss rather than the divorce itself (Sayer, 2006).

WRITING PROMPT

What are some of the reasons that divorce has a larger economic impact on women than on men?

▶ The response entered here will appear in the performance dashboard and can be viewed by your instructor.

Submit

5.7: The Effect of Variations in Timing

5.7 **Discuss the timing of social roles in adulthood**

Social timing refers to the roles we occupy, how long we occupy them, and the order in which we occupy them. It also depends on the culture we live in and what expectations our society has for role transitions (Elder, 1995). For example, to become a parent at 15 may be expected in some societies and may even happen frequently in our society, but it is considered "off-time" by mainstream U.S. norms. Similarly, a 45-year-old man who does not want to get involved in marriage or parenthood because he values his independence is similarly considered off-time. Both these behaviors would be acceptable, or "on-time," at other ages. The extent that one's roles are on-time or off-time is hypothesized to be of prime importance to one's social development and well-being (McAdams, 2001).

WRITING PROMPT

Think of the roles you currently occupy. Which ones are on-time, and which are off-time? Write a brief response that will be read by your teacher. Be sure to explain the reasoning behind your answers.

▶ The response entered here will appear in the performance dashboard and can be viewed by your instructor.

[Submit]

The concept of a social clock becoming important in adulthood was first proposed by sociologist Bernice Neugarten and her colleagues (Neugarten, Moore, & Lowe, 1965). They viewed this as an important distinction between children and adults in that adults were capable of viewing their lives both in the past and in the future, comparing their past selves with their present selves and anticipating their future selves. It also allows us to compare our own life cycles with those of others. Neugarten believed that we form a mental representation of the "normal, expectable life cycle" and use this to evaluate our own lives and the lives of others.

Young adults who continue living at home with their parents, not having a serious romantic relationship or making efforts to become financially independent, are no doubt aware of their off-time development. Middle-aged adults are likewise aware that the time has come to either reach their career goals or disengage. Likewise, older adults fare better when they are able to make age-appropriate role transitions in their lives (such as accepting care from their children). Psychologist Jette Heckhausen (2001) theorizes that the stronger the correlation a person's social role sequence has with developmental norms, the less stress he or she will have in life.

To my thinking, the idea of a social clock adds another dimension to the roles we move into during adulthood. It's not only important to assume the expected roles and fulfill them well, but also to assume them at the right time and in the right order. This is not always within our control, as exemplified by the 27-year-old woman who is a widow because her husband died in an auto accident, or the 75-year-old grandmother who is raising her school-aged grandchildren (and her 77-year-old husband who has gone back to work to support them). However, it is accurate to predict that people who are off-time with the social clock of their culture are more apt to have difficulty in their roles and less apt to report high levels of life satisfaction.

As in earlier chapters, I have pulled together the various patterns of change with age in a review table (Table 5.2) so that you can begin to build a composite picture of the qualities and experiences of adults in different age groups. The key point to be reemphasized is the one with which I began this chapter: Despite all the variations in timing and sequence, the basic shape of the pattern of role transitions seems to be similar for most adults. We move into more roles in early adulthood, renegotiate and make transitions into different roles in middle adulthood, and make still more transitions in late adulthood. Some of the roles are ruled by the biological clock and some by the social clock, but there is a similar basic itinerary for most adults.

Table 5.2 Review of Social Roles Throughout Adulthood

ⓧ 18–24 Years

- Social roles of emerging adults are a mixture of childhood and adult roles, and transitions are fluid as they move in and out of roles.

- Gender role differences are moderate.

- Most live in parents' home and are financially dependent to some extent.

- Role of partner is usually one of dating or cohabiting.

- Small percentage take on parental role during this time.

ⓧ 25–39 Years

- Busiest time for role transitions as young adults enter the workforce and establish careers.

- Maximum gender-role differences, especially after the transition to parenthood.

- Roles with parents involve assistance and advice from them.

- Most marry during this time, although many cohabit or remain single. Marriages often end in divorce.

- Transition to parent role.

ⓧ 40-64 Years

- Roles become more intense as children get older, jobs become more important, and community involvement often involves leadership responsibilities.

- Gender role differences remain strong while children are in the home.

- Roles with parents are more equal than at other times of life. Some move into care giving role with parents.

- Role of spouse is central, though divorce and remarriage may occur.

- Role with children is central, most become grandparents.

ⓧ 65–74 Years

- Roles have less content as children become more independent and retirement arrives. Roles of volunteer worker and great-grandparent become important.

- Gender roles expand to allow for more freedom, but do not cross over.

- Role with surviving parents usually involves some level of care giving.

- Role of spouse for many has changed to role of widower, or role of remarried widower.

- Role with children remains important, though nonparents have social networks with siblings and their children, close friends, stepchildren.

ⓧ 75+ Years

- Roles are highly individualized depending on health, marital status, and personal preferences.

- Gender roles remain expanded.

- Role with parents is over. Role with surviving siblings becomes extremely strong.

- Many are widowed, especially women.

- Adjustment to care-receiver role takes place. Role with children is central as they assume caretaking in varying degrees. Those without children receive care from other relatives, friends, or stepchildren.

Summary: Social Roles

LISTEN TO THE AUDIO:

1. Despite many variations today in the timing and sequence of roles, adulthood is still largely structured by the patterns of roles adults take on and the role transitions they experience.

2. Gender roles are fairly diverse and describe what people really do within their roles as men and women; gender stereotypes are shared beliefs about what men and women have in common. The stereotypes for women usually center around communal qualities (being nurturing and intuitive); the stereotypes for men usually center around instrumental qualities (being adventurous and competitive).

3. Learning-schema theory states that gender roles are based on distorted views that exaggerate gender differences. Social role theory states that gender roles are based on observations of male and female behavior. Evolutionary psychology states that gender roles are based on inherited traits men and women have that were critical to survival and reproduction for our primitive ancestors. The biosocial perspective states that gender roles are an interaction of hereditary biases and current social and cultural influences.

4. The transition from emerging adult to young adult is a change in roles from dependent child to independent adult. It can include moving out of the parental home, entering college or military service, entering into a marriage or cohabitation relationship, becoming financially independent, and becoming a parent. These roles are not taken on in a single typical sequence, and many young adults move in and out of them several times before viewing themselves as totally adult.

5. Adults in the United States are marrying at later ages, and a greater percentage are cohabiting before marriage. This is true in developed countries throughout the world. However, marriage remains the preferred form of committed relationship.

6. Although gender roles are egalitarian within early committed relationships, men and women divide household tasks along gender stereotypical lines. Married women do more hours of housework than married men, even when both work full time.

7. Married men and women are mentally and physically healthier than those who are not currently married, giving rise to the "healthy marriage effect." However, when the unmarried are divided into never-married, divorced, separated, and widowed, those who never married are almost as healthy as those who are married, giving rise to the "marital crisis" effect, suggesting that the health difference is due to the crises associated with divorce, separation, and death of a spouse.

8. Adults are delaying the transition to parenthood in the United States and other developed countries. The percentage of children born to unmarried parents has increased, with over 40% of all births in the United States being to unmarried parents. However, about 60% of these were born to parents who were cohabiting at the time of the birth.

9. When men and women become parents, their gender roles become more traditional. The amount of child care and housework that fathers do is increasing, but mothers still do more child care, even when they have full-time jobs.

10. In the middle years of adulthood, the role of parent changes from a day-to-day role to a more distant one as children move out of the house and start their own families, but the role of parent does not end. Most parents find this transition to be positive and use the new freedom to restructure their own lives.

11. Middle age is the time of life when most people become grandparents. This role can take many forms. For a growing number of grandparents, it means returning to the role of parent or returning to full-time work to care for their grandchildren.

12. Another role in the middle years is that of caregiver for aging parents. About a third of middle-aged men and women have at least one parent in poor health who requires care. Although spouses are usually the first-line caregivers, many family members help out, especially daughters and daughters-in-law. Many people with multigenerational responsibilities report that their roles are important and satisfying. When the burden of caregiving is extreme and long lasting, it can lead to depression, marital problems, and physical illnesses.

13. Social role transitions in late life include learning to live alone, more common for women than for men,

and becoming the receiver of care, which can be a difficult transition. However, informal care from family, friends, and neighbors can keep older adults living in their own homes and feeling in control of their lives.

14. Not everyone fits the preceding discussion. Some people never marry (about 4% of people over 65 in the United States). Those who have close relationships with friends and relatives report being as happy and fulfilled as their married peers with children, and they have better health than those who are divorced, separated, or widowed. A growing number of adults in the United States over 40 (about 20%) have no children. Among older adults, the childless are as happy as those with children. And among older adults who need assistance, those without children receive as much help from their social networks than those who have children.

15. About one third of couples marrying today will divorce within 10 years. Most will remarry, causing a number of role transitions, such as ex-spouse, stepmother, and stepfather.

16. Although we have a lot of flexibility today in the timing of social roles, life is still easier when the roles are moved through on-time instead of off-time.

SHARED WRITING: SOCIAL ROLES

Consider this chapter's discussion of role transitions. What role transitions have you experienced in the last few years? What kind of adaptations did they require and why? Write a short response that your classmates will read. Be sure to discuss specific examples.

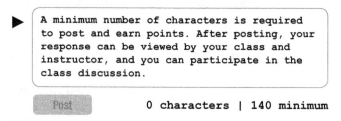

A minimum number of characters is required to post and earn points. After posting, your response can be viewed by your class and instructor, and you can participate in the class discussion.

Post   0 characters | 140 minimum

Chapter 5 Quiz: Social Roles

Chapter 6
Social Relationships

Learning Objectives

6.1 Explain various theories of social relationships in adulthood

6.2 Explain intimate relationship between married couples, and cohabiting relationships between both with heterosexual and same-sex partners

6.3 Interpret the term "Family" and relationships between members of the family

6.4 Define the term "friendship" and explain various types of friends at various stages in life

LISTEN TO THE AUDIO:

▶ ●━━━━━━━━━ 03:42 🔇 ●━━━

THERE ARE NOT many developmental psychology jokes, but this is one a student in my human development class told me many years ago:

A child psychologist was sitting in his office writing a textbook when he heard an annoying sound, "Squeak, squeak, squeak." He looked outside and saw a little child on a tricycle riding across his newly surfaced driveway. He ran outside and yelled angrily at the boy to get off his property and take his tricycle with him. A neighbor observed this and said to him, "How can you call yourself a developmental psychologist and write books on child development when you are so intolerant of little children?" The psychologist replied, "Because, madam, I like children in the abstract, not in the concrete."

Besides it being a very bad pun, I also like this joke because it helps me keep my priorities straight. I do most of my writing in my office at home, and while I am writing this chapter on relationships, I have a lot of "relating" going on around me, especially of the family variety. It is spring break, and my school-age grandsons, Brendan and Shayne, are just getting out of the pool and will soon want to use my computer to play video games. The fact that I'm using it to write a textbook doesn't seem to carry much weight with them. In 3 days, their 21-year-old twin cousins, Alese and Aaron, will arrive from college, perhaps with some friends, and they will be hungry for home-cooked meals. Just when I am ready to say, "Please leave me alone so I can write this section on grandparent–grandchild relationships," I remember the joke about the developmental psychologist and laugh.

If I sound a little authoritarian in this chapter on relationships, it is because I am living it as I write—not in the abstract, but smack dab in the concrete.

This chapter deals with **social relationships**—dynamic, recurrent patterns of interactions with other individuals and how they change over the course of adulthood. In this chapter I will discuss changes in the give-and-take interactions between people and how such changes affect them (and the people they give to and take from).

If you think about your own social relationships—with your parents, your friends, your spouse or partner, your coworkers—it's clear immediately that these relationships are not all the same, either in intensity or in quality. And if you think back a few years, it should also be clear that each of your relationships has changed somewhat over time. This is the dynamic quality of social interactions—each give-and-take changes each participant, which, in turn, changes the relationship. The topic is highly personal and complex. A fairly new field, it is difficult to study scientifically, but I think you will find it interesting and important on several levels. As one set of researchers put it, social relationships are "the wellspring from which our daily lives emerge, accumulating into our life experiences. These relationships play a major role in how the life course is experienced and evaluated" (Cate, Levin, & Richmond, 2002, p. 261).

I plan to start this chapter with a discussion of some current theories about the development of relationships, then cover what we know about specific relationships within partnerships, families, and friendships.

6.1: Theories of Social Relationships

6.1   **Explain various theories of social relationships in adulthood**

The study of social relationship development in early childhood is a prominent topic of research and theory, but only recently has attention been focused on social relationships in adulthood. As you will see, attachment theory has been extended from early childhood into adulthood. Evolutionary psychology deals primarily with the young adult years and intimate partnerships, though it has recently expanded into grandparenthood. Socioemotional selectivity theory addresses older adulthood, and the convoy model seems to apply across the life span.

6.1.1: Attachment Theory

One of the oldest and best-known theories of social relationships is **attachment theory**. The concept of **attachment** is most commonly used to describe the strong affectional bond formed by an infant to his or her major caregiver. These bonds are considered part of an innate regulatory system that evolved in our primitive ancestors, presumably because they aided survival of young children, who are born with few abilities to care for themselves. Psychiatrist John Bowlby (1969) and developmental psychologist Mary Ainsworth (Ainsworth, Blehar, Waters, et al., 1978), two of the major theoretical figures in this area, have both made a clear distinction between the attachment itself, which is an invisible, underlying bond, and **attachment behaviors**, which are the ways an underlying attachment is expressed. Because we cannot see the attachment bond, we have to infer it from the attachment behavior. In securely attached infants, we see it in their smiles when their favored person enters the room, in their clinging to the favored person when they are frightened, in their use of the favored person as a safe base for exploring a new situation. The three key underlying features are (a) association of the attachment figure with feelings of security, (b) an increased likelihood of attachment behavior when the child is under stress or threat, and (c) attempts to avoid, or to end, any separation from the attachment figure (Weiss, 1982).

In adults, of course, many of these specific attachment behaviors are no longer seen. Most adults do not burst into tears if their special person leaves the room; adults maintain contact in a much wider variety of ways than what we see in young children, including the use of phone calls, e-mail, text messages, social networking, and imagery. But if we allow for these changes in the attachment behavior, it does appear that the concept of attachment is a useful way to think about many adult relationships.

First of all, we appear to form strong new attachments in adulthood, particularly to a spouse or partner, and we usually maintain our attachment to our parents as well. Social psychologists Mario Mikulincer and Philip R. Shaver (2009) have listed three kinds of support that people of all ages seek from attachment figures in time of need: proximity (comfort that comes from the close physical or psychological presence of the attachment figure), a safe haven (help and support when a threat is present), and a secure base (support in pursuing personal goals).

Attachment theorists propose that each person has formed an **internal working model** of attachment relationships, which are a set of beliefs and assumptions about the nature of all relationships, such as whether others will respond if you need them and whether others are trustworthy. Based on early childhood experiences, this internal working model has components of security or insecurity. The behavior that reflects the internal working model is an **attachment orientation**—patterns of expectations, needs, and emotions one exhibits in interpersonal relationships that extend beyond the early attachment figures.

Adults with secure attachment orientations believe that the world is a safe place, and they welcome the challenges that life presents to them. They know they can rely on others when they need protection and support. They are able to explore the world, meet new people, and learn new things without the fear of failure. This doesn't mean that they never feel threatened or discouraged, and it doesn't mean that they will always succeed, but they enter into interactions knowing that they are able to summon help and encouragement from their support system—sometimes in person and sometimes with a phone call or text message. It is also possible to receive comfort by simply recalling the support one has received reliably in the past.

To complement the attachment orientation, theorists believe that we have also evolved a **caregiving orientation**, a system that is activated in adults when they interact with infants and young children. Most adults will respond to the appearance and behavior of younger members of the species (and often other species) by providing security, comfort, and protection. Many evolutionary psychologists believe that we also use this caregiving orientation in our relationships with adult friends, romantic partners, and elderly parents. Some believe it is also used by teachers in their devotion to their students, nurses with their tender loving care of patients, and therapists with their deep concern for clients.

Now if everyone has some degree of secure or insecure attachment orientation and also some degree of caregiving orientation, you can see how it plays out in social relationships in adulthood. There are individual differences in how much support a person needs, how well they are able to let others know that they need it, and how able the other person is to understand their needs and provide the asked-for support. All these individual differences have their roots, according to Bowlby (1973), in the parent–child relationship in infancy. If we had caregivers in infancy and childhood who were available, responsive, and supportive of our needs, we are more apt to have secure attachment orientations and effective caregiving orientations in adulthood. We can solicit social support from our spouses, partners, family members, and friends with confidence that they will provide it. We can tell when important people in our lives need caregiving, and we are able to give that care.

Attachment theory has been backed up by empirical research showing that an infant's attachment classification tends to remain stable into young adulthood (Waters, Merrick, Albersheim, et al., 1995) and studies showing that parents' attachment classifications correspond to their children's attachment classifications (van IJzendoorn, 1995). Attachment theory also has been applied to the formation of intimate relationships, which will be discussed later in this chapter.

6.1.2: The Convoy Model

Another approach to relationships in adulthood comes from developmental psychologist Toni Antonucci and her colleagues (Antonucci, 1990; Kahn & Antonucci, 1980), who use the term **convoy** to describe the ever-changing network of social relationships that surrounds each of us throughout our adult lives. "Convoy relationships serve to both shape and protect individuals, sharing with them life experiences, challenges, successes, and disappointments" (Antonucci, Akiyama, & Takahashi, 2004, p. 353). These relationships affect how the individual experiences the world. They are reciprocal and developmental; as the individual changes and develops through time, the nature of the relationships and interactions is also likely to change.

In her research using the convoy model, Antonucci (1986) developed a mapping technique. She asked respondents to report on three levels of relationships and write the names of the people within three concentric circles. The inner circle is for names of people who are so close and important to the respondent that he or she could hardly imagine life without them. The middle circle is for people who are also close, but not as close as those in the inner circle. And the outer circle is for names of people who are part of the respondent's personal network but not as close as the other two groups. The entire structure is referred to as a *social network*.

Critical Thinking

Who is in the inner circle of your convoy? What about the middle and outer circles? What changes would you predict 10 years from now?

Ongoing research is investigating the role of social networks as buffers against stress and how the support a person perceives that they get from their social network affects their health. Plans have been made for longitudinal studies that may lead to better health through preventative measures and intervention programs. Is it possible to make changes in social networks with the goal of improving health? These are some of the topics being covered by researchers using the convoy model to explore social networks (Ertel, Glymour, & Berkman, 2009).

6.1.3: Socioemotional Selectivity Theory

Yet another explanation of social relationship changes in adulthood comes from psychologist Laura Carstensen (1995; Carstensen, Mikels, & Mather, 2006). Known as **socioemotional selectivity theory**, it states that as we grow older, we tend to prefer more meaningful social relationships. This results in our social networks becoming smaller but more selective as we devote our limited emotional and physical resources to a smaller group of relationships that are deeply satisfying emotionally. In other words, the quantity of social relationships declines with age, but the overall quality remains the same (or even better).

Carstensen explains that younger adults perceive time as open-ended, measuring it by how long they have been on this earth. They are motivated to pursue information, knowledge, and relationships. In contrast, older adults perceive time as constrained, measuring it in terms of how long they have left on this earth. They are motivated to pursue emotional satisfaction, deepening existing relationships and weeding out those that are not satisfying. Research findings have backed this up by showing distinct age differences in social relationships and also the topics people are most likely to attend to and remember (Kryla-Lighthall & Mather, 2009).

6.1.4: Evolutionary Psychology

The final theory to be discussed is based on the belief that social relationships had an important role in human evolution, perhaps the central role in the design of the human mind (Buss & Kenrick, 1998). This is based on the premise that our early ancestors banded together in small social groups as an important survival strategy (Caporeal, 1997). Social relationships provided protection from predators, access to food, and insulation from the cold. Simply put, according to **evolutionary psychology**, individuals who carried genes for cooperativeness, group loyalty, adherence to norms, and promotion of social inclusion were more apt to survive in the primal environment and pass on these genes to their descendants (and ultimately to us). These genes continue to affect our social and cognitive behavior and are reflected in the ways we form and maintain social relationships in today's environment.

According to this theory, today's members of our species have biological systems that foster the formation and maintenance of social relationships, and this is manifested in a universal "need to belong." This need drives us to engage in frequent and pleasurable social interactions with a small number of familiar people who care about us and depend on us to care about them. Members of all human societies respond to distress and protest when they are separated from their social group or when a close relationship ends (Baumeister & Leary, 1995). The need to belong is observed in all human societies and in many other primate social species (de Waal, 1996).

Our species' ability to form social bonds and be loyal and cooperative within our "tribe" may be due to genetic inheritance from our primitive ancestors, who found these abilities crucial to survival in their environment.

A WORD ABOUT THEORIES OF SOCIAL RELATIONSHIPS You have no doubt noticed that these theories have a lot of similarities. In fact, the proponents of convoy theory are now writing about attachment as the "glue" that holds the convoys together. Both evolutionary psychologists and attachment theorists are referring to attachment as an evolved mechanism to ensure the survival of infants. It seems pretty clear that the theories have more similarities than differences.

Psychologist Cornelia Wrzus and her colleagues (Wrzus, Hänel, Wagner, et al., 2013) examined the results of 227 studies of social relationships from adolescence to late adulthood and found that both the convoy model and socioemotional selectivity theory explain the changes that were found. As you can see in Figure 6.1, they found that all social networks expand in adolescence, then reach a plateau in the 20s and 30s,

Figure 6.1 Meta-analysis

A meta-analysis of 227 studies of social relationships over the life span show that the total number of people in one's social network increases for emerging adult and young adults, then gradually declines. Within that total, the number of family relationships stay stable, whereas the number of close friends and acquaintances decline.

SOURCES: Based on Hazan, C., & Shaver, P. (1990); Bartholomew, K., & Horowitz, L.M. (1991).

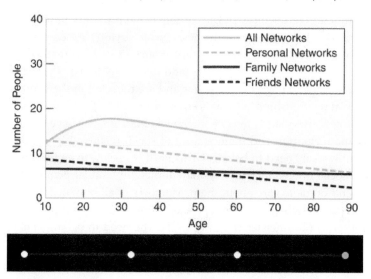

decreasing afterward until late adulthood. When subtypes of social networks are examined, both the personal network of close, intimate friends and the friendship network of less close friends and acquaintances follow this same pattern from adolescence through late adulthood. In contrast, the size of family networks remain stable throughout life.

According to socioemotional selectivity theory, adolescence and young adulthood is the time that we look to the future, seeking information and new relationships, and these results demonstrate that our personal networks and friendship networks expand during those years. In contrast, later adulthood is a time that we reflect back over our lives and concentrate on fewer, but deeper relationships. These results demonstrate that decrease in personal and friendship relationships. The convoy model explains that we travel along the road of life with a group of fellow travelers, and that is exactly what happens with the family network. The names may change over adulthood, but the size of our family social network remains the same from adolescence to the end of life.

I think you will see even more evidence of this convergence as I use these theories to discuss specific types of relationships, beginning with intimate partnerships.

6.2: Intimate Partnerships

6.2 **Explain intimate relationship between married couples, and cohabiting relationships between both with heterosexual and same-sex partners.**

One social relationship that almost all adults experience is the intimate partnership. Most of the research on this topic involves married couples, but I will also discuss cohabiting relationships, both with heterosexual and same-sex partners. Although it seems like a variety of topics, I think you will find that romantic partners in committed relationships, whatever the nature of the relationship, have more similarities with each other than differences.

6.2.1: Establishing an Intimate Relationship

The process of choosing a life partner and formalizing the relationship is found in every known culture; 90% of people in the world will marry at some point in their lives (Campbell & Ellis, 2005). How such partnerships are arrived at has been the interest of researchers for some time, and in recent studies this process has been referred to as **mate selection**. The majority of people in the world select their own mates and do it on the basis of a combination of subjective feelings that include "euphoria, intense focused attention on a preferred individual, obsessive thinking about him or her, emotional dependency on and craving for emotional union with this beloved, and increased energy" (Aron, Fisher, Mashek, et al., 2005, p. 327). Anthropologist Helen L. Fisher (2000, 2004) suggests that mate selection depends on three distinct emotional systems: lust, attraction, and attachment. Each of these systems has its own neurological wiring. The *lust system* causes men and women to experience sexual desire and seek out sexual opportunities. The *attraction system* directs men and women to attend to specific potential mates and to desire an emotional relationship with them. The *attachment system* drives men and women to be close to the target of attraction (and lust) and to feel comfortable, secure, and emotionally dependent with that person. Fisher's theory of relationship formation seems like a good one to me, and it makes a good model for viewing the components of the process of partnership formation.

LUST This system should be familiar to all psychology majors, not because of their torrid personal lives but because it was the cornerstone of Freud's classic psychoanalytic theory. Freud believed that **libido**, or sexual desire, was the foundation of all intimate relationships, and that one's experience of such relationships depends on how much sexual desire one feels for the other person, whether one is consciously aware of it or not (Jones, 1981). Lust is certainly part of romantic love, but it can also operate independently. Most adults are familiar with feelings of lust toward someone they have no romantic involvement with and also the inverse—no feelings of sexual desire toward someone they do have a romantic involvement with. The lust system is powered by androgens in both men and women. Using an automobile analogy, lust could be viewed as the accelerator of romantic love.

ATTRACTION   If lust is the accelerator in Fisher's theory, then attraction is the steering wheel, determining where the lust will be directed. The experience of attraction is also known as romantic love, obsessive love, passion (Sternberg 1986), passionate love (Hatfield, 1988), and limerence, which is described as thinking of the other person all the time, even when you are trying to think of other things, and feeling exquisite pleasure when the other person seems to return your feelings (Tennov, 1979). Mate-attraction behavior is observed in every known human culture (Jankowiak & Fischer, 1992) and in all mammals and birds (Fisher, 2000). The attraction system is associated with increased levels of dopamine and norepinephrine and decreased levels of serotonin, all neurotransmitters in the brain.

In a study of brain activity, young men and women who reported being in love for 1 to 7 months were shown a photo of their loved one and asked to think about a pleasurable event that had occurred when they were together (Aron, Fisher, Mashek, et al., 2005). As a control, they were shown a photo of a neutral person in their lives and asked to think about pleasurable events with that person. Results showed that viewing a photo of their loved one and thinking about a pleasant interaction with him or her activated regions of the brain that are rich in dopamine receptors, regions that are associated with the motivation to acquire a reward. These regions were not activated when the participants turned their attention and thoughts to a neutral person. Furthermore, the length of time a person had been in love caused different activation patterns; the more recent the relationship, the stronger the activation. The authors emphasize that the patterns of brain activation for new romantic love are different from those associated with the sex drive (or lust system, as Fisher calls it), indicating that they are distinct systems. Some evidence suggests that the hormones responsible for attachment may decrease the levels of androgen, causing sexual desire to decline as attachment increases.

The topic of what attracts one person to another, or two people to each other, was traditionally explained by **filter theory**, which states that we begin with a large pool of potential mates and gradually filter out those who do not fit our specifications (Cate & Lloyd, 1992). An alternative explanation was **exchange theory**, which says that we all have certain assets to offer in a relationship, and we try to make the best deal we can. Research has shown that people tend to have partners who match them on physical attractiveness. However, characteristics such as education level, pleasing personalities, and good grooming can help offset unattractive features such as obesity (Carmalt, Cawley, Joyner, et al., 2008). Sense of humor is also "exchanged" for physical attractiveness (McGee & Shevlin, 2009).

Evolutionary psychologists have a somewhat different explanation of mate selection, although their conclusions are similar. Their explanation is based on our ancient ancestors' need to increase their chances of reproducing and providing for their children until they were old enough to fend for themselves. Men, who needed someone to bear and feed their children, looked for signs of good health and fertility—such as youth, low waist-to-hip ratio, clear skin, lustrous hair, full lips, good muscle tone, sprightly gait, and absence of sores or lesions. Women, who needed someone to care for their needs during pregnancy and to provide for them and their infants during the first few years after birth, looked for men with qualities that signal economic resources, such as social status, self-confidence, slightly older age, ambition, and industriousness. They also needed someone to contribute healthy genes and protect them and their infants, so they preferred men who were brave, were athletic, and had a high shoulder-to-hip ratio (Buss, 2009). According to evolutionary psychology, these preferences are genetically based, and those members of our species who acted on these preferences were more apt to survive and pass them on to their offspring. Those who did not were less apt to survive or to have healthy offspring.

These preferences in potential mates have been demonstrated in studies across cultures. For example, psychologist Todd Shackelford and his colleagues examined data from over 9,000 young adults living in 37 different cultures around the world and found sex differences on three out of four universal dimensions of mate preference for long-term relationships. As predicted by evolutionary psychology, women value social status and financial resources more than men do and also dependability, stability, and intelligence. Men value good looks, health, and a desire for home and children more than women do (Shackelford, Schmitt, & Buss, 2005). Studies of online dating sites show that these preferences are present across the life span, even when reproduction is not an issue, with adults from 20 to 75 year or more expressing similar preferences— men prefer women who are physically attractive, and women prefer men with status (Alterovitz & Mendelsohn, 2011).

Other research on mate selection has shown that men and women have different preferences for mates depending on whether they are interested in a long-term or short-term relationship. Women also show different preferences depending on whether they are ovulating or not, their age, their life stage, and their own value as a mate (Buss, 2009). According to evolutionary psychology, all these preferences are explained by our species' drive to survive and to reproduce successfully.

In the past decade or so, there has been a growing use of social media to find potential romantic partners, and at the rate this trend is going, online dating sites will soon account for the majority of relationship initiations (Aron, 2012). Because the quality of our romantic relationships is extremely important to our overall well-being, not to mention health and longevity, it is important to evaluate how well these websites work. According to psychologist Eli Finkel and his colleagues (Finkel, Eastwick, Karney, et al., 2012), Internet dating sites claim to provide access, communication, and matching with potential romantic partners. How valid are these claims? Access to a large number and wide range of potential partners is valid; there are an estimated 2 billion Internet users today, and that potential is almost limitless. However, the downside is that these websites reduce three-dimensional people to two dimensions and can leave out important cues to a person's compatibility that might be apparent in more conventional social interactions. And the sheer number of potential partners one is presented with can lead to difficulty narrowing down the pool to a manageable size.

Communication with potential partners makes it convenient to chat online without actually having a face-to-face meeting, but again the downside is that the longer people communicate online, the more they overinterpret the few social cues available. Once they meet in "reality," the experience may be far from what they are expecting. Generally, the sooner people meet face-to-face, the better. Finally, the matchmaking claims of online dating sites that their mathematical algorithms match people on similarity and complementarity are lacking in evidence that these features affect the long-term relationship outcomes. First, they are based on self-reports, and second, they are operating in a vacuum by considering one person's traits and preferences without considering the dynamics of a second person in the mix.

The researchers (Finkel, Eastwick, Karney, et al., 2012) suggest that people using these sites consider the following to benefit from online dating and avoid the pitfalls:

- Limit yourself to a manageable number of potential partners at a time.
- Try to go beyond candidates who look good "on paper."
- Try not to compare the candidates or rate them. Instead, imagine how to have a positive interaction with each person individually.

- Be open-minded about candidates who do not fulfill your entire wish list of desired characteristics.
- Try not to be influenced by the most-mentioned characteristics or traits if they aren't on your wish list.
- Avoid too much online contact with a potential partner. The sooner you have a face-to-face meeting the better.
- Don't create exaggerated expectations before meeting someone in person.
- Write your profile carefully to highlight aspects of yourself that are not what everyone else is highlighting.
- Log in frequently.
- Don't pay too much for a website's matching ability.

ATTACHMENT   Fisher's attachment system has some similarity to its namesake, Bowlby's attachment theory, discussed earlier in this chapter. Although Bowlby initially formulated his theory to explain parent–infant relationships, he believed that attachment was a lifelong process and that the quality of relationship one had with parents was the base for later attachments, including romantic partnerships. More recent attachment theorists have suggested that attachment between romantic partners is a mechanism that evolved to keep parents together long enough to raise their children. Men and women who are able to feel secure together and lonely when apart are more apt to be committed to each other and to the task of raising their child safely into adulthood. Interestingly, the hormone oxytocin plays a central role in mother–infant attachment and also in women's romantic attachment to a mate (Campbell & Ellis, 2005).

Another link between early childhood attachment relationships with one's parents and adult attachment relationships with one's intimate partners is the topic of a large portion of adult attachment research. As mentioned before, extensions of Bowlby's attachment theory have been used to suggest that adult romantic relationship styles are reflections of the attachment bond the adults had with their parents in childhood (Bartholomew, 1990; Hazan & Shaver, 1987).

When adults were given questionnaires asking them to choose a description that best characterized the way they felt about romantic relationships, they fell into categories that were similar to Ainsworth's secure and insecure categories, and the proportion of adults falling into each category was similar to that of infants (Feeney & Noller, 1996; Hazan & Shaver, 1990; Mikulincer & Orbach, 1995). Later researchers confirmed these results with participants from the ages of 15 to 54 (Michelson, Kessler, & Shaver, 1997) and over a period of several years (Feeney & Noller, 1996), suggesting that styles of adult romantic attachments reflect internal working models of attachment established in early childhood. In longitudinal research, 2-year-olds who showed secure attachment to their mothers were better able, at age 20 or 21 years, to resolve and rebound from romantic relationship conflicts than former 2-year-olds who were insecurely attached. In addition, the *partners* of securely attached 20-year-olds rebound faster, too, from relationship conflict regardless of their own attachment history (Simpson, Collins, & Salvatore, 2011).

An extension of Hazan and Shaver's model has been proposed that has four categories of attachment styles based on a person's model of the self and others (Bartholomew & Horowitz, 1991). Based on self-reported ratings of how well different statements describe their own attitudes toward relationships, people are classified as secure (having a positive model of both self and others), dismissing (having a positive model of self and a negative model of others), preoccupied (negative model of self and positive model of others), or fearful (negative model of both self and others). The descriptions used in this study are shown in Table 6.1, along with the attachment classifications that correspond to each. Using this relationship questionnaire with young adults, the researchers found that almost half

Table 6.1 Adult Romantic Attachment Styles

Attachment Type	Description
Secure	"It is relatively easy for me to become emotionally close to others. I am comfortable depending on others and having others depend on me. I don't worry about being alone or having others not accept me."
Preoccupied	"I want to be completely emotionally intimate with others, but I often find that others are reluctant to get as close as I would like. I am uncomfortable being without close relationships, but I sometimes worry that others don't value me as much as I value them."
Fearful	"I am somewhat uncomfortable getting close to others. I want emotionally close relationships, but I find it difficult to trust others completely or to depend on them. I sometimes worry that I will be hurt if I allow myself to become too close to others."
Dismissing	"I am comfortable without close emotional relationships. It is very important to me to feel independent and self-sufficient, and I prefer not to depend on others or have others depend on me."

Hide All Cells	Show All Cells

SOURCES: Adapted from Hazan & Shaver (1990); Bartholomew & Horowitz (1991).

rated themselves as secure, whereas the other half was equally distributed among the remaining three categories.

It is still not clear what direct role infant attachment plays in adult romantic relationships. Some argue that infant attachment affects peer competence in primary school, which affects friendship security in adolescence, which in turn affects romantic relationships (Simpson, Collins, & Salvatore, 2011). Psychologist R. Chris Fraley and his colleagues (Fraley, Roisman, Booth-LaForce, et al., 2013) examined data from over 700 emerging adults who had been participants in an ongoing longitudinal study since shortly after birth. They found that the various adult attachment styles they exhibited at the age of 18 years could be traced to their early caregiving environments (early maternal sensitivity, changes in maternal sensitivity, father absence, maternal depression), changes in social competence, and quality of relationships with best friends.

Another set of studies shows that attachment styles in young adults change within the same individual depending on their ongoing experiences in romantic relationships. Instead of having participants to fill out an adult attachment questionnaire, researchers asked them to keep a daily diary (Pierce & Lydon, 2001). They found more variation of attachment patterns within the diaries than they did from person to person. When things were going well in their relationships, the participants reported feelings of secure attachment; when there were problems, they reported less secure feelings in their diaries. The authors suggest that we should consider proximal causes (events taking place today) as well as distal causes (early childhood experiences) when looking for the sources of adult attachment styles.

Which romantic attachment style best describes you? Do you see a correspondence between your adult attachment type and the relationship you had with your parents as a young child? Explain why. Write a brief response that will be read by your instructor.

▶ The response entered here will appear in the performance dashboard and can be viewed by your instructor.

Submit

6.2.2: Successful Marriages

The preceding discussion has covered different thinking on how partners select each other, but what happens after that? As you well know, not all couples who marry or otherwise commit to a partnership end up living happily ever after. Some do, but others drift into empty relationships, some divorce, and some live together in a constant war zone. What makes the difference? This is both an academic question and a personal one. Almost all of us wind up in partnerships of one kind or another, and it's safe to say that almost all of us want them to be happy and long-lasting. But what is the secret to successful marriages? We have the benefit of several longitudinal studies that provide some answers.

Psychologist Howard J. Markman and colleagues (Clements, Stanley, & Markman, 2004) studied 100 couples from before marriage until well past their 13th anniversaries. This study was unusual not only because of its duration, but also because it included data from both members of the couples, it did not rely only on self-report data, and it consisted of a group of young couples from the general population and not couples who were in marriage counseling or otherwise considered at risk.

Before marriage, the couple was interviewed and participated in discussions about problem areas in their relationships. They were given a number of standardized tests of relationship satisfaction, interaction, and problem solving. This was repeated 10 times in the next 13 years, and at the end of that time, the 100 couples were divided into three categories—those who had divorced (20 couples), those who remained happily married (58 couples), and those who had experienced a period of distress at several assessment points (22 couples). Comparisons were made among the groups based on the data gathered at the beginning of the study, and it was clear that the three groups differed even before the marriage took place. For example, the groups that experienced divorce or marital distress had exhibited negative interactions with each other in their first interviews, expressing insults toward each other, showing lack of emotional support, and making negative and sarcastic comments about their partners. Markman and his colleagues described the process as "erosion" and said that these negative interactions before marriage and in the early years of marriage wear down the positive aspects of the relationship and violate the expectation that one's partner will be a close friend and source of support. Subsequent studies with different groups of couples have yielded similar findings (Markman, Rhoades, Stanley, et al., 2010; Markman, Stanley, & Blumberg, 2010). Markman and his colleagues concluded that there are a number of risk factors for unhappy marriages and divorce, some of which can be changed and some of which cannot. These risk factors include aspects of personal history that cannot be changed (having divorced parents, different religious backgrounds, children from previous relationships); individual personality traits (being defensive when personal problems arise, having negative styles of interacting with others, not being able to communicate during disagreements); and different ideas about the future (unrealistic beliefs about marriage, different priorities, and less than total commitment to each other).

MARRIAGE AND NEGATIVE INTERACTIONS   The eroding power of negative interactions has also been found in the results of longitudinal studies by psychologist John Gottman and his colleagues. For example, Gottman and Notarius (2000) found that couples who will eventually divorce can be identified years ahead of time by looking at the pattern of positive and negative exchanges. In fact, Gottman claims that he is able to interview a couple for a few hours and predict with 94% accuracy whether they will be divorced or still together 4 years later (Gottman, 2011). Gottman asks couples to tell him "the story of us." He listens for five key components and evaluates whether they are positive or negative. If the positive outweighs the negative, then the couple will almost certainly be together 4 years later. These are the key components Gottman evaluates during the interview:

(x) **Fondness and admiration**

Is the couple's story full of love and respect? Do they express
positive emotional like warmth, humor, and affection? Do they
emphasize the good times? Do they compliment each other?

(x) **"We-ness" versus "me-ness"**

Does the couple express unity in beliefs, values, and goals? Do
they use "us" and "we" more than "I" and "me?"

(x) **Love maps**

Does the couple describe the history of their relationship in
vivid detail and with positive energy? Are they open with
personal information about themselves and their partner?

(x) **Purpose and meaning instead of chaos**

Do couples talk about their life together in terms of pride over
the hardships they have overcome? Do they talk about shared
goals and aspirations?

(x) **Satisfaction instead of disappointment**

Do couples say that their partner and their marriage have
exceeded their expectations? Are they satisfied and grateful for
what they have in each other? Do they speak positively about
marriage?

Fortunately, negative patterns in marriage can be changed. Therapists who work with couples have found that marital satisfaction can be increased significantly by teaching couples how to understand each other better, increase affection, attend to each other and influence each other more, practice healthy conflict resolution, and create shared meaning within their relationship. It is possible for couples whose relationships have grown distant or hostile to acquire new skills or relearn earlier patterns of interaction through relationship education courses (Markman & Rhodes, 2012). Recently, these courses have been given successfully to high-risk couples online (Loew, Rhoades, Markman, et al., 2012).

Other researchers have studied couples in long-term marriages to find out how they feel about each other and what the differences are in couples who have positive feelings about each other versus those who do not. Although some theories discussed earlier in this chapter suggest that passionate love occurs mostly in early years of a relationship and then is replaced by companionate love, little research has been done with long-term married couples to see if this is true. Recently, psychologist K. Daniel O'Leary and his colleagues surveyed almost 300 married adults who had been married an average of 20 years (O'Leary, Acevedo, Aron, et al., 2012). The central question they asked was, "How in love are you with your partner?" They were asked to rate their love on a scale from 1 to 7, with "Very intensely in love" being 1 and "Not at all in love" being 7. Unexpectedly, the researchers found that the most frequent response was 1—over 46% of the men and women in this sample reported being very intensely in love with their partners. Those who reported intense love for each other were also apt to report high levels of thinking positively about their partner, affectionate behaviors and sexual intercourse with their partners, sharing novel and challenging activities with their partners, and having a general feeling of life happiness.

Another study looked at unhappy long-term marriages. Sociologists Daniel N. Hawkins and Alan Booth (2005) examined over 12 years of data from couples in low-quality marriages. The study showed that people who remain in unhappy marriages experience a reduction in life satisfaction, self-esteem, psychological well-being, and overall health. Furthermore, people who stay in unhappy marriages are less happy than those who divorce and remarry, and they have lower levels of life satisfaction, self-esteem, and overall health than those who divorced and remained single. For this sample of people at least, there was no benefit to remaining in unhappy marriages instead of divorcing.

The lesson from studying various types of marriages is that a happy marriage is a huge plus in the partners' lives, and that an unhappy marriage is a huge minus. Not all beginning marriages are happy and healthy, and not all long-term marriages are cooled down and companionable; a lot still sizzle. Unhappy relationships can be helped with family therapy or relationship education classes. And divorce is not the worst thing that can happen to a couple.

6.2.3: Cohabitation and Marriage

The role transition from single adult to cohabiting partner is becoming increasingly common in the United States and other developed countries. I would like to add a note about the relationships that are formed between cohabiting couples and what effect they have on subsequent marriages.

WRITING PROMPT

Before you read on, what are your thoughts about cohabitation? Do you believe it is helpful for a couple to live together so that they can get all their problems worked out before marriage? Do you think couples who cohabit before marriage have better marriages than those who move in together after marriage?

▶ The response entered here will appear in the performance dashboard and can be viewed by your instructor.

Submit

The majority of cohabiting couples eventually marry. How do these marriages fare? One popular notion, which I hear often from my students and young adult relatives, is that cohabitation is a trial run for marriage, and that couples who marry after living together will have better marriages because they "know what they are getting into" and "have all the problems ironed out." However, that doesn't turn out to be true. A large body of research in the United States, Australia, Canada, and England has consistently found that "people who cohabit before marriage have an increased likelihood of separation than those who do not cohabit" (Hewitt & de Vaus, 2009, p. 353).

Why would this be true? Some have argued that there is a *selection effect*—those who are more mature and have stronger relationships follow the traditional path to marriage, whereas those with doubts and troubled relationships opt for cohabitation first (Woods & Emery, 2002). Others believe that the experience of cohabiting changes the couple's attitudes about marriage (Magdol, Moffitt, Caspi, et al., 1998). However, studies by psychologist Howard Markman and his colleagues (Kline, Stanley, Markman, et al., 2004; Rhoades, Stanley, & Markman, 2009; Stanley, Rhoades, Amato, et al., 2010) show that there are two distinct types of cohabitation relationships that lead to marriage; *engaged cohabitation*—in which the couple becomes engaged before moving in together, and *preengaged cohabitation*, in which the couple becomes engaged after moving in together. The former tends to lead to marriages as successful as those of couples who did not cohabit before marriage; the latter tends to lead to less successful marriages. Why? The authors conclude that couples who become engaged before moving in together have made a formal commitment to each other, and their relationships are more similar to those of couples who marry before living together than to those of couples who cohabit without that commitment.

Another factor in the success of cohabitating couples is how well it is accepted in one's culture—their family and religion. Sociologist Kristen Schultz Lee and Hiroshi Ono (2012) investigated the happiness of over 25,000 married and cohabiting couples in 27 countries. They assigned scores to each country indicating the relative strength of traditional gender beliefs (how they view mothers of young children who work outside the home) and religious context (how important religion is in personal lives). Results showed that there was little difference for men's happiness in any country whether they were cohabiting or married, but in countries where traditional gender beliefs and religious context is high, there is a "happiness gap" between married women and cohabiting women. In countries where the traditional gender beliefs and religious context is low, there is no difference in happiness between married and cohabiting women. Apparently, women's relative unhappiness in more gender-restrictive, religious countries is a reaction to the negative connotations cohabitation has in their culture. Although these findings were for people living in these countries today, they would also apply to people who were cohabiting in the United States a few decades ago when the practice was not so accepted (Loving, 2011).

COHABITING VS MARRIED FAMILIES   Given the recent increase in births to cohabiting couples, researchers have also begun to look into such matters as the differences between cohabiting families and married families and the effect of the parents' marital status on the children. In one such study, developmental psychologists Stacey Rosenkrantz Aronson and Aletha Huston (2004) compared mother–infant relationships in three types of families: single-mother families, two-parent cohabiting families, and two-parent married families. They found that the mother–infant relationships were better in the two-parent married families than the other groups, with single-mother families and two-parent cohabiting families showing the same low level of mother–infant attachment. A closer look revealed that selection effects accounted for most of the differences. Single mothers and cohabiting mothers were similar in that they were younger and less educated. Surprisingly, such factors as family income, the time the mother spent with the infant, and the social support the mother received from friends and family did not make a difference in the mother–child relationship. The researchers concluded that there are problems involved with being a single mother with no partner in the home, but the problem is *not* simply the absence of the child's father; the problems are within the parents themselves and their relationships. Individual factors of the mothers (and no doubt the fathers) who choose to marry contribute to better mother–infant relationships than the factors of those who choose to remain single or to cohabit. The authors warn us against believing that family problems can be solved simply by adding the father's presence to the single-mother family without commitment from the couple.

My interpretation of these findings is that marriage is something young adults today take very seriously, in contrast to members of my generation, who often viewed it as a "piece of paper" needed to have a sexual relationship or move out of their parents' homes (and saw divorce as another "piece of paper" necessary to get out of a relationship that wasn't working). Today's young adults (perhaps in reaction to their parents' high divorce rates) are more cautious about committing to a lifetime together. They have several intimate relationships before committing to another person and often live together after making that commitment before they take the next step to marriage. That seems to be working well for them. Hopefully they will give that same level of deliberation to parenthood.

6.2.4: Same-Sex Partnerships

Long-lasting, committed relationships between same-sex partners are very common today, and it is possible for gay and lesbian partners to be married in most of Europe, all of Canada, and most of the United States. However, same-sex marriages are not yet recognized by all branches of the U.S. federal government, and as a result, same-sex married couples do not have all the rights and protections that opposite-sex married couples have (U.S. General Accounting Office, 2004). In addition, although more people in the United States now support same-sex marriages than oppose them (Pew Research Center, 2013a), these relationships are still openly condemned by some political and religious leaders and some individuals who feel that they threaten our society. For this reason, research on same-sex partnerships has been slow in getting started, but as lesbian, gay, bisexual, and transgendered (LGBT) people become increasingly visible and accepted, the data on these couples are being included in the U.S. Census surveys and also is being gathered in separate databases such as the National Study of Gay and Lesbian Parents (Johnson & O'Connor, 2002), making more research projects possible. The last decade has brought forth a rapid expansion of findings on LGBT couples (Biblarz & Savci, 2010).

What proportion of us fit into the LGBT category? We don't know. Although the U.S. Census Bureau recently included "same-sex partners" in their questionnaires, we don't know about those who live alone or those who do not want to share that information. There is also the problem about how to define these terms. When the definition is limited to those who identify solely as gay or lesbian, the prevalence is between 1% and 4% of the population. Figure 6.2 shows the results of nine surveys asking adults if they identify as lesbian, gay, or bisexual. When the definition is broadened to include people who have had any same-sex sexual experience or who find people of the same sex attractive, it goes up to as high as 6%. Then there are those who identify as bisexual—somewhere between 1 and 4%, and transgender—around 0.3% (Gates, 2011). However, we do know that about 8% of the 7.7 million unmarried-couple households in the United States today report that they are same-sex couples (Lofquist, Lugalia, O'Connell, & Feliz, 2012). About half of the same-sex households are males and half are females, and about 10% are 65 years of age or older (Gates, 2013).

Figure 6.2 The percent of people in the United States who identify as lesbian, gay, or bisexual differs substantially de̶ ̶ ̶ ̶ ̶ ̶ on the sample surveyed and the wording of the survey questions. In ni̶ ̶ ̶ ̶ ̶ ̶ ̶ ̶s, somewhere between 1.2% and 5.6% identify as belon̶ ̶ ̶ ̶

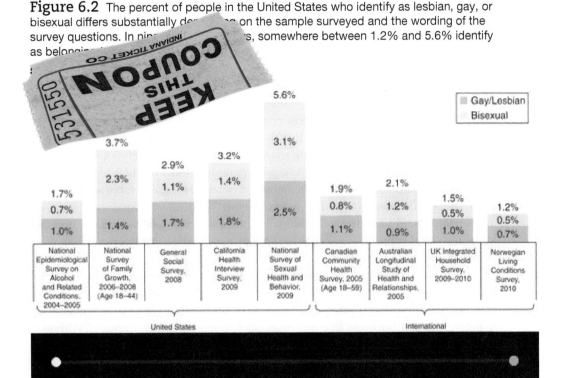

Critical Thinking

What are some of the reasons you can suggest that the percentages of gay, lesbian, and bisexual people in Figure 6.2 are different from survey to survey?

Same-sex couples and different-sex couples are similar in many ways. They fall in love, worry about the long-term outcome of their relationships, and desire legal status as a recognized couple. Both partners probably work outside the home, and they divide up the household chores and financial responsibilities. Regardless of couple type, the one who makes the most money usually does the least around the house. The stereotypes that same-sex partners take on "male" and "female" roles or distinguish themselves by their preferred sexual positions (top versus bottom) have not been supported by research (Harman, 2011).

In the early years of a relationship, the amount of sex a couple has generally depends on how many males are in the relationship. Gay men have the most, followed by heterosexual couples, followed by lesbian couples. After 10 years or so, the frequency of sex declines for everyone, but the heterosexual partners have sex more often than the same-sex partners. Men in same-sex relationships are more likely to cheat on their partner than individuals in heterosexual marriages or women in same-sex relationships. However, men in same-sex relationships often have a more open partnership or nonexclusive agreement (Bonello & Cross, 2010).

THE IMPLICATIONS OF OPENNESS IN SAME-SEX RELATIONSHIPS There are differences in the degree of openness same-sex partners express about being gay and being in a relationship. In one study, researchers interviewed gay and lesbian couples about how they presented their relationships to friends, family members, and coworkers and how satisfied they were with their partners. Then they asked the couples to discuss a problem area in their relationships. They found that couples who were more open about their relationships reported greater satisfaction with their partners and also treated each other with more positive emotions when they discussed problem areas in their relationships (Clausell & Roisman, 2009). This research illustrates another way that same-sex couples differ from opposite-sex couples; few heterosexual people feel a need to hide their sexual orientation or their intimate partnerships from others. The resulting loss of social support and contact with important friends and family members seemingly takes a toll on same-sex relationships that may not be present for opposite-sex couples.

One more difference in same-sex relationships is contending with physical violence. One study showed that in comparison with their heterosexual siblings, gay and lesbian adults reported experiencing more violence over their lifetimes—more childhood psychological and physical abuse by parents, more childhood sexual abuse, more psychological and physical victimization in adulthood, and more sexual assault in adulthood (Balsam, Rothblum, & Beauchaine, 2005). Clearly studies of same-sex partnerships need to address discrimination, victimization, health concerns, and lack of family social support—topics that are not present in the same degree in heterosexual relationships (Green, 2004).

Although these studies by no means present a complete picture of gay and lesbian partnerships, they feature creative, solid research that gives us valuable information about this topic. Perhaps the most important finding is that homosexual relationships are far more like heterosexual relationships than different. Although long-term committed relationships are probably less common in the gay and lesbian community, such commitments, when made, involve love and strong attachment. Many last a lifetime. Because same-sex relationships, by definition, involve two people who share the same biological and social gender characteristics, there are some differences in the dynamics of the relationships compared to heterosexual partnerships. But the human urge to commit to another person in an intimate relationship (and perhaps to raise children together) is as evident in gay relationships as it is in heterosexual relationships.

6.3: Relationships with Other Family Members

6.3 Interpret the term "Family" and relationships between members of the family

Defining "family" is not an easy task. Each time I find a definition, I realize that it doesn't apply to my particular family group, or to the family that lives next door to me. It's not that we are so unusual, but that family is a hard concept to pin down into a definition that includes all the people we consider family. We have biological relatives, adopted relatives, and step- and half-relatives. Some of us have close friends who function as family members. Then there is the situation of ex-family members, and who knows what will happen when surrogate mothers and sperm-donor fathers are considered! However, I do like the solution suggested by gerontologist Rosemary Blieszner (2000), who writes that when it comes to researching family relationships, "It is not possible to identify family members via external observation. Rather, individuals must specify the members of their own families" (p. 92). Presumably, like beauty, family is in the eye of the beholder.

My guess is that your version of "family" may be complicated too. Unfortunately, research on family relationships in adulthood has not yet caught up to this complexity. Most attention has been directed to parent–child relationships, with less emphasis on sibling relationships or grandparent–grandchild links. There is essentially no information available on relationships between step-siblings or in-laws (let alone former in-laws). In the future I hope we will see explorations of a broader array of "family" connections and their effects on adult development.

6.3.1: General Patterns of Family Interaction

When my youngest child moved out of the house at 18, I admit that I experienced a few moments of panic. Would he ever come back to see us? Why would he? He had a comfortable apartment, he was a good cook, he knew how to do his own laundry, and he had a good income. But Sunday rolled around, and there he was sitting at the dining room table with my husband and me, his grandparents, his sister and her husband, and his 2-year-old nephew. And he has been there almost every Sunday since, for over 30 years, first bringing his girlfriend (who later became his wife), and then his children. For a number of years he was a single dad raising two sons, and the three of them graced our dinner table. Recently he has added a new fiancé to the group and her son. And I know why. Because we are family, and once a week we touch base, catch up on the news, and recharge our batteries for the coming week.

During the 1970s and 1980s, social scientists grappled with the idea that **nuclear families** (parents and their children) in the United States were in danger of being isolated from their **extended families** (grandparents, aunts and uncles, cousins). The reason for their concern was that young families had become more mobile than ever before, moving across the country to seek out job opportunities that were not available in their hometowns. But closer examination showed that although the mobility was a fact of family life, the isolation was not. Families had begun using communication technology—cell phones, text messaging, e-mail, video conferencing, digital cameras—to keep in touch with each other and to keep their family relationships strong (Williams & Nussbaum, 2001).

Sociologists have theorized that the quality of family relationships can be evaluated on six dimensions (Bengtson & Schrader, 1982). Click below to learn what the **intergenerational solidarity theory** states that family relationships depend on.

ⓧ Intergenerational solidarity theory statement about family relationships

Associational solidarity—how often family members interact with each other and what type of activities they do together.

Affectional solidarity—how positive the sentiments are that family members hold for each other and whether those sentiments are returned.

Consensual solidarity—how well family members hold the same values, attitudes, and beliefs.

Functional solidarity—how much family members do for each other in terms of services or assistance.

Normative solidarity—how much family members feel a part of the family group and identify with each other.

Intergenerational family structure—how many family members there are, how they are related, and how close they live to each other.

According to this theory, family members can be very close if they have frequent interactions, feel a great deal of affection toward each other, share basic attitudes and opinions, help each other when help is needed, agree with the basic beliefs of the family unit, and have the means to interact with each other (either living close together or having access to communication technology). To the extent that any of these factors is not present, the relationships will be less close.

6.3.2: Parent–Child Relationships in Adulthood

One big question in the study of parent–child relationships in adulthood is, "What happens to the attachment bond from childhood?" Does it end, leaving independent adult children ready to form new and different relationships with their parents? Or does it continue, with adjustments made for the adult status of the child? Bowlby (1969) claimed that attachment diminished during adolescence and then disappeared, except in times of illness or extreme distress, being transferred to romantic partners. One attachment theorist puts it this way: "If children are eventually to form their own households, their bonds of attachment to the parents must become attenuated and eventually end. Otherwise, independent living would be emotionally troubling. The relinquishing of attachment to parents appears to be of central importance among the individuation-achieving processes of late adolescence and early adulthood" (Weiss, 1986, p. 100).

More recent theorists have suggested that attachment between parents and their children does not decline in adolescence, but changes slightly in form (Cicirelli, 1991). Instead of physical proximity being the key, communication becomes important. In adulthood, children and parents are capable of substituting symbols of each other (memories, photos, family heirlooms) for their physical presence and communicating through phone calls, text messages, occasional visits, and other communications. I think my experiences and probably yours fit this explanation, and so do the data from recent studies.

Most adult children and their parents live near each other, have frequent contact, report feeling emotionally close, and share similar opinions. Recent studies of middle-aged adults have shown that the younger cohort of these parents—the baby boomers—has significantly more frequent contact with their adult children and give significantly more support of all kinds than earlier cohorts of parents. In a study of 633 middle-aged individuals, their spouses, adult children, and living parents, developmental psychologist Karen L. Fingerman and her colleagues found that the middle-aged parents give emotional support to their adult children an average of once a week, advice an average of once a month, and financial/material support several times a year (Fingerman, Miller, Birditt, et al., 2009). And if you wonder what the result is of all this attention, their adult children show better adjustment and well-being than earlier cohorts (Fingerman, Cheng, Tighe, et al., 2011).

These findings are remarkable when you consider that the baby-boomer cohort of parents has aging parents themselves who are living longer with more chronic conditions than any generation of elders in history. In addition, they have adult children who came of age during the worst economic time since the Great Depression (Fingerman, Pillemer, Silverstein, et al., 2012).

Baby boomers are more involved with their adult children than they are with their parents and more involved with their adult children than their parents were with them. They give more to adult children who need more and also to those who show potential of being successful—perhaps because they see these children as their legacies. African-American baby boomers give more assistance of all types to their parents than white baby boomers, but it is not because their parents have more need or disability but because of their personal beliefs about parent–child obligation (Fingerman, VanderDrift, Dotterer, et al., 2011).

Baby boomers do not give across-the-board emotional and material support to parents; it seems to depend on the emotional bonds that were present in childhood. This can be a problem for divorced fathers who were not involved in their children's early years, especially if the fathers have not remarried and do not have a spouse or stepchildren to provide support in their later years (Fingerman, Pillermer, Silverstein, et al., 2012).

According to Bengston's theory of intergenerational solidarity, affection is an important component in family relationships. Mutual expressions of affection between family members are often seen as a measure of how close the relationship is and how it is progressing. For example, young children often perceive their parents' affection as a finite resource, and when they observe their parents expressing affection to their siblings, they fear that there won't be enough left for themselves. This implicit belief is thought to fade away as the child becomes more cognitively mature and realizes that a parent's love is not a concrete, tangible commodity and that the old saying is true, that "parents' hearts expand to hold all their children." However, a study by communication researchers Kory Floyd and Mark T. Morman (2005) shows that remnants of this belief still can be found in emerging adulthood.

Middle-aged fathers (average age 51) and their adult sons (average age 23) were asked how much affection the fathers expressed for their sons through either verbal statements (such as saying, "I love you"), direct nonverbal gestures (such as hugging or kissing), or supportive behaviors (doing favors for them). The sons' responses depended on how many siblings they had—those who had no siblings reported receiving the most affection from their fathers, and those with many siblings reported receiving the least. In contrast, the fathers' reports of affection expressed toward their sons were not affected by the number of children in the family. Does this show that parental love is spread too thin when one has several children? Not really. What it more likely shows is that there can be real differences between children's perceptions of relationship quality and that of their parents—and that those who have to share a parent can perceive that they are being slighted.

Another important component of intergenerational solidarity, according to Bengtson, is consensual solidarity, agreeing on values, attitudes, and beliefs. It is presumed that children will learn these lessons from their parents, but there is also evidence that parents' values, attitudes, and beliefs can be broadened by their adult children. A longitudinal study of older adults in the Netherlands demonstrated that the lifestyles and experiences the adult children introduce to their parents have an effect on the parents' attitudes in late adulthood. Sociologists Ann-Rist Poortman and Theo van Tilburg (2005) surveyed 1,700 men and women who were between 70 and 100 years of age, asking them about their beliefs concerning gender equality and moral issues. They also asked questions about unconventional life experiences of their own parents (whether their mothers had been employed outside the home or either parent had previously been divorced) and their children (whether they had cohabited or divorced, whether their daughters worked or their sons did not work). Older people whose children had cohabited or divorced tended to be more progressive in their beliefs about gender role equality and their moral attitudes toward voluntary childlessness, abortion, and euthanasia than those whose adult children had not cohabited or divorced. Interestingly, the older adults were not influenced by how unconventional their own parents had been, or else they were no longer under the influence of childhood experiences that had occurred 70 or 80 years earlier.

The authors of this study suggested that parents whose adult children are demonstrating unconventional behavior, such as cohabiting or divorcing, face the decision to either change their attitudes or risk distancing themselves from their child. In a larger sense, the authors suggested, the influence young adults have on their parents in this respect is an important mechanism of social change whereby younger members of society, who are more apt to be influenced by cultural change, can pass their attitudes on to the older members of the society, thus bringing greater progress to the overall group.

THE EFFECTS OF LATE-LIFE DIVORCE Although the overall divorce rate in the United States has remained stable or even dropped over the last two decades, the divorce rate among middle-aged and older adults has doubled during that time (Amato, 2010). In fact, one of every four people who divorced in 2010 was aged 50 or older (Brown & Lin, 2012). We are familiar with the effects of divorce on young children, but what happens to adults when their parents divorce? The popular concept is that children suffer less from parental divorce the older they are, but some researchers have argued that this is not true; adult children are as affected emotionally by parental divorce as young children (Cooney, Hutchinson, & Leather, 1995).

One of the effects of parental divorce for adult children is the relationship they have with their parents. In a qualitative study of 40 young and middle-aged adults who had experienced the divorce of their parents when they were 18 to 24 years of age, sociologist Joleen Loucks Greenwood (2013) found that about half of her group had experienced a change in their relationships with one or both parents following their divorces. The most common reasons given were because they blamed one parent for "wronging" the other, they felt their parents were using them as mediators, or they felt their parents had reversed roles—turning to them for social and emotional support instead of giving it. Interestingly, those whose parents had divorced within the past 5 years were more apt to report a strained relationship than those whose parents had divorced more than 5 years ago. When the researcher asked the participants to talk about their relationships with their divorced parents over time, she found that they viewed the strained relationships as stages or temporary situations they needed to work through, and most did with time.

In Greenwood's study, about half of the participants who had experienced parental divorce in their young adult years reported no changes in their relationships. They reported that they always had a close relationship with their parents and that the parents did not involve them in any negativity surrounding the divorce. Some respondents reported that they now felt closer to their parents because the divorce brought out a more human, vulnerable side of them.

There are practical problems when adults' parents divorce, such as financial problems if the children are in college or still dependent on their family for support. And even when parents have not been providers for their adult children, their divorce disrupts the traditions and symbols that were the center of the extended family. The family home is often sold as a result of the parents' divorce, and holidays are split between "Mom's house" and "Dad's house." The roles the parents filled have changed, and if either parent remarries, there are changes brought by new family members. Parental divorce often leads to adult daughters becoming confidants for the mother and family social director for the father (reminding him of family birthdays, conveying family news, making sure he has a place to go for Thanksgiving dinner). Adult children of divorce are more reluctant to enter marriage themselves and are at elevated risk for marriage problems and divorce if and when they do marry (Murray & Kardatzke, 2009).

WRITING PROMPT

What advice would you give a friend or classmate whose parents are divorcing? What advice would you give the parents? Write a brief response that will be read by your instructor.

 The response entered here will appear in the performance dashboard and can be viewed by your instructor.

Submit

One additional effect of having divorced parents is that unmarried older parents need more assistance sooner than married ones. For example, before their recent deaths, my parents were happily married for over 65 years, and even though they had some health problems, they were still working together as a team. My father's memory was bad, and my mother was in a wheelchair, but he could push her wheelchair, and she could remember the way to the music room or the dining room of their skilled care facility. They enjoyed each other's company, so my sisters and I didn't have the responsibility to visit every day. I can't help but compare this to friends who have elderly divorced parents they provide care for in two separate households. I'm sure the situation will become more common as the divorce-prone baby boomers get older. It is clear that the effects of divorce on children don't necessarily end when they reach adulthood.

PROBLEM CHILDREN IN ADULTHOOD   Unfortunately, not all children outgrow their childhood problems, and others acquire problems in adulthood. What effect does this have on older parents? Is there an age that parents can quit feeling responsible for their children's problems? Apparently not, at least not for most parents. A major cause of late-life distress for older adults is the problems their adult children are having (Pillemer, Suitor, Mock, et al., 2007). Children's problems are a primary cause for depressive symptoms and worry in older adults (Hay, Fingerman, & Lefkowitz, 2007), especially when those problems stem from the adult child's own behavior and lifestyle such as substance abuse or incarceration (Birditt, Fingerman, & Zarit, 2010).

Developmental psychologist Karen L. Fingerman and her colleagues investigated the cumulative effects of multiple adult children on older parents for both positive and negative events (Fingerman, Cheng, Birditt, et al., 2012). One general question was whether having a successful child caused an increase in well-being that matched the distress caused by a problem child. The answer was that successful children did not have the same positive impact on their parents' lives as problem children had in the negative direction. In other words, parents tend to react to negative events concerning their children more than to positive events. Another question concerned what cumulative effect problem children and successful children had on their parents. The researchers found that just one problem child had an effect on the parents' well-being, but that one successful child did not have the same effect—it takes many successful children to have impact on parents' well-being. Fingerman and her colleagues concluded that the old adage is correct: *Parents are only as happy as their least happy child.*

Recently researchers have adopted a more complex outlook on this situation. Instead of simply asking about positive or negative feelings parents have toward their adult children, they have investigated feelings of *ambivalence*—mixed feelings or feelings of being torn in two directions. In these studies, they find that anywhere between half and two thirds of older parents (mostly mothers) report experiencing these feelings. The factors that contribute to parents' ambivalence are in several categories: The first is adult children who have not attained independent status. This includes not being married, not completing their educations, and continuing to require care and financial support from parents well into adulthood. Second are adult children who have experienced serious problems in adulthood, whether they caused the problems themselves (criminal charges or substance abuse) or not (health problems or being laid off from work). And third, older parents have ambivalent feelings when they give more to their adult child than their child gives back to them (Pillemer, Suiter, Mock, et al., 2007).

As the parent of several adult children (and some adult grandchildren, too), I can attest to the complexity of emotions described in these studies. It's seldom a case of either positive or negative feelings, but often ambiguous ones. Furthermore, I have found that it changes as the situations change, which is another dimension that should be investigated.

6.3.3: Grandparent–Grandchild Relationships

Families have fewer children today than in generations past and more older adults are living into late adulthood, which means that today's grandchildren and grandparents can enjoy a very special, long-lasting relationship (Antonucci, Jackson, & Biggs, 2007). However, these relationships can differ a lot depending on the age of the grandchildren, the health of the grandparents, the distance between their residences, and many other factors. Still, there is some general information we have about these special relationships.

We know that grandparents spend more time with younger grandchildren, but discuss more personal concerns with older grandchildren (Kemp, 2005). Grandparents report the same affection for their granddaughters as for their grandsons (Mansson & Booth-Butterfield, 2011). Married grandfathers have more interaction with their grandchildren than widowed grandfathers (Knudsen, 2012). About one of four grandparents name at least one adult grandchild in the innermost circle of their social convoy, most often a grandchild that they had an intense relationship with when they were a child (Geurts, van Tilburg, & Poortman, 2012). In recent decades, grandfathers seem to have joined grandmothers in having nurturing relationships with their grandchildren. This can include being a surrogate parent, financial provider, playmate, advice giver, and family historian (Bates & Goodsell, 2013). Not only is this of benefit to the grandchildren, but it also benefits the grandfather's own mental health and well-being (Bates & Taylor, 2012).

In a study that included interviews with both grandparents and adult grandchildren, sociologist Candace Kemp (2005) found that adult grandchildren and their grandparents view their relationships as a safety net—a potential source of support that provides security even though it may never be tapped. Both generations reported that they "just knew" that if they needed help, the other would be there for them. Actual help was common also, with grandparents providing college tuition and funds to help adult grandchildren buy homes, and grandchildren helping with transportation and household chores. Adult grandchildren represent the future to their grandparents and give them a feeling of accomplishment; grandparents represent the past to their grandchildren, holding the keys to personal history and identity. It seems clear that adult grandchildren and their grandparents are able to build on their early years and develop unique relationships together in adulthood.

Another factor that is important for grandparenting in the United States is racial/ethnic group. African-American grandparents view their relationships with their grandchildren as more central to the family than do white grandparents. They believe they have a responsibility for caregiving and providing security, cohesion, and structure within the family. They have higher status within the family and carry more authority than white grandparents, especially grandmothers. When African-American grandparents serve as surrogate parents for their grandchildren, they are often able to draw on their own experiences of being raised by grandparents and to receive social support from friends who are in the same situation. This may be one reason why African-American grandparents who have taken on this role report significantly less caregiver burden than those in other groups (Pruchno, 1999).

Hispanic grandparents in the United States have different relationships with their grandchildren than non-Hispanic grandparents. The families are typically large and include several generations living close together, reporting strong feelings of emotional closeness, but the grandparent–grandchild relationship does not include high levels of exchange and support. This seems to be due, in part, to language differences within the family. It is not unusual for grandparents to speak only Spanish and grandchildren to speak (or prefer to speak) only English, causing a gap between the generations that is hard to bridge (Brown & Roodin, 2003).

In a study several years ago, college students were asked to rank their grandparents according to the time they spent with them, the resources they shared with them, and the emotional closeness they felt to them. For all three categories, students ranked their mother's mothers the highest, followed by their mother's fathers, their father's mothers, and their father's fathers (DeKay, 2000). The results are shown in Figure 6.3. The same pattern has been found in many similar studies, and I don't think anyone would find it very surprising—in fact I would have responded the same way about my grandparents at that age. However, psychologists W. Todd DeKay and Todd Shackelford (2000) explained these data using an evolutionary psychology perspective. They argue that the grandparents' rankings reflect the relative confidence each grandparent has, although not always conscious, that the grandchild is truly his or her biological descendant and as a result will carry their genes into a new generation.

Figure 6.3 College students rate their maternal grandmothers highest on time spent together, resources provided, and emotional closeness, followed by maternal grandfathers, paternal grandmothers, and last, paternal grandfathers.

SOURCE: DeKay (2000).

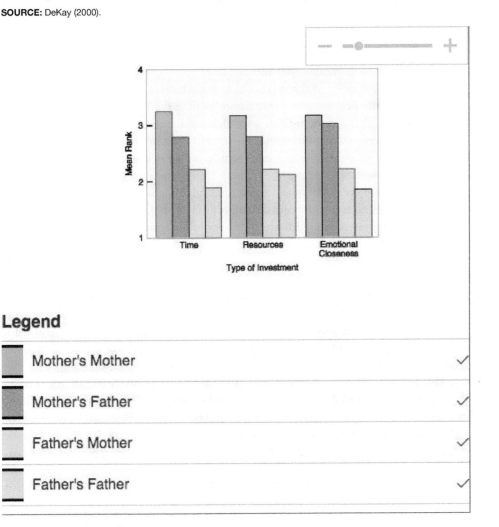

Considering that the rate of error in parentage (charmingly known as the *cuckold rate*, from an old English word for a man whose wife has been unfaithful) is about 10 to 15% in modern cultures (Cerda-Flores, Barton, Marty-Gonzales, et al., 1999), a good number of grandparents stand to invest time, resources, and emotional attachment in grandchildren who are not biological relatives. The reasoning goes like this: A mother is sure her child is her biological descendant; a father is not so sure. Taking this a step further, a mother's mother (or maternal grandmother) is also sure that the grandchild is her biological relative and thus carries her genes. The mother's father is not so sure; the child is surely his daughter's child, but is his daughter truly his child? He can't be sure, so he invests less than his wife in the relationship. The paternal grandmother knows that the child's father is her biological son, but she is not so sure about the grandchild being her son's biological child. Chances are that if she has a daughter, she will invest more in grandchildren from that branch of the family. Finally, the paternal grandfather has a lot of doubts. Is his son truly his biological descendant? And if he is, is the grandson the child of his son? According to DeKay and Shackelford, this explains the low investment on the part of the paternal grandfathers.

WRITING PROMPT

Using an evolutionary psychology perspective, would you be closer to nieces and nephews who are your sisters' children or those who are your brothers' children? Why? Write a short response that will be read by your teacher.

▶ The response entered here will appear in the performance dashboard and can be viewed by your instructor.

Submit

Of course I can generate other reasons to explain why the mother's parents are perceived to invest more in the relationship with their grandchildren. Perhaps the young couple settled closer to the wife's parents than the husband's parents and it is due to proximity. Perhaps the mother, as kinkeeper, is more attuned to promoting the relationship between her children and her parents than her husband is with his parents. Perhaps the younger family is more similar to the maternal grandparents in traditions, social practices, and family customs because the wife usually promotes these things. Or perhaps we do base our emotional relationships on the probability that some grandchildren carry our genes and others may not.

Increasing numbers of grandparents take over the residential care of their grandchildren when the parents are not able to, but many grandparents also serve as informal caregivers when their grandchildren live in single-parent families or families in which both parents work. Although official numbers aren't available for this, one study of over 1,400 adolescents in England and Wales showed that grandparents were more involved in providing informal care for this generation of young people than in generations before, probably due to the greater number of hours parents spent at work and the greater number of grandchildren living in single-parent homes (Tan, Buchanan, Flouri, et al., 2010).

This is quite common in my neighborhood, and probably in yours, too. I often pick up my 10-year-old grandson at school, and I notice that the "parent pickup line" can easily be taken for the "grandparent pickup line." Many of the cars waiting for the bell to ring are driven by people my age. And on Lunch with Parents Day these same grandparents are there to have lunch with their grandchildren—most because the parents are at work some distance away and the grandparent is either retired or, in my case, has a more flexible schedule. This is considered *informal care* because the children don't live with us full time, and we don't get paid (at least not in money).

ROLE OF GRANDPARENTS IN TIMES OF FAMILY CRISES   Recently attention has turned to the role of grandparents in time of family crisis. Can grandparents "level the playing field" when grandchildren are at risk for social and emotional problems due to the divorce of their parents or subsequent remarriage? And, more timely, can grandparents help fill the gap that occurs when their unmarried daughters have children? In a study of over 900 grandchildren who were emerging adults (18 to 23 years of age), researchers found that those who had lived with a single parent or in stepparent homes had fewer depressive symptoms when they had a strong relationship with a grandparent (Ruiz & Silverstein, 2007). Another study of 324 emerging adults showed that the quality of their relationships with maternal grandmothers predicted their psychological adjustment following their parents' divorce (Henderson, Hayslip, Sanders, et al., 2009).

In a similar study, social work researcher Shalhevet Attar-Schwartz and her colleagues (Attar-Schwartz, Tan, Buchannan, et al., 2009) questioned over 1,500 high school students in England and Wales, asking about the contact they had with their grandparents and their family structure. Information was also gathered about problems with school conduct and with peers. The kids in single-parent homes had the same level of involvement with their grandparents as kids in two-parent homes. However, when the problems of students in single-parent homes were compared to those of students in two-parent homes, the level of contact with the grandparents became important. Figure 6.4 shows that adolescents in single-parent homes with low levels of involvement with grandparents had more difficulties with school conduct and peers than those who had high levels of involvement with grandparents. According to this research, it is possible for grandparents to "level the playing field," at least for kids who are at risk for social problems as a result of living in single-parent homes.

In the cited studies of high-risk grandchildren faring better when they had a close relationship with grandparents, it is important to reiterate that there was no difference

Figure 6.4 Teenagers who live in single-parent homes have fewer difficulties and distress with school and peers if they have a close relationship with their grandparents. Those in two-parent homes showed few differences in difficulties based on grandparent involvement.

SOURCE: Attar-Schwartz, Tan, Buchanan, et al. (2009).

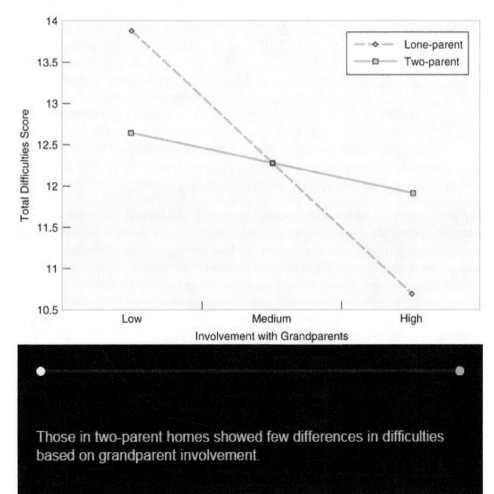

Those in two-parent homes showed few differences in difficulties based on grandparent involvement.

between the grandparent–grandchild relationships for single-parent families and two-parent families. The difference was in the benefits of these relationships in time of trouble. Adolescents and emerging adults from single-parent homes who had close relationships with grandparents were more apt to have fewer social problems than kids from those single-parent homes who were not close to their grandparents.

These last studies are good illustrations of a hypothesis offered by evolutionary psychologists and evolutionary anthropologists called the **grandmother effect** (Hawkes, O'Connell, & Blurton-Jones, 1997). This suggests that the presence of grandmothers (especially maternal grandmothers) has been a predictor of children's survival throughout recorded history. This hypothesis states that the trait of longevity (especially for women) has been favored in our species by natural selection because social groups that had more grandparents had an advantage in that the older members of the group helped with the birthing of the babies and the child care (nest-tending tasks) and also provided knowledge and wisdom to the younger members of the group, making their survival more likely (Coall & Hertwig, 2011).

One current-day example of the grandmother effect comes from a longitudinal study in the Netherlands that followed three generations of families for 10 years (Kaptin, Thomese, Van Tilburg, et al., 2010). They found that parents who received child-care assistance from the children's grandparents were more apt to have more children in the next 10 years than parents who did not have this assistance. Because the Netherlands has such a low birthrate, these results were of particular interest in that country, but it also shows how older men and women, past reproductive age themselves, can have an effect on the birthrate of their group.

Another study showed how older people impart important knowledge and wisdom to the younger people in their cultural group. In 2004, a tsunami struck near Thailand and Burma, and the Moken people, who lived on islands near the coast, were able to survive because their elders knew how to read the signs of the sea and urged the group to flee to high ground, thus avoiding disaster (Greve & Bjorklund, 2009).

Anthropologist Sarah B. Hrdy (2011) contends that we mothers have never raised our children alone, that we have always had help by members of our social group, and I believe this is true. Although these helpers are not always kin, one type of related helper who is often available and willing to help is the children's grandmother. Hrdy described a grandmother as "a mother's ace in the hole." I know this describes my grandmother, and I hope my daughters-in-law will say that it describes me.

6.3.4: Relationships with Brothers and Sisters

The great majority of adults have at least one living sibling, and this relationship in adulthood is becoming the topic of increased research interest as the baby boomers get older. (One benchmark of this generation is that they have more siblings than children.) Descriptions of sibling relationships in everyday conversation range from exceptional closeness, to mutual apathy, to enduring rivalry. Although rivalry and apathy certainly both exist, moderate emotional closeness is the most common pattern. It is really quite unusual for a person to lose contact completely with a sibling in adulthood.

Sibling relationships are important in early adulthood in that they can help compensate for poor relationships with parents. Psychologist Avidan Milevsky (2005) surveyed over 200 men and women between the ages of 19 and 33, asking questions about their relationships with their siblings, their parents, and their peers. They were also given questions to measure their loneliness, depression, self-esteem, and life satisfaction. Those who had low support from their parents had significantly higher well-being scores if they were compensated with high levels of social support from their siblings. Figure 6.5 shows the well-being scores for the participants who had low parental support. Those with high sibling support scored significantly lower on the depression and loneliness measures and significantly higher on the self-esteem and life-satisfaction measures than participants who had low sibling support.

Young adult siblings also provide direct support to their younger brothers and sisters; in fact, they are the third line of defense for child rearing, after parents and grandparents (Derby & Ayala, 2013). They demonstrate a high degree of ability to function as surrogate parents, especially if they have help from friends and neighbors.

Figure 6.5 Young adults with low levels of parental support score better on four measures of well-being when they have high levels of support from their siblings.

SOURCE: Data from Milevsky (2005).

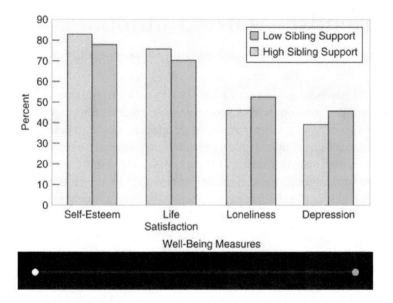

Relationships with siblings decline in importance during the child-rearing years. It is suggested that during this time, adults concentrate on their children and their careers, leaving little time or energy to foster relationships with siblings. But even when these relationships are not foremost in adults' minds, they remain positive and supportive (Neyer, 2002).

LATER ADULTHOOD   In later adulthood, siblings become central to each other again, intensifying their bonds and offering each other support in their later years. Sociologist Deborah Gold (1996) interviewed a group of older adults about their relationships with their sisters and brothers over their adult years. The respondents were 65 years of age or older, had at least one living sibling, had been married at some point in their lives, had children, and were living independently in the community.

Gold asked about how various life events during adulthood might have contributed to the change in closeness between the sibling pairs. She found that events in early adulthood, especially marriage and the arrival of children, resulted in distance between siblings. In middle adulthood, events tended to bring siblings closer together, especially the deaths of their parents. Late adulthood further increased closeness. Retirement brought more free time to spend together and reunited some siblings whose jobs had required them to live far apart. Loss of spouse or illness brought siblings to help "fill in the blanks." Finally, in older adulthood, some siblings reported being the only surviving members of their family of origin and the only ones to share family memories.

To be fair, 18% of the respondents reported becoming more emotionally distant from their siblings with time. Some went through the typical distancing in early adulthood and never got back together; others had hoped life events would bring renewed closeness and were disappointed that they did not, especially when they had anticipated more help during bad times such as widowhood or illness.

What type of sibling relationships are the closest? People who are single and those who have no children tend to have stronger relationships with their siblings (Campbell, Connidis, & Davies, 1999). And, if you are a woman who is lucky enough to have a sister (I have three!), it will be no surprise to you that two sisters are the closest, followed by a brother-and-sister pair and then by two brothers. Once again, it is women—mothers, wives, sisters—who are the kinkeepers and who provide the family with nurturance and emotional support.

6.4: Friendships in Adulthood

6.4 Define the term "friendship" and explain various types of friends at various stages in life

Developmental psychologist Dorothy Field (1999) defines **friendship** as "a voluntary social relationship carried out within a social context" (p. 325). She goes on to stress the discretionary aspect of friendship—unlike other relationships, it depends not on proximity or blood ties or institutionalized norms, but on personal reasons that vary from individual to individual. As vague as the concept of friendship may be, it is still an important one, and although most of the developmental attention has been focused on friendships in childhood and adolescence, there have been a number of studies in the last decade or so that examine this topic in adulthood.

6.4.1: Friendship Networks

As mentioned in the section on social convoys, family networks stay stable in size over adulthood, but friendship networks increase in emerging adulthood and young adulthood as we seek out friends to explore our identities, establish ourselves in the work world, and establish a family of our own. But once middle age arrives and we are focused on our partners and children, the number of people in our friendship networks start declining, and that continues until the end of life. Not only do older adults have smaller friendship networks, but they also have less contact with their friends (Antonucci, Burditt, & Akiyama, 2009).

Other factors that influence friendships in adulthood are gender, race, and education. Women have larger friendship networks than men at all age levels, and women are more often named as friends by both other women and men. When asked which friends they receive support from, women name a number of people; men name their wives. African-American people have smaller friendship groups that contain more family members, but they have more contact with them than white people do. People in higher socioeconomic groups have larger numbers of overall friends, but the same number of close friends as people in lower socioeconomic groups. And men with professional jobs have friends from a wider geographic area than men who are skilled workers (Ajrouch, Blandon, & Anotnucci, 2005).

Researchers have found that friendships are not totally positive and worry-free. Although it is not a surprise that people would feel ambivalent about some family relationships, or even about one's spouse because those are generally constant members of one's social convoy, some people report that friends can cause mixed feelings, especially when they give unasked-for support and unsolicited advice. These feelings are not bad enough to end the friendship, but can be a source of stress in a relationship that should serve as protection from stress.

One final note—we have seen that unhappy marriages are related to lower levels of well-being. Can having one high-quality close friend make up for being in an unhappy marriage? No, but having two high-quality close friends provides feelings of well-being, regardless of the state of one's marriage.

6.4.2: Pets as Friends

Some of my students have urged me to include a section on pets as friends, and although I am not currently a pet owner, I am well aware of the growing importance of pets to people. (In fact, 62% of households in the United States now include at least one pet, so I am definitely in the minority.) Pets are service animals for people with disabilities, but also provide companionship and are considered friends (or family members) by many of their owners. Can pets provide social support in the same way friends do? Can a pet provide happiness, well-being, and good health the way a friend can?

Psychologist Allen McConnell and his colleagues (McConnell, Brown, Shoda, et al., 2011) gathered data from 217 adults, of whom 25% were pet owners. Pet owners turned out to have more self-esteem, get more exercise, be in better physical shape, and be less lonely than the non–pet owners. Pet owners were just as close to their friends as nonowners were, showing that the pets were not taking the place of other friends. Pet owners reported their pets to be as close to them as their siblings and closer than their best friends and parents. Pet owners who reported receiving more social support from their pets had higher feelings of well-being and also reported greater support from others.

The problem seems to come with **anthropomorphizing** pets, which means giving them human thoughts, feelings, and motivations. People who do this, whether they have high levels of human support or not, are apt to report higher levels of stress and depression (Duvall Antonacopoulos & Pychyl, 2010).

WRITING PROMPT

What are some examples of how pet owners might anthropomorphize their pets? Write a brief response that will be read by your instructor.

▶ The response entered here will appear in the performance dashboard and can be viewed by your instructor.

Submit

6.4.3: Facebook Friends

Another type of friendship is through social media, of which the largest site is currently Facebook. Two thirds of people in the United States who have Internet access use Facebook. Similar to other social channels, women use it more than men, and younger people use it more than older people (Brenner, 2013). Figure 6.6 shows Facebook users by age.

People of different ages use Facebook for different purposes. Emerging adults and young adults use it to meet potential mates (McAndrew & Jeong, 2012). It seems to benefit college students with low self-esteem and low life satisfaction (Johnston, Tanner, & Lalia, 2013). Students with a large number of friends who estimate that a lot of people read their status updates have higher levels of life satisfaction and perceive more social support than those with smaller numbers and lower estimates (Manago, Taylor, & Greenfield, 2012). Facebook seems to provide a way to maintain permanent relationships in a geographically mobile world; college students who have more former high school friends as Facebook friends perceive more social support. At the same

Figure 6.6 The percent of Internet users who are on Facebook decreases with age, but almost a third of those aged 65 and older are among the users.

SOURCE: Data from Brenner (2013).

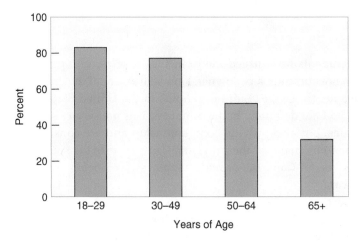

time, college students also report using Facebook to create a new sense of self and independence from family (Stephenson-Abetz & Holman, 2012).

Some younger adults report being "frazzled" by Facebook, especially college females who, compared to college males, report spending more time than intended on Facebook, losing sleep because of Facebook, feeling closer to Facebook friends than "real-life" friends, and generally feeling addicted (Thompson & Lougheed, 2012). More than half of all Facebook users report having voluntarily taken a break from using Facebook for several weeks or more (Rainie, Smith, & Duggan, 2013). However, researchers who examined a group of emerging adults found no relationship between amount of time spent on social media and any type of depression (Jelenchick, Eickhoff, & Moreno, 2013).

Middle-aged adults often use Facebook to feel close to their young adult children, and although that sounds intrusive, a recent study showed that most adult children did not consider it an invasion of their privacy and felt that it actually enhanced the closeness between the parent and adult child (Kanter, Afifi, & Robbins, 2012). More skeptical researchers suggested that adult children accept their parents' friend requests because they can't easily decline due to the power differential between parent and child. Some even suggest that the increase in the number of young people using Twitter is due to the increase of parents using Facebook (Wiederhold, 2012).

Older adults do use Facebook, but similar to the content of social convoys, their friends list contains fewer friends and more family members. In a twist, researchers questioned nonusers of Facebook from the ages of 19 to 76 and compared them to Facebook users of the same ages. They found that the nonusers were older, more shy and lonely, less socially active, and less prone to sensation-seeking activities (Sheldon, 2012). This says to me that Facebook is not simply a way that shy and lonely people can have social interactions without face-to-face contacts. People who are social enjoy face-to-face contacts *and* social networking. People who are not social do neither.

In a larger sense, social satisfaction seems to be something inside people and is not affected much by whether or not one's social network contains members of another species or friends in cyberspace.

As in previous chapters, I have included a review table of changes that occur in major types of relationships over the adult years (see Table 6.2).

Table 6.2 Review of Changes in Relationships over Adulthood

18–24 Years	25–39 Years	40–64 Years	65–74 Years	75+ Years
Intimate relationships take the form of dating or cohabitation. Partners are chosen based on strong feelings of lust and attraction, and also suitability for short-term mate. Early attachment styles may influence romantic relationships.	Long-term partners are chosen based on physical attractiveness (by men) and resources and status (by women). Many cohabitation relationships become marriages. Negative interactions between spouses can result in unhappy marriages and divorce. Cohabitation after commitment often leads to happy marriages, especially if the culture has progressive ideas about women and religion.	Many couples in long-term marriages report still being intensely in love. Couples in unhappy long-term marriages have worse health and well-being than those who have divorced. Divorce is common, as is remarriage.	Marriages are highest in satisfaction and psychological intimacy, lowest in conflict in the empty-nest years. Divorce rate is low, although many start new relationships after death of spouse.	Many are widowed, especially women, but most have adjusted by increasing friendship group and family relationships.
Social networks include mothers and friends from school. Other social support comes from pets and social media.	Social networks include parents and other family members, spouses, neighbors, colleagues from work, children, pets, and social media.	Social networks narrow somewhat to include family, closer friends and coworkers, and pets. Grandparenting begins for many.	Social networks no longer include parents and coworkers for most. Grandchildren are prominent.	Social networks are small but close and consist mostly of family members, often adult grandchildren who were close as children.
Family relations are similar to childhood. Physical distance is not far, and parents are active in the lives of emerging adults. Siblings provide support for each other when parents do not.	Family relations are strong even if physical distances between members are far. Young adult children continue to learn from their parents, and parents change their attitudes based on their children's lifestyles.	Siblings are more distant during the parenting years.	Siblings regain some closeness, especially when parents die and when sisters are involved. Widowed siblings, ever-single siblings, and those with no children are especially close.	Remaining family members, especially siblings are important.

Relationship problems stem from romantic breakups and failures to understand each other.	Relationship problems include disagreements about children, infertility, divorce, work/family interface, and parents' divorces.	Relationship problems come from parenting issues with adolescent children, aging parents, divorce, work/family interface.	Relationship problems come from death of spouse, adult children's financial and marital problems, grandchildren's problems, parents' declining health.	Relationship problems come from adjusting to care-receiving role with children and in asserting independence. Adult children who continue to be problems cause distress and ambivalence.
⟳	⟳	⟳	⟳	⟳

Hide All Cells   Show All Cells

Summary: Social Relationships

LISTEN TO THE AUDIO:

07:03

1. Attachment theory was originally formulated to explain the relationship between infants and their parents. Subsequent hypotheses suggested that the attachments formed in infancy were relatively permanent and were reflected in other relationships later in life.

2. Other theories of social relationships include the convoy model, which considers the group of significant people who travel with us in our lives at different points in time. Socioemotional theory states that as people grow older, they prefer to have a few close, emotional relationships instead of many more casual relationships. Another explanation of the importance of social relationships is provided by evolutionary psychology, stating that the tendency to bond together with similar people is a genetic mechanism passed down from our primitive ancestors because it contributed to their survival and reproductive success.

3. Almost all adults experience relationships with intimate partners, and the formalization of intimate partnerships is found in all cultures. Most people of the world select their own partners. Some social scientists hypothesize that establishing an intimate partnership is a process that includes the lust system, the attraction system, and the attachment system, each involving a separate neurotransmitter system and pattern of brain activity.

4. The relationship with an intimate partner is typically the most central relationship in adulthood. The process

of partner selection has been explained traditionally by filter theory and exchange theory. More recently, evolutionary psychology suggests that people are attracted to others based on physical signs of good health and potential reproductive success.

5. Attachment theory has also been used to explain success in creating romantic relationships. People who are classified as secure in their attachment will also have longer lasting, happier romantic relationships than those who are in other, less secure categories.

6. Longitudinal studies of couples that begin before marriage show early predictors of problem marriages, even during the engagement period. These include negative interactions, insults, lack of emotional support, and sarcasm, which result in unhappy relationships and ultimate divorce.

7. Many couples cohabit before marriage, and they have higher divorce rates and lower levels of marital happiness than couples who marry without cohabiting. However, when couples commit to marry and then cohabit as an engaged couple, they have marriages as happy and long-lasting as couples who marry without cohabiting. The difference in happiness between married and cohabiting couples depends on how the culture views women's roles and religion.

8. About 1 to 4% of the population identifies themselves as gay or lesbian. Recently same-sex couples have been able to marry in some countries and some parts of the United States, and others have participated in commitment ceremonies to formalize their intimate partnership. Recent research on the relationships of same-sex couples shows that there are more similarities than

differences when they are compared to opposite-sex couples.

9. Interactions with adults and their parents occur at high and relatively constant levels throughout adulthood. Most adults have at least weekly contact with their parents.

10. Late-life divorces are increasing, and a new issue for young and middle-aged adults is dealing with their parents' divorce. The problem has proved to be a serious one for many due to the loss of the family home and holiday traditions, the addition of stepparents and adult stepsiblings, and the need to care for elderly divorced parents.

11. The problems of one's children are always a cause for concern, even when the children are adults. Major causes of distress for older parents are children's divorces, financial problems, and drug or alcohol problems. Even one problem child causes late-life distress.

12. For the present generation, the grandparenting role is very broad and depends on many factors, such as the age of the grandparent and grandchild, the distance between homes, and the relationship of the grandparents and the children's parents. Maternal grandparents are usually closer than paternal grandparents, especially if parents divorce. African-American grandparents, especially grandmothers, have a more central role in the family than white grandparents.

13. The relationship with maternal grandmothers is considered closest by their grandchildren, followed by maternal grandfathers, paternal grandmothers, and paternal grandfathers. This is interpreted by evolutionary psychology as reflecting the probability that the grandchildren are truly biological descendants of the grandparent.

14. Studies have shown that good relationships with grandparents can level the playing field for emerging adults who are at risk for social problems. Evolutionary psychology suggests a grandmother effect, pointing out that children with living grandmothers have been more apt to survive into adulthood throughout recorded history.

15. Although relatively constant over the life span, relationships with siblings appear to be strongest in late adulthood. Changes in sibling relationships seem to be related to life events, with events occurring later in life (death of parents, retirement) making siblings closer than events occurring in early adulthood.

16. Friendships are important in emerging adulthood and young adulthood. Family relationships take precedence in the later years, as the numbers of personal friends and acquaintances decline. Many adults of all ages consider their pets to be central figures in their social networks, as close as family members. Emerging adults and young adults count Facebook friends as part of their social networks. Middle-aged adults and older adults use social media to interact with family members.

SHARED WRITING: MAJOR CAREGIVERS

Consider this chapter's discussion of role transitions. What role transitions have you experienced in the last few years? What kind of adaptations did they require and why? Write a short response that your classmates will read. Be sure to discuss specific examples.

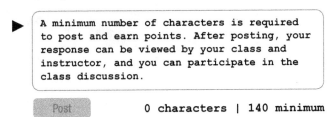

▶ A minimum number of characters is required to post and earn points. After posting, your response can be viewed by your class and instructor, and you can participate in the class discussion.

Post   0 characters | 140 minimum

Chapter 6 Quiz: Social Relationships

Chapter 7
Work and Retirement

Learning Objectives

7.1 Explain the importance of careers in adult life and gendered career patterns

7.2 Explain various career selection theories with reference to gender, family influence, and genetics

7.3 State effects of age-related declines in cognitive abilities, reaction time, physical strength, and sensory abilities

7.4 Relate work to the individual, relationships, and family

7.5a Discuss retirement in terms of reasons, timings, and effects

7.5b List reasons for retirement

7.6 Summarize retirement planning to be the most important for a happy retired life

LISTEN TO THE AUDIO:

▶ ━━━●━━━━ 02:41 🔈●━━━━

THE REVEREND WILLIAM Augustus Johnson is a working man. He is 93 years old and lives in a retirement home, confined to a wheelchair ever since his left foot was amputated, but he still works at his church, where he serves as pastor emeritus. He spends about 5 hours each day calling church members, writing letters, and reading church literature—trying to keep up with the times. "Things are moving so swiftly these days, I have to stay up nights to catch up with them" (Terkel, 1995, p. 209). He also writes a sermon each week, although his church has several other pastors. He wants to be ready on Sunday in case he is needed.

How did Reverend Johnson choose his career? He didn't. Like many Baptist ministers, the career chose him. He was "called" one day when he was 25 years old. "I wanted to be a lawyer like Perry Mason," he explained. But instead he heard a voice asking him to preach. At first he said no. "I'd just started to learn to dance and was enjoying it. But I was a Christian and a deacon in the church and I woke up to the fact that you don't tell God 'no'" (Terkel, 1995, pp. 211–212). That was the beginning of a career spanning almost seven decades and three generations of parishioners.

Retirement? "I'd just like to go in one Sunday morning and say, 'Beloved, this is my last sermon. May the Lord be with you.' Go out, get my hat, and be taken home. I can't see the pressure of seeing people I knew as babies, grown men now, saying to me 'Pastor, why did you leave us?' None of that" (Terkel, 1995, p. 214).

And what about a legacy? Reverend Johnson sums it up: "I just want to be remembered as someone who cried with you when your baby was sick, who went to the cemetery with you. I was there. I don't send somebody else unless I just can't make it in the snow with this one leg" (Terkel, 1995, p. 214).

Although not many of us can identify fully with the Reverend Johnson, I think there is some common ground we can recognize in his attitude toward work. Most of us have made changes in our initial career paths; we strive to do our jobs well, feel gratified when our efforts are recognized, and hope that our work has made some difference in the world. Even if your "job" at the moment is being a student, we all have a basic need to be good at what we do and to think of it as important. This chapter is about work—its importance in our lives, how we choose careers, how careers are affected by age, how we incorporate career and personal life, and how we plan for and adjust to retirement.

7.1: The Importance of Work in Adulthood

7.1 Explain the importance of careers in adult life and gendered career patterns

For most of us, our jobs occupy a hefty portion of our time, our thoughts, and our emotions. They determine in large part where we live, how well we live, and with whom we spend time—even after working hours. On another level, our jobs provide a good deal of our identity and self-esteem. The role of worker is not a static one; over the years changes take place in the economy, technology, workforce composition, and social climate. Individuals change too; we go from intern to full-fledged professional as a result of attaining a degree. We go from full-time paid worker to full-time unpaid caregiver as the result of new parenthood. We go from work to retirement as a function of age. We go from retirement to part-time work when we find that the days are too long or the expenses of retirement are higher than we thought. These various work situations over the years of adulthood can be summed up in the term **career**, the patterns and sequences of occupations or related roles held by people across their working lives and into retirement.

I start this chapter with a discussion of two major theories, one on the centrality of careers to adult life, and one on how we select careers. Then I go on to cover how patterns of work are different for men and women, and how the work experience changes with age. Then I will cover the interaction of work and personal life. Finally, I will discuss retirement, which, it may surprise you to find out, is not simply the opposite of work.

7.1.1: Super's Theory of Career Development

Vocational psychologist Donald Super was the author of the best-known theory in the study of careers—the **life-span/life-space theory**, based on the concept that individuals develop careers in stages, and that career decisions are not isolated from other aspects of their lives. Although this theory was first proposed some 45 years ago (Super, 1957), it has been frequently revised and updated to keep pace with changes in workers and the workplace (Super, Savickas, & Super, 1996; Super, Starishevsky, Matlin, et al., 1963).

Not only is Super's theory influential to researchers and other theoreticians, it is also useful in applied settings for vocational counselors in high schools and colleges, and for human resource officials in businesses (Hartung & Niles, 2000). Super created a number of career-development tests to assess individuals' career adjustment, interests, and values. If you have ever taken the Adult Career Concerns Inventory (ACCI), the Career Development Inventory (CDI), or the Work Values Inventory (WVI), you have had your career trajectory evaluated according to Super's theory.

The first component of Super's theory, the *life span,* is divided into five distinct career stages, each with specific developmental tasks and issues to resolve. The five stages are displayed in Table 7.1, along with approximate ages for each. These stages are the major developmental pathway of the life span, according to Super, and our task is to make our way through them. However, we also cycle back through some of the stages at various times in our careers when we change jobs or leave the workplace to go back to school or to retire.

Table 7.1 Super's Five Stages of Career Development

Stage	Approximate Age	Tasks and Issues to be Faced
Growth	4–14	Identify with significant others and develop self-concepts. Spontaneously learn about the world. Develop work-related attitudes, such as orientation toward the future, establishing control over life, developing sense of conviction and purpose, attaining attitudes and competencies for work.
Exploration	15–24	Crystallize career preference. Specify and implement an occupational choice.
Establishment	25–44	Stabilize in a job. Consolidate job. Advance in a job.
Maintenance	45–65	Hold achieved job. Update and innovate tasks. Perhaps reevaluate and renew.
Disengagement	65+	Decelerate workloads and productivity. Plan for and implement retirement. Shift energy to other aspects of life.

SOURCES: Adapted from Hartung & Niles (2000); Super, Savickas, & Super (1996).

Super acknowledged that the work role is not the only role people have in their lives and thus cannot be considered in isolation from other roles. In fact, he goes so far as to say that the work role is best perceived in terms of its importance relative to other roles an individual plays (Super, 1990). The second component of his theory, the *life space,* deals with these roles. Researchers and vocational counselors (not to mention individuals who are evaluating their own career paths) need to also consider the relative importance of school, work, home, family, community, and leisure. Their importance is measured by tests assessing *role salience*—the degree of one's participation, commitment, and value expectation in the roles in each of these five areas.

WRITING PROMPT

Which of Super's five stages best describes you today? Which do you think will describe you 10 years from now?

> The response entered here will appear in the performance dashboard and can be viewed by your instructor.

Submit

7.1.2: Gender Differences in Career Patterns

The first big distinction in career patterns is between men's and women's work lives. Although women are now represented in all major areas of work, gender is still a big factor in almost all aspects of careers. Men and women may perform their jobs equally well, but they are not the same, and knowing a person's gender predicts a lot about their career pattern. There are three major differences in the career paths of men and women.

First, *more men work full time than women*. This is illustrated by Figure 7.1, which shows the number of men and women over 16 in the United States who hold full-time jobs. As you can see, fewer women hold full-time jobs than men, but the difference is becoming smaller—about 70% of men and about 57% of women in recent years (U.S. Bureau of Labor Statistics, 2013c).

Figure 7.1 A greater number of men than women hold full-time jobs, but the gap is closing because of an increase in the percent of women who work outside the home.

SOURCE: Data from U.S. Bureau of Labor Statistics (2013c).

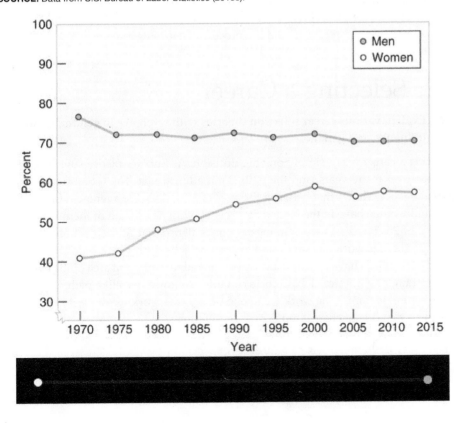

Why do more men work full time than women? It's partly because of demographics; older people aren't as apt to work full time as younger people, and there are more women in this age group than men. Another reason is a combination of biological and social factors—it is difficult for both parents of young children to work full time, and the wife is usually the spouse to quit her job or reduce her work schedule when a child is born or while children are young.

This leads us to a second gender difference; *men stay in full-time jobs longer than women do.* Men start their work careers with full-time jobs and usually keep working full time until they retire. If their career is interrupted, it is usually due to being laid off and unable to find another job. Women, on the other hand, are more apt to start working full time, leave the workforce when a child is born, go back to part-time work when the child is a few years old, perhaps stop again for a second child, and then go back to full-time work when the children are older. Women are also more apt to leave their own jobs when their spouses are transferred to another location, a situation that often leads to a period of unemployment for the women until they find a new job.

The third gender difference is that *women are more apt to work in part-time jobs than men.* This type of nonstandard work schedule is almost exclusively filled by women in the United States and worldwide. In the United States, 26% of women who work hold part-time jobs, and only 13% of men do (U.S. Bureau of Labor Statistics, 2013e). This type of work schedule may seem ideal for women who want to combine work and family, but the downside is that most of these jobs are in the service sector and feature lower wages and fewer benefits (Rix, 2011).

One of the major impacts of the two genders having different career paths is that women's career discontinuities result in lower salaries and lack of job advancement. Thanks to these (and other) factors, women earn less money than men even when they work full time. According to the U.S. Bureau of Labor Statistics (2013e), women's salaries average only 81% of men's.

Having jobs with lower salaries, fewer benefits, and less chance for advancement, combined with moving from full time to part time jobs to unpaid leaves of absence, has an obvious effect on women's career paths and financial security (and of course their family's financial security), but it also has a delayed effect, which I will cover later in this chapter when I write about women and retirement. But first let us look at the beginnings of a career path and the process of choosing a career.

7.2: Selecting a Career

7.2 Explain various career selection theories with reference to gender, family influence, and genetics

Selecting a career is not simply one big decision. As Super's theory suggests, careers develop over many years, and the path is not a linear one. The U.S. Bureau of Labor Statistics (2012) shows that between the ages of 18 and 46, the average number of jobs men and women have in the United States is 11, with nearly half of them being before the age of 25. Teenagers work in jobs of convenience that fit their school schedules. College students work weekends and at seasonal jobs during semester breaks. Adults find that their jobs have been outsourced or moved to a different area of the country, so they retrain for a different job. Careers can often follow a mazelike path, but there are some central features. The work we like to do and the work we do best are aspects of ourselves that do not change much over our lifetimes.

7.2.1: Theories of Career Selection

Vocational psychologist John Holland (1958, 1997) has been a major voice in the area of career selection for several decades. His basic argument is that people seek work

environments that fit their **vocational interests**, which are defined as personal attitudes, competencies, and values (Hartung & Niles, 2000). Holland believes that
there are six basic vocational interests: social, investigative, realistic, enterprising,
artistic, and conventional, sometimes abbreviated as SIREAC types. These interests
are displayed in Figure 7.2, along with the traits for each type and the preferred
work environments.

Figure 7.2 Holland's six basic types of vocational interests (attitudes, abilities,
and values).

Many tests used by career counselors and vocational psychologists are based on this model.

SOURCE: Holland (1992).

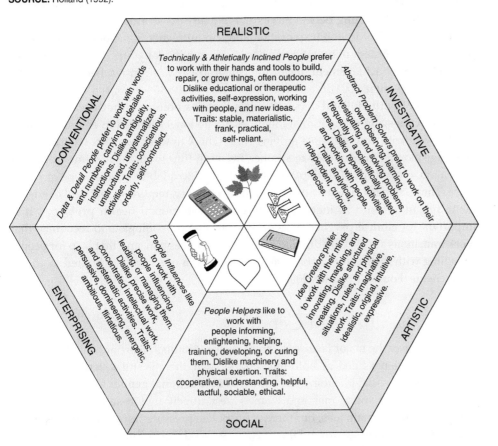

A number of tests can be used to determine a person's vocational interest type
according to Holland's theory, some given by vocational counselors, some given
over the Internet for about $10. These tests all ask you to tell whether you like,
dislike, or are indifferent to a long list of school subjects, activities, amusements,
situations, types of people, and jobs. Your answers are converted into six scores, one
for each type. The top three scores define your vocational interest type. For example, if you score highest on social (S), investigative (I), and artistic (A) factors, your
vocational type would be identified as "SIA." This would help you (or your career
planner) to steer you toward a career that would be a good fit with your vocational
interests.

Holland's theory has been extremely well researched over the years since it was
introduced in the 1950s, and the findings have generally supported Holland's conten-
tion that vocational interest types affect career choices (Helms, 1996; Holland, 1996).
Some critics of Holland's theory argue that finding a job that fits one's vocational interests may lead to greater job satisfaction, but it does not predict that one will advance in
the job or stay with it over the long term (Schwartz, 1992).

Another theory of career selection comes from developmental psychologist James E. Marcia (1966, 1980), who considered career selection as part of the identity achievement that takes place in adolescence and emerging adulthood. This is an extension of Erikson's theory of psychosocial development, which will be discussed in the next chapter. After interviewing many young people in this age group, Marcia theorized that four stages lead to career identity—diffusion, foreclosure, moratorium, and commitment. In the *diffusion* stage, young people have not decided on a future career and aren't interested in thinking about it (no exploration, no commitment). In the *foreclosure* stage, a career is chosen without much thought—usually following parents' expectations—and other options are closed off (commitment, no exploration). *Moratorium* follows and involves a large amount of exploration of possible careers with no commitment to a particular one (exploration, no commitment). The last stage is *achievement,* in which the young person has explored many possibilities for careers and has made a commitment to one (exploration and commitment). Some developmentalists point out that the stage of moratorium has been extended for young people today, and that full identity achievement, including career identity, is not reached much before the age of 30 (Arnett, 2004).

Critics of both Holland's and Marcia's theories point out that decisions about career selections and occupational identities are no longer limited to emerging adulthood. Along with young people moving from school to work, we now have adults of every age moving from one job to another, from full-time work to part-time work, and from a job in one type of workplace to no job at all to a job in another type of workplace. These changes, whether voluntary or involuntary, require a great deal of adjustment and may result in increased stress and even mental health problems. It is important for clinical psychologists and vocational psychologists to recognize that work transitions are part of adult life throughout the life span, and that help for people grappling with their career options and decisions is a need not just limited to young adult clients (Fouad & Bynner, 2008).

7.2.2: The Effects of Gender

Gender is one of the major factors in career choice. Although there are few if any occupations that are not filled by both men and women, there is still a stereotype of "his and her" jobs, a social phenomenon known as **occupational gender segregation**. This doesn't mean that young men and women are routinely told in so many words that they should take certain jobs, but there is unspoken pressure from many directions to conform to what they see around them (Eagly & Wood, 2012). This is a particular problem for women, and it is a prime factor contributing to women's lower earnings (Bayard, Hellerstein, Neumark, et al., 2003) and their lack of resources in the retirement years (Costello, Wight, & Stone, 2003). The traditional male jobs are typically higher in both status and income than the traditional women's jobs. They are also more likely to offer healthcare benefits and pensions. Although women over 25 make up about 45% of the labor force, they make up 66% of minimum wage and lower-than-minimum-wage workers (U.S. Bureau of Labor Statistics, 2013a).

Most of the occupations filled predominantly by women are pink-collar jobs, such as secretarial and clerical jobs, retail sales positions, and service jobs. They are low in status and pay, offer few benefits, and give little chance for advancement (Mastracci, 2003). Another category of occupations that is traditionally filled by women is in professions like teaching and nursing. These require college degrees, but do not have the income or chances for advancement that male-dominated professions have.

Included in the male-dominated occupations are careers in the physical sciences, technology, engineering, and mathematics—known as the STEM areas. Twice as many men work in mathematics and physical sciences than women, four times as many men work in computer sciences than women, and five times as many men work

Vocational interests seem to be established well before adulthood, and young people of all ages benefit from early guidance and exposure to possible careers.

in engineering than women (Su, Rounds, & Armstrong, 2009). Not only does this contribute to salary inequities for women, but it also means that our country (and others) is not benefiting from the potential contributions in these important fields from over half the population. At a time that science and technology is being called on to solve problems such as global temperature change, food resource scarcity, and our dependence on fossil fuel, we could use the full talents of both genders.

Needless to say, this continuation of occupational gender segregation, despite laws against gender discrimination in the workplace and sexual harassment, an increase in the number of women graduating from college, and research showing few gender-specific job abilities, has been a puzzle to vocational psychologists and others. Why are young men and women still choosing to go into "his and hers" jobs?

One possibility is that men and women have different career interests. There may not be much difference in work-related skills and abilities, but perhaps there is a difference in work-related interests. Vocational psychologist James Rounds and his colleagues (Su, Rounds, & Armstrong, 2009) conducted a meta-analysis of the results of vocational preference tests for over 500,000 people and found that women are more interested in working with people, and men are more interested in working with things. Using the vocational interests categories that Holland devised (see Figure 7.2 earlier in this chapter), Rounds and his colleagues found that the largest differences were that women scored higher on the social (S) factors, and men scored higher on the realistic (R) factors. There were smaller but significant gender differences on the artistic (A) and conventional (C) factors in favor of women and the investigative (I) and enterprising (E) factors for men. This does not necessarily mean that there are innate gender differences in vocational interests, but it could also be interpreted as showing that by the time young people reach emerging adulthood and start thinking about their careers, they have internalized the gender stereotypes presented by their families, teachers, and friends. Rounds and his colleagues point out that vocational interests are formed early and that parents, teachers, and counselors need to start addressing the topic in the lower grades of school before children's vocational interests stabilize.

A second possibility for occupational gender segregation is that men and women anticipate different career patterns, as was discussed earlier in this chapter. One difference between men's and women's career decisions is that men plan to work steadily until retirement, and women plan to move in and out of the paid workforce as they have children. Women also choose jobs that have regular hours and fewer demands that would interfere with family life. For example, even though women are graduating from medical school and law school at record numbers, they are choosing specialties within those fields—anesthesiology, dermatology, real estate law, family law—that feature more regular work schedules but often lower salaries.

A third possible explanation for occupational gender segregation is that men and women who have vocational interests for nontraditional jobs are not being encouraged to enter them (or are being discouraged). For example, data on vocational interest tests show that a number of women are interested in the STEM jobs, and some men are interested in working with people instead of things. Are they ending up in those jobs, or do they bow to pressure and enter jobs that are more traditional for their genders?

GENDER AND NONTRADITIONAL CAREERS   In a review of research findings on women in nontraditional careers, counseling psychologists Julia A. Ericksen and Donna E. Palladino Schultheiss (2009) reported that women in trades (such as painters, plumbers, and electricians) and construction jobs report having family members and mentors who encouraged them. Others felt they had a natural ability for this type of work and were independent enough not to be discouraged by other people's opinions. Not surprisingly, many of the women had very a strong sense of self; they were confident, self-assured, and comfortable with their career choices.

Critical Thinking

What do you think are some of the reasons why women in nontraditional jobs might express higher levels of job satisfaction than women in traditional jobs?

Other research has shown that some of the reasons men go into nontraditional occupations mirror women's reasons: They have skills and interests that are showcased by those jobs. Other reasons are unique to men, such as wanting to escape the stress and competition in traditional male occupations. Stay-at-home dads have been the topic of a number of studies, and the findings have been generally positive. They report low levels of stress and high levels of life satisfaction. These nontraditional dads acknowledged that stigma is attached to their career choices, but they cited strong social support from their families and almost unanimously reported their gratitude at the opportunity to be in this role with their children as they grew and developed (Heppner & Heppner, 2009).

As a strong believer in personal choice, it is difficult for me to view occupational gender segregation as a problem if men and women are making free and informed choices. Rather, I think the problem arises when these young people are, instead, bowing to social pressures to conform to gender stereotypes. It seems that some good suggestions have been offered by researchers in this area. Expose children to vocational possibilities at younger ages, encourage parents and educators to foster children's interests and talents regardless of gender, and make the workplace more family friendly so that women (and men) don't have to choose between being a good parent and following their career dreams.

7.2.3: Family Influences

Families affect occupational choice in at least two ways. First, families can have a profound effect on educational attainment. Middle-class parents are far more likely than working-class parents to encourage their children to attend college and to provide financial support for education. This is not just an ability difference in disguise. Even when you compare groups of high school students who are matched in terms of grades or test scores, it is still true that the students from middle-class families are more likely to go on to further education and better-paying, higher-prestige jobs than their working-class peers (Foskett, Dyke, & Maringe, 2008).

When parents actively support higher education, their children achieve more in their future careers.

Most of the young women today who are facing career choices have grown up with a working mother. Studies show that these young women have different ideas about gender and job selection than their peers who had mothers who did not work outside the home. For example, across many ethnic groups, young women with working mothers face their own futures with better self-esteem, higher educational goals, and aspirations toward more prestigious careers (Beal, 1994). Some of this difference certainly comes from having a resident role model, but there are other differences in these families than the simple fact that the mothers work outside the home. Women who work have different attitudes, personalities, and behaviors that have an influence on their children (and so do their husbands). Families with working mothers have different child-rearing practices and different division of chores. The result is often more responsibility and independence for the children, especially the daughters.

Aside from modeling positive gender roles in the workplace, mothers also have a more direct effect on their daughters when they hold stereotypical beliefs about gender differences in abilities. For example, mothers who believe that girls are not as good at math as boys produce daughters whose own math performance is lowered when they are reminded of their gender before doing math problems. This demonstration of *stereotype threat* was found for girls as young as 5 years of age, whereas girls whose mothers did not hold those beliefs were not affected by being reminded of their gender (Tomasetto, Alparone, & Cadinu, 2011). Although girls this age are far from entering careers, they seem to be old enough to be picking up attitudes from adults around them concerning what school subjects girls are good at and what subjects are best "left to the boys."

Another area in which the family influences the careers of adolescents and young adults is the marital status of the parents. A number of studies have shown that single parents do not provide the same level of encouragement and financial support as married parents to children preparing for careers. And this is true even when the income of the parents is considered. Young people living in stepfamilies do not fare much better, unless the parent and stepparent have had biological children together. This fact seems to turn the whole household into a "reconstituted family," and all the children benefit (Aquilino, 2005).

Why should divorced parents be less supportive of their children? One reason is that noncustodial parents may not have the same contact with and closeness to their children as they would if they lived together. Another reason is that child support after high school is not required in most states, and many divorced parents feel that if they contribute to their child's college expenses, it will lessen the obligation the custodial ex-spouse might feel. This is not a surprising finding considering that divorced couples have probably never had a good history of cooperating with each other and working toward common goals, but as a result, young adults with divorced parents are less likely to receive financial support from their parents just at a time when they are beginning to develop their careers.

7.2.4: The Role of Genetics

There is evidence that career choice is also influenced by genetics. If you consider that various cognitive strengths and physical abilities are inherited, it should come as no surprise that people end up in occupations that showcase these traits. Looking at a family tree, it is not uncommon to find generations of people in the same occupation. My grandfather and two of his brothers were plumbers, and my father's generation produced even more (including my father). But was this because there is a "plumbing gene" in our family, or because tradition called for fathers to train their sons in their trades and pass down the family business? Genetic epidemiologist Paul Lichtenstein and his colleagues (Lichtenstein, Hershberger, & Pedersen, 1995) offer some insight into this question. They gathered occupational histories of 118 pairs of monozygotic twins and 180 pairs of dizygotic twins who ranged in age from 26 to 87 years and were part of the Swedish Twin Registry. The researchers evaluated the participants' career histories and assigned each twin a score based on occupational status, using a standard Swedish socioeconomic scale. The five categories were (a) unskilled and semiskilled worker, (b) skilled worker, (c) assistant nonmanual employee, (d) intermediate nonmanual employee, and (e) employed and self-employed professionals, higher civil servants, and executives. For the males, the monozygotic twins' occupational status scores correlated significantly higher than the scores for the dizygotic twins. In other words, if one identical twin was a level 2 on the socioeconomic scale (skilled worker), there was a significantly greater chance that his twin would also be a level 2 than if they were fraternal twins, indicating a genetic influence for occupational status.

In contrast, the women twins did not show this genetic effect, but rather showed a stronger environmental effect. Considering that this sample had a mean age of almost 60, a sizable number of these women belonged to a cohort in which women were restricted to certain jobs or worked with their husbands in a family business. Neither of these situations would reflect an inherited genetic ability or interest. And to back this up, when the women's data were analyzed by age groups, the younger women were more apt to show the male pattern of genetic influence than were the older women. This supports earlier predictions that in countries that have social welfare programs to promote equal access to higher education, there would be an increase in the magnitude of genetic effects with time—thus younger women who had more opportunity to obtain education and job training compatible with their talents, interests, and competencies would show stronger genetic effects in the careers they developed.

In the study of Swedish twins described here, the researchers also had a group of farmers in their sample, but removed them because there were too few to analyze. If there had been enough, which type of twin pairs do you think would be more apt to both be farmers, monozygotic or dizygotic? Why? Write a brief response that will be read by your instructor.

▶ The response entered here will appear in the performance dashboard and can be viewed by your instructor.

Submit

7.3: Age Trends in Work Experience

7.3 State effects of age-related declines in cognitive abilities, reaction time, physical strength, and sensory abilities

Actual work performance is one area where older people hold their own, and the same is true for job satisfaction. When skill sets of older workers become obsolete, retraining is possible with the right methods. How can we reconcile these findings with the information in earlier chapters about age-related decline in cognitive and physical abilities? This is an interesting dilemma, and one that has some *very* real implications for the near future. As sociologist John C. Henretta (2001) reminds us, with all the hoopla about baby boomers reaching retirement age in the near future, we seem to forget that before they retire, they will spend a good amount of time being older members of the workforce. What can we anticipate from this "graying of the workplace"?

7.3.1: Job Performance

Early research concluded that performance on the job does not appear to change with age; that older workers are as good as younger workers by most measures (Clancy & Hoyer, 1994; Warr, 1994). This is a little surprising because we also know from previous chapters that lab studies typically show age-related declines in abilities that are central to many jobs, such as reaction time, sensory abilities, physical strength and dexterity, and cognitive flexibility. Psychologists Timothy Salthouse and Todd Maurer (1996) reviewed this paradox in the research literature and suggested several explanations. One idea is that we consider job performance as made up of two factors: general ability and **job expertise**, or job experience. General ability may decline with age, but job expertise increases, perhaps enough to compensate for the decline, an **ability/expertise trade-off**.

An example of the ability/expertise trade-off is demonstrated in a classic study of typing ability among women who ranged in age from 19 to 72 years (Salthouse, 1984). Two tasks were used, one that measured reaction time (ability) and one that measured typing speed (experience). Not surprisingly, reaction time decreased with age; older women took more time to react to visual stimuli. However, typing speed was the same regardless of age. How did this happen? Researchers explained that the older women relied on their increased job experience to compensate for their decreased general ability. As they typed one word, they read the next few words and were ready to type those words sooner than their younger colleagues, who processed the words one at a time. Similar effects were demonstrated with groups of musicians (Krampe & Ericsson, 1996), airline pilots (Hardy & Parasuraman, 1997), clinical psychologists, and college professors (Smith, Staudinger, & Baltes, 1994). Clearly, older workers in jobs that involve knowledge-based, crystallized abilities and highly-practiced abilities have less job-related decline and are able to swap expertise for any physical or cognitive slowdown they might experience (Czaja & Lee, 2001).

Workers in jobs that require manual skills and fluid cognitive abilities may show declines with age, but the declines are usually gradual, and there is a lot of variation in the abilities of older workers. Industrial and organizational psychologist Michael A. McDaniel and his colleagues (McDaniel, Pesta, & Banks, 2012) caution that decisions about hiring or retaining workers should not be based on chronological age. Often the workers themselves will leave jobs that are beyond their abilities or transfer to jobs with fewer demands. And because of our aging workforce, it might be a good idea for employers to consider restructuring jobs to take advantage of the skills older workers have retained.

Most of us who have had jobs know that core performance is not the whole story. There are many aspects of the job other than the major task you were hired for. How does this whole package of abilities and attitudes change with age? Organizational behavior researchers Thomas W. H. Ng and Daniel C. Feldman (2008) conducted a meta-analysis of studies correlating the age of workers with job performance on a number of dimensions, including core task performance. Like other researchers, they found that age was not related to core task performance, but they also found that age is not related to on-the-job creativity either. Furthermore, older workers demonstrate more citizenship behaviors (compliance to norms, not complaining about trivial matters, helping fellow workers) and more on-the-job safety behaviors. Older workers also engage in fewer counterproductive work behaviors (workplace aggression, on-the-job substance abuse, tardiness, and voluntary absences from work).

These findings are particularly relevant today, considering that the average age of workers is steadily growing older throughout the world. For example, the largest segment of the U.S. workforce in 1980 was young adults 20 to 24 years of age; today it is middle-aged adults 50 to 54 (U.S. Bureau of Labor Statistics, 2013c). This has brought about concern based on the stereotypes of older workers being less able to perform the jobs required and more difficult to get along with in the workplace. According to the studies cited earlier, these stereotypes are not supported by research, and in fact, for many aspects of job performance, workers get better with age.

7.3.2: Job Training and Retraining

To revisit Super's theory of career development for a moment, recall the stages he outlined: growth, exploration, establishment, maintenance, and disengagement, and recall also his notion that people may go back through some of these stages from time to time during their careers, a process he calls **career recycling**. As career paths become more flexible, this recycling process has become more common, especially for the stages of exploration and establishment. As things change in the workplace (businesses closing, downsizing, automation) and in workers' lives (young children starting school, older children completing college, job-related stress builds up), individuals explore career options and often decide to retrain. For example, if you are in a college classroom at the moment, there is a good chance you are a **nontraditional student**, one who is over the age of 25 and engaged in career recycling. If you are not in this category, there is an excellent chance that the person seated next to you is.

About 38% of college students today are 25 years of age or older (U.S. Census Bureau, 2012a). Most of them have been in the workforce or have been working in the home raising their children and are now back for retraining to take the next step in their careers. Add to them the workers who are being retrained within their companies and the workers picking up new skill sets using Internet courses at home, and the total is a considerable proportion of adults of all ages who are engaged in job retraining. Research shows that younger workers have a slight edge when learning new job-related skills, but that some of that benefit could be explained by the related finding that older workers lack confidence in these learning situations. Older workers over 55 years of age are also slightly less willing to participate in training and career development (Ng & Feldman, 2012), possibly because they are reaching the end of their careers and don't feel they will reap the benefits of additional training. Still, it might be worthwhile for employers to skip the retraining for valuable older workers and reassign them to work they still do well (McDaniel, Pesta, & Banks, 2012).

7.3.3: Job Satisfaction

Studies show that older workers are more satisfied with their jobs than younger workers (Clark, Oswald, & Warr, 1996), and this might be a partial explanation of why job performance does not always decline as workers get older. Why would work satisfaction rise with age? In part, this pattern seems to be explained by time-in-job rather than age itself. Older workers have typically been in their jobs longer, which usually means that they have reached a level with more intrinsically challenging or interesting jobs, better pay, more job security, and more authority. This is an important point to keep in mind because as people change jobs more often, as women move in and out of the labor market, many people will not accumulate large amounts of time-in-job and so may not experience the rise in satisfaction that is normally correlated with age. Similarly, if women move into the job market for the first time in their 30s or 40s, they may experience the peak of job satisfaction in their 50s rather than in their 40s. (This may be why women who don't begin to work outside the home until after their children are older often work past traditional retirement age, as I will discuss a little later in this chapter.)

Still, time-in-job cannot account for all of what we see. There are also "young" jobs and "old" jobs. Young people are much more likely to hold physically difficult, dirty, or less complex and less interesting jobs. In addition, there is undoubtedly some selective attrition operating here. Workers who really dislike some line of work tend not to stay in it long enough to become dissatisfied older workers. Older workers in any given occupation are thus likely to be people who choose to stay in that line of work because it gives them a good match to their personality or their interests.

Older workers may also have a more realistic attitude toward work. As my friend explained to her 16-year-old son, who was complaining about how much he disliked his summer job bagging groceries, "That's why they call it 'work' and not 'entertainment,' and that's why they pay you to do it and not charge admission." I'm sure that none of the retirees who work with him at the supermarket in the same job would need that explanation spelled out for them. Whether this is a cohort effect (the older generation had to work harder because times were rough when they were young) or an effect of increased wisdom, the lower expectations of older workers can lead to higher job satisfaction.

Industrial and organizational psychologists Eric E. Heggestad and Ashley M. Andrew (2012) reviewed the research literature on age-related changes in job satisfaction and found a "U-shaped" function with job satisfaction being highest in the 20s and at retirement and lowest in the mid-20s and 30s. The authors explain that part of this curve is due to age changes in work attitudes, but part is also because people who dislike their jobs usually move on into something they like better.

7.4: Work and Personal Life

7.4   Relate work to the individual, relationships, and family

Freud said that the defining features of life were work and love, and nowhere does this ring truer than in the intersection almost everyone experiences as we merge our jobs and personal lives. There is a bidirectional effect between work and the individual, work and committed relationships, and work and family. We may be more aware of the effects our personal lives have on our work, but our jobs also have profound effects on our personal lives. I will start with work and the individual, then discuss work and various relationships—marriage, children, older family members who need care. And I will even cover household labor, a frequent topic of discussion in many homes.

7.4.1: Work and the Individual

Although older people are more satisfied with their jobs than younger people, workers of any age can experience the effects of heavy workplace demands. One example is **job burnout**, a combination of exhaustion, depersonalization, and reduced effectiveness on the job. This is especially common among workers whose jobs involve expressing emotion or being empathetic, such as nurses and social workers. Burnout has commonalities with depression, but the symptoms of burnout are specific to the job environment, whereas depression is more pervasive. Techniques used to relieve job burnout include a combination of helping the individual with coping strategies and making changes within the organization (Maslach, Schaufeli, & Leiter, 2001).

Not everyone in a difficult job responds to it with adverse reactions. For example, those who have strong social support from family and friends (Huynh, Xanthopoulou, & Winefield, 2013), greater job satisfaction, better general health, and higher levels of life satisfaction will fare better when working in a stressful situation (Kozak, Kersten, Schillmöller, et al., 2013). Several traits and coping styles have been identified that relate to job stress and burnout: low levels of hardiness (being uninvolved in daily activities and resistant to change), external locus of control (attributing events to chance or powerful others instead of to one's own abilities and efforts), and avoidant coping style (dealing with stress in a passive and defensive way; Semmer, 1996). Also, individuals who need to validate their own self-worth by achieving on the job are more apt to experience burnout (Blom, 2012).

In the last decade or so, industrial and organizational psychologists have been investigating the concept of **work engagement**, which is an active, positive approach to work characterized by vigor, dedication, and absorption (Kahn, 1990; Schaufeli & Bakker, 2004). This is similar to job satisfaction, only more active and sustained. And it seems to me that it is the opposite of job burnout. Workers who are engaged in their work are more productive and creative (Bakker, 2011). Work engagement comes from a combination of resources from the job (social support, feedback, skill variety, autonomy, and learning opportunities) and resources within the worker (self-efficacy, self-esteem, and optimism).

WRITING PROMPT

What other jobs would you predict have high rates of job burnout? What about work engagement? Write a brief response that will be read by your teacher. Be sure to explain your reasoning.

▶ The response entered here will appear in the performance dashboard and can be viewed by your instructor.

Submit

A timely topic for many is **unemployment**, the state of being without a paid job when you are willing to work. In 2012, about 7% of the workforce in the United States over the age of 25 was unemployed. Unemployment is not distributed randomly through the population. Education is a significant factor. People in the United States with a bachelor's degree have a lower rate of unemployment (4.5%) than those with only a high school diploma (8.3%). Race and gender are factors, too; white people have lower unemployment (6.1%) than black people (11.5%), and black men have a higher rate of unemployment (12.3%) than black women (10.6%; U.S. Bureau of Labor Statistics, 2013d).

Although unemployment may occur for several reasons (relocation, recent graduation from college), most of the research on this topic concerns **job loss**—paid employment being taken away from an individual. Job loss can be the result of a business closing, jobs being outsourced overseas, or a slowdown in the market for some product or service. Job loss and the subsequent period of unemployment are strongly related to poor physical health and mental health problems such as anxiety, depression, and alcoholism (Nelson, Quick, & Simmons, 2001). The negative effects increase the longer the person has been unemployed. Surprisingly, women who have experienced job loss have higher rates of mental health problems and lower levels of life satisfaction than men in the same situation (McKee-Ryan, Song, Wanberg, et al., 2005). This could be because women are more apt to suffer from depression, or it could reflect the fact that job loss represents a larger financial problem for women than for men.

In early 2008, the economy of the United States (as well as the economies of other developed countries) experienced a recession with record job losses. The unemployment rate in the United States doubled the first 2 years of the recession, leaving over 15 million adults without jobs. This had an effect on workers in terms of finances and also more personal aspects of their lives. The most extreme effect of increased unemployment may have been an increase in suicides. Sociologist Aaron Reeves and his colleagues (Reeves, Stuckler, McKee, et al., 2012) tracked suicide rates in the United States over the recent economic recession to compare the actual rate with the rate that would be expected based on previous years' data. They found that 2007 marked the beginning of an acceleration in suicides—amounting to an estimated 4,750 excess suicide deaths from 2007 to 2010. Even greater acceleration of the suicide rates have been found in European countries such as Greece and Italy, which have experienced greater job loss. The economy seems to be improving again, and the future looks better, but it is important to look beyond the unemployment figures and consider the complex human toll of job loss.

Losing one's job is difficult for anyone, but there are some age differences. It is difficult for a young person just leaving school to be unemployed because it interferes with establishing a career and an identity as an adult (McKee-Ryan, Song, Wanberg, et al., 2005). It is difficult for older workers because of the problems they have finding new jobs and adjusting to new work conditions. A good number of older people take early retirement after losing their jobs because they have little hope of getting new ones. However, being laid off is worst for middle-aged adults. Usually they have reached a middle or high level in the company structure and have problems finding a job with comparable pay and prestige, but they are also too young to retire with a pension or benefits.

THE THREAT OF JOB LOSS   Not surprisingly, it is not only the actual job loss that causes problems but also the threat of job loss. Sociologist Leon Grunberg and his colleagues (Grunberg, Moore, & Greenberg, 2001) found that workers who are exposed to layoffs among friends or coworkers experience significantly lower job security, higher levels of depression, and more symptoms of poor health than workers who have not been exposed to layoffs. This topic of **job insecurity**, or the anticipation of job loss by currently employed workers, has received a considerable amount of research attention in recent years due to the large numbers of mass layoffs of workers around the world.

Psychologists Grand Cheng and Darius Chan (2008) performed a meta-analysis on 133 studies of job insecurity and reported that workers who felt higher levels of job insecurity reported lower levels of job satisfaction, commitment to the company, work performance, trust in the employer, and workplace involvement. They reported higher levels of health problems and higher levels of intentions to leave the job than workers who felt less job insecurity. The workers' ages and number of years on the job were significant mediators of the effects of job insecurity. The older the workers were and the longer they had been on the job, the more likely they were to report health problems. However, it was the younger workers and those who had been on the job less time who were more likely to be thinking about changing jobs, probably because they had less invested in the job, had fewer financial obligations, and had a better chance of finding a similar job somewhere else. The picture that emerges from these studies is that unemployment affects not only the workers who are forced off the job, but the remaining workers, too. Their high levels of job insecurity result in low productivity and morale.

7.4.2: Work and Marriage

There is ample evidence that work has an influence on relationship commitment—that is, having a job, being out of school, having a good income, and being settled in a career are often prerequisites for entering into marriage or a committed partnership. However, it also seems that the partnership, in turn, has an effect on the work life of each partner. A number of studies show that married men earn higher wages than unmarried men, even when genetic endowment and family background are held constant (Antonovics & Town, 2004), and the same is true for women's incomes (U.S. Bureau of Labor Statistics, 2009).

Sociologist Elizabeth Gorman (2000) investigated the differences in attitude toward work between married and never-married adults. She found that married men and women are significantly more interested in the income potential of a job than single individuals. In addition, married men and women are less satisfied with their current incomes than single individuals. Gorman believes that the attitudes expressed by the married participants in her study lead to more productive behaviors in the workplace and higher evaluations of job success, whether it be measured by income, promotions, or number of days on the job per year.

There is also plenty of evidence that aspects of the job can affect relationship quality. Sociologist Harriet B. Presser (2000) has looked at the timing of work for both husbands and wives, specifically the nonstandard work schedules, or **shift work**, including evening shifts, night shifts, and rotating shifts. A preliminary look at labor statistics shows that shift work is becoming more and more common in the United States as business is conducted around the world in various time zones. About 15% of the workforce is shift workers (McMenamin, 2007). If both spouses have jobs, there is a one-in-four chance that one of them will be a shift worker, and if they have children, the likelihood goes up to one in three. Usually these irregular schedules are not the choice of the workers but are determined by the employers. When employees choose shift work, it is usually for better pay, to reduce child care costs, or to be able to attend school during the daytime.

What do irregular work schedules do to marriages? When children are present, having one spouse who works a night shift significantly increases the chance of divorce or separation. If it is the husband who works the night shift, the chance of divorce or separation is over six times higher than for husbands who work days, and if it is the wife who works the night shift, it is almost three times higher. Presser suggests that night shifts bring lack of sleep, stress from being out of sync with other family members, and loss of intimacy and social life together.

Critical Thinking

Some parents of young children choose to work different shifts to eliminate the need for day care. If you had friends considering this path, what advice would you give them?

In another study, couples who had families and worked the night shifts were compared to similar couples who worked the day shifts. Those who worked the night shifts reported more marital instability, more job-related family problems, and more family-related job problems than their coworkers who worked the day shifts (Davis, Goodman, Piretti, et al., 2008). The authors suggest that it would be good management policy to reduce work-shift stressors and the resulting family problems they can cause, if for no other reason than the fact that family problems can reduce productivity and increase negativity among the workers. They suggest giving workers more flexibility in choosing their shift hours and in contacting their families during work hours. They also suggest that for some workers who are in career positions, shift work is less problematic or even preferred, such as for those who are single or attending college during the day.

7.4.3: Work and Parenthood

In the United States, approximately 59% of married couples with children are considered "dual-career" families, meaning that both parents are employed (U.S. Census Bureau, 2013b). In addition, a large number of single parents combine family and paid work. However, as discussed earlier in this chapter, it is more typical for men to remain in the labor force and for women to move into and out of employment due to family obligations. Almost all fathers are employed (96%), whereas mothers' rates of employment depend on their marital status and the age of the children (see Table 7.2). As you can see from this table, age of children is a bigger factor than marital status. The number of years women spend in the workplace during their careers depends on the number of children they have; the more children a woman has, the less time she spends in the workplace.

Table 7.2 Percent of Mothers in the Labor Force

Age of Youngest Child	Married Mothers	Single Mothers
6 to 17 years	70%	72%
Under 6 years	60%	60%

SOURCE: Data from U.S. Bureau of Labor Statistics (2013b).

Early studies showed that being a parent did not reduce the working hours of men, and it was concluded that parenthood did not have an effect on men's careers (Hyde, Essex, & Horton, 1993; Presser, 1995). More recently, researchers have argued that it is not accurate to measure the effects of parenthood on men's and women's careers using the same ruler. Some point out that men's roles in the family have traditionally been those of provider, and that men respond to parenthood with a greater commitment to their careers, not in providing less (Kaufman & Uhlenberg, 2000). We saw in the last section that men who are married are more motivated to work hard and increase their incomes, so it stands to reason that these men would be even more motivated when they become fathers. This is supported in a study by sociologists Gayle Kaufman and Peter Uhlenberg (2000), who examined data from the National Survey of Families consisting of almost 4,000 married men and women under 50 living in the United States. An interesting dichotomy appeared; men were more likely to be employed if they were fathers and to work more hours the more children they had. Women, on the other hand, were *less* likely to work if they had children, and they worked *fewer* hours the more children they had.

"Career choice" for many women means leaving their paid jobs for a number of years when they have young children and working full time as caregivers for their families.

Similar findings come from a study by economists Robert Lerman and Elaine Sorensen (2000), who analyzed data gathered over 13 years as part of the National Longitudinal Survey of Youth. Their group of interest was unwed fathers, men who had various degrees of contact with their children. The researchers were interested in determining what factors predict change in the pattern of contact between the fathers and their children. One of the strongest predictors of increased contact was higher income, but the timing of the effect was a surprise: Fathers who increased contact with their children during any year of the study showed a subsequent increase in the number of hours worked and the amount of income earned during the following years. It seems that once a father becomes more involved in his child's life, he starts working more hours and making more money, not vice versa.

To summarize, parenthood has an effect on the careers of both men and women. Parents are different workers than nonparents. Mothers are more apt to change their career pattern to accommodate their roles as mothers, and men are more apt to become more committed to their roles as traditional breadwinners for their families. But does work have an effect on the parenting roles of men and women? That is the topic I will take up next.

Critical Thinking

Before you read on, what have you heard about children of working mothers? Have you heard that day care has negative effects on children's behavior and later academic success? Do you think it is always best for mothers to stay home with their preschoolers unless they absolutely need the income?

THE INCREASE OF MOTHERS IN THE WORKFORCE The increase of mothers in the workforce has been one of the biggest social changes in the United States over the last three generations. Early concerns about neglected children haven't materialized; the fact that a mother has a job outside the home, in and of itself, has no effect on her children's well-being. Instead, factors such as home environment, quality of day care, parents' marital status, and the stability of mother's employment determine the outcome for her children (Gottfried, 2005). To the contrary, a mother in the workforce can be a benefit to her children if she has good support at home and at work; when mothers are willingly in the workforce, their children have increased academic achievement and fewer behavior problems than children whose mothers are not in the workforce—or who are there unwillingly (Belsky, 2001). When children of working mothers grow up, they have more egalitarian attitudes (Riggio & Desrochers, 2005). The daughters of working mothers consider more options when choosing careers, and the sons are more apt to share in the household work when they marry (Gupta, 2006).

One effect of maternal employment is that fathers' involvement in the lives of their children increases. Fathers spend more time with their children than their own fathers spent with them, and married, working parents spend an average of 1 hour more a day with their children than parents did 25 years ago (Bond, Thompson, Galinsky, et al., 2002).

In my usual search for balance, I don't want to paint too rosy a picture of the world of dual-earner families. First, the U.S. workplace is not friendly to families. The rules were set in 1938, and although there have been adjustments, they still reflect the family structure of that time (Halpern, 2005). For example, the United States is one of only a handful of countries in the world that does not offer paid maternity leave to its workers (United Nations Statistics Division, 2009). Another example is that it is legal in the United States for employers to pay part-time employees (most of whom are women) less per hour than full-time employees doing the same job and to deny them medical benefits, sick leave days, and paid vacation days. Taking unpaid time off to care for a new baby or an aging parent, working part time at greatly reduced pay while children are young, forgoing promotions because the new job would interfere with family responsibilities—all these are trade-offs parents frequently must make.

The American Psychological Association (Halpern, 2005) reviewed the situation faced by U.S. parents in the workforce and made recommendations for policy makers, employers, schools, and communities. Some of these ideas are to provide paid family and medical leave and to support job training and parent training for young fathers. Other recommendations involve support for after-school and summer programs for children and alignment of school and work calendars. (This latter one would be a big help for my students who are also parents. Our university calendar does not fit our district school system calendar, so parents and children have different holidays and spring breaks.)

The fact that a mother works outside the home has no negative effect on the well-being of her child and can have long-term positive effects.

WRITING PROMPT

If you are combining college with parenting, what changes in the college rules and schedules would be most helpful to you? Why? Write a brief response that will be read by your instructor.

 The response entered here will appear in the performance dashboard and can be viewed by your instructor.

Submit

7.4.4: Work and Caregiving for Adult Family Members

Caring for children is not the only family responsibility that many men and women need to combine with their careers. An increasing number of working adults have caregiving responsibilities for adult family members—parents or parents-in-law who are frail or ill, spouses with dementia or other chronic disabilities, or adult children or siblings who are disabled and can't care for themselves. A survey by the National Alliance for Caregiving and AARP (2009) showed that 29% of adults in the United States provide care for at least one adult family member, and a fifth of these provide more than 40 hours of care per week. Almost 60% of caregivers combine their caregiving with full-time jobs. The proportion of men involved in caregiving is increasing steadily—about 40% of caregivers are now men, although women contribute more hours of caregiving per week and do more hands-on caregiving tasks.

In this same study, over 1,000 men and women were interviewed who provided unpaid care to adult relatives or friends who were unable to take care of themselves (National Alliance of Caregivers and AARP, 2009). The topic of interest for this study was how the economic downturn had affected their caregiving roles. These caregivers reported that they had experienced their work hours or their salaries cut (43%), had lost their jobs or been laid off (16%), and were working more hours or had taken a second job to keep up with the expense of being a caregiver (33%). In addition, the respondents told about how caregiving costs had gone up, and that they had compensated for that by saving less for retirement (60%), using up their savings (43%), and borrowing money or increasing their credit card debt (43%). Still, over three quarters of caregivers reported that the quality of their caregiving to their loved ones had not decreased.

Interestingly, another study included dual-earner couples who care for both children and dependent adult family members. These "extreme caregivers" make up about 10% of the population today, and that number is expected to increase. Researchers interviewed the participants twice over a 12-month period. One surprising result was that the couples doing the most caregiving for the most people had less depression and that the wives reported higher levels of life satisfaction than those with fewer responsibilities. The authors suggest that we look at the strengths of families and not just study the problems. Taking care of family members brings a sense of agency to a family and can strengthen a couple's relationship and give a sense of confronting challenges together and developing successful coping strategies (Neal & Hammer, 2007).

The role of caregiver is very demanding when it is combined with one's career. Hopefully employers will create more family-friendly policies in the workplace for both parents of young children and caregivers of adult family members such as offering flextime, work-at-home options, job sharing, counseling, and dependent-care accounts.

7.4.5: Household Labor

Housework, unpaid family work, housekeeping, domestic engineering, family chores—whatever you want to call **household labor**—few people enjoy doing it, but we all need it done. The topic of who does the meal preparation and cleanup, the grocery shopping, the laundry, the child care, the household repairs, and the housecleaning is a common one in discussions among people who live together. In the past decade, household labor division has become the topic of over 200 research articles and books. Why should serious scholars be interested in household labor? One reason is that it is embedded in complex patterns of social relations. According to sociologist Scott Coltrane, the division of household labor is "related to gender, household structure, family interaction, and the operation of both formal and informal market economies" (Coltrane, 2000, p. 1208).

Critical Thinking

If you live with others, how is the household labor divided? Is it distributed according to gender, time availability, or relative resources?

Household labor takes place in the privacy of the home, so it is difficult to know who does what. The best we can do is look at survey data, in which working couples are asked how they spend their time. Figure 7.3 shows the results of a survey done by the Pew Research Center (2013b). Parents who are either married or living together and who have at least one child under the age of 18 report that the mothers spend an average of 16 hours a week on household labor while the fathers spend 9. Mothers also report spending more time on child care than the fathers. However, fathers spend more on paid work, and when housework, child care, and paid work are combined, the total is very close (59 hours for mothers and 58 hours for fathers).

Figure 7.3 Working mothers and fathers contribute differently to household labor, paid work, and child care, but the total time spent is almost the same.

SOURCE: Pew Research Center (2013).

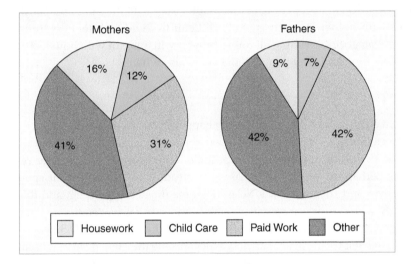

One last note, though, is that there is more involved here than just who does the dishes and who goes to the office. When women limit their time in paid labor, they also limit their lifetime incomes, their Social Security benefits and pensions, and their earning potentials. The bottom line is that these preferences and choices often lead to reduced financial security in the later years, when women are more apt than men to be widowed and to have chronic illnesses. I don't recommend that women turn their backs on household labor, but I do strongly recommend that they consider these long-term consequences and make arrangements now that will compensate for their personal pattern of labor force participation. This issue is about more than equality between the genders or being there for the children; it's about the long-term financial security of women, and we will come back to that yet again later in this chapter.

7.5: Retirement

7.5a Discuss retirement in terms of reasons, timings, and effects

7.5b List reasons for retirement

The concept of **retirement**, or the career stage of leaving the workforce to pursue other interests, such as part-time work, volunteer work, or leisure interests, is relatively new. My grandfather was the first person in his family to retire. He was the eldest son, and his father (as well as his grandfather) had been farmers who continued working until they died. Even if they had worked in salaried jobs, there was no Social Security until 1935 (and then it was called "old age survivors' insurance").

My grandfather worked for the city water department, and when he turned 65 in 1949, he was given a gold watch and a picture of himself shaking hands with the mayor. He began collecting Social Security, and several years later, so did my grandmother, who had never worked outside the home. Workers my grandfather's age were pioneers; they had no role models for retirement and may have felt a little sheepish about leaving the job while they were still able-bodied and had all their wits about them. It is hard to imagine today how much our retirement behavior and expectations have changed since that time.

Today retirement is quite different. Many people spend 20 years or more in this stage, and many look forward to it. They spend these years doing a variety of things; they travel, take classes at the university, and become political activists. Another difference today is that retirement is seldom an all-or-nothing state. People retire from one career after 20 years and then begin a second one or take a part-time job. Others start collecting a pension at 62 and spend their days in leisure activities. And some, like Reverend Johnson in the opening of this chapter, stay with the same company, but take positions with lighter loads. It is really difficult to divide adults into "retired" and "working" categories. Keeping all this in mind, I will jump in with both feet and write about when, how, and why people retire—and also where.

7.5.1: Preparation for Retirement

Retirement is not something that suddenly happens to us on some random date. Barring an unexpected illness, disability, or job layoff, the vast majority of adults who retire do so after some period of planning and expectation. Some adults prepare for retirement beginning perhaps as early as 15 or 20 years ahead. They talk with their spouses, talk with relatives and friends, read articles, do some financial planning, and think about where they will live. These activities seem to increase fairly steadily as the expected retirement date draws closer. However, 56% of a random sample of U.S. workers report that they have not tried to calculate how much income they will need in retirement, and only 14% feel confident that they will be able to retire comfortably (Employee Benefit Research Institute, 2012). At the same time, retired people report that income is an important factor in their feelings of well-being after leaving the workforce.

Critical Thinking

Before you read on, what age do you consider to be "retirement age"? At what age will you be eligible for full Social Security benefits? (If you haven't checked recently, you might be surprised.)

There is a gender difference in preparing for retirement. Women are not as likely to plan for retirement as men are. Women are less likely than men to participate in employer-sponsored pension plans and are more likely to cash out accumulated pension assets when they change jobs. This gender difference remains in force even when men and women in similar jobs are compared. Women are twice as likely to have no retirement income except Social Security. Many depend on their husbands to "take care of things," but not even those who are recently divorced or widowed make the effort to prepare for retirement that their male coworkers do (Hardy & Shuey, 2000). This lack of planning contributes to significant gender differences in retirement income.

7.5.2: Timing of Retirement

Just as planning varies, so does the actual timing of retirement. We tend to think of 66 as "retirement age" because that is the age at which people in the United States are able to start receiving full Social Security benefits. However, many people retire earlier, and many keep working past that age. Figure 7.4 shows the proportions of adults of various ages who are in the **labor force**, meaning they are either working or actively looking for jobs. These data extend back to 1990 and are projected to 2020. If you examine the figure, you will see that a little over 80% of adults between the ages of 25 and 54 years of age are currently in the labor force. Likewise, almost 65% of those from 55 to 64 years of age are in the labor force, a little over 25% of those 65 to 74 years of age, and about 7% of those over 75 are in the labor force. Looking back to 1990 and forward to 2020, you can see that although the younger group has remained stable, the older three groups have increased in labor force participation and are expected to continue this increase into the next decade, with the sharpest increase for those 65 years of age and older (Toossi, 2012).

Figure 7.4 The percent of people in the U.S. workforce has remained about the same since 1990 for those 24 to 54 years of age, but increased for older workers.

SOURCE: Data from Toossi (2012).

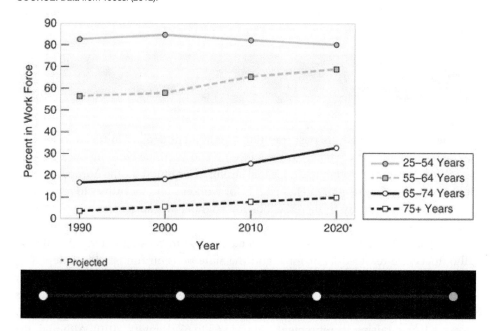

* Projected

One reason for the increase in older workers is that each year the group of people reaching retirement age is healthier, on average, than the group before, so more of them are able to work if they choose to. Also, mandatory retirement was ended for most jobs in the United States in 1986, making it possible for older workers to continue in their jobs if they so desired. The number of physically demanding jobs has declined from 20% in 1950 to 7.5% in the 1990s, making it easier for older adults to do the work required in many jobs. In addition, as of 2000, there is no longer a penalty for people 66 and older who collect Social Security and continue to receive a paycheck (Clark, Burkhauser, Moon, et al., 2004). Finally, women make up larger parts of the older groups, and their workforce participation has increased steadily.

This picture of an abundance of older workers in the labor force is not found in other developed countries. Figure 7.5 shows the proportion of adults between 65 and 69 who are part of the labor force in Germany, France, Italy, and Greece compared to the United States. As you can see, the proportions are lower for those four European countries, and they declined until 2000, when France, Germany, and Italy began increasing the proportion of older adults in the workforce. Greece has continued to decline, reflecting its tenuous economic situation (United Nations Economic Commission for Europe, 2013).

Figure 7.5 The percent of workers past traditional retirement age (65–69 years) has increased considerably in the United States in the last few decades. In contrast, it declined in several European countries until 2000, when most began to increase also.

SOURCE: Data from United Nations Economic Commission for Europe (2013).

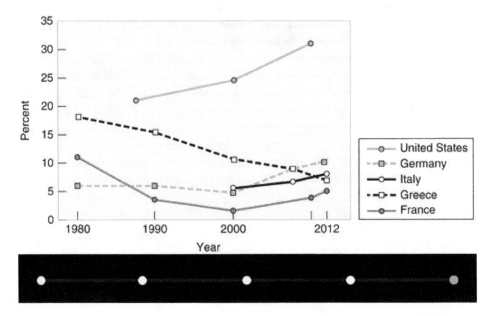

One reason fewer adults past traditional retirement age are in the workforce in Europe is that higher taxes take away the incentive to continue working once they are eligible for pensions. Another reason is that strong labor unions in the European countries have won generous retirement benefits for workers, and incentives to retire early have been used as a way to increase jobs for younger workers (Alesina, Glaeser, & Sacerdote, 2005).

Many European countries are concerned that the increasing elderly population will outpace the reduced labor force and the state pension funds will be depleted. Some are slowly increasing the age at which full benefits will be paid for retirees. For example, in 2011, France started raising its mandatory retirement age of 60 by 4 months every year until 2018, when French workers will be required to retire at 62. In 2012, Germany began raising its retirement age from 65 to 67 (Reuters, 2010). Although the situation is not as grave in the United States, with its higher level of participation in the workforce, the age at which full benefits will be paid to retirees is slowly increasing here also, reducing some of the financial incentive for retirement (Clark, Burkhauser, Moon, et al., 2004).

7.5.3: Reasons for Retirement

As was discussed in earlier sections of this chapter, retirement is not always a voluntary decision. A good number of older workers find themselves unemployed due to company layoffs, mergers, or bankruptcies and have difficulty finding another job at the same level and salary. A viable option for some of these individuals is to retire early. However, for most people, the decision of when to retire is more complex and depends on the interaction of a number of factors.

RETIREMENT AND FINANCE   Economists and other social scientists have found that the biggest determinant in the decision to retire is the value a worker receives from staying on the job compared to the value he or she would receive from retiring. **Work-related value** is not only the worker's salary, but also the increase in pension and Social Security benefits to be received later if he or she continues working.

For example, full Social Security benefits are currently available when workers reach 66 years of age; if they decide to retire between 62 and 66, they receive less than full benefits for the rest of their lives. If they retire between 66 and 70, they receive more than full benefits for the rest of their lives. Clearly, the longer a worker stays on the job, the higher the Social Security benefits will be. Some private pension plans work the same way. In addition, there are other values related to staying on the job, such as health insurance coverage for the worker and his or her family and other incentives the employer might offer for continued employment (Clark, Burkhauser, Moon, et al., 2004).

Workers weigh this package of value for staying on the job with the **retirement-related value**. In this package is personal wealth—how much is in savings, investments, home equity, and other assets. With the stock market downturn in 2008 and the dip in housing prices and sales, many people approaching retirement who were depending on returns from these investments decided to stay on the job, which helps explain the increase in the percentage of older men and women in the workforce. Retirement-related value also includes how much the worker would receive in Social Security and pension benefits, as well as what might be earned from other work, such as a part-time job or consulting work. The cost of health insurance coverage is also part of this package. Medicare, the national medical coverage for workers, is not available until a person reaches 65, but some employers continue health insurance for retirees. Making these decisions is even more complex in many instances because the situation of a spouse must be added to the equation.

RETIREMENT FOR PERSONAL ISSUES   Another important factor in the timing of retirement is health. Again, this is not a simple matter. Health can affect the decision to retire in two ways. Increased medical expenses and the need for health-care insurance can increase the chances that workers will stay on the job—and this involves not only the individual worker's health, but also that of his or her spouse and other family members (Clark, Burkhauser, Moon, et al., 2004). The second effect is that poor health can make working difficult and lead to a lower salary or transfer to a lower-paying position, making retirement more attractive. This is especially common in physically demanding jobs (Johnson, 2004). Alternatively, the poor health of a spouse or family member can lead to increased caregiving responsibilities and subsequent retirement. About 3% of people who try to combine caregiving and careers solve the problem by taking early retirement (Family Caregiver Alliance, 2012).

FAMILY   Children can play a role in deciding when to retire. With parenthood coming later and retirement opportunities coming earlier, having children still in the home might be a reason to remain in the workforce. And even if the children are out of the home, parents may want to provide college tuition and other types of support. In addition, an increasing number of grandparents are raising grandchildren, often without much financial help from the parents or the state. The consequence is that many grandfathers (and some grandmothers) delay retirement to support another generation of their families.

Family is one of the most-mentioned reasons women cite for retiring. Many decide to retire early because their husband (who is typically older) has retired, but this companionable-sounding statistic can be misleading. Many of these wives report that they feel pressured by their husbands to retire before they are ready to leave their jobs (Szinovacz & DeViney, 2000). Other couples resolve this dilemma when the husband remains in the labor force until the wife retires, believing that "solitary leisure" is not worth the reduction of income (Rix, 2011).

CAREER COMMITMENT   The reasons for retiring cannot all be evaluated with dollar amounts. Some people find their jobs unpleasant and stressful, and they count the days until they can retire. Others could not imagine life without their jobs and plan to stay as long as possible. This factor is *career commitment*; those who are self-employed and highly committed to their careers retire later than those who work for others or are less committed. Workers who have lower standards for their work output, less identification with the company, and more dissatisfaction with their jobs and supervisors are more apt to retire early, compared to those who do not share these attitudes.

LEISURE-TIME INTERESTS Another nonfinancial reason to retire is that life outside the workplace is calling. Workers who have hobbies, recreation interests, and active social lives are apt to retire earlier than those who do not. In addition, those who enjoy travel and doing home-improvement projects are more eager to retire.

7.5.4: Effects of Retirement

Once an adult has retired, what happens? Does life change totally? Does health decline? The striking fact is that for most adults, retirement itself has remarkably few effects on lifestyle, health, activity, or attitudes.

CHANGES IN INCOME Adults in the United States who are 65 and older have a variety of income sources, the major one being Social Security, which makes up about 37% of the average income for retirees. Figure 7.6 shows the proportion of income that comes from various sources (Federal Interagency Forum on Aging-Related Statistics, 2012). *Earnings* are from jobs they hold. *Pensions* are from private companies; state, local, or federal government; the military; or personal retirement accounts such as 401(k)s. *Asset income* is interest from savings, dividends from stock, and income from rental property.

Figure 7.6 Social Security is the largest source of income for people in the United States aged 65 and older, accounting for 37% of their income.

SOURCE: Data from Federal Interagency Forum on Aging-Related Statistics (2012).

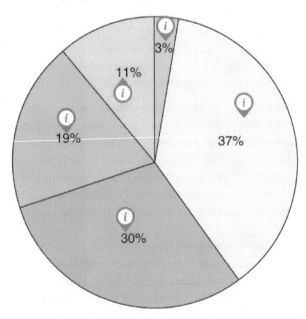

However, this doesn't tell us how the incomes of retired adults compare to their preretirement incomes. We know that income typically drops when retirement begins, but this may not have a negative effect on the retiree's lifestyle. Many own their homes free and clear and thus no longer have to make mortgage payments, their children are launched, they are eligible for Medicare and thus have potentially lower payments for health care, and they are entitled to many special senior-citizen bene-fits. When you include all these factors in the calculation, you find that many retirees have fewer expenses after they retire. In the United States, incomes for some older adults actually increase after retirement because the combination of Social Security and other government benefits is greater than the salaries they earned in their working years.

This upbeat report on the economic status of American elderly is possible primarily because of improvements in Social Security benefits in the United States over the past several decades. Indeed, the financial position of America's elderly has improved more than that of any other age group in recent years. As you can see in Figure 7.7, the percentage of people 65 and over who were living in poverty in 1966 was 28.5%; in 2010, the most recent year for which we have data, the number was 9% (Federal Interagency Forum on Age-Related Statistics, 2012).

But just as the figures on the drop in income with retirement are misleadingly pessimistic, the figures on the rate of poverty for retired persons are misleadingly optimistic. Although the number living below the official poverty line (which was $11,490 a year in 2013 for a person living alone) has indeed dropped, there are still a large percent-age in the category referred to as the "near poor," those whose incomes are between the poverty threshold and 25% above the poverty thresh-old (or $14,363 a year). In fact, this group is made up predominantly of older adults (U.S. Department of Health and Human Services, 2013). And because these older adults are ineligible for many special pro-grams designed to provide support for those whose incomes are below the poverty line, they are in many ways the worst off financially of any subset of the elderly.

Women have even more need than men to plan for retirement; at retirement age they have typically worked fewer years at lower salaries and have more years to live than their male counterparts.

Figure 7.7 The percent of older adults (65 years and older) living in poverty has declined slowly since the mid 1970s, whereas the percent of children (younger than 18 years) has increased. The percent of working age adults (18–64 years) have remained fairly stable.

SOURCE: Federal Interagency Forum on Age-Related Statistics (2012).

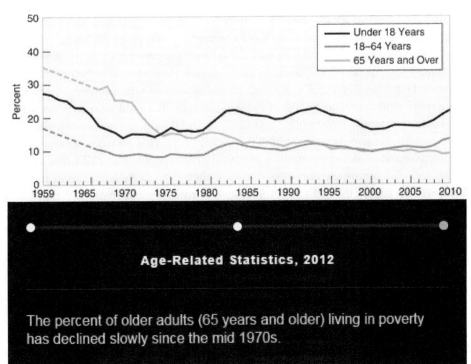

Age-Related Statistics, 2012

The percent of older adults (65 years and older) living in poverty has declined slowly since the mid 1970s.

Like other social ills, poverty in old age is not equally distributed across ethnic groups or gender. Older women are about twice as likely to be poor as older men, and black and Hispanic elders are considerably more likely to be poor than white elderly adults. Combining these two factors, we find that the group most likely to be poor is African-American women who are 65 and older living alone. Among this group, 43% live below the poverty line, and 54% are in the "twilight zone" of having incomes 25% above the poverty line. Finally, because women live longer than men, which means there are many more older women than men, we find that roughly two thirds of all the elderly poor are women (Costello, Wight, & Stone, 2003).

This **feminization of poverty**, in which we find a larger proportion of women than men among the poor, especially among older adults, has many causes. An obvious one is that so many older women are widowed. In the United States, the Social Security rules are such that when a woman becomes a widow, she is entitled to either her own Social Security benefits or 100% of her husband's Social Security benefits, whichever is higher. That may seem like a good deal, but in fact it results in a substantial drop in household income. When the husband was still alive, both spouses received pension support; after he dies, there is only one pension check, and the widow's total income will be somewhere between half and two thirds of the previous household income, even though many of her expenses, such as housing and taxes, stay the same. This drops a great many women into poverty (Gonyea & Hooyman, 2005).

It is too simple to attribute older women's greater likelihood of poverty simply to widowhood or living alone. The gendering of poverty in old age flows from a whole string of gender differences that women have experienced over their lifetimes and that come home to roost in their later years. Current cohorts of older women were much less likely to work throughout their adult years, less likely to be involved in private pension plans if they did work, and more likely to work at lower wages than their male peers, all of which affect their incomes at retirement. Add to this the facts I've already presented about women moving into and out of the labor force to raise children or to care for elderly family members. The result is that the women are less likely to receive pensions, and if they do, the amounts are lower than men receive. This leads to gender differences in personal income.

Some consolation is that married women this age can share their husbands' greater personal income, but almost half of women who enter retirement are widowed, divorced, or never married, making this "sharing" a moot point for them. Another consolation for younger women is that these figures represent a cohort of women whose roles did not necessarily include working outside the home or being involved in financial decisions. Hopefully, coming cohorts of women will reach retirement age with a more equitable distribution of personal income. It would be nice if we had a state-supported family-leave policy and other financial help for women who are the kinkeepers for so many, but the outlook is not optimistic. Women who choose to limit their income and career opportunities for family reasons, whether child care or caregiving for adult family members, need to look ahead and make adjustments in their financial plans so that they will be compensated fairly in their later years. Perhaps the feminization of poverty will be ancient history when young adults of today reach retirement age.

Many of the statistics I've given you are quite discouraging and give a very negative impression of the financial status of the elderly. But let us not lose sight of two bits of information I gave you at the beginning of this section: On average, the effective income of older adults declines only slightly at the time of retirement, and the elderly in the United States are better off financially now than ever in the past.

RETIREMENT AND CHANGES IN RESIDENCE Another effect of retirement for many adults is an increase in choices about where to live. When you are no longer tied to your job, you can choose to live nearer to one of your children or move south for sunnier weather. How many people this age move? The most recent report from the U.S. Census Bureau shows that between 2005 and 2010, about 15% of people who were 60 years of age or older moved, and the majority of those moved to residences within the same county. Only about 20 percent of those who moved went to another state, and just 2 percent moved out of the country to new residences abroad (Ihrke & Faber, 2012). Although this is a small group, it still represents a major decision and a life-changing event for these older adults.

Among those who engaged in **domestic migration**, about 19% made a move to another state or another region of the country. The states losing the most older adults to domestic migration were New York, Illinois, and California; the top destinations were Florida, Arizona, and Nevada. Most of the domestic migration can be explained by weather; older people are moving where the climate is warmer. In Europe, the same holds true; people of retirement age migrate to the south, and with travel restrictions between the European Union countries being relaxed, there has been a large increase in northern Europeans moving to southern Europe, especially people from Great Britain moving to Spain, Portugal, Greece, and Malta (Longino & Bradley, 2006).

Sociologist Charles Longino (2001) refers to the act of moving toward warmer weather and outdoor activities as an *amenity move*. In contrast, older retirees who move usually are going "back home," closer to their children and familiar surroundings, a process known as a *kinship move* and undertaken by about 18% of those who earlier made amenity moves. Finally, for some, there is a move to an assisted-living facility or some type of nursing home within the community. In Longino's terms, this is called an *institutional move*.

One large group that doesn't show up in the census figures are those who take part in **seasonal migration**, or "the snowbirds," as we in south Florida affectionately call them. These are retired people like my in-laws, who enjoyed the warm winters of the south and southwest but didn't want to make a complete break from home. They split the difference by spending winters in the sunshine and the summers in their home states. These seasonal migrants tend to be white, healthy, educated, in their 70s, and married. Almost all are homeowners back north, and surprisingly, over 80% own their winter residences also. About two thirds of the snowbirds in Florida have made the annual migration for at least 10 years (Smith & House, 2005).

What happens when snowbirds get older? They stay "back home" year-round. Only a small number relocate permanently to their vacation homes; most shorten their visits as their health declines and then reluctantly end their seasonal stays when they can no longer make the move, or when one of them dies.

7.5.5: Alternatives to Full Retirement

Sociologist Sara E. Rix (2011) tells us that today, older workers do not fit the stereotype of working full time until retirement and then not working at all. Instead, most workers now go from full-time work to full-time retirement in stages that consist of various types of transitional employment. The following section tells about some of these alternatives to full retirement.

SHUNNING RETIREMENT We all hear about middle-aged people who claim to enjoy work so much that they plan to keep working when they reach retirement age, even if they have comfortable pensions. If you are like me, you might be skeptical about these forecasts, but, about one third of people 65 and over are still in the labor force (Toosi, 2012). These "retirement shunners" are often highly educated individuals in professions like academia, where their personal lives blend into their professional lives, and they are highly motivated and involved in their work. Many have spouses who are in similar professions and share their dedication to work. Another group that continues working as long as possible is at the other end of the spectrum—lower-income workers who have little education and low wages. Often they have no retirement pensions except Social Security, so simply cannot afford to retire.

RETURNING TO THE WORKFORCE   A number of workers retire and then reenter the labor market at some point after their retirement, either in a different job or in a similar job with a different company. My grandfather, whom I used as an example of retirement earlier in this chapter, did just this. A few years after receiving his gold watch, he returned to work for my father in his new plumbing business. He worked with my dad for 8 years, helping him get the business up and running, and then retired again. The practice of going back to work after retirement is done by about 25% of older workers who exit the labor force (Maestas, 2007). Again, the reasons are myriad—need for income, loneliness, need to feel useful, restlessness. A few even make another attempt at retirement and then go back to work for a third time!

GRADUAL RETIREMENT   Another nontraditional exit from the labor force is to retire and take a **bridge job**, which can be a part-time job or a less stressful full-time job. This is done by about 45% of retired men, especially those who retire at early ages from jobs such as police work, the military, and other government jobs. Often the job is related to their careers—for instance, police officers who take jobs as security guards or as police officers in smaller towns. Others take their knowledge and expertise into the classroom and become teachers. Some enjoy the social interaction that comes with being supermarket baggers or discount store greeters.

The downside of these bridge jobs are that they typically pay less and have fewer benefits than full-time work. Research shows that older adults who remain in the labor force are better educated, healthier, and wealthier than younger workers, but are paid less—perhaps because they have traded good pay for shorter hours and flexibility (Johnson, Kawachi, & Lewis, 2009).

A popular option for retirees is self-employment. A large number of self-employed workers start up their businesses after the age of 50, presumably as a bridge job or as a way to turn a hobby into an income-producing activity (Rix, 2011). My father-in-law, for example, retired from his job with the police force in a small New England town and started a lawn service in his neighborhood. He had always enjoyed doing yard work, but with a large family to support, it was never a career option. Once he retired, he spent several days a week during spring and summer on "his lawns" in Massachusetts. When fall came he raked the leaves one last time and then headed for Florida until it was time to go back north for the spring fertilizer sale.

VOLUNTEER WORK   If you have visited a hospital, a school, or a museum lately, you have no doubt had contact with a retired person who donates his or her time to your community. Over a quarter of adults over the age of 55 years in the United States, the majority of them being retired, contribute their time to various community services (U.S. Bureau of Labor Statistics, 2015). To give you an idea of the contribution these people make, the volunteer force of the National Senior Services Corps (which includes the Foster Grandparents Program, the Retired and Senior Volunteer Program—RSVP, and the Senior Companion Program) consists of over 337,000 persons 55 years of age and older. They tutor, counsel, care for, and mentor children; provide social support and instrumental support for the frail and elderly; and staff community projects such as blood drives and health-awareness seminars (National Senior Services Corps, 2012).

Volunteering in retirement is a two-way street. Numerous cross-sectional and lon-gitudinal studies have shown that older adults who do volunteer work receive increases in all sorts of well-being: happiness, life satisfaction, self-esteem, self-control, physical health, and longevity (Cutler, Hendricks, & O'Neill, 2011). Other studies show similar results for elders in Japan (Sugihara, Sugisawa, & Harada, 2008), Australia (Windsor, Anstey, & Rodgers, 2008), and Israel (Shmotkin, Blumstein, & Modan, 2003). The benefits older adults receive from volunteering is greater than the benefits received by people of other ages, and some speculate that it is because it helps compensate for the loss of other roles in their lives, such as hands-on par-ent, spouse, or worker (Greenfield & Marks, 2004).

PHASED RETIREMENT   Phased moves from full-time work to permanent retire-ment are usually designed by the employer and offered as an option for senior employees. This practice is more common in Japan and some European countries than in the United States. In Japan, where companies set mandatory retirement ages, workers reaching that age are given a lump-sum retirement settlement and have the option of (a) exiting the workforce completely, (b) joining a family business or start-ing their own business, or (c) taking a part-time job with the same company at lower wages (Usui, 1998).

The benefits of this retirement plan for workers are obvious. They have their retirement cake and eat it too. They have the lump-sum payment, but are not shut out of the workforce. They can still feel the pride and social support that come from hav-ing a job, plus more free time and a part-time salary. The employers have top-level workers at reduced salaries who can be placed in whatever section of the company that needs the help, often serving as mentors or troubleshooters. And there is the over-all benefit of keeping valued seniors in the workplace while still freeing up full-time jobs for younger workers.

The closest thing we have to this is something called **phased retirement**, a situa-tion in which an older person is working for an employer part time as a transition to retirement. In these situations, the worker may be receiving some retirement benefits while still employed. However, there are all sorts of tax problems involved, and workers usually have to officially retire and be hired back in the new capacity, thus risking the loss of employee benefits. Surveys show that workers would favor phased retirement if it meant they could collect pension benefits while remaining on the payroll in a reduced capacity, so this may become easier for U.S. companies in the near future.

7.6: A Concluding Note on Work and Retirement

7.6   **Summarize retirement planning to be the most important for a happy retired life**

I have reviewed changes in careers over the years of adulthood in Table 7.3, and I would like to conclude this chapter with some words of wisdom. When retired men and women were surveyed about which stage of their lives had been the best, 75% of those who had done extensive planning for their retirement years responded with "the best is now." Only 45% of those who had not done much planning rated their current stage as best (Quick & Moen, 1998). Considering all we have covered on this topic, it seems clear to me that (to paraphrase an old joke) the three most important factors for successful retirement are planning, planning, and planning.

Table 7.3 Review of Changes in Careers over Adulthood

18–24 Years	25–39 Years	40–64 Years	65–74 Years	75+ Years
Vocational interests are present as early as the teen years for some emerging adults. Identity is achieved in stages, which includes vocational interests.	Vocational interests are acted on in selections of first jobs, college majors, or vocational training. Changes are made until a good job–vocational interest fit is reached and career is established.	Middle-aged adults usually remain in the same career but change employers as they advance. Some workers retrain for new jobs due to layoffs in the 40s and early 50s. In late 50s and early 60s, they tend to take early retirement if laid off.	A growing number of workers continue their careers well past traditional retirement age. Some leave their major jobs and take bridge jobs that are less stressful or involve fewer hours. Others lend their skills and expertise as volunteer workers. Some workers this age retire and then return to work again, sometimes several times, depending on their health and expenses.	A small number keep working into their late 70s and later because they enjoy their work or they need the income.
Both males and females have part-time or entry-level jobs that may not be related to adult vocations.	Men tend to move into the full-time labor force and remain until retirement. Women move into and out of the full-time labor force as they have children and care for them.	The departure of children from home leads women to start new careers or take on new responsibilities in existing jobs.	Women retire at an earlier age than men. They are more apt to be widows and have lower retirement income and more chronic health conditions than men. They are more apt to live at or below the poverty line, especially black women.	This age group is predominantly widowed women. Many reap the results of a lifetime of gender inequality at this stage. Others with good financial resources and generous families do better.
Variable job performance.	Job performance increases with experience and, for men, as family obligations increase.	Job performance remains high despite declines in physical and cognitive abilities, probably due to expertise.	Job performance remains high for experts and those who maintain a high level of practice.	Most who are working do adequate jobs, but show a slowing down and lack of stamina compared to younger workers.

The beginnings of job–family interactions.	Job–family intersection is difficult during this time as most couples combine careers, marriages, and children.	Job–family intersection is easier, but now can include caregiving for elderly parents or surrogate parenting of grandchildren.	Family responsibilities seldom interfere with work, although some older workers leave work to become caregivers for their spouses.	Too few are working to make an evaluation.
Little thought of retirement.	A few begin long-term financial planning.	Preparation for retirement begins in the 40s and early 50s, especially for men.	People this age are eligible for Social Security and Medicare, but the average senior depends on other sources for 60% of his or her income. Women have less retirement income than men their age from every source.	Many this age have retired once (or twice) already.
Moves involve college or military involvement.	Residential moves at this age are usually related to career moves (or spouses' career moves).	Some early-retired people make amenity moves to areas with warm weather and leisure activities. Others become "snowbirds."	Some who are in good health continue to live in retirement areas or commute in the winter. Those in declining health move to be closer to family.	Some enter assisted-living communities or skilled care facilities. Most remain in their homes.

Hide All Cells Show All Cells

Summary: Work and Retirement

LISTEN TO THE AUDIO:

05:22

1. For most adults, career is a lifelong pattern of full-time and part-time work, time out for family responsibilities and retraining, and ultimately retirement pursuits. It occupies a central part of our time, thoughts, personal identity, and self-esteem.

2. The major theory in the field of vocational psychology for decades has been the life-space/life-span theory of Donald Super. His model shows the stages of career and the tasks that must be done at each stage. It takes into account that career must be integrated with other roles in life.

3. There are gender differences in the typical career paths of men and women. Women are less apt to work

full time, more apt to move into and out of the labor force, and more apt to work part time than men. The result for women is lower income, less chance for advancement, fewer benefits during the work years, and less retirement income than men.

4. The best-known theory of career selection is that of John L. Holland, who suggests that people are happiest in job environments that fit their vocational interests. Holland devised tests to evaluate people on five types of vocational interests.

5. Emerging adulthood is a time of identity achievement, as young people go through the stages of identity diffusion, foreclosure, moratorium, and commitment, with career decisions being a large part of this identity.

6. Gender is a big factor in career selection. Both men and women tend to select careers that are stereotypically defined as gender-appropriate. Unfortunately, the "female" jobs usually pay less and have fewer benefits and chances of advancement than the "male" jobs. Studies of men and women who have chosen nontraditional jobs are giving some useful insight into the career-selection process. Other factors are family influences and genetics.

7. Although physical, sensory, and cognitive declines accompany age, measures of actual job performance show no age-related declines. One explanation is that the expertise of older adults compensates for decline in abilities.

8. Older workers express more satisfaction in their work lives than younger workers. There are many explanations for this, including attrition, cohort effects, and types of jobs each age group has.

9. Job stress can have negative effects on the individual, including burnout, but not having a job can be even worse. Unemployment is a serious life crisis for most adults, and even more serious for middle-aged workers than for those of other ages. Even the possibility of job loss can cause stressful reactions.

10. Marriage seems to increase work performance and goals for both men and women. Work conditions can affect marriage stability. Divorce rates are related to situations in which one partner works a night shift or the wife works a rotating shift.

11. Men are apt to work more hours the more children they have. Women are apt to work fewer hours the more children they have. Whether a mother works outside the home does not influence the well-being of her children one way or another. More important factors are the home environment, day care quality, the parents' marriage, and the stability of the mother's employment. The workplace could be changed in a number of ways to fit the realities of today's families.

12. Over one fourth of all workers are also caregivers for a frail or disabled adult family member. The workplace could also be changed in a number of ways to fit this reality.

13. Mothers who work full time outside the home spend slightly more time on child care and housework than their husbands, who spend slightly more time on work and work-related activities. When one partner works part time or does not work outside the home at all, the gender division is more traditional.

14. There are many factors that influence the decision to retire. Among them are finances, health, family, career commitment, and leisure-time interests.

15. For most people, retirement brings slightly lower incomes but also lower expenses. More women live in poverty after retirement than men, partly due to women's greater longevity, but also because of lower lifetime earnings, pensions, and savings.

16. For some, retirement brings a change of residence to another part of the country, or the beginning of a pattern of seasonal migration to warmer parts of the country.

17. Nontraditional ways to leave the labor force include shunning retirement, taking a less stressful job, working part time, and working as a volunteer.

SHARED WRITING: CAREER SELECTION

Consider this chapter's discussion of career selection and how your career goals have fluctuated since childhood. What role did factors such as gender and family place in these changing career goals? How have these factors changed since your parents' generation (for better or worse)? Write a short response that your classmates will read. Be sure to discuss specific examples.

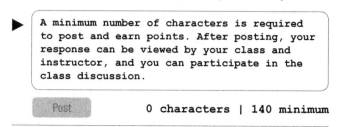

► A minimum number of characters is required to post and earn points. After posting, your response can be viewed by your class and instructor, and you can participate in the class discussion.

Post   0 characters | 140 minimum

Chapter 7 Quiz: Work and Retirement

Chapter 8
Personality

Learning Objectives

8.1 Explain the trait theory of personality stability during adult years

8.2 State the factors that influence personality traits

8.3 Explain the early theories of personality development

LISTEN TO THE AUDIO:

`▶ ●━━━━━━ 02:05 ◀×●`

GROWING UP IN a large extended family is like having instant access to longitudinal information about a variety of human behaviors. One may not have observed all the "participants" through all the stages of their lives, but there are always older relatives to provide the missing "data." For example, as children my sister Rose and I always enjoyed spending time with our grandmother's older sister, Aunt May. She was a retired teacher, had no children, and had never married, but her home was designed for children's visits. She had a chess board, a Scrabble game, and a set of dominoes tucked under her sofa. There was a huge porch swing, an endless supply of homebaked cookies, and a workroom devoted to pottery complete with a potter's wheel and kiln—the site of many "mud parties" she hosted for the kids in the family.

After one particularly fun-filled visit to her house, we commented to our mother that Aunt May was probably so patient and so much fun in her old age because she missed having children herself, but our mother laughed and said, "Oh no, Aunt May has always been good with children and a lot of fun. Age doesn't change a person's basic qualities. She was having 'mud and cookie' parties when I was your age and she was in her 40s. And your grandmother said May was like a second mother to her—always watching out for the younger kids in the family and making up games to amuse them."

Although our mother was not a research psychologist, she was voicing the basic concept of personality stability within an individual over the life span. I think most of us have our own theories about personality and age, some based on personal experience within our own families and some based on stereotypes. This chapter delves into this complex topic and should sort things out a bit, sometimes supporting our personal theories and sometimes replacing them with others.

8.1: Personality Structures

8.1 Explain the trait theory of personality stability during adult years

Personality consists of a relatively enduring set of characteristics that define our individuality and affect our interactions with the environment and other people. The study of personality psychology encompasses a large range of interesting topics—traits, motivations, emotions, the self, coping strategies, and the like. In fact, before you took your first psychology course, this is probably what you thought the field was all about. It is one of the oldest specialties in psychology and has been a very active forum in the study of adult development. The main question is: What happens to personality as we go through adulthood and into old age? There appear to be only two possible answers to this question: Either personality is continuous or it changes. However, research over four decades has shown that the answer is not so simple. A better answer is, "It depends." First, it depends on which type of continuity or change is being studied. Then, it depends on which personality factor we are interested in. And furthermore, it depends on the age of the adults being studied, their life experiences, genetic makeup, and the way the data are gathered (Alea, Diehl, & Bluck, 2004). So if you like mental roller-coaster rides, hang on!

My plan of attack for this topic is to cover research based on trait theory that argues generally for personality stability across most of the adult years. Then, I will tackle some recent research based on traditional developmental theories that argues for a good deal of change in personality over adulthood. I will add a section on positive psychology and, finally, try to tie it all together.

8.1.1: Personality Traits and Factors

The early formulations of personality come from people whose names are familiar to you, such as Freud, Jung, and Erikson, developmental theorists whose ideas were based on the premise that many aspects of adult life, including personality, are dynamic and evolving throughout the life span in predictable ways. Many of these theories were based on specific changes at specific ages brought about by resolution of tension between competing forces in life. (I will discuss some of these theories in more detail later in this chapter along with some current research based on their concepts of personality.) About 25 years ago, a new generation of personality psychologists began arguing that it wasn't enough to have a popular theory that was enthusiastically endorsed; it was also important for a personality theory to be empirically tested and validated (McCrae & Costa, 1990). Therefore, it was necessary to define personality more precisely. One of the biggest problems was deciding just what the "enduring characteristics" were that should be studied empirically. What are the basic **personality traits**, or patterns of thoughts, feelings, and behaviors exhibited by our human species?

A good example of a personality trait is how a person typically behaves in social situations. Some people are retiring, and some are outgoing. If you think of several people you know well and consider how they usually act around other people, you can probably arrange them along a continuum from most outgoing to most retiring. The continuum represents a personality trait, and the position each of your friends occupies along that dimension between outgoing and retiring illustrates how they rate on this trait. I use the term *typically* here so as not to confuse personality traits with **personality states**, which are more short-term characteristics of a person. If you go to a party after an argument with your best friend, your usual outgoing *trait* may be eclipsed by your withdrawn *state*, but your trait is still outgoing.

WRITING PROMPT

Think of what your closet looks like today. Where would that put you on the "orderly—messy" continuum? Does this reflect a trait for you or a state? Write a brief response that will be read by your instructor. Be sure to explain your reasoning and use specific examples.

► ┌───┐
  │ The response entered here will appear in the performance dashboard │
  │ and can be viewed by your instructor.   │
  └───┘

  [Submit]

Personality traits were not new to psychology in 1990. To the contrary, there were too many of them: "Thousands of words, hundreds of published scales, and dozens of trait systems competed for the researcher's or reviewer's attention. How could one make any generalization about the influence of age on personality traits when there appear to be an unlimited number of traits?" (Costa & McCrae, 1997, p. 271). The solution was to narrow down the great number of personality traits into a small number of **personality factors**, groups of traits that occur together in individuals. For example, if people who score high in modesty also score high in compliance (and those who score low in one also score low in the other), it stands to reason that tests that evaluate modesty and compliance are probably tapping into the same well. The basic question was: How many different wells (or factors) are there?

Personality psychologists Robert McCrae and Paul Costa (1987) started with two dimensions that had been long agreed on, Neuroticism (N) and Extraversion (E). By using a procedure called factor analysis, they found evidence for three more factors: Openness (O), Agreeableness (A), and Conscientiousness (C). The result of this work was the **Five-Factor Model (FFM)** of personality (also known as the "Big Five Model," although to my knowledge, neither Costa nor McCrae has ever used this term). Since that time, they have devised and revised a test instrument, the latest version of which is called the Revised NEO Personality Inventory. This inventory has been translated into many languages and been administered with similar results to people representing a large number of backgrounds. Basically, researchers have found that no matter what the ages of the individuals tested or what their gender or cultural background, people's personality traits fell into patterns around these five factors, or personality structures. These five factors are shown in Table 8.1 along with some of the traits that are clustered within them.

Table 8.1 Five Factors of Personality and the Traits They Include

⊗ Neuroticism (N)

- Anxiety
- Angry hostility
- Depression
- Self-consciousness
- Impulsivity
- Vulnerability

⊗ Conscientiousness (C)

- Competence
- Order
- Dutifulness
- Achievement striving
- Self-discipline
- Deliberation

⊗ Extraversion (E)

- Warmth
- Gregariousness
- Assertiveness
- Activity
- Excitement seeking
- Positive emotions

⊗ Agreeableness (A)

- Warmth
- Trust
- Straightforwardness
- Altruism
- Compliance
- Modesty
- Tender-mindedness

⊗ Openness (O)

- Fantasy
- Aesthetics
- Feelings
- Actions
- Ideas
- Values

SOURCE: Adapted from McCrae & John (1992).

The Five-Factor Model is not the only factor analysis model of personality, and the NEO Personality Inventory is not the only test used to evaluate personality traits. There are also the familiar Minnesota Multiphasic Personality Inventory (MMPI), the California Psychological Inventory (CPI; Gough, 1957/1987), the Sixteen Personality Factor Questionnaire (16PF; Cattell, Eber, & Tatsuoka, 1970), and others. Currently, the Five-Factor Model is the standard, and when other tests are used, their factors are often converted to the terminology of the NEO Personality Inventory. But regardless of the test used, researchers had defined a limited set of personality factors and the traits that fell within them to begin scientific research on the question of what happens to personality over the course of adulthood.

Critical Thinking

In Table 8.1, look over the traits listed under the personality factor Neuroticism. How might high levels of each contribute to the demise of romantic relationships? What relationship effects might the traits in the Agreeableness factor have?

8.1.2: Differential Continuity

Now that the history and methodology have been covered, what does the study of personality factors tell us about personality continuity and change? One way of conceptualizing what happens to personality over adulthood is to investigate **differential continuity**, which refers to the stability of individuals' rank order within a group over time. In other words, do the most extraverted participants at Time 1 (for example, age 20) remain among the most extraverted participants at Time 2 (for example, age 50)? And do the lowest-ranked participants still score in the lowest ranks of Extraversion 30 years later? This type of question is usually answered by correlating the ranking order for the group of participants at Time 1 with their rankings at Time 2. If the correlation coefficient is positive and sufficiently high, it means the group generally stays in the same rank order, and that the personality factor (in this case, Extraversion), is considered moderately stable. More interesting, comparisons can be made between intervals in young adulthood (for example, age 20 to age 30) and then again in older adulthood (for example, age 50 to age 60), assessing whether this personality factor is more stable at one time of life than another.

Using this method, we know that personality traits remain moderately stable throughout adulthood and that their stability increases with age (we get "stabler and stabler"). This is even true when the time period from childhood to early adulthood is included, which has long been thought to be a time of life-changing roles and identity decisions. Figure 8.1 shows the rank-order correlations from childhood to late adulthood, reflecting data from 152 studies of personality (Roberts & DelVecchio, 2000). As you can see, there is an increase in rank-order stability from age 6 to age 73. Other things we know about rank-order stability are that these patterns don't differ much from one personality factor to another, show no gender differences, and are very similar no matter what type of assessment method is used (Caspi, Roberts, & Shiner 2005).

Figure 8.1 Differential continuity is demonstrated in results from 152 studies showing that individuals' correlations from age to age in scores on various personality tests remain high from early childhood through late adulthood and increase in middle adulthood. People ranking high in some personality trait at one age tend to rank high in that trait on tests given to them at later ages, and the same is true for people who are in the middle or lower ranks.

SOURCE: Roberts & DelVecchio (2000).

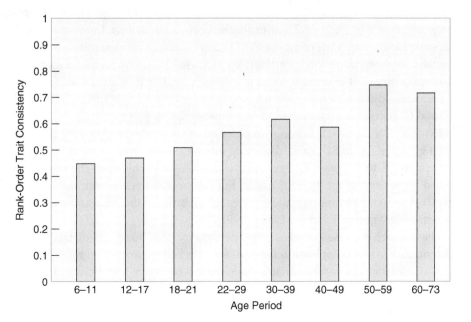

In summary, personality traits are surprisingly stable during childhood and throughout adulthood, increasing steadily until about age 50 and then leveling off. Even in the oldest groups, there is a correlation coefficient of around 0.70, which means that total stability has not been reached (as it would if the coefficient were 1.00), showing that there are still some changes taking place in rank order.

WRITING PROMPT

In your high school class, the guy who drove too fast and always left studying until the last possible moment would probably have ranked among the highest of your group in "excitement seeking." If he maintained that top ranking in your group, what behaviors might you expect of him at your 20-year class reunion? And if your class decided to retire together to a condo community in Florida in your 60s, what behaviors would you anticipate from him at that age? Write a brief response that will be read by your instructor. Be sure to give specific examples and explain your reasoning.

▶ The response entered here will appear in the performance dashboard and can be viewed by your instructor.

Submit

8.1.3: Mean-Level Change

The concept of **mean-level change** refers to changes in a group's average scores over time. If your first-year college class was tested on some personality measure (for example, Conscientiousness) and then tested again in your senior year, would the averages of the group change significantly? And if so, why? Mean-level change is attributed to such factors as maturation (such as menopause for women at midlife) or cultural processes shared by a population (such as the normative changes of completing school, starting a career, and leaving the parental home).

In a cross-sectional study of participants from five different cultures, those over 30 showed higher mean-level scores for Agreeableness and Conscientiousness, and those under 30 showed higher scores for Extraversion, Openness, and Neuroticism (McCrae, Costa, Pedroso de Lima, et al., 1999). In a similar study, researchers divided Extraversion into two components, Social Dominance and Social Vitality. Then, in a review of three cross-sectional studies and three longitudinal studies, they showed that Social Dominance increases with age between 20 and 80 years, whereas Social Vitality decreases (Helson & Kwan, 2000).

In a meta-analysis of 92 studies, researchers found that personality factors not only changed with age, but also showed distinct patterns of change. These patterns of change are shown in Figure 8.2. For example, Conscientiousness, Emotional Stability, and Social Dominance (one component of Extraversion) showed significant increases, especially in young adulthood. Participants increased in Openness and Social Vitality (a second component of extraversion) in adolescence, but then decreased in old age. Agreeableness did not increase much from adolescence to middle age, but did increase at 50 and 60 years (Roberts, Walton, & Viechtbauer, 2006).

Evidence for mean-level change in older adults is similar; personality trait scores from a group of 74- to 84-year-old participants were compared to an older group of participants 85 to 92 years of age, and researchers reported that the older group showed higher scores for Agreeableness. Furthermore, 14 years later, the "younger" group had shown an increase in these traits, which brought them up to the level of the original "older" group (Field & Millsap, 1991).

The message from these studies is that personality does change predictably with age and continues to change at least to the age of 92. We become more and more agreeable, more conscientious, more emotionally stable (or less neurotic), and more socially dominant. We become more open and socially vital in young adulthood, but then decline in old age. These patterns seem to be independent of gender and cultural influences.

Figure 8.2 Cumulative change for six personality traits show distinct patterns across the life span.

SOURCE: Roberts, Walton, & Viechtbauer (2006).

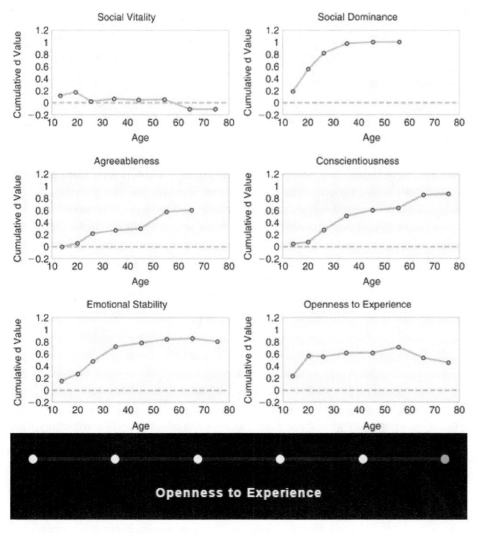

8.1.4: Intra-Individual Variability

Another way to chart the progress of personality traits over adulthood is to look at **intra-individual variability**, or in other words, find out whether the personality traits of an individual remain stable over the years or change. This is done by giving personality tests to individuals at several points in time and then correlating each person's scores from Time 1 with the scores for Time 2, and so on. This is not the same as differential stability because you are correlating the actual scores, not the rank order. One of the few studies of this type was an examination of self-confidence measures in women over a 30-year period. Researchers found several patterns of increase and decline during those years (Jones & Meredith, 1996). Another study of intra-individual variability correlated five-factor scores for men between the ages of 43 and 91, finding that most showed declines in Neuroticism and no changes in Extraversion with age. However, this was not true for all the participants, and many showed different patterns of individual variability even in very late adulthood (Mroczek & Spiro, 2003). More recent studies have shown that scores on all five factors of personality show "unmistakable variability" in the rate and direction of change for individuals (Roberts & Mroczek, 2008).

Another important question addressed by researchers is: can personality be changed intentionally? For example, psychologist Carol Dweck (2008) argued that personality is based on beliefs about the self and that it is possible to change some of those beliefs and, as a result, change personality. One set of beliefs that Dweck used in her research involved what people believe about their own intelligence. Those who believe that their intelligence is malleable, that it can be improved, tend to be more open to learning, more willing to face challenges and persevere, and more resilient after failure—all traits that are important in school and adult life. People who believe that their intelligence is fixed tend not to demonstrate those characteristics. In a number of experiments, people with fixed beliefs about their intelligence changed their way of thinking after receiving information about the brain and how new connections can be made when learning takes place. Once they believed that their intelligence was malleable, they began showing traits of openness, perseverance, and resilience similar to those who expressed malleable beliefs at the beginning of the study (Blackwell, Trzesniewski, & Dweck, 2007).

A similar study targeted African-American college students who were entering historically white institutions. When the students were taught that their feelings of apprehension were normal, but would not last long, and were given personal testimonies from second-year African-American students telling them about their positive experiences, they reported better feelings of acceptance, took more challenging courses the following semester, were more apt to reach out to their professors for help, and made better grades than students in a control group (Walton & Cohen, 2007). Not only do aspects of personality seem to change over time, but it is also possible to devise methods of changing maladaptive traits using fairly simple interventions.

8.1.5: Continuity, Change, and Variability Coexist

How do human personality structures within a group show differential continuity, mean-level change, and intra-individual variability over time? It's quite possible to understand if you consider it in terms of something more familiar, such as exam scores. For example, I generally give three exams in my class on adolescent psychology. The class shows differential continuity because those who are the top students on the first exam are usually the top students on the second and third exams too, whereas those at the bottom of the grading scale tend to remain in that rank order. However, there is also considerable mean-level change. The average score for the first exam is always significantly lower than the later exams. Some students don't take the subject matter seriously and are shocked to see questions about genetics, brain structures, and research findings. Others explain that they need to take one exam in a class before they know what to study for the next ones. Whatever the reason, almost everyone improves on the second exam, showing mean-level change for the class alongside differential continuity. And there is also intra-individual variability. Although most students follow the patterns described thus far, there are exceptions each semester. A student can start off strong with a top grade on the first exam, then get inundated with work as the semester goes on, floundering on the later exams as a result of trying to burn the candle at both ends. Another can start out strong, get frazzled at midterm, and then buckle down to pull up the grade on the final. The result is differential continuity, mean-level change, and intra-individual variability, all in the same class. And the same is true for personality traits across adulthood.

8.1.6: What Do Personality Traits Do?

As discussed already in this chapter, researchers have identified five major personality factors and a large number of traits associated with one factor or another, and they have explained the patterns of stability and change across adulthood, but recently work has been done on just what personality traits do other than define our uniqueness. Three areas have been identified that are shaped by personality: relationships, achievement, and health (Caspi, Roberts, & Shiner, 2004).

PERSONALITY AND RELATIONSHIPS   Personality traits are important in the development of intimate relationships in adulthood. Neuroticism and Agreeableness in particular are strong predictors of relationship outcome. The higher a person is in Neuroticism and the lower in Agreeableness, the more apt he or she is to be in conflicted, dissatisfying, and abusive relationships, and the more quickly the relationships will dissolve (Karney & Bradbury, 1995). In a longitudinal study that followed the relationships of adolescents into adulthood, researchers found that high levels of Neuroticism predicted that the individual would repeat the same negative experiences from relationship to relationship (Ehrensaft, Moffitt, & Caspi, 2004).

The influence of personality on intimate relationships happens in at least three ways. First, personality helps determine with whom we choose to have a relationship, often someone with a similar personality. For example, a person who is high in Neuroticism would tend to seek a relationship with a person who shares that trait. Second, personality helps determine how we behave toward our partners and how we react to our partner's behavior. A person high in Neuroticism who is in a relationship with a similar person will express negative behavior toward the partner and will meet the partner's negative behavior with further escalation of negativity. And third, personality evokes certain behaviors from one's partners. For example, people high in Neuroticism and low in Agreeableness express behaviors that are known to be destructive to relationships: criticism, contempt, defensiveness, and stonewalling, behaviors that psychologist John Gottman (2011) has identified as very good predictors of future breakup or divorce.

Research in this area is currently limited to intimate partnerships, but personality could be useful in exploring relationship dynamics between parents and children, friends, employers and employees, and within groups.

PERSONALITY AND ACHIEVEMENT   The personality traits that make up the factor of Conscientiousness are the most important predictors of a number of work-related markers of achievement, such as occupational attainment and job performance (Judge, Higgins, Thoreson, et al., 1999). The traits included in this factor include competence, order, dutifulness, and self-discipline. In fact, if you look around your classroom, you will probably see a lot of Conscientiousness being displayed because it also predicts academic achievement. These traits are integral to completing work effectively, paying attention, striving toward high standards, and inhibiting impulsive thoughts and behavior.

The traits involved in Conscientiousness could affect job achievement in several ways. First, people choose niches (jobs) that fit their personality traits. We feel comfortable doing things we are good at and get pleasure from. Second, people who display these behaviors are singled out by others to be given jobs and promotions. Third are selection processes; people who are not conscientious leave high-achievement jobs (or are asked to leave). And fourth is the obvious fact that people who are high in Conscientiousness actually do the job better (Caspi, Roberts, & Shiner, 2004).

Researchers have shown that all five of the personality factors predict good job performance if the job is a good match for the personality (Judge, Higgins, Thoreson, et al., 1999).

I also want to point out that these findings about personality traits and achievement depend on gender expectations and sociocultural contexts of the times. What is valid for today's adults may not have been the same for earlier cohorts of women. Psychologist Linda K. George and her colleagues (George, Helson, & John, 2011) examined longitudinal data on the Mills College women, born between 1935 and 1939 and found that women high in Conscientiousness during the college years were not more likely to be involved in careers than their classmates because they were adhering to their culturally defined roles of wife and mother. In fact, women high in Conscientiousness were more apt to report high commitment to their family roles all through their adult years. They had lower divorce rates, and their lack of career involvement did not handicap them financially in retirement because they had been conscientious about selecting a spouse who was a good provider. Clearly the same personality trait that drives a young woman today to attend college and excel at her chosen career might have driven her great-grandmother to take cooking lessons and work hard to keep her marriage strong.

PERSONALITY TRAITS AND HEALTH   The most dramatic finding about personality is that it is closely related to health and longevity. People who have high levels of Conscientiousness (Hill, Turiano, Hurd, et al., 2011) and low levels of Neuroticism (Danner, Snowdon, & Friesen, 2001) tend to live longer. Other studies show that people low in Agreeableness (having high levels of anger and hostility) are at higher risk for heart disease (Miller, Smith, Turner, et al., 1996), and those who are high in Neuroticism report lower levels of mental and physical health (Löckenhoff, Sutin, Ferrucci, et al., 2008).

This link between personality traits and health can take place in a number of ways. First, personality can directly affect the functioning of the body, as seems to be the case with the link between hostility and heart disease. The physiological reactions summoned by hostility act directly as pathogens to cause disease. Second, personality can lead to behaviors that either promote health or undermine health. People who are high in Agreeableness are more likely to have close relationships with supportive people, a factor known to be a buffer against stress-related diseases. People high in Neuroticism are more likely to smoke and indulge in other high-risk health behaviors, whereas those high in Conscientiousness are more likely to have regular checkups, watch their diets (Caspi, Roberts, & Shiner, 2004), and follow their doctors' orders (Hill & Roberts, 2011). And fourth, personality may be linked with the type of coping behaviors there are in one's repertoire and which ones a person chooses to use when confronted with stress (Scheier & Carver, 1993).

In a meta-analysis of 194 studies, psychologist Brent Roberts and his colleagues (Roberts, Walton, & Bogg, 2005) correlated scores on Conscientiousness-related traits (review Table 8.1) and nine different health behaviors, such as drug use, risky driving, and unsafe sex practices. Conscientiousness was significantly correlated with each of them, meaning that knowing a person's score on Conscientiousness would allow you to predict his or her likelihood of engaging in these health behaviors. The results are shown in Figure 8.3. As you can see, drug use, violence, risky driving, and excessive alcohol use show the largest correlations. The lower one's Conscientiousness score, the

---

Figure 8.3 Conscientiousness is negatively correlated with a number of health-related behaviors. The higher the Conscientiousness score, the less likely a person will engage in drug use, violence, risky driving, excessive alcohol use, and other unhealthy behaviors.

SOURCE: Roberts, Walton, & Bogg (2005).

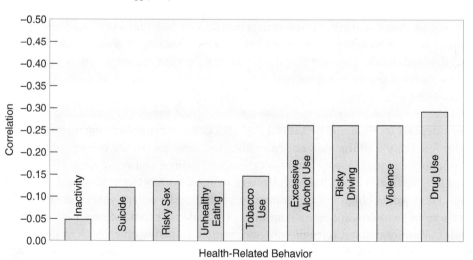

more likely one is to engage in those behaviors. Other behaviors shown in Figure 8.3 had smaller correlations, but were still significantly predicted by Conscientiousness. As the authors stated, "People who are not conscientious have quite a number of ways to experience premature mortality. They can die through car accidents, through acquisition of AIDS via risky sexual practices, through violent activities such as fights and suicides, and through drug overdoses. People can still suffer from an attenuated life span in middle age through not eating well, not exercising, and smoking tobacco, which all lead to heart disease and cancer" (Roberts, Walton, & Bogg, 2005, p. 161).

An additional way personality traits can influence health was suggested by Roberts and his colleagues (Roberts, Smith, Jackson, et al., 2009). Using data from over 2,000 older adults, the researchers found that Conscientiousness contributes not only to one's own good health, but also to the good health of one's spouse. Men who had wives with high scores on Conscientiousness reported better health than those with low-scoring wives, and the same was true for women who had husbands with high scores in Conscientiousness. The reasons seem clear—within a long-term marriage, conscientious persons take care of their own health and also that of their spouse.

Personality traits also contribute to one's subjective health when in the role of an informal caregiver, a role many people will face during late middle age. In a study of over 500 informal caregivers, those who were high in Conscientiousness and Extraversion, and low in Neuroticism, reported better mental and physical health. In addition, Agreeableness was associated with better mental health, and Openness was associated with better physical health. However, the way these personality traits worked seemed to be that they affected the person's sense of self-efficacy—the belief that they can achieve their goals. And if those goals were caregiving for a family member, they did it better than those whose personality traits were at the other ends of the scales (Löckenhoff, Duberstein, Friedman, et al., 2011).

8.2: Explanations of Continuity and Change

8.2 State the factors that influence personality traits

We know that there is evidence of both continuity and change in various personality traits, but what is less clear is why. What factors influence these features of personality? The explanations may sound familiar by now—genes and environment. There is also an explanation from evolutionary psychology that uses the interaction of both.

8.2.1: Genetics

To what extent do our genes determine our personalities? The short answer is "quite a lot." In fact, about 40 to 60% of the variance in personality types is heritable. Furthermore, the five major factors are influenced by genetics to about the same extent, and there seem to be few gender differences.

Studies comparing the personality scores of monozygotic twins and dizygotic twins illustrate the extent of this genetic influence. Psychologist Rainer Riemann and his colleagues (Riemann, Angleitner, & Strelau, 1997) compiled personality data for nearly 1,000 pairs of adult twins in Germany and Poland to investigate the heritability of the Five-Factor Model of personality. Each participant completed a self-report questionnaire, and then the twins' scores were correlated with their cotwins' scores. As you can see in Figure 8.4, the identical-twin pairs, who shared the same genetic makeup, had significantly higher correlations than the fraternal-twin pairs, who shared only about 50% of their genes, suggesting that all five of these personality trait structures are moderately influenced by genetics.

Figure 8.4 Monozygotic twins' scores for five personality factors show higher correlations that scores for dizygotic twins, suggesting that there is a genetic influence for personality structures.

SOURCE: Based on data from Riemann, Angleitner, & Strelau (1997).

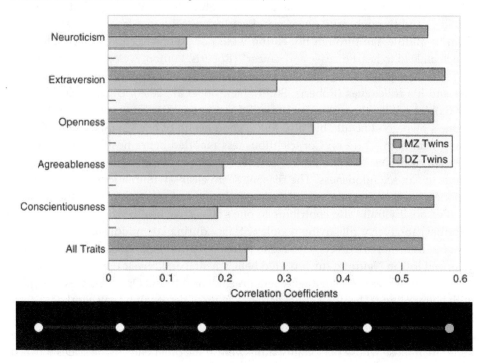

In an interesting twist, Riemann and his colleagues also gave questionnaires to two friends of each twin and asked them to respond about the twin's personality, providing an objective rating to compare with the self-reports. The two friends agreed with each other substantially (the correlation coefficient was 0.63), and the means of their scores agreed with the twins' self-reports moderately (the correlation coefficient was 0.55), all adding evidence to the heritability of personality traits.

Critical Thinking

Which related pairs would you predict to have the most similar personality scores, grandparents and grandchildren or first cousins? Or would it be the same? Why?

8.2.2: Environmental Influences

As important as genetic influences are on personality, the environment has an effect also, both directly and in combination with genetic factors. Although individuals' personality measures tend to remain stable in rank-order positions through adulthood, there is room for some change (as shown back in Figure 8.1), even in the later years, presumably due to environmental influences. Longitudinal studies of twins show that personality change is more influenced by genetics in childhood than in adulthood, meaning that environmental influences are more prominent in adulthood (Plomin & Nesselroade, 1997).

Changes in mean-level measures of personality are common and tend to occur mostly in young adulthood, a time that is very dense in role transitions (leaving home, starting careers, entering committed partnerships, becoming parents). For example, measures of social dominance, conscientiousness, and emotional stability all increase in mean level during young adulthood, leading some researchers to believe that "life experiences and life lessons centered in young adulthood are the most likely reasons for the patterns of development we see" (Roberts, Walton, & Viechtbauer, 2006, p. 18). All cultures support these role transitions for young adults and have expectations for the content of these roles. This might explain why these traits develop universally at this time of life (Helson, Kwan, John, et al., 2002).

In addition, different cohorts show different mean levels of personality traits. For example, more recent cohorts show higher scores on measures of social dominance, conscientiousness, and emotional stability, perhaps showing the effects of changing social values and child-rearing practices (Roberts, Walton, & Viechtbauer, 2006).

We also have evidence that the environment works in combination with genetic factors to maintain differential stability. Psychologist Avshalom Caspi and his colleagues (Caspi, 1998; Caspi & Roberts, 1999) suggest that individuals' genetic endowment and environmental factors combine to maintain personality traits over the years of adulthood, a concept known as **person–environment transactions**.

Person–environment transactions can be conscious or unconscious and happen in a variety of ways. *Reactive transactions* take place when we react to, or interpret, an experience in a way that is consistent with our own personality or self-concept. If a friend calls you 2 days after your birthday to congratulate you and have a nice long chat, you can either interpret it as meaning that you are not important enough to be called on your birthday or that you are so important that your friend waited 2 days until there was time for a long talk. Either reaction would tend to perpetuate your established way of thinking about yourself.

Evocative transactions are those in which we behave in a way that elicits reactions from others that confirm our own personality or self-concept. People who have low self-esteem often reject compliments or overtures of friendship and, as a result, end up even more convinced that they are not valued by others.

Proactive transactions occur when we select roles and environments that best fit our personalities and self-concept. If you are not high on extraversion, you will probably not make career decisions that put you into a job that involves working directly with people. Not only will you be happier in a more solitary work environment, but this choice will also serve to maintain your introverted traits.

Finally, *manipulative transactions* are those strategies in which we attempt to change our current environments by causing change in the people around us. An example is an extraverted manager who is transferred into a quiet office and proceeds to motivate his coworkers to be more outgoing. To the extent that this maneuver is successful, the manager is creating an environment that serves to reinforce his or her own personality traits.

8.2.3: Evolutionary Psychology Explanations

If personality structure has substantial genetic components and is similar in many cultures, it probably evolved over generations along with our other human traits. Evolutionary psychologist David Buss (1997) argued that personality traits are based on the most important features of the social groups our early ancestors lived in. It was important for our species to have indicators of who was good company (Extraversion), who was kind and supportive (Agreeableness), who put in sustained effort (Conscientiousness), who was emotionally undependable (Neuroticism), and who had good ideas (Openness). According to Buss, these differences (and the ability to perceive them in others) have been important to the survival of our species.

Buss also contended that personality traits have led to important individual differences linked to status, sexuality and survival—all contributors to reproductive success (Buss, 2012). For example, scores on Extraversion measures are related to access to sexual partners (Eysenck, 1976), and Conscientiousness is related to work and status

(Lund, Tamnes, Moestue, et al., 2007). The suggested mechanisms for this is **reactive heritability**, a process whereby individuals use the qualities they have inherited, such as strength or attractiveness, as a basis to determine strategies for survival and reproduction, such as developing a personality high in Extraversion (Tooby & Cosmides, 1990; Lukaszewski & Rooney, 2010).

8.2.4: Cultural Differences

As I discussed earlier in this chapter, the Five-Factor Model was constructed by factor analysis of personality traits found in the U.S. population and then tested on people in other cultures with the goal of showing universality in underlying personality constructs, and it has been found to be stable across many cultures (McCrae, Terracciano, et al., 2005). However, cultural and language differences have appeared (De Raad, Barelds, Levert, et al., 2010; Cheung, Cheung, Zhang, et al., 2008), causing researchers to take a different approach and construct alternative models of personality structures based on other cultures and other languages. These bottom-up, indigenous psychologies are being developed in areas of Latin America, Europe, and Asia and have covered constructs such as the selfless-self in Eastern religions (Verma, 1999) and the concepts of "face," harmony, reciprocity in relationships, predestined relationships, and mother–child attachments (Cheung, van de Vijver, & Leong, 2011). For example, the Chinese Personality Assessment Inventory was developed using these methods and consists of four personality factors: Social Potency/Expansiveness, Dependability, Accommodation, and Interpersonal Relatedness (Cheung, Cheung, Zhang, et al., 2008).

Studies comparing the Chinese Personality Assessment Inventory with the NEO-Five-Factor Inventory have shown that the Chinese factor of Interpersonal Relatedness did not correspond to any of the NEO five factors, and that the NEO factor of Openness did not correspond with any of the Chinese factors. The Chinese Personality Assessment Inventory has since been translated into various languages including Korean, Japanese, and Vietnamese, and studies have shown that its personality constructs, especially Interpersonal Relatedness, are found in these collectivist cultures (Yang, 2006). The point of all this is that the NEO-Five Factor Model was a great start, but now researchers are developing alternative models to learn more about what is universal about personality and what is particular to a given culture. With globalization, it is important for all of us—clinical psychologists, college professors, travelers, even good neighbors—to understand better "what makes others tick."

8.2.5: Summing Up Personality Structure

In this section I have covered research based on personality structures, mainly the Five-Factor Model that was defined by Costa and McCrae in the 1990s. Using the NEO Personality Inventory, researchers are able to assign scores to each factor, giving each participant in the study a numerical personality profile. These studies are usually done as self-reports and with very large groups of people. Once the scores are computed, the patterns can be analyzed to find out how personality changes over time, whether there are cultural differences, and the like. It is quick and relatively easy, and it is empirical. We have learned a lot about human personality from these studies—that is, personality of humans living in Western, individualistic cultures. And we are beginning to learn about personality in Eastern, collectivist cultures. However, these factor-analysis studies lack something in the depth and richness that we know reside within ourselves and the people we know well. To try to tap into these dimensions of personality, I will now make a 180-degree turn and discuss theories of personality development.

8.3: Theories of Personality Development

8.3 **Explain the early theories of personality development**

Another approach to changes in personality across adulthood is to conduct research based on some of the early theories of personality development, most of which had their roots in Freudian psychoanalytic theory. Full explanations of these theories comprise a whole course in itself, and I'm sure you are familiar with the basic concepts from your other classes, so I will only briefly describe them before going on to the current research findings. Although these researchers use different terminology and research methods, many of their findings fit well with the trait theory findings, as I will explain in a summary at the end.

8.3.1: Psychosocial Development

One of the most influential theories of personality development is that of psychoanalyst Erik Erikson, who proposed that psychosocial development continues over the entire life span and results from the interaction of our inner instincts and drives with outer cultural and social demands (Erikson, 1950, 1959, 1982). For Erikson, a key concept is the gradual, stepwise emergence of a sense of identity. To develop a complete, stable personality, the person must move through and successfully resolve eight crises or dilemmas over the course of a lifetime. Each stage, or dilemma, emerges as the person is challenged by new relationships, tasks, or demands. As you can see in Table 8.2, each stage is defined by a pair of opposing possibilities, such as trust versus mistrust, or integrity versus despair. Erikson also talked about the potential strengths to be gained

Table 8.2 Erikson's Stages of Psychosocial Development

Approximate Age (Years)	Stage	Potential Strength to Be Gained	Description
0–1	I. Basic trust versus mistrust	Hope	The infant must form a first, loving, trusting relationship with the caregiver or risk a persisting sense of mistrust.
2–3	II. Autonomy versus shame and doubt	Will	The child's energies are directed toward the development of key physical skills, including walking, grasping, and sphincter control. The child learns autonomy but may develop shame if not handled properly.
4–5	III. Initiative versus guilt	Purpose	The child continues to become more assertive and take more initiative, but may be too forceful and injure others or objects, which leads to guilt.
6–12	IV. Industry versus inferiority	Competence	The school-aged child must deal with the demands to learn new, complex skills or risk a sense of inferiority.
13–18	V. Identity versus role confusion	Fidelity	The teenager (or young adult) must achieve a sense of identity—both who he or she is and what he or she will be—in several areas, including occupation, gender role, politics, and religion. If not, the result is role confusion.
19–25	VI. Intimacy versus isolation	Love	The young adult must risk the immersion of self in a sense of "we," creating one or more truly intimate relationships, or suffer feelings of isolation.
25–65	VII. Generativity versus self-absorption and stagnation	Care	In early and middle adulthood, each must satisfy the need to be generative, to support the next generation, to turn outward from the self toward others. The alternative is stagnation.
65+	VIII. Ego integrity versus despair	Wisdom	If all previous stages have been dealt with reasonably well, the culmination is an acceptance of oneself as one is. If not, the result is despair.

SOURCE: Adapted from Erikson (1950, 1959, 1982).

from a healthy resolution of each dilemma, which are also listed in the table. A healthy resolution, according to Erikson, is finding a balance between the two possibilities.

Four dilemmas describe adulthood, beginning with Stage V, *identity versus role confusion,* which is the central task of adolescence and those in the early 20s. In achieving **identity**, the young person must develop a specific ideology, a set of personal values and goals. In part, this is a shift from the here-and-now orientation of the child to a future orientation; teenagers must not only consider what or who they are but also what or who they will be. Erikson believed that the teenager or young adult must develop several linked identities: an occupational identity (what work will I do?), a gender or gender-role identity (how do I go about being a man or a woman?), and political and religious identities (what do I believe in?). If these identities are not developed, the young person suffers from a sense of confusion, a sense of not knowing what or who one is.

Stage VI, *intimacy versus isolation,* builds on the newly forged identity of adolescence. **Intimacy** is the ability to fuse your identity with somebody else's without fear that you're going to lose something yourself (Evans, 1969). Many young people, Erikson thought, make the mistake of thinking they will find their identity in a relationship, but in his view, it is only those who have already formed (or are well on the way to forming) a clear identity who can successfully enter the fusion of identities that he calls intimacy. For those whose identities are weak or unformed, relationships will remain shallow, and the young person will experience a sense of isolation or loneliness.

The next stage of personality development, Stage VII, is *generativity versus self-absorption and stagnation.* **Generativity** is concerned with establishing and guiding the next generation. It encompasses procreation, productivity, and creativity. The bearing and rearing of children is clearly a key element in Erikson's view of generativity, but it is not the only element. Serving as a mentor for younger colleagues, doing charitable work in society, and the like are also expressions of generativity. Adults who do not find some avenue for successful expression of generativity may become self-absorbed or experience a sense of stagnation. The strength that can emerge from this stage, according to Erikson, is care, which implies both taking care of and caring for or about others or society.

Erikson's final proposed stage, or Stage VIII, is *ego integrity versus despair.* **Ego integrity** is achieved when people look back over their lives and decide whether they find meaning and integration in their life review or meaninglessness and unproductivity. If they see that they have resolved well the conflicts that arose in each previous stage, they are able to reap the fruit of a well-lived life, which Erikson labels "wisdom."

In many work settings, middle-aged people demonstrate generativity by serving as mentors for their younger colleagues.

FURTHER IMPLICATIONS OF DEVELOPMENT   Erikson was a good thinker. He had a combination of formal training in psychoanalysis and informal training in a variety of arenas—as an art student, in his work with Native American tribes, and in his studies of the lives of a diverse group of individuals such as Mahatma Ghandi, Martin Luther, and Adolf Hitler. His theory makes sense intuitively—it fits the way we think about our own lives and those of others. But how does it hold up under scientific scrutiny? A number of researchers have found ways to test Erikson's theory, with mixed results.

Psychologist Susan Krauss Whitbourne and her colleagues devised a test instrument, the Inventory of Psychosocial Development (IPD), which provides numerical scores for Erikson's psychosocial stages (Walaskay, Whitbourne, & Nehrke, 1983–1984). In a sequential study of men and women, they found that scores for Stage V (identity versus role confusion) increased significantly when participants were between the ages of 20 and 31, but remained stable between the ages of 31 and 42. The mean scores for this group are depicted in Figure 8.5 by the black line marked Cohort 1. This supports Erikson's views that adolescence and early adulthood is a time to question and explore alternative possibilities for adult identity. Eleven years later, the researchers repeated the testing on a new group of 20-year-olds, following them until they were 31. They found the same results, depicted in Figure 8.5 by the blue line labeled Cohort 2, showing that this was probably not an effect of just one particular cohort (Whitbourne, Zuschlag, Elliot, et al., 1992).

Figure 8.5 Mean scores for Erikson's Stage V (Identity) for two cohorts. Scores for both increase significantly between the ages of 20 and 31, but not at later ages.

SOURCE: Adapted from Whitbourne, Zuschlag, Elliot, et al. (1992).

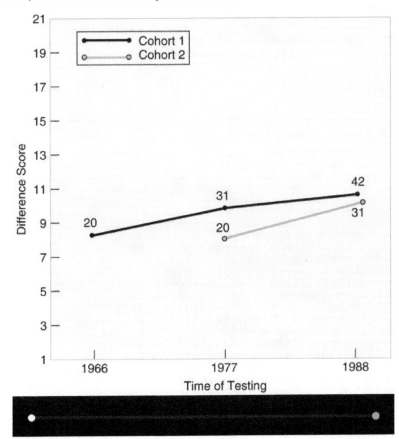

An important component of identity is sexual orientation. Psychologist Jerel P. Calzo and colleagues (Calzo, Antonucci, Mays, et al., 2011) interviewed over 1,200 gay, lesbian, and bisexual adults between the ages of 18 and 84, asking, among other things, how old they were when they self-identified as gay, lesbian, or bisexual. The average age was 19.7 years, regardless of age cohort, showing that the formation of this type of identity also tends to occur around the same age as other types.

Whitbourne and her colleagues (Whitbourne, Sneed, & Sayer, 2009) followed two cohorts of men and women from the age of 20 to the age of 54, evaluating their progress in Erikson's stages of psychosocial development. They found slow increases in all stages, with cohort differences in ego integrity and gender differences in intimacy. Interestingly, individuals who were late in establishing their careers, entering into intimate relationships, or having children, and were at a disadvantage in psychosocial development in early adulthood, were able to catch up and show favorable outcomes by the time they reached middle age.

Erikson's Stage VII (generativity versus stagnation) is the stage that has been studied the most. For example, psychologists Kennon Sheldon and Tim Kasser (2001) measured the personality development of a group of adults by asking them to list their current goals, or some of the things they are typically trying to do in their everyday lives that they may or may not be successful at. These goals were then coded according to which Eriksonian stage they best typified. Strivings that involved giving to others or making one's mark on the world were coded as Stage VII (generativity versus stagnation). Results showed that older persons were more concerned with generativity than identity, supporting Erikson's belief that this is a major task in later years.

WRITING PROMPT

What are your current goals? What are some of the things you are trying to do in your everyday life? Make a list and see which of Erikson's stages seem to best describe your goals. Write a brief response describing your findings that will be read by your instructor. Are you surprised by the results? Why or why not?

▶ The response entered here will appear in the performance dashboard and can be viewed by your instructor.

Submit

Table 8.3 Loyola Generativity Scale

How well do each of the following statements apply to you? (Rate each item on a scale from 0 to 3, where 0 = never applies to me, and 3 = applies to me very often. Items marked with * are reverse scored.)

1. I try to pass along the knowledge I have gained through my experiences.
2. I do not feel that other people need me.*
3. I think I would like the work of a teacher.
4. I feel as though I have made a difference to many people.
5. I do not volunteer to work for a charity.*
6. I have made and created things that have had an impact on other people.
7. I try to be creative in most things that I do.
8. I think that I will be remembered for a long time after I die.
9. I believe that society cannot be responsible for providing food and shelter for all homeless people.*
10. Others would say that I have made unique contributions to society.
11. If I were unable to have children of my own, I would like to adopt children.
12. I have important skills that I try to teach others.
13. I feel that I have done nothing that will survive after I die.*
14. In general, my actions do not have a positive effect on other people.*
15. I feel as though I have done nothing of worth to contribute to others.*
16. I have made many commitments to many different kinds of people, groups, and activities in my life.
17. Other people say that I am a very productive person.
18. I have a responsibility to improve the neighborhood in which I live.
19. People come to me for advice.
20. I feel as though my contributions will exist after I die.

SOURCE: McAdams & de St. Aubin (1992).

Interestingly, Sheldon and Kasser also found that adults of all ages reported having intimacy goals, or in other words, listed personal goals that increased the quality of relationships. The researchers interpreted these findings as supporting Erikson's

Figure 8.6 Adult in the midlife group (Age 37 to 42) score higher on three measures of Erikson's Stage VII (Generativity) than either younger or older groups.

SOURCE: McAdams, Hart, & Maruna (1998).

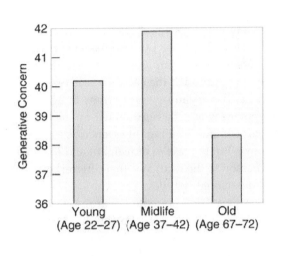

assumptions of lifelong development and the order in which the stages present themselves to individuals across the life span, but the lack of reduction of intimacy goals with age "raises the possibility that once mature psychosocial themes become salient within a person's life, they tend to remain important rather than fade away, to be replaced by new themes" (Sheldon & Kasser, 2001, p. 495). Considering the importance that close connections with others have throughout life, it stands to reason that once an individual develops the ability to form intimate bonds, it will remain a priority in his or her list of goals.

Another test instrument that measures generativity is the Loyola Generativity Scale (LGS), which consists of 20 statements that participants rate according to how well each applies to them personally (McAdams & de St. Aubin, 1992). These statements are given in Table 8.3 and reflect an overall orientation or attitude regarding generativity in one's life and social world. Psychologist Dan McAdams and his colleagues (McAdams, de St. Aubin, & Logan, 1993; McAdams, Hart, & Maruna, 1998) gave the LGS, along with several other generativity measures, to 152 men and women who made up a stratified random sample of citizens living in Evanston, Illinois. The participants represented three age groups of adults: young (22 to 27), midlife (37 to 42), and old (67 to 72). Results showed that adults in the midlife group, as predicted by Erikson's theory, scored higher on generativity than both the younger and the older groups (see Figure 8.6).

Interestingly, male participants who were not fathers scored significantly lower on generativity than fathers and women in general. The researchers speculate that fatherhood may have a dramatic impact on men's generativity, increasing their concern for the next generation. (To be fair, one could also argue that experiencing an increase in generativity inspires men to become fathers.)

In summary, empirical studies have shown that there is good evidence for Erikson's adult stages of psychosocial development. Although the ages do not always match Erikson's "optimal ages" for a stage, there is ample evidence that young adulthood is a time of emphasis on identity concerns. Midlife seems to be a time of forming generativity goals. Intimacy is important in young adulthood, as Erikson stated, but is also a concern at other ages. However, Erikson's theory held that stages are never "over," but are just replaced by new dilemmas, so it is not surprising that so important an aspect of life as intimacy is a concern throughout adulthood.

8.3.2: Ego Development

A second theory with Freudian roots comes from psychologist Jane Loevinger (1976), who suggested a number of stagelike levels of ego development. Like Erikson, Loevinger believed that each level was built on the level that preceded it, but unlike Erikson's theory, a person must complete the developmental tasks in one stage before moving to the next. Although the early stage is typically completed in childhood, the stages have only very loose connections to ages. Thus a wide range of stages of ego development would be represented among a group of adults of any given age. What Loevinger is describing, in essence, is a pathway along which she thinks we all must move. But the rate of movement and the final stage achieved differ widely from one person to the next, and that difference, according to Loevinger, is the basis of different personality types.

A number of stages have been presented over the 30 years or so this theory has been part of the field of developmental psychology. Some earlier stages are difficult to gather data on because they are most likely to be found in very young children. Later stages are also difficult because so few people have reached them.

IMPULSIVE STAGE The earliest stage that can be measured is the *impulsive stage*. This occurs in small children when they become aware of themselves as separate entities from those around them. This separateness is verified when they experience impulses, but they don't have control over them at first, and their emotional range is narrow. There are egocentric and dependent in their interactions with others, and preoccupied with bodily feelings. "In small children this stage is charming; when it persists into adolescence and adulthood, it is at best maladaptive and in some cases psychopathic" (Loevinger, 1997, p. 203).

SELF-PROTECTIVE STAGE During the next stage, the *self-protective stage*, the child becomes aware of his or her impulses and gains some control over them to secure at least an immediate advantage. In young children it is natural to be egocentric and self-protective, but in adolescence and adulthood, this becomes exploitation and manipulation of others. In this stage, there is a preoccupation with taking advantage of others and of others taking advantage of oneself, and this is often expressed in hostile humor. Unlike those in the impulsive stage, adults in the self-protective stage are capable of very adaptive behavior and can be very successful.

CONFORMIST STAGE People in Loevinger's next stage, the *conformist stage*, are able to identify themselves with their reference group, whether it is family, peer group, or work group. They are very concerned with rules and deal with others using cooperation and loyalty. There is a preoccupation with appearances and outward behavior. They think in terms of stereotypes and are rather limited emotionally to standard clichés—they report being happy, sad, mad, glad, and so on.

SELF-AWARE STAGE The *self-aware stage* is characterized by awareness that there are allowable exceptions to the simple rules the conformists live by. People are aware that they don't always live up to the group's professed standards (and neither do other members of their group). They realize that they have an existence that is separate from their group, and this can be the basis of some loneliness and self-consciousness. It may not surprise you to know that this stage is the one most common in late adolescents and emerging adults.

CONSCIENTIOUS STAGE At the *conscientious stage*, people have formed their own ideals and standards instead of just seeking the approval of their group. They express their inner life using rich and varied words to describe their thoughts and emotions.

Interpersonal relationships are intense. They have long-term goals and may even be overly conscientious. This stage may seem similar to Erikson's stage of identity versus role confusion, but Loevinger argues that it can occur well past adolescence and continue far into adulthood.

INDIVIDUALISTIC STAGE The next stage is called the *individualistic stage,* and this is the time people take a broad view of life as a whole. They think in terms of psychological causes and are able to consider their own developmental processes. Their interpersonal relationships are mutual and they are preoccupied with a sense of individuality.

AUTONOMOUS STAGE People in the *autonomous stage* begin to see the multifaceted nature of the world, not just the good and the bad. Life is complex, and situations don't have simple answers or even one best answer. There is a lessening of the burden taken on at the conscientious stage and a respect for the autonomy of others, even one's own children. And there is the ability to see one's own life in the context of wider social concerns. (Another stage, the integrated stage, is very rare and is not included in most discussions. In this stage the ego is completely integrated.)

EGO DEVELOPMENT IN ADULTS Loevinger's theory deals with the integration of new perspectives on the self and others, and the stages, or levels, are measured by the Washington University Sentence Completion Test of Ego Development (Hy & Loevinger, 1996). In this test, participants are asked to complete 18 sentence stems, such as "My mother and I …," "A man's job …," and "Rules are …" Each response is scored according to guidelines, and then a total score is computed that corresponds to a particular stage or level of ego development.

The sentence-completion test is used to assess the ego development of adults across the life span. For example, young adults' ego development stage was found to be a reflection of problems experienced in childhood and adolescence. Those who had a history of externalizing disorders (attention problems or aggressive behavior) were below the conformist level at age 22, indicating that they had not reached a stage that involves respect for rules. Those who had a history of internalizing disorders (anxiety or depression) had not advanced beyond the conformist level at age 22, indicating that although they had respect for rules, they had not reached the self-aware level (Krettenauer, Urlich, Hofmann, et al., 2003).

Psychologists Jack Bauer and Dan McAdams (2004) interviewed middle-aged adults who had been through either a career change or a change in religion, asking questions about personal growth. They also computed their ego development stage according to the Washington University sentence-completion test described earlier. Participants who were at higher levels of ego development on the sentence-completion test were more apt to describe their career change and religion change in terms of *integrative themes* (having new perspectives on the self and others). These adults described their personal growth as increased self-awareness, better understanding of relationships, and a higher level of moral reasoning—all themes that reflect more complex thinking about one's life and meaningful relationships.

Researchers in adult education Janet Truluck and Bradley Courtenay (2002) gave older adults (55 to 85 years of age) the Washington University sentence-completion test to assess their ego development. There were no gender differences or age effects, but as shown in Figure 8.7, educational level was positively related to ego development. The proportion of people who scored in the self-aware stage was higher for those with only a high school education and declined for people with some college, for college graduates, and then for those with a postgraduate education. The proportion of those in the conscientious and individualistic stages generally increased with educational attainment. Although some researchers have found that educational level is related to ego development in earlier adulthood (Labouvie-Vief & Diehl, 1998), these findings of lifelong effects of education on ego development are interesting, especially considering that the older participants' education had been attained decades earlier.

Figure 8.7 In older adults (55 to 85 years of age), higher education is related to higher levels of ego development.

SOURCE: Based on data from Truluck & Courtenay (2002).

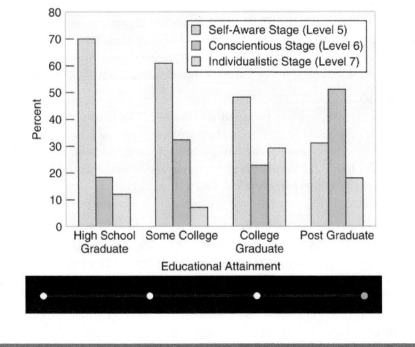

The simplest explanation of how college education contributes to ego development is that people learn important lessons in college and remember them all their lives. What is another explanation? Write a brief response that will be read by your instructor. Be sure to explain your reasoning.

▶ The response entered here will appear in the performance dashboard and can be viewed by your instructor.

Submit

8.3.3: Mature Adaptation

A theory that seems to be a cross between Erikson's and Loevinger's theories is that of psychiatrist George Vaillant (1977, 1993). He begins by accepting Erikson's stages as the basic framework of development, but inserts an additional stage between Erikson's stages of intimacy and generativity at some time around the age of 30. Vaillant calls this stage *career consolidation*, the stage when young adults are intent on establishing their own competence, mastering a craft, or acquiring higher status or a positive reputation.

Like Loevinger, Vaillant describes a direction in which personality growth or development may occur, but he does not assume that everyone moves the same distance in this direction. In particular, Vaillant is interested in *mature adaptation*, potential progressive change in the ways adults adapt psychologically to the trials and tribulations they face. The major form of adaptation he discusses is the **defense mechanism**, Freud's term for a set of normal, unconscious strategies used for dealing with anxiety. Everyone has some anxiety, so everyone uses defense mechanisms of some kind. All of them involve some type of self-deception or distortion of reality. We forget things that make us uncomfortable or remember them in a way that is not so unpleasant; we give ourselves reasons for doing something we know we shouldn't do; we project our unacceptable feelings onto others rather than acknowledge them in ourselves. What Vaillant has added to Freud's concept is the notion that some defense mechanisms are more mature than others. In general, mature defenses involve less distortion of reality.

They reflect more graceful, less uncomfortable ways of coping with difficulties. Vaillant's central thesis is that an adult's defense mechanisms must mature if he or she is to be able to cope effectively with the slings and arrows of normal life.

VAILLANT'S SIX DEFENSE MECHANISMS Vaillant arranged defense mechanisms into six levels, with the first level as the most mature. The six levels, along with examples of each, are shown in Table 8.4. Vaillant believed that people use defense mechanisms from several levels at any point in their lives and, at times of stress, may regress to lower levels. However, in the course of life maturation, adults add more and more adaptive defense mechanisms to their psychological toolboxes and use fewer and fewer of the less mature defense mechanisms. So instead of this being a stage theory with discreet steps of development, Vaillant considered his theory as more of a slope, with those who use more mature defense mechanisms having more integrated personalities and being more successful in their lives (Vaillant, 2002).

Table 8.4 Vaillant's Six Levels of Defense Mechanisms

Level	Defense Mechanism	Example
I. High Adaptive Level	Altruism	Dealing with stress over health by participating in a race to raise funds for researching a disease.
II. Mental Inhibition Level	Repression	Dealing with stress over childlessness by expelling thoughts and wishes from conscious awareness.
III. Minor Image Distorting Level	Omnipotence	Dealing with stress over military assignment by glorifying one's special training and high-tech equipment.
IV. Disavowal Level	Denial	Dealing with stress over marital problems by refusing to acknowledge that a hurtful incident, apparent to others, occurred.
V. Major Image Distorting Level	Autistic Fantasy	Dealing with stress over potential layoffs by daydreaming about an ideal job instead of taking action to find a new one.
VI. Action Level	Help-rejecting Complaining	Dealing with stress over money problems by complaining, but then rejecting offers of help and advice.

Hide All Cells   Show All Cells

SOURCE: Adapted from the American Psychiatric Association (2000).

Vaillant based many of his ideas on data from the Harvard Men's Study, a longitudinal study that began with 268 men of the 1922 graduating class of Harvard College and followed them throughout their lives (Heath, 1945). Although Vaillant was not born when the study began, he joined the research group in its 30th year and is still gathering data on the surviving participants. (Interestingly, his father, who died when Vaillant was 13, was an original participant in the study.)

Vaillant's theory was based on data from numerous interviews, personality tests, and other measurements that were given to the men in the Harvard study over the years. When personality factors research began to take center stage in the study of personality, he and his colleagues adapted the concept of the Five-Factor Model to fit the longitudinal study of Harvard men. By reviewing early interviews and test results, the researchers were able to assign scores for the five major personality factors to the men at age 22, some 45 years earlier. Then they gave the Five-Factor Personality Inventory (NEO-PI) to the 163 surviving participants and compared the early scores with the later scores. The results showed low but significant intra-individual stability for three factors, Neuroticism, Extraversion, and Openness, despite the cards stacked against the study, such as the very long interval between tests, the use of different tests, and Time 1 being at such a young age (Soldz & Vaillant, 1999).

In addition to looking at individual stability over a 45-year interval, Soldz and Vaillant also investigated other details of these men's lives to see if their early personality traits were related to actual events and outcomes over the life course. Some of the results were that Extraversion at the age of 22 predicted maximum income during one's working years; the higher a participant scored on this trait, the more money he made. Openness at 22 predicted creative accomplishments during the men's lifetimes, and early Conscientiousness scores predicted good adult adjustment and low levels of depression, smoking, and alcohol abuse. (Recall earlier in this chapter that Conscientiousness is also related to good health.)

8.3.4: Gender Crossover

Psychoanalyst Carl Jung (1933) believed that the second half of life was characterized by exploring and acknowledging the parts of oneself that had been hidden during the first half of life. Men allowed the softer, more nurturant parts of their personalities to emerge, whereas women became more independent and planful. Influenced by Jung's psychoanalytic thought about aging, anthropologist David Gutmann (1987) believed that adult gender differences in personality begin in young adulthood when both men and women accentuate their own gender characteristics and suppress the opposite-gender characteristics to attract mates and reproduce. After the parenting years are over and these roles are not paramount in their lives, according to this theory, they are able to relax the suppression and allow some of the "other-gender" characteristics to emerge.

Gutmann referred to this relaxation of gender roles at midlife as **gender crossover**. He believed that aging does not represent a loss at this time but, rather, a gain in personal freedom and new roles within the "tribe." Gutmann also found support for his ideas in his experiences among the Mayan, Navajo, and Druze societies showing that men move from active mastery, which involves making changes in external circumstances, to accommodative mastery, which is making changes in one's inner self; and that women move from accommodative to active mastery.

Psychologist Ravenna Helson and her colleagues (Helson, Pals, & Solomon, 1997) reviewed data from three longitudinal studies of different cohorts of college students. They found support for Gutmann's theory in the responses of the women participants, most of whom expressed interest in marriage and family. The difference in cohorts was that the earlier cohorts (who were young adults in the 1930s and 1940s) were concerned about choosing between a career and a family, and the more recent ones (who were young adults in the 1980s) were concerned about combining both a career and a family. The males in the study seldom expressed those concerns.

Helson explored the reasons for change and ruled out the narrow interpretation of stereotypical gender traits as important for parenting; the dramatic increase in women's competence, independence, and self-confidence at midlife was evident whether the women were mothers or had remained childless. Furthermore, it depended on what opportunities were available for women at the time they were going through these age-related changes.

There seems to be evidence of men's and women's personalities blending in middle and late adulthood, but this does not constitute a true "crossover," in which women become more masculine than men and men become more feminine than women. What the research findings show is best described as an increased openness to the expression of previously unexpressed parts of the self. The cause for this blending does not strictly seem to be parenthood because it is not limited to those who have had children. The change seems to be stronger for women than for men. Helson suggests that we are viewing a complex biosocial phenomenon that involves hormones, social roles, historical changes, and economic climate. However, it is strong enough to show up in these studies and in similar studies in other cultures, so it seems to be a worthwhile research topic for the future.

8.3.5: Positive Well-Being

Another approach that has its roots in psychoanalytic theory comes from psychologist Abraham Maslow (1968/1998), who traced his theoretical roots to Freud and offered some highly original insights. As a humanistic psychologist, Maslow's most central concern was with the development of motives or needs, which he divided into two main groups: deficiency motives and being motives. *Deficiency motives* involve instincts or drives to correct an imbalance or to maintain physical or emotional homeostasis, such as getting enough to eat, satisfying thirst, or obtaining enough love and respect from others. Deficiency motives are found in all animals. *Being motives*, in contrast, are distinctly human. Maslow argued that humans have unique desires to discover and understand, to give love to others, and to push for the optimum fulfillment of their inner potentials.

In general, Maslow believed that the satisfaction of deficiency motives prevents or cures illness, and re-creates homeostasis (inner balance). In contrast, the satisfaction of being motives produces positive health. The distinction is like the "difference between fending off threat or attack, and positive triumph and achievement" (Maslow, 1968/1998, p. 32). But being motives are quite fragile and do not typically emerge until well into adulthood, and then only under supportive circumstances. Maslow's well-known needs hierarchy (shown in Figure 8.8) reflects this aspect of his thinking. The lowest four levels all describe different deficiency needs, whereas only the highest level, the need for **self-actualization**, is a being motive. Further, Maslow proposed that these five levels emerge sequentially in development and tend to dominate the system from the bottom up. That is, if you are starving, the physiological needs dominate. If you are being physically battered, the safety needs dominate. The need for self-actualization emerges only when all four types of deficiency needs are largely satisfied.

Instead of studying people with mental health problems, Maslow sought to understand the personalities and characteristics of those few adults who seemed to have risen to the top of the needs hierarchy and achieved significant levels of self-understanding and expression, people such as Eleanor Roosevelt, Albert Schweitzer, and Albert Einstein. Some of the key characteristics of self-actualized people, as

Figure 8.8 Maslow's hierarchy of needs proposes that lower needs dominate the individual's motivations and that higher needs become prominent only late in life and when the lower needs are satisfied.

SOURCE: From Maslow (1968/1998).

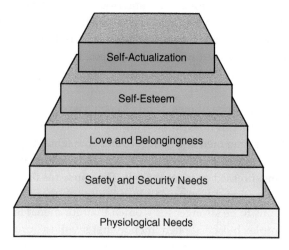

Maslow saw them, are having an accurate perception of reality, being involved in deep personal relationships, being creative, and having a good-natured sense of humor. He described self-actualized individuals as having **peak experiences**—feelings of perfection and momentary separation from the self when one feels in unity with the universe.

Maslow and other humanistic psychologists such as Carl Rogers (1959) had their major influence in clinical psychology and self-help movements. In some of the later adaptations and applications of these ideas by others, the need for self-actualization has become more self-centered and less centered on the collective well-being of humankind than Maslow had envisioned. One reason is that Maslow's theory had little empirical testing; it was not stated very scientifically, and there were no means developed for assessing the dominance of the various motives he proposed. For some reason this theory did not attract the attention of research psychologists who might have picked up the ball and advanced it further down the field. However, there is something about Maslow's theory that is appealing to us; it fits our gut-level feeling of what life is all about. We can experience its truth in our lives almost every day. When we feel endangered by terrorist attacks, we are not too concerned about whether we will be graduating next year with two gold braids on our shoulders or just one.

There has been a renewed interest in humanistic psychology and new attempts to use it as a basis for empirical studies. Foremost among this movement has been the appeal by psychologists Martin Seligman and Mihaly Csikszentmihalyi (2000) for a new focus that turns away from a disease model of human behavior that is fixated on curing or preventing negative conditions such as mental illness, crime, failure, victimization, abuse, brain damage, negative effects of stress, and poverty. Instead, they offered the following focus on **positive psychology**:

> The field of positive psychology at the subjective level is about valued subjective experiences: well-being, contentment, and satisfaction (in the past); hope and optimism (for the future); and flow and happiness (in the present). At the individual level, it is about positive individual traits: the capacity for love and vocation, courage, interpersonal skill, aesthetic sensibility, perseverance, forgiveness, originality, future mindedness, spirituality, high talent, and wisdom. At the group level, it is about the civic virtues and the institutions that move individuals toward better citizenship: responsibility, nurturance, altruism, civility, moderation, tolerance, and work ethic. (Seligman & Csikszentmihalyi, 2000, p. 5)

SELF-ACTUALIZATION One result of this movement is a personality theory that has some components of Maslow's theory of self-actualization. This theory, formulated by psychologists Richard Ryan and Edward Deci (2000; Deci & Ryan, 2008b), is known as **self-determination theory**. It holds that personality is based on individuals' evolved inner resources for growth and integration. Ryan and Deci believe that the need for personal growth and personality development is an essential part of human nature. The extent to which we succeed in this endeavor is the basis of our personalities, much as in Loevinger's theory of ego development described earlier in this chapter. Ryan and Deci stress how important it is for individuals to experience what they call *eudaimonia*— a sense of integrity and well-being similar to Maslow's concept of self-actualization. They believe that too much emphasis is placed on *hedonia*—happiness that involves the presence of positive feelings and the absence of negative feelings (Deci & Ryan, 2008a). In contrast, they say that eudaimonia entails the basic needs for competence, autonomy, and relatedness. They theorize that individuals cannot thrive without satisfying all three of these needs—and thus an environment that fosters competence and autonomy but not relatedness, for example, will result in a compromised sense of well-being.

Competence, according to Ryan and Deci's theory, is the feeling of effectiveness as one interacts with one's environment. It's not necessary to be the best, but in terms of the U.S. Army slogan, it's important to "be all that you can be." It's feeling challenged and seeing the results of your efforts. This can be difficult during late adulthood, but the authors caution that competence doesn't mean being better than before; sometimes it means modifying the environment, selecting which activities to perform, and redirecting extra resources to doing those activities well—a strategy they refer to as "having a choice over challenges."

The need for *autonomy* means that we need to feel that our actions are being done by our own volition. We are making decisions to act, and our actions reflect our true inner selves and not someone else's rules or guidelines. It means that a person is acting due to internal controls and not external ones. This is not always easy for independent adults, but it is much more difficult at other stages of life, such as childhood, adolescence, and the later years of adulthood when people are dependent on others to a greater degree. However, Ryan and LaGuardia (2000) believe that dependence does not rule out autonomy. In fact, they found that dependent patients in nursing homes that allow them to make many of their own decisions are both physically and psychologically healthier than patients in homes that allow less autonomy.

WRITING PROMPT

What does your college or university do to foster feelings of autonomy, relatedness, and competence in its students? Are these measures successful? Can you suggest any other measures that could be taken to promote a sense of eudaimonia in students?

▶ The response entered here will appear in the performance dashboard and can be viewed by your instructor.

Submit

Relatedness, in self-determination theory, refers to the feeling of being connected to, cared about, and belonging with significant others in one's life. It's the feeling that others are standing behind you with love and affection. Like the other basic needs, this one changes with age. In the later years, the quality of contact with friends and family members takes precedence over the quantity of contact. Kasser and Ryan (1999) found that the quality of relatedness and social support felt by nursing-home residents along with the sense of autonomy (and the support they felt for being autonomous) predicted positive outcomes, such as lower incidence of depression, higher satisfaction with life, and higher self-esteem.

Psychologist Christopher P. Niemiec and his colleagues (Niemiec, Ryan, & Deci, 2009) applied the concepts of self-determination theory to recent college graduates to see if the types of goals and aspirations they had attained 2 years after graduation were related to their psychological well-being. They found that the graduates who expressed intrinsic goals (personal growth, close relationships, community involvement) and had attained those goals 2 years after graduation showed better psychological well-being than those who had expressed extrinsic goals (money, fame, and image) and who had attained those goals. In fact, those who had attained extrinsic goals showed more indicators of psychological ill-being. The authors summed up their study with a quotation from Aristotle (around 350 BCE): "[Happiness] belongs more to those who have cultivated their character and mind to the uttermost, and kept acquisition of external goods within moderate limits, than it does to those who have managed to acquire more external goods than they can possibly use, and are lacking goods of the soul. ... Any excessive amount of such things must either cause its possessor some injury, or, at any rate, bring him no benefit" (Aristotle, 1946, pp. 280–281).

Summary: Personality

LISTEN TO THE AUDIO:

▶ ●────────── 08:19 🔊● ────

1. Early ideas about adult personality were based on grand theories of development that were popular and enthusiastically endorsed but not empirically tested and validated.

2. One of the first methods of testing and validating ideas about personality was the trait structure approach, in which a small number of trait structures were identified through factor analysis. The most prominent of these models is Costa and McCrae's Five-Factor Model (FFM), which identifies Neuroticism, Extraversion, Openness to experience, Agreeableness, and Conscientiousness as the basic factors of human personality.

3. Differential continuity has been found for the major five factors of personality through childhood and adulthood. People tend to keep their rank orders within groups regardless of gender. The level of stability increases with age through the 70s, but never becomes totally stable, showing that personality can change throughout life.

4. What happens to personality traits as people get older? We become more agreeable and conscientious, less neurotic and open.

5. Personality trait structures can be stable in some ways (differential continuity) and change in others (mean-level changes). The former is relative to others in your age group, the latter is your group in comparison to a different age group. You can be the most conscientious

person in your age group throughout your life, but the average level of scores for that trait may increase as you (and your age-mates) get older.

6. Personality traits are related to the development of intimate relationships, career success, and health in adulthood. People who are high in Agreeableness and low in Neuroticism have relationships that last longer and are more satisfying than those who are lower in these traits. Those who have high levels of Conscientiousness are more apt to do their jobs well and advance quickly in their careers than those who are lower in these traits. High levels of Conscientiousness and low levels of Neuroticism predict better health and longevity.

7. The five major personality structures have a significant genetic component, but there are mixed findings about the primary factors. The genetic influence is found to be greater in childhood than in adulthood, when environmental influences are stronger.

8. People work together with their environments to keep their personalities stable by the way they interpret events, the way they act toward others that elicits responses compatible with their personalities, the way they select situations that fit and reinforce their personalities, and the way they make changes in surroundings that are incompatible with their personalities.

9. Evolutionary psychologists argue that personality traits give us important survival cues about the people in our environment and, as a result, have been selected for throughout our evolutionary history. Furthermore, personality traits may develop

to complement inherited physical characteristics to ensure survival and reproductive success.

10. Researchers have been finding subtle cultural differences in personality traits and factors among Chinese, Korean, and Vietnamese groups and are developing alternative models and scales to measure personality traits in collectivist cultures.

11. Erikson's theory of psychosocial development states that personality development takes place in distinct stages over the life span. Each stage represents a conflict the individual must try to resolve. Each resolution attempt brings the potential for a new strength gained. Four stages take place in adulthood as individuals attempt to establish identities, form intimate partnerships, tend to the next generation, and find meaning at the end of their lives. Although Erikson's theory was not data based or scientifically tested before it was presented, recent research has shown that establishing an identity is a concern for younger adults but not for middle-aged adults, and that this is true for intimacy also. Other studies have shown that middle-aged adults are more concerned with generativity goals than younger adults.

12. Loevinger's theory of ego development parted with Erikson's theory on the concept of stages. She believed that adults make their way along the incline from one stage to the other, but don't have to complete the whole progression. Personality depends on which stage a person ultimately attains. The stages represent movement toward interdependence, values, attitudes toward rules, and evaluations of the self. Recent research has shown that Loevinger's test of ego development predicts how people will describe personal outcomes of life events, and that ego development increases with education.

13. Vaillant's theory of mature adaptation is based on levels of defense mechanisms—normal, unconscious strategies we use for dealing with anxiety. He posed six levels, beginning with the most mature and proceeding on to those that involve more and more self-deception, suggesting that we use several levels, but the ones we use the most determine the maturity of our adaptations. Recent research has incorporated trait-theory tests with more traditional personality evaluations on a group of older Harvard men who have been studied longitudinally since they were undergraduates. Vaillant has found stability in Neuroticism, Extraversion, and Openness over a 45-year period; some factors at the age of 22 predicted later outcomes in health and career.

14. Gutmann's theory of gender crossover explains that young adults strive to display accentuated gender traits to attract mates and raise children. After the parenting years are over, they are able to express the hidden sides of their personalities by displaying the gender traits of the opposite sex. Studies show that there is a tendency for both men and women to incorporate characteristics of the other gender, but it's more of a blending than a true crossover, and it seems to be independent of being a parent.

15. Maslow's theory of self-actualization consists of stages of a sort, in the form of a needs hierarchy, with the most-pressing biological needs coming first; once they are satisfied, the individual turns his or her attention to higher-level needs. The highest is self-actualization, which Maslow believed was seldom achieved. A recent reformulation of this theory is found in self-determination theory, which states our basic needs as being competence, autonomy, and relatedness. Research based on this idea has shown that fulfilling all three needs is necessary for high scores on a number of indicators of well-being, such as career success, good health, and life satisfaction.

SHARED WRITING: PERSONALITY TRAITS

Consider this chapter's discussion of personality traits. What are the basic personality traits, or patterns of thoughts, feelings, and behaviors exhibited by humans? Why do you think these have become so fundamental to us as humans? How do they distinguish us from other animals? Write a short response that your classmates will read. Be sure to discuss specific examples.

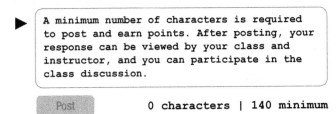

▶ A minimum number of characters is required to post and earn points. After posting, your response can be viewed by your class and instructor, and you can participate in the class discussion.

Post   0 characters | 140 minimum

Chapter 8 Quiz: Personality

Chapter 9
The Quest for Meaning

Learning Objectives

9.1 List reasons for the quest for self-transcendence

9.2 Appraise the directly proportionate relationship between spirituality and age with reference to gender and race

9.3 Discuss spiritual development in terms of moral reasoning and faith

9.4 Review of stages of personality, morality, and faith development

9.5 Explain the transition process from one stage of faith and equilibrium to another

9.6 Discuss life as a journey from the known to the unknown

LISTEN TO THE AUDIO:

▶ ●———————— 04:03 🔊 ●————

My grandparents lived next door throughout my childhood, and their search for meaning began and ended at the Presbyterian church. It was the center of their lives and the answer to all their questions. My grandfather began Sunday mornings teaching Sunday School to a group of teenage boys—most of whom were in the Boy Scout troop he led. Then he attended morning church service, where my grandmother played the organ. Wednesday nights were for Prayer Meeting. During the week, at least during their retirement years, they visited the sick and helped out in the food and clothing bank the church ran. Most of their friends and neighbors attended the same church. Ten percent of their income went to the church, and they did not drink alcohol, use tobacco, or dance. The Holy Bible (King James version) was part of their home décor, and it was well read. Before every meal around their table, we expressed appreciation for our food with a prayer beginning, "God is great, God is good. Let us thank Him for our food."

Today life is more complicated, and the search for meaning in our family has gone in new directions. I no longer attend church services, and only one of my three sisters does—and it is not the Presbyterian church of our childhood. We contribute to our community through civic donations and volunteer work, not through the church. Our talk about spiritual matters takes place in book clubs, at Sunday dinner, or at cocktail parties (where we drink alcohol and sometimes dance!). Around our dining room table are family members who seek meaning through yoga, psychotherapy, mindfulness, meditation, and science. Frequent guests include a friend who is a devout Catholic, a colleague who is Muslim, and a neighbor who believes that the answer to everything can be found in the teachings of AA. Two young adult grandchildren are currently vocal atheists. Instead of a prayer, meals around our dinner table begin with "Bon appétit!"

Critical Thinking

Is your quest for meaning similar to or different from that of your grandparents? In what ways?

Sometimes, I think that my late grandparents would be horrified to see what kind of family I have created. But then I realize that we are all searching for the same thing. Trying to find out why we are here, what the best way is to spend this lifetime, and how to prepare for what happens next (if anything does).

Spirituality is a common characteristic of our species. Burial sites that date back 30,000 years reveal bodies buried with food, pots, and weapons, seemingly provisions for the afterlife. And today, in the midst of nanotechnology and biomedical advances, 92% of people in the United States state that they believe in God (Harris Poll, 2011). This **quest for meaning**, also known as **spirituality**, is the self's search for ultimate knowledge of life through an individualized understanding of the sacred (Wink & Dillon, 2002). Whether through the practice of traditional religion or a personal quest to find self-enlightenment, the search for meaning is an integral part of the human experience.

In my grandparents' day, a personal quest for meaning was the realm of theology; today science has become interested. Some of the questions being asked are: Is there a gene for spirituality? Is there a difference between religiosity and spirituality? Is there a health benefit to being spiritual or religious? Is a belief in a Supreme Being an evolved trait in our species? Although it may seem strange to apply scientific testing to these topics, the geneticists and psychologists are saying the same thing as the anthropologists who found the ancient burial sites: The quest for meaning is a common characteristic of our species. This chapter addresses that quest and how it unfolds over the adult years.

9.1: Why a Chapter on the Quest for Meaning?

9.1 List reasons for the quest for self-transcendence

Elsewhere, I talked about age-related changes in personality and the progression toward self-actualization, which are certainly aspects of inner growth in adulthood. But there is another aspect to inner development—perhaps more speculative, but certainly no less vital to most of us—that touches on questions of meaning. As we move through adulthood, do we interpret our experiences differently? Do we attach different meanings, understand our world in new ways? Do we become wiser, or less worldly, or more spiritual?

Certainly, a link between advancing age and increasing wisdom has been part of the folk tradition in virtually every culture in the world, as evidenced by fairy tales, myths, and religious teachings (Campbell, 1949/1990). Adult development, according to these sources, brings an increased storehouse of worldly knowledge and experience. It also brings a different perspective on life, a different set of values, and a different worldview, a process often described as **self-transcendence**, or coming to know oneself as part of a larger whole that exists beyond the physical body and personal history. What I am interested in knowing is whether this process is part of—or potentially part of—the normal process of adult development.

You may well think that the answers to such questions lie in the province of religion or philosophy, not psychology. Despite the increasing number of psychologists over the years interested in the psychology of religion, in wisdom, and in adults' ideas about life, you are not likely to find a chapter on this subject in any other textbook on adult development. So perhaps my first task here is to explain to you why I think this is important. Why talk about meaning? There are three reasons.

- **IT IS THE MEANING WE ATTACH TO EXPERIENCE THAT MATTERS, RATHER THAN THE EXPERIENCE ITSELF.** Most fundamentally, psychologists have come to understand that individual experiences do not affect us in some uniform, automatic way; rather, it is the way we interpret an experience, the meaning we give it, that is really critical. There are certain basic assumptions individuals make about the world and their place in it, about themselves and their capacities that affect their interpretations of experiences. Such a system of meanings is sometimes referred to as an *internal working model* that determines how we experience the world. I've touched on other aspects of the same point in earlier chapters . Elsewhere, I covered attachment theory and explained how we form internal working models of the attachment relationships we had with our parents, and how these models influence the way we approach relationships with other people. If my internal model includes the assumption that "people are basically helpful and trustworthy," that assumption is clearly going to affect not only the experiences I will seek out, but also my interpretation of those experiences. The objective experiences each of us have are thus filtered through various internal working models before they convey meaning to us. I would argue that the ultimate consequence of any given experience is largely (if not wholly) determined by the meaning we attach and not the experience itself. To the extent that this is true, then, it is obviously important for us to try to understand the meaning systems that adults create.

Critical Thinking

How might the exact same experience, such as the eruption of a volcano, be interpreted very differently by people who have differing meaning systems? What other examples can you think of?

- **THE QUEST FOR MEANING IS A BASIC HUMAN CHARACTERISTIC.** A second reason for exploring this rather slippery area of adult development is that the quest for meaning is a central theme in the lives of most adults. This is echoed in the writings of many clinicians and theorists. Psychoanalyst Erich Fromm (1956) listed the need for meaning as one of the five central existential needs of human beings. Psychiatrist Viktor Frankl (1984) argued that the "will to meaning" is a basic human motive. Theologian and psychologist James Fowler has made a similar point: "One characteristic all human beings have in common is that we can't live without some sense that life is meaningful" (1981, p. 58). Thus, not only do we interpret our experiences and in this way "make meaning," but it may also be true that the need or motive to create meaningfulness is a vital one in our lives. More recently, evolutionary psychologist Jesse Bering (2006) wrote that a sense of spirituality is an important component of our species' social cognitive system.

- **MOST CULTURES SUPPORT THE TRADITION THAT SPIRITUALITY AND WISDOM INCREASE WITH AGE.** There has always been anecdotal evidence of **gerotranscendence**, the idea that meaning systems increase in quality as we age, beginning with myths and fairy tales about wise elders (Tornstam, 1996). Early theorists in psychology explained the development of meaning as a growth process. For example, psychoanalyst Carl Jung (1964) proposed that young adulthood was a time of turning outward, a time to establish relationships, start families, and concentrate on careers. But at midlife, when adults become aware of their own mortality, they turn inward and strive to expand their sense of self. In this way, the outward focus of the first half of life is balanced by the inward focus of the second half, completing the process of self-realization. Similarly, psychologist Klaus Riegel (1973) proposed that cognitive development extends to **postformal stages** that appear in midlife when adults are able to go beyond the linear and logical ways of thinking described in Piaget's formal operations stage. In this postformal stage, adults are able to view the world in a way that adds feelings and context to the logic and reason proposed by Piaget and use their cognitive abilities in a quest for meaning (Sinnott, 1994).

The second half of life brings a change from outward to inward concerns and from physical to spiritual values.

No matter whether changes in meaning systems over age are a function of normal development or the result of lifetime experience, it is generally agreed that the development of meaning systems in adulthood is a real phenomenon and worthy of scientific attention.

9.2: The Study of Age-Related Changes in Meaning Systems

9.2 **Appraise the directly proportionate relationship between spirituality and age with reference to gender and race**

Assuming that I have persuaded you that this subject is worth exploring, we now come to the equally sticky/tricky question of method. How do we explore something so apparently fuzzy? An obvious idea is to look at **religiosity**, the outward signs of spirituality, such as participation in religious services or being a member of a religious organization. Quantitative studies of such matters attempt to answer questions like: Do adults attend religious services more (or less) as they get older? Is there some kind of age-linked pattern? One body of research is based on this line of reasoning, and I'll look at the evidence it presents in a moment. However, there are other approaches that also have to be discussed.

Some theologians and psychologists believe that we need to dig deeper than observable behavior and use a measure of personal, individualized spirituality to answer questions about age-related changes in meaning systems. We all know of people who go through the motions of religiosity but cannot be described as spiritual. Some researchers use questionnaires asking about personal beliefs, and others use personal interviews, asking essay-type questions that give more depth but are more difficult to analyze. These studies of individualized spirituality are very fruitful because they have shown that personal beliefs about the quest for meaning are not necessarily related to religiosity.

Yet another approach is to use a qualitative method, such as reviewing case studies drawn from biographies or autobiographies, personal reports by well-known adults (politicians, saints, philosophers, mystics) about the steps and processes of their own inner development. Collections of such data have been analyzed, perhaps most impressively by William James (a distinguished early American psychologist) in his book *The Varieties of Religious Experience* (1902/1958) and by theologian and philosopher Evelyn Underhill in her book *Mysticism* (1911/1961). Of course, personal reports do not fit with our usual notion of "scientific evidence." The participants being studied are not representative of the general population, and the "data" may not be objectively gathered. Still, information from such sources makes a valuable contribution to theories of age-related changes in meaning systems. They tell us something about what may be possible or about the qualities, meaning systems, or capacities of a few extraordinary adults who appear to have explored the depths of the human spirit. Yet, even if we accept such descriptions as valid reports of inner processes, it is a very large leap to apply the described steps or processes to the experiences of ordinary folks. I am going to take that leap in this chapter. You will have to judge for yourself whether it is justified.

I need to make one further preparatory point: It is surely obvious (but nonetheless worth stating explicitly) that I bring my own meaning system to this discussion. Of course, that statement is true about the entire book (or anyone else's book). I approach this subject with a strong hypothesis that there are "higher" levels of human potential than most of us have yet reached, whether they are expressed in Maslow's terms as self-actualization, in Loevinger's concept of the integrated personality, or in any other terms that express advanced progress in the quest for meaning. When I describe the various models of the development of meaning systems, I am inevitably filtering the theories and the evidence through this hypothesis. There is no way I can avoid this, any more than you can avoid filtering this chapter through your own assumptions, your own meaning system. Keep this in mind as you read further.

I will begin with some empirical research on the search for meaning in adulthood and then add some discussion of the development of moral thinking, which is a manifestation of spirituality. And finally, I will discuss some qualitative work, some case studies of the quest for meaning by prominent writers and historical figures. Then I will try to tie together the evidence I have presented into a meaningful whole or at least a framework that will guide your thinking on this important topic.

9.2.1: Changes in the Quest for Meaning

Let us begin with the empirical research on religion and spirituality. There has been a surge of research on these two topics in the last few decades. Out of curiosity, I checked the listings in the PsycINFO database for empirical journal articles with the keywords "religion" or "spirituality" since 1973. My results are shown in Figure 9.1. As you can see, the number of articles has increased from zero in the first decade to over 3,500 in the most recent decade. And one of the most-studied topics within this area has been age-related changes in religion and spirituality.

Figure 9.1 The number of empirical journal articles on religion or spirituality has increased from zero to over 3,500 in the past 4 decades.

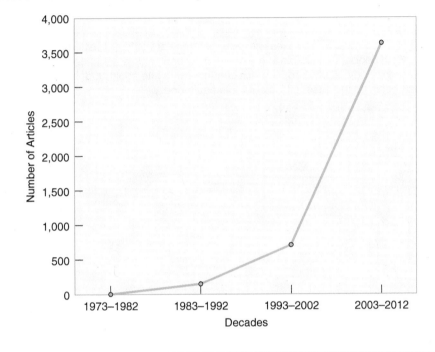

Critical Thinking

What explanations could you suggest for women attending religious services more frequently than men? How does this fit with other gender differences you have studied in this book?

Overall attendance and membership in religious organizations have dropped in the United States over the last 50 years, but cross-sectional data show that attendance at religious services is higher for adults 65 years of age and older than for younger adults (Pew Research Center, 2010). The few longitudinal studies on this topic show a decline in religious participation in very late life, but it is related to declining health and functional ability (Benjamins, Musick, Gold, et al., 2003). In general, the consensus seems to be that there is an increase in religiosity over the life course, with a short period of health-related drop-off at the end of life (Idler, 2006). In addition, data show that women attend religious services at higher rates than men for all ages and in all religions and countries studied (Miller & Stark, 2002). Religious participation is higher in the United States than in most European countries.

When it comes to religious beliefs and private religious activities such as engaging in prayers, meditating, or reading sacred texts, cross-sectional studies show that older adults participate in private religious behavior more than younger people (Pew Research Center, 2010). And a longitudinal study that showed a drop-off in attendance at religious services in very late adulthood also showed stable or even increased levels of private religious practices for this age group at the same time (Idler, Kasl, & Hays, 2001). The conclusion from these studies is that there is an increase in religious beliefs and private religious activities over adulthood, with a period of stability at the end of life (Idler, 2006).

In a longitudinal study that spanned 40 years, psychologist Paul Wink and sociologist Michele Dillon (2002) analyzed data from the Institute for Human Development longitudinal study to evaluate participants on their level of spirituality over the course of the study. The study included over 200 men and women, and most were interviewed four times between the ages of 31 and 78. In addition, the participants represented two cohorts, the younger born in 1927 and the older in 1920. The results are shown in Figure 9.2. As you can see, there was an increase in spirituality for women from middle to late-middle to older adulthood and an increase for men from late-middle to older adulthood.

Figure 9.2 Spirituality increases with age, but there are different patterns for the two genders. Both genders are stable in their spirituality until middle adulthood. Women begin an increase in middle adulthood, and this continues into late adulthood. In comparison, men don't begin an increase until late-middle adulthood.

SOURCE: Wink & Dillon (2002).

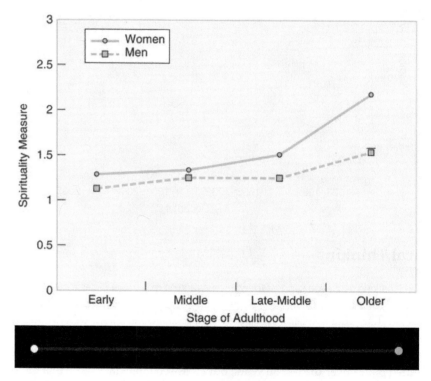

When the younger and older cohorts were compared, Wink and Dillon found different patterns of spiritual development, as shown in Figure 9.3. The younger cohort increased significantly throughout their adult lives, whereas the older cohort, although significantly more spiritual in early adulthood, only increased in the last stage, between late-middle and older adulthood. Wink and Dillon concluded that there is a tendency for men and women to increase in spirituality between the mid-50s and mid-70s. They become more involved with the quest for meaning as they become increasingly aware that their lives will end at some point in the future. The years from early to middle adulthood were more varied, depending on the gender and the cohort being studied. Women typically begin their quest for meaning in their 40s (but not before). In addition, people born less than a decade apart may show the same general increase in spirituality over adulthood, but they may show different patterns of spirituality. Wink and Dillon speculated that the younger cohort, who showed greater spirituality in their 30s, were living in the 60s when the "Age of Aquarius" was in its prime, and they were at an age that was more responsive to cultural changes than the older cohort, who were in their 40s at the time. So to answer the question of whether there is an increase in spirituality during adulthood, the answer is yes, but the timing depends on age, gender, and also the cultural conditions that prevail when adults are at certain critical ages.

Figure 9.3 The age-related increase in spirituality is different for two cohorts born seven years apart. The older cohort (born in 1920) did not show an increase in spirituality until late-middle adulthood. In comparison, the younger cohort (born in 1927) showed an increase in spirituality throughout adulthood, from early adulthood until late adulthood.

SOURCE: Wink & Dillon (2002).

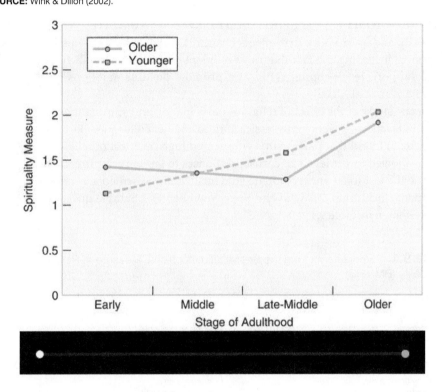

Psychologist Padmaprabha Dalby (2006) performed a meta-analysis on recent studies of changes in spirituality over the adult years and found an age-related increase in certain aspects of spirituality, such as integrity, humanistic concern, positive relationships with others, concern for the younger generations, relationship with a higher power, self-transcendence, and acceptance of death. However, these increases seemed to be responses to the adversities of later adulthood, such as poor health, disability, one's own impending death, and the loss of loved ones, rather than related to age itself. This has been suggested as an alternative to the idea that an accumulation of general life experience brings forth self-transcendence, but as Dalby pointed out, there are no studies comparing people of the same ages who differ in health and other measures of adversity.

9.2.2: Religion, Spirituality, and Health

In the past decade, a large number of studies in a variety of scientific fields, including psychology, epidemiology, and medicine, have explored the relationship religion and spirituality have with health. In general, consistent and robust findings have shown that people who attend religious services live longer than people who do not (Chida, Steptoe, & Powell, 2009), and that this result is stronger for women than for men (Tartaro, Lueken, & Gunn, 2005). Other studies have shown that religious involvement serves a protective role regarding mental health for European Americans, African Americans, and Asian Americans (Ai, Huang, Biork, et al., 2013). Spirituality and religiosity are related to lower levels of anxiety and depression (Brown, Carney, Parrish, et al., 2013). A meta-analysis showed that attendance at religious services was associated with lower levels of cardiovascular deaths (Chida, Steptoe, & Powell, 2009). Even when studies are controlled for healthy behaviors, socioeconomic factors, and health factors, religious practices and spirituality remain significant factors (Masters & Hooker, 2012).

In addition, meditation has been linked to both lower cortisol levels and lower blood pressure levels (Seeman, Dubin, & Seeman, 2003). It has been demonstrated that people who possess the personality trait of hardiness, who are committed to finding meaning in their lives, are more resilient to the effects of stress than those who have lower levels of this trait. They have confidence that they will be able to cope with whatever situations life hands them and will find meaning in the process (Maddi, 2005).

WHY RELIGIOSITY AND SPIRITUALITY AFFECTS HEALTH   What is it about religiosity and spirituality that affects health? A number of mechanisms have been suggested, including the fact that most religions promote healthy behavior, provide social support, teach coping skills, and promote positive emotions (McCullough, Hoyt, Larson, et al., 2000).

In one study of the effect of religious participation and spirituality on physiological stress reactions, psychologist Jessica Tartaro and her colleagues (Tartaro, Lueken, & Gunn, 2005) found that participants who scored high on a test of religiosity and spirituality showed lower levels of cortisol responses to lab-induced stress. The researchers gave the test to 60 undergraduate students who represented a variety of religious affiliations, including 22% who had their "own beliefs." Sample questions from this test are shown in Table 9.1.

Table 9.1 Sample Items from the Brief Multidimensional Measure of Religiousness/Spirituality (BMMRS)

I find strength and comfort in my religion

- many times a day.
- every day.
- most days.
- some days.
- once in a while.
- never or almost never.

I am spiritually touched by the beauty of creation

- many times a day.
- every day.
- most days.
- some days.
- once in awhile.
- never or almost never.

I feel a deep sense of responsibility for reducing pain and suffering in the world.

- Strongly agree
- Agree
- Disagree
- Strongly disagree

I have forgiven those who hurt me.

- Always or almost always
- Often
- Seldom
- Never

How often do you go to religious services?

- More than once a week
- Every week or more often
- Every month or so
- Once or twice a month
- Once or twice a year
- Never

How often do you pray privately in places other than at church or synagogue?

- More than once a day
- Once a day
- A few times a week
- Once a week
- A few times a month
- Once a month
- Never

I think about how my life is part of a larger spiritual force

- a great deal.
- quite a bit.
- somewhat.
- not at all.

I try hard to carry my religious beliefs over into all my other dealings in life.

- Strongly agree
- Agree
- Disagree
- Strongly disagree

SOURCE: Adapted from Underwood (1999).

Later, the students' cortisol levels were measured before and after performing two computer tasks that had been shown to induce physiological indicators of stress reactivity. (Cortisol is a hormone released as part of the stress response and is related to decreases in immune system response.) Results are shown in Figure 9.4.

Figure 9.4 Young adults who described themselves as "not being religious at all" had greater stress reactivity than those who described themselves as being "slightly," "moderately," or "very" religious.

SOURCE: Tartaro, Luecken, & Gunn (2005).

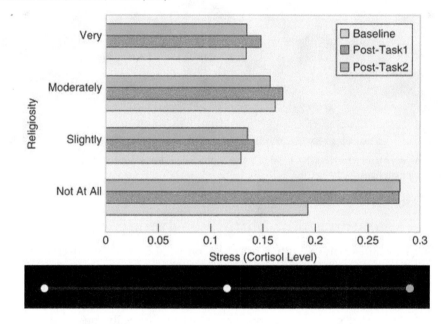

For the question, "To what extent do you consider yourself a religious person?" those who responded, "not at all," showed significantly higher cortisol response levels than those who responded that they were "slightly," "moderately," or "very" religious. When responses to the specific religious or spiritual practices were examined, two areas were found to be associated with the cortisol response—forgiveness and frequency of prayer. The researchers concluded that religious practices and spiritual beliefs, especially forgiveness and prayer, may serve to protect individuals from the damaging effects of stress.

9.3: Theories of Spiritual Development

9.3   Discuss spiritual development in terms of moral reasoning and faith

For several reasons, I want to start this exploration with a look at psychologist Lawrence Kohlberg's theory of the development of **moral reasoning**—reasoning about what is right and wrong and how to judge the rightness or wrongness of an act. Although the questions Kohlberg addressed touch on only a corner of the subject I am examining, his basic theoretical model is the foundation of much of the current thinking about adults' evolving worldviews or meaning systems. Kohlberg's theory has been tested extensively with empirical research and is widely accepted by developmental psychologists, so it provides a relatively non-controversial jumping-off point.

Participating in religious services is related to better coping skills, less severe stress reactions, better health, and longer lives.

9.3.1: Development of Moral Reasoning

Faced with a conflict between different values, on what basis do we decide what is morally right, fair, or just? Kohlberg argued, as an extension of Jean Piaget's theory of cognitive development, that we move through a sequence of stages in our moral reasoning, each stage growing out of, but superseding, the one that came before. In this view, each stage reflects a meaning system or model, an internally consistent and pervasive set of assumptions of right and wrong (Kohlberg, 1981, 1984).

Kohlberg made an important distinction between the decision one makes and the reason behind that decision. The issue is not whether a person thinks, for example, that stealing is wrong, but why he or she thinks it is wrong. Kohlberg searched for developmental changes in the reasoning about moral questions, just as Piaget searched for developmental changes in broader forms of logic.

THE MEASUREMENT PROCEDURE Kohlberg assessed a person's level or stage of moral reasoning by means of a moral judgment interview in which the subject is asked to respond to a series of hypothetical moral dilemmas. In each dilemma, two different principles are in conflict. For example, in the now-famous Heinz dilemma, the subject must grapple with the question of whether a man named Heinz ought to steal a drug to save his dying wife if the only druggist who can provide it is demanding a higher price than he can pay. In this instance, the conflicting principles are the value of preserving life and the value of respecting property and upholding the law. This story of Heinz is the best known of these moral dilemmas:

> In Europe a woman was near death from a special kind of cancer. There was one drug that doctors thought might save her. It was a form of radium that a druggist in the same town had recently discovered. The drug was expensive to make, but the druggist was charging $2,000, or 10 times the cost of the drug, for a small (possibly lifesaving) dose. Heinz, the sick woman's husband, borrowed all the money he could, about $1,000, or half of what he needed. He told the druggist that his wife was dying and asked him to sell the drug cheaper or to let him pay later. The druggist replied, "No, I discovered the drug, and I'm going to make money from it." Heinz then became desperate and broke into the store to steal the drug for his wife. Should Heinz have done that? Why or why not?

The following responses are examples of people operating in different stages of moral development:

ⓧ Level 1: Preconventional morality

Stage 1: Punishment and obedience orientation

Yes, Heinz should take the drug. *Why?* Because if he lets his wife die, he could be responsible for it and get into trouble.

No, Heinz should not take the drug. *Why?* Because it is stealing. It doesn't belong to him and he can get arrested and punished.

Stage 2: Naive hedonism orientation

Yes, Heinz should take the drug. *Why?* Because he really isn't hurting the druggist, and he wants to help his wife. Maybe he can pay him later.

No, Heinz shouldn't take the drug. *Why?* The druggist is in business to make money. That's his job. He needs to make a profit.

ⓧ Level 2: Conventional morality

Stage 3: Good-boy or good-girl orientation

Yes, Heinz should take the drug. *Why?* Because he is being a good husband and saving his wife's life. He would be wrong if he didn't save her.

No, Heinz should not take the drug. *Why?* Because he tried to buy it and he couldn't, so it's not his fault if his wife dies. He did his best.

Stage 4: Social order maintaining orientation

Yes, Heinz should take the drug. *Why?* Because the druggist is wrong to be interested only in profits. But Heinz also must pay for the drug later and maybe confess that he took it. It's still wrong to steal.

No, Heinz should not take the drug. *Why?* Because even though it is natural to want to save your wife, you still need to obey the law. You can't just ignore it because of special circumstances.

ⓧ **Level 3: Postconventional (or principled) morality**

Stage 5: Social contract orientation

Yes, Heinz should take the drug. *Why?* Although the law says he shouldn't, if you consider the whole picture, it would be reasonable for anyone in his situation to take the drug.

No, Heinz should not take the drug. *Why?* Although some good would come from him taking the drug, it still wouldn't justify violating the consensus of how people have agreed to live together. The ends don't justify the means.

Stage 6: Individual principles of conscience orientation

Yes, Heinz should take the drug. *Why?* When a person is faced with two conflicting principles, they need to judge which is higher and obey it. Human life is higher than possession.

No, Heinz should not take the drug. *Why?* Heinz needs to decide between his emotion and the law—both are "right" in a way, but he needs to decide what an ideally just person would do, and that would be not to steal the drug.

THE STAGES   Based on many subjects' responses to such dilemmas, Kohlberg concluded that there are three basic levels of moral reasoning, each of which can be divided further into two stages, resulting in six stages in all, summarized in Table 9.2.

Another way to look at the shifts from preconventional to conventional to post conventional levels of reasoning is to see them as a process of **decentering**, a term Piaget used to describe cognitive development more generally as a movement outward from the self. At the preconventional level, the children's reference points are themselves—the consequences of their own actions, the rewards they may gain. At the conventional level, the reference point has moved outward away from the center of the self to the family or society. Finally, at the postconventional level, the adult searches for a still broader reference point, some set of underlying principles that lies behind or beyond social systems. Such a movement outward from the self is one of the constant themes in writings on the growth or development of meaning systems in adult life.

KOHLBERG'S RESEARCH   Only longitudinal data can tell us whether Kohlberg's model is valid. If it is, not only should children and adults move from one step to the next in the order he proposes, but they should also not show regression to earlier stages.

THE DATA   Kohlberg and his colleagues tested these hypotheses in three samples, all interviewed repeatedly, and each time asked to discuss a series of moral dilemmas: (a) 84 boys from the Chicago area first interviewed when they were between 10 and 16 in 1956, and some of whom were reinterviewed up to five more times (the final interview was in 1976–1977, when they were in their 30s; Colby, Kohlberg, Gibbs, et al., 1983); (b) a group of 23 boys and young men in Turkey (some from a rural village and some from large cities), followed over periods of up to 10 years into early adulthood

Table 9.2 Kohlberg's Stages of Moral Development

Stages	Description
Preconventional Level	Typical of most children under age 9 but is also found in some adolescents and in some adult criminal offenders. At both stages of this level, one sees rules as something outside oneself. In stage 1, the *punishment-and-obedience orientation*, what is right is what is rewarded or what is not punished; in stage 2, right is defined in terms of what brings pleasure or serves one's own needs. Stage 2 is sometimes described as the *naive hedonism orientation*, a phrase that captures some of the flavor of this stage.
Conventional Level	The characteristic of most adolescents and most adults in our culture, one internalizes the rules and expectations of one's family or peer group (at stage 3) or of society (at stage 4). Stage 3 is sometimes called the *good-boy or good-girl orientation*, whereas stage 4 is sometimes labeled as the *social order maintaining orientation*.
Postconventional Level	This is found in only a minority of adults, involves a search for the underlying reasons behind society's rules. At stage 5, which Kohlberg calls the *social contract orientation*, laws and regulations are seen as important ways of ensuring fairness, but they are not perceived as immutable, nor do they necessarily perfectly reflect more fundamental moral principles. Because laws and contracts are usually in accord with such underlying principles, obeying society's laws is reasonable nearly all the time. But when the underlying principles or reasons are at variance with some specific social custom or rule, the stage 5 adult argues on the basis of the fundamental principle, even if it means disobeying or disagreeing with a law. Civil rights protesters in the early 1960s, for example, typically supported their civil disobedience with stage 5 reasoning. In addition, stage 5 moral reasoning is related to concerns for the environment in college students, presumably because it is necessary to be able to consider the perspective of the other when dealing with competing interests and rights (**Karpiak & Baril, 2008**). Stage 6, known as the *individual principles of conscience orientation*, is simply a further extension of the same pattern, with the person searching for and then living in a way that is consistent with the deepest set of moral principles possible.

Hide All Cells   Show All Cells

SOURCE: Based on Kohlberg (1976, 1984).

(Nisan & Kohlberg, 1982); and (c) 64 male and female subjects from kibbutzim (collective communities) in Israel, who were first tested as teenagers and then retested once or twice more over periods of up to 10 years (Snarey, Reimer, & Kohlberg, 1985).

Figure 9.5 gives two kinds of information about the findings from these three studies. In the top half of the figure are total "moral maturity scores" derived from the interviews. These scores reflect each subject's stage of moral reasoning and can range from 100 to 500. As you can see, in all three studies the average score went up steadily with age, although there are some interesting cultural differences in speed of movement through the stages. In the bottom half of the figure are the percent of answers to the moral dilemmas that reflected each stage of moral reasoning for the participants at each age. These data are for the Chicago sample only because it has been studied over the longest period of time. As we would expect, the number of stage 1 responses drops out quite early, whereas conventional morality (stages 3 and 4) rises rapidly in the teenage years and remains high in adulthood. Only a very small percent of answers, even of respondents in their 30s, shows stage 5 reasoning (postconventional reasoning), and none show stage 6 reasoning.

Figure 9.5 The upper panel shows that scores of four diverse samples of boys on a moral reasoning test show a general increase from middle childhood through young adulthood. The lower panel shows the percent of responses given that reflect the different stages of moral development. It is clear that Stage 4 responses increase with age and that Stage 2 responses decrease.

SOURCE: Data from Colby, Kohlberg, Gibbs, et al., 1983; Nisan & Kohlberg, 1982; and Snarey Reimer, & Kohlberg (1985).

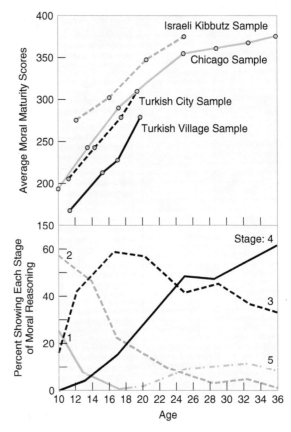

Both analyses show the stages to be strongly sequential. The sequential pattern is supported by the fact that in none of these three studies was there a single participant who skipped a stage, and only about 5% showed regression. Each participant also showed a good deal of internal consistency at any one testing, using similar logic in analyzing each of several quite different moral problems. The same patterns were found in both shorter-term longitudinal studies (Walker, 1989) and in studies using a questionnaire method of measuring moral judgment rather than the more open-ended interview (Rest & Thoma, 1985).

Unfortunately, no equivalent longitudinal data exist for any adults past midlife. Cross-sectional results show no age differences in overall level of moral judgment between young, middle-aged, and older adults (Lonky, Kaus, & Roodin, 1984; Pratt, Golding, & Hunter, 1983). Such findings might be taken to mean that the level of reasoning achieved in early adulthood remains relatively stable throughout adulthood.

But the longitudinal data do not support such an assertion, at least not through the middle 30s. Among Kohlberg's sample were quite a few people who shifted from stage 3 to stage 4 while in their 20s and a few who moved to stage 5 while in their 30s. At least some adults may thus continue to develop through Kohlberg's stages throughout adulthood. The only way to know this for sure would be to assess moral reasoning longitudinally over the full years of adult life.

STAGE 6, AND THE POSSIBILITY OF STAGE 7 In his early work Kohlberg suggested that a fair number of college students reached stage 6. In his later writings, however, he changed his mind and concluded that this universalistic stage is extremely uncommon (Colby & Kohlberg, 1987). The longitudinal data suggest that stage 5 may be the typical "endpoint" of the developmental progression. Adults who reach stage 6 (about 15% of those in their 30s in Kohlberg's samples) do indeed operate on some broad, general principles. What they lack, however, is "that which is critical for our theoretical notion of Stage 6, namely, the organization of moral judgment around a clearly formulated moral principle of justice and respect for persons that provides a rationale for the primacy of this principle" (Kohlberg, 1984, p. 271). In other words, at stage 5 one develops some broad principles that go beyond (or "behind") the social system; at stage 6, the rare person develops a still broader and more general ethical system in which these basic principles are embedded. Among those Kohlberg listed as apparently stage 6 thinkers were Martin Luther King, Jr., and Mahatma Gandhi.

WRITING PROMPT

What do you know about Martin Luther King, Jr. or Mahatma Gandhi that is consistent with Kohlberg's stage 6 moral reasoning? Write a brief response that will be read by your instructor.

▶ The response entered here will appear in the performance dashboard and can be viewed by your instructor.

Submit

Kohlberg and his colleagues also speculated about the existence of a still higher stage, Stage 7, a *unity orientation*, which they thought might emerge only toward the end of life, after an adult has spent some years living within a principled moral system.

According to Kohlberg's theory, only a few individuals, such as Martin Luther King, Jr. (left) and Mahatma Gandhi (right), reach the highest level of moral reasoning.

It is the confrontation of one's own death that can bring about this transition. As they ask the fundamental questions, "Why live?" and "How do I face death?" some people transcend the type of logical analysis that typifies all the earlier forms of moral reasoning and arrive at a still deeper or broader decentering. It is a sense of unity with being, with life, or with God (Kohlberg, Levine, & Hewer, 1983).

EVALUATION AND COMMENT   The body of evidence that has accumulated concerning the development of moral reasoning provides strong support for several aspects of Kohlberg's theory:

- There do appear to be stages that children and adults move through in developing concepts of fairness and morality.
- At least up to stage 5, these stages appear to meet the tests of a hierarchical stage system: They occur in a fixed order, each emerging from and replacing the one that preceded it, and together forming a structural whole.
- The stage sequence appears to be universal. The specific content of moral decisions may differ from one culture to the next, but the overall form of logic seems to move through the same steps in every culture in which this has been studied—a list that includes 27 different countries, Western and non-Western, industrialized and nonindustrialized (Snarey, 1985).

The stages have relevance for real life as well as theory. For example, researchers in one study found that adults who reason at the principled level are more able than are those at the conventional level to deal positively and constructively with significant losses in their lives, such as the death of a family member or the breakup of a relationship (Lonky, Kaus, & Roodin, 1984).

At the same time, a number of critics have pointed out that Kohlberg's theory is relatively narrow, focusing almost exclusively on the development of concepts of justice or fairness. Other aspects of moral/ethical reasoning, other facets of meaning systems, are omitted.

The most eloquent of the critics is psychologist Carol Gilligan (1982). She argued that Kohlberg was interested in concepts of justice and not concepts of care, so his theory and research largely ignore an ethical/moral system based on caring for others, on responsibility, on altruism or compassion. In particular, Gilligan proposed that women more often than men approach moral and ethical dilemmas from the point of view of responsibilities and caring, searching not for the "just" solution, but for the solution that best deals with the social relationships involved. She argues that men, in contrast, use a morality of justice more often than women.

This aspect of Gilligan's argument is not strongly supported by research findings. In studies in which boys and girls have been compared on stage of moral reasoning using Kohlberg's revised scoring system, no gender differences are typically found (Smetana, Killen, & Turiel, 1991), although several studies of adults do show the difference that Gilligan hypothesizes (Lyons, 1983). What is clear from the research to date is that girls and women can and do use moral reasoning based on principles of justice when they are presented with dilemmas in which that is a central issue.

9.3.2: Development of Faith

Faith is a set of assumptions or understandings about the nature of our connections with others and the world in which we live. Using this definition, it follows that each of us has a faith, whether or not we belong to a church or religious organization. Moral reasoning is a part of faith, but faith is broader.

Theologian and developmental psychologist James Fowler (1981) goes beyond questions of moral reasoning with his theory of faith development. At any point in our lives, he argues, each of us has a master story, which is "the answer you give to the questions of what life is about, or who's really in charge here, or how do I live to make my life a worthy, good one. It's a stance you take toward life" (Fowler, 1983, p. 60).

Critical Thinking

Do you have a master story? Has it changed in the last 10 years? What do you think caused the change?

Like Kohlberg, Fowler is interested not in the specific content of one's faith, but in its structure or form. A Christian, a Hindu, a Jew, a Muslim, and an atheist may all have faiths that are structurally similar but sharply different in content. And like Kohlberg, Fowler hypothesizes that each of us develops through a shared series of faith structures (or worldviews, broad internal working models, meaning systems, or whatever we choose to call them) over the course of childhood and adulthood. Like Piaget, he believes that "the structural stage sequence is sequential, invariant, and hierarchical" (Fowler, 2001, p. 171). Two of the six stages he proposed occur primarily in childhood, and I won't describe them here; the remaining four can be found among adults.

THE STAGES OF FAITH   The first of the adult forms of faith, which Fowler calls *synthetic-conventional faith*, normally appears first in adolescence and then continues well into early adulthood for most of us. Like Kohlberg's level of conventional morality, conventional faith is rooted in the implicit assumption that authority is to be found outside oneself.

Many adults remain within this form of faith throughout their lives, defining themselves and interpreting their experiences within the meaning system of a group or a specific set of beliefs.

Let me give you an example from Fowler's own interviews that may make the point clearer. Mrs. H. is a 61-year-old southern woman who grew up on a tenant farm. At the time Fowler interviewed her, she had recently rededicated herself to the Baptist Church after many years away from church activity. At one point she said,

> I feel very sad and ashamed for the way I have wasted my life. I do know that God has forgiven me for every wrong that I've done, and that He loves me. I feel very close to God most of the time, now that I am active in the work of the church again. Of course there are times that I don't feel as close to Him as I'd like to, but I know that I am the one who moves away, not He. I've learned that we all have so much to be thankful for, if we only stop and count our blessings. (Fowler, 1981, p. 172)

It is precisely this reliance on external authority that changes when an adult moves to the next proposed stage, which Fowler calls *individuative-reflective faith*. This move requires an interruption of reliance on an external source of authority—a relocation of authority from external to internal. In making this shift, many adults reject or move away from the faith community to which they belong. Often, there is also a rejection of ritual or myth and an embracing of science or rationality. But the transition can occur without such rejections. The key is that the person not only reexamines old assumptions but also takes responsibility in a new way.

It is hard to convey just how profound a change this is. The metaphor I have found most helpful is one I have adapted from the writings of mythologist Joseph Campbell (1949/1990). It is as if in the stage of conventional faith we experience ourselves as like the moon, illuminated by reflected light. We are not ourselves the source of light (or knowledge) but are created by outside forces. In the stage of individuative faith, we experience ourselves as like the sun, radiating light of our own. We are no longer defined by the groups to which we belong; rather, we choose the groups, the relationships, based on our self-chosen beliefs or values. Thus, even if the specific beliefs we choose at this point are the same ones with which we have grown up, the underlying meaning system is changed.

Rebecca, a woman in her mid-30s, seems clearly to have made this transition:

> I know I have very defined boundaries and I protect them very carefully. I won't give up the slightest control. In any relationship I decide who gets in, how far, and when. What am I afraid of? I used to think I was afraid people would find out who I really was and then not like me. But I don't think that's it anymore. What I feel now is—"that's me. That's mine. It's what makes me. And I'm powerful. It's my negative side, maybe, but it's also my positive stuff—and there's a lot of that. What it is is me, it's my self—and if I let people in maybe they'll take it, maybe they'll use it—and I'll be gone." … This "self," if I had to represent it I think of two things: either a steel rod that runs through everything, a kind of solid fiber, or sort of like a ball at the center that is all together. (Kegan, 1982, pp. 240–241)

The next stage in Fowler's model, *conjunctive faith,* requires an opening outward from the self-preoccupation of the individuative reflective level. There is an openness here to paradox, a moving away from fixed truth toward a search for balance, not only of self and other, but also of mind and emotion, of rationality and ritual. The person who lives within this meaning system, which is not typically found before midlife, accepts that there are many truths, that others' beliefs, others' ideas, may be true for them—a point of view that not only brings far greater tolerance toward others but also very commonly brings the person to an interest in service or commitment to the welfare of others.

Critical Thinking

Does Fowler's stage of conjunctive faith remind you of one of Erikson's stages of psychosocial development?

Here's one illustrative voice, that of Miss T., a 78-year-old woman who had been variously a Unitarian, a Quaker, and a follower of Krishnamurti and other Eastern teachers. When asked if there were beliefs and values everyone should hold, she said,

> If somebody asked me that and gave me just two minutes to answer it, I know what I'd say. It's a line from George Fox, the founder of Quakerism. It's old-fashioned English and it seems to me to have the entire program of anybody's life. It's a revolution, it's an enormous comfort, it's a peace maker. The line is: "There is that of God in every man." Now, you can start thinking about it. You can see that if you really did believe that, how it would change your relationships with people. It's far-reaching. It applies nationally and individually and class-wise; it reaches the whole. To anyone that I loved dearly I would say, "Put that in your little invisible locket and keep it forever." (Fowler, 1981, p. 194)

Other statements by Miss T. make it clear that the content of her faith at this point involves a kind of return to some of the elements of her earlier religious teachings, but she has reframed it, casting it in language that has meaning for her now and that focuses on finding fulfillment in service to others—all of which are significant elements of conjunctive faith.

The final proposed stage in Fowler's system is *universalizing faith*. Like Kohlberg's stage 6, reaching this stage is a relatively rare achievement, but Fowler argues that it is the next logical step. To some extent, it involves a step beyond individuality. In the stage of conjunctive faith, the person may be "open" and "integrated" but is still struggling with the paradox of searching for universality while attempting to preserve individuality. In the stage of universalizing faith, the person lives the principles, the imperatives, of absolute love and justice. Because such people live their lives based on such basic outward-oriented principles, they are heedless of their own self-preservation, much as Mother Theresa continued caring for the dying up until the end of her own life. They may even be seen by others as subversive to the structures of society or traditional religion because they do not begin with the assumption that society or religion is necessarily correct in its institutions or customs.

9.3.3: Some Basic Points about Fowler's Stages

Some key points need emphasis. First, like Kohlberg, Fowler assumes that these stages occur in a sequence, but that the sequence is only very roughly associated with age, especially in adulthood. Some adults remain within the same meaning system, the same faith structure, their entire lives; others make one or more transitions in their understanding of themselves and their relationships with others.

Second, Fowler nonetheless contends that each stage has its "proper time" of ascendancy in a person's lifetime, a period at which that particular form of faith is most consistent with the demands of life. Most typically, the stage of conventional faith is in its ascendance in adolescence or early adulthood, and the stage of individuative-reflective faith in the years of the late 20s and 30s, whereas a transition to the stage of conjunctive faith, if it occurs at all, may occur around midlife. Finally, the stage of universalizing faith, if one can reach it, would be the optimal form of faith in old age, when issues of integrity and meaning become still more dominant.

Third, Fowler conceives of each stage as wider or more encompassing than the one that preceded it. And this greater breadth helps to foster both a greater capacity for a sense of sureness and serenity and a greater capacity for intimacy—with the self as well as with others.

RESEARCH FINDINGS   I am not aware of any longitudinal studies that have tested the sequential aspect of Fowler's theory. However, Fowler (1981) has reported some cross-sectional data that show the incidence of the stages of faith at each of several ages. He asked over 300 adolescents and adults open-ended questions about their faith and had raters assign a stage to each person based on these interviews. The results fit the theory relatively well, showing that conventional faith is most common in the teenage years, individuative-reflective faith among people in their 20s, and conjunctive faith emerging only in the 30s. Furthermore, only one person fit the category of universalizing faith, a man in his 60s.

Another study that offers consistent evidence comes from psychologist Gary Reker, who has developed a very similar model of the emergence of meaning systems over the years of adulthood. Reker (1991) argued that an adult can find meaning in life through any of a variety of sources, such as leisure activities, personal relationships, personal achievement, traditions and culture, altruism or service to others, or enduring values and ideals. Reker suggested that these various sources of meaning can be organized into four levels: *self-preoccupation*, in which meaning is found primarily through financial security or meeting basic needs; *individualism*, in which meaning is found in personal growth or achievement, or through creative and leisure activities;

collectivism, which includes meaning from traditions and culture and from societal causes; and *self-transcendence,* in which meaning is found through enduring values and ideals, religious activities, and altruism.

Reker's work does not provide a direct test of Fowler's model, but it is consistent with the basic idea that there may be systematic changes over the years of adulthood in the framework that adults use to define themselves and find meaning in their lives.

A PRELIMINARY ASSESSMENT   Theories like Fowler's and research like Reker's supplement our thinking about adulthood in important ways, if only to help us focus on the importance of meaning systems and their possible sequential change with age. But it is still very early in our empirical exploration of this and related theories. The greatest immediate need is for good longitudinal data, perhaps initially covering the years that are thought to be transitional for many adults, but ultimately covering the entire adult age range.

9.4: Integrating Meaning and Personality: A Preliminary Theoretical Synthesis

9.4   Review of stages of personality, morality, and faith development

Some of the parallels between these theories and the ones you have studied elsewhere may have already struck you. The surface similarities are obvious, as you can see in Table 9.3.

Table 9.3 Review of Stages of Personality, Morality, and Faith Development

General Stage	Loevinger's Stages of Ego Development	Maslow's Levels of Needs Hierarchy	Kohlberg's Stages of Moral Reasoning Development	Fowler's Stages of Faith Development
Conformist; Culture-bound Self	Conformist; Self-Aware Stages	Love and Belongingness Needs	Good-Boy or Good-Girl Orientation; Social Order Maintaining Orientation	Synthetic-Conventional Faith
Individuality	Conscientious; Individualistic Stages	Self-Esteem Needs	Social Contract Orientation	Individuative-Reflective Faith
Integration	Autonomous; Integrated Stages	Self-Actualization	Individual Principles of Conscience Orientation	Conjunctive Faith
Self-transcendence		Peak Experiences	Unity Orientation	Universalizing Faith

Loevinger's conformist stage in her theory of ego development certainly sounds like both Kohlberg's conventional morality and Fowler's conventional faith. There seems to be agreement that in adolescence and early adulthood, people tend to be focused on adapting to the demands of the roles and relationships society imposes on them and assume that the source of authority is external.

Loevinger's conscientious and individualistic stages are a great deal like Maslow's layer of esteem needs, Kohlberg's social contract orientation, and Fowler's individuative-reflective faith. All four theorists agree that the next step involves a shift in the central source of meaning or self-definition from external to internal, accompanied by a preoccupation with the self and one's own abilities, skills, and potentials.

Loevinger's autonomous and integrated stages are similar to Fowler's conjunctive faith, possibly related to self-actualization needs as described by Maslow. All speak of a shift away from self-preoccupation toward a search for balance, a shift toward greater tolerance toward both self and others.

Finally, there seems to be agreement about a still higher stage that involves some form of self-transcendence: Kohlberg's unity orientation, Fowler's stage of universalizing faith, or Maslow's peak experiences.

Of course, we are not dealing with four independent visions here. These theorists all knew of each other's work and were influenced by each other's ideas. This is particularly true in the case of Fowler and Kohlberg because Fowler's theory is quite explicitly an extension of Kohlberg's model. So the fact that they all seem to agree does not mean that we have uncovered "truth" here. However, my confidence in the validity of the basic sequence these theorists describe is bolstered by three additional arguments.

First, although they have influenced one another, there are still three quite distinct theoretical heritages involved. Kohlberg's and Fowler's work are rooted in Piaget's theory and in studies of normal children's thinking; Loevinger's work is rooted in Freud's theory and in clinical assessments of children and adults, including those with emotional disturbances; and Maslow's theory, although influenced by psychoanalytic thought, is based primarily on his own observations of a small number of highly unusual, self-actualized, adults. The fact that one can arrive at such similar views of the sequence of emergence of meaning systems from such different roots makes the convergence more impressive.

Second, in the case of both Kohlberg's and Loevinger's models, we have reasonably strong supporting empirical evidence, especially concerning the first step in the commonly proposed adult sequence, of a move from conforming/conventional to individualistic stages. Transitions beyond that are simply much less well studied, in part because longitudinal studies have not yet followed adults past early midlife, perhaps in part because the later transitions are simply less common. Still, this is not all totally speculative stuff. We can anchor at least part of the commonly proposed basic sequence in hard data.

Finally, this basic model seems plausible to me because the sequence makes sense in terms of a still more encompassing developmental concept proposed by Robert Kegan.

9.4.1: A Synthesizing Model

Psychologist Robert Kegan (1982) proposes that each of us has two enormously powerful and equal desires or motives built in. On the one hand, we deeply desire connection, the state of being joined or integrated with others. On the other hand, we equally desire independence, the state of being differentiated from others. No accommodation between these two is really in balance, so whatever *evolutionary truce* (as Kegan calls each stage) we arrive at, it will lean further toward one than toward the other. Eventually, the unmet need becomes so strong that we are forced to change the system, to change our understanding. In the end, what this creates is a fundamental alternation, a moving back and forth of the pendulum, between perspectives or meaning systems centered on inclusion or union and perspectives centered on independence or separateness.

The child begins life in a symbiotic relationship with the mother or mother figure, so the pendulum begins on the side of connection and union. By age 2 the child has pulled away and seeks independence, a separate identity. The conformist or conventional meaning system that we see in adolescence and early adulthood (if not later) is a move back toward connection, with the group, while the transition to the individualistic meaning system is a return to separation and independence. The term *detribalization* fits nicely with Kegan's basic model (Levinson, 1978). In shifting the source of authority from external sources to one's own resources, there is at least initially a pushing away of the tribe and all its rituals and rules.

Do you identify the competing drives of connection and independence in your own life? Have there been stages in your life during which they have alternated? Write a brief response that will be read by your teacher. Explain your reasoning.

> ▶ | The response entered here will appear in the performance dashboard and can be viewed by your instructor.

Submit

If the model is correct, the step after this ought to be another return toward connection, which seems to me to be precisely what is proposed by most of the theorists I have described. As I see it, most of them talk about two substeps in this shift of the pendulum, with Fowler's conjunctive faith or Kohlberg's individual principles of conscience orientation being intermediate steps on the way toward the more complete position of union or community represented by Fowler's universalizing faith or Kohlberg's unity orientation.

Although my explanation here describes the process with the image of a pendulum moving back and forth, clearly Kegan is not proposing that movement is simply back and forth in a single groove. Instead, he sees the process as more like that of a spiral in which each shift to the other side of the polarity is at a more integrated level than the one before.

If such a basic alternation, such a spiral movement, really does form the underlying rhythm of development, why should we assume that it stops even at so lofty a point as Kohlberg's unity orientation? When I first understood this aspect of Kegan's theory, I had one of those startling "ah ha!" experiences, for I realized that the stages of the mystical journey described in case studies by Evelyn Underhill and by William James could be linked seamlessly with the sequence Kegan was describing.

I am well aware that a discussion of such subjective mystical experiences here will seem to some to be going very far afield, perhaps totally outside the realm of psychology. But to me the risk is worth it, not only because in this way perhaps I can make a case for my own basic assumptions regarding the immense potential of the individual human spirit, but also because the pattern that emerges fits so remarkably well with the research evidence and the theories I have discussed thus far.

9.4.2: Stages of Mystical Experience

The stages I am describing here were suggested by theologian and philosopher Evelyn Underhill (1911/1961), based on her reading of autobiographies, biographies, and other writings of the lives of hundreds of people from every religious tradition, all of whom described some form of **mysticism**, or self-transcendent experience, in which they know that they are part of a larger whole and that they have an existence beyond their own physical body and personal history. They did not describe all the steps or stages listed, but Underhill reported that there was a remarkable degree of unanimity about the basic process, despite huge differences in historical period and religious background.

STEP 1   Step 1 in this process, which Underhill calls *awakening*, seems to me to correspond to the usual endpoint in theories like Kohlberg's or Fowler's. It involves at least a brief self-transcendent experience, such as the peak experiences that Maslow describes. In Kegan's model, this step is clearly represented on the "union" end of the polarity; it is an awakening to the possibility of stepping outside one's own perspective and understanding the world from a point of deep connection.

STEP 2   Step 2, which Underhill calls *purification*, is clearly a move back toward separateness. The person, having seen himself or herself from a broader perspective, also sees all his or her own imperfections, fruitless endeavors, and flaws. As St. Teresa of

Ávila, one of the great mystics of the Christian tradition, put it, "In a room bathed in sunlight not a cobweb can remain hidden" (1562/1960, p. 181). To understand and eliminate the flaws, the cobwebs, the person must turn inward again. At this stage many people are strongly focused on self-discipline, including special spiritual disciplines such as regular prayer or meditation and fasting.

STEP 3 Step 3 clearly moves us back toward union. Underhill calls this *illumination.* It involves a much deeper, more prolonged awareness of light, or greater reality, or God, and may in fact encompass some of what Kohlberg refers to as stage 7.

STEPS 4 AND 5 But even this illumination is not the end of the journey. Underhill finds two other steps described by many mystics that appear to lie beyond. The first of these, stage 4, often called the *dark night of the soul,* involves a still further turn inward, back toward separateness. At stage 3, illumination, the person still feels some personal satisfaction, some personal pleasure or joy in having achieved illumination. According to mystics who have described these later stages, if one is to achieve ultimate union, even this personal pleasure must be abandoned. And the process of abandonment requires a turning back to the self, to awareness, and exploration, of all the remaining ways in which the separate self has survived. Only then can the person achieve the endpoint, stage 5, which is *unity*—with God, with reality, with beauty, with the ultimate—however, this may be described within a particular religious tradition.

I cannot say, of course, whether this sequence, this spiral of inner human progress, reflects the inevitable or ultimate path for us all. I can say only that the developmental analyses of stages of morality, or stages of faith or personality, that have been offered by many psychologists, for which we have at least some preliminary supporting evidence, appear to form a connected whole with the descriptions of stages of mystical illumination. For example, Jung (1917/1966) described similar stages in his journey to discover his own inner world through psychoanalysis. At the very least, we know that a pathway similar to this has been trod by a long series of remarkable individuals, whose descriptions of their inner journeys bear striking similarities. There may be many other paths or journeys. But the reflections of these remarkable few point the way toward the possibility of a far vaster potential of the human spirit than is apparent to most of us in our daily lives.

9.5: The Process of Transition

9.5 **Explain the transition process from one stage of faith and equilibrium to another**

Coming down a bit from these lofty heights, but still assuming for the moment that there is some basic rhythm, some developmental sequence, in the forms of meaning we create, let me turn to a question that may be of special personal importance: What is the process by which transitions or transformations from one stage to the next take place? What triggers them? What are the common features of transitions? How are they traversed?

Most developmental psychologists who propose stages of adult development have focused more on the stages than on the transition processes. But some common themes are repeated in the ways transitions are described.

A number of theorists have described transitions in parallel terms, with each shift from one level or stage to the next seen as a kind of death and rebirth—a death of the earlier sense of self, of the earlier faith, of the earlier equilibrium (James, 1902/1958; Kegan, 1980). The process typically involves first some glimpses or precursors or premonitions of another stage or view, which are then followed by a period (which may be brief or prolonged) in which the person struggles to deal with the two "selves" within. Sometimes the process is aborted and the person returns to the earlier equilibrium. Sometimes the person moves instead toward a new understanding, a new equilibrium.

The middle part of this process, when the old meaning system has been partially given up but a new equilibrium has not yet been reached, is often experienced as profoundly dislocating. Statements such as "I am beside myself" or "I was out of my mind" may be used (Kegan, 1980). The process of equilibration may be accompanied by an increase in physical or psychological symptoms of various kinds, including depression.

Kegan perhaps best summarized the potential pain of the process: "Development is costly—for everyone, the developing person and those around him or her. Growth involves a separation from an old system of meaning. In practical terms this can involve both the agony of felt meaninglessness and the repudiation of commitments and investment.... Developmental theory gives us a way of thinking about such pain that does not pathologize it" (1980, p. 439). Such transitions may emerge slowly or may occur rapidly; they may be the result of self-chosen activities such as therapy or exercise, the happenstances of ordinary life, or unexpected experiences. In Table 9.4, I have suggested some of the stimuli for such transitions, organized around what appear to be the three most frequent adult transitions: (1) from conformity to individuality, (2) from individuality to integration or conjunctive faith, and (3) from integration to self-transcendence. I offer this list quite tentatively. We clearly lack the longitudinal evidence that might allow us to say more fully what experiences may or may not stimulate a transition.

Table 9.4 Transitions from One Stage to Another: Some Possible Triggering Situations of Experiences That May Assist in Passing Through a Transition

Specific Transition	Intentional Activities That May Foster That Transition	Unintentional or Circumstantial Events That May Foster That Transition
From conformist to individualistic	Therapy; reading about other religions or faiths	Attending college; leaving home for other reasons, such as job or marriage; usual failures or reversals while "following the rules"; development of personal or professional skills
From individualistic to integrated	Therapy; introspection; short-term programs to heighten self-awareness (e.g., Gestalt workshops)	Illness or prolonged pain; death in the family or prolonged crisis; peak experiences
From integrated to self-transcendent	Meditation or prayer; various forms of yoga; self-disciplines	Near-death experience; transcendent experiences such as peak or immediate mystical experiences

You can see in the table that I am suggesting that somewhat different experiences may be involved in each of these three transitions. Attending college or moving away from home into a quite different community seem to be particularly influential in promoting aspects of the transition to individuality. For example, in longitudinal studies, both Kohlberg (1973) and Rest and Thoma (1985) have found a correlation between the amount of college education completed and the level of moral reasoning. Principled reasoning was found only in those who had attended at least some college. This transition, then, seems to be precipitated by exposure to other assumptions, other faiths, other perspectives. Such a confrontation can produce disequilibrium, which may be dealt with by searching for a new, independent, self-chosen model.

Critical Thinking

College-educated people tend to make moral decisions at higher levels than those who have not attended college. Some suggest it is the education they receive, and some argue it is the exposure to diverse classmates and ideas. How would you design a study to answer this question?

I have also suggested that therapy may play some role in triggering or assisting with either of the first two transitions. In fact, helping a client to achieve full integration is the highest goal of many humanistically oriented therapies, such as those based on the work of Carl Rogers (1961/1995) or Fritz Perls (1973). But my hypothesis is that traditional forms of therapy do little to assist the transition from integrated person to a level of self-transcendence. This transition, I think, requires or is assisted by a different form of active process, such as meditation or other forms of yoga or systematic prayer.

Both painful experiences and transcendent ones can also be the occasion for a new transition. The death of a child or of a parent may reawaken our concern with ultimate questions of life and death. A failed marriage or discouragement at work may lead to questioning or to a loss of the sense of stability of one's present model. Peak experiences, too, by giving glimpses of something not readily comprehensible within a current view, may create a disequilibrium. Most adults who have had a near-death experience, for example, report that their lives are never again the same. Many change jobs or devote their lives to service in one way or another. Other forms of peak experiences or religious rebirth may have the same effect.

The transition from college to first job can be a triggering situation for new growth in meaning systems.

I have been consistently using the word *may* in the last few paragraphs to convey the fact that such life changes do not invariably result in significant reflection or decentering. In an argument reminiscent of the concept of scheduled and unscheduled changes, psychologists Patricia Gurin and Orville Brim (1984) have offered an interesting hypothesis to explain such differences in the impact of major life changes. In essence, they argued that widely shared, age-linked changes are not likely to trigger significant reassessments of the sense of self precisely because expected changes are interpreted differently than unexpected ones. Shared changes are most often attributed to causes outside oneself, for which one is not personally responsible. In contrast, unique or off-time life changes are more likely to lead to significant inner reappraisals precisely because it is difficult to attribute such experiences to outward causes. If everyone at your job has been laid off because the company has gone out of business during a recession, you need not reassess your own sense of self-worth. But if you are the only one fired during a time of expanding economy, it is much more difficult to maintain your sense of worth.

Some shared experiences, such as college, may commonly trigger reappraisals or restructuring of personality, moral judgment, or faith. But most age-graded experiences can be absorbed fairly readily into existing systems. It may then be the unique or mistimed experiences that are particularly significant for changes in meaning systems. This hypothesis remains to be tested but raises some intriguing issues.

9.6: Commentary and Conclusions

9.6 Discuss life as a journey from the known to the unknown

For me, one of the striking things about the information I have presented in this chapter is that it is possible to find such similar descriptions emerging from such different traditions. But let me say again that the fact that there is a great deal of apparent unanimity in the theoretical (and personal) descriptions of the development of moral judgment, meaning systems, motive hierarchies, and spiritual evolution does not make this shared view true.

It does seem fair to say that most adults are engaged in some process of creating or searching for meaning in their lives. But this is not necessarily—perhaps not commonly—a conscious, deliberate process. Some adults, such as my dinner guests who appeared in the opening of this chapter, spend many years of adulthood in a conscious search, and their descriptions of the process are remarkably similar. But as I pointed out earlier, this may or may not mean that such a search, or even a non-conscious, or nonintentional, sequence of faiths, is a "natural" or essential part of adult development. A good number of equally spiritual adults, such as my grand-parents, find meaning in their lives in quiet, conventional ways. They follow their childhood religions and find great richness in meaning as they delve deeper into the teachings and then teach it to young people themselves, never feeling the need to search alternative pathways.

Furthermore, it is important to realize that all of what I have said and all of what these various theorists have said is based on a single metaphor of development, the metaphor of "life as a journey." We imagine the adult trudging up some hill or along some road, passing through steps or stages as he or she moves along. Implicit in this metaphor is the concept of a goal, an endpoint or *telos* (a Greek word from which our word *teleological* comes, meaning "having purpose or moving toward a goal"). This is a journey going somewhere. And if the purpose of the journey is thought of as personal growth, we must have some concept of an endpoint, of some highest level of personal growth.

The linearity and teleology of the journey metaphor may well limit our thinking about changes in adult meaning systems. Philosopher and television producer Sam Keen (1983) has suggested several other ways we might think of the process, two of which I find particularly appealing:

- "When we think of this eternal dimension of our being, the circle is more appropriate than the line. If life is a journey, then, it is not a pilgrimage but an odyssey in which one leaves and returns home again" (Keen, 1983, p. 31). Each step may be a circling back, a remembering of the "still point" within (to use poet T. S. Eliot's phrase). Progressively, we understand or know ourselves and our world differently with each movement of the circle, but there is no necessary endpoint.

- We can also think of the entire process as "musical themes that weave together to form a symphony; the themes that are central to each stage are anticipated in the previous stage and remain as resonant subthemes in subsequent stages" (Keen, 1983, p. 32). Another metaphor for this is that of life as a tapestry in which one weaves many colors. A person who creates many different meaning systems or faiths is weaving a tapestry with more colors, but it may be no more beautiful or pleasing than a tapestry woven intricately of fewer colors.

The basic point I am trying to make here is a simple one, although often hard to absorb thoroughly: Our theories of the quest for meaning are based in part on metaphors. We begin our search for understanding of adult development with a metaphor, and it colors all of what we choose to examine and all of what we see. The journey metaphor has dominated most of the current thinking, but it is not the only way to think about the process.

If we are to understand this process further, if we are to choose among the several metaphors, what we need is a great deal more empirical information to answer questions like the following. First, is there a longitudinal progression through Fowler's stages of faith or through equivalent sequences proposed by others, such as Loevinger's stages of ego development? A number of cross-sectional studies and several longitudinal studies suggest that some indicators of spiritual growth increase with age. But as we discussed in the first chapter of this book, age alone does not cause much of anything except the number of candles on one's cake. We need to ask: Is it due to the collected wisdom that comes from experience, from some kind of biological change in the nervous system, from facing the adversities of late adulthood, or something else? There has been a very large increase in research in this area, and I am confident that answers to this question are forthcoming.

Second, what are the connections, if any, between movement through the several sequences described by the various theorists? If we measure a given person's moral reasoning, the stage of ego development in Loevinger's model, and the type of faith he or she holds, will that person be at the same stage in all three? And when a person shifts in one area, does the shift occur across the board? Alternatively, might integration occur only at the final steps, at the level of what Loevinger calls the "integrated person?" These questions have been explored for many years in children's stages of cognitive development and should be explored within the context of the quest for meaning in adulthood.

Third, assuming that longitudinal data confirm that there are stages of meaning making, we need to know what prompts a shift from one to the next. What supports a transition? What delays it? Finally, we need to know more about the possible connection between stages of faith (or models of meaning, or constructions of the self) and a sense of well-being, or greater physical health, or greater peace of mind. My own hypothesis is that one experiences greater happiness or satisfaction with one's life when it exists within a meaning system that lies at the "union" end of the dichotomy than when it is embedded in any of the more self-oriented stages.

Answers to some of these questions may be forthcoming in the next decades because researchers have begun to devise measuring scales for spirituality and to explore various components of the quest for meaning. The recent evidence of a connection between health and religious practices is a promising start to further investigations that include other forms of spirituality. And the work on genetic coding for spirituality brings its own intrigue to the mix. For now, much of what I have said in this chapter remains tantalizing and intriguing speculation—but speculation that nonetheless points toward the potential for wisdom, compassion, even illumination within each adult.

Summary: The Quest for Meaning

LISTEN TO THE AUDIO:

▶ ●————————— 07:46 ◀× ●

1. The quest for meaning, or spirituality, is an integral part of the human experience, with signs of its existence found in archaeological sites, in all cultures today, and even as a genetic trait in humans.

2. Psychology has long held that it is the meaning we attach to our experiences rather than the experiences themselves that defines reality for us. We filter experience through a set of basic assumptions we have each created, known as internal working models or meaning systems.

3. The idea of gerotranscendence, or the growth of meaning systems as we go through adulthood, is well known in literature, mythology, and psychological theories, although there is no agreement on what experiences in life cause the changes in meaning systems.

4. Empirical study of religion and spirituality has increased dramatically in the last 4 decades, and most of the studies address the question of whether this trait changes as we age. Religious participation is greater in older adults than younger adults, but there is a drop-off in late adulthood, possibly due to poor health. More women attend religious services and belong to religious organizations than men, and this gender difference is even greater for African Americans and Mexican Americans.

5. Rates of private religious practices, such as prayer and reading sacred texts, also increase with age, but remain steady into late adulthood, when participation in religious services drops off. It is suggested that people in late adulthood retain their spiritual beliefs and private practices, even though they are no longer able to attend services.

6. Two groups that were followed longitudinally show an increase in spirituality during the adult years, but women begin the increase earlier in adulthood than men. Those in a younger cohort showed a different pattern of increase than those in an older cohort,

indicating that events we experience during our lifetimes also have an impact on changes in spirituality over time.

7. It is as yet uncertain whether the experience of living for many years causes changes in spirituality, or whether the changes are due to the adversity older adults have to cope with. This will be an important topic of future research.

8. People, especially women, who attend religious services live longer than those who do not. One reason is that spirituality is related to lower levels of cortisol response during stressful situations. Cortisol has been implicated in many of the negative physiological effects of stress reactions, such as lowered immune function. This finding has been replicated in a number of populations and for a number of measures of spirituality, especially forgiveness and frequency of prayer.

9. One theory of the development of meaning systems is Kohlberg's theory of the development of moral reasoning. Based on Piaget's theory of cognitive development, this theory consists of six stages of moral reasoning, evaluating the level of moral reasoning by the explanations people give for their responses to moral dilemmas. At the first level, preconventional, reasoning reflects the punishment and obedience orientation in which what is moral is simply behavior that is rewarded, and the naive hedonism orientation in which the moral choice is the one that brings pleasure. At the second level, conventional, moral decisions are explained by following rules of the family or society. The third level, postconventional, chooses moral responses based on a search for underlying reasons for rules and laws.

10. Kohlberg's theory has been evaluated and refined over the years. For example, Carol Gilligan has pointed out that Kohlberg based his theory on interviews with boys, who use a system of justice, whereas girls base their moral decisions on a system of caring.

11. A second theory of spiritual development is Fowler's theory of faith development. Like Kohlberg, Fowler was interested in the individual search for meaning, not in specific beliefs. In Fowler's first stage, synthetic-conventional faith, meaning comes from an authority outside oneself. In the second stage, individuative-reflective faith, the individual takes responsibility for his or her own meaning system. In the third stage, conjunctive faith, an individual opens up to others' beliefs and welfare. Finally there is universalizing faith, the full opening of a person to disregard personal concerns.

12. There are similarities between the theories that seek to explain the development of spirituality over the adult years. There are also similarities between the theories of spiritual development and the personality theories discussed in previous chapters. One theory that seems to encompass all of them is Kegan's Synthesizing Model, which proposes that we move between the need to be part of the group and the need to be individuals.

13. Autobiographies, biographies, and case histories offer valuable information about individuals' search for meaning and thoughts about spiritualism. Underhill studied the accounts of many diverse individuals who described their quests for meaning, and she found commonalities in these quests that made up five possible stages. The first stage is awakening to a self-transcendence experience. This is followed by purification, in which the person is made aware of his or her faults and imperfections. The third stage is illumination, in which the person is made even more aware of the presence of a higher power. In the fourth stage, the person undergoes the dark night of the soul, turning inward for more critical self-examination. Stage 5 is unity, in which the individual feels one with the universe.

14. This process described by Underhill has been described similarly by many people from different eras and fields of interest, for example, American psychologist William James in the early 20th century, Spanish nun St. Teresa of Ávila in the 16th century, and Swiss-born American psychoanalyst Carl Jung in the mid-20th century.

15. The question of what factors lead to changes in meaning systems over adulthood is a relatively new topic of research. It is known that these changes may be triggered by unique life changes, by adversity, by peak experiences, and by intentionally pursuing self-knowledge and spiritual growth.

SHARED WRITING: QUEST FOR MEANING

Consider this chapter's discussion of the quest for meaning. How is your own quest for meaning different from that of your parents' generation, and their parents' generation? What are the implications of these changes (for better or worse)? Write a short response that your classmates will read. Be sure to discuss specific examples.

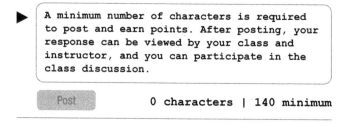

▶ A minimum number of characters is required to post and earn points. After posting, your response can be viewed by your class and instructor, and you can participate in the class discussion.

Post   0 characters | 140 minimum

Chapter 9 Quiz: The Quest for Meaning

Chapter 10
Stress, Coping, and Resilience

⌄ Learning Objectives

10.1a Define stress, stressors, and stress reactions

10.1b Discuss response-oriented viewpoint and stimulus-oriented viewpoint

10.2 Describe the characteristics of stressors and the characteristics of individuals which determines their daily well being

10.3 Analyze the physical and emotional effects of stress and individual differences in stress reactions

10.4 Relate stress coping with personal traits, behavior, and social support

10.5 Explain resilience, its relation to trauma and individual differences in resilience

LISTEN TO THE AUDIO:

▶ ●━━━━━━ 03:26 ◀× ●

MIGUEL LEFT CUBA for Miami in an unusual way; he took a boat west to Mexico and then bought his way across the border into Texas. He was only 15. The other people in the group were eight pregnant women who were trying to get into the United States to have their babies in American hospitals—not so much for the medical care but so they would have U.S. citizenship. Despite being promised a safe journey across the border, Miguel and the women were left on the riverbank to make their own way across. Suddenly gunshots rang out from somewhere. Miguel helped woman after woman cross the shallow river and finally made it to safety himself before realizing he had been shot in the thigh. He ended up in the hospital with two of the women who had gone into labor during the river crossing.

This is an exciting story, and to the best of my knowledge it is true. I heard it from Miguel himself and saw the scar from the bullet wound in his thigh. He showed me photos of the two Mexican-American teenagers, now living in Texas, whose mothers he had helped cross the river. They were named Miguel, after him, and he keeps in touch with their families. The amazing part of the story, to me, is that today he is so similar to my younger son, Derek. They are both American citizens, and they work together as civil engineers. They drive their trucks to work, go out in the field together, go home at night to their wives and children, and plan their vacations to Disney World or Las Vegas or the Bahamas. You would not notice any difference between Miguel and Derek except that Miguel has a touch of a Cuban accent (and a scar on his thigh). And yet my son grew up in a middle-class home and was riding a skateboard and playing Senior League baseball when he was 15. When I think about Miguel, I look around at the students in my classes, the people who work in my neighborhood grocery store, the woman who delivers my mail, and I wonder what their stories are. The more I get to know my fellow south Floridians, the more stories I hear like Miguel's. We have people who have come to our state on rafts made out of inner tubes and styrofoam coolers, people who have fled their country one step ahead of rebel troops, people who survived concentration camps and people who liberated concentration camps after World War II, people who have seen their family and neighbors killed, people who have survived earthquakes and hurricanes, and people who have been in prison for their political and religious beliefs. Adversity is not just in history books in our part of the country, and I'm sure the same is true of yours.

This chapter is about stress, coping, and resilience. The main theme is how people face the adversities of life, whether these entail making one's way across a river to freedom or being caught in a traffic jam on the interstate highway with a crying baby buckled into the car seat behind you. How does stress affect us? What resources do we have to deal with it on a daily basis? And how do we cope with large-scale adversity and then get on with our lives? I will begin with some of the leading theories and research on the effects of stress. Then I will present some information on social support and other coping mechanisms. Finally, I will turn to an examination of the most common response to stressful events, resilience.

10.1: Stress, Stressors, and Stress Reactions

10.1a Define stress, stressors, and stress reactions

10.1b Discuss response-oriented viewpoint and stimulus-oriented viewpoint

Stress is a set of physical, cognitive, and emotional responses that humans (and other organisms) display in reaction to demands from the environment. These environmental demands are known as **stressors**. The scientific study of stress (and stressors) is a very old field, going back to the early 1900s, and has been "claimed" by medical researchers and social scientists alike (Dougall & Baum, 2001). It seems that every new research tool or technological advance results in more knowledge about stress and its antidote, **coping**.

The best-known explanation of the stress response is that of medical researcher Hans Selye (1936, 1982), who first coined the term *stress* and then developed the concept of the **general adaptation syndrome**. According to Selye, there are three stages to this response. The first is the *alarm reaction,* in which the body quickly responds to a stressor by becoming alert and energized, preparing for "fight or flight." If the stressor continues for a longer time, the body goes into the second stage, *resistance,* in which it attempts to regain its normal state. One notable physical change in this stage is that the thymus gland, which is involved in immune responses, decreases in size and function. Thus, in this phase, the person is able to control the initial alarm reaction to the stressor but does so at the expense of the immune function. If the stressor continues long enough (and many chronic stressors do continue over very long periods of time), the resistance phase cannot be sustained, and the person reaches the third stage, *exhaustion,* when some of the alarm-stage responses reappear. If the stressor is severe enough, according to Selye, exhaustion is accompanied by physical illness or even death.

Selye postulated that the "return to rest" after the stressor has stopped and the general adaptation syndrome is terminated is never complete. One almost gets back to one's former state, but not quite, leading some to suggest that the process of aging may thus simply be the accumulation of the effects of many years of stress.

Selye's theory was one of the earliest demonstrations of the link between psychological reactions and physical illnesses. He was careful not to claim that stress itself *caused* physical changes, but that our reaction to stress (which he called "distress") was the culprit, leaving the door open for others to suggest preventative measures, such as coping mechanisms and social support, which will be discussed later in this chapter.

In the half century since Selye's theory was published, hundreds of studies have been done on the effects stress reactions have on the human immune system. Selye's idea of stress leading to a general suppression of the immune system has been refined to postulate two separate types of immune responses: a *natural immunity,* which is a quick defense against pathogens in general, and a *specific immunity,* which is slower and requires more energy because the body needs to identify specific pathogens and form matching lymphocytes to combat them. Ordinarily the two systems work in balance, but a stress reaction results in the natural immune system going quickly into overdrive and the specific immune system being suppressed, to conserve energy. Stressful events of longer duration, such as bereavement, lead to a decline in the natural immune system over time and an increase in the specific immune system. And when stress is chronic, such as caregiving for a relative with dementia, being a refugee, or being unemployed for a long period of time, both immune systems eventually decline in function (Segerstrom & Miller, 2004).

Evolutionary psychologists suggest that the reaction to acute stress (the fight-or-flight response) is an adaptive mechanism that enabled our primitive ancestors to summon optimal levels of energy (increased adrenaline and increased blood supply to the heart and large muscles) while at the same time preparing the body for accelerated healing of wounds and prevention of infection from whatever antigens entered through them (natural immunity). Modern humans seldom need this set of responses because the types of stressors we encounter do not often have physical consequences, nor do they require us to defend ourselves physically. However, as with many other evolved mechanisms, the stress response reflects the demands of more primitive environments, resulting in a mismatch of physical responses to psychological events (Flinn, Ward, & Noone, 2005).

RESPONSE-ORIENTED AND STIMULUS-ORIENTED VIEWPOINTS Selye's theory took a **response-oriented viewpoint**, meaning that it was focused on the physiological reactions within the individual that resulted from exposure to stressors. Other researchers have focused on the stressors themselves. To do this, it is necessary to evaluate events in the environment to determine whether they are stressors and, if they are, the relative magnitude of the stress they cause. The earliest evaluation method came from psychiatrists Thomas Holmes and Richard Rahe (1967), who devised a checklist to rate the level of a person's stressors based on **life-change events**. This rating scale consists of 43 events with points assigned to each event depending on how much stress it causes. For example, death of a spouse is the most stressful at 100 points, being fired is 47 points, and getting a speeding ticket is 11 points. The researchers focused on life *changes*, not just negative events, and included some positive events, such as pregnancy (40 points), outstanding personal achievement (28 points), and vacation (13 points). Holmes and Rahe hypothesized that the more points a person had accumulated in the recent past, the higher the stress level and the greater the chances of illness in the near future.

Holmes and Rahe approached the topic of stress from a **stimulus-oriented viewpoint**, meaning that their focus was on the stressors themselves, the stimuli that trigger the stress reactions, or more specifically, life events. Their rating scale, along with similar measures of life stressors, proved to be a fairly accurate predictor of physical illness and psychological symptoms. Most of the research today on stress reactions uses some form of a life-event rating scale. At the same time, serious questions have been raised about this definition of stress and this method of measurement. First of all, it is not so obvious that life changes all produce stress in the same way. Are positive life changes and negative life changes really equally stressful? And even among life changes that may be classed as negative, perhaps some subvarieties are more stress producing or more likely to lead to illness than others. And what about events that can be positive in one situation (pregnancy to a long-married couple who have been trying to conceive for years) and negative in another (pregnancy to an unprepared teenage girl)?

10.2: Types of Stress

10.2 **Describe the characteristics of stressors and the characteristics of individuals which determines their daily well being**

With these questions in mind, several researchers have suggested subcategories of stressors or life-change events that may help answer some of the preceding questions. For example, sociologist Leonard Pearlin (1980) made a distinction between *short-term life events*, which are stressors that may cause immediate problems but have a definite beginning and end, and *chronic life strains*, which are continuous and ongoing. He explained that chronic life strains were the type of stressors that caused the most health problems and also eroded social relationships (ironically, the very interactions that help alleviate stress).

Another distinction is made between types of job-related stressors. *Work stress* is what a worker experiences on a job with high demands but a good amount of control and sense of personal accomplishment. *Work strain* results from situations in which a worker is faced with high demands but low control, no sense of personal accomplishment, and low reward (Nelson & Burke, 2002).

Life-span developmental psychologist David Almeida (2005) distinguishes between *major life events*, such as divorce and death of a loved one, and *daily stressors*, the routine challenges of day-to-day living, such as work deadlines, malfunctioning computers, and arguments with children. Daily stressors also include more chronic challenges such as caring for a sick spouse or balancing the roles of a single, working parent (Almeida, Piazza, Stawski, et al., 2011). Although he acknowledges that major life events may be associated with prolonged physiological reactions, he believes that daily stressors, which occur far more frequently, also have serious effects on one's well-being. Almeida contends that the daily stressors not only have direct and immediate effects on emotional and physical functioning, but also accumulate over time to create persistent problems that may result in more serious stress reactions.

Daily stressors are difficult to measure because they are small issues that are not easily recalled over time, so Almeida used a diary method to follow the daily stressors of about 1,500 adults, part of a nationally representative sample of people in the United States participating in the National Study of Daily Experiences (NSDE). Instead of requiring participants to keep their own diaries (and perhaps fail to fill them out on a regular basis), he had telephone interviewers call each person in the study each evening during an 8-day period. And instead of using a checklist, the interviewers asked semistructured questions that allowed the participants to tell about their daily stressors and their subjective appraisals of the events (Almeida, 2005).

Almeida and his colleagues found that adults in the United States typically experienced at least one stressor on 40% of the days studied and more than one on 10% of the days. The most common stressors were interpersonal arguments and tensions, which accounted for half of the reported stressful events. The types of stressors are shown in Figure 10.1 along with the frequency with which they were reported. Interestingly, the subjective appraisal of the severity of stressful events overall was "average," whereas the objective appraisals, given by expert coders, were "low." In other words, we tend to perceive our own stressful events as more severe than they are perceived by a noninvolved rater (Almeida & Horn, 2004).

Figure 10.1 U.S. adults from 25 to 74 years report that the largest proportion of their daily stressors arise from interpersonal tensions, followed by stressful events that happen to other people in their networks and events that happen at work or school.

SOURCE: Data from Almeida (2005).

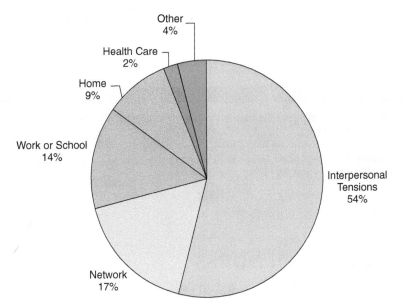

Almeida's model of the factors involved in the buildup of daily stressors is shown in Figure 10.2. If you look at the box on the left, you will see a number of factors within the individual that may affect the stress/well-being connection, such as age, marital status, personality traits, and chronic health problems. The box on the right shows characteristics of the stressor, such as frequency and the subjective severity. If you are a young woman in good health, living with your parents and attending school, and you are faced with transportation problems on a regular basis because your car is not dependable, it may be a daily hassle to ask a friend for a ride to class or to take your mother to work and borrow her car, but even if this continues for the whole semester, chances are it won't have a negative effect on your well-being. It's just an inconvenience and a regular hassle. However, if you are a middle-aged man living on disability benefits and need dialysis 2 days a week, transportation problems may pose a very different set of stressors (such as not getting vital medical treatment and feeling helpless and hopeless). These drains on daily well-being would feed back to the individual factors and cause them to decline even more. In the case of the young college student, the fact that her friends are there for her and that her mother is so helpful may actually increase her ability to handle stress.

Figure 10.2 Characteristics of the individual determine whether they will be exposed to certain stressors and what their reaction will be, resulting in a potential effect on daily well-being.

SOURCE: Adapted from Almeida (2005).

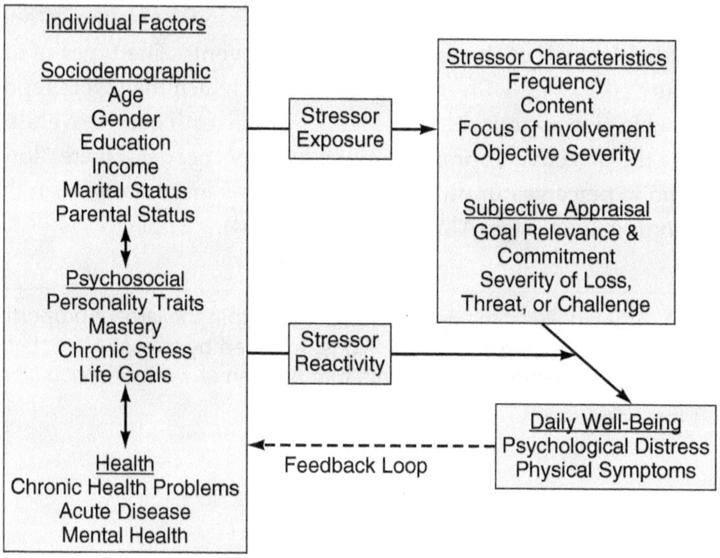

WRITING PROMPT

List your top 10 sources of stress. Do they fit the ratios in Figure 10.1? Write a brief response that will be read your instructor.

> The response entered here will appear in the performance dashboard and can be viewed by your instructor.

Submit

10.3: Effects of Stress

10.3 Analyze the physical and emotional effects of stress and individual differences in stress reactions

If you recall Selye's theory, stressors cause physiological stress reactions that lead to lowered immune function and ultimately may cause physical disease and mental health disorders. Early studies showed a significant relationship between self-rated life-change events and a number of health problems, but the effects were very small and it was difficult to know which came first, the stressors or the health problems. Also, there is the problem of stress causing unhealthy behaviors, such as tobacco and alcohol use and overeating, and certain common factors, such as poverty, that cause both a high number of stressors and poor health. Recent researchers have controlled for many of these confounds to concentrate on the areas that have the most promise for unwrapping the stress/disease package and finding effective treatment and prevention measures.

10.3.1: Physical Disease

Stressors seem to contribute to the progression of heart disease, the risk of diabetes, and the onset of some cancers. For example, a longitudinal study of over 10,000 women in Finland showed that accumulation of stressful life events (such as divorce or separation, death of a husband, personal illness or injury, job loss, death of a close friend or relative) was associated with an increased risk of breast cancer. Women were surveyed in the initial stage of the study and asked to report stressful life events they had experienced over the previous 5 years. Fifteen years later, 180 incidents of breast cancer had been reported for women in the study (doctors are required to report all cancer diagnoses to the Finnish Cancer Registry). Grouping the women by how many stressful life events they reported (none, one, two, or three or more), researchers found a linear relationship, as shown in Figure 10.3, between the number of stressful events and the incidence of breast cancer in the subsequent 15 years (Lillberg, Verkasalo, Kaprio, et al., 2003). The greater the number of stressful events they reported, the greater the women's chance of having breast cancer, and because the surveys had been done years before the cancer appeared and not after the fact, this is very strong support that stressors are related to subsequent physical illness.

Figure 10.3 Women who reported one, two, or three or more major life events in the previous 5 years were significantly more likely to be diagnosed with breast cancer during the next 15 years than those who reported no major life events. The more events reported, the greater incidence of breast cancer.

SOURCE: Adapted from Lillberg, Verksalo, Kaprio, et al. (2003).

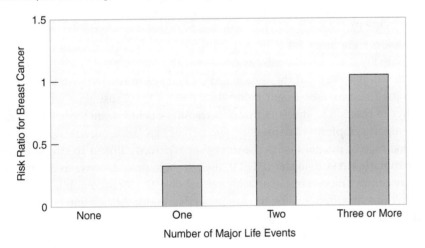

Other studies have shown a link between stress and heart disease. Researchers followed almost 13,000 men for 15 years and demonstrated that work-related stress (such as being fired or laid off, not being able to work because of a disability, failure of a business) was related to an increased risk of death from heart disease. Men were given physical examinations and surveys annually for 6 years. Nine years after the study was completed, death records were examined along with causes of death. When the men were grouped according to the number of job stressors they had reported during the study, researchers found a linear relationship between the number of stressful events and the incidence of death due to heart disease in the 9 years since the study ended. The greater the number of stressful events, the higher the risk of death from heart disease (Mathews & Gump, 2002).

Another group of researchers examined the relationship between stressful life events and subsequent risk for heart disease and diabetes. The 149 male participants filled out the Holmes and Rahe questionnaire (described earlier in this chapter), reporting the life-change events they had experienced in the previous 5 years. Then they were tested for various markers of risk for cardiovascular disease and diabetes (high blood pressure, high HDL cholesterol, obesity, high levels of glucose in the blood). Men who were at the highest risk for cardiovascular disease and diabetes had significantly higher scores on their life-change events questionnaires than those at low risk (Fabre, Grosman, Mazza, et al., 2013). These studies, and many more, provide support that life stressors and a variety of physical illnesses are strongly related.

10.3.2: Mental Health Disorders

Stressful life events are associated with the onset of various mental disorders, such as depression and anxiety, and this relationship has been demonstrated in a number of studies, though the effect is relatively small, showing that many other factors are at work than just the stressors one is exposed to. However, one's reaction to those stressors seems to have a more substantial effect on which of us will develop a mental health disorder and which will not. For example, you probably know someone who has broken up with their girlfriend or boyfriend, spent a few sad days moping around in their pajamas, and then was back to their usual demeanor, perhaps even telling you that it was a learning experience never to date someone so self-centered or so much older than they are or a vegan. And you probably know another person who had a similar breakup but was incapacitated the rest of the semester. The difference is how they reacted to the stressful event.

In the diary study described earlier, in which 1,500 adults of all ages were called every evening for 8 consecutive days to report on the stressors in their day, they were also asked to report on their overall moods (Almeida, 2005). Ten years later, over half of the original participants were contacted again to find out about their current emotional health. Participants who had reported high levels of negativity on days they had no stressors were more apt to have symptoms of mood disorders 10 years later than those with lower levels of negativity on days with no stressors (Charles, Piazza, Mogle, et al., 2013). It seems that these participants' long-term reactivity to earlier stressors was a predictor of subsequent mood disorders in that those who were still feeling negative in reaction to stressors that occurred days before were those who were most apt to report symptoms of depression, anxiety, or bipolar disorder.

One type of mental health disorder that is directly linked to stressful events is **posttraumatic stress disorder (PTSD)**, the psychological response to trauma, such as military combat, rape, terrorist attacks, natural disasters, or automobile accidents. This disorder was first identified by the American Psychiatric Association in 1980, although it has been described throughout history as battle fatigue, shell shock, nervous breakdown, and other nonscientific terms. Symptoms of PTSD include re-experiencing the event in intrusive thoughts and dreams, numbing of general responses and avoiding stimuli associated with the event, and increased arousal of physiological stress mechanisms. Unlike other stress reactions, PTSD does not decline over time and is not alleviated by social support (American Psychiatric Association, 2000). **Posttraumatic stress symptoms** is the term used for reactions to trauma that are severe, but do not fit the full diagnosis criteria.

Treatment for PTSD includes counseling, during which patients are helped to understand that their condition is a normal reaction to trauma and not a sign of weakness or a character flaw. Once a trusting relationship is formed between the patient and the therapist, work can begin on confronting painful memories and rebuilding thoughts of trust and safety. Other treatment includes problem-focused cognitive behavior therapy. Medication, such as antianxiety and antidepressant drugs, is often helpful. Still, much needs to be learned about the most effective treatment of people who have experienced trauma (Forneris, Gartlehner, Brownley, et al., 2013).

Researchers often accompany first responders after traumatic incidents, such as the explosion of the space shuttle *Challenger* in 1986, the Oklahoma City bombing in 1995, the terrorist attacks on the World Trade Center and the Pentagon on September 11, 2001, Hurricane Katrina in 2005, and the 2010 earthquake in Haiti, ready to gather data on the victims, the bystanders, and the rescue workers. Around the world, researchers have tagged along with rescuers in war zones, at the sites of genocide and mass rape, in areas where famine has occurred, and in refugee camps. Although it may seem cold-hearted to be using victims as research participants during these difficult times, a lot of knowledge has been gained from such projects.

For example, because of this research, we know that about one third of people will show symptoms of PTSD immediately after a traumatic event, and about 10% will continue showing those symptoms a year later (Gorman, 2005). We also know that the most valuable help mental health providers can give to people exposed to trauma is to promote feelings of safety, calmness, self-efficacy, community connectedness, and hope. Survivors need their practical needs attended to first, such as medical care, information about family members, food, clothing, and shelter. The time for therapy comes later, if at all. For most survivors, symptoms of PTSD are short-lived, and resilience is the norm (Watson, Brymer, & Bonanno, 2011).

When therapy is needed for PTSD, it should address the feelings of vulnerability and powerlessness that are the effects of traumatic stress. The best remedy is to examine the source of the fear and correct exaggerated beliefs, but when part of the syndrome is to avoid thoughts of the trauma, this is not possible. The feelings of vulnerability and powerlessness may be accompanied by horror, anger, sadness, humiliation, and guilt. The biological effects seem to involve more than just extreme general-anxiety reactions. For example, the physical responses to stress in patients with PTSD are different from those in normal people—the hormone levels are different, and different areas of the brain are involved in the responses. In addition, patients with PTSD often have structural alterations in two areas of the brain, the amygdala and the hippocampus. All this evidence leads us to believe that extreme trauma causes long-lasting alterations in the brain and nervous system that lead to changes in the stress reaction mechanism causing the intrusive thoughts, the numbing of responses, and the increased reactivity of stress response mechanisms (Yehuda, 2002).

One in three survivors of Hurricane Katrina showed signs of PTSD a month after the tragedy; 1 in 10 continued to have symptoms a year later.

10.3.3: Individual Differences in Stress-Related Disorders

Everyone is exposed to stressors on a daily basis, and everyone meets them with stress reactions, but not everyone suffers from physical disease and mental disorders as a result. In fact the majority of people handle stress very well. Of course the type of stress and the amount of stress can make a difference, but researchers have found that other factors affect an individual's susceptibility to stress-related health problems, such as gender, age, racial discrimination, and environment–gene interactions.

GENDER When it comes to daily stressors, women report more days with at least one stressor than men do. Women and men also report different sources of stress. Men are more apt than women to report daily stressors related to work or school, whereas women are more apt than men to report experiencing daily stressors as a result of things that happened to people in their social or family networks. Men are more apt to report stressors that threaten them financially; women are more apt to report stressors that threaten the ways others feel about them (Almeida, 2005).

Some researchers argue that Selye's theory of fight or flight applies only to men, and that women have a totally different reaction to stressors. Social psychologist Shelley Taylor (2002) argued that males and females have evolved different survival and reproductive behaviors, and that females may have developed a response to stress that differs from the one typically seen in studies of males. Instead of fight or flight, Taylor suggested that women have a genetic response to stress that involves "tend and befriend." Instead of being based on either fleeing the dangerous situation or defeating an aggressor, as is the case with males, this response in females is aimed at tending to one's immature offspring and seeking support from others, especially other females. As Taylor and her colleagues explained, "We suggest that females respond to stress by nurturing offspring, exhibiting behaviors that protect them from harm and reduce neuroendocrine responses that may compromise offspring health (the tending pattern), and by befriending, namely affiliating with social groups to reduce risk" (Taylor, Klein, Lewis, et al., 2000, p. 411). These researchers believe that female responses to stress are based on the attachment-caregiving process and may be regulated, in part,

Women have the role of kinkeeper in almost all cultures. This may cause them to react to stress by "tending and befriending" instead of "fighting or fleeing."

by sex hormones (Taylor, Gonzaga, Klein, et al., 2006), a topic that merits further study, especially the effects of age-related decline in these hormones (Almeida, Piazza, Stawski, et al., 2011).

This research fits well with other findings on gender differences in social behavior. Women have larger social networks, have deeper and more emotional friendships, and are more apt to respond to emotional events by seeking out friends and talking. They are the kinkeepers and caregivers in families. It has been well demonstrated that men and women do not react with the same intensity to stress and the stressors that bring on stress reactions. Why not differences in the role of stressors in their lives?

There are also gender differences in PTSD. Men are more exposed to trauma than women during their lifetimes, but women are more likely to experience PTSD as a result of trauma. Figure 10.4 shows the number of traumatic events men and women report and the incidence of PTSD for both genders. However, this does not tell the whole story. Some events are more apt to lead to PTSD for one gender than another. For example, women are much more likely to experience rape than men (9% versus 1%), but men are more likely to suffer from PTSD as a result (65% versus 46%). Men have a higher rate of experiencing physical assault than women (11% versus 6%), but women's rates of developing PTSD as a result are higher than men's (21% versus 2%). Clearly the likelihood of developing PTSD as the result of a traumatic experience depends on more factors than just the objective severity of the event (Yehuda, 2002).

Figure 10.4 Men experience more trauma in their lifetimes, but women are more likely to develop PTSD.

SOURCE: Data from Yehuda (2002).

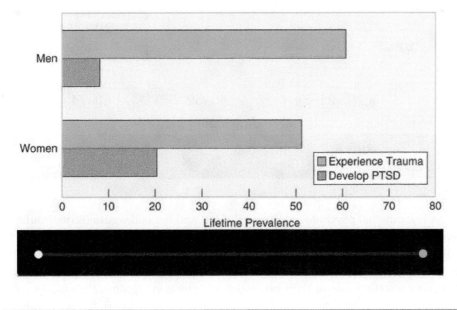

Critical Thinking

What have you learned about gender differences so far that might account for the greater prevalence of traumatic events in men's lives versus women's? What about the differences in PTSD?

AGE In general, stress decreases with age. The highest amount of stress is reported by young adults, and the lowest is reported by older adults (Almeida, Piazza, Stawski, et al., 2011). There are several reasons suggested for this. First, younger people have more complex lives than older people, thus more potential sources of stress. Older people have more experience with stressful events and, presumably, have developed some expertise in coping with situations that might become stressors. Although older people often have more chronic health problems and experience more loss in their lives, they often compare their own situation with that of others their age and consider themselves to be doing well. A large number of older adults consider themselves to be in excellent or very good health, but at the same time report a number of chronic health conditions.

In the diary study I described earlier, participants ranged in age from 25 to 74. Approximately half were men and half were women. As seen in Figure 10.5, the proportion of days that people reported experiencing any stressors declined after middle adulthood, and women reported more days with stressors than men at all ages (Almeida & Horn, 2004).

Figure 10.5 Men and women report having fewer days with stressors as they go from middle to older adulthood, and men report fewer days with stressors than women at all ages.

SOURCE: Adapted from Almeida & Horn (2004).

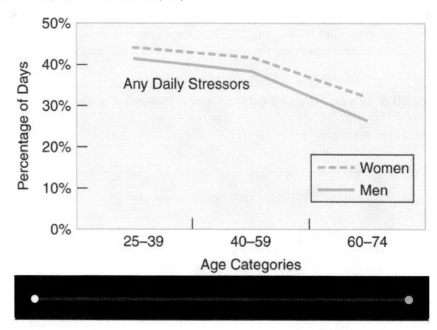

Developmental psychologist Stacey B. Scott and her colleagues (Scott, Poulin, & Silver, 2013) examined changes in reactions to the terrorist attacks of September 11, 2001, over a 3-year period. The 2,340 participants, ranging in age from 18 to 101 years, filled out Web-based surveys at several points in time during that period, answering questions about their posttraumatic stress symptoms, their general distress, and their fear of future attacks. For adults in all age groups, the posttraumatic stress symptoms, general distress, and fear of future attacks were lower 3 years after the World Trade Center attack, but there were different patterns of decline for different age groups. For example, in Figure 10.6, you will see that people 75 years of age and older had more posttraumatic stress symptoms during the year following the attack than younger age groups, but beyond that 1-year mark, these symptoms had declined for all age groups.

Figure 10.7 shows the survey responses for the amount of fear the participants felt concerning future attacks. Older groups reported more fear than younger groups throughout the 3 years studied. Interestingly, fear levels for all age groups rose and fell together around the dates of historic milestones such as the first anniversary of the attacks and the beginning of the Iraq war (Scott, Poulin, & Silver, 2013).

Figure 10.6 Adults 75 years of age and older who lived in the vicinity of the World Trade Center showed more incidence of posttraumatic stress in the first 12 months, but then declined in symptoms.

SOURCE: Scott, Poulin, & Silver (2013).

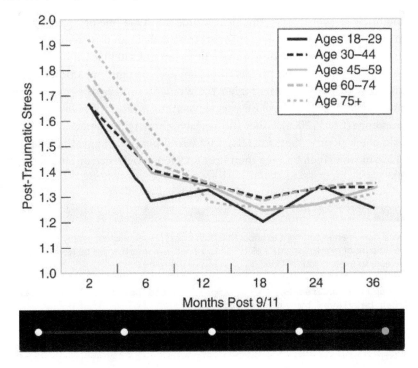

Figure 10.7 Adults 65 years of age and older continue to express fear of future terrorism more than younger adults. This fear starts to peak on the anniversaries of the attack for all ages.

SOURCE: Scott, Poulin, & Silver (2013).

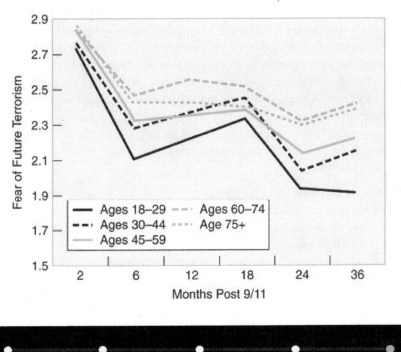

DISCRIMINATION It has long been known that black adults in the United States have greater incidence of high blood pressure and stroke than other racial/ethnic groups. On the surface, this seems to be an example of a genetic predisposition, but with evidence of the vast genetic variability among people of African descent (Cavalli-Sforza & Cavalli-Sforza, 1995), some researchers have investigated more plausible factors that might be responsible for this health problem. One line of investigation has focused on racial discrimination as a chronic stressor that can elevate blood pressure and increase the risk of stroke. For example, in a study of 110 black college women, a relationship was found between perceived racism and changes in blood pressure following a public-speaking task. The higher the women's reports of perceived racism, the more their systolic blood pressure was elevated as a result of giving a short talk before an audience (Clark, 2006). Other studies have shown that hypertension is higher for Hispanic black people than for Hispanic white people, suggesting that health disparities are more driven by race than immigration experience or language group (Borrell, 2009).

WRITING PROMPT

How would you design an experiment to show that high blood pressure is not simply a condition related to the amount of pigment in one's skin? Write a brief response that will be read by your instructor. Be sure to explain your reasoning.

▶ The response entered here will appear in the performance dashboard and can be viewed by your instructor.

Submit

Health-related effects of discrimination have been demonstrated in groups of U.S. citizens of Irish, Jewish, Polish, and Italian descent. Those who perceive chronic discrimination against their groups were two to six times more likely to show high-risk markers for cardiovascular disease than people in those same groups who do not perceive discrimination (Hunte & Williams, 2009).

Still other studies show that people in minority groups react differently to stressors than those in majority groups. One study examined Jewish-Israeli and Arab-Israeli residents in five cities in Israel that had been affected by terrorism. The Arab-Israeli participants showed higher levels of PTSD and depressive symptoms than the Jewish-Israeli participants, even though they were equally at risk for victimization. Researchers suggested that being part of an ethnic and economic minority in Israel brings with it a lower level of coping resources (Somer, Maguen, Or-Chen, et al., 2009).

This line of research suggests to me that discrimination seems to be the opposite of social support in times of stress. Groups who are targets of discrimination often have lower incomes and lack of opportunities, and adding the effects of discrimination to the mix may help explain the inordinate amount of stress-related health problems found in these groups.

ENVIRONMENT–GENE INTERACTIONS In the last decade, researchers have become aware that the differences in genetic expression between two people were due more to the environment they lived in than their gender and ancestry (Slavich & Cole, 2013). In other words, the expression of our genes can be influenced by the external social conditions we experience, especially how we subjectively perceive those conditions. This emerging field of research is known as **human social genomics**, the study of changes in gene expression due to subjective perceptions of the social environment.

One of the first studies to show the effect of social environment on gene expression was conducted by biopsychologist Steve W. Cole and his colleagues (Cole, Hawkley, Arevalo, et al., 2007), using a group of socially isolated individuals and a control group who were more socially integrated. Earlier research had shown that people who are socially isolated have more incidences of illness and die at earlier ages than those who are more socially integrated in their communities. The researchers discovered two types of immune response genes that differentiated the groups—one that responded to bacteria and one that responded to viruses. When the genomes of the participants were examined, they found that the altered genes were those involved in regulating inflammation, a key symptom of many of the diseases socially isolated individuals develop.

Similar genetic changes have been found in groups experiencing other types of stress, such as ongoing interpersonal difficulties (Murphy, Slavich, Rohleder, et al., 2013), low socioeconomic status (Chen, Miller, Kobor, et al., 2011), and posttraumatic stress disorder (O'Donovan. Sun, Cole, et al., 2011). This is also a possible explanation of how discrimination can affect health, as discussed in the previous section. These studies show that our long-standing belief that one's biological makeup is set at conception (or at birth) and is not affected by the social environment is inaccurate. Individual differences in adulthood have been shaped by our perceptions of the social environment, and those differences have altered the way our genes express on an individual basis.

10.3.4: Stress-Related Growth

Popular folk wisdom holds that the Chinese word for "crisis" is made up of two characters—one meaning "danger" and one meaning "opportunity." Other cultures have equivalent words of wisdom to express the idea that "what doesn't kill us makes us stronger." The same idea is what has motivated a wave of research examining **stress-related growth**—the positive changes that follow the experience of stressful life events. Indeed, this idea is not a new one. Many theories of development, such as Erikson's, include the concept that crisis, or stress, can make useful changes in the individual, and that personal growth may result from facing difficult life events.

Some early studies examining the negative effects of stress also found some positive effects. One study of middle-aged adults whose parents had recently died showed that although the participants reported typical symptoms of emotional distress, many also reported that they had experienced personal growth as a result of the loss, in that they finally felt they were complete adults with increased self-confidence and a sense of maturity. They also reported that they had learned to value personal relationships more (Scharlach & Fredrickson, 1993). Similar results have been noted in studies of divorce (Helson & Roberts, 1994) and widowhood (Lieberman, 1996). More recent studies of the aftermath of the terrorist attacks on September 11, 2001, revealed positive and prosocial reactions to the tragedy, including reports of interpersonal closeness and an increase in blood donations, charitable giving, and volunteerism (Morgan, Wisneki, & Skitka, 2011).

A study of stress-related growth in World War II veterans involved surveys of over 600 men who served in the military during that time and whose average age was now 74. Researchers found that those who had been exposed to moderate levels of stress in combat and who believed that there were benefits to serving in the military showed higher levels of wisdom than those who reported otherwise. Researchers concluded that how one appraises and copes with problems may be the key to deriving benefits from stressful experiences (Jennings, Aldwin, Levenson, et al., 2006).

Stress-related growth has also been studied in breast cancer survivors (Connerty & Knott, 2013), Palestinian adults living in Gaza (Kira, Abou-Median, Ashby, et al., 2012), Israeli ex-prisoners of war (Dekel, Ein-Dor, & Solomon, 2012), and low-income mothers who survived Hurricane Katrina (Lowe, Manove, & Rhodes, 2013), among other groups. The findings generally agree that, depending on the stressful event itself,

Older people who experienced stressful events in their younger years may show personal growth and wisdom in later years as a result.

the personal beliefs of the individual, and the support available, people in the most dire circumstances are able to later report personal growth, increased wisdom, growth in relationships with others, a new appreciation for life, a new sense of maturity, a stronger religious belief, or a greater sense of self-efficacy and self-confidence.

10.4: Coping with Stress

10.4 Relate stress coping with personal traits, behavior, and social support

There has been a shift recently in psychology from the "illness" model of stress, which catalogs symptoms, probabilities, and groups more prone to stress-related disorders, to a "wellness" approach, which involves prevention, preparation, and early intervention immediately after trauma occurs (Friedman, 2005). These priorities emphasize the importance of **resistance resources**, the personal and social resources that may buffer a person from the impact of stress. Central among these are individual coping responses, a sense of personal control, and the availability of social support.

10.4.1: Types of Coping Behaviors

At the top of the list of protections against the effects of stressors in our lives are **coping behaviors**, an all-purpose term that refers to anything you might think, feel, and do to reduce the effects of stressful events. Suppose that you received a rejection letter from a graduate program you had been working hard to get into. Or suppose that your apartment was damaged by a fire and most of your belongings were lost. How would you cope with these stressors? There are a number of behaviors you might employ, and some of them are found in Table 10.1, which lists styles of coping and examples of each from the Brief COPE Inventory (Carver, 1997).

These are not the only ways of coping. Many theorists and investigators have made their own lists and organized them into useful subcategories. One way of doing this is to divide coping mechanisms into four categories: problem focused, emotion focused, meaning focused, and social coping (Folkman & Moskowitz, 2004).

Table 10.1 Styles of Coping and Examples from the Brief COPE Inventory

Style of Coping	Example
Self-distraction	"I've been turning to work or other activities to take my mind off things."
Active coping	"I've been concentrating my efforts on doing something about the situation I'm in."
Denial	"I've been saying to myself, 'This isn't real.'"
Substance use	"I've been using alcohol or other drugs to make myself feel better."
Use of emotional support	"I've been getting comfort and understanding from someone."
Use of instrumental support	"I've been getting help and advice from other people."
Behavioral disengagement	"I've been giving up trying to deal with it."
Venting	"I've been saying things to let my unpleasant feelings escape."
Positive reframing	"I've been looking for something good in what is happening."
Planning	"I've been trying to come up with a strategy about what to do."
Humor	"I've been making jokes about it."
Acceptance	"I've been learning to live with it."
Religion	"I've been praying or meditating."
Self-blame	"I've been criticizing myself."

Hide All Cells   Show All Cells

SOURCE: Adapted from Carver (1997).

Problem-focused coping directly addresses the problem causing distress. If you were not accepted into your first-choice grad school, calling the school for more information would be an example of problem-focused coping. You might inquire about whether you could reapply for midyear acceptance or ask if it would be helpful to retake your admission exams. For the problem of having a fire in your apartment, calling the insurance company would be an example of a problem-focused coping strategy, as would taking an inventory of the things that were damaged and making plans about how to replace them.

The second category of coping mechanisms is **emotion-focused coping**, which includes ways that people try to ameliorate the negative emotions associated with the stressful situation. Dealing with the rejection from graduate school by going out and running for an hour is a good example. Using alcohol or drugs to blunt the stress is also emotion-focused, but is not a good example because it can lead to even more stress in your life. Distancing oneself from the problem emotionally can be helpful in some cases and maladaptive in others.

The use of drugs and alcohol as a coping mechanism may not be an effective one, but for college students, substance abuse of all kinds is related to stress levels. Interestingly, this relationship differs by gender and by race. In a large study of over 1,500 students at a large midwestern university in the United States, general college-life stress (such as problems with professors, grades, relationships) was associated with increased alcohol use for all groups except black males. Traumatic stress (such as being victimized or witnessing violence) was related to alcohol problems for white students only and with binge drinking for white female students only. Although this was only one university, and the sample was not a representative one, the authors suggested that university counselors consider the larger finding that substance-abuse problems can be symptoms of underlying stress (Broman, 2005).

In the study described earlier that was done in the aftermath of the DC sniper, a number of emotion-focused coping strategies were reported in addition to the problem-focused strategies shown in Figure 10.8. These included taking medication, disconnecting, watching the news, blaming the government, and blaming the terrorists. Unlike the problem-focused strategies discussed earlier, there were no gender differences in these ways of coping (Zivotofsky & Koslowsky, 2005).

Figure 10.8 Men and women in Washington, DC, used problem-focused coping with the DC sniper attacks by restricting their usual activities in many areas. Women reduced activities significantly more than men for all types of activities except socializing with friends (a source of social support).

SOURCE: Data from Zivotofsky & Koslowsky (2004).

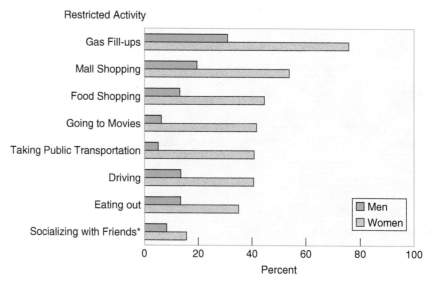

*No Significant Gender Difference

Meaning-focused coping includes ways that people find to manage the meaning of a stressful situation. Telling yourself that you would probably be happier at a different grad school that doesn't have such a rigorous program (or is closer to home, or where your best friend is going) is an example of decreasing the stress by reframing the stressful situation of being rejected. Dealing with the fire in your apartment, you could tell yourself that the loss was only material things and it's good no one was hurt, or you could tell yourself that everything happens for a reason—both would be meaning-focused ways to cope. Such coping is especially useful in chronic stress situations like caregiving, where people often report that they are simply following religious teachings or fulfilling their marriage vows.

The fourth category of coping strategies, **social coping**, involves seeking help from others, both instrumental and emotional support. If you call your best friend to share your bad news about the grad school, and he or she offers kind words of support, you are indulging in social coping. And if you ask your parents to help you replace the belongings you lost in the fire (and they do), that's more of the same. In the study discussed earlier of mechanisms people used to cope with the stress of a sniper at large, one of the more-reported ways of coping was to call or be in touch with relatives or friends. And although women reported using this form of social coping more than men, the numbers were high for both—92% of the women and 68% of the men (Zivotofsky & Koslowsky, 2004). This was also seen after the terrorist attacks on September 11, 2001, when the number of phone calls and Internet messages reached a record high all over the world. When we are stressed, whether as individuals or as a nation, we seek comfort in contacting those in our support networks.

EVALUATING THE EFFECTIVENESS OF COPING   Which coping mechanisms are the best in a given situation? Sometimes, it depends on whether you feel that you are in control of the problem. If you feel in control, then problem-focused coping is usually the most effective. An example would be a student who has an exam coming up and feels stressed. Problem-focused coping would include reviewing notes or meeting with a study group. But in a situation that offers little feeling of control, such as dealing with chronic illness, emotion-focused coping gives greater stress relief. Some examples would be distancing and finding other activities to keep one's mind occupied.

Two abilities are important in dealing with the stressors one encounters in life. First is the ability to use a variety of coping skills, depending on the situation, known as *coping flexibility*. The other is the ability to match the appropriate coping skill with the situation at hand, known as *goodness of fit* (Folkman & Moskowitz, 2004).

PROACTIVE COPING   Most coping research has been concerned with how people cope with situations that happened in the past (bereavement) or are happening at present (chronic illness), but a few researchers have investigated **proactive coping**, the ways people cope in advance to prevent or mute the impact of a stressful event that will happen in the future, such as a scheduled medical procedure or an impending layoff at work (Aspinwall & Taylor, 1997). They consider five interrelated components of proactive coping:

- Building a reserve of resources
- Recognizing potential stressors
- Initial appraisal of stressors
- Preliminary coping efforts
- Seeking feedback about one's success and acting on it

For example, in the 11 years we have lived in this house, our family has prepared for hurricanes six times. In our garage we have big steel shutters for all the windows and doors, and we have gone through the chores of bolting each one into its separate spot, bringing in all outdoor furniture and potted plants, filling our cars up with gas, getting cash from the ATM, checking out our generator, our battery-powered radio, our food supply, our water supply, and hunkering down to ride out the storm. Three of those six times, we experienced major hurricanes with trees uprooted, property damage, and electricity cut off for more than a week. Three times we had only tropical storms and felt quite lucky. As a result of these stressful experiences, we now engage in proactive coping in anticipation of the next season. Each year we build a reserve of resources (canned food, batteries, bottled water), and we have recognized potential stressors (putting up shutters, riding out the hurricane itself, losing electricity and water supply to the house, being unable to leave the immediate neighborhood, and being unable to contact others in the family for several days). We have already made preliminary coping efforts by buying a generator and long-range walkie-talkies. We often talk to neighbors and family members about our preparedness and our concerns, getting feedback and acting on their suggestions. On the wooden racks where the shutters are stored we have listed the names of the storms and the dates. It is a nice reminder of the success we have experienced. Although the next storm will still be stressful, it will be less so because of our proactive coping.

Another area that has attracted research attention is **religious coping**, in which a person relies on religious or spiritual beliefs to reduce stress. This type of coping ranges from finding meaning in suffering, achieving a sense of control by trusting in God, and gaining social solidarity with others who have similar beliefs. One way of viewing religious coping is to categorize it as either positive or negative. Positive religious coping includes people trusting that God will take care of their problems and believing that there is a higher purpose for their suffering. Negative religious coping involves people wondering whether God has abandoned them or questioning whether God loves them. Generally speaking, positive religious coping leads to positive adjustment to stress, and negative religious adjustment is related to negative adjustment (Ano & Vasconcelles, 2005). For example, one study that examined the effect of religious coping on health showed that reporting negative religious thoughts was related to increased risk of death in older hospitalized patients (Pargament, Koenig, Tarakeshwar, et al., 2001).

10.4.2: Social Support

Social support refers to affect, affirmation, and aid received from others. But how should we measure such support? In many early studies, it was measured only by objective criteria like marital status and frequency of contact with friends and relatives. Now we know that subjective measures are often more valuable. A person's *perception* of the quality of his or her social contacts and emotional support is more strongly related to physical and emotional health than are most objective measures (Feld & George, 1994), just as subjective measures of stress have turned out to be more accurate predictors of stress responses than mere listings of life-change events. It is not the actual amount of contact with others that is important, but how that contact is understood or interpreted.

However it is measured, it is clear that adults who have adequate social support have lower risk of disease, death, and depression than adults with weaker social networks or less supportive relationships (Uchino, Cacioppo, & Kiecolt-Glaser, 1996). Similar patterns have been found in other countries, including Sweden (Rosengren, Orth-Gomér, Wedel, et al., 1993) and Japan (Sugisawa, Liang, & Liu, 1994), so the link between social contact and physical hardiness is not restricted to the United States, or even to Western cultures.

THE BUFFERING EFFECT OF SOCIAL SUPPORT The beneficial effect of social support is even clearer when a person is under high stress. That is, the negative effect of stress on health and happiness is smaller for those who have adequate social support than for those whose social support is weak. This pattern of results is usually described as the **buffering effect** of social support, meaning that it won't keep stressors from entering one's life, but it will provide some protection against the harm they do. It may not be a coincidence that many of the top-rated life changes on the Holmes and Rahe list involve the loss of social support, such as divorce, separation, death of a loved one, and loss of a job.

Research has shown that women who fill multiple roles of parent, wife, worker, and caregiver of elderly parents suffer greater effects of stress when they don't have adequate social support in their own lives (Stephens, Franks, & Townsend, 1994). The buffering effect of social support is not limited to women. For example, in a study of men and women veterans who had been exposed to war-zone stress 10 years earlier (during the Gulf War of 1990–1991), the amount of encouragement and assistance they perceived from other unit members, unit leaders, and the military in general was related to the amount of depression they reported since their return from the war. For both men and women, the less social support they perceived receiving the higher level of depression they reported. These findings indicate that social support in a high-stress situation may serve as a buffer against later stress reactions such as depression, and that social support is an important buffer against negative mental health consequences of stress and trauma (Vogt, Pless, King, et al., 2005).

Another interesting gender difference in the giving and receiving of social support comes from a longitudinal study of over 700 adults in Finland. Researchers measured their "intimate reciprocity" at the beginning of the study, finding out how much social support they received from people close to them and how much of this they gave. Then they followed the participants' work records for 9 years, taking note of the number of days each was absent from work due to sickness. The men who had the best record of attendance on the job were the ones who *received* the most social support from their family and friends; the women with the best records were the ones who *gave* the most social support to those close to them. The authors concluded that men benefit the most from receiving social support, and women benefit the most from giving it, presumably because women gain in self-esteem when they are able to give support (Väänänen, Buunk, Kivimäki, et al., 2005).

Social support also reduces the negative impact of stressful experiences among the elderly. In a study of people 65 years of age and older who had experienced major negative life events, those who showed the most resilience (low depressive symptoms, high life satisfaction) were those who had larger social networks and happier marriages (Fuller-Iglesias, Sellars, & Antonucci, 2008).

SOCIAL SUPPORT AND COPING   Social support can also help in times of stress by aiding with active coping. Social network members can help a person define the source of stress and plan a solution. They can give advice about coping behaviors and give feedback about the results. This dimension of social support is especially helpful for older adults because they often have problems maintaining a sense of meaning in life when faced with stressful events or a buildup of chronic stress. Having a good friend or close relative who helps the older person reflect on his or her past life and come to terms with the distressing circumstances can be a great asset (Krause, 2006).

SOME NEGATIVE EFFECTS OF SOCIAL NETWORKS   Lest I give the impression that there is nothing but sweetness and light in the world of social relationships, let me quickly add that there are also costs associated with them. Network systems are generally reciprocal. Not only do you receive support, but you give it as well. At some points in the life course, such as the early parenting years, the giving side of the equation seems to be more heavily weighted than the receiving side, a situation that may increase stress.

Everyday social interactions can also be a significant source of hassles. Most of us have at least some regular interactions with people we do not like or who irritate us to distraction. When these negative social interactions involve anger, dislike, criticism, or undermining, especially when the negative feelings come from people who are central to our social convoy, they have a substantial negative effect on one's overall feeling of well-being (Antonucci, 1994).

Social support can operate in a negative way even if it is well intentioned—for example, when the support given is not what is needed, or the offer of support is perceived as criticism, or intrusion, or an insult to our independence. When this occurs, instead of buffering, the misdirected social support can result in our losing the desire to cope, reducing our efforts to cope, or making our coping efforts less effective (DeLongis & Holtzman, 2005).

Social support at a time of chronic strain, such as financial problems or long-term caregiving, can also have negative effects, especially in the late years of adulthood. Support providers may not have the resources to sustain their support over the long periods of time required and may begin to feel resentful and frustrated as a result. In addition, the care receivers may not have the wherewithal to reciprocate and may feel as though they are losing what little independence they have left (Krause, 2006).

10.4.3: Personality Traits and Coping

Another major buffer against the impact of stress is a sense of optimism. You'll recall that whether we measure this trait by assessing internal versus external locus of control or optimism versus pessimism or helplessness, those who have a stronger sense of optimism are less likely to become physically ill or depressed. A sense of control also serves as a buffer against stress, in much the same way that social support acts as a buffer. That is, among people facing some major life change or chronic stressor, those who approach the problem with a strong sense of self-efficacy or optimism are less likely to develop physical or emotional symptoms and more likely to recover quickly from physical problems.

One example is shown in a study of women who had been diagnosed and treated for breast cancer. Those who were more optimistic after their treatment was completed had higher scores of well-being at the end of the study, some 5 to 13 years later (Carver, Smith, Antoni, et al., 2005). In another study that may hit closer to home, college students who reported higher levels of optimism at the beginning of their first semester of college had smaller increases in stress and depression over the semester and more perceived social support than those lower in optimism (Brisette, Scheier, & Carver, 2002).

10.5: Resilience

10.5 Explain resilience, its relation to trauma and individual differences in resilience

I have covered various stressors and stress reactions, ways that people can cope with stress once it sets in, and how people may gain personal growth from their stressful experiences, but as you can tell from the statistics for different stress reactions, not everyone who is exposed to stress, even traumatic stress, suffers its effects. Recently, in an effort to emphasize the positive outcomes in psychology, researchers have been investigating **resilience**, the maintenance of healthy functioning following exposure to potential trauma.

Resilience is not the same as recovery and is quite different from chronic and delayed posttraumatic stress reactions and recovery. Figure 10.9 shows the trajectories of resilience compared to these three other outcomes. As you can see, chronic stress symptoms, which are experienced by 10–30% of people exposed to trauma, are severe reactions immediately after the traumatic event and remain severe 2 years afterward.

Delayed-stress reactions, which account for 5–10% of reactions, begin moderate but have increased to severe 2 years after the trauma. Recovery, reported by 15–35%, begins with moderate-to-severe reactions but has become mild 2 years after trauma. Resilience is a reaction that may involve slightly increased disruption at the time of the trauma, but never leaves the mild range. According to psychologist George Bonanno, resilience is the most common response to traumatic stress, found in 35–55% of people who are exposed to a traumatic event (Bonanno, 2005).

Figure 10.9 Of four outcomes people can have after exposure to trauma, the most prevalent is resilience. Others, such as chronic stress reaction, delayed stress reaction, and recovery, are not as typical as resilience.

SOURCE: Bonanno (2005).

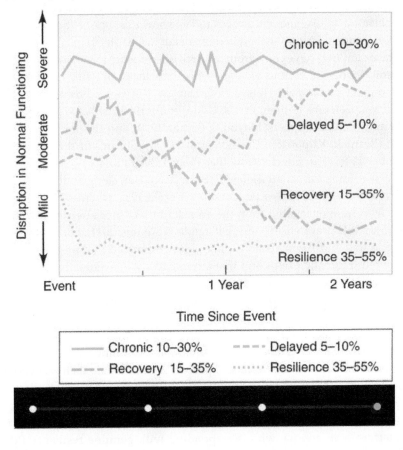

10.5.1: Reactions to Trauma

In studies of a variety of traumatic events, resilience is the most common outcome, not recovery or PTSD. Studies that investigate the responses of widows or widowers after the death of their spouses show that reactions of resilience are near 50% (Bonanno & Keltner, 1997; Mancini, Robinaugh, Shear, et al., 2009). Contrary to popular belief, there is no evidence that these individuals will later suffer from "delayed grief," or that they were only superficially attached to their spouses. In a longitudinal study of older married couples, those who became widowed in the course of the study were followed for 18 months after the deaths of their spouses, and almost half the survivors showed only low levels of depression and had relatively few sustained symptoms of grief. When the marital histories of these resilient widowed individuals were examined, there were no signs of marital problems or of cold, distant personalities. They did have high scores on acceptance of death, belief in a just world, and having a strong support network. And they did have moments of intense sadness and yearning for their spouses, but these grief symptoms did not interfere with their ability to continue with their lives, including their ability to feel positive emotions (Bonanno, Wortman, Lehman, et al., 2002).

Researchers are challenging the concept of "grief work," the Freudian-based idea that everyone experiencing traumatic loss must "work through" the negative feelings and "let it all out." This concept labels resilient people (often the majority) as pathological—either in denial or showing abnormal detachment. In light of the research findings on resilience, not only does grief work seem unnecessary, but it may even be harmful to many individuals (Bonanno & Kaltman, 1999). One study of grief-work therapy showed that 38% of people receiving this type of postbereavement help actually got worse when compared to a control group who had no treatment (Neimeyer, 2000). Clearly, for resilient people who have experienced the death of a loved one, therapy that expects you to express emotions you do not feel, and then questions your mental health or your attachment to the deceased loved one, is a classic example of adding insult to injury, and it is understandable how this type of "help" could result in secondary trauma. This is covered in more detail in Chapter 11.

Similar findings have come from research on exposure to violent and life-threatening events. Studies of various violent events show levels of PTSD ranging from 7% to 10% during the Los Angeles riots in 1992 (Hanson, Kilpatrick, Freedy, et al., 1995), 13% for Gulf War veterans (Sutker, Davis, Uddo, et al., 1995), 17% for hospitalized survivors of auto accidents (Ehlers, Mayou, & Bryant, 1998), and 18% for victims of physical assault (Resnick, Kilpatrick, Dansky, et al., 1993). Studies of the aftermath of the September 11 terrorist attacks show that about 13% of those who had direct exposure to the World Trade Center attack had PTSD 2 years later, along with about 4% of those who lived in the vicinity. Rescue workers reported 12%, whereas Pentagon staff and people who were evacuated from the World Trade Center after the attack reported about 15% PTSD prevalence (Neria, DiGrande, & Adams, 2011). For military personnel serving in Iraq and Afghanistan (or both), it is estimated that most have personally experienced traumatic events and that around 10% will eventually develop PTSD or related disorders (Hoge, Castro, Messer, et al., 2004).

Although these rates are disturbing, they support the findings that resilience is the most common response to trauma of many kinds. Intervention is important for those who will sustain or eventually develop extreme levels of chronic stress, but the current practice of giving all exposed individuals psychological treatment may actually undermine their natural resilience processes and impede their recovery (Mayou, Ehlers, & Hobbs, 2000). Some researchers are proposing that first-response personnel develop a screening device that would quickly identify people at high risk of PTSD (such as those who have experienced prior trauma and have low social support), and not interfere with anyone who is responding with genuine resilience (Mancini & Bonanno, 2009).

WRITING PROMPT

If you were in charge of developing a short screening test for first responders to use, based on what you have learned about stress, coping, and resilience, what five questions would you include? Write a response that will be read by your instructor.

▶ The response entered here will appear in the performance dashboard and can be viewed by your instructor.

Submit

10.5.2: Individual Differences in Resilience

We know a little about people who are prone to PTSD, but what about the people who are prone to resilience? A few factors have been identified, such as hardiness, self-identity, and positive emotion.

HARDINESS This personality construct describes people who are committed to finding meaning in life, believe that they can control their own surroundings and the outcome of events, and believe that all life experiences bring growth and knowledge (Maddi, 2005). With this way of thinking, hardy individuals approach difficult situations with less fear and with confidence that they will cope and maybe even benefit from the experience. Not surprisingly, hardy individuals use more coping skills and have more social support than those who do not fit this type (Florian, Mikulincer, & Taubman, 1995).

SELF-IDENTITY When trauma occurs, whether a natural disaster or the death of a loved one, it often results in having one's world "turned upside down." The familiar becomes strange, routines are disrupted, and usual sources of comfort are not available. People who have a strong sense of self appear to experience less stress at these times than people who do not. Resilient people feel a continuity of the self and are better able to cope with the changes around them (Mancini & Bonanno, 2009).

POSITIVE EMOTION (AND EVEN LAUGHTER) Although it has long been thought to be a symptom of unhealthy denial, recent evidence shows that people who respond to aversive events with positive emotion (gratitude, concern for others, love) have better adjustments than those who are more negative. In addition, this behavior brings out more positive responses from family and others in their social support network. For example, bereaved spouses who spoke about their loss with stories that were accompanied with smiles and genuine laughter showed better adjustment over several years after the loss of their loved one.

These findings about resilience are centered on reactions to traumatic events, but it stands to reason that the lessons here can be generalized to reactions most of us have to daily stressors at home or at work. Sure, the number of stressors and their intensity make a difference in our reactions, but not all of us will succumb to health problems and mental disorders as a result. In fact, most of us will deal successfully with them, hopefully finding some positive benefits in the experiences. To reiterate, stress is life, and most of us have what it takes to not only deal with it, but to also embrace it and grow from our experiences.

10.5.3: Resilience in Military Combat and Deployment

Proponents of positive psychology, working with the U.S. Army, have proposed a way to identify individual soldiers who are susceptible to PTSD and provide special interventions as part of their training procedure (Cornum, Matthews, & Seligman, 2011). Treating mental fitness similar to physical fitness, these researchers devised the General Assessment Tool (GAT) that compares each soldier with the Army norms for emotional, social, family, and spiritual fitness (Peterson, Park, & Castro, 2011). Figure 10.10 shows results from a male lieutenant who answered the 110-item test. As you can see, this soldier is relatively cheerful and optimistic. He values family and friends. However, he is not strongly engaged in Army work and does not have a strong sense of meaning and purpose in life. He does not use active methods of coping and is not a flexible thinker. Based on this information, the researchers consider this particular soldier to be unable to handle adversity very well. They recommend that he might benefit from training on flexible thinking skills and active problem solving and also some type of training that helps him see the bigger picture concerning his life and his work with the Army. They also suggest that his strengths in relationships with friends and family might be used to help increase his fitness in other areas (Park, 2011).

There is no estimate of when this program may be used on a large scale in the military, but the focus of evaluating soldiers on attributes that affect coping and resilience, and then providing training in low-scoring areas, is a much different approach than waiting until symptoms of PTSD are diagnosed after exposure to trauma and

Figure 10.10 Once a soldier has answered a computerized questionnaire, a profile is devised showing their strengths and weaknesses in four areas of mental fitness: emotional (the top 12 bars), social (the bars labeled "trust" and "friendship"), family, and spiritual. This profile comes from the responses of a male lieutenant compared to Army-wide norms.

SOURCE: Peterson, Park, & Castro (2011).

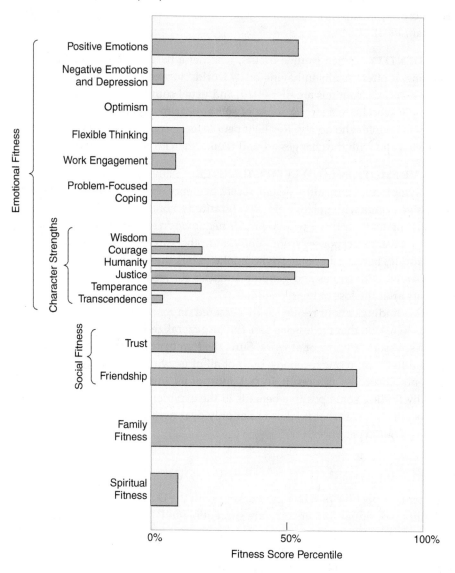

then trying to remedy that. This is a valuable application of positive psychology and could be of benefit for the 1.1 million men and women serving in active duty in the U.S. military today as well as their families.

10.5.4: A Final Word on Stress and Resilience

Our lives are full of stressors, and they tend to increase as we move through adulthood and take on more and more roles. In the best of all possible worlds there would be no hostile drivers on the road, no natural disasters, no terrorist attacks, and no wars, but we live here in reality, and those things exist. The secret to a happy and productive life seems to be three pronged: managing our reactions to stressors before they affect our health, strengthening effective coping skills, and building up resilience. This seems to be one area in which we gain expertise with age, and it might be wise to take some cues from the elders in our lives and how they handle stressors.

Summary: Stress, Coping, and Resilience

1. The best-known theory of stress response is Selye's general adaptation syndrome, in which we meet stressors with alarm reactions, followed by resistance and exhaustion if the stressor is still present. This sequence of events has an effect on the body's immune system and can lead to an increase in natural immunity at the expense of specific immunity, resulting in a lowered defense against specific diseases.

2. Types of stressors have been studied, and scoring systems have been proposed to rate the number and intensity of stressors in a person's life. Early studies showed that there was a relationship between the number and intensity of stressors and some health outcomes.

3. The most common types of stressors are interpersonal tensions, followed by things that happen to other people in one's family or social network and things that happen at work or school.

4. Longitudinal studies have linked stress with the occurrence of breast cancer, death from heart disease, and risk of diabetes. Stress, especially long-lasting negative reactions to stressors, has also been shown to be one of several factors in the onset of some mental health disorders.

5. Posttraumatic stress disorder (PTSD), a long-lasting, extreme reaction to acute stress, is a mental health disorder strongly related to stress. From examining people who have been exposed to a variety of disasters, researchers know that about one third of people will develop PTSD either immediately after the traumatic event or in the weeks following. About 10% will continue to have PTSD a year after the event. PTSD causes alterations in the brain and changes in the brain function. Treatment is counseling and medication.

6. Individuals who have severe reactions to trauma but do not meet the criteria for PTSD are considered to have posttraumatic stress symptoms.

7. Men and women have different sources of stress and different reactions. Evolutionary psychologists suggest that the response systems of men developed differently from those of women due to the types of threats each gender was exposed to in our primitive ancestors' time. Men respond with "fight or flight," women with "tend and befriend." Men are exposed to more trauma, but women are more likely to develop PTSD.

8. Daily stressors decline over the adult years, and older people react less to them. Older people may be more affected by trauma initially, but they recover more quickly.

9. Stress, such as social isolation, can change our biological makeup by altering specific genes that affect our immune responses.

10. Some researchers have suggested that racial discrimination is a form of chronic stress, and that the greater incidence of high blood pressure and stroke among African Americans is a result of this stress. This has also been found for other racial and ethnic minorities who feel discriminated against.

11. Along with the negative effects of stress, there is evidence that some people experience personal growth, increased wisdom, new appreciation for life, and a stronger religious belief.

12. The measures we take to reduce stress are known as coping. Problem-focused coping directly addresses the source of the stress. Emotion-focused coping is an attempt to reduce the emotional reactions. Meaning-focused coping is used to help us make sense of the situation, and social-focused coping is seeking help from others close to you.

13. All categories of coping skills are useful if implemented at the right time. It is important to have a wide repertoire of coping skills and to know when to use which one.

14. New ideas in coping research involve proactive coping, or coping with something before it happens, and religious coping, which is using one's religious or spiritual beliefs to cope.

15. Social support is an important antidote for stress because it serves as a buffer to provide some protection against the negative effects of stress. Social networks can also be a source of stress, if the interactions are difficult or the support offered is not welcome or what is needed. Other protectors against stress are having a sense of personal control and optimism.

16. The most common reaction to stress is resilience, maintaining healthy functioning. Even with extreme trauma such as the September 11th terrorist attacks, most of the people involved did not suffer disruption of their normal functioning.

17. Resilience has been misdiagnosed as "delayed PTSD" in trauma victims and "denial" in bereaved spouses. The popular idea that it is necessary for a person to experience debilitating stress reactions to trauma or the death of a loved one is not supported by research. Engaging these people in "grief work" may undermine their resilience.

18. One feature of resilient people is hardiness. They show commitment, control, and a quest for meaning in their lives. Other features are a strong sense of self-identity and positive emotion.

19. Psychology researchers and military leaders have devised a way to assess the mental fitness of soldiers with the intent of fostering resilience and preventing PTSD. The attributes being evaluated are emotional, social, family, and spiritual fitness.

SHARED WRITING: STRESS

Consider someone you know who is good at coping with stress and someone who struggles to cope with stress. How do their strategies differ? What are the positive and negative implications of these strategies? Write a short response that your classmates will read. Be sure to discuss specific examples.

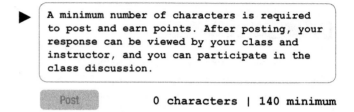

▶ A minimum number of characters is required to post and earn points. After posting, your response can be viewed by your class and instructor, and you can participate in the class discussion.

Post   0 characters | 140 minimum

Chapter 10 Quiz: Stress, Coping, and Resilience

Chapter 11
Death and Bereavement

Learning Objectives

11.1a Appraise the meanings of death

11.1b List factors that affect death anxiety

11.2a List the stages of reactions to death

11.2b Explain individual choices of personal death

11.3 Explain after death rituals and their significance

11.4 Express the inevitability of death and the need to come to terms with it for a happy adulthood

LISTEN TO THE AUDIO:

DAVID TASMA WAS a young man with inoperable cancer who was dying in a hospital in England, alone with no family. His native language was Polish, and he did not fully understand the English conversations that surrounded him. He was a Jew and did not feel comforted by the Anglican priests who visited the ward. Although his medical care was skilled and efficient, he faced death feeling frustrated and distressed. His only consolation was a young woman social worker who visited him and patiently listened as he struggled with English to talk about his childhood, his family, and his thoughts about death. For 2 months she sat with him daily as he went through the physical and mental process of dying. His greatest fear, he told her, was that he would leave this earth without making a mark on it. He was young and had no children. He had never written a book or built a house or planted a field of corn. Perhaps they fell in love; we don't know. When he died, he left her all that he had, about 500 pounds, and the seed of an idea—that dying involves much more than physical pain; there is also the social pain of leaving loved ones, the mental pain of trying to know the unknowable, the spiritual pain of finding meaning in the life-and-death process, and the emotional pain of fear, disappointment, frustration, and regret. The medical community had nothing to offer the dying.

The young social worker was Cicely Saunders, founder of the modern hospice movement. The event recounted took place in 1948, and as a tribute to Tasma, Saunders dedicated her life to finding ways for society to minister to its members at the end of their lives. She was one of the few women to become a medical doctor in England in the 1950s, and the first medical doctor of either gender to specialize in the treatment of dying patients. Ten years later, she opened St. Christopher's Hospice in London in memory of her young Polish friend, David Tasma, showing that he had indeed made his mark on the world—inspiring over 8,000 hospice centers in more than 100 countries. These centers all give the same message that defined Saunders's long career, "You matter because you are you, and you matter to the last moment of your life." Dame Cicely died at the age of 82 at the hospice she had founded (Field, 2005).

This chapter is about death—how we think about it at different ages, how we cope with the death of loved ones, and how we face the reality of our own death. This has long been a central topic in psychoanalytic theory and clinical psychology, but recently it has become a topic of interest for researchers in many other fields. I will begin by discussing how we think about death, then will explore the process of death, and finally will consider how we cope with the death of a loved one. This is a difficult topic, but one that must be included in a course on adulthood and aging.

11.1: Achieving an Understanding of Death

11.1a Appraise the meanings of death

11.1b List factors that affect death anxiety

Death has a significant impact on individuals, families, and the community. The meaning of death changes with age and goes well beyond the simple understanding of inevitability and universality. Most broadly, death has important social meaning. The death of any one person changes the roles and relationships of everyone else in a family. When an elder dies, everyone else in that particular lineage moves up one step in the generational system. Beyond the family, death also affects other roles; for instance, it makes opportunities for younger adults to take on significant tasks. Retirement serves some of the same functions because the older adult "steps aside" for the younger, but death brings many permanent changes in social systems.

11.1.1: Meanings of Death

Four meanings that death may have for adults have been identified. Typically, they are all present in any person's meaning system.

- **DEATH AS AN ORGANIZER OF TIME.** Death defines the endpoint of one's life, so the concept of "time until death" may be an important one for a person trying to organize his or her life. In fact, sociologist Bernice Neugarten suggests that one of the key changes in thinking in middle age is a switch in the way one marks one's own lifetime, from time since birth to time until death. Her interviews with middle-aged adults frequently yielded statements like the following: "Before I was 35, the future just stretched forth. There would be time to do and see and carry out all the plans I had…. Now I keep thinking, will I have time enough to finish off some of the things I want to do?" (Neugarten, 1970, p. 78).
- **DEATH AS PUNISHMENT.** Children are quite likely to think of death as punishment for being bad—a kind of ultimate Stage 1 of Kohlberg's moral reasoning theory. But this view and its reverse (that long life is the reward for being good) are still common in adults. Such a view is strengthened by religious teachings that emphasize a link between sin and death.
- **DEATH AS TRANSITION.** Death involves a transition—from life to some sort of life after death, or from life to nothingness. In surveys, 74% of people in the United States said that they believed in an afterlife, meaning that they would exist after death with some sort of consciousness (Pew Research Center, 2010), and 27% believed in reincarnation, meaning that they had lived before and will live again in another body after death (Harris Poll, 2005).
- **DEATH AS LOSS.** Perhaps most pervasively, death is seen by most of us as a loss—loss of the ability to complete projects or carry out plans; loss of one's body; loss of experiencing, of taste, smell, and touch; loss of relationships with people. Unlike beliefs in an afterlife, in this domain there are age differences. In particular, the specific losses that adults associate with death appear to change as they move through the adult years. Young adults are more concerned about loss of opportunity to experience things and about the loss of family relationships; older adults may be more concerned with the loss of time to complete some inner work (Kalish, 1985).

11.1.2: Death Anxiety

The most studied aspect of attitudes toward death is **death anxiety**, or fear of death. This fear is strongly linked to the view of death as a loss. If we fear death, it is, in part, because we fear the loss of experience, sensation, and relationships. Fear of death may also include fear of the pain or suffering or indignity often involved in the process of death, fear that one will not be able to cope well with such pain or suffering, fear of whatever punishment may come after death, and a fundamental fear of loss of the self.

AGE   Researchers have quite consistently found that middle-aged adults show the greatest fear of death, and older adults the least (De Raedt, Koster, & Ryckewaert, 2013), with young adults falling somewhere in between (Thorson & Powell, 1992). These results are consistent with the idea that one of the central tasks of midlife is to come to terms with the inevitability of death. The greater awareness of body changes and aging that is part of this period, coupled perhaps with the death of one's parents, breaks down the defenses we have all erected against the knowledge of and fear of death. In particular, the death of one's parents may be especially shocking and disturbing, not only because of the specific loss to be mourned but also because you must face the realization that you are now the oldest generation in the family lineage and thus "next in line" for death. So in midlife we become more aware of the fear, more preoccupied with death and its imminence. In these years, many adults grope toward new ways of thinking about death, eventually accepting it in a different way, so that the fear recedes in old age. This does not mean that older adults are unconcerned about death. On the contrary, they are more likely to talk about it and think about it than younger adults. But although death is highly salient to the elderly, it is apparently not as frightening as it was in midlife.

RELIGIOSITY   Age is not the only element in fear of death. Several other personal qualities have been nominated as factors. First, a likely factor would be **religiosity**, the degree of one's religious or spiritual belief. Presumably, there would be a negative correlation, the more religiosity one expresses, the less fear of death one should have. However, research findings show that there is no direct relationship between religiosity and fear of death. For example, in a study of older adults (70–80 years of age), those who were low in religiosity and those who were high in religiosity feared death less than participants who were moderate in their religious and spiritual beliefs. It was an inverted U-shaped function. The researchers suggest that those who are high in religiosity are not anxious about death because they believe that there is an afterlife and they have earned a place there. Those low in religiosity are not anxious about death because they don't believe there is an afterlife and aren't worried about missing out on any rewards. It's just those in the middle, the moderately religious, who are anxious about death because they believe there may be an afterlife and they may not have earned a place in it (Wink & Scott, 2005).

Religiosity can be divided into two separate factors: *extrinsic religiosity* is practiced by people who use religion for social purposes and as an arena for doing good deeds; *intrinsic religiosity* is practiced by people who live their lives according to their religious beliefs and seek meaning in life through their religion. In a study of older adults, extrinsic religiosity was positively related to death anxiety—those who scored higher on measures of extrinsic religiosity had higher fears of death. In addition, intrinsic religiosity had a strong positive relationship with anticipation of a better existence after death (Ardelt & Koenig, 2006).

Researchers suggest that extrinsic religiosity might be useful for middle-aged adults whose focus is social support and opportunities for generative activities, such as volunteer work within the religious community. In later years, however, intrinsic religiosity has a purpose because this is a time when actively participating in religious activities becomes difficult and the need is more for finding answers to fundamental questions of life, such as, Where did we come from? Where are we going? Why are we here? (McFadden, 2000).

GENDER   Death anxiety is also linked with gender. A number of studies from various cultures show that women have higher levels of death anxiety than men. This gender difference was found for a group of Episcopal parishioners in New York (Harding, Flannelly, Weaver, et al., 2005); young adults in Egypt, Kuwait, and Syria (Abdel-Khalek, 2004); and college students in Malaysia, Turkey, and the United States (Ellis, Wahab, & Ratnasingan, 2013). However, it has been suggested that this may be an artifact of the higher rates of anxiety disorders of all kinds for women. However, a recent study of over 400 college students showed that females report higher levels of death anxiety than males, even when controlling for depression and other possible confounds (Eshbaugh & Henninger, 2013).

DEATH ANXIETY AND PERSONALITY TRAITS   Certain personality traits seem to be factors in people's attitudes toward death. Self-esteem has been related to death anxiety, with high levels of self-esteem seeming to serve as a buffer against the fear of death (Xiangkui, Juan, & Lumei, 2005). Another study investigated the link between death anxiety and a **sense of purpose in life**, the extent to which individuals feel they have discovered satisfying personal goals and believe that their lives have been worthwhile. Psychologists Monika Ardelt and Cynthia Koenig (2006) studied a group of adults who were 61 years of age and older (some healthy and some hospice patients). Those who had a higher sense of purpose in life had lower death anxiety. This was especially interesting because general religiosity, for this sample, was not related to death anxiety. A sense of purpose in life has also been linked to lower levels of death anxiety in young adults (Rasmussen & Johnson, 1994). Related to this is the finding that regrets are linked to death anxiety. People who feel a great deal of regret, both for things they have done (or not done) in the past and things they may not do in the future, have higher levels of death anxiety (Tomer & Eliason, 2005).

WRITING PROMPT

What would you predict about students' fear of death in the United States versus that of students in Israel or in one of the other Middle Eastern countries, where suicide bombers are a fact of life? Would that make young adults have higher death anxiety scores or lower? Write a brief response that will be read by your instructor. Be sure to explain your reasoning.

▶ The response entered here will appear in the performance dashboard and can be viewed by your instructor.

Submit

Such findings suggest that adults who have successfully completed the major tasks of adult life, adequately fulfilled the demands of the roles they occupied, and developed inwardly are able to face death with greater equanimity. In contrast, adults who have not been able to resolve the various tasks and dilemmas of adulthood face their late adult years more fearfully, more anxiously, and with what Erikson describes as despair. Fear of death may be merely one facet of such despair.

In some sense, then, all adult life is a process of moving toward death. Adults' attitudes toward death, and their approaches to it, are influenced by many of the same qualities that affect the way they approach other life changes or dilemmas.

11.1.3: Accepting the Reality of One's Eventual Death

Coming to grips with one's eventual death is known as **finitude**. It is a process that occurs over time and at many levels (Johnson, 2009). At a practical level, for example, you can make out a will or obtain life insurance. Such preparations become more common with increasing age, especially in late middle age and thereafter. For example, older people are more apt to have life insurance than younger people. They are also more likely to prepare for death by making a will; only about 55% of all adults in the United States have done so, but among adults who are 65 years of age or older, 83% have done so (Harris Poll, 2007).

At a somewhat deeper level, adults may start making preparations for death through some process of **reminiscence**, or reviewing their memories. This is often done by writing a memoir or autobiography, or seeking out old friends and relatives to talk with about the past. We have little evidence that older adults typically or necessarily go through such a review process. But for some, a life review may be an important aspect of "writing the final chapter" or legitimizing one's life in some fashion (Birren & Feldman, 1997).

One type of planning for eventual death that has become increasingly popular recently is the **living will**, a document that takes effect if you are no longer able to express your wishes about end-of-life decisions. These documents (which may differ from state to state) give people the opportunity to decide, while they are still healthy, which specific treatments they would accept or refuse if they had a terminal illness or permanent disability and were not able to communicate their wishes. Living wills can be prepared with the assistance of an attorney or by using forms available on the Internet. For adults of all ages in the United States, 29% have a living will, but for adults 65 and over, 54% do (Pew Research Center, 2009).

Living wills help alleviate the fear that dying will be a long and painful process. A person writing one can take responsibility for his or her own end-of-life decisions and not burden family members. And they help avoid situations in which various family members hold different strong beliefs about end-of-life decisions.

Another way people accept the reality of their eventual death is to become an **organ transplant donor**, agreeing that at the time of death, their usable organs and other tissue can be transplanted to people who have been approved to receive them. The technology of organ transplantation has advanced faster than the concept of being a donor has been accepted by the public. At the moment thousands of people are waiting for donated organs. The process of becoming an organ donor varies by area, but in many states it can be done quickly when you renew your driver's license. Recently, Facebook allowed members to display their organ donor status on their timelines under Health and Fitness.

Who chooses to be an organ transplant donor? One study of young adults in Israel showed that it is typically a person who knows other potential donors, has a lot of information about organ transplantation, and has low levels of death anxiety (Besser, Amir, & Barkan, 2004). Many people view their decision to be an organ donor as a way to give back to others and to gain a little immortality.

11.2: The Process of Death

11.2a List the stages of reactions to death

11.2b Explain individual choices of personal death

Death and mourning have always been part of the human experience, but the thoughts people have about death and the way mourning is expressed differ from culture to culture and from era to era. For example, 50 years ago, no textbook about adult development or gerontology would have included a chapter like this one. Science and medicine have long been fixated on life and lifesaving treatment. Death was viewed as a failure of science; dying people were isolated in hospital wards, and every attempt was made to "cure" them. The idea of welcoming death or even accepting it was not discussed. This mind-set was changed largely through the writings of physician Elisabeth Kübler-Ross (1969), whose book *On Death and Dying* was acclaimed for having "brought death out of the darkness."

11.2.1: Stages of Reactions to Death

Kübler-Ross's book was based on her work with terminally ill adults and children and is probably best known for describing five stages of dying: denial, anger, bargaining, depression, and acceptance. Although she later wrote that these stages are not experienced by all people and do not necessarily occur in this order, her terminology is still used to describe the reactions to impending death of both the person who is dying and those who are bereaved (Kübler-Ross, 1974). I will describe these stages because they are often used to describe the constellation of reactions to impending death (see Table 11.1).

Table 11.1 Stages in Preparation for Death

Scenarios	Reactions
When confronted with a terminal diagnosis, the first reaction most patients report is some form of "No, not me!" "It must be a mistake," "The lab reports must have been mixed up," "I don't feel that sick, so it can't be true," "I'll get another doctor's opinion." All these are forms of denial. Kübler-Ross argued that denial is a valuable, constructive first defense. It gives the patient a period of time in which to marshal other strategies of coping with the shock.	DENIAL
The classic second reaction, so Kübler-Ross argued, is "Why me?" The patient resents those who are healthy and becomes angry at whatever fate put him or her in this position. This may be reflected in angry outbursts at nurses, family members, doctors—anyone within reach.	ANGER
At some point, Kübler-Ross saw anger being replaced by a new kind of defense. The patient now tries to "make a deal" with doctors, with nurses, with God. "If I do what I'm told and don't yell at everyone, then I'll be able to live till Christmas." She described one woman with terminal cancer who wanted to live long enough to attend the wedding of her oldest son.	BARGAINING
Bargaining only works for so long, however, and as disease processes continue and the signs of the body's decline become more obvious, patients typically become depressed. This is a kind of mourning—for the loss of relationships as well as of one's own life.	DEPRESSION
The final step, according to this theory, is a quiet understanding, a readiness for death. The patient is no longer depressed but may be quiet, even serene. In a widely quoted passage, newspaperman Stewart **Alsop (1973)**, who was dying of leukemia, described his own acceptance: "A dying man needs to die as a sleepy man needs to sleep, and there comes a time when it is wrong, as well as useless, to resist" (p. 299).	ACCEPTANCE

Hide All Cells	Show All Cells

Since the publication of Kübler-Ross's *On Death and Dying* in 1969, the way we treat the process of dying has been changed in many ways. Patients with terminal conditions are considered to be whole people with wishes and needs, not just failures of medical science. The vast majority do not want to die in a hospital ward, but prefer to be at home in their familiar surroundings. Most reach a point when they choose not to continue with heroic measures that might give them a few more days or weeks of life at the expense of their comfort and dignity. But refusing medical treatment does not mean that they don't need professional care. There is still a need for pain management, spiritual counseling, and accurate information about their condition and the time they have left. From loved ones there is a need for social support, listening, forgiving, and even laughter.

Perhaps more important than her stage theory, Kübler-Ross identified three key issues: The dying are still alive and have unfinished needs they may want to address. We need to listen actively to the dying and identify with their needs to provide effectively for them. And we need to learn from the dying to know ourselves better and our potential for living (Corr, 1993).

Critical Thinking

Why would it be important for a physician who deals with terminal diseases to be familiar with the various reactions to impending death? Which reactions would they be most likely to witness in their patients?

11.2.2: The Importance of Farewells

One aspect of the process of dying that is not reflected in Kübler-Ross's stages or in most research on dying, but that is clearly a significant feature for the dying person and his or her family, is the process of saying farewell. A study in Australia by sociologists Allan Kellehear and Terry Lewin (1988–1989) gave us a first exploration of such goodbyes. They interviewed 90 terminally ill cancer patients, all of whom had been told they were within a year of death, and a smaller group of 10 patients, who were in hospice care and thought to be within 3 months of death. Most had known they had cancer for over a year before the interview but had only recently been given a specific short-term prognosis. Subjects were asked whether they had already said some goodbyes or intended future farewells to family or friends and, if so, when and under what circumstances. The minority (19 of the 100) said they did not plan any farewells at all. The rest had either already begun to say goodbye (22 of the 100) or had planned their farewells for the final days of their lives—deathbed goodbyes, if you will.

The early farewells had often been in the form of a letter or a gift, such as giving money to a child or grandchild, or passing on personal treasures to a member of the family who might especially cherish them. One woman made dolls that she gave to friends, relatives, and hospital staff. Another knit baby clothes to give to each of her daughters for babies they planned to have someday.

More commonly, both planned and completed farewells were in the form of conversations. One subject asked her brother to come for a visit so that she could see and talk to him one last time; others arranged with friends for one last get-together, saying goodbye quite explicitly on these occasions. Those who anticipated saying farewell only in the last hours of their conscious life imagined these occasions to be times when loving words would be spoken or a goodbye look would be exchanged.

All such farewells, whether spoken or not, can be thought of as forms of gifts. By saying goodbye to someone, the dying person signals that that person matters enough to warrant a farewell. Saying goodbye also serves to make the death real, to force the imminent death out of the realm of denial into acceptance by others as well as by the dying person. And finally, as Kellehear and Lewin pointed out, farewells may make the dying easier, especially if they are completed before the final moments of life. They may make it easier for the dying person to disengage, to reach a point of acceptance.

11.2.3: Individual Adaptations to Dying

The process of dying varies hugely from one person to the next, not only in the emotions expressed (or not expressed), but also in the physical process. Some experience a long, slow decline; others die instantly, with no "stages" or phases at all. Some experience great pain; others little or none. Similarly, the way each person handles the process also varies. Some fight hard against dying; others appear to accept it early in the process and struggle no further. Some remain calm; others fall into deep depression. The question that researchers have begun to ask is whether such variations in the emotional response to impending or probable death have any effect at all on the physical process of dying.

In an early study, psychiatrist Steven Greer and his colleagues (Greer, 1991; Pettingale, Morris, Greer, et al., 1985) followed a group of 62 women diagnosed with early stages of breast cancer. Three months after the original diagnosis, each woman was interviewed at some length, and her reaction to the diagnosis and to her treatment was classed in one of five groups:

Table 11.2 Adaptations to Dying

Reactions	Term
Patient rejects the diagnosis and the evidence presented to her.	POSITIVE AVOIDANCE (DENIAL)
Patient shows optimism and actively searches for more information about her diagnosis. Expresses the desire to fight the disease in any way possible.	FIGHTING SPIRIT
Patient acknowledges the diagnosis, but does not seek further information and continues with her normal life.	STOIC ACCEPTANCE (FATALISM)
Patient is overwhelmed by the diagnosis and considers themselves gravely ill and without hope.	HELPLESSNESS/HOPELESSNESS
Patient responds to the diagnosis with extreme anxiety and interprets additional information pessimistically. She interprets all body sensations as possible recurrence.	ANXIOUS PREOCCUPATION

Hide All Cells   Show All Cells

Greer checked on the survival rates of these five groups 15 years later. Only 35% of those whose initial reaction had been either positive avoidance (denial) or fighting spirit had died of cancer, compared to 76% of those whose initial reaction had been stoic acceptance, anxious preoccupation, or helplessness/hopelessness. Because the five groups had not differed initially in the stage of their disease or in treatment, these results support the hypothesis that psychological response contributes to disease progress, just as coping strategies more generally affect the likelihood of disease in the first place.

In a more recent study, medical psychology researcher, Johan Denollet and colleagues (Denollet, Martens, Nyklíc̆ek, et al., 2008) assessed the coping styles of 736 cardiac patients and identified 159 as having repressive coping styles. This was defined as a tendency to minimize distress and to avoid negative emotions in response to their diagnosis and treatment. On tests of coping mechanisms, these patients reported low levels of depression, anxiety, anger, sadness, or fear. Approximately 6 years later, the outcome for these patients was examined. Patients who exhibited repressive coping styles were more apt to have died of any cause, died of heart disease, or experienced a nonfatal heart attack during the intervening time period than patients who exhibited other coping styles.

The researchers concluded that even though these patients were not reporting any negative emotion (distress, anxiety, anger, depression), they were experiencing physiological signs of distress (such as increased blood pressure) and low adherence to their physicians' recommendations. And as a result of their appearance of healthy coping, they were considered to be low risk by their health-care professionals, whereas, in truth, they were at increased risk of heart attack or death in the next 5–10 years.

Similar results have emerged from studies of AIDS patients (Reed, Kemeny, Taylor, et al., 1994; Solano, Costa, Salvati, et al., 1993). In general, those who report less hostility, more stoic acceptance, and more helplessness and who fail to express negative feelings die sooner (O'Leary, 1990). Those who struggle the most, who fight the hardest, who express their anger and hostility openly, and who find some sources of joy in their lives live longer. In some ways, the data suggest that "good patients"—those who are obedient and not too questioning, who don't yell at their doctors or make life difficult for those around them—are, in fact, likely to die sooner.

Furthermore, there are studies linking these psychological differences to immune system functioning. A particular subset of immune cells called NK cells, thought to be an important defense against cancer cells, have been found to occur at lower rates among patients who report less distress and seem better adjusted to their illness (O'Leary, 1990). And among AIDS patients, one study shows that T-cell counts declined more rapidly among those who respond to their disease with repression (similar to the stoic acceptance or helplessness groups in the Greer study), whereas those showing fighting spirit had a slower loss of T cells (Solano, Costa, Salvati, et al., 1993).

LIMITATION TO THE FIGHTING SPIRIT   Despite the growing body of results of this type, two important cautions are nonetheless in order before we leap to the conclusion that a fighting spirit is the optimum response to any disease. First, in some careful studies, no link has been found between depression/stoic acceptance/helplessness and more rapid death from cancer (Richardson, Zarnegar, Bisno, et al., 1990). Second, it is not clear that the same psychological response is necessarily optimum for every form of disease. Consider heart disease, for example. There is a certain irony in the fact that many of the qualities that appear to be optimum for cancer patients could be considered reflections of a type A personality. Because the anger and hostility components of the type A personality are a risk factor for heart disease, it is not so obvious that a fighting-spirit response that includes those components would necessarily be desirable.

One of the major difficulties in all this research is that investigators have used widely differing measures of psychological functioning. Greer and his colleagues have found quite consistent results with their category system; others, using standardized measures of depression or hopelessness, have not necessarily found the same patterns. My own reading of the evidence is that there is indeed some link between psychological responses to stress (including a fatal diagnosis) and prognosis, but that we have not yet zeroed in on just what psychological processes may be critical for which disease. Fortunately, this is an area in which a great deal of research is under way, giving some hope that clearer answers may emerge before long.

Another important ingredient in a person's response to imminent death is the amount of social support that he or she may have available. High levels of social support are linked to lower levels of pain, fewer depressive symptoms, and longer survival times. For example, patients with heart failure survive longer and adhere to medication regimen better if they have social support (Wu, Frazier, Rayens, et al., 2013) and those with significant levels of atherosclerosis live longer if they have a confidant than if they do not (Williams, 1992). The latter study involved a sample of African Americans, suggesting that the connection is not unique to Anglo culture.

WRITING PROMPT

When people learn that a friend is dying, they sometimes stay away because they don't know what to do or to say. How can this decision be harmful? What are some helpful things they can do and say? Write a brief response that will be read by your instructor. Be sure to give specific examples.

> ▶ The response entered here will appear in the performance dashboard and can be viewed by your instructor.

Submit

11.2.4: Choosing Where to Die

In the United States and other industrialized countries today, the majority of adults report that they would prefer to die in their homes, but the fact is that the great majority die in hospitals and nursing homes. For example, patients' preferences for place of terminal care and place of death were gathered for 96 end-stage cancer patients in Denmark. More than three fourths of them (84%) wished to be cared for at home, and 71% wished to die at home. Of those who expressed these wishes, only half were cared for and died at home. What made the difference? Two major factors were having a spouse or partner at home and being in contact with a palliative care team (Brogaard, Neergaard, Sokolowski, et al., 2012).

In a large study that surveyed family members of individuals who had died recently of chronic disease, physician Joan Teno and her colleagues (Teno, Clarridge, Casey, et al., 2004) asked about the details of the deaths. The sample, which consisted of over 1,500 families, was selected to be representative of the 1.97 million deaths from chronic illnesses that occurred that year in the United States. Respondents were asked about their deceased family members' last place of care; the results showed that one third died at home, and two thirds died in an institution, either a hospital or a nursing home. However, the critical difference in quality of care was not whether they died at home or not, but whether they received home-care nursing services, or **hospice care**, which is care focused on pain relief, emotional support, and spiritual comfort for the dying person and his or her family. When asked about the quality of care the deceased family member had received at the end of life, the responses indicated that there was little difference between dying at home with nursing services, dying in a nursing home, and dying in a hospital—fewer than half of the respondents reported that their family members who had spent their last days in these situations received "excellent" care. In contrast, over 70% of the respondents whose family members had died at home with hospice care evaluated this care as "excellent." Unfortunately, the number of people whose family members died at home with hospice care represented only about 16% of the total survey respondents.

Figure 11.1 shows some of the problem areas survey respondents reported in this study, divided by whether their loved ones died at home with home-care nursing services, at home with hospice care, in a nursing home, or in a hospital. As you can see, the biggest concern was lack of emotional support for the patient, which was reported by twice as many respondents whose family members had their final care at home with home nursing care (70%) than at home with hospice care (35%). The same ratio is shown for lack of emotional support for the family, with families of those dying at home with home health nursing reporting this problem twice as often (45%) as those at home with hospice care (21%).

Figure 11.1 After the death of a loved one, family members report concerns about last place of care.

SOURCE: Data from Teno, Clarridge, Casey, et al. (2004).

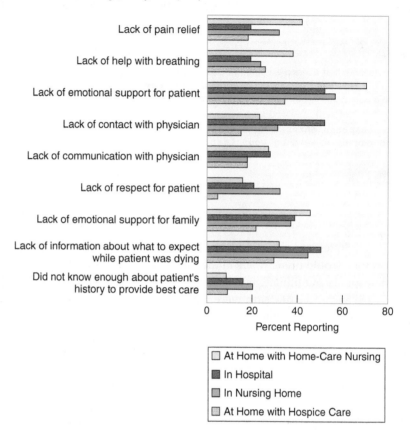

The authors of the study concluded that although the study only tapped the respondents' perceptions of their family members' care and, at that, only after some time had passed, it is still appropriate to be alarmed about the problems associated with end-of-life care in the United States. The authors were especially concerned about the problems reported with nursing homes, which are more apt to be the last places of care for the very old. We will have more and more elderly people requiring end-of-life care in the years to come, at a time when nursing homes are receiving less and less federal support. In addition, hospitals are unable to keep terminally ill patients, so are increasingly transferring them to nursing homes.

What exactly does hospice care consist of? I talked about the beginnings of the hospice movement in the story that opened this chapter, but what exactly is it today, and why is it so successful in providing "excellent" services to dying people and their families?

The hospice movement was given a good deal of impetus by Kübler-Ross's writings because she emphasized the importance of **a good death**, meaning a death with dignity, with maximum consciousness and minimum pain, and with the patient and the patient's family having full information and control over the process. Hospice care began in England in the 1960s. It started in the 1970s in the United States as a grassroots movement to give terminal cancer patients an alternative to continued aggressive treatment. By 1982, the idea had gained so much support that Congress was persuaded to add hospice care to the list of benefits paid for by Medicare. Today there are more than 3,000 hospice programs in the United States, serving about a half million terminally ill patients and their families each year (Wilkinson & Lynn, 2001).

HOSPICE PHILOSOPHY AND SERVICES   The philosophy that underlies the **hospice approach** has several aspects:

- Control over the care and the care-receiving setting should belong to the patient and family.

- Medical care provided should be *palliative,* not curative, meaning that pain should be alleviated and comfort maximized, but a minimum of invasive or life-prolonging measures should be undertaken.

- Death should be viewed as a normal, inevitable part of life, not to be avoided but to be faced and accepted.

- A multidisciplinary team is involved, which can include a physician, nurses, social workers, therapists, and chaplains or other spiritual leaders (Torpy, Burke, & Golub, 2012).

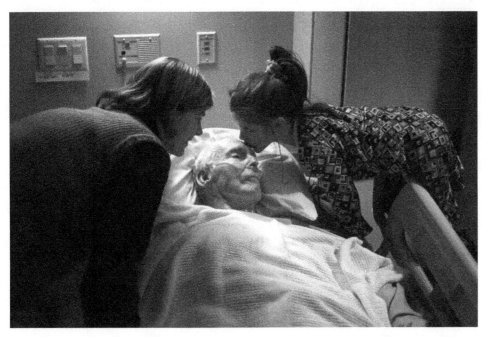

Hospice care is based on the belief that when death is inevitable, professional caregivers should focus on helping the patient and family accept it as a natural part of the life process.

In real terms, this philosophy translates into a constellation of services available to the dying person and his or her family and friends. These services are listed and described in Table 11.3. Over 44% of deaths in the United States currently take place under the care of a hospice program. The most common condition patients seek hospice care for is terminal cancer (38%). Although hospice is designed to provide care during the last 6 months of a person's life, the average length of care is under 2 months, primarily because of the difficulty of predicting the course of many terminal illnesses (National Hospice and Palliative Care Association, 2012). The reason families don't use hospice services is because of the increasing number of patients dying of heart disease and Alzheimer's disease (which are not as predictable), the psychological blocks patients and family have against accepting death as imminent, and the difficulty some physicians (and family members) have in ceasing aggressive treatment. The result is that although hospice care is a positive move toward allowing people to have a "good death," it is still used by a small number of people and for a short period of time.

Table 11.3 What Is Hospice Care?

- An interdisciplinary team of physicians, nurses, social workers, counselors, home health aides, clergy, therapists, and trained volunteers who care for the patient based on their areas of expertise to relieve symptoms and provide support to the patient and his or her family.

- Pain and symptom control that helps the patient be comfortable yet in control of his or her life.

- Spiritual care for the patient and his or her family, based on their individual beliefs, to help the patient find meaning, say goodbye, or perform religious rituals.

- Home care for those who are able to stay in their own homes, but also inpatient care in hospitals or nursing homes when needed.

- Respite care for family caregivers.

- Family conferences to enable family members to learn about the patient's condition and to share feelings, talk about expectations, learn about dying, and ask questions.

- Bereavement care from counselors and clergy to help family members through the grieving process with visits, phone calls, and support groups.

- Coordinated care provided by the interdisciplinary team to communicate with the physicians, home- care agency, and community professionals such as pharmacists, clergy, and funeral directors.

SOURCE: Adapted from American Cancer Society (2013).

11.2.5: Choosing When to Die

Another way of looking at the advances of modern medicine is that instead of extending life, it prolongs death. Today about 90% of the people who die each year do so after experiencing prolonged illnesses and steady decline. Many believe that there is a fundamental right to die a good death and to choose when, how, and where it will occur.

In 1976, California passed the first law in the United States concerning living wills, documents discussed earlier, which allow individuals to legally express the wish that if they are in a condition with no hope of recovery, no heroic measures should be taken to extend their lives. Living wills are now valid in all 50 states of the United States and in many other countries. In 1990 the U.S. Supreme Court ruled that Americans have the right to refuse medical treatment, even if refusing it will result in death.

In 1997 voters in Oregon passed the Death with Dignity Act, which allows for **physician-assisted suicide**, meaning that under certain circumstances, physicians are allowed to assist patients to obtain medication that will end their lives. Among other requirements, the patient must request the medication voluntarily, be terminally ill, and be mentally competent, and these points must be confirmed by a second physician. There is a waiting period of 15 days, and the prescription must be registered with the state. Despite the warnings by opponents of this law, not many terminally ill patients have requested physician-assisted deaths. The first year this option was available, 24 people received prescriptions, and 16 used them to end their lives. In 2012, 115 people received prescriptions, and 77 used them to end their lives (Oregon Department of Human Services, 2013).

Oregon keeps careful records of requests and prescriptions for physician-assisted suicides. In 2012, the 115 prescriptions were written by 61 different doctors, and the average age of the patient was 69. The large majority were white (97%), had at least a bachelor's degree (43%), had cancer (75%), died at home (97%), and were in hospice care (97%). All (100%) had some form of health insurance, meaning that they were not choosing this outcome because of the inability to pay for further treatment of their diseases. The most frequent reasons given for the decisions to end their lives were first, loss of autonomy, followed by decreasing ability to participate in activities that made life enjoyable for them and loss of dignity (Oregon Department of Human Services, 2013). As of this writing, the states of Washington, Montana, and Vermont also have physician-assisted suicide provisions, as do the countries of Luxembourg, the

Netherlands, and Switzerland. Belgium allows euthanasia, which involves the physician administering the lethal drug, not the patient.

Physician and bioethicist Ezekial Emanuel and his colleagues (Emanuel, Fairclough, & Emanuel, 2000) surveyed almost 1,000 terminally ill patients about their attitudes toward physician-assisted suicide. Although a majority (60%) of the patients supported it hypothetically, only about 10% seriously considered it for themselves. Those who were more likely to consider physician-assisted suicide had depressive symptoms, had substantial caregiving needs, and were in pain. Those who were less likely to consider it felt appreciated, were 65 years of age or older, and were African American. Interestingly, about 4 months later, the surviving patients were interviewed again, and about half of each group had changed their minds. Those who now favored physician-assisted suicide were more likely to have developed depressive symptoms or breathing difficulties.

This is an interesting study for several reasons. It is the first study I have seen that actually interviewed terminally ill patients about physician-assisted suicide, making a distinction between the hypothetical construct and the actual application to oneself. It is also interesting because it showed that the key indicators in this decision were more social than medical. It followed up on the patients and showed that the wish to be assisted in suicide was not consistent over time for about half of the patients. These findings show the importance of evaluating patients for depression, unrelieved pain and breathing difficulties, and the feeling that they are a burden or unappreciated when considering physician-assisted suicide. And it also reinforces the idea of having a waiting period between requesting the medication and receiving it.

Certainly the advances we have made in medicine and health care have given us a whole host of blessings. It is very unusual for a woman to die in childbirth or a toddler not to live to adulthood. Many of us reach middle age with all our siblings and our parents still in our lives. Our children often have four grandparents and probably a few great-grandparents, too. But there is a downside, and that is our diminished opportunity to die a "good death," as described this way:

> Humans have faced all manner of challenges over time. As things go, the challenge of having the opportunity to grow old and die slowly is not such a bad thing. However, it is a challenge. Society has simply never been in this position before. We have to work on language, categories, framing, meanings, rituals, habits, social organization, service delivery, financing, and community commitment. Much remains to be learned and done. The burgeoning numbers of persons living into old age and coming to the end of life makes the need for that learning and implementing all the more urgent (Wilkinson & Lynn, 2001, p. 457).

11.3: After Death Occurs: Rituals and Grieving

11.3 Explain after death rituals and their significance

Whether a death is sudden or prolonged, anticipated or unexpected, it leaves survivors who must somehow come to terms with the death and eventually pick up the pieces of their lives.

11.3.1: Ritual Mourning: Funerals and Ceremonies

All human cultures participate in **ritual mourning**, a set of symbolic rites and ceremonies associated with death. Far from being empty gestures, these rituals have clear and important functions. As sociologists Victor Marshall and Judith Levy put it, "Rituals provide a... means through which societies simultaneously seek to control the disruptiveness of death and to make it meaningful.... The funeral exists as a formal means to accomplish the work of completing a biography, managing grief, and building new social relationships after the death" (1990, pp. 246, 253).

One way in which rituals accomplish these goals is by giving the bereaved a specific role to play. The content of the role differs markedly from one culture to the next, but the clarity of the role in most cases provides a shape to the days or weeks immediately following the death of a loved person. In our culture, the rituals prescribe what one should wear, who should be notified, who should be fed, what demeanor one should show, and far more. Depending on one's religious background, one may need to arrange to sit shiva, or gather friends and family for a wake, or arrange a memorial service. One may be expected to respond stoically or to wail and tear one's hair. But whatever the social rules, there is a role to be filled that provides shape to the first numbing hours and days following the death of someone important to us.

Every culture has funeral rituals that help its members mark the passing of one of their own and console those who are bereaved.

The rituals surrounding death can also give some meaning to the death by emphasizing the meaning of the life of the person who has died. It is not accidental that most death rituals include testimonials, photographs, biographies, and witnessing. By telling the story of the person's life, by describing that life's value and meaning, the death can be accepted more readily. And of course, ceremonies can also provide meaning by placing the death in a larger philosophical or religious context.

The United States, which is known as a nation of immigrants, has a very diverse collection of funeral and mourning rituals. There are many subgroups, and Table 11.4 shows the practices of some of the major ones. As you can see, there are very large differences in the ways people express their loss and pay tribute to their loved ones.

Table 11.4 Funeral Rituals and Practices among U.S. Cultural Groups

Cultural Group	Predominant Religious Beliefs	Mourning Traditions	Funeral Traditions
African American (in the south)	Protestant. Believe that all will be reunited in heaven and that events in life are in accordance with God's plan.	Open and emotional grief by men and women. Many wear black to signify mourning.	Viewing of the body at home; large gathering of family and community members; funeral in church with support for mourners from church "nurses." Burial in cemetery, often with favorite belongings of the deceased in the casket, such as CDs, sports uniforms, trophies, and photos.
African American (immigrants from Western Africa and Caribbean West Indies)	Mostly Catholic mixed with African folk-medicine beliefs, some Protestant.	Long period of mourning and elaborate ceremonies, including prayers, drumming, and singing. Photographs are taken of the deceased. Children are included in all parts of mourning to instill respect for ancestors.	Traditional, formal funeral ceremonies conducted by males in native dialects passed down from elders. Paid for by the community and extended family. No embalming or cremation. Usually burial, but cremation sometimes allowed if remains are returned to homeland.
U.S. Latinos (Cuban, Puerto Rican, and Dominican descent)	Catholic. Believe that death is entry to heaven and that there is a continued relationship between the living and the dead.	Women express grief openly; men control emotions and remain "strong."	Open-casket wake for two days as family gathers with food, prayers, candles. Funeral is traditional mass, and burial is in a Catholic cemetery.
U.S. immigrants from Muslim countries (Caribbean islands, Asian and African countries)	Islam. Believe that the purpose of life is to prepare for eternity. At death the soul is exposed to Allah for judgment.	Crying is acceptable, but no extreme emotional displays, such as wailing.	Burial must take place within 24 hours. Imam directs funeral. No viewing of remains, no embalming, no cremation. Deceased is buried facing Mecca. Women are not allowed to visit cemeteries.

(Continued)

Asian immigrants from China	Mixture of Taoism, ancestor worship, veneration of local deities, Buddhism.	The more mourners and the more emotion expressed, the more the person was loved. After the funeral, the family observes a 100-day period of mourning during which they wear a piece of colored cloth signifying their relationship to the deceased.	Determined by the age of the deceased. Children and young adults without children do not have full funeral rites. Wake takes place in the home with traditional rules about what colors different family members must wear and where people must sit. Guests donate money to help pay the expenses. Coffin goes from home to cemetery, which is on a hill. The higher the gravesite, the more prestige. The eldest son brings . back earth from the grave to be used at home in a shrine to the deceased family member.
Asian immigrants from Thailand, Vietnam, Myanmar, and Cambodia	Buddhism. Believe that death is an opportunity for improvement in the next life.	Deep mourning, sometimes with somatic (bodily) symptoms.	Wake with open casket in home for 1–3 days. Family wears white clothing or headbands. Funeral includes altar with flowers, fruit, incense, water, and candles. Ceremony begins with 1 hour of chanting by priests. Mourners place pinch of ashes in a bowl and say personal prayer for the deceased. Private cremation witnessed by a priest.
Indian	Hindu. Believe that birth and death are part of a cycle. Good actions in life (karma) lead to final liberation of the soul.	Mourning is done to let the soul know that it should depart and to let the family say goodbye.	Body is bathed and dressed in new clothes, then cremated before the next sunrise to ensure the soul's transition to the next world. Family conducts rituals for 10 days, and on the 11th, the soul leaves the earth. No burial, no embalming. Children participate in all parts of the ceremony. Remains are sent to India or scattered over a river in the U.S. along with flowers.

(Continued)

Native American (Navajo and related tribes)	Navajo tradition mixed with Catholic and Protestant. Believe that the soul is present in the products the person created (pottery, blankets).	Mourners sprinkle dirt on the casket before burial.	Deceased is wrapped in Navajo blankets and placed in the casket. Broken pots or frayed blankets are included to help the release of the soul from these products. Also in the casket are an extra set of clothing, food, water, and personal items. Services are in English and Navajo. Burial is facing east to west. No footprints are left in the dirt around the grave to confuse spirit guide.
European Americans, Christian faith	Believe in afterlife, that friends and family will be reunited in heaven.	Mourners wear black clothing or black armbands. Some put dark wreath on the door of the deceased person's home.	Gathering in a funeral home or church in the days before the funeral to console each other and pay final respects to the deceased. Sometimes the casket is open so mourners can view the body. Funeral is at church or funeral home. The clergy conducts a service with prayers and songs. Friends and family members eulogize the deceased. Catholics celebrate mass. Burial takes place after service with a short graveside ceremony. Mourners gather at the home of the deceased or close relative to have a meal and continue consolation. Cremation is more common for Protestants than Catholics.
European Americans, Jewish faith	Believe that one's good works live on in the hearts and minds of others. No specific teachings on the afterlife. Funeral is celebration of the life of the deceased.	Family "sits shiva" for a week in the home and mourns by sitting on low stools, covering mirrors, not attending to clothing or appearance, and wearing a black ribbon or torn clothes. Friends bring food to the house and attend to the needs of the family.	Funeral and burial take place soon after death. Deceased is buried in plain shroud and simple casket to symbolize that all were created equal by God. Earth from Israel may be sprinkled on casket during burial. Family says traditional prayers for 1 year, after which a headstone can be put on the grave.

Hide All Cells	Show All Cells

SOURCE: Adapted from Hazell (1997), Lobar (2006), Santillanes (1997), Techner (1997).

Does Table 11.2 describe the experiences you have had with mourning and funeral rites in your family or community? What are the differences?

▶ The response entered here will appear in the performance dashboard and can be viewed by your instructor.

Submit

11.3.2: The Process of Grieving

When the funeral or memorial service is over, what do you do then? How does a person handle the grief of this kind of loss, whether it be of a spouse, a parent, a child, a friend, or a lover? The topic of grief was dominated for many years by stage theories of various kinds, such as the ones proposed by Kübler-Ross (described earlier in the chapter) and John Bowlby. Although Kübler-Ross softened the stagelike progression in her theory, Bowlby and others did not. These neo-Freudian theories describe the reaction to the death of a loved one as a series of stages and state that everyone must go through all the stages in a fixed order. At any given moment in the process, the bereaved person is either in one stage or another, never in two at once. According to these theories, one cannot skip stages or return to a stage once one has left it. The result of this "grief work" is that at the end of the stages, the bereaved have adjusted to the loss and regained their normal lives.

Bowlby's theory has four stages: numbness, yearning, disorganization, and despair, followed by a time of reorganization (1980). Kübler-Ross's five stages were described earlier in this chapter. Research does not support the claim that these stages are experienced in the stated order or even experienced by all bereaved individuals. For example, one critic wrote:

> We are discovering that just as there are multitudinous ways of living, there are numerous ways of dying and grieving.... The hard data do not support the existence of any procrustean stages or schedules that characterize terminal illness or mourning. This does not mean that, for example, Kübler-Ross's "stages of dying" and Bowlby's "phases of mourning" cannot provide us with implications and insights into the dynamics and process of dying and grief, but they are very far from being inexorable hoops through which most terminally ill individuals and mourners inevitably pass. We should beware of promulgating a coercive orthodoxy of how to die or mourn. (Feifel, 1990, p. 540)

Some argue that it would be better to think in terms of themes or aspects rather than stages, such as themes of numbness, yearning, anger, disorganization, and despair. In the first few days or weeks after the death of a loved one, the dominant theme is likely to be numbness, with yearning coming later but perhaps not replacing numbness totally. Exhaustion may be a later theme, although yearning could also occur at that time. Like Kübler-Ross's stages of death acceptance, Bowlby's stages of mourning are perhaps best viewed as descriptors of human emotions that many people experience in bereavement, but not in totality and not in this specific order.

However, for many decades Bowlby's theory was the basis for professional understanding of grief by psychologists, counselors, healthcare professionals, and clergy. In fact, the dominant belief was that failure to experience trauma and the proper stages of grief was a sign that normal, healthy grieving had not taken place and that some pathology was present, such as repression or denial (Rando, 1993). In these cases, clinical intervention was recommended to help the person work through hidden, unresolved grief feelings (Jacobs, 1993). The obvious alternative was that the loved one must not have been truly "loved" (Fraley & Shaver, 1999). More recently, researchers have found that many bereaved people do not follow any particular set of stages. In fact the most common reaction to grief is *resilience*, the maintenance of healthy functioning after a potentially traumatic event.

STUDIES OF GRIEF In a study of participants who had recently experienced the death of their spouses, almost half failed to show even mild symptoms of depression following the loss (Zisook, Paulus, Shuchter, et al., 1997). Other studies have shown that positive emotions, including genuine smiling and laughter, are not only present when the bereaved discuss their recent losses, but seem to promote well-being (Bonanno & Kaltman, 1999; Bonanno & Keltner, 1997).

In a longitudinal study, gay men who had been caregivers for their partners with AIDS were interviewed shortly after their partners' deaths. The bereaved partners' appraisals of the experience were more positive than negative; many said that they had experienced feelings of personal strength and self-growth, and that their relationships had become stronger. Twelve months later, the individuals who had been the most positive in their appraisals of the caregiving experience were more likely to show high levels of psychological well-being (Moskowitz, Folkman, & Acree, 2003). These studies and others with similar findings show that the experiences of actual bereaved people do not follow traditional theory; the typical reaction to the death of a spouse or partner was not all-encompassing negative thoughts and feelings occurring in predictable stages. Furthermore, the participants who did not follow the theory were not maladjusted or in need of clinical intervention. To the contrary, those who showed the most positive thoughts and affect were the best adjusted a year later. One problem remained—how genuine was their grief? Did they truly have a close and loving relationship with the deceased person, or did the lack of negative grief simply indicate that there wasn't much to mourn? Asking a person about a relationship with a recently deceased partner may not bring forth an honest answer.

To investigate this possibility, psychologist George Bonanno and his colleagues (Bonanno, Wortman, Lehman, et al., 2002) conducted a longitudinal study that covered the time before bereavement. They recruited 1,500 older married couples and interviewed them over the course of several years about their relationships, attachment styles, coping mechanisms, and personal adjustment. During this time 205 participants experienced the death of their spouse. Using the preloss data, researchers were able to evaluate the quality of the marriage before the death occurred along with the adjustment of the widowed spouse for 18 months afterward. The researchers were able to distinguish five patterns of adjustment and the preloss factors that predicted each pattern.

The results are illustrated in Figure 11.2. The most common pattern of adjustment following the death of a spouse was resilience (46%), followed by chronic grief (16%), common grief (11%), depressed-improved (10%), and chronic depression (8%). When the quality of the marriage was compared to the grief response, there were no differences between the top three groups (resilience, chronic grief, common grief). The one group that showed significantly low quality-of-marriage scores was the depressed-improved group, which, as you can see in the figure, had high levels of depression before the death of their spouse and improved after the spouse died. This strongly suggests that the popular view that the relative absence of grief shown by bereaved individuals is due to poor relationships before their loss is only appropriate for about 10% of cases.

More recently, Bonanno and his colleagues (Bonanno, Moskowitz, Papa, et al., 2005) conducted a similar study with a population of bereaved spouses, bereaved parents, and bereaved gay men and found similar levels of resilience. They also found no association between the reaction to bereavement and the quality of relationship or the caregiver burden before death. However, there was an association between reaction to

Figure 11.2 Bereaved spouses studied before loss, at the time of loss, and 18 months after loss show five distinct patterns of grief, the most common being resilience.

SOURCE: Bonanno, Wortman, Lehman, et al. (2002).

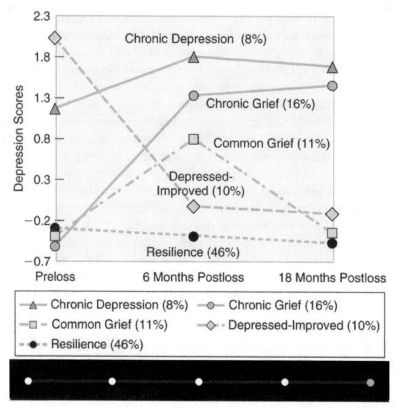

bereavement and personal adjustment, with participants who were rated more positively and better adjusted by close friends being more apt to react to the loss of a loved one with resilience.

In summary, recent research has shown that the stage theories of bereavement, such as those proposed by Bowlby and Kübler-Ross, are helpful in defining possible reactions people may have to the death of a loved one, but do not describe the common path that grief takes for the majority of bereaved individuals. Grief is highly personal and individualized. It is also complex. No doubt bereaved individuals run the gamut of reactions described by theorists, but most are not overwhelmed by their grief or unable to function in their usual roles. They have moments of yearning and despair, but they also have moments of positive feelings—of appreciation to those who offer support, words of comfort for others who share their loss, fond memories of their loved one, and even some funny stories and jokes. Grief is not an altered state of consciousness to be feared. The death of a loved one is painful, and a departed loved one will never be forgotten, but for most people, death becomes part of life, and life goes on.

How to help someone cope who has become widowed? Like many other questions in this book, the answer is, "It depends." For those who are deeply distressed or depressed, you could suggest a support group or counseling. Don't tell them to cheer up or push them to get back into "life as usual." But if they seem to be coping well and not showing high levels of grief, consider that it might be a normal, healthy reaction, and don't be shocked if they host a dinner party for a small group of friends 2 months after the funeral. Or if a widower begins to date before the traditional year of mourning is over, don't automatically think that his marriage must not have been a good one. When people are coping well, don't suggest that they need to "let it all out" or "take time to grieve." As usual, the best way to be helpful to a person dealing with such a loss is to be highly attentive to the signals you are receiving, rather than to impose your own ideas of what is normal or expected.

Finally, let us not lose sight of the fact that loss can also lead to growth. Indeed, the majority of widows in one study said not only that they changed as a result of their husband's death, but also that the change was in the direction of greater independence and greater skill (Wortman & Silver, 1989). Like all crises and all major life changes, bereavement can be an opportunity as well as, or instead of, a disabling experience. How we respond is likely to depend very heavily on the patterns we have established from early childhood: our temperament or personality, our internal working models of attachment and self, our intellectual skills, and the social networks we have created.

11.4: Living and Dying: A Final Word

11.4 Express the inevitability of death and the need to come to terms with it for a happy adulthood

Our understanding of death and its meaning, our attitude toward the inevitability of death, and the way we come to terms with that inevitability affect not only the way we die but also the way we choose to live our lives throughout adulthood. David Steindl-Rast, a Benedictine monk, made this point: "Death… is an event that puts the whole meaning of life into question. We may be occupied with purposeful activities, with getting tasks accomplished, works completed, and then along comes the phenomenon of death—whether it is our final death or one of those many deaths through which we go day by day. And death confronts us with the fact that purpose is not enough. We live by meaning" (Steindl-Rast, 1977, p. 22).

An awareness of death is thus not something we can put off until one day we hear a diagnosis of our own impending demise. It can, instead, help to define and give meaning to daily life. My grandmother's funeral was ended with the statement: "Let us go forth and celebrate life!" It is a good ending for any discussion of death.

Summary: Death and Bereavement

LISTEN TO THE AUDIO:

`▶ ●━━━━━━━━━ 06:21 ◀× ●`

1. Death is an inevitable fact of life, and the way we think about it, how we cope with the deaths of loved ones, and how we come to terms with the reality of our own ultimate deaths are topics of interest for those concerned with adult development.

2. Death has various meanings. To some it is an organizer of time, to others it is punishment (and long life is a reward). Most believe that death is a transition either to an afterlife or to a new life through reincarnation. The most pervasive meaning of death is loss—of opportunity, of relationships, of time.

3. Death anxiety has been studied extensively. We know that it occurs most strongly in middle-aged adults and

people of midlevel religiosity. Middle age is a time when the effects of aging become noticeable. Older adults think more about death, but have less fear. Those who are midlevel in religious beliefs seem to fear death more because presumably they believe there may be an afterlife but have not prepared for it. Women express more death anxiety than men, but that might reflect higher rates of anxiety in general. Those who feel a sense of purpose in life and few regrets are less likely to fear death.

4. People accept the reality of their own eventual death by purchasing life insurance, making wills, collecting memories, and reminiscing about their lives. In recent years, as medical technology has become able to extend life, many people have come to fear the dying process more than they fear death itself. They also

have concerns about leaving family members to make the difficult decisions about such matters. A good number of adults have drawn living wills that express the limits they want in end-of-life care. Another way people accept the eventuality of their own death is by becoming an organ transplant donor.

5. Physician Elisabeth Kübler-Ross was the first to write about the personal acceptance of death some 40 years ago. Before that time, the focus was on extending life, not accepting death. She described five stages of death reactions, and although not everyone goes through these stages, and they do not always occur in the same sequence, her descriptions are accurate, and her terminology is used in every field that deals with death. The stages are denial, anger, bargaining, depression, and acceptance.

6. Elisabeth Kübler-Ross identified three key issues about the dying process: Those who are dying are still alive and have unfinished needs, we need to listen to them to be able to provide the care they need, and we need to learn from the dying how to live ourselves.

7. Dying people can accept the reality of their death by giving farewell messages to their loved ones. These can be conversations, letters, or gifts.

8. Psychological responses to disease seem to have an effect on the course of the illness. Those who react to a diagnosis of a potentially terminal disease with positive avoidance (denial), with a fighting spirit, and even with hostility are more apt to survive than those who show anxiety, depression, or fatalism. Another factor in a person's response to death is the amount (and quality) of social support they have.

9. Most people express the wish to die at home in familiar surroundings, but the majority die in hospitals and nursing homes. An alternative for those who have predictable terminal conditions, such as cancer, is hospice care. A hospice provides a team of professionals and volunteers who focus on pain relief, emotional support, and spiritual comfort for the patient and family, usually in their own home. The goal of hospice is not to cure the patient but to provide a good death. Families of people who have died in hospice care report significantly fewer concerns about their care than those whose family members died in hospitals, nursing homes, or at home with home nursing care.

10. A good number of people believe that they have the right to control when they die, and several countries, along with the states of Oregon, Washington, Montana,

and Vermont, have enacted laws that allow physicians, under certain conditions, to assist dying patients in ending their lives. In 2012, this option was used by 77 people in Oregon; they tended to be younger, more educated, and more apt to have cancer than other people who died in that state in 2012.

11. A defining characteristic of our species is that we have ritual ways of dealing with the death of a member of our community. The earliest evidence of human habitations usually consists of ancient graves with decorative objects placed around the remains. Each culture has its own traditions, and in the United States, a nation of immigrants from many cultures, there are many ways of expressing loss and grief. The only common bond is that we feel loss and grief when someone dies who has touched our lives, either directly or as a public figure.

12. There are also many ways of feeling personal grief. There is no set of stages or processes that everyone experiences, and the way one feels grief does not reflect one's bond with the deceased.

13. The most common reaction to the death of a loved one is resilience. Most people are able to function in a healthy way despite their genuine feelings of loss and sorrow. These feelings are accompanied by fond memories, concern for others, appreciation of social support, and even laughter. The pattern of bereavement is not related to the quality of the relationship before death in most cases. It is related to the quality of the bereaved person's overall adjustment.

14. The death of a loved one can lead to gains, and bereavement can lead to personal growth.

SHARED WRITING: CHOOSING WHEN TO DIE

Consider this chapter's discussion of "choosing when to die." How much control should a person have over when they die? How much control should family members have? Write a short response that your classmates will read. Be sure to give concrete reasons in your discussion.

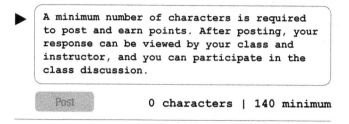

> A minimum number of characters is required to post and earn points. After posting, your response can be viewed by your class and instructor, and you can participate in the class discussion.

Post   0 characters | 140 minimum

Chapter 11 Quiz: Death and Bereavement

Chapter 12
The Successful Journey

∨ Learning Objectives

12.1 Describe the events and activities that typically classify each stage of adulthood

12.2 List distinct parameters that classify individual life

LISTEN TO THE AUDIO:

▶ ●━━━━━━━ 04:34 🔇 ●━

HANK WAKES UP every morning and makes himself a glass of fresh-squeezed orange juice, commenting to the world in general, "Ah, this is the life!" He is just short of his 80th birthday and has not had an easy life. He has scars on his chin and upper lip from having an incoming shell blow up in his face as he and his regiment of Marines stormed Peleliu Island in World War II. He has scars on his chest from coronary-bypass surgery and discolored places on his arms and legs due to the blood thinner he takes to ward off more heart trouble. He has a pacemaker and defibrillator implanted in his chest and needs surgery to have his batteries changed from time to time. He tells his great-grandsons that Grandma B. has a remote control device in her handbag, and if he gets "out of line," she will turn it on and make him behave. They think this is the funniest thing they have ever heard.

Hank and his wife raised five kids and supported them by always working at least two jobs. He married after the war and lived in his in-laws' house while he and his father built a house next door for the new family. Two years after they moved in, his father-in-law lost his eyesight (and his job), and the in-laws moved in with the new family, who now had three sons—a 2-year-old and a new pair of twins. Within 3 years of leaving the Marines, he was 26 and the head of a household of seven people.

When I first met Hank, he was a 60-year-old police officer—a job he did not like, but that had good pay and medical insurance, plus a chance for overtime. On Saturday nights he would turn on the TV a little before 8:00 and wait for the Lotto drawing. He would pat the phone on the table next to him and say, "If I win, the first thing I will do is call the chief and put in my two-weeks' notice." Then he would talk about what he would do with the winnings—buy a mansion on the hill for his wife, take a cruise around the world, send all his grandchildren to college, buy a vacation home on the beach in Florida.

Well, Hank never won the lottery, but he did leave his job when he retired a few years later, and he did buy a new house for his wife, smaller and newer than the family homestead. He started a lawn service and gave the college-aged grandkids jobs in the summer to help with their tuition. He bought a condo in Florida. He took a cruise to the Bahamas. He lives on a budget, watches his diet carefully, follows his doctor's orders strictly, and gets plenty of exercise on the small golf course near his condo. He and his wife go to concerts at the community center on Friday nights and out for pizza on Wednesdays (coupon night). He attends church and plays cards with the neighbors. He has a new cell phone with unlimited long-distance calls, so he talks to all his children and grandchildren every Sunday evening, wherever they are.

By most yardsticks, Hank's journey of adulthood has been a good one. He served his country, took care of his family, launched successful children, nurtured grandchildren, sustained a happy marriage for over 60 years, and is loved and respected by everyone who knows him. But by his own yardstick, he is the luckiest guy in the world. Hank happens to be my father-in-law, but over the years I have met many men and women like him. Despite the headlines in the papers and the lead stories on the nightly news, the vast majority of people in this country and in developed countries all over the world are satisfied with their lives and view themselves as successful adults. This chapter is about the journeys of people like Hank and the millions of other adults of every age who greet the world each morning saying, "Ah, this is the life!"

I plan to start this chapter with a summary of the major themes of development that describe the typical person's experience on the journey of adulthood. In the earlier chapters of this book I have carved up adulthood into different topics to examine them more closely; in this chapter I will put them back together again into a chronological review that readers can relate to a little better. Our lives are not neatly sliced up in separate topics. As you have no doubt sensed throughout the text, the topics merge into each other. I'd like to present whole lives in this chapter and how we evaluate our progress on the journey of adulthood.

12.1: Themes of Adulthood Development

12.1 Describe the events and activities that typically classify each stage of adulthood

In many of the earlier chapters I presented a review table to illustrate the major trends and age changes, so I will end the text with a mega-table showing a chronological review that spans from emerging adulthood (18 to 24 years) to late adulthood (75 years and over).

As always, these ages are approximate. Also note that the table describes the typical sequence of events for an adult who follows the culturally defined order of role transitions at the appropriate ages. I'll have more to say about individual pathways later in this chapter. For now, though, it is important to think about the typical or average. The normative pattern is to marry and have one's first child in the 20s. The children then typically leave home by the time one is about 50. Most people make major career changes in their mid-60s when they retire, change to part-time work, or become volunteer workers. Each row of the table represents a highly condensed version of one facet of the change that we might see over the lifetime of a person who follows such a modal pattern.

Table 12.1 Review of Changes in Eight Different Domains of Adult Functioning

	Emerging Adulthood (18–24 Years)	Early Adulthood (25–39 Years)	Middle Adulthood (40–64 Years)	Older Adulthood (65–74 Years)	Late Adulthood (75+ Years)
Physical change	Peak functioning in most body systems and physical abilities; optimal reproductive years; health habits established now will create pattern of later well-being. Bone mass is still increasing. Obesity is present for some, and many do not follow diet and exercise recommendations.	High levels of functioning continue (except for top athletes in most sports). Slight decline in sensory functioning appear. Weight and girth increase. Bone mass begins slight decline.	Noticeable signs of physical decline in some areas (e.g., near vision, stamina, muscle, and cardiovascular functioning). Climacteric ends reproduction for women suddenly around 50, and diminishes it gradually for men. Weight and girth increase. Bone mass shows sharp decline for women.	Physical decline more noticeable, but rate of decline is still relatively slow; reaction time slows. Weight decreases for many as bone and muscle mass decrease. More decline in sensory systems.	Acceleration in decline of physical abilities and sensory functioning.
Cognitive change	Peak period of cognitive skill on most measures, fastest reaction time. Most depend on parents for important decisions. Driving safety is low, and electronics use is high and skilled.	Most memory abilities show slight but gradual declines except crystallized abilities, semantic and procedural memory. Decision making increases. Driving safety increases. Electronic use is integral part of lives.	Small declines continue for all except crystallized abilities (which peak), semantic and procedural memory. Decision making increases due to experience. Driving safety is good. Electronic use is variable.	More slow decline for memory systems except crystallized abilities and procedural memory. Decision making remains good. Driving begins to decline, but may be helped with training. Electronic use can be valuable to help with day-to-day tasks.	All systems have gradual decline, including crystallized abilities, but not procedural memory. Decision making can be affected by cognitive loss and health disorders (and prescription drugs). Driving safety declines sharply. Electronic use continues to be helpful if started at earlier age.
Family and gender roles	Family roles are mixture of childhood and adult roles, and young people move in and out of them.	Major family roles are acquired (e.g., spouse, parent). Advances in these areas dominate life. Clear separation of gender roles.	Launch children; postparental phase; for many, added role of caregiver for elderly family members. Grandparent role begins for most.	Grandparent role continues in importance; significantly less dominance of gender roles.	Participation in family roles declines as activities are restricted. Role of care receiver begins for some.
Relationships	Family relationships are similar to childhood; peers are important socially. Romantic relationships consist of short-term dating for most.	Emphasis on forming new friendships, cohabitation, and marriage. Continued relationship with parents, siblings, and often grandparents. When children arrive, the focus turns toward parenting and away from other relationships.	Increased marital satisfaction as focus turns from parenting to other relationships. Adult children remain important. Increased importance of relationships with siblings and friends.	High marital satisfaction for those who have spouses; friendships and sibling relationships may become more intimate. Relationships with adult children frequent but not central to well-being. Relationship with grandchildren is important.	Majority are widowed; small network of close friends and siblings remain important.

(Continued)

Table 12.1 *(Continued)*

	Emerging Adulthood (18–24 Years)	Early Adulthood (25–39 Years)	Middle Adulthood (40–64 Years)	Older Adulthood (65–74 Years)	Late Adulthood (75+ Years)
Work roles	Vocational interests present for most. Jobs are part time or entry level and not related to vocational interests. Job performance is variable. Little thought of retirement plans. Residential moves are for college or military service.	Emphasis on choosing career, changing jobs, and establishing oneself in a career.	Peak years of career success and income for most, also work satisfaction. Slight physical and cognitive decline is compensated for by increases in job expertise.	Most leave their full-time jobs and take less stressful or part-time jobs, do volunteer work, or retire entirely.	Work roles unimportant for most. Some continue to volunteer.
Personality and meaning	Establish identity in areas of occupation, gender role, political, and religious beliefs. Begin to see the self as separate from the group. Accentuate own gender characteristics and repress opposite-gender characteristics.	Establish intimacy in relationships. Increased individuality (self-confidence, independence, autonomy). Form own ideas and standards. Gender differences remain high.	Establish generativity within family or workplace. Some sign of a softening of the individuality of the earlier period; fewer immature defenses; possibly autonomous level. Increase in spirituality for some, especially women. Gender differences begin to soften as children leave home.	Task of ego integrity; perhaps more interiority; a few may reach integrated level. Increase in spirituality for most.	Continuation of previous pattern. Increase in spirituality for most, even if outward signs decrease.
Major tasks	Establish self as an adult by completing education or job training, become independent from parents financially, make own decisions, become an autonomous member of community.	Renegotiate relationship with parents; form intimate partnerships; begin family, begin career, create individual identity, strive for success in both personal and professional life.	Guide children into adulthood; cope with death of parents; strengthen marriage; redefine life goals; achieve individuality; care for aging family members.	Find alternative to lifelong job; cope with health problems of self and spouse; redefine life goals and sense of self.	Come to terms with one's own life, possibly through reviewing memories or writing a memoir. Cope with the deaths of loved ones and the eventuality of own death. Value remaining family members and friends, and other remaining joys in life.

Of the seven horizontal rows in the table, four seem to me to describe genuinely maturational or developmental sequences. Clearly, the physical and mental changes described in the first two rows are strongly related to highly predictable and widely shared physical processes. Although the rate of change is affected by lifestyle and habits, the sequences appear to be maturational. More tentatively, I have argued that the sequences of change in personality and in systems of meaning may also be developmental in the sense I have used that term throughout the text. These are not strongly age-linked changes, but there is at least some evidence that they are sequential and not merely a function of particular or culture-specific changes in roles or life experiences. The remaining three rows, covering roles, tasks, and relationships, seem to describe sequences that are common insofar as they are shared by many adults in a given cohort and a given culture. If the timing or the sequence of these roles or tasks changes in any particular culture, however, the pattern described in the table will change as well.

A second way to look at the table is to read down the columns rather than across the rows. This gives some sense of the various patterns that may occur simultaneously.

12.1.1: Emerging Adulthood (Ages 18 to 24)

Although we have always had adults in this age group, of course, they have become a distinct group, sufficiently different from the 25- to 39-year-old group to merit their own category—*emerging adults.* Developmental psychologists attribute this phenomenon to the increased time it takes adolescents to become full-fledged adults. No longer do young people graduate from high school and move directly into adult roles in the workforce, the military, or as stay-at-home mothers as they did several generations ago. Slowly this transition has increased until what we consider "full adulthood" doesn't occur until the mid-twenties for most. Developmental psychologist Jeffrey Arnett (1994, 2000, 2007) began to write about this group in the 1990s, coining the term "emerging adults" a few years later. Researchers who worked with young people this age held their first conference in 2003, and since then, the stage of emerging adulthood has been included in journals, textbooks, classroom curricula, and the popular press.

What is involved in the stage of emerging adulthood? According to Arnett, the major tasks of this period are:

- **IDENTITY EXPLORATION.** This entails looking at the possibilities for their lives in a variety of areas, especially love and work. Determining what kind of adult life they will have, what they will believe in, and what they will value. In what way will they be like their parents, and in what way will they be different? This is similar to the psychosocial stages of *identity versus role confusion* and *intimacy versus isolation* theorized by Erik Erikson (1950, 1959), and also the identity development theory of James Marcia (1966, 1980).

- **POSITIVE INSTABILITY.** This type of instability involves young people finding their way by trial and error—starting in one direction and then changing course if that is not a good way for them. This happens in choosing majors in college, deciding where to live, determining who will be their long-term partner, and other parts of their life plan.

- **FOCUSING ON THE SELF.** At no other time of life is a person more self-focused than during emerging adulthood. They are between the age that they are subject to their parents' rules and the age that they are constrained by marriage, family, and workplace rules. The result is wide-open options on everything from what to have for breakfast to whether to drop out of college or not. And the decision is largely up to the emerging adult himself or herself.

- **FEELING IN-BETWEEN.** If adulthood means being responsible for yourself, making your own decisions, and being financially independent, most emerging adults feel like they have one foot in childhood and one in adulthood. These aspects of adulthood come gradually, and it is not surprising that the in-between, ambiguous feeling is part of this time of life.

- **IMAGINING POSSIBILITIES.** In adolescence, a young person's environment is determined largely by parents, but during emerging adulthood, many possibilities become evident. Those who grew up in difficult circumstances can make changes so their lives will be better. This can be a time of seeking new friends and new role models. And for those who grew up in more positive environments, there are still possibilities to imagine and changes that can be made before the responsibilities of young adulthood take place (Arnett, 2004).

The years of emerging adulthood feature peak physical condition. All systems are at their best, and top athletes will never perform better. Neuronal development is finally complete. Death and disease rates are both low. All cognitive processes are at peak except crystallized intelligence, which depends on education and experience. Yet with all this good health and top thinking skills, there are the harbingers of later problems. A significant proportion of emerging adults are overweight and obese; they do not eat healthy or exercise at the recommended level for continued good health. They smoke, and they subject their hearing apparatus to loud noises at sports events and concerts. Those of us who are past this age are of two minds—first, we want to lecture about valuing good health and youth, and second, we remember our own emerging adulthood years with great pleasure and remember our own reactions to advice from our elders.

Emerging adults move into young adulthood at different rates of development. They also enter some areas (such as starting a career) and not others (such as finding a partner or starting a family). But the social clock is ticking.

12.1.2: Young Adulthood (Ages 25 to 39)

Anyone who has been this age has probably been told by older people to enjoy it, that it is "the prime of life." This can be a frightening thought for the typical young adult, who is struggling to balance school, work, and family obligations. The truth is that although young adulthood may be a time of top performances in physical and cognitive abilities, it also is the period of adult life with the most changes. Consider that during these years, most young adults:

- Move into more major roles than at any other time in their lives: a work role, marriage, and parenthood.
- Have jobs that are the most physically demanding, least interesting, least challenging, and lowest paying than at any other time in their careers.
- Form romantic partnerships and select long-term partners for marriage or cohabitation relationships.
- Become parents of one or more children, participating in marathon child care during the early years.

Fortunately, young adults have a number of striking assets to help them deal with these high levels of demand. Most obviously, like emerging adulthood, these are years in which body and mind are at top performance. Neurological speed is at maximum, so physical and mental reaction time is swift; new information is learned easily and recalled easily; the immune system is highly efficient, so one recovers quickly from disease or injury; and the cardiovascular system is similarly at its best, so sports can be played with speed and endurance.

Young adults deal with the changes by creating a network of friendships and other close relationships—part of what Erik Erikson talks about as the stage of intimacy versus isolation. Friendships are not only numerous but also particularly important in these years; those who have small friendship networks report more loneliness and depressive symptoms than socially isolated people at other stages of adulthood.

Young adulthood brings the greatest number of role transitions and highest levels of demands than any other stage, but this is also a time for peak physical and mental abilities and large social networks.

Perhaps because the role demands are so powerful, the young adult's sense of himself or herself, the meaning system with which he or she interprets all these experiences, seems to be dominated by rules, by conformity, by a sense that authority is external to the self. We think of these years as a time when the young person is becoming independent, but in becoming independent of their parents, most young adults are not becoming individualized in the sense that I have used the term elsewhere. Most are still locked into a conformist view, seeing things in black-and-white terms, looking to outside authority to tell them the rules. The years of young adulthood are a time of maximal *tribalization*. We define ourselves by our tribe and our place in the tribe.

EMERGING ADULTHOOD   The years of emerging adulthood are typically spent on periods of dependence and searching (for the right career, the right major in school, the right girlfriend or boyfriend), but young adulthood is spent in overdrive. Once the course of the journey of adulthood is set, young adults usually waste no time settling into their myriad roles and working at being successful spouses, workers, and parents.

WRITING PROMPT

How would you design an experiment to test the hypothesis that workers with greater individual skills would have more individualistic worldviews?

▶ | The response entered here will appear in the performance dashboard and can be viewed by your instructor.

Submit

At the same time, the conventional worldview they entered adulthood with slowly begins to give way to a more individualistic outlook. This change comes over time and seems to happen for several reasons. Among other things, we discover that following the rules doesn't always lead to reward, a realization that causes us to question the system itself. Neither marriage nor having children, for example, leads to unmitigated bliss, as evidenced by the well-replicated drop in marital satisfaction after the birth of the first child and during the period when the children are young. For those who married in their early or middle 20s, this drop in satisfaction occurs in their late 20s and 30s, contributing to a kind of disillusionment with the entire role system. A second reason for the change in perspective, I think, is that this is the time in which we develop highly individualized skills. In conforming to the external role demand that we find work and pursuing it, we also discover our own talents and capacities, a discovery that helps to turn our focus inward. We become more aware of our own individuality, more aware of the parts of ourselves that existing roles do not allow us to express.

Critical Thinking

How do you stand in relationship to your "tribe"?

But although the individualization process begins in our 30s, it is nonetheless true that this period of young adulthood, like the period from 18 to 25, is dominated by the social clock. In our 30s, we may begin to chafe at the strictures of the roles in which we find ourselves; we may be less and less likely to define ourselves solely or largely in terms of the roles we occupy, but the role demands are still extremely powerful in this period. This fact tends to make the lives of those in young adulthood more like one another than will be true at any later point. To be sure, some adults do not follow the normative pattern, and their lives are less predictable. But the vast majority of adults do enter into the broad river of family and work roles in their mid-20s and are moved along with the common flow as their children grow older and their work status progresses. One of the key changes as we move into middle adult life is that the power of these roles declines; the social clock begins to be less audible, less compelling.

12.1.3: Middle Adulthood (Ages 40 to 64)

Although the change is usually gradual rather than abrupt, the period of middle adulthood is really quite distinctly different from the years that come before. As Elizabeth Barrett Browning said in another context, "Let me count the ways."

BIOLOGICAL AND SOCIAL CLOCKS   Most obviously, the biological clock begins to be audible because it is during these years that the first signs of physical aging become apparent—the changes in the eyes that mean most adults require glasses for reading; loss of elasticity in the skin that makes wrinkles more noticeable; the diminished reproductive capacity, most noticeable for women but present for men as well; the heightened risk for major diseases, such as heart disease or cancer; the slight but measurable slowing in reaction time or physical stamina; perhaps some slowing in the speed of bringing names or other specific information out of long-term memory.

The early stages of this physical aging process normally don't involve much functional loss. Mental skills may be a trifle slower but not enough slower that you can't do your job well or learn something new, such as using an iPhone. In fact, the expertise gained from experience compensates for the physical and cognitive slowing. Achieving and maintaining fitness may take more work, but it's still quite possible. If you've been out of shape, you can even improve significantly by running faster or doing more pushups than you could when you were 30. But as you move through these middle years toward older adulthood, the signs of aging become more and more apparent and less and less easy to overcome.

At the same time, the social clock becomes much less significant. If you had your children in your 20s, then by your late 40s or early 50s they are likely to be on their way to independence. And in your work life you are likely to have reached the highest level that you will achieve. You know the role well, and the drive to achieve may peak and then decline. You may find satisfaction in the achievement of young colleagues you have mentored rather than in your own accomplishments.

If young adulthood is a time of *tribalization,* the middle years bring *detribalization,* perhaps part of a deeper shift in personality or meaning systems toward a more individualistic view. The greater openness to self that emerges at this time includes an openness to unexpressed parts of the self, parts that are likely to be outside the prescribed roles. The change is thus both external and internal.

If you think about the relationship of these two clocks over the years of adulthood, you might visualize them as something like the pattern in Figure 12.1. The specific point of crossover of these two chronologies is obviously going to differ from one adult to another, but it is most likely to occur sometime in this middle-adulthood period.

WRITING PROMPT

Find your position on the graph shown in Figure 12.1. Can you give examples of how the biological and social clocks are influencing you at your age? Write a brief response that will be read by your instructor.

▶
> The response entered here will appear in the performance dashboard and can be viewed by your instructor.

Submit

Figure 12.1 One way to think about the different phases or stages of adulthood is in terms of the relative potency or importance of the biological and social clocks. Except for the issue of childbearing for women, the biological clock is relatively unimportant until some time in midlife, after which it becomes increasingly important. The social clock follows an opposite pattern.

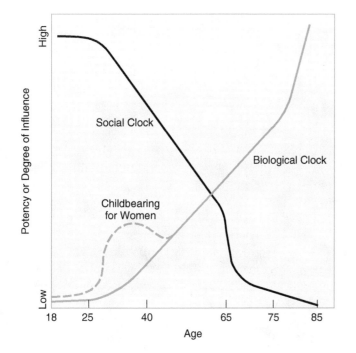

WORK AND MARRIAGE   One of the ironies is that the decline in the centrality of work and relationship roles in midlife is often accompanied by greater satisfaction with both work and relationships. Both marital and work satisfaction rise in the years of middle adulthood. As always, there are undoubtedly many reasons for the rise, including the fact that the actual work one is doing in these years is likely to be less physically demanding, more interesting, and more rewarded than was true in young adulthood, and that once the children are older and require less hands-on parenting, one of the major strains on a marriage declines. But the improvement in satisfaction with both work and relationships may also be a reflection of the inner shift of perspective I have been talking about. Adults who experience the world from a more individualist or conscientious perspective take responsibility for their own actions, so they may find ways to make their work and relationships more pleasant. Or they may choose to change jobs or partners.

It is precisely this sense of choice that seems to me to be a key aspect of this age period. There are certainly still roles to be filled; one does not stop being a parent just because the children have been launched; one still has work roles to fill, relationships with one's own parents, with friends, with the community. But adults in middle life have more choices about how they will fill these roles, both because the roles of this age have more leeway and because we now perceive roles differently, as being less compellingly prescriptive.

Is this picture too rosy? For those who have not been there yet, midlife sounds like the best of all worlds. And as someone who is there already, I tend to agree. In midlife we have more choices; our work and marital satisfaction is likely to rise, and there is a likelihood of some inner growth or transformation as well. To be sure, there is also the growing awareness of physical aging, but for most of us such an awareness is not dominant. We still feel fit and capable. It sounds as if these years, when both the biological and the social clocks are ticking away quietly in the background, are the best of all worlds.

But isn't this also the time when the infamous midlife crisis is supposed to hit? In this more negative view of midlife, "midlife men [are seen] as anxious, conflicted, and going through a crisis. The women are menopausal, fretful, and depressed" (Hunter & Sundel, 1989, p. 13). Can these two views be reconciled? I have discussed bits and pieces of this in earlier chapters; now I need to face it more squarely.

Middle age brings greater career satisfaction than young adulthood, sometimes through major job changes.

MIDLIFE CRISIS: FACT OR MYTH?   An interesting part of our popular culture involves the **midlife crisis**, portrayed as a time when the responsible middle-aged person (usually a man who has a lot of responsibilities) makes a 180-degree turn on the road of life and suddenly becomes irresponsible. Movies, novels, and TV shows have entertained us with stories of staid bankers who suddenly trade in their gray sedans for red sports cars and start coloring their hair. Often these crises involve leaving one's long-term spouse and becoming involved with a younger person who has a more care-free lifestyle—perhaps acquiring a trophy wife. We may even know of middle-aged people who have had a "breakdown" of some kind and made drastic lifestyle changes as a result. But is this something that happens to a great number of people in middle age? Is it something that is more apt to happen in middle age than at other times of life? Is the midlife crisis predictable?

Scholars became interested in these questions several decades ago, and perhaps the best-known writing on the subject was presented in journalist Gail Sheehy's 1976 book, *Passages.* Using survey data from a sample of people, Sheehy reported that many middle-aged adults experience a midlife crisis, which can result in either damaging or positive changes in their lives. Her book opened the topic up to the public as well as researchers. It was followed by a number of books and articles by clinicians giving accounts of their middle-class, middle-aged patients who experienced problems and unrest at this time of life. But more recently, research has shown that the general population of middle-aged individuals is not more likely to suffer breakdowns and crises than adults of other ages. In fact, middle-aged people, as a group, report an increase in positive moods and a decrease in negative emotions (Mroczek & Kolarz, 1998).

For example, a survey of over 700 adults between 28 and 78 years of age showed that 26% of the respondents (both male and female in equal numbers) claimed they had experienced a midlife crisis (Wethington, 2000). When questioned more closely, the events they described were not crises, nor had they occurred at midlife. Instead, the term *midlife crisis* seems to have come to mean coping successfully with some threatening situation in one's adult life and making personal changes as a result. People reported that these events had taken place at almost any age during adulthood, though they considered them "midlife crises."

Other research evidence also casts doubt on the notion of midlife crisis. For example, researchers developed a midlife-crisis scale that included items about a sense of inner turmoil, a sense of failing power, marital dissatisfaction, and job dissatisfaction. When this scale was used in a cross-sectional study of over 500 men aged 35 to 70, they could find no age at which scores were particularly high. Some men at each age reported feelings of crisis (McCrae & Costa, 1984).

Of course, this is all cross-sectional evidence. Studies such as these may tell us that there is no specific age at which some kind of upheaval is common, but they don't tell us whether each person, as he or she passes through the decades of midlife, is likely to have an upheaval at some time. Because the span of years we are calling *midlife* is fairly broad, it might still be that some kind of crisis is common between 40 and 64, but that it happens at different times for different adults, depending on the timing of various life changes, such as the topping out of one's career or the children leaving home.

Longitudinal evidence is obviously the best antidote to this problem. Yet here, too, there is little support for the expectation of widespread midlife crises. For instance, in an analysis of the subjects in the Berkeley and Oakland longitudinal studies, researchers found no indication of a widespread upheaval in midlife. Those who experience a genuine upheaval at this period of life, and perhaps 5% of the population do, are likely to be people who have experienced upheavals at other times as well (Haan, 1981).

In George Vaillant's life-long study of Harvard men, he noted that difficulties such as divorce, depression, and job loss happen at all ages throughout adulthood, but when they occur in midlife, we say, "Ah-ha! The midlife crisis, the dirty forties, menopausal depression!" (Vaillant, 1995, p. 80). In contrast, Vaillant found in his study that the Harvard men considered the period from 35 to 49 years to be the happiest time of their lives and 21 to 35 years as the unhappiest.

That is, the midlife crisis (along with its cousin, the empty-nest syndrome) is, to some extent, an aspect of individual personality rather than a characteristic of this particular age period. And, as sociologist Glen Elder, Jr. (1979) would remind us, it can also be a product of the cultural and historical events we experienced at earlier stages of our lives.

12.1.4: Older Adulthood (Ages 65 to 74)

In many ways people in this group are more like middle-aged adults than like those in late adulthood. So why make a division at age 65? From a physical point of view there is nothing notable about age 65 that would suggest that some new stage or phase has begun. Certainly, some adults in this age range experience significant disease or chronic disability. But the norm is rather that small—albeit noticeable—physical changes or declines continue to accumulate at roughly the same rate as was true in one's middle years. Hearing loss is now more likely to become a problem, as is arthritis; one is likely to have an increased sense of being a bit slower. But for most adults (in developed countries at least) the rate of physical or mental change does not appear to accelerate in these years. What makes this 10-year period unique is the rapid drop in role demands that accompanies retirement, a drop that once again changes the balance between what I have been calling the social clock and the biological clock, as I illustrated in Figure 12.1.

Explain why the family role of parent declines in older adulthood while the role of sibling becomes more central.

▶ The response entered here will appear in the performance dashboard and can be viewed by your instructor.

Submit

There is certainly little evidence that this change is marked by any kind of crisis. Research on retirement shows no increase in illness, depression, or other distress that can be linked causally to the retirement itself. For those who must retire because of ill health, the picture is rather different; for this subgroup retirement is linked with further declines in health and perhaps depression. But for the majority, every indication is that mental health is as good—or perhaps better—in this age group than at younger ages.

Older adulthood can be a time of independence and exploration as responsibilities diminish and the rules and norms become more flexible.

What does mark this change is the loss of the work role, which is of course accompanied by a continuing decline in the centrality of other roles. Spousal roles continue, of course, for those whose spouse is still living; there is still some parental role, although that too is less demanding and less clearly defined; the roles of friend and of brother or sister to one's aging siblings may actually become more central. But even more than was true in middle life, these roles are flexible and full of choices.

12.1.5: Late Adulthood (Age 75 and Older)

The fastest-growing segment of the U.S. population is the group in late adulthood. As life expectancy increases, more and more of us are living well past what we once considered "old age." And as health has improved, it is often not until these years that the processes of physical and mental aging begin to accelerate. It is at this point that the functional reserve of many physical systems is likely to fall below the level required for everyday activities (Pendergast, Fisher, & Calkins, 1993), creating a new level of dependence or disability.

I do not want to make too big a deal of the age of 75. The demarcation point between the period of older adulthood and late adulthood is more a function of health than of age. Some adults may be frail at 60; others may still be robust and active at 85. But if you look at the norms, as I have been doing in this chapter, it appears that age 75 is roughly where the shift begins to take place, at least in today's cohorts in the United States and other developed countries.

Our knowledge of late adulthood is growing. Only in recent years have there been large numbers of adults in this group; only quite recently has the Census Bureau begun to divide some of its statistics for the elderly into decades rather than merely lumping everyone over age 65 into a single category. But we do have some information that points to a qualitative change that takes place at roughly this time.

Go back and look again at , for example. You'll see that longitudinal studies show that the acceleration in the decline in total mental ability scores starts at about 70 or 75. There is decline before that, but the rate of decline increases in late adulthood. And as one moves into the 80s and beyond, the incidence of physical and mental frailty rises rapidly (Guralnik & Simonsick, 1993). Psychologist Edwin Shneidman (1989), writing about the decade of one's 70s, puts it this way: "Consider that when one is a septuagenarian, one's parents are gone, children are grown, mandatory work is done; health is not too bad, and responsibilities are relatively light, with time, at long last, for focus on the self. These can be sunset years, golden years, an Indian Summer, a period of relatively mild weather for both soma and psyche in the late autumn or early winter of life, a decade of greater independence and increased opportunities for further self-development" (p. 684). But what is it that adults in this period of early old age, of Indian Summer, choose to do with their lives? Do they remain active and involved, or do they begin to withdraw, to turn inward toward self-development or reminiscence? If there is controversy about this age period, it has centered on some variant of this question. The issue is usually framed in the terms of disengagement in old age.

Over 50 years ago, the term **disengagement** was proposed by gerontologists Elaine Cumming and William Henry (1961) to describe what they saw as a key psychological process in old age. This process was seen as having three features or aspects: (a) adults' social "life space" shrinks with age, a change especially noticeable in the period from 75 on when we interact with fewer and fewer others and fill fewer and fewer roles as we move through late adulthood; (b) in the roles and relationships that remain, the aging person becomes more individualized, less governed by rules and norms; and (c) the aging person anticipates this set of changes and actively embraces them, disengaging more and more from roles and relationships (Cumming, 1975).

Few would disagree with the first two of these points. In late adulthood, most people do show a decline in the number of social activities they engage in, they occupy fewer roles, and their roles have fewer clear prescriptions. Adults of this age participate in fewer clubs or organizations, go to religious services less often, and have a smaller network of friends.

But the third of Cumming and Henry's points about disengagement is in considerable dispute. They argued that disengagement is not only natural but also optimally healthy in late adulthood, so that those who show the most disengagement are going to be the happiest and healthiest. And this is simply not supported by the research. There is no indication that those who show the greatest decline in social activity (who "disengage" the most) are happier or healthier. On the contrary, the common finding is that the least disengaged adults (or the most engaged adults) report greater satisfaction with themselves and their lives, are healthiest, and have the highest morale (Adelmann, 1994; Bryant & Rakowski, 1992). The effect is not large, but the

Reduced mobility in late adulthood often results in more limited activities and smaller social networks.

direction of the effect is consistently positive: More social involvement is linked to better outcomes.

The picture is not totally one-sided. On the other side of the ledger is a significant body of work pointing to the conclusion that solitude is quite a comfortable state for many older adults. Note, for example, that among all age groups, loneliness is least common among the elderly. Indeed, some older adults clearly find considerable satisfaction in an independent, socially isolated (highly disengaged) life pattern. Clearly it is possible to choose and to find contentment in a largely disengaged lifestyle in these older years. But does this mean that disengagement is necessary for mental health? On the contrary, most of the evidence says exactly the opposite. For most older adults, social involvement is both a sign of, and probably a cause of, higher levels of satisfaction. Those who do not have satisfactory contact with others, particularly with friends, are typically less satisfied with their lives. These changes appear to be part of a more general adaptive process.

RESERVE CAPACITY AND ADAPTING TO LIMITATIONS   Psychologists Paul Baltes and Margaret Baltes (1990) suggested that one of the key features of late adulthood is that the person operates much closer to the edge of reserve capacity than is the case for younger or middle-aged adults. To cope with this fact, and with the fact of various physical declines, one must use a process that they call **selective optimization with compensation**. Older adults *select* the range of activities or arenas in which they will operate, concentrating energy and time on needs or demands that are truly central. They *optimize* their reserves by learning new strategies and keeping old skills well practiced. And when needed, they *compensate* for losses.

The very fact that such selection, optimization, and compensation are necessary in later adulthood is a crucial point. Reserve capacities are reduced, but it is also crucial to realize that many adults in this age group can and do compensate and adjust their lives to their changing circumstances.

WRITING PROMPT

Select a sport and then tell how an aging athlete would use selective optimization with compensation to continue their participation.

▶ The response entered here will appear in the performance dashboard and can be viewed by your instructor.

Submit

LIFE REVIEW   Finally, let me say just a word about another process that may be involved in the process of adaptation in late life. In Erikson's theory, the stage Erikson proposes for late adulthood is *ego integrity versus despair*. One of Erikson's notions was that to achieve wisdom, which is the potential strength to be gained at this stage, older adults must think back over their lives and try to come to terms with the person they once were and the one they are now.

Some years ago, professor of geriatric medicine Robert Butler (1993) expanded on Erikson's idea. Butler proposed that in old age, all of us go through a process he called a **life review**, in which there is a "progressive return to consciousness of past experience, and particularly, the resurgence of unresolved conflicts" (p. 53). Butler argued that in this final stage of life, as preparation for our now clearly impending deaths, we engage in an analytic and evaluative review of our earlier life. According to Butler, such a review is a necessary part of achieving ego integrity, and the wisdom that results from it, at the end of life.

This is an attractive hypothesis. Clinicians who work with the elderly have devised life-review interventions for use with older adults. Gerontologist James Birren recommends that older adults form autobiography groups and discuss various stages and turning points in their lives to determine how to best spend their remaining years (Birren & Feldman, 1997). And indeed, several studies show that a process of structured reminiscence may increase life satisfaction or self-esteem among older adults (Haight, 1992). However, at this point we do not know whether reminiscence is actually more common in the elderly than among the middle-aged or any other age group. We are left with many unanswered questions: Is some form of reminiscence really more common among the elderly than at other ages? How much do the elderly vary in the amount of reminiscence they engage in? How much of reminiscence is really integrative or evaluative, rather than merely storytelling for amusement or information? Is reminiscence a necessary ingredient in achieving some form of integration in late life?

On the whole, I think there is good reason to doubt the validity of Butler's hypothesis that life review is a necessary part of late adulthood. At the same time, it is clear that some kind of preparation for death is an inevitable, or even central, part of life in these last years. Although death certainly comes to adults of all ages, most younger adults can continue to push the idea of death away: that's something for later. But in the years past 75, the imminence of death is inescapable and must be faced by each of us. Life review may be one of the ways this is done.

12.2: Variations in Successful Development

12.2 List distinct parameters that classify individual life

The study of adult development is based on the means of large groups of people. It gives us information on the *typical* person's life changes and the *average* type of behavior. It is important information and very useful to professionals and to the layperson who wants to learn some general truths about the development of adults in general. But for the individual reflecting on his or her own life, it is less useful. Few of us fit the average; few of us are on the typical journey of adulthood.

I opened this book with a description of my own adult journey, and as you could see, I have not practiced what I preach as typical adult development. I married early and had three children before I was 25. I spent my young adulthood as a stay-at-home mom, tending to the children and volunteering at the neighborhood library. Once they were all in school, I enrolled at the local community college, and by the time the kids were in middle school, I was writing magazine articles on parenting and teaching part-time at the university where I had received my master's degree in developmental psychology. This is certainly not the typical career path (and not a typical career). As you know from this book, I was *off-time*—younger than the parents of my children's friends and older than my fellow students.

I became a divorced mother when my youngest was still at home, and then within one wonderful year I remarried and became a grandmother for the first time. What a combination of new roles! Fortunately my new husband, a professor of child development, saw instant grandfatherhood as a bonus. At 50, I enrolled in a Ph.D. program and 3 years later marched down the aisle to Elgar's *Pomp and Circumstance* at the University of Georgia to be hooded in red and black, with four generations of relatives applauding.

Since that time I have taught a variety of developmental psychology courses at a satellite campus of our local state university. Two years ago I acted on an impulse and accepted a challenge to teach a group of bright high school students in the summer, going through an entire college course in just 3 weeks. It was great fun, and I have continued doing that each year. I also branched out and started teaching a forensic psychology course last year after giving myself a crash course at the local state attorney's office, fire department, police department, and juvenile detention center. Many women my age have taken early retirement, but I feel off-time yet again and have just hired a grad student to help me brush up on my computer skills so I can embed YouTube segments in my classroom lectures for the fall. Since the last edition of this textbook, I have lost both my in-laws and my parents—all having lived long and happy lives. I keep involved with my three sisters, my adult children, and my grandchildren—all nine of them.

My own version of the journey of adulthood has been interesting, but it was not easy. I am tempted to add the warning: *Do not try this yourselves!* But few of us have master plans for our lives. Most of us make one small decision at a time, and sometimes we are a bit surprised when we look back and see what the big picture looks like.

WRITING PROMPT

Think of two people you know of similar ages whose journeys of adulthood have been vastly different so far. How do you think they will compare in the future?

> ▶ The response entered here will appear in the performance dashboard and can be viewed by your instructor.

Submit

No doubt your own journey of adulthood has aspects that do not fit the typical. Knowing all about the means and the norms of adult development still leaves some questions. To fully understand the process of adult development and change, we also have to understand the ways in which individuals' lives are likely to differ, the variations in their reactions to the stresses and challenges they will encounter, and the eventual satisfaction or inner growth they may achieve.

Reaching such understanding is as immense a task as the diversity is great. But let me offer two approaches, beginning with an exploration of the literature explaining individual differences in what has come to be called *quality of life* (Achenbaum, 1995) or its close cousins, *subjective well-being* (Pinquart & Soerensen, 2000) and *successful aging* (Baltes & Baltes, 1990; Rowe & Kahn, 1998), and concluding with my own attempt at a model of both normative and individual aging.

12.2.1: Individual Differences in Quality of Life

- **HEALTH AND SOCIOECONOMIC STATUS.** The strongest predictor of quality of life for adults under 65 is socioeconomic status (income and education). The strongest predictor for adults over 65 is health, with socioeconomic status coming in second. When these factors are considered, quality-of-life differences between other groups become weaker. In this sense, socioeconomic status and health are *proximal predictors;* they play intervening roles between quality of life and other more *distal predictors,* such as age, gender, race/ethnicity, and marital status (George, 2006). This will be explained in more detail next.

- **AGE.** Recent research has shown consistently that the older one is, the better one's quality of life. This has been found in both cross-sectional and longitudinal studies, although longitudinal studies show a peak at age 65 and a slight decline afterward (Mroczek & Spiro, 2005). However, this can be explained by the increase in chronic health problems after 65 and the decrease in income for some people in this age group.

- **GENDER.** Women under 65 report higher quality of life than men in this age group, but women 65 and over report lower quality of life than their male counterparts (Pinquart & Soerensen, 2001). This, again, can be partially explained by economic differences (women have lower incomes than men in older adulthood) and health (women in older adulthood have more chronic illnesses), and also the fact that women in older adulthood are more apt to experience the death of their spouse.

- **RACE AND ETHNICITY.** These factors do not relate to quality of life, and when some relationship is shown, it can usually be accounted for by socioeconomic status (Krause, 1993).

- **MARITAL STATUS.** Married people have better quality of life than unmarried people, and this has been found for adults in 45 different countries (Diener, Gohm, Suh, et al., 2000; Pinquart & Soerensen, 2001). This can be partially explained by socioeconomic differences (married people have higher incomes than single people). When these data are examined by age, though, this is stronger among young and middle-aged adults than those in older or late adulthood. In fact, researchers report that widows experience a 1- to 2-year decline in quality of life following the death of their husbands, with a return to their prewidowhood quality of life afterward (Lucas, Clark, Georgellis, et al., 2003).

- **ACTIVITIES.** In a nutshell, quality of life is related to any kind of activity—physical, social, or any combination of the two. And these results are found in cross-sectional (Warr, Butcher, & Robertson, 2004) and longitudinal studies (Menec, 2003). People who participate in more activities enjoy a higher quality of life than those who are more sedentary and isolated.

- **SOCIAL INTEGRATION.** Adults who have multiple roles report higher levels of well-being than those who have few roles, unless their roles bring additional stress, such as becoming a caregiver for a spouse or parent (Pinquart & Soerensen, 2003). And as reported in Chapter 9, attending religious services is a strong predictor of positive well-being and quality of life in adults (Kirby, Coleman, & Daley, 2004). Several longitudinal studies show that doing volunteer work contributes to the quality of life in adults, especially those 65 and older (George, 2006). And not surprisingly, a meta-analysis of almost 300 studies shows that social support is strongly related to quality of life, both in the number of significant others in one's support system and the quality of the relationships (Pinquart & Soerensen, 2000).

- **PSYCHOSOCIAL FACTORS.** Adults who have a strong *sense of control* over their lives (also expressed as mastery, self-efficacy, and cognitive hardiness) enjoy a better quality of life at every age than those who do not share this feeling (George, 2006). As discussed in Chapter 9, people who have a strong sense of meaning (also expressed as sense of coherence, a perception of life as predictable and manageable) report a better quality of life than others (Ardelt, 2003).

- **SOCIAL COMPARISONS.** It seems to be part of our human character to compare ourselves to others, especially on aspects of ourselves that aren't easily measured, such as quality of life. This may be one of the reasons that older adults consider themselves as enjoying a high level of well-being and good health, even though their health is not as good as it was in earlier adulthood and their activities and social circles are limited. The trick seems to be comparing oneself with others in the same age group. "Compared to others my age, I'm doing great!" This was demonstrated in several studies of older adults that showed they were more apt to compare themselves to others who are less advantaged than they are (Gana, Alaphilippe, & Bailey, 2004; Beaumont & Kenealy, 2004). Young and middle-aged adults were more likely to compare themselves to others who are more advantaged (thus deflating their quality-of-life assessments).

- **CULTURAL DIFFERENCES.** Surveys conducted in the United States over the past 50 years have shown that a stable 85% of people rate their lives as "satisfying" or "very satisfying" (Diener & Diener, 1996). This stability has been found for European countries as well, with more affluent countries (such as Germany and Denmark) showing larger percentages of satisfied or very satisfied people and less affluent countries (such as Portugal and Greece) with smaller percentages (Fahey & Smyth, 2004).

Psychologist Bruce Kirkcaldy and his colleagues (Kirkcaldy, Furnham, & Siefen, 2004) examined data from 30 developed and developing countries to determine what factors were responsible for the differences in well-being reported by people in those countries. They examined economic factors (e.g., economic growth and gross national product indices), health indicators (e.g., life expectancy and disability rates), and educational attainment (e.g., literacy). The strongest predictor of well-being was literacy. The countries that had the highest scores on tests of reading, science, and math literacy were the ones in which the people reported the highest levels of well-being and happiness. Conversely, the countries that scored the lowest on these three literacy measures were more apt to have the lowest levels of well-being and happiness. (The top-performing countries on the literacy measures were Japan, South Korea, Finland, Canada, and New Zealand; the lowest were Brazil, Mexico, Luxembourg, Latvia, and Greece.) Economic and health factors were not valid predictors of well-being for either developed or developing countries. The researchers concluded that the finding that people living in countries with prosperous economies report greater levels of well-being is due more to the better educational systems and higher literacy rates than the gross national product or healthcare systems of those countries.

And finally, in a study that examined cross-cultural quality of life for adults of various ages, researchers found that older adults report the same levels of well-being and happiness as younger adults, regardless of what political structures they live in and their country's economic resources (Diener & Suh, 1998).

In summary, quality of life in adulthood is determined largely by health, income, education, and the people we choose to compare ourselves with. Another contributing factor is having a sense of control, meaning, or purpose in one's life. It is probably more informative to list the factors that don't matter much: age, race and ethnicity, and living in a country with a healthy economy. And factors that matter somewhat (but are probably part of health, income, and education) are gender, marital status, activities, and religious participation. I look forward to a comprehensive study that will take all these factors into account and give us a model showing the proximal and distal effects of quality of life in adulthood.

12.2.2: Other Measure of Life Success

The quality of life that individuals report is one of the best measures of success in the adult years. But there are other ways of defining successful adulthood that rely on professional assessments of psychological health or on objective measures of life success. Two approaches, both involving analyses of rich longitudinal data, are particularly interesting.

Researchers working with the Berkeley longitudinal data have developed a measure of ideal adult adjustment that they call *psychological health*. In this research, psychotherapists and theorists agreed that the pattern of qualities of an optimally healthy person includes the capacity for work and satisfying relationships, a sense of moral purpose, and a realistic perception of self and society. According to this view, adults who are psychologically healthy show a great deal of warmth, compassion, dependability and responsibility, insight, productivity, candor, and calmness. They value their independence and autonomy as well as their intellectual skill and behave in a sympathetic and considerate manner, consistent with their personal standards and ethics (Peskin & Livson, 1981).

In one study, the participants received scores evaluating their psychological health. When this measure was correlated with self-reports of satisfaction with work, family life, and marriage, participants who had been rated by the professionals as having higher levels of psychological health were found to have reported themselves as more satisfied with their lives.

Psychiatrist George Vaillant and social worker Caroline Vaillant (1990) approached the definition of successful aging somewhat differently in their studies of the Harvard men included in the Grant study. They searched for a set of reasonably objective criteria reflecting what they call *psychosocial adjustment* and then investigated what factors in the men's childhood or adult lives predict good or poor psychosocial adjustment.

Despite their quite different strategies for measuring successful aging, the findings from the Berkeley and Grant studies are reasonably consistent and lead to some intriguing suggestions about the ingredients of a healthy or successful adult life. Both studies show that the most successful and well-adjusted middle-aged adults had grown up in warm, supportive, intellectually stimulating families. In the Berkeley study, researchers found that those who were higher in psychological health at age 30 or 40 had grown up with parents who were rated as more open-minded and more intellectually competent, with good marital relationships. Their mothers had been warmer, more giving and nondefensive, more pleasant and poised (Peskin & Livson, 1981). Similarly, the men who were rated as having the best adjustment at midlife had come from warmer families and had had better relationships with both their fathers and mothers in childhood than had the least well-adjusted men (Vaillant, 1974).

Both studies also show that well-adjusted or successful middle-aged adults began adulthood with more personal resources, including better-rated psychological and physical health at college age, a practical, well-organized approach in college (Vaillant, 1974), and greater intellectual competence (Livson & Peskin, 1981). Both of these sets of findings are pretty much what we might expect. To put it most directly, those who age well are those who start out well. To be sure, none of the correlations is terribly large, so even among the midlife subjects there were some who began with two strikes against them but nonetheless looked healthy and successful at 45 or 50, and some who started out with many advantages but did not turn out well. But in general, the findings point to a kind of consistency up until midlife.

Yet when the researchers looked at their subjects again at retirement age, a very different picture appeared. Among these 173 men, no measure of early family environment remained a significant predictor of psychosocial adjustment at 63, nor did any measure of early-adult intellectual competence. Those who turned out to be "successful" 63-year-olds had been rated as slightly more personally integrated when they were in college, and they had had slightly better relationships with their siblings. But other than that, there were simply no childhood or early-adulthood characteristics that differentiated those who had turned out well and those who had turned out less well (Vaillant & Vaillant, 1990).

What does predict health and adjustment at age 63 among these men is health and adjustment at midlife. The least successful 63-year-olds were those who had used mood-altering drugs at midlife (primarily prescribed drugs intended to deal with depression or anxiety), abused alcohol or smoked heavily, and used mostly immature defense mechanisms in their 30s and 40s.

These findings come from only a single study, one that only included men, and only very well-educated professional men at that. So we shouldn't make too many huge theoretical leaps from this empirical platform. Still, the pattern of results suggests one (or both) of two possibilities:

⊗ Possibility 1

It may be that each era in adult life simply calls for different skills and qualities, so that what predicts success or healthy adjustment at one age is simply not the same as what predicts it at another age. As one example, college-aged intellectual competence may be a better predictor of psychosocial health at midlife simply because at midlife adults are still in the midst of their most productive working years, when intellectual skill is more central. By retirement age, this may not be so critical an ingredient.

⊗ Possibility 2

Alternatively, we might think of a successful adult life not as something foreordained by one's childhood or early-adult qualities, but as something created from the resources and opportunities available over the course of the decades. Those who start out with certain familial and personal advantages have a greater chance of encountering still further advantages, but it is what one does with the experiences—stressful as well as constructive—that determines the long-term success or psychosocial health one achieves. The choices we make in early adulthood help to shape the people we become in midlife; our midlife qualities in turn help to shape the kind of older people we become—a process I might describe as cumulative continuity. Early-childhood environment or personal qualities such as personality or intellectual competence are not unimportant, but by age 65 their influence is indirect rather than direct.

It seems likely that both of these options are at least partially true, but it is the second possibility that I find especially compelling. It helps to make sense of a series of other facts and findings.

One relevant fragment comes from yet another longitudinal study in which George Vaillant has been involved, in this case of a group of 343 Boston men, all white, and nearly all from lower-class or working-class families. As teenagers, these men had been part of a nondelinquent comparison group in a major study of delinquency originated by criminologists Sheldon Glueck and Eleanor Glueck (1950, 1968). They had been interviewed at length when they were in early adolescence and were then reinterviewed by the Gluecks when they were 25 and 31, and by Vaillant and his colleagues when they were in their late 40s. In one analysis by the Vaillant group (Snarey, Son, Kuehne, et al., 1987), the researchers looked at the outcomes for those men who had not had children at the normative time to see how they had handled their childlessness.

Of the group of childless men, those independently rated at age 47 as clearly generative in Erikson's terms were likely to have responded by finding someone else's child to parent, such as by adopting a child, joining an organization like Big Brothers/Big Sisters, or becoming an active uncle. Those childless men who were rated low in generativity at 47 were much less likely to have adopted a child; if they had chosen a substitute it was more likely a pet. Among the childless men, the generative and the nongenerative had not differed at the beginning of adult life in either social class or level of industry, so the eventual differences in psychosocial maturity do not seem to be the result of differences that existed at age 20. Rather, they seem to be a result of the way the men responded to or coped with an unexpected or nonnormative event in early adult life, namely childlessness.

The central point is that there are many pathways through adulthood. The pathway each of us follows is affected by the departure point, but it is the choices we make as we go along, and our ability to learn from the experiences that confront us, that shape the people we become 50 or 60 years later. If we are going to understand the journey of adulthood, we need a model that will allow us to make some order of the diversity of lifetimes that results from such choices and such learning or lack of it. So as a final step in the synthesis I have been attempting in this final chapter, let me try my hand at a more general model.

12.2.3: A Model of Adult Growth and Development: Trajectories and Pathways

Let me offer a set of four propositions. The first takes us back to many of the points I made earlier in this chapter as I summarized the information we have on normative or common pathways.

Proposition 1: There are shared, basic sequential physical and psychological developments occurring during adulthood, roughly (but not precisely) age linked.

Whatever other processes may influence adult life, it is clear that the entire journey occurs along a road that has certain common features. The body and the mind change in predictable ways with age. These changes, in turn, affect the way adults define themselves and the way they experience the world around them. I place the sequence of changes in self-definition or meaning system in the same category. The difference is that unlike physical and mental changes, the process of ego development or spiritual change is not an inevitable accompaniment of aging, but a possibility or potentiality.

Within the general confines of these basic processes and sequences of development, however, there are many individual pathways—many possible sequences of roles and relationships, many different levels of growth or life satisfaction or "success," which brings me to the second major proposition.

Proposition 2: Each adult's development occurs primarily within a specific pathway or trajectory, strongly influenced by the starting conditions of education, family background, ethnicity, intelligence, and personality.

I can best depict this individuality by borrowing biologist Conrad Waddington's image of the epigenetic landscape, a variation of which is shown in Figure 12.2 (Waddington, 1957). Waddington introduced this idea in a discussion of the strongly "canalized" development of embryos, but the same concept can serve for a discussion of adult development. The original Waddington image was of a mountain with a series of gullies running down it. He demonstrated how a marble placed at the top had an almost infinite number of possibilities for its final destination at the bottom of the mountain, due to the many possible intersections of gullies and ravines. However, because some of the gullies are deeper than others, some outcomes have a greater probability than others. In my version of this metaphor, the bottom of the mountain represents late adulthood, and the top of the mountain represents young adulthood. In our adult years, each of us must somehow make our way down the mountain. Because we are all going down the same mountain (following the same basic path of physical, mental, and spiritual development), all journeys will have some features in common. But this metaphor also allows for wide variations in the specific events and outcomes of the journey.

Figure 12.2 One way to illustrate the journey of adulthood is with the image of a mountain landscape. One begins the journey at the top and follows along in the ravines and gullies toward the bottom. There are many options and alternative paths, and the landscape changes as cultural and social changes occur.

SOURCE: Adapted from Waddington (1957).

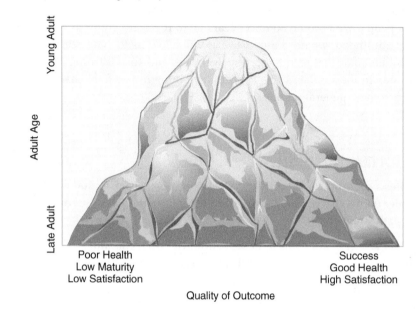

Imagine a marble placed in one of the gullies at the top of the mountain. The pathway it follows to the bottom of the mountain will be heavily influenced by the gully in which it starts. If I also assume that the main pathways are deeper than the side tracks, then shifting from the track in which one starts is less probable than continuing along the same track. Nonetheless, the presence of choice points or junctions makes it possible for marbles starting in the same gully to end up in widely varying places at the bottom of the mountain. From any given starting point, some pathways and some outcomes are much more likely than others. But many possible pathways diverge from any one gully. In addition, the landscape is constantly shifting in response to environmental changes, such as cultural or historical influences and changes in health.

This model or metaphor certainly fits with the general findings from Vaillant's long-term study of the Grant study men. The gully one starts in certainly does have an effect on where you are likely to be on the mountain at midlife. But the eventual end-point is much more strongly linked to where you were at midlife than where you started out. One might depict this idea using the mountain-and-gully model by showing the main gullies becoming deeper and deeper (harder to get out of) as you trace them down the mountain.

WRITING PROMPT

Give an example of a deep main pathway you have been on and a choice point you reached to change paths. How would you describe the effort involved in moving from a deep gully to an alternative pathway? Write a brief response that will be read by your instructor.

▶ The response entered here will appear in the performance dashboard and can be viewed by your instructor.

The model also fits with another finding I mentioned earlier in this chapter, that there is an increase in the variability of scores on various measures of health, mental skills, personality, and attitudes with increasing age. In early adulthood, the various alternative gullies are more like each other (closer together) than is true 40 or 60 years later.

Still another feature implicit in Figure 12.2 as I have drawn it is significant enough to state as a separate proposition.

Proposition 3: Each pathway is made up of a series of alternating episodes of stable life structure and disequilibrium.

In the mountain-and-gully metaphor, the stable life structures are reflected in the long, straight stretches between junction points; the junctions represent the disequilibria. I conceive of each stable life structure as the balance one achieves among the collection of role demands one is then facing, given the skills and temperamental qualities at one's command. This balance is normally reflected in a stable, externally observable life pattern: getting up at a particular time every day to get the kids off to school, going off to your job, doing the grocery shopping on Saturday, having dinner with your mother every Sunday, going out to dinner with your spouse every Valentine's Day. It is also reflected in the quality and specific features of relationships and in the meaning system through which we filter all these experiences. These patterns are not totally fixed, of course. We all make small adjustments regularly, as demands or opportunities change. But there do appear to be times in each adult's life when a temporary balance is achieved.

12.2.4: The Relationship of Stable Periods and Age

These alternating periods of stability and disequilibrium or transition appear to be related to age. I have suggested a rough age linkage in Figure 12.2 by showing more choice points at some levels of the mountain than at others. It seems to me that the content of the stable structures at each approximate age, and the issues dealt with during each transition, are somewhat predictable. After all, we are going down/along the same mountain. There is a set of tasks or issues that confront most adults in a particular sequence as they age, as I outlined in Table 12.1. In early adulthood this includes separating from one's family of origin, creating a stable central partnership, bearing and beginning to rear children, and establishing satisfying work.

In middle adulthood the tasks include launching one's children into independence, caring for aging parents, redefining parental and spousal roles, exploring one's own inner nature, and coming to terms with the body's aging and with the death of one's parents. An adult who follows the modal "social clock" will thus be likely to encounter transitions at certain ages and to deal with shared issues at each transition. But I am not persuaded that there is only one order, or only one set of ages, at which these tasks are or can be confronted. In this respect the mountain-and-gully model is misleading because it does not convey the variability in the timing of major choice points, such as what happens when an adult does not marry, does not have children until his or her 30s or 40s, or becomes physically disabled or widowed or ill in the early adult years, or the like. But whatever the variations in timing, it still appears to me to be valid to describe adult life as alternating between periods of stability and transition.

TURNING POINTS   The periods of disequilibrium, which we might think of as turning points in individual lives, may be triggered by any one or more of a whole series of events. There is no way to depict these in the mountain-and-gully model, so I have to turn to a more common kind of two-dimensional diagram, the (very complicated!) flowchart or path diagram shown in Figure 12.3.

Figure 12.3 I know this is complicated, but take a crack at it anyway. This is a model of disequilibrium and its resolution. I am suggesting that such a process occurs repeatedly during adulthood, with the effects of these transitions accumulating over time. Each such transition affects the pathway (the gully) along which the adult then moves.

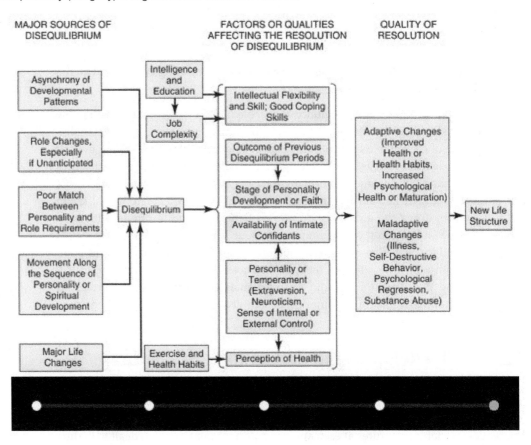

The major sources of disequilibrium, listed on the left-hand side of the figure, are the following:

- **ASYNCHRONY OF DEVELOPMENTAL PATTERNS** in the several different dimensions of adult change or growth. When physical development, mental development, or role patterns are out of sync, there is tension or disequilibrium in the system. Being significantly off-time in any one dimension of adulthood automatically creates asynchrony and is thus associated with higher rates of stress. Having a first child in your late 30s is not only a role change but also an asynchronous role change, which should increase the likelihood of a major disequilibrium, just as will the failure to have children at all, as among the childless men in the Glueck/Vaillant study of working-class men mentioned earlier. The general rule, as I have indicated, is that on-time role changes seldom trigger major crises or self-reexamination precisely because they are shared with one's peers. You can easily explain both the change and the strain it may cause as originating "outside" yourself. Nonnormative changes, by contrast, are difficult to explain away except with reference to your own choices or failures or successes. These more individual experiences, then, are far more likely than the normative ones to bring about reassessment or redefinition of the self, of values, of systems of meaning.

- **ROLE TRANSITIONS**, such as becoming a spouse or a parent, the departure of the last child from home, retirement, and changes in jobs.

- **POOR MATCH BETWEEN PERSONALITY AND ROLE REQUIREMENTS.** This is, in some sense, another kind of asynchrony. For example, research shows that adults who looked psychologically healthy at 50 but had shown signs of distress or disturbance at 40 were likely to have had qualities as teenagers that didn't match the then-prevalent gender roles. The less social and more intellectual young women in this group tried to fit into a mold of full-time homemaking and found it distressing; the more creative and emotional men tried to fit into the mold of the gray-flannel-suit society and were disturbed at 40. Both groups went through a process in their 40s of freeing themselves of the constraints of those early, ill-fitting roles and emerged at 50 looking very much put together (Livson, 1981).

- **PERSONALITY OR SPIRITUAL DEVELOPMENT** can trigger disequilibrium, such as any movement along the dimensions described by Erikson or by Fowler's stages of faith. Such inner changes typically occur in response to the disequilibrium-causing agents I have just described. But once begun, a transition, say from conformist to conscientious ego structure, or from individuative to conjunctive faith, carries its own disequilibrium. Any new stable life structure that emerges at the end of the disequilibrium period must be built on the new sense of self, or faith, that has evolved.

- **MAJOR LIFE CHANGES,** particularly losses in relationships, such as the death of a close family member or friend or the loss of a friendship or love relationship. Although unanticipated or off-time changes may be the most difficult in most instances, anticipated changes that involve such relationship losses, such as the death of your parents when you are in your 40s or 50s, still call for significant reassessment and reorganization.

Whether a person will experience a disequilibrium period as a crisis or merely as a rather transitory phase seems to depend on at least two things: the number of different sources of disequilibrium and the individual's own personality and coping skills. When there is a pileup of disequilibrium-producing events within a narrow span of years, such as changes in roles, major relationship losses, and asynchronous physical changes, anyone is likely to experience a major transition. But the tendency to respond to this pileup as a crisis may also reflect relatively high levels of neuroticism, low levels of extraversion, or the lack of effective coping skills.

In the model I am proposing here, it is our response to these disequilibrium periods that determines our pathway down the mountain, which leads me to the fourth basic proposition.

Proposition 4: The outcome of periods of disequilibrium may be either positive (psychological growth, maturity, improved health), neutral, or negative (regression or immaturity, ill health).

What kind of outcome occurs at any choice point—which channel one follows—is determined or affected by the wide range of variables listed in the third column of Figure 12.3. Intellectual flexibility or skill seems to be an especially critical ingredient in leading to the "higher" stages of maturity and growth that Vaillant and Loevinger describe. Our adult intellectual flexibility, in turn, is influenced by the complexity of the environments in which we live, particularly the complexity of job (either a job outside the home or even the complexity of housework). Sociologist Janet Giele (1982) put it well:

> It is the degree of social complexity on the job or in other aspects of everyday life that appears critical. Those who must learn a great deal and adapt to many different roles seem to be the most concerned with trying to evolve an abstract self, conscience, or life structure that can integrate all these discrete events. By contrast, those with a simple job, limited by meager education and narrow contacts, are less apt to experience aging as a process that enhances autonomy or elaborates one's mental powers. (p. 8)

And, of course, job complexity is itself partially determined by the level of education we have attained. Well-educated adults are more likely to find complex jobs and are thus more likely to maintain or increase their intellectual flexibility. Linkages such as these help create the pattern of predictability between early adulthood and midlife, but because none of these relationships is anywhere near a perfect correlation, there is a good deal of room for shifts from one gully to another. Some blue-collar jobs, for example, are quite complex, whereas some white-collar jobs are not, and such variations may tend to push people out of the groove in which they started.

Underlying temperamental tendencies are another key ingredient. Adults who are high in what Costa and McCrae call *Neuroticism* appear to be more likely to respond to disequilibrium by increases in substance abuse, illness, depression, or regressive patterns of defense. Adults with less neurotic or more extraverted temperaments, in contrast, respond to disequilibrium by reaching out to others, by searching for constructive solutions.

The availability of close supportive confidants is also a significant factor, clearly not independent of temperament. Adults who lack close friends or the supportive intimacy of a good marriage are more likely to have serious physical ailments in midlife or to have significant emotional disturbances, to drink or use drugs, and to use more immature forms of defense. Friendless or lonely adults more often come from unloving and unsupportive families, but a poor early environment can be overcome more readily if the adult manages to form at least one close, intimate relationship. Vaillant (1977) described several men in the Grant study who had grown up in unloving or highly stressful families and were withdrawn or even fairly neurotic as college students, but nonetheless went on to become successful and emotionally mature adults. One of the common ingredients in the lives of these men, especially compared to those with similar backgrounds who had poorer outcomes, was the presence of a "healing" relationship with a spouse. Similarly, sociologist David Quinton and his colleagues looked at the adult lives of several groups of young people in England, some of whom had had teenage histories of delinquency (Quinton, Pickles, Maughan, et al., 1993). They found that a continuation of problem behavior (such as criminality) was far less likely when the person had a nondeviant, supportive partner than when the problem teen later joined up with a nonsupportive or problem partner. Thus early maladaptive behavior can be redirected, or "healed," through an appropriately supportive partner relationship. Health may also make some difference in the way an adult responds to a period of disequilibrium. Poor health reduces options; it also reduces your level of energy, which affects the range of coping strategies open to you or the eventual life structures you can create.

Cumulative Effects of Transitions.   As a final point, I would argue that the effects of these several disequilibrium periods are cumulative, a process that sociologist Gunhild Hagestad and psychologist Bernice Neugarten (1985) described as the "transition domino effect." The cumulative effect of earlier stages or transitions is a key element in Erikson's theory of development. Unresolved conflicts and dilemmas remain as unfinished business—excess emotional baggage that makes each succeeding stage more difficult to resolve successfully. Vaillant and others who have studied adults from childhood through midlife have found some support for this notion. Harvard men in the Grant study who could reasonably be described as having failed to develop trust in their early childhood did have many more difficulties in the first few decades of adulthood. They were more pessimistic, self-doubting, passive, and dependent as adults and showed many more maladaptive or unsuccessful outcomes compared to those with more trusting childhoods.

Other forms of cumulative effect operate as well. One major off-time experience early in life, for example, may trigger a whole series of subsequent off-time or stressful experiences. The most obvious example is the impact of adolescent parenthood, which often leads to early school departure, which in turn affects the complexity of the job one is likely to find, which affects intellectual flexibility, and so on through the years.

Adaptive or Maladaptive Outcomes versus Happiness. It is important to emphasize that the range of possible outcomes I have labeled adaptive and maladaptive changes are not identical to happiness and unhappiness. Maladaptive changes such as illness, substance abuse, suicide attempts, or depression obviously are correlated with unhappiness. But such adaptive changes as improved health habits, increased social activity, or movement along the sequence of stages of ego or spiritual development are not uniformly associated with increases in happiness. For example, McCrae and Costa (1983) did not find that adults at the conscientious or higher levels of ego development reported any higher life satisfaction than did adults at the conformist stage. Thus profound changes can result from a disequilibrium period without being reflected in alterations of overall happiness or life satisfaction. Instead, a change in ego development stage may alter the criteria of happiness one applies to one's life. As McCrae and Costa say:

> We suggest that the quality and quantity of happiness do not vary with levels of maturity, but that the circumstances that occasion happiness or unhappiness, the criteria of satisfaction or dissatisfaction with life, may vary with ego level. The needs and concerns, aspirations and irritations of more mature individuals will doubtless be different—more subtle, more individualistic, less egocentric. The less psychologically mature person may evaluate his or her life in terms of money, status, and sex; the more mature, in terms of achievement, altruism, and love. (1983, p. 247)

Maturing does not automatically make an adult happy, as demonstrated by (among other things) the lack of correlation between age and happiness. Maturing and other adaptive changes alter the agenda and thus alter the life structures we create and the way we evaluate those life structures.

I am sure it is clear to you already that the model I have sketched in this chapter, complex as it is, is nonetheless too simplistic. It is doubtless also too culture specific, although I have tried to state the elements of the model broadly enough to encompass patterns in other cultures. It may also be quite wrong in a number of respects. Among other things, I have assumed throughout this discussion that something like Loevinger's sequence of ego development stages actually exists, and that all adults mature in this pattern if they mature at all. But that assumption is based on slim evidence.

Despite these obvious limitations, however, the model may give you some sense of the rules or laws that seem to govern the richness and variety of adult life. In the midst of a bewildering array of adult patterns there does appear to be order, but the order is not so much in fixed, age-related sequences of events as in process. To understand adult development, it is useful to uncover the ways in which all the pathways, all the gullies, are alike. But it is equally important to understand the factors and processes that affect the choices adults will have and the way they will respond to those choices as individuals. Perhaps the most remarkable thing about this journey is that, with all its potential pitfalls and dilemmas, most adults pass through it with reasonable happiness and satisfaction, acquiring a modicum of wisdom on the way to pass along to those who travel behind them.

May your journey be successful!

Summary: The Successful Journey

LISTEN TO THE AUDIO:

▶ ●————————— 04:33 🔇 ●————

1. To understand adult development, it is important to divide it into topics, as is done in the earlier chapters of this book. But it is also important to put it back together again and view people as wholes.

2. Emerging adulthood is the time of peak physical and cognitive abilities. This is a newly identified stage of adulthood defined by identity exploration, positive instability, focusing on the self, feeling in-between, and imagining possibilities.

3. Young adulthood is the time of continued high levels of physical and cognitive abilities. Some decline begins as early as 30, but it is not noticeable except for top-performing athletes. This period is the time of peak role transitions, relationship formation, and tribalization (a sense of belonging to a group).

4. Middle adulthood is the time in which the biological clock begins to tick noticeably. The first signs of physical aging appear, and the first signs of cognitive decline, though it is slight. Reproductive ability declines for both men and women, and then ends for women. The social clock becomes less loud. There is more flexibility in family roles and careers. There is time to question the rules and actions of the tribe and to become more of an individual.

5. Although middle adulthood is known as a time of crisis, this myth does not stand up to empirical research.

6. The hallmark of older adulthood is retirement. There is little biological difference between this group and those in middle adulthood, but the social differences can be significant if retirement is considered. The end of one's regular work life can have major financial and social effects, although there is no evidence that retirement has an effect on physical or mental health. Most older adults spend this stage adapting to a new lifestyle and finding new roles to fill now that the role of worker is finished.

7. Late adulthood is the fastest-growing age group in the United States and in all developed countries. As a result, we know more about this age than ever before. The slow decline in physical and cognitive abilities that began back in early adulthood speeds up in late adulthood. This is accompanied by a decrease in social activities and social networks. However, most people this age enjoy fewer but closer relationships. The hypothesis that those who disengage from the world are mentally healthier has not held up to close examination.

8. Late adulthood is a time for reviewing one's life and perhaps coming to grips with one's eventual death. Some adults in this time of life write memoirs or mend fences with former friends and family members.

9. Although this book emphasizes the typical pathways through adulthood, there are many variations that can lead to success and well-being.

10. Quality of life for adulthood in the United States depends highly on socioeconomic status and health. These two factors explain many of the more distal predictors, such as race and gender. Another factor is age, with older adults reporting greater quality of life than middle-aged or young adults. Those who are happily married, participate in physical and social activities, feel they have control over their lives, and base their comparisons on others their age also report higher quality of life.

11. Despite the variability in adult development, most of us have similarities in our journeys of adulthood, and these journeys are strongly influenced by our education, family background, intelligence, and personality.

12. The developmental pathways we travel along are made up of alternating stable times and times of disequilibrium. The periods of disequilibrium can result in positive change, negative change, or neutral outcomes.

13. Most adults pass through adulthood with reasonable happiness and satisfaction, picking up some wisdom along the way and passing it along to those who come behind them.

SHARED WRITING: SUCCESS IN LIFE

Consider this chapter's discussion of "success in life." How do you measure success in life and why does this matter? How do your measurements of success compare to those of your parents' generation? Write a short response that your classmates will read. Be sure to give concrete reasons in your discussion.

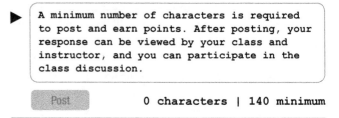

▶ A minimum number of characters is required to post and earn points. After posting, your response can be viewed by your class and instructor, and you can participate in the class discussion.

| Post | 0 characters | 140 minimum |

Chapter 12 Quiz: The Successful Journey

Glossary

a good death   death with dignity, with maximum consciousness and minimum pain.

ability/expertise trade-off   observation that as general ability declines with age, job expertise increases.

accommodate   ability of the lens of the eye to change shape to focus on near or far objects, or small print.

acute conditions   short-term health disorders.

adaptive nature of cognition   how cognitive abilities adapt to life changes across a lifetime.

ADLs (activities of daily living)   basic self-care activities.

adult development   changes that take place within individuals as they progress from emerging adulthood to the end of life.

ageism   discrimination against those who are in a later (or earlier) period of adulthood.

alternative medicine providers   healthcare providers whose treatments are not supported by scientific data.

Alzheimer's disease   progressive, incurable deterioration of key areas of the brain.

anthropomorphizing   giving human thoughts, feelings, and motivations to non-human animals and objects, such as pets.

antibodies   proteins that react to foreign organisms such as viruses and other infectious agents.

antioxidants   substances that protect against oxidative damage from free radicals.

anxiety disorders   category of mental health disorders that involves feelings of fear, threat, and dread when no obvious danger is present.

atherosclerosis   process by which fat-laden deposits called plaques form in the artery walls.

attachment   strong affectional bond an infant forms with his or her caregivers.

attachment behaviors   outward expressions of attachment.

attachment orientation   patterns of expectations, needs, and emotions one exhibits in interpersonal relationships that extend beyond the early attachment figures.

attachment theory   Bowlby's theory that infants form strong affectional bonds with their caregivers that provide basic security and understanding of the world and serve as a foundation for later relationships.

attrition   dropout rate of participants during a study.

atypical   not typical; unique to the individual.

B cells   cells of the immune system produced in the bone marrow that manufacture antibodies.

balance   ability to adapt one's body position to change.

behavior genetics   study of the contributions genes make to individual behavior.

bioecological model   model of development proposed by Bronfenbrenner that points out that we must consider the developing person within the context of multiple environments.

biological age   measure of an individual's physical condition.

biological clock   patterns of change over adulthood in health and physical functioning.

biosocial perspective   viewpoint that gender-role bias is based on both biological differences and current social and cultural influences.

body mass index (BMI)   number derived from a person's weight and height; a standard indicator of body composition.

bone mass density (BMD)   measurement of bone density used to diagnose osteoporosis.

bridge job   part-time job or less stressful full-time job usually taken after retirement.

buffering effect   pattern of results that cushion the outcomes of a distressing situation.

caloric restriction (CR)   diet in which calories are severely reduced, but containing essential nutrients; found to slow down aging in animal studies.

cancer   disease in which abnormal cells undergo rapidly accelerated, uncontrolled division and later move into adjacent normal tissues.

cardiovascular disease   disorder of the heart and blood vessels that occurs more frequently with age.

career   patterns and sequences of occupations or related roles held by people across their working lives and into retirement.

career recycling   in vocational psychology, the notion that people may go back and revisit earlier stages of career development.

caregiver burden   symptoms of decline in mental and physical health common among caregivers.

caregiving orientation   system that is activated in adults when they interact with infants and young children, causing them to respond to the appearance and behavior of younger members of the species (and often other species) by providing security, comfort, and protection.

cataracts   visual disorder characterized by gradual clouding of the lens of the eye.

change   slow and gradual movement in a predictable direction.

chronic conditions   long-term health disorders.

chronic traumatic encephalopathy (CTE)   type of dementia that has increased prevalence for individuals who have suffered traumatic brain injury (TBI).

chronological age   number of years that have passed since birth.

climacteric   time of life for men and women that involves the reduction of sex hormone production resulting in the loss of reproductive ability.

cochlea   small shell-shaped structure in the inner ear containing auditory receptor cells.

cohabitation   living together in an intimate partnership without marriage.

cohort   group of people who share a common historical experience at the same stage of life.

commonalities   aspects that are typical of adult life.

communal qualities   personal characteristics that nurture and bring people together, such as being expressive and affectionate; stereotypical female qualities.

community dwelling   living in one's own home either with a spouse or alone.

comorbid relationship of two or more health disorders that occur in an individual at the same time.

comparison of means statistical analysis that allows researchers to determine whether the difference in measurements taken on two groups are large enough to be considered statistically significant.

complementary medicine providers healthcare providers whose treatments are not supported by scientific data.

contextual perspective approach to cognition that considers the context within which thought processes take place.

continuous property of development that is slow and gradual, taking us in a predictable direction.

convoy ever-changing network of social relationships that surrounds each of us throughout our lives.

coping ways to reduce the effects of stress reactions.

coping behaviors thoughts, feelings, and actions that serve to reduce the effects of stressful events.

correlational analysis statistical analysis that tells us the extent to which two sets of scores on the same individuals vary together.

cross-sectional study in the study of development, research method in which data is gathered at one time from groups of participants who represent different age groups.

crossover of gender roles hypothesized change in gender roles at midlife causing women to become masculine and men to become feminine.

crystallized intelligence learned abilities based on education and experience, measured by vocabulary and by verbal comprehension.

cultures large social environment in which development takes place.

cyclic GMP substance released by the brain during sexual arousal.

dark adaptation ability of the pupil of the eye to adjust to changes in the amount of available light.

death anxiety fear of death.

decentering cognitive movement outward from the self.

declarative memory knowledge that is available to conscious awareness and can be assessed by recall or recognition tests.

defense mechanism in Vaillant's theory of mature adaptation, the set of normal, unconscious strategies used for dealing with anxiety.

dementia category of various types of brain damage and disease that involve significant impairment of memory, judgment, social functioning, and control of emotions.

depressive symptoms feelings of sadness or hopelessness that are not as severe or long-lasting as major depression; subclinical depression.

descriptive research type of data gathering that defines the current state of participants on some measure on interest.

developmental psychology field of study that deals with changes that take place in behavior, thoughts, and emotions of individuals as they go from conception to the end of life.

developmental-origins hypothesis explanation that events during the fetal period, infancy, and the early years of childhood are significant factors in subsequent adult health.

dexterity skill and grace in physical movement, especially in the use of the hands.

DHEA (dehydroepiandrosterone) hormone involved in the production of sex hormones for both males and females.

diabetes disease in which the body is not able to metabolize insulin.

differential continuity stability of individuals' rank order within a group over time.

digit-span task test in which the participant hears a list of digits and is asked to recall them in exact order.

disengagement early hypothesis which held that late adulthood is a time when people withdraw from activities and relationships in preparation for the end of life.

distal causes factors that were present in the distant past.

DNA methylation chemical process by which genes are modified in epigenetic inheritance.

domestic migration moving one's residence from one county to another or to a different state within the United States.

economic exchange theory explanation of gender roles stating that men and women form intimate partnerships based on an exchange of goods and services.

egalitarian roles roles based on equality between genders.

ego integrity in Erikson's theory of psychosocial development, the tendency older adults develop to review their life for meaning and integration.

emerging adulthood period of transition from adolescence to young adulthood (approximately 18 to 25 years of age).

emotion-focused coping stress-reducing technique that directly addresses the emotions causing stress.

empirical research scientific studies of observable events that are measured and evaluated statistically.

epigenetic inheritance process in which the genes one receives at conception are modified by subsequent environmental events that occur during the prenatal period and throughout the life span.

episodic memory in information processing, the segment of the long-term store that contains information about sequences of events.

erectile dysfunction (ED) the inability for a man to have an erection adequate for satisfactory sexual performance.

estrogen female sex hormone.

evolutionary psychology field of psychology that explains human behavior in terms of genetic patterns that were useful in our primitive ancestors for survival and reproduction success.

exchange theory theory that we select mates by evaluating the assets we have to offer in a relationship and the assets the potential mates have to offer, and try to make the best deal.

executive function in cognition, the process involved in regulating attention and coordinating new and old information.

expansion of gender roles change in gender roles at midlife causing men and women to broaden their gender roles to include more attributes of the opposite gender.

experimental design empirical study that has a high level of experimental control.

extended families grandparents, aunts and uncles, cousins, and other relatives beyond the nuclear family of parents and children.

faith a set of assumptions or understandings about the nature of our connections with others and the world in which we live.

feminization of poverty term used to describe the trend that an increasingly larger proportion of people living in poverty are women.

filter theory theory that we select mates by using finer and finer filtering mechanisms.

finitude process of coming to grips with one's eventual death.

Five-Factor Model inventory of five basic personality factors first demonstrated by Costa and McCrae.

fluid intelligence basic adaptive abilities, measured by tests of digit span, response speed, and abstract reasoning.

Flynn effect   term for the increase shown in IQ scores over the last century, due mainly to changes of modern life.

free radicals   molecules or atoms that possess an unpaired electron; by-products of cell metabolism.

friendship   voluntary interpersonal relationship carried out within a social context.

functional age   measure of how well an individual is functioning in various aspects of adulthood.

g   general intellectual capacity, which influences the way we approach many different tasks.

gender crossover   relaxation of gender roles that is hypothesized to occur in men and women when the parenting years are over.

gender roles   actual behaviors and attitudes of men and women in a given culture during a given historical era.

gender stereotypes   sets of shared beliefs or generalizations about how men and women in a society ought to behave.

general adaptation syndrome   in Selye's theory, three stages of symptoms that occur in response to stress: alarm reaction, resistance, and exhaustion.

generativity   in Erikson's theory of psychosocial development, the tendency middle-aged adults develop to help establish and guide the next generation.

genotype   individual's complement of genes.

gerotranscendence   idea that meaning systems increase in quality as we age.

GH   synthetic version of human growth hormone that is prescribed for a limited number of conditions but widely used as an anti-aging drug.

glaucoma   visual disorder characterized by a buildup of pressure inside the eye that can lead to blindness if not treated.

grandfamilies   families formed when grandparents take grandchildren into their home and care for them without the presence or assistance of their parents.

grandmother effect   suggestion that the presence of grandmothers (especially maternal grandmothers) has ensured children's survival through recorded history.

Hayflick limit   maximum number of times cells are programmed to divide for a species.

hookups   casual sex without commitment.

hormone replacement therapy (HRT)   therapy in which women take estrogen and progestin at menopause to replace hormones once produced by the ovaries; relieves menopause symptoms.

hospice approach   philosophy that underlies hospice care. Specifically that death is an inevitable part of life, that the dying person and the family should be involved in as much of the care as possible and have control over the setting, and that no life-prolonging measures should be taken.

hospice care   end-of-life care focused on pain relief, emotional support, and spiritual comfort for dying patients and their families.

hostility   negative cognitive set against others.

household labor   unpaid work done in the home for oneself and family that includes meal preparation and cleanup, grocery shopping, laundry, and housecleaning.

human social genomics   study of changes in gene expression that result from subjective perceptions of the environment.

IADLs (instrumental activities of daily living)   complex everyday tasks.

identity   in Erikson's theory of psychosocial development, the set of personal values and goals a young adult develops pertaining to gender, occupation, and religious beliefs.

impulse-control disorders   mental health disorders that affect a person's judgment or ability to control strong and often harmful impulses.

individual differences   aspects that are unique to the individual, not part of the whole group.

inner changes   internal alterations not apparent to the casual observer.

insomnia   inability to have normal sleep patterns.

instrumental qualities   personal characteristics that have an active impact, such as being competitive, adventurous, and physically strong; stereotypical male qualities.

intelligence   visible indicator of the efficiency of various cognitive processes that work together behind the scenes to process information.

interactionist view   idea that genetics influence how one interacts with the environment and the environment one chooses.

intergenerational effects   prenatal experiences that affect the female fetus in adulthood and also her subsequent offspring.

intergenerational solidarity theory   extent to which family members of different generations are close to each other.

internal working model   in Bowlby's attachment theory, the set of beliefs and assumptions a person has about the nature of all relationships based on specific experiences in childhood.

intimacy   in Erikson's theory of psychosocial development, the ability young adults develop that allows them to enter into intimate relationships without losing their own sense of self.

intra-individual variability   stability or instability of personality traits within an individual over time.

IQ (intelligence quotient)   score on an intelligence test that reflects general intellectual capacity.

job burnout   job-related condition that is a combination of exhaustion, depersonalization, and reduced effectiveness.

job expertise   high level of skill that results from years of experience at a certain job.

job insecurity   anticipation of job loss by currently employed workers.

job loss   having paid employment taken away from an individual.

labor force   those who are officially working at paid jobs.

learning-schema theory   explanation of gender roles stating that children are taught to view the world and themselves through gender-polarized lenses that make artificial or exaggerated distinctions between what is masculine and what is feminine.

lens   transparent structure in the eye that focuses light rays on receptors in the retina.

libido   sexual desire.

life-change events   in Holmes and Rahe's theory, events that alter the status quo of an individual's life; when accumulated can lead to stress reactions.

life-span developmental psychology approach   idea that development is lifelong, multidimensional, plastic, contextual, and has multiple causes.

life-span/life-space theory   in vocational psychology, Super's theory that careers develop in stages and cannot be studied in isolation from other aspects of a person's life.

living will   legal document that states a person's end-of-life decisions.

long-term store   in information processing, the third step of memory processing, in which information is stored—both facts (in the semantic memory) and events (in episodic memory).

longitudinal study research method in which data is gathered over a period of time from the same group of people as they age.

macular degeneration visual disorder of the retina, causing central vision loss.

major depression mood disorder that involves long-term, pervasive sense of sadness, helplessness, and hopelessness; clinical depression.

marital crisis effect explanation that married people have not been through the crises involved in divorce or widowhood and, as a result, have better mental and physical health.

marital resources effect explanation that married people have more financial and social resources, so have better mental and physical health.

marital selection effect statistical effect in which healthier people are more apt to marry and stay married, producing the appearance that marriage benefits health.

mate selection process of choosing a long-term partner for an intimate relationship.

mean-level change changes in a group's average scores over time.

meaning-focused coping stress-reducing technique that refers to anything you might think, feel, and do to give a positive meaning to a stressful situation.

medication adherence ability of patients to follow their physicians' instructions about taking their prescribed medication in the right dosages, at the right time, and for the right length of time.

memory ability to retain or store information and retrieve it when needed.

menopause cessation of women's menstrual periods, occurring 12 months after the final menstrual period; climacteric.

meta-analysis analysis of data from a large number of studies that deal with the same research question, yielding in more powerful results.

midlife crisis popular myth that portrays middle age as a time of unstable and unpredictable behavior.

mild cognitive impairment (MCI) condition in which patients show some cognitive symptoms, but not all those necessary for a diagnosis of Alzheimer's disease.

mood disorders category of mental health disorders that involves loss in the sense of control over emotions, resulting in feelings of distress.

moral reasoning analyzing what is right and wrong, judging the rightness or wrongness of an act.

morbidity rate illness rate.

mortality rate probability of dying in any one year.

myelin fatty substance that insulates and protects the neuronal axons and is a major component of the white matter of the brain.

mysticism self-transcendent experience.

name-retrieval failures inability to recall a name that is known but momentarily absent.

neurogenesis growth of new neurons.

neurons cells in the brain and nervous system.

nondeclarative (procedural) memory memory system responsible for learning and retaining new skills.

nonnormative life events aspects that influence one's life that are unique to the individual.

nontraditional student in college, a student who is older than 25.

normative age-graded influences common effects of age that are experienced by most adults.

normative history-graded influences effects connected to historical events and conditions that are experienced by everyone within a culture at that time.

nuclear families parents and their children.

obesity condition in which one's weight-to-height ratio increases to a point that has an adverse effect on health; usually measured in terms of body mass index (BMI).

obsessive-compulsive disorder anxiety disorder that involves guilt and anxiety over certain thoughts or impulses.

occupational gender segregation separation of jobs into stereotypical male and female categories.

olfactory membrane specialized part of the nasal membrane that contains olfactory receptor cells.

onset first occurrence.

optimism positive outlook on life.

organ transplant donor individual who agrees to the transplantation, at the time of death, of his or her usable organs and other tissue to approved recipients.

osteoarthritis condition caused by loss of cartilage that protects the bones at joints; can involve pain, swelling, and loss of motion.

osteoporosis severe loss of bone mass.

outer changes external alterations visible and apparent to those we encounter.

parental imperative genetically programmed tendency for new parents to become more traditional in their gender roles.

parental investment theory in evolutionary psychology, the explanation that men and women evolved different behaviors and interests because the women have more invested in each child than the men.

peak experiences in Maslow's theory of positive well-being, the feeling of perfection and momentary separation from the self when one feels in unity with the universe.

person-environment transactions combinations of genetic endowment and environmental factors that maintain the stability of personality traits over time.

personal interview research method in which the experimenter meets with the participant and gathers data directly, often through open-ended and follow-up questions.

personality enduring set of characteristics that define our individuality and affect our interactions with the environment and other people.

personality factors groups of personality traits that occur together in most individuals.

personality states short-term patterns of thoughts, feelings, and behaviors.

personality traits stable patterns of thoughts, feelings, and behaviors.

phased retirement situation in which an older person continues to work for an employer part time as a transition to retirement.

phobias anxiety disorders that involve fears and avoidance out of proportion to the danger presented.

physician-assisted suicide situation in which physicians are legally allowed to assist patients, under certain circumstances, to obtain medication that will end their lives.

plaques fat-laden deposits formed in the coronary artery walls as a result of inflammation.

plasticity in neurons, the ability to form new connections or grow new extensions.

positive psychology emphasis of psychology research to turn away from negative outcomes, such as mental illness and crime, and toward positive outcomes, such as well-being, optimism, and spiritual growth.

positivity bias tendency for older adults to remember emotionally positive stimuli over emotionally negative stimuli.

postformal stages adult stage of cognitive development that involves thinking beyond the linear and logical ways.

posttraumatic stress disorder (PTSD) psychological response to a traumatic experience. Symptoms include re-experiencing the event in intrusive thoughts and dreams, numbing of general responses, avoiding stimuli associated with the event, and increased arousal of the physiological stress mechanisms.

posttraumatic stress symptoms term used to describe reactions to trauma that are severe, but do not fit the full diagnosis criteria of posttraumatic stress disorder.

presbyopia visual condition caused by loss of elasticity in the lens, resulting in the inability to focus sharply on nearby objects.

prevalence proportion of people experiencing a certain disorder at a given time.

primary aging physical changes that are gradual, shared, and largely inevitable as people grow older.

primary memory in information processing, the segment of the short-term store that holds information in place for immediate recall.

proactive coping stress-reducing techniques done in advance of a potentially stressful event.

problem-focused coping stress-reducing techniques that directly address the problem causing stress.

progesterone female sex hormone.

prospective memory ability to remember to do something later on or at a specific time in the future.

proximal causes factors present in the immediate environment.

pruning ability to shut down neurons that are not needed in order to "fine-tune" the system and improve functioning of the remaining neurons.

psychological age measure of an individual's ability to deal effectively with the environment.

psychometrics field of psychology that studies the measurement of human abilities.

pupil opening in the eye that changes in diameter in response to available light.

qualitative research research without numerical data, such as case studies, interviews, participant observations, direct observations, and exploring documents, artifacts, and archival records.

quantitative research research with numerical data.

quest for meaning search for ultimate knowledge of life through an individualized understanding of the sacred.

reactive heritability process whereby individuals use the qualities they have inherited as a basis to determine strategies for survival and reproduction.

reliability extent to which a test instrument gives the same results repeatedly under the same conditions.

religiosity outward expression of spiritual beliefs.

religious coping stress-reducing techniques that involve relying on religious or spiritual beliefs.

reminiscence review of one's personal memories.

replicative senescence state in which older cells stop dividing.

resilience ability to maintain healthy functioning following exposure to potential trauma.

resistance resources personal and social resources that may buffer a person from the impact of stress.

response-oriented viewpoint explanations of stress that focus on the physiological reactions within the individual.

retina structure at the back of the eye that contains receptor cells.

retirement career stage in which an older worker leaves the full-time workforce to pursue other interests, such as part-time work, volunteer work, or leisure interests.

retirement-related value in retirement decisions, the amount of personal wealth one has, plus Social Security and pension benefits, salary from part-time jobs, and health insurance benefits available if one retires; can be weighed against work-related value.

ritual mourning set of symbolic rites and ceremonies associated with death and bereavement.

role transitions changes in roles due to changes in the individual or in his or her life circumstances.

seasonal migration moving one's residence to another location temporarily, usually to spend the winter in a warmer climate, and then returning home in the spring.

secondary aging physical changes that are sudden, not shared, and often caused by disease, poor health habits, and environmental events as people grow older.

selective optimization with compensation process described by Baltes and Baltes in which older people cope with limitations by selecting their activities, optimizing their strategies, and compensating for their losses.

self-actualization in Maslow's theory, the drive to become everything that one is capable of being. It is reached when more basic needs are met.

self-determination theory explanation of personality based on individuals' evolved inner resources for growth and integration.

self-transcendence knowing the self as part of a larger whole that exists beyond the physical body and personal history.

semantic memory in information processing, the segment of the long-term store that contains factual information.

sense of purpose in life discovery of satisfying personal goals and the belief that one's life has been worthwhile.

sensorineural hearing loss inability to discriminate between loud and soft sounds caused by damage to receptors in the inner ear.

sensory store in information processing, the first step of memory processing, in which information is detected by the senses and processed briefly by the perceptual system.

sequential study series of several longitudinal studies begun at different points in time.

shift work jobs with nonstandard work schedules, including evening shifts, night shifts, and rotating shifts.

short-term store in information processing, the second step of memory processing, in which information is held "in mind" for immediate recall (primary memory) or for active processing (working memory).

sleep apnea pause in breathing during sleep due to constriction of the airway.

social age measure of the number and type of roles an individual has taken on at a specific point in his or her life.

social clock patterns of change over adulthood in social roles; time schedule of the normal sequence of adult life experiences.

social coping stress-reducing technique that involves seeking both instrumental and emotional support from others.

social relationships dynamic, recurrent patterns of interactions with other individuals.

social role theory explanation of gender roles based on children viewing the gender divisions around them and then modeling their behavior on those divisions.

social roles expected behaviors and attitudes that come with one's position in society.

social support   positive affect, affirmation, and aid received from others at stressful times.

social timing   pattern of when we occupy certain roles, how long we occupy them, and the order in which we move from one to another.

sociobiographical history   level of professional prestige, social position, and income that one experiences throughout one's life.

socioeconomic status (SES)   combined rating of income level and educational attainment.

socioemotional selectivity theory   according to Carstensen, the explanation that people emphasize more meaningful, emotionally satisfying social relationships as they become older because they are more aware of the end of life than younger people.

spirituality   an individual's personal quest for meaning; an inner process often distinguished from religiosity, which involves outward signs of a quest for meaning.

stability   having little or no change for significant periods of time.

stages   parts of the life span when there seems to be no progress for some time, followed by an abrupt change.

stamina   ability to sustain moderate or strenuous activity.

standardized tests   established instruments that measure a specific trait or behavior.

stem cells   immature undifferentiated cells that can multiply easily and mature into many different kinds of cells.

stereotype threat   anxiety that arises when members of a group are put in positions that might confirm widely held, negative stereotypes about themselves. This anxiety often results in confirmation of that stereotype.

stimulus-oriented viewpoint   explanations of stress that are focused on the stressors themselves, the stimuli or life events, that trigger the stress reactions.

stress   set of physical, cognitive, and emotional responses that humans (and other organisms) display in reaction to stressors, or demands from the environment.

stress-related growth   positive changes that follow the experience of stressful life events.

stressors   environmental demands that lead to stress reactions.

substance abuse disorders   mental health disorders that involve abuse or dependence on drugs or alcohol.

survey questionnaire   written form that participants can fill out on their own consisting of structured and focused questions.

T cells   cells of the immune system produced in the thymus gland that reject and consume harmful or foreign cells.

taste buds   receptor cells for taste found on the tongue, mouth, and throat.

telomeres   lengths of repeating DNA that chromosomes have at their tips.

testosterone   major male sex hormone.

transition to adulthood   period during which young people take on the social roles of early adulthood.

traumatic brain injury (TBI)   head injury severe enough to result in loss of consciousness; increases risk of dementia, especially chronic traumatic encephalopathy (CTE).

twin studies   studies that compare similarities of monozygotic twin pairs with dizygotic twin pairs on some behavior or trait of interest; results can give information on the extent of genetic contribution to that behavior or trait.

type A behavior pattern   state of being achievement-striving, competitive, and involved in one's job to excess.

typical   common to most people.

unemployment   state of being without a paid job when you are willing to work.

useful field of view (UFOV)   area of the visual field that can be processed in one glance.

validity   extent to which a test instrument measures what it claims to measure.

visual acuity   ability to perceive detail in a visual pattern.

vocational interests   in vocational psychology, personal attitudes, competencies, and values a person has relating to his or her career; basis of Holland's theory of career selection.

word-finding failures   failure to recall a word that is known but momentarily unavailable.

work engagement   approach to work that is active, positive, and characterized by vigor, dedication, and absorption.

work-related value   in retirement decisions, the amount of salary, pension, and Social Security benefits a worker will receive later if he or she continues working; can be weighed against retirement-related value.

working memory   in information processing, the segment of the short-term store that performs cognitive operations on information.

Suggested Readings

Chapter 1

Reading for Personal Interest

Segal, N. L. (2012). *Born together—reared apart: The landmark Minnesota Twin Study.* Cambridge, MA: Harvard University Press.

Psychologist Nancy Segal is a twin researcher in several senses of the word; she is a twin herself, and she has spent her career studying twins, beginning as a post doc with the Minnesota Twin Study, in which twins separated at birth were reunited and studied to investigate the influence of shared genes and unshared environments. Professor Segal has the ability to explain complex ideas in a very warm and interesting way. She reports the findings of the research, but also tells the human side of the twins who participated in this landmark study.

Snowdon, D. (2008). *Aging with grace: What the Nun Study teaches us about leading longer, healthier, more meaningful lives.* New York: Bantam Books.

Retired epidemiologist David Snowdon tells the story of his research project of 678 Roman Catholic nuns and how they are aging. His inquisitiveness and their enthusiasm shine through in this book and provide a good picture of successful aging. It is also a very good account of how a young researcher stumbled onto a gold mine of information in the convent archives and how he nurtured his relationship with these very private women to establish a career-long research project.

Classic Work

Elder, G. H., Jr. (1974). *Children of the Great Depression.* Chicago: University of Chicago Press.

This is the classic study by sociologist Glen Elder, Jr., of people who had been children of different ages during the Great Depression in the United States, showing how their developmental trajectories were changed by how they experienced these years.

Neugarten, B. L. (1979). Time, age and the life cycle. *American Journal of Psychiatry, 136,* 887–894.

Sociologist Bernice Neugarten was the first to write about the biological and social clocks and how they influence our lives.

Vaillant, G. E. (1977). *Adaptation to life.* Boston: Little Brown.

Psychiatrist George Vaillant writes about the Grant longitudinal study of Harvard men from college years through age 55.

Contemporary Scholarly Work

Schaie, K. W. (2011). Historical influences in aging and behavior. In K. W. Schaie & S. L. Willis (Eds.), *Handbook of the psychology of aging* (7th ed.), pp. 41–55. San Diego, CA: Academic Press.

Using Bronfenbrenner's concept of the chronosphere, Schaie explains some of the cohort differences found in cognitive processes and health, citing various historical changes that may have been responsible, such as the G.I. Bill, the changes in teaching methods, the war on poverty, and immigration.

Friedman, H. S., & Martin, L. R. (2012). *The longevity project: Surprising discoveries for health and long life from the landmark eight-decade study.* New York: Plume.

You have probably heard in your psychology classes about the Terman study that started in 1921 in San Francisco, a longitudinal study that began with gifted and talented children and followed them throughout their lives. But you probably don't realize that the data from that study is still being analyzed and is a treasure trove of developmental information. This book summarizes some of the findings that answer questions such as "What determines health and long life? What are the long-term effects of parental divorce? What was the effect of the war years on these kids?" It compiles the results from hundreds of research articles into a very interesting and readable book.

Salkind, N. (2012). *Tests and measurements for people who (think they) hate tests and measurements* (2nd ed.). Thousand Oaks, CA: Sage.

and

Salkind, N. (2012). *Statistics for people who (think they) hate statistics* (4th ed.). Thousand Oaks, CA: Sage.

If your background in research methods and statistics is not very strong, these two books offer a good way to get up to speed. Professor Salkind writes clearly in a nonintimidating, noncondescending way.

Chapter 2

Reading for Personal Interest

Cave, S. (2012). *Immortality: The quest to live forever and how it drives civilization.* New York: Crown.

Stephen Cave is a philosopher who believes that the driving force behind our civilization is the desire to live forever. He says that there are four ways we do this—fight disease, embrace religion, believe that there is an immortal spirit in everyone, and find a way to be remembered after our deaths through some legacy. This is a novel way of thinking, but he backs up his beliefs by giving examples of how this has been practiced in different cultures, including stories about Nefertiti, St. Paul, Alexander the Great, and the Dalai Lama.

Cohen, P. (2012). *In our prime: The invention of middle age.* New York: Scribner.

New York Times reporter, Patricia Cohen, writes that middle age is a relatively new stage in life and that it has only recently been investigated scientifically. She reviews the research with wisdom and humor, showing that these years can be the best years of life.

Horstman, J. (2012). *The Scientific American healthy aging brain: The neuroscience of making the most of your mature mind.* San Francisco: Jossey-Bass.

If you are an older adult, or just curious about what's going on with your parents, this is a good book that tells about the normal development of the brain during adulthood, what can go wrong, and how to optimize the brain that you have. It dispels a lot of myths and gives some good news, too.

Classic Work

Harman, D. (1956). Aging: A theory based on free-radical and radiation chemistry. *Journal of Gerontology, 2,* 298–300.

The free-radical theory of aging was first introduced in this article.

Hayflick, L. (1965). The limited in vitro lifetime of human diploid cell strains. *Experimental Cell Research, 37,* 614–636.

This is biologist Leonard Hayflick's early publication indicating that human cells grown in the lab have a limit to the number of times they replicate.

McCay, C., Crowell, M., & Maynard, L. (1935). The effect of retarded growth upon the length of life and upon ultimate size. *Journal of Nutrition, 10,* 63–79.

This article is one of the first studies to suggest that slowing growth might increase longevity.

Contemporary Scholarly Work

Filley, C. (2012). *The behavioral neurology of white matter.* New York: Oxford University Press.

Researchers have recently turned attention to the white matter of the brain, due in part to advances in neuroimaging. The author, a professor of neurology and psychiatry, reviews the role of white matter in the development of the brain, discussing both the normal functioning and the dysfunctioning. Clinical discussions include Alzheimer's disease, multiple sclerosis, HIV, migraines, and shaken-baby syndrome, all in terms of underlying white matter. The book is comprehensive, is timely, and reads easily—quite a nice combination.

Florido, R., Tchkonia, T., & Kirkland, J. L. (2011). Aging and adipose tissue. In E. J. Masoro & S. N. Austad (Eds.), *Handbook of the biology of aging,* 7th ed. (pp. 119–139). San Diego, CA: Academic Press.

The authors explain the connection between the changes in adipose tissue (fat) that occur in primary aging and the increased risk of metabolic diseases, such as diabetes.

Fontana, L., Colman, R. J., Holloszy, J. O., et al. (2011). Caloric restriction in nonhuman and human primates. In E. J. Masoro & S. N. Austad (Eds.), *Handbook of the biology of aging,* 7th ed. (pp. 447–461). San Diego, CA: Academic Press.

This article gives some more details on the effects of caloric restriction on various lab animals and humans, including longer lives, less obesity, and fewer illnesses (such as diabetes, heart disease, and cancer).

Chapter 3

Reading for Personal Interest

Mukherjee, S. (2010). *The emperor of all maladies: A biography of cancer.* New York: Scribner.

This book is about cancer from the earliest recorded diagnoses to the most recent treatments involving genome mapping. The author, a practicing oncologist, tells the stories of patients, researchers, surgeons, and other practitioners who have been involved with this disease and who have contributed to the gains we have made. The writing brings out the human side of this dreaded disease and leaves the reader with optimism that a cure will be found.

Genova, L. (2009). *Still Alice.* New York: Gallery.

Strange to recommend a novel in a textbook, but this one is written by a neuroscientist, and it gives a very good picture of how early-onset Alzheimer's disease affects the lives of one woman and her family.

Classic Work

Friedman, M., & Rosenman, R. H. (1959). Association of a specific overt behavior pattern with increases in blood cholesterol, blood clotting time, incidence of arcus senilis and clinical coronary artery disease. *Journal of the American Medical Association, 169,* 1286–1296.

This paper was the first time "type A" was introduced to the scientific world. The authors described an "action-emotion complex" that consisted of striving for achievement, being overly involved in one's job, being extremely competitive and hostile, and experiencing urgency in time-related matters. Friedman and Rosenman showed that this type of behavior pattern was related to certain physical symptoms of coronary heart disease.

Peterson, C., & Seligman, M. (1987). Explanatory style and illness. *Journal of Personality, 55,* 237–265.

These two scientists first suggested that a person's way of explaining the world (optimism or pessimism) has an effect on her or his physical health.

Contemporary Scholarly Work

Finch, C. (2011). Inflammation in aging processes: An integrative and ecological perspective. In E. J. Masaro & S. N. Austad (Eds.), *Handbook of the biology of aging* (7th ed., pp. 275–296). San Diego, CA: Academic Press.

This article is a nice explanation of the major role inflammation has in many age-related disorders. It includes a very clear section on epigenetic inheritance, specifically how the environment today can determine the health of generations to come via infectious disease and pollution.

Karel, M. J., Gatz, M., & Smyer, M. A. (2012). Aging and mental health in the decade ahead: What psychologists need to know. *American Psychologist, 67,* 184–198.

Anyone planning to work in a clinical setting should read this article, which tells about how the increase in older adults in our population will affect the type of services needed for mental health care in the United States.

American Psychiatric Association. (2013). *Diagnostic and statistical manual of mental disorders* (5th ed.). Washington, DC: American Psychiatric Association.

This book is what most professionals use as the authority on diagnosing mental disorders. The APA revises this manual about every 6 to 10 years, and it includes the most recent descriptions of various mental disorders—the symptoms, prevalence, and variations, plus the all-important diagnosis numbers. If you are planning a career in clinical psychology, medicine, mental health counseling, or any related field, this is a must for your bookshelf. If you are just interested in psychology and mental disorders, you might enjoy owning it also.

Chapter 4

Reading for Personal Interest

Strauch, B. (2010). *The secret life of the grown-up brain: The surprising talents of the middle-aged mind.* New York: Penguin.

If you are leaving young adulthood and find yourself forgetting names and not being able to come up with the right word at the right time, this is a book for you. Science writer Barbara Strauch has the good news that despite those pesky symptoms, the middle-aged brain is at its peak, and it stays there for much longer than we ever thought (or hoped). She tells about new research using imaging techniques and does it all in a very conversational and understandable way.

Flynn, J. R. (2012). *Are we getting smarter? Rising IQ in the twenty-first century.* New York: Cambridge University Press.

The author explores the effect he discovered and that carries his name, the *Flynn effect*—the rising IQ over the past 100 years. In this, his latest book, he includes some discussion about gender differences in IQ, reasons for the IQ increase in developing countries, and a thought-provoking discussion about the death penalty in regard to one's intellectual ability to stand trial.

Stokes, A. (2012). *Is this thing on? A computer handbook for late bloomers, technophobes, and the kicking and screaming.* New York: Workman.

This is a nice introduction for older adults to computers, smartphones, e-books, Skype, Facebook, and other electronic devices. The author has taught over 140,000 people, mostly seniors, how to use electronic equipment. In this book she covers how to buy a computer, sign up for e-mail, connect with the Internet, how to use search engines, and many more important skills. She covers how to safely use online banking and Internet shopping with credit cards. If you are a reluctant e-user or your parents (or grandparents) are, this book will teach all the basics in a reassuring, jargon-free way.

Classic Work

Horn, J. L., & Cattell, R. B. (1966). Refinement and test of the theory of fluid and crystallized intelligence. *Journal of Educational Psychology, 57,* 253–270.

This paper justified the bifurcation of general intelligence into two distinct types of abilities. Although other cognitive psychologists have had other terminology and definitions for similar theories, this is the one that caught on and is still in use today.

Contemporary Scholarly Work

Rodrigue, K. M., & Kennedy, K. M. (2011). The cognitive consequences of structural changes to the aging brain. In K. W. Schaie & S. L. Willis (Eds.), *Handbook of the psychology of aging* (7th ed., pp. 73–91). San Diego, CA: Academic Press.

The authors discuss cortical thinning, white matter integrity, and beta-amyloid deposits and how they relate to age-related changes in the cognitive functioning.

Moye, J., Marson, D., Edelstein, B., et al. (2011). Decision making capacity. In K. W. Schaie & S. L. Willis (Eds.), *Handbook of the psychology of aging* (7th ed., pp. 367–379). San Diego, CA: Academic Press.

This chapter presents guidelines about assessing the legal capacities of older adults based on their cognitive capacities. For example, it tells how to evaluate a person's ability to manage finances, consent to medical treatment, drive, and live independently. Although it is based on cognitive research findings, it applies that knowledge to real issues many of us face with older parents and grandparents.

Chapter 5

Reading for Personal Interest

Arnett, J. J., & Fishel, E. (2013). *When will my grown-up kid grow up? Loving and understanding your emerging adult.* New York: Workman.

This book is advertised as the parenting guide for parents who no longer thought they needed one. Arnett, the developmental psychologist who first wrote about "emerging adulthood," gives practical advice to parents whose kids are past "childhood" but are still living at home and depending on their parents for much of their support. The message for parents is that it is OK, you are not alone, but you also need to take care of yourself.

Klinenberg, E. (2012). *Going solo: The extraordinary rise and surprising appeal of living alone.* New York: Penguin Group.

The author is a sociologist who states that the recent increase in the number of people living alone is the biggest social change that has taken place in our lifetimes, and that the numbers are even greater in Europe and Japan. His second statement is that people who live alone are not necessarily lonely, anti-social, or introverted, but often well-adjusted people with friends and community involvement. In a combination of research accounts and interviews with people who live alone, Klinenberg gives a good picture of this recent phenomenon and suggests some changes that could be made by society to adjust.

Solomon, A. (2012). *Far from the tree: Parents, children, and the search for identity.* New York: Scribner.

Many people prepare for the role of parent, planning on their child to be similar to themselves. But for some parents, that role turns out to be something very different when they find that their child is deaf, autistic, transgendered, a prodigy, or has another condition that make them very different from their parents. Solomon combines facts about each condition, the history of how society has dealt with each, and interviews with parents who are coping with their unexpected roles. It is very clear from these chapters that we do not "reproduce" when we become parents, but we create a child different from ourselves and sometime very different.

Classic Work

Eagly, A. H. (1987). *Sex differences in social behavior: A social role interpretation.* Hillsdale, NJ: Erlbaum.

Social psychologist Alice Eagly put forth her social role theory of gender differences in this book.

Gutmann, D. (1975). Parenthood: A key to the comparative study of the life cycle. In N. Datan & L. H. Ginsberg (Eds.), *Life-span developmental psychology: Normative life crises* (pp. 167–184). New York: Academic Press.

Anthropologist David Gutmann collected data about parenthood practices from a number of cultures to show that there are many similarities, specifically that when young adults become parents, they adopt more traditional gender roles than they had as nonparents. His interpretation is a genetic one—that these behaviors are preprogrammed to ensure the best chances of the survival of the children.

Contemporary Scholarly Work

Eagly, A. H., Eaton, A., Rose, S. M. (2012). Feminism and psychology: Analysis of a half-century of research on women and gender. *American Psychologist, 67,* 211–230.

The authors trace the progression of research articles on gender from feminist-specialty journals to mainstream psychology journals and give some predictions for the future.

Golant, S. M. (2011). *The changing residential environments of older people.* In R. H. Binstock & L. K. George (Eds.), *Handbook of aging and the social sciences* (7th ed., pp. 207–220). San Diego, CA: Academic Press.

The author introduces the concept of environmental gerontology and tells how the spaces that older people occupy can be optimized to keep them as independent as possible for as long as possible. Several model neighborhoods and communities are discussed.

Chapter 6

Reading for Personal Interest

Psychology professors who do research often get very frustrated when so little of their findings ever filter down to practical use. The authors of this book are a dozen or so relationship researchers who decided to write a "how-to" book based on real research and not just personal opinion (like most books on relationships). And they wrote it for young adults. It applies social psychology, developmental psychology, evolutionary psychology, and other social sciences to answer questions like "What makes some hot and some not?" and "Does love last forever?" I have used this as supplemental reading in my social psychology class, and the students like it a lot.

I wrote a lot about the research of Howard J. Markman and his colleagues in the section on successful marriages. This is a "how-to" book they have written that applies their research findings to practical matters that couples face when problems arise. I routinely lend out my copy of this to students who are having relationship problems, and they report good results.

Tannen, D. (2011). *That's not what I meant: How conversational style makes or breaks relationships.* New York: HarperCollins.

Deborah Tannen is another serious researcher who has written some good "how-to" books. In this one, her most recent, she writes about how small details of our personal conversation styles can cause serious problems in interpersonal relationships. Tannen is a professor of linguistics, so her message is sound, but she is also a talented writer, so her delivery of the message is fun to read.

Classic Work

Psychologist Daniel Levinson studied 40 men over the period from young adulthood through middle age and concluded that there are stages (or seasons) that most men experience and that they are defined by relationships with others, a spouse, children, social groups, and coworkers. This was pioneering work in the field of adult development and inspired studies of many other groups.

This is the first of three books by psychoanalyst John Bowlby that were the foundation for attachment theory. They have very strong Freudian tones and reflect Bowlby's experiences during World War II working with children's evacuation and resettlement in war zones.

These two social psychology researchers extended childhood attachment theory to romantic relationships in adulthood.

Contemporary Scholarly Work

I have discussed the work of psychologist John M. Gottman in some detail in the section of this chapter dealing with successful marriages. This is his most recent book, written for marriage counselors and researchers, and it takes the reader through his couples' therapy sessions, explaining the exercises he uses with couples and what he looks for in terms of positive and negative interactions. He also talks about how he helps couples make changes that put their relationships back on the right track.

Fingerman, K. L. & Birditt, K. S. (2011). Relationship between adults and their aging parents. In K. W. Schaie & S. L. Willis (Eds.), *Handbook of the psychology of aging* (7th ed., pp. 219–232). San Diego, CA: Academic Press.

This chapter reviews the research on the exchange of support between adults and their aging parents, and also the benefits both receive in terms of well-being.

Antonucci, T. C., Birdidtt, K. S., & Ajrouch, K. J. (2013). Social relationships and aging. In R. M. Lerner, M. A. Easterbrooks, J. Mistry, et al., (Eds.), *Handbook of psychology, Vol. 6: Developmental psychology* (2nd ed., pp. 459–514). Hoboken, NJ: Wiley.

This chapter reviews the literature on social relationships from young adulthood to middle adulthood and especially older adulthood, with an emphasis on the convoy model, which provides an organizing framework for the research findings. It includes the latest research in this area and discusses social relationships that influence stress, health, and well-being.

By the time you read this, the most common way for couples to meet romantic partners will be by using an online dating site. Yet not much is known about how these companies work, whether they live up to their claims, or what single people can do to make the most of their online dating experiences. This article answers those questions and gives one of the few research-based accounts of this fairly new mate-selection method.

Shaver, P. R., & Mikulincer, M. (2012). Attachment theory. In P. A. M. Van Lange, A. W. Kruglanski, & E. T. Higgins (Eds.), *Handbook of theories of social psychology* (Vol. 2, pp. 160–179). Los Angeles, CA: Sage.

These authors are pioneers in the field of adult attachment, and in this article, they trace the development of attachment theory from its beginning to current applications. It is concise and easy to read.

Chapter 7

Reading for Personal Interest

Bolles, D. (2014). *What color is your parachute? A practical manual for job-hunters and career-changers.* Berkeley, CA: Ten Speed Press.

The cover of the newest edition of this book proclaims that it is "the best-selling job-hunting book in the world," and that is true. It has sold 10 million copies over the last 40 years. No matter your age or your college major, this book is for you. The Library of Congress recently included it in the top 25 books that have changed people's lives, along with *War and Peace* and *On Walden Pond.* It is continually updated and gives adults a way to evaluate their abilities, their career situations, and their options. I have given at least a dozen copies of this book to relatives who graduated from high school, college, or are just thinking about a career change.

Spooner, J. D. (2014). *No one ever told us that: Money and life, letters to my grandchildren.* New York: Business Plus.

Written by a respected financial advisor, this book tells young people important lessons about work, investing, and life in general. This is a perfect book for the college student who is dealing with college loans, credit cards, and perhaps a part-time job. This book doesn't preach or lecture. The author talks to the reader with affection and, like a grandfather, often imparts his wisdom through stories.

Milne, D. (2013). *The psychology of retirement: Coping with the transition from work.* Malden, MA: Wiley-Blackwell.

Clinical psychologist Derek Milne bases this book on psychological theory, research, and case studies from his patients who faced problems with retirement. It is clear and engaging, and would be a very big help to anyone approaching this stage of life.

Classic Work

Super, D. E. (1957). *The psychology of careers.* New York: Harper & Row.

This book recounts the early formulation of Super's life-span/life-space theory.

Holland, J. L. (1973). *Making vocational choices: A theory of careers.* Englewood Cliffs, NJ: Prentice Hall.

Holland's career theory was first introduced in this book.

Contemporary Scholarly Work

Reno, V. P., & Veghte, B. (2011). Economic status of the aged in the United States. In R. H. Binstock & L. K. George (Eds.), *Handbook of aging and the social sciences* (7th ed., pp. 175–191). San Diego, CA: Academic Press.

This chapter is an overview of the economic situation of older adults in the United States, how the recession of 2007 affected this age group, how older adults in the United States compare to similar groups globally, and what the future holds for this generation.

Rix, S. E. (2011). Employment and aging. In R. H. Binstock & L. K. George (Eds.), *Handbook of aging and the social sciences* (7th ed., pp. 193–206). San Diego, CA: Academic Press.

The author of this chapter notes the recent trend of older workers to remain in the workforce or to return to the workforce after initial retirement. She explains the reasons this is happening, the types of jobs older workers tend to fill, and the changes that this trend will bring about in the workplace.

Chapter 8

Reading for Personal Interest

Seligman, M. E. P. (2012). *Flourish: A visionary new understanding of happiness and well-being.* New York: Atria.

Psychologist Martin Seligman, one of the founders of positive psychology, moves beyond the quest for happiness and writes about how people can be fully engaged in their lives—being more self-disciplined, wiser, stronger, and more generous to others. The author bases his advice on his own research and other recent work in the field of positive psychology.

Vaillant, G. E. (2009). *Spiritual evolution: How we are wired for faith, hope, and love.* New York: Harmony Books.

Psychiatrist George Vaillant is known for his ideas about mature adaptation and defense mechanisms. This book draws on neuroscience, ethology, social psychology, and human development to explain that humans have evolved positive emotions such as forgiveness, compassion, and gratitude because they are essential to our survival. This is a good example of the scientific examination of the quest for meaning.

Classic Work

Erikson, E. H. (1985/1994). *The life cycle completed: A review.* New York: Norton.

Erikson, E. H. (1980/1994). *Identity and the life cycle.* New York: Norton.

Psychoanalyst Erik Erikson wrote several books explaining his theory of psychosocial development using examples from his own life as well as from other cultures.

Anthropologist David Gutmann spells out his ideas about changes in gender roles over the years of adulthood. He draws on his vast knowledge of roles in other cultures, such as the Navajo, the Maya, and the Druze.

Psychologist Jane Loevinger explains her theory of ego development.

This book describes Maslow's ideas of self-actualization and the hierarchy of needs in a simple, straightforward style.

This article is an early discussion of the Five-Factor Model of personality.

The 40-year report on the Grant study of Harvard men is described. These 268 men were followed through their careers and into retirement, and psychiatrist George Vaillant used the results to formulate a personality theory of mature adaptation. An interesting and very readable account of the study results.

Contemporary Scholarly Writing

Jensen, L. A., & Arnett, J. J. (2012). Going global: New pathways for adolescents and emerging adults in a changing world. *Journal of Social Issues, 68*, 473–492.

The authors review theory and research on cultural identity formation in emerging adulthood and the implications of globalization, such as cultural identity confusion, gender roles, and national identity formation.

Kandler, C. (2012). Nature and nurture in personality development: The case of neuroticism and extraversion. *Current Directions in Psychological Science, 21*, 290–296.

Research in the stability and rank-order continuity of personality traits shows that personality follows a developmental pattern that unfolds across the life span. However, we are not clear on what drives these patterns. In this paper, the authors review research on the genetic and environmental sources involved and the times of life that each has an impact.

Chapter 9

Reading for Personal Interest

Sacks, J. (2012). *The great partnership: Science, religion, and the search for meaning.* New York: Schocken Books.

The author of this book is the Chief Rabbi of the United Hebrew Congregations of Great Britain, and he writes this book to teach us that science and religion should not be in conflict, but that we need both perspectives to view the world in three-dimensional depth. He combines discussions of neuroscience, evolutionary psychology, biochemistry with faith, search for meaning, and history. If you have problems merging science with your personal beliefs, this may help you combine the two.

Dalai Lama. (2011). *Beyond religion: Ethics for a whole world.* New York: Houghton Mifflin Harcourt.

The 14th Dalai Lama, leader of the Tibetan people and the incarnation of the Buddha of Compassion, wrote this book to propose moving beyond ethics based on religious principles and follow a path toward ethical and happy life in a global human community based on understanding and mutual respect. He writes of compassion, justice, mindfulness, meditation, and happiness.

Classic Work

I find this a delightful book, remarkably free of the convoluted style that otherwise seems to be common in this area.

Lawrence Kohlberg explains his ideas about moral development proceeding in stages.

St. Theresa was a Spanish nun. Many experts consider her description of her inner spiritual journey the most complete and comprehensible account of the mystical experience. I found it beautifully written, provocative, and stimulating.

Philosopher Evelyn Underhill combined and distilled reports of hundreds of mystics and other teachers from all religious traditions into a single coherent account of the human quest for meaning. Her style is clear and straightforward.

Contemporary Scholarly Work

Churchland, P. S. (2012). *Braintrust: What neuroscience tells us about morality.* Princeton, NJ: Princeton University Press.

This book, by philosophy professor Patricia Churchland, blends her field with neuroscience and genetics to form "neurophilosophy." Her main message is that we can find the basis of our morality and ethics in brain chemicals and DNA. She begins with attachment and bonding to show that our sense of morality does not come from a set of laws or religious teachings, but from within.

Parker, S. (2011). Spirituality in counseling: A faith development perspective. *Journal of Counseling and Development, 89*, 112–119.

The author describes how Fowler's faith development theory is used effectively when therapists recognize the crises that accompany transitions from one stage to another and how they interact with other life crises.

Chapter 10

Reading for Personal Interest

Hillenbrand, L. (2010). *Unbroken: A World War II story of survival, resilience, and redemption.* New York: Random House.

This book is the biography of Louie Zamperini, who spent his adolescent years as a streetfighter and hellraiser. In his teen years he started running and became one of the best athletes in the world, competing in the 1936 Berlin Olympics. He was closing in on the 4-minute mile when World War II broke out, and he enlisted in the Army Air Corps. Serving as a bombardier, he was shot down over the Pacific and spent 47 days in a life raft with two other crew members, only to be rescued by a Japanese ship. He spent 2-1/2 years in one of the cruelest POW camps in Japan and came home to the United States in the clutches of PTSD. Still, he not only overcame all this, but triumphed as he began to reach out to other soldiers with PTSD and to find forgiveness for his captors. This is an excellent example of how resilient the human mind and body can be.

Sheridan, T. (2011). *Buddha in blue jeans: An extremely short simple Zen guide to sitting quietly.* Create Space Independently Publishing Platform.

If you are new to meditation and mindfulness, this is a good place to start. In this short book, you can learn to sit quietly, accept your feelings, listen to others, live gratefully, do no harm, and several other important lessons. The message in the title is that you don't need to go to a special place or put on a special outfit—just sit down in your blue jeans and get started. Bonus is that the book is free on your e-reader.

Bonanno, G. A. (2010). *The other side of sadness: What the new science of bereavement tells us about life after loss.* New York: Basic Books.

Psychologist George A. Bonanno is cited prominently in this text along with his research on bereavement and his new ideas that resilience is the typical response to trauma. This book goes behind the research findings and tells stories about the people Bonanno interviewed and the lessons he learned from them. If you have experienced the death of a loved one, this book will help you with your loss. Since I last revised this book, I have lost both my parents, so this topic is very close to my heart at this time.

Classic Work

Cannon, W. B. (1914). The interrelations of emotions as suggested by recent physiological researches. *American Journal of Physiology, 25*, 256–282.

Cannon, W. B. (1932). *The wisdom of the body.* New York: Norton.

These two works are considered the beginning of modern stress theories. In the first, physiologist Walter Cannon suggested that certain events cause the sympathetic nervous system to react, and that this reaction leads to disequilibrium in the body. This theory was innovative because it stated that stressors had a psychological component—they had to be recognized as threatening before they could elicit a stress response. In the second selection, Cannon reviewed his work and his ideas about physiological reactions to stress, including the "fight-or-flight" concept.

Although the link between stress and illness is well known today, in 1967 it was a radical idea. This was the article that started the ball rolling. Not only was it important in its day, but it is still regularly cited in research. The SRRS remains a favorite measurement instrument in studies of stress.

Selye, H. (1956/1984). *The stress of life (Rev. ed.).* New York: McGraw-Hill.

Hans Selye is considered the major pioneer of stress research, and his focus is on the almost universal physiological response to almost all types of stress. This book summarizes his contribution to the field.

Contemporary Scholarly Work

Almeida, D. M., Piazza, J. R., Stawski, R. S., et al. (2011). The speedometer of life: Stress, health, and aging. In K. W. Schaie & S. L. Willis (Eds.), *Handbook of the psychology of aging* (7th ed., pp. 191–206). San Diego, CA: Academic Press.

This handbook article reviews the current research on stress from the viewpoint of David Almeida and his colleagues, who are leading researchers in this field.

MacDermid Wadsworth, S. M. (2010). Family risk and resilience in the context of war and terrorism. *Journal of Marriage and Family, 72,* 537–556.

As director of the Military Family Research Institute at Purdue University, this author has gathered research findings on how war and terrorism has affected families, including the effect of combat deployment on service members, the effect of deployment on families, the effect of war on families living in combat zones, the effect of mass violence and refugee status on families, and the effect of children serving in combat themselves. She also writes about how families cope and grow in the aftermath of violence.

Knight, B. G., & Losada, A. (2011). Family caregiving for cognitively or physically frail older adults: Theory, research, and practice. In K. W. Schaie & S. L. Willis (Eds.), *Handbook of the psychology of aging* (7th ed., pp. 353–365). San Diego, CA: Academic Press.

This handbook chapter deals with caring for the caregivers—the 40 million or so adults who provide care for older family members, giving potential physical and mental health outcomes and the factors that influence those outcomes. It also covers the topic of grief after caregiving, which can be a complicated type of bereavement.

Chapter 11

Reading for Personal Interest

Bell, K. W. (2011). *Living at the end of life: A hospice nurse addresses the most common questions.* New York: Sterling Ethos.

Hospice nurse Karen Bell wrote this book for families and friends of people who are approaching the end of their lives. Drawing on her 16 years of experience, she writes straightforward information about choosing a hospice, what to expect, and what can be done to make sure the patients' final months are peaceful, comfortable, and meaningful. She illustrates her practical advice with empathetic accounts of families she has worked with.

Konigsberg, R. D. (2011). *The truth about grief: The myth of its five stags and the new science of loss.* New York: Simon & Schuster.

The author of this book, a veteran science writer, describes the five-stage theory of Kübler-Ross and tells how the more current theories, which are based on empirical research done with bereaved people, give a better picture of the resilience most people exhibit after the loss of a loved one.

Classic Work

Kübler-Ross, E. (1969). *On death and dying.* New York: Macmillan.

This is the original book by Kübler-Ross that significantly changed the way many physicians and other health professionals view death. It is full of case material and reflects Kübler-Ross's great skill as a listener and a clinician. Although this theory has been supplemented and augmented by more current researchers, she was the first to put the patient's interests in the forefront of the dying process.

Contemporary Scholarly Work

Gold, D. (2011). Late-life death and dying in 21st-century America. In R. H. Binstock & L. K. George (Eds.), *Handbook of aging and the social sciences* (7th ed., pp. 235–247). San Diego, CA: Academic Press.

The author gives a good overview of the various definitions involved in the death process in older adults and then discusses changes that have taken place in the practices surrounding death. Finally, she reviews the social factors that are involved in different attitudes toward death.

Chapter 12

Reading for Personal Interest

Pestalozzi, T. (2013). *Life skills 101: A practical guide to leaving home and living on your own* (5th ed.). New York: Stonewood.

The author offers emerging adults a helpful guide to living on their own, including how to read contracts, do laundry, keep a car running, open a bank account, and equip a kitchen.

Bainbridge, D. (2013). *Middle age: A natural history.* London, UK: Portobello Books.

What does a veterinarian do with his spare time when he turns 40? Bainbridge decided to indulge his interest in evolutionary zoology to explore the physical, cognitive, and emotional changes that he and his age-mates were experiencing. This book gives a little different viewpoint of middle age, but it's good science and good writing.

Vaillant, G. E. (2012). *Triumphs of experience: The men of the Harvard Grant Study.* Cambridge, MA: Belknap Press.

George Vaillant based this book on findings from the Harvard Grant Study, which is the longest longitudinal study of developmental psychology. The participants began as undergraduates and are now in their 90s. Vaillant tells us what their lives are like now and what factors have contributed to this outcome. For example, an unhappy childhood can be overcome, but a happy childhood stays with us throughout our lives. Also, our physical condition after 80 depends more on our earlier lifestyles than our genes. As our older population increases, this information has become important to anyone with older family members or who plans to work with people this age.

Lyubomirsky, S. (2013). *The myths of happiness: What should make you happy but doesn't; what shouldn't make you happy but does.* New York: Penguin Press.

If you have ever had thoughts that you would be happy "if only"—you finished college, married the right person, had children, or had more money, this book, written by a social psychologist and based on scientific evidence, offers you the real secrets to happiness (and unhappiness). She points out that we have been given false promises that every milestone we reach in life will bring the best (or the worst) outcomes, and we forget about looking inward and seeing our own growth potential.

Classic Work

Cummings, E., & Henry, W. E. (1961). *Growing old.* New York: Basic Books.

Disengagement theory is formulated and discussed in detail in this book.

Sears, R. R. (1977). Sources of life satisfaction of the Terman gifted men. *American Psychologist, 32*, 119–128.

Pioneer developmentalist Robert Sears interviewed in old age the men who had been child participants in Terman's famous longitudinal study of gifted children.

Waddington, C. H. (1957). *The strategy of the genes.* London, UK: Allen & Son.

Embryologist Conrad Waddington used an epigenetic landscape model to describe the idea that the development of an organism can take many paths on its way to differentiation. His model has since been borrowed by other developmental scientists to describe the transactional properties of the influences people encounter during their lifetimes.

Contemporary Scholarly Work

Ardelt, M. (2011). Wisdom, age, and well-being. In K. W. Schaie & S. L. Willis (Eds.), *Handbook of the psychology of aging* (7th ed., pp. 279–291). San Diego, CA: Academic Press.

Although it is common knowledge in most cultures that wisdom increases with age, the empirical study of this ability has not resulted in a uniform definition, a general method of measurement, or any methods to foster wisdom in the family or in schools. Yet we know that wisdom is positively related to well-being and happiness in some groups of older adults. This chapter is a good summary of what we know and what we need to find out.

References

AARP. (2012). *AARP policy book 2011–2012*. Retrieved May 10, 2013, from http://www.aarp.org/content/dam/aarp/about_aarp/aarp_policies/2011_04/pdf/Chapter4.pdf

Abdel-Khalek, A. M. (2004). The Arabic Scale of Death Anxiety (ASDA): Its development, validation, and results in three Arab countries. *Death Studies, 28,* 435–457.

Achenbaum, W. A. (1995). *Crossing frontiers: Gerontology emerges as a science.* Cambridge, MA: Cambridge University Press.

Ackerman, P. L. (2008). Knowledge and cognitive aging. In F. I. M. Craik & T. A. Salthouse (Eds.), *The handbook of aging and cognition* (3rd ed., pp. 443–489). New York: Psychology Press.

Adams, C., Smith, M. C., Pasupathi, M., et al. (2002). Social context effects on story recall in older and younger women: Does the listener make a difference? *Journals of Gerontology: Psychological and Social Sciences, 57,* 28–40.

Adelmann, P. K. (1994). Multiple roles and physical health among older adults: Gender and ethnic comparisons. *Research on Aging, 16,* 142–166.

Adler, N., Stewart, J., Cohen, S., et al. (2007). *Reaching for a healthier life: Facts on socioeconomic status and health in the U.S.* Chicago: MacArthur Foundation.

Ai, A. L., Huang, B., Biorck, J., et al. (2013). Religious attendance and major depression among Asian Americans from a national database: The mediation of social support. *Psychology of Religion and Spirituality, 5,* 78–89.

Ainsworth, M. D. S., Blehar, M., Waters, E., et al. (1978). *Patterns of attachment.* Hillsdale, NJ: Erlbaum.

Ajrouch, K. J., Blandon, A. Y., & Antonucci, T. C. (2005). Social networks among men and women: The effects of age and socioeconomic status. *Journals of Gerontology: Psychological and Social Sciences, 60,* 311–317.

Albanesius, C. (2011). Apple unveils updated iPod nano touch. *PC Magazine.* Retrieved May 4, 2012, from http://www.pcmag.com/article2/0,2817,2394061,00.asp

Alea, N., Diehl, M., & Bluck, S. (2004). Personality and emotion in late life. *Encyclopedia of Applied Psychology, 1–10.* San Diego, CA: Elsevier.

Alesina, A., Glaeser, E., & Sacerdote, B. (2005). Work and leisure in the U.S. and Europe: Why so different? *Harvard Institute of Economic Research.* Discussion paper number 2068. Retrieved March 20, 2006, from http://www.colorado.edu/economics/morey/4999Ethics/AlesinaGlaeserSacerdote2005.pdf

Allman, J., Rosin, A., Kumar, R., et al. (1998). Parenting and survival in anthropoid primates: Caretakers live longer. *Proceedings of the National Academy of Sciences of the United States of America, 95,* 6866–6869.

Almeida, D. M. (2005). Resilience and vulnerability to daily stressors assessed via diary methods. *Current Directions in Psychological Science, 14,* 64–68.

Almeida, D. M., & Horn, M. C. (2004). Is daily life more stressful during middle adulthood? In O. G. Brim, C. D. Ryff, & R. C. Kessler (Eds.), *How healthy are we? A national study of well-being at midlife* (pp. 425–451). Chicago: University of Chicago Press.

Almeida, O. P., Waterreus, A., Spry, N., et al. (2004). One-year follow-up study of the association between chemical castration, sex hormones, beta-amyloid, memory, and depression in men. *Psychoneuroendocrinology, 29,* 1071–1081.

Alsop, S. (1973). *Stay of execution.* New York: Lippincott.

Alterovitz, S. S.-R., & Mendelsohn, G. A. (2011). Partner preferences across the life span: Online dating by older adults. *Psychology of Popular Media Culture, 1,* 89–95.

Alzheimer's Association. (2012). *Fact sheet.* Retrieved November 28, 2012, from http://www.alz.org/documents_custom/2012_facts_figures_fact_sheet.pdf

Alzheimer's Association. (2013). *Early signs and symptoms of Alzheimer's.* Retrieved January 3, 2013, from http://www.alz.org/alzheimers_disease_10_signs_of_alzheimers.asp\#typical

Amato, P. R. (2010). Research on divorce: Continuing trends and new developments. *Journal of Marriage and Family, 72,* 650–666.

American Academy of Orthopedic Surgeons. (2011a). Retrieved May 5, 2012, from http://orthoinfo.aaos.org/topic.cfm?topic=A00389

American Academy of Orthopedic Surgeons. (2011b). Retrieved May 5, 2012, from http://orthoinfo.aaos.org/topic.cfm?topic=A00377

American Cancer Society. (2013). *What does hospice care provide?* Retrieved May 4, 2013, from http://www.cancer.org/treatment/findingandpayingfortreatment/choosingyourtreatmentteam/hospicecare/hospice-care-services

American Diabetes Association. (2011). *Diabetes statistics.* Retrieved November 27, 2012, from http://www.diabetes.org/diabetes-basics/diabetes-statistics/

American Diabetes Association. (2012). *Diabetes basics.* http://www.diabetes.org/diabetes-basics/prevention/risk-factors/

American Hair Loss Association. (2010). *Hair loss fact sheet.* Retrieved May 8, 2012, from http://www.americanhairloss.org/

American Heart Association. (2012). *High blood pressure: Statistical fact sheet.* Retrieved November 6, 2012, from http://www.heart.org/idc/groups/heart-public/@wcm@sop@smd/documents/downloadable/ucm_319587.pdf

American Nutrition Association. (2011). USDA defines food deserts. *Nutrition Digest.* Retrieved October 18, 2012, from http://american-nutritionassociation.org/newsletter/usda-defines-food-deserts

American Psychiatric Association. (2000). *Diagnostic and statistical manual of mental disorders* (4th ed.). Washington, DC: American Psychiatric Association.

American Psychological Association. (2004). *Public policy, work, and families: The report of the APA presidential initiative on work and families.* Retrieved March 14, 2006, from http://www.apa.org/work-family/fullreport.pdf

American Society of Plastic Surgeons. (2012). *2011 Plastic surgery statistics report.* Retrieved April 25, 2012, from http://www.plasticsurgery.org/News-and-Resources/2011-Statistics.html

American Speech-Language-Hearing Association. (2012). *Unsafe use of portable music players may damage your hearing.* Retrieved May 4, 2012, from http://www.asha.org/About/news/atitbtot/Unsafe-Usage-of-Portable-Music-Players-May-Damage-Your-Hearing/

Andresen, E. M., Malmgren, J. A., Carter, W. B., et al. (1994). Screening for depression in well older adults: Evaluation of a short form of the CES-D. *American Journal of Preventive Medicine, 10*, 77–84.

Ano, G. G., & Vasconcelles, E. B. (2005). Religious coping and psychological adjustment to stress: A meta-analysis. *Journal of Clinical Psychology, 61*, 461–480.

Antonovics, K., & Town, R. (2004). Are all the good men married? Uncovering the sources of the marital wage premium. *American Economic Review, 94*, 317–321.

Antonucci, T. C. (1986). Social support networks: A hierarchical mapping technique. *Generations, 3*, 10–12.

Antonucci, T. C. (1990). Social supports and social relationships. In R. H. Binstock & L. K. George (Eds.), *Handbook of aging and the social sciences* (3rd ed., pp. 205–226). San Diego, CA: Academic Press.

Antonucci, T. C., Akiyama, H., & Takahashi, K. (2004). Attachment and close relationships across the life span. *Attachment and Human Development, 6*, 353–370.

Antonucci, T. C., Birditt, K. S., & Akiyama, H. (2009). Convoys of social relations: An interdisciplinary approach. In V. Bengston, M. Silverstein, N. Putney, et al. (Eds.), *Handbook of theories of aging* (pp. 247–260.). New York: Springer.

Antonucci, T., Jackson, J. S., & Biggs, S. (2007). *Intergenerational relations: Theory, research, and policy.* Malden, MA: Blackwell.

Aquilino, W. S. (2005). Impact of family structure on parental attitudes toward the economic support of adult children over the transition to adulthood. *Journal of Family Issues, 26*, 143–167.

Ardelt, M. (2003). Effects of religion and purpose in life on elders' subjective well-being and attitudes toward death. *Journal of Religious Gerontology, 14*, 55–77.

Ardelt, M., & Koenig, C. S. (2006). The role of religion for hospice patients and relatively healthy older adults. *Research on Aging, 28*, 184–215.

Ardila, A., Ostrosky-Solis, F., Rosselli, M., et al. (2000). Age related decline during normal aging: The complex effect of education. *Archives of Clinical Neuropsychology, 15*, 495–513.

Aristotle. (1946). *The politics of Aristotle* (E. Barker, Trans.). London, England: Oxford University Press. (Original work written around 350 BCE.)

Arnett, J. J. (2000). Emerging adulthood. *American Psychologist, 55*, 469–480.

Arnett, J. J. (2004). *Emerging adulthood: The winding road from late teens through the twenties.* Oxford, England: Oxford University Press.

Arnett, J. J. (2007). Emerging adulthood: What is it, and what is it good for? *Child Development Perspectives, 1*, 68–73.

Aron, A. (2012). Online dating: The current status—and beyond. *Psychological Science in the Public Interest, 13*, 1–2.

Aron, A., Fisher, H., Mashek, D., et al. (2005). Reward, motivation, and emotion systems associated with early-stage intense romantic love. *Journal of Neurophysiology, 93*, 327–337.

Arterburn, D. E., Bogart, A., Sherwood, N. E., et al. (2012). A multisite study of long-term remission and relapse of type 2 diabetes mellitus following gastric bypass. *Obesity Surgery, 23*, 93–102.

Aspinwall, L. G., & Taylor, S. E. (1997). A stitch in time: Self-regulation and proactive coping. *Psychological Bulletin, 121*, 417–436.

Atchley, P., & Dressel, J. (2004). Conversation limits the functional field of view. *Human Factors: The Journal of the Human Factors and Ergonomics Society, 46*, 664–673.

Attar-Schwartz, S., Tan, J.-P., Buchanan, A., et al. (2009). Grandparent and adolescent adjustment in two-parent biological, lone-parent, and step-families. *Journal of Family Psychology, 23*, 67–75.

Ault-Brutus, A. A. (2012). Changes in racial-ethnic disparities in use and adequacy of mental health care in the United States, 1900–2003. *Psychiatric Services, 63*, 531–540.

Austad, S. N. (2011). Sex differences in longevity and aging. In E. J. Masoro & S. N. Austad (Eds.), *Handbook of the biology of aging* (7th ed., pp. 479–495). San Diego, CA: Academic Press.

Aviv, A. (2011). Leukocyte telomere dynamics, human aging, and life span. In E. J. Masoro & S. N. Austad (Eds.), *Handbook of the biology of aging* (7th ed., pp. 163–176). San Diego, CA: Academic Press.

Azaola, M. C. (2012). Becoming a migrant: Aspirations of youths during their transition to adulthood in rural Mexico. *Journal of Youth Studies, 15*, 875–889.

Bäckman, L., & Nilsson, L. G. (1996). Semantic memory functions across the adult life span. *European Psychologist, 1*, 27–33.

Bäckman, L., Small, B. J., & Wahlin, Å. (2001). Aging and memory: Cognitive and biological perspectives. In J. E. Birren & K. W. Schaie (Eds.), *Handbook of the psychology of aging* (5th ed., pp. 349–377). San Diego, CA: Academic Press.

Bäckman, L., Small, B. J., Wahlin, Å., et al. (2000). Cognitive functioning in very old age. In F. I. M. Craik & T. A. Salthouse (Eds.), *The handbook of aging and cognition* (pp. 499–558). Hillsdale, NJ: Erlbaum.

Baddeley, A. D. (1986). *Working memory.* Oxford, England: Oxford University Press.

Bailey, H., Dunlosky, J., & Hertzog, C. (2009). Does differential strategy use account for age-related deficits in working memory performance? *Psychology and Aging, 24*, 82–92.

Bakker, A. B. (2011). An evidence-based model of work engagement. *Current Directions in Psychological Science, 20*, 265–269.

Baldwin, C. L., & Ash, I. K. (2011). Impact of sensory acuity on auditory working memory span in young and older adults. *Psychology and Aging, 26*, 85–91.

Balsam, K. F., Rothblum, E. D., & Beauchaine, T. P. (2005). Victimization over the life span: A comparison of lesbian, gay, bisexual, and heterosexual siblings. *Journal of Consulting and Clinical Psychology, 73*, 477–487.

Baltes, P. B. (1987). Theoretical propositions of life-span developmental psychology: On the dynamics between growth and decline. *Developmental Psychology, 23*, 611–626.

Baltes, P. B., & Baltes, M. M. (1990). Psychological perspectives on successful aging: The model of selective optimization with compensation. In P. B. Baltes & M. M. Baltes (Eds.), *Successful aging: Perspective from the behavioral sciences* (pp. 1–34). Cambridge, MA: Cambridge University Press.

Baltes, P. B., & Lindenberger, U. (1997). Emergence of a powerful connection between sensory and cognitive function across the adult life span: A new window to the study of cognitive aging? *Psychology and Aging, 12*, 12–21.

Baltes, P. B., & Mayer, K. U. (Eds.). (1999). *The Berlin aging study: Aging from 70 to 100.* Cambridge, England: Cambridge University Press.

Baltes, P. B., & Staudinger, U. M. (1993). The search for a psychology of wisdom. *Current Directions in Psychological Science, 2*, 75–80.

Baltes, P. B., Reese, H. W., & Lipsitt, L. P. (1980). Life-span developmental psychology. *Annual Review of Psychology, 31*, 65–110.

Barker, D. J. (2004). Developmental origins of adult health and disease. *Journal of Epidemiology and Community Health, 58*, 114–115.

Barker, D. J., Winter, P. D., Osmond, C., et al. (1989). Weight in infancy and death from ischaemic heart disease. *Lancet, 2*, 577–580.

Barnes, P. M., & Schoenborn, C. A. (2012). *Trends in adults receiving a recommendation for exercise or other physical activity from a physician or other health professional.* Retrieved February 18, 2013, from http://www.cdc.gov/nchs/data/databriefs/db86.pdf

Bartholomew, K. (1990). Avoidance of intimacy: An attachment perspective. *Journal of Social and Personal Relationships, 7,* 147–178.

Bartholomew, K., & Horowitz, L. M. (1991). Attachment styles among young adults: A test of a four-category model. *Journal of Personality and Social Psychology, 61,* 226–244.

Bates, J. S., & Goodsell, T. L. (2013). Male kin relationships: Grandfathers, grandsons, and generativity. *Marriage and Family Review, 49,* 28–50.

Bates, J. S., & Taylor, A. C. (2012). Grandfather involvement and aging men's mental health. *American Journal of Men's Health, 6,* 229–239.

Bauer, J. J., & McAdams, D. P. (2004). Personal growth in adults' stories of life transitions. *Journal of Personality, 72,* 573–602.

Baumeister, R. F., & Leary, M. R. (1995). The need to belong: Desire for interpersonal attachments as a fundamental human motivation. *Psychological Bulletin, 117,* 497–529.

Baun, M. M., & Johnson, R. A. (2010). Human/animal interaction and successful aging. In A. H. Fine (Ed.), *Handbook on animal-assisted therapy: Theoretical foundations and guidelines for practice* (3rd ed., pp. 283–300). San Diego, CA: Academic Press.

Bayard, K., Hellerstein, J., Neumark, D., et al. (2003). New evidence on sex segregation and sex differences in wages from matched employee–employer data. *Journal of Labor Economics, 21,* 887–922.

Beal, C. R. (1994). *Boys and girls: The development of gender roles.* New York: McGraw-Hill.

Beaumont, J. G., & Kenealy, P. M. (2004). Quality of life perceptions and social comparisons in healthy old age. *Aging and Society, 24,* 755–769.

Becker, G. (1981). *A treatise on the family.* Cambridge, MA: Harvard University Press.

Beers, M. H. (2004). *Merck manual of health and aging.* Whitehouse Station, NJ: Merck Research Labs.

Belsky, J. (2001). Emmanuel Miller Lecture: Developmental risks (still) associated with early child care. *Journal of Child Psychology and Psychiatry, 42,* 845–859.

Belsky, J., & Kelly, J. (1994). *The transition to parenthood: How a first child changes marriage. Why some couples grow together and others apart.* New York: Dell.

Belsky, J., Spanier, G. B., & Rovine, M. (1983). Stability and change in marriage across the transition to parenthood. *Journal of Marriage and the Family, 45,* 567–577.

Bem, S. L. (1981). Gender schema theory: A cognitive account of sex typing. *Psychological Review, 88,* 354–364.

Bem, S. L. (1993). *The lenses of gender: Transforming the debate on sexual inequality.* New Haven, CT: Yale University Press.

Bengtson, V. L., & Schrader, S. S. (1982). Parent–child relations. In D. Mangen & W. Peterson (Eds.), *Research instruments in social gerontology* (pp. 114–128). Minneapolis, MN: University of Minnesota Press.

Bengtson, V. L., Gans, D., Putney, N. M., et al. (2009). Theories about age and aging. In V. L. Bengtson, D. Gans, N. M. Putney, et al. (Eds.), *Handbook of theories of aging* (2nd ed., pp. 3–23). New York: Springer.

Bengtsson, T., & Lindström, M. (2003). Airborne infectious diseases during infancy and mortality in later life in southern Sweden, 1766–1894. *International Journal of Epidemiology, 32,* 286–294.

Benjamins, M. R., Musick, M. A., Gold, D. T., et al. (2003). Age-related declines in activity level: The relationship between chronic illness and religious activities. *Journals of Gerontology: Psychological and Social Sciences, 58,* 377–385.

Berdasco, M., & Esteller, M. (2010). Aberrant epigenetic landscape in cancer: How cellular identity goes awry. *Developmental Cell, 19,* 698–711.

Berg, C. A., & Sternberg, R. J. (2003). Multiple perspectives on the development of adult intelligence. In J. Demick & C. Andreoletti (Eds.), *Handbook of adult development* (pp. 103–119). New York: Kluwer.

Bering, J. M. (2006). The folk psychology of souls. *Behavioral & Brain Sciences, 29,* 453–498.

Besser, A., Amir, M., & Barkan, S. (2004). Who signs an organ transplant donor card? A study of personality and individual differences in a sample of Israeli university students. *Personality and Individual Differences, 36,* 1709–1723.

Biblarz, T. J., & Savci, E. (2010). Lesbian, gay, bisexual, and transgender families. *Journal of Marriage and Family, 72,* 480–497.

Bielak, A. A. M., Gerstorf, D., Kiely, K. M., et al. (2011). Depressive symptoms predict decline in perceptual speed in older adulthood. *Psychology and Aging, 26,* 576–583.

Birditt, K. S., Fingerman, K. L., & Zarit, S. (2010). Adult children's problems and successes: Implications for intergenerational ambivalence. *Journals of Gerontology: Psychological and Social Sciences, 65,* 146–153.

Birkhill, W. R., & Schaie, K. W. (1975). The effects of differential reinforcement of cautiousness in intellectual performance among the elderly. *Journals of Gerontology: Psychological and Social Sciences, 30,* 578–583.

Birren, J. E., & Feldman, L. (1997). *Where to go from here.* New York: Simon & Schuster.

Bissig, D., & Lustig, C. (2007). Who benefits from psychological training? *Psychological Science, 18,* 720–726.

Bjerkeset, O., Nordahl, H. M., Mykletun, A., et al. (2005). Anxiety and depression following myocardial infarctions: Gender differences in a 5-year prospective study. *Journal of Psychosomatic Research, 58,* 153–161.

Blackwell, L., Trzesniewski, K., & Dweck, C. S. (2007). Implicit theories of intelligence predict achievement across an adolescent transition: A longitudinal study and an intervention. *Child Development, 78,* 246–263.

Blanchard-Fields, F. (2007). Everyday problem solving and emotion: An adult developmental perspective. *Current Directions in Psychological Science, 16,* 26–31.

Blanchard-Fields, F., Mienaltowski, A., & Seay, R. B. (2007). Age differences in everyday problem-solving effectiveness: Older adults select more effective strategies for interpersonal problems. *Journals of Gerontology: Psychological and Social Sciences, 62,* 61–64.

Blieszner, R. (2000). Close relationships in old age. In C. Hendrick & S. S. Hendrick (Eds.), *Close relationships: A sourcebook* (pp. 85–95). Thousand Oaks, CA: Sage.

Blom, V. (2012). Contingent self-esteem, stressors, and burnout in working women and men. *Work: Journal of Prevention, Assessment and Rehabilitation, 43,* 123–131.

Bloom, B. (2005). Public health in transition. *Scientific American, 293,* 92–99.

Bonanno, G. A. (2005). Resilience in the face of potential trauma. *Current Directions in Psychological Science, 14,* 135–138.

Bonanno, G. A., & Kaltman, S. (1999). Toward an integrative perspective on bereavement. *Psychological Bulletin, 125,* 760–776.

Bonanno, G. A., & Keltner, D. (1997). Facial expressions of emotion and the course of conjugal bereavement. *Journal of Abnormal Psychology, 106,* 126–137.

Bonanno, G. A., Moskowitz, J. T., Papa, A., et al. (2005). Resilience to loss in bereaved spouses, bereaved parents, and bereaved gay men. *Journal of Personality and Social Psychology, 88,* 827–843.

Bonanno, G. A., Wortman, C. B., Lehman, D. R., et al. (2002). Resilience to loss and chronic grief: A prospective study from pre-loss to 18 months post-loss. *Journal of Personality and Social Psychology, 83,* 1150–1164.

Bond, J. T., Thompson, C., Galinsky, E., et al. (2002). *The 2002 national study of the changing workforce.* New York: Families and Work Institute.

Bonello, K., & Cross, M. C. (2010). Gay monogamy: I love you but I can't have sex with only you. *Journal of Homosexuality, 57,* 117–139.

Bookwala, J. (2009). The impact of parental care on marital quality and well-being in adult daughters and sons. *Journals of Gerontology: Psychological and Social Sciences, 4,* 339–347.

Borrell, L. N. (2009). Race, ethnicity, and self-reported hypertension. *American Journal of Public Health, 99,* 313–319.

Bouchery, E. E., Harwood, H. J., Sacks, J. J., et al. (2011). Economic costs of excessive alcohol consumption in the U.S., 2006. *American Journal of Preventive Medicine, 441,* 516–524.

Bowlby, J. (1969). *Attachment and loss: Vol. 1. Attachment.* New York: Basic Books.

Bowlby, J. (1973). *Attachment and loss: Vol. 2. Separation: Anxiety and anger.* New York, Basic Books.

Bowlby, J. (1980). *Attachment and loss: Vol. 3. Loss, sadness, and depression.* New York: Basic Books.

Brault, M. (2012). *Americans with disabilities, 2010: Household economic studies.* Retrieved November 19, 2012, from http://www.census.gov/prod/2012pubs/p70-131.pdf

Brébion, G., Smith, M. J., & Ehrlich, M. F. (1997). Working memory and aging: Deficit or strategy differences? *Aging, Neuropsychology, and Cognition, 4,* 58–73.

Brehmer, Y., Li., S.-C., Müller, V., et al. (2007). Memory plasticity across the life span: Uncovering children's latent potential. *Developmental Psychology, 43,* 465–478.

Brenner, J. (2013). *Pew Internet: Social networking.* Retrieved April 22, 2013, from http://pewinternet.org/Commentary/2012/March/Pew-Internet-Social-Networking-full-detail.aspx

Breslau, J., Lane, M., Sampson, N., et al. (2008). Mental disorders and subsequent educational attainment in a U.S. national sample. *Journal of Psychiatric Research, 42,* 708–716.

Brisette, I., Scheier, M. F., & Carver, C. S. (2002). The role of optimism and social network development, coping, and psychological adjustment during a life transition. *Journal of Personality and Social Psychology, 82,* 102–111.

Brogaard, T., Neergaard, M. A., & Sokolowski, T. (2012). Congruence between preferred and actual place of care and death among Danish cancer patients. *Palliative Medicine, 27,* 155–164.

Broman, C. L. (2005). Stress, race, and substance abuse in college. *College Student Journal, 38,* 340–352.

Bromberger, J. T., Schott, L. L., Kravitz, H. M., et al. (2010). Longitudinal change in reproductive hormones and depressive symptoms across the menopausal transition: Results from the Study of Women's Health Across the Nation (SWAN). *Archives of General Psychiatry, 67,* 598–607.

Brondolo, E., Hausmann, L. R. M., Jhalani, J., et al. (2011). Perceived racism and self-reported health in a diverse sample. *Annals of Behavioral Medicine, 42,* 14–28.

Bronfenbrenner, U. (1979). *The ecology of human development.* Cambridge, MA: Harvard University Press.

Bronfenbrenner, U., & Morris, P. A. (2006). The bioecological model of human development. In W. Damon & R. M. Lerner (Eds.), *Handbook of child psychology: Vol. 1. Theoretical models of human development* (6th ed., pp. 793–828). New York: John Wiley.

Brown, D. R., Carney, J. S., Parrish, M. S., et al. (2013). Assessing spirituality: The relationship between spirituality and mental health. *Journal of Spirituality and Mental Health, 15,* 107–122.

Brown, L. H., & Roodin, P. A. (2003). Grandparent–grandchild relationships and the life course perspective. In J. Demick & C. Andreoletti (Eds.), *Handbook of adult development* (pp. 459–474). New York: Kluwer.

Brown, S. L., & Lin, I.-F. (2012). The gray divorce revolution: Rising divorce among middle-aged and older adults, 1990–2010. *Journals of Gerontology: Psychological and Social Sciences, 67,* 731–741.

Bryant, S., & Rakowski, W. (1992). Predictors of mortality among elderly African-Americans. *Research on Aging, 14,* 50–67.

Buchner, D. M., Beresford, S. A. A., Larson, E. B., et al. (1992). Effects of physical activity on health status in older adults: II. Intervention studies. *Annual Review of Public Health, 13,* 469–488.

Buman, M. P., Hekler, E. B., Bliwise, D. L., et al. (2011). Moderators and mediators of exercise-induced objective sleep improvements in midlife and older adults with sleep complaints. *Health Psychology, 30,* 579–587.

Burack, O. R., & Lachman, M. E. (1996). The effects of list-making on recall in young and elderly adults. *Journals of Gerontology: Psychological and Social Sciences, 51,* 226–233.

Buring, J., & Lee I.-M. (2012). *Women's Health Study : Going strong for 18 years!* Retrieved October 12, 2012, from http://whs.bwh.harvard.edu/methods/html

Buss, D. M. (1997). Evolutionary foundations of personality. In R. Hogan, J. Johnson, & S. Briggs (Eds.), *Handbook of personality psychology* (pp. 317–344). San Diego, CA: Academic Press.

Buss, D. M. (2012). *Evolutionary psychology: The new science of the mind* (4th ed.). Boston: Allyn & Bacon.

Buss, D. M., & Kenrick, D. T. (1998). Evolutionary social psychology. In D. T. Gilbert, S. T. Fisk, & G. Lindzey (Eds.), *The handbook of social psychology* (4th ed., Vol. 2, pp. 982–1026). New York: McGraw-Hill.

Butler, R. N. (1993). The importance of basic research in gerontology. *Age and Ageing, 22,* S53–S55.

Calder, N., & Aitken, R. (2008). An exploratory study of the influences that comprise the sun protection of young adults. *International Journal of Consumer Studies, 32,* 579–587.

Calzo, J. P., Antonucci, T. C., Mays, V. M., et al. (2011). Retrospective recall of sexual orientation identity development among gay, lesbian, and bisexual adults. *Developmental Psychology, 47,* 1658–1673.

Campbell, J. (1949/1990). *Hero with a thousand faces.* Princeton, NJ: Princeton University Press.

Campbell, L. D., Connidis, I. A., & Davies, L. (1999). Sibling ties in later life: A social network analysis. *Journal of Family Issues, 20,* 114–148.

Campbell, L., & Ellis, B. J. (2005). Commitment, love, and mate retention. In D. M. Buss (Ed.), *The handbook of evolutionary psychology* (pp. 419–442). New York: Wiley.

Campbell, P., Wright, J., Oyebode, J., et al. (2008). Determinants of burden in those who care for someone with dementia. *International Journal of Geriatric Psychiatry, 23,* 1078–1085.

Caporeal, L. R. (1997). The evolution of truly social cognition: The core configuration model. *Personality and Social Psychology Review, 1,* 276–298.

Cappell, K. S., Gmeindl, L., & Reuter-Lorenz, P. A. (2010). Age differences in DLPFC recruitment during verbal working memory depend on memory load. *Cortex, 46,* 462–473.

Carmalt, J. H., Cawley, J., Joyner, K., et al. (2008). Body weight and matching with a physically attractive romantic partner. *Journal of Marriage and Family, 70,* 1287–1296.

Carr, D., & Springer, K. W. (2010). Advances in families and health research in the 21st century. *Journal of Marriage and Family, 72,* 743–761.

Carskadon, M. A. (2009). Sleep, adolescence, and learning. *Frontiers of Neuroscience, 3,* 470–471.

Carstensen, L. L. (1995). Evidence for a life span theory of socioemotional selectivity. *Current Directions in Psychological Science, 4,* 151–156.

Carstensen, L. L., & Mikels, J. A. (2005). At the intersection of emotion and cognition: Aging and the positivity effect. *Current Directions in Psychological Science, 14,* 117–121.

Carstensen, L. L., Isaacowitz, D. M., & Charles, S. T. (1999). Taking time seriously: A theory of socioemotional selectivity. *American Psychologist, 54,* 165–181.

Carstensen, L. L., Mickels, J. A., & Mather, M. (2006). Aging and the intersection of cognition, motivation, and emotion. In R. H. Binstock & L. K. George (Eds.), *Handbook of aging and the social sciences* (6th ed., pp. 343–362). San Diego, CA: Academic Press.

Carver, C. S. (1997). You want to measure coping but your protocol's too long: Consider the Brief COPE. *International Journal of Behavioral Medicine, 4,* 92–100.

Carver, C. S., Smith, R. G., Antoni, M. H., et al. (2005). Optimistic personality and psychosocial well-being during treatment predict psychosocial well-being among long-term survivors of breast cancer. *Health Psychology, 24,* 508–516.

Caspi, A. (1998). Personality development across the life course. In W. Damon (Series Ed.) & N. Eisenberg (Vol. Ed.), *Handbook of child psychology: Vol. 3. Social, emotional, and personality development* (pp. 311–388). New York: Wiley.

Caspi, A., & Roberts, B. W. (1999). Personality continuity and change across the life course. In L. A. Pervin & O. P. John (Eds.), *Handbook of personality psychology: Theory and research* (pp. 300–326). New York: Guilford Press.

Caspi, A., Roberts, B. W., & Shiner, R. L. (2004). Personality development: Stability and change. *Annual Review of Psychology, 56,* 453–484.

Cate, R. M., & Lloyd, S. A. (1992). *Courtship.* Newbury Park, CA: Sage.

Cate, R. M., Levin, L. A., & Richmond, L. S. (2002). Premarital relationship stability: A review of recent research. *Journal of Social and Personal Relationships, 19,* 261–284.

Catoni, C., Peters, A., Schaefer, H. M. (2008). Life history trade-offs are influenced by the diversity, availability and interactions of dietary antioxidants. *Animal Behaviour, 76,* 1107–1119.

Cattell, R. B. (1963). Theory of fluid and crystallized intelligence: A critical experiment. *Journal of Educational Psychology, 54,* 1–22.

Cattell, R. B., Eber, H. W., & Tatsuoka, M. M. (1970). *Handbook for the Sixteen Personality Factor Questionnaire.* Champaign, IL: Institute for Personality and Ability Testing.

Cavalli-Sforza, L. L., & Cavalli-Sforza, F. (1995). *The great human diasporas: The history of diversity and evolution.* Reading, MA: Addison-Wesley.

Cejka, M. A., & Eagly, A. H. (1999). Gender-stereotypic images of occupations correspond to the sex segregation of employment. *Personality and Social Psychology Bulletin, 25,* 413–423.

Centers for Disease Control and Prevention (CDC). (2009). *Difference in prevalence of obesity among black, white and Hispanic adults—United States, 2006–2008.* Retrieved June 24, 2012, from http://www.cdc.gov/mmwr/preview/mmwrhtml/mm5827a2.htm

Centers for Disease Control and Prevention (CDC). (2011a). *Arthritis related statistics.* Retrieved October 30, 2012, from http://www.cdc.gov/arthritis/data_statistics/arthritis_related_stats.htm

Centers for Disease Control and Prevention (CDC). (2011b). *Body mass index for adults and children.* Retrieved October 30, 2012, from http://www.cdc.gov/healthyweight/assessing/bmi/

Centers for Disease Control and Prevention (CDC). (2011c). *Breast cancer rates by race and ethnicity.* Retrieved January 20, 2013, from http://www.cdc.gov/cancer/breast/statistics/race.htm

Centers for Disease Control and Prevention (CDC). (2011d). *Cancer prevention and control.* Retrieved November 26, 2012, from http://www.cdc.gov/cancer/dcpc/prevention/

Centers for Disease Control and Prevention (CDC). (2012a). *An estimated 1 in 10 U.S. adults report depression.* Retrieved January 4, 2013, from http://www.cdc.gov/Features/dsDepression/

Centers for Disease Control and Prevention (CDC). (2012b). *Health: United States, 2011: With special feature on socioeconomic status and health.* Retrieved January 29, 2013, from http://www.cdc.gov/nchs/data/hus/hus11.pdf

Centers for Disease Control and Prevention (CDC). (2012c). *National program of cancer registries, 1999–2009 incidence results.* Retrieved November 26, 2012, from http://wonder.cdc.gov/controller/datarequest/D75

Centers for Disease Control and Prevention (CDC). (2012d). *Summary health statistics for U.S. adults: National Health Interview Survey, 2011.* Retrieved February 13, 2013, from http://www.cdc.gov/nchs/data/series/sr_10/sr10_256.pdf

Centers for Disease Control and Prevention (CDC). (2012e). *Underlying causes of death 1999–2010.* Retrieved January 20, 2013, from http://wonder.cdc.gov/controller/datarequest/D76;jsessionid=16267A63499929D48152365C6FD1D666

Centers for Disease Control and Prevention (CDC). (2012f). *Women and heart disease.* Retrieved November 26, 2012, from http://www.cdc.gov/women/heart/

Centers for Disease Control and Prevention (CDC). (2012g). *World Heart Day 2012: Women and children at risk.* Retrieved November 26, 2012, from http://www.cdc.gov/Features/WorldHeartDay/

Centers for Disease Control and Prevention (2013). Vision health initiative. Retrieved August 18, 2013 from http://www.cdc.gov/visionhealth/

Centofanti, M. (1998). Fear of Alzheimer's undermines health of elderly patients. *APA Monitor, 29,* 1, 33.

Cepeda, N. J., Kramer, A. F., & Gonzalez de Sather, J. C. M. (2001). Changes in executive control across the life-span: Examination of task switching performance. *Developmental Psychology, 37,* 715–730.

Cerda-Flores, R. M., Barton, S. A., Marty-Gonzales, L. F., et al. (1999). Estimation of nonpaternity in the Mexican population of Neuvo Leon: A validation study of blood group markers. *American Journal of Physical Anthropology, 109,* 281–293.

Chang, E., Wilbur, K. H., & Silverstein, M. (2010). The effects of childlessness on the care and psychological well-being of older adults with disabilities. *Aging and Mental Health, 14,* 712–719.

Charles, S. T., Mather, M., & Carstensen, L. L. (2003). Aging and emotional memory: The forgettable nature of negative images for older adults. *Journal of Experimental Psychology: General, 132,* 310–324.

Charles, S. T., Piazza, J. R., Mogle, J., et al. (2013). The wear and tear of daily stressors on mental health. *Psychological Science, 24,* 733–741.

Charness, N. (1981). Visual short-term memory and aging in chess players. *Journals of Gerontology: Psychological and Social Sciences, 36,* 615–619.

Chen, E., Miller, G. E., Kobor, M. S., et al. (2011). Maternal warmth buffers the effects of low early-life socioeconomic status on pro-inflammatory signaling in adulthood. *Molecular Psychiatry, 16,* 729–737.

Cheng, G. H.-L., & Chan, D. K.-S. (2008). Who suffers more from job insecurity? A meta-analytic review. *Applied Psychology: An International Review, 57,* 272–303.

Cherkas, L. F., Hunkin, J. L., Kato, B. S., et al. (2008). The association between physical activity in leisure time and leukocyte telomere length. *Archives of Internal Medicine, 168,* 154–158.

Cherlin, A. J. (2013). Health, marriage, and same-sex partnerships. *Journal of Health and Social Behavior, 54,* 64–66.

Cheung, F. M., Cheung, S. F., Zhang, J. X., et al. (2008). Convergent validity of the Chinese Personality Assessment Inventory and the Minnesota Multiphasic Personality Inventory-2: Preliminary findings with a normative sample. *Journal of Personality Assessment, 82,* 92–103.

Cheung, F. M., van de Vijver, F. J. R., & Leong, F. T. L. (2011). Toward a new approach to the study of personality in culture. *American Psychologist, 66,* 593–603.

Chida, Y., & Hamer, M. (2008). Chronic psychosocial factors and acute physiological responses to laboratory-induced stress in healthy populations: A quantitative review of 30 years of investigations. *Psychological Bulletin, 134,* 829–885.

Chida, Y., Steptoe, A., & Powell, L. H. (2009). Religiosity/spirituality and mortality. *Psychotherapy and Psychosomatics, 78,* 81–90.

Chin, L., & Quine, S. (2012). Common factors that enhance the quality of life for women living in their own homes or in aged care facilities. *Journal of Women & Aging, 24,* 269–279.

Chiou, W.-B., Yang, C.-C., & Wan, C.-S. (2011). Ironic effects of dietary supplementation: Illusory invulnerability created by taking dietary supplements licenses health-risk behaviors. *Psychological Science, 22,* 1081–1086.

Christensen, K., Iachina, M., Rexbye, H., et al. (2004). Looking old for your age: Genetics and mortality. *Epidemiology, 15,* 251–252.

Cicirelli, V. G. (1991). Attachment theory in old age: Protection of the attached figure. In K. Pillemer & K. McCartney (Eds.), *Parent–child relations throughout life* (pp. 2–42). Hillsdale, NJ: Erlbaum.

Clancy, S. M., & Hoyer, W. J. (1994). Age and skill in visual search. *Developmental Psychology, 30,* 545–552.

Clark, A. E., Oswald, A. J., & Warr, P. B. (1996). Is job satisfaction U-shaped in age? *Journal of Occupational Psychology, 69,* 57–81.

Clark, C. M., Schneider, J. A., Bedell, B. J., et al. (2011). Use of Florbetapir-PET for imaging β-amyloid pathology. *Journal of the American Medical Association, 305,* 275–283.

Clark, R. (2006). Perceived racism and vascular reactivity in black college women: Moderating effects of seeking social support. *Health Psychology, 25,* 20–25.

Clark, R. L., Burkhauser, R. V., Moon, M., et al. (2004). *The economics of an aging society.* Malden, MA: Blackwell.

Clarkson-Smith, L., & Hartley, A. A. (1990). The game of bridge as an exercise in working memory and reasoning. *Journals of Gerontology: Psychological and Social Sciences, 45,* 233– 238.

Clausell, E., & Roisman, G. I. (2009). Outness: Big Five personality traits and same-sex relationship quality. *Journal of Social and Personality Relationships, 26,* 211–226.

Cleary, P. D., Zaborski, L. B., & Ayanian, J. Z. (2004). Sex differences in health over the life course. In O. G. Brim, C. D. Ryff, & R. C. Kessler (Eds.), *How healthy are we? A national study of well-being at midlife* (pp. 37–63). Chicago: University of Chicago Press.

Clements, M. L., Stanley, S. M., & Markman, H. J. (2004). Before they say "I do": Discriminating among marital outcomes over 13 years. *Journal of Marriage and Family, 66,* 613–626.

Clunis, D. M., Fredriksen-Goldsen, K. I., Freeman, P. A., et al. (2005). *Lives of lesbian elders: Looking back, looking forward.* New York: Hayworth.

Coall, D. A., & Hertwig, R. (2011). Grandparental investment: A relic of the past or a resource for the future? *Current Directions in Psychological Science, 20,* 93–98.

Cohen, P. (2012). *In our prime: The invention of middle age.* New York: Scribner.

Colby, A., & Kohlberg, L. (1987). *The measurement of moral judgment: Vol. 1. Theoretical foundations and research validation.* Cambridge, MA: Cambridge University Press.

Colby, A., Kohlberg, L., Gibbs, J., et al. (1983). A longitudinal study of moral judgment. *Monographs of the Society for Research in Child Development, 48* (1–2, Serial No. 200).

Colcombe, S., & Kramer, A. F. (2003). Fitness effects on the cognitive function of older adults: A meta-analytic study. *Psychological Science, 14,* 125–130.

Colcombe, S., Erickson, K. I., Raz, N., et al. (2003). Aerobic fitness reduces brain tissue loss in aging humans. *Journals of Gerontology: Biological and Medical Sciences, 58,* 176–180.

Cole, S. W., Hawkley, L. C., Arevalo, J. M., et al. (2007). Social regulation of gene expression in human leukocytes. *Genome Biology, 8,* R189.

Colman, R. J., Anderson, R. M., Johnson, S. C., et al. (2009). Caloric restriction delays disease onset and mortality in rhesus monkeys. *Science, 325,* 201–204.

Coltrane, S. (2000). Research on household labor: Modeling and measuring the social embeddedness of routine family work. *Journal of Marriage and the Family, 62,* 1208–1233.

Compton, D. M., Bachman, L. D., Brand, D., et al. (2000). Age-associated changes in cognitive function in highly educated adults: Emerging myths and realities. *International Journal of Geriatric Psychiatry, 15,* 75–85.

Connerty, T. J., & Knott, V. (2013). Promoting positive change in the face of adversity: Experiences of cancer and posttraumatic growth. *European Journal of Cancer Care, 22,* 334–344.

Cooney, T. M., Hutchinson, K., & Leather, D. M. (1995). Surviving the breakup? Predictors of parent–adult child relations after parental divorce. *Family Relations, 44,* 63–84.

Copen, C. E., Daniels, K., Vespa, J., et al. (2012). *First marriages in the United States: Data from the 2006–2010 national survey of family growth.* Retrieved March 16, 2013, from http://www.cdc.gov/nchs/data/nhsr/nhsr049.pdf

Coren, S. (2010). Foreword. In A. H. Fine (Ed.), *Handbook on animal-assisted therapy* (3rd ed., pp. xv–xviii). San Diego, CA: Academic Press.

Cornum, R., Matthews, M. D., & Seligman, M. E. P. (2011). Comprehensive soldier fitness. *American Psychologist, 66,* 4–9.

Corr, C. A. (1993). Coping with dying: Lessons we should and should not learn from the work of Elisabeth Kubler-Ross. *Death Studies, 17,* 69–83.

Costa, P. T., Jr., & McCrae, R. R. (1997). Longitudinal stability of adult personality. In R. Hogan, J. Johnson, & S. Briggs (Eds.), *Handbook of personality psychology* (pp. 269–290). San Diego, CA: Academic Press.

Costello, C. B., Wight, V. R., & Stone, A. J. (2003). *The American woman 2003–2004.* New York: Palgrave Macmillan.

Couzin, J. (2005). To what extent are genetic variation and personal health linked? *Science, 309,* 81.

Cowan, C. P., & Cowan, P. A. (1995). Interventions to ease the transition to parenthood: Why they are needed and what they can do. *Family Relations, 44,* 412–423.

Craig, J., & Foster, H. (2013). Desistance in the transition to adulthood: The roles of marriage, military, and gender. *Deviant Behavior, 34,* 208–223.

Craik, F. I. M. (2000). Age related changes in human memory. In D. Park & N. Schwarz (Eds.), *Cognitive aging: A primer* (pp. 75–92). Philadelphia, PA: Taylor & Francis.

Craik, F. I. M., & Byrd, M. (1982). Aging and cognitive deficits: The role of attentional resources. In F. I. M. Craik & S. Trehub (Eds.), *Aging and cognitive processes* (pp. 191–211). New York: Plenum.

Crawford, D. W., & Huston, T. L. (1993). The impact of the transition to parenthood on marital leisure. *Personality and Social Psychology Bulletin, 19,* 39–46.

Cullum, S., Huppert, F. A., McGee, M., et al. (2000). Decline across different domains of cognitive function in normalageing: Results of a longitudinal population-based study using CAMCOG. *International Journal of Geriatric Psychiatry, 15,* 853–862.

Cumming, E. (1975). Engagement with an old theory. *International Journal of Aging and Human Development, 6,* 187–191.

Cumming, E., & Henry, W. E. (1961). *Growing old.* New York: Basic Books.

Cutler, S. J., Hendricks, J., & O'Neill, G. (2011). Civic engagement and aging. In R. H. Binstock & L. K. George (Eds.), *Handbook of aging and the social sciences* (7th ed., pp. 221–233). San Diego, CA: Academic Press.

Czaja, S. J., & Lee, C. C. (2001). The Internet and older adults: Design challenges and opportunities. In N. Charness & D. C. Parks (Eds.), *Communication, technology, and aging: Opportunities and challenges for the future* (pp. 60–78). New York: Springer.

Dalby, P. (2006). Is there a process of spiritual change or development associated with ageing? A critical review of research. *Aging and Mental Health, 10,* 4–12.

Danner, D. D., Snowdon, D. A., & Friesen, W. V. (2001). Positive emotions in early life and longevity: Findings from the Nun Study. *Journal of Personality and Social Psychology, 80,* 804–813.

Davis, K. D., Goodman, W. B., Perretti, A. E., et al. (2008). Nonstandard work schedules, perceived family well-being, and daily stressors. *Journal of Marriage and Family, 70,* 991–1003.

De Raad, B., Barelds, D. P. H., Levert, E., et al. (2010). Only three factors of personality description are fully replicable across languages: A comparison of 14 trait taxonomies. *Journal of Personality and Social Psychology, 98,* 160–173.

De Raedt, R., Koster, E. H. W., & Ryckewaert, R. (2013). Aging and attentional bias for death-related and general threat-related information: Less avoidance in older as compared with middle-aged adults. *Journals of Gerontology: Psychological and Social Sciences, 68,* 41–48.

de Waal, F. (1996). *Good natured: The origins of right and wrong in humans and other animals.* Cambridge, MA: Harvard University Press.

Deary, I. J., Batty, G. D., Pattie, A., et al. (2008). More intelligent, more dependable children live longer: A 55-year longitudinal study of a representative sample of the Scottish nation. *Psychological Science, 19,* 874–880.

Deci, E. L., & Ryan, R. M. (2008a). Hedonia, eudaimonia, and well-being: An introduction. *Journal of Happiness Studies, 9,* 1–11.

Deci, E. L., & Ryan, R. M. (2008b). Self-determination theory: A macrotheory of human motivation, development, and health. *Canadian Psychology, 49,* 182–185.

DeKay, W. T. (2000). Evolutionary psychology. In W. C. Nichols, N. A. Pace-Nichols, D. S. Becvar, et al. (Eds.), *Handbook of family development and intervention* (pp. 23–40). New York: Wiley.

DeKay, W. T., & Shackelford, T. K. (2000). Toward an evolutionary approach to social cognition. *Evolution and Cognition, 6,* 185–195.

Dekel, S., Ein-Dor, T., & Solomon, Z. (2012). Posttraumatic growth and posttraumatic stress: A longitudinal study. *Psychological Trauma: Theory, Research, Practice, & Policy, 4,* 94–101.

DeLamater, J. (2012). Sexual expression in later life: A review and synthesis. *Journal of Sex Research, 49,* 125–141.

DeLamater, J., & Moorman, S. M. (2007). Sexual behavior in later life. *Journal of Aging and Health, 19,* 921–945.

DeLongis. A., & Holtzman, S. (2005). Coping in context: The role of stress, social support, and personality in coping. *Journal of Personality, 73,* 1633–1656.

Denollet, J., Martens, E. J., Nyklicek, I., et al. (2008). Clinical events in coronary patients who report low distress: Adverse effect of repressive coping. *Health Psychology, 27,* 302–308.

Derby, R. W., & Ayala, J. (2013). Am I my brother's keeper? Adult siblings raising younger siblings. *Journal of Human Behavior in the Social Environment, 23,* 193–210.

Desrichard, O., & Köpetz, C. (2005). A threat in the elder: The impact of task instructions, self-efficacy and performance expectations on memory performance in the elderly. *European Journal of Social Psychology, 35,* 537–552.

Diekman, A. B., Eagly, A. H., Mladinic, A., et al. (2005). Dynamic stereotypes about women and men in Latin America and the United States. *Journal of Cross-Cultural Psychology, 36,* 209–226.

Diener, E., & Diener, C. (1996). Most people are happy. *Psychological Science, 7,* 181–183.

Diener, E., & Suh, E. (1998). Measuring quality of life: Economic, social, and subjective indicators. *Social Indicators Research, 40,* 189–216.

Diener, E., Gohm, C. L., Suh, E., et al. (2000). Similarity of the relations between marital status and subjective well-being across cultures. *Cultural Psychology, 31,* 419–436.

Dixon, R. A. (2000). Concepts and mechanisms of gains in cognitive aging. In D. Park & N. Schwarz (Eds.), *Cognitive aging: A primer* (pp. 23–42). Philadelphia, PA: Taylor & Francis.

Dixon, R. A., de Frias, C. M., & Maitland, S. B. (2001). Memory in midlife. In M. E. Lachman (Ed.), *Handbook of midlife development* (pp. 248–278). New York: Wiley.

Dougall, A. L., & Baum, A. (2001). Stress, health and illness. In A. Baum, T. A. Revenson, & J. E. Singer (Eds.), *Handbook of health psychology* (pp. 321–337). Mahwah, NJ: Erlbaum.

Douglass, C. B. (2007). From duty to desire: Emerging adulthood in Europe and its consequences. *Child Development Perspectives, 1,* 101–108.

Duvall Antonacopoulos, N. M., & Pychyl, T. A. (2010). An examination of the potential role of pet ownership, human social support, and pet attachment in the psychological health of individuals living alone. *Anthrozoö, 23,* 37–54.

Dweck, C. S. (2008). Can personality be changed? The role of beliefs in personality and change. *Current Directions in Psychological Science, 17,* 391–394.

Dykiert, D., Der, G., Starr, J. M., et al. (2012). Sex differences in reaction time mean and intraindividual variability across the life span. *Developmental Psychology, 48,* 1262–1276.

Eagly, A. H. (1987). *Sex differences in social behavior: A social role interpretation.* Hillsdale, NJ: Erlbaum.

Eagly, A. H. (1995). The science and politics of comparing men and women. *American Psychologist, 50,* 145–158.

Eagly, A. H., & Wood, W. (1999). The origins of sex differences in human behavior: Evolved dispositions versus social roles. *American Psychologist, 54,* 408–423.

Eagly, A. H., & Wood, W. (2011). Feminism and the evolution of sex differences and similarities. *Sex Roles, 64,* 758–767.

Eagly, A. H., & Wood, W. (2012). Social role theory. In P. A. M. Van Lange, A. W. Kruglanski, & E. T. Higgins (Eds.), *Handbook of theories of social psychology* (Vol. 2, pp. 458–476). Los Angeles, CA: Sage.

Earles, J. L., Kersten, A. W., Curtayne, E. S., et al. (2008). That's the man who did it, or was it a woman? Actor similarity and binding errors in event memory. *Psychonomic Bulletin Review, 15,* 1185–1189.

Edwards, B. K., Brown, M., Wingo, P. A., et al. (2005). Annual report to the nation on the status of cancer, 1975–2002, featuring population-based trends in cancer treatment. *Journal of the National Cancer Institute, 97,* 1407–1427.

Eheman, C., Henley, S. J., Ballard-Barbash, R., et al. (2012). Annual report to the nation on the status of cancer, 1975–2008, featuring cancers associated with excess weight and lack of sufficient physical activity. *Cancer, 118,* 2338–2366.

Ehlers, A., Mayou, R. A., & Bryant, B. (1998). Psychological predictors of chronic posttraumatic stress disorder after motor vehicle accidents. *Journal of Abnormal Psychology, 107,* 508–519.

Ehrensaft, M., Moffitt, T. E., & Caspi, A. (2004). Clinically abusive relationships in an unselected birth cohort: Men's and women's participation and developmental antecedents. *Journal of Abnormal Psychology, 113,* 258–270.

Einstein, G. O., & McDaniel, M. A. (2005). Prospective memory: Multiple retrieval processes. *Current Directions in Psychological Science, 14,* 286–290.

Elder, G. H., Jr. (1979). Historical change in life patterns and personality. In P. B. Baltes & O. G. Brim, Jr. (Eds.), *Lifespan development and behavior* (Vol. 2, pp. 117–159). New York: Academic Press.

Elder, G. H., Jr. (1995). The life course paradigm: Social change and individual development. In P. Moen, G. H. Elder, Jr., & K. Luscher (Eds.), *Examining lives in context: Perspectives on the ecology of human development* (pp. 101–139). Washington, DC: American Psychological Association.

Elder, G. H., Jr. (2001). Life course: Sociological aspects. In N. J. Smelser & P. B. Baltes (Eds.), *International encyclopedia of the social and behavioral sciences* (Vol. 13, pp. 8817–8821). Oxford, England: Elsevier.

Ellis, B. J., & Ketelaar, T. (2000). On the natural selection of alternative models: Evaluation of explanations in evolutionary psychology. *Psychological Inquiry, 11,* 56–68.

Ellis, L., Wahab, E. A., & Ratnasingan, M. (2013). Religiosity and fear of death. *Mental Health, Religion, and Culture, 16,* 179–199.

Ellis, M. J., Ding, L., Shen, D., et al. (2012). Whole genome analysis informs breast cancer response to aromatase inhibition. *Nature, 486,* 353–360.

Emanuel, E. J., Fairclough, D. L., & Emanuel, L. L. (2000). Attitudes and desires related to euthanasia and physician-assisted suicide among terminally ill patients and their caregivers. *Journal of the American Medical Association, 284,* 2460–2468.

Emery, C. F., & Gatz, M. (1990). Psychological and cognitive effects of an exercise program for community-residing older adults. *The Gerontologist, 30,* 184–192.

Emery, C. F., Finkel, D., & Pedersen, N. L. (2012). Pulmonary function as a cause of cognitive aging. *Psychological Science, 23,* 1024–1032.

Employee Benefit Research Institute. (2012). *The 2012 retirement confidence survey: Job insecurity, debt weigh on retirement confidence, savings.* Retrieved May 10, 2013, from http://www.ebri.org/pdf/briefspdf/EBRI_IB_03-2012_No369_RCS2.pdf

Epel, E. S., Blackburn, E. H., Lin, J., et al. (2004). Accelerated telomere shortening in response to life stress. *Proceedings of the National Academy of Sciences U.S.A., 101,* 17312–17315.

Epelbaum, E. (2008). Neuroendocrinology and aging. *Journal of Neuroendocrinology, 20,* 808–811.

Ericksen, J. A., & Schultheiss, D. E. P. (2009). Women pursuing careers in trades and construction. *Journal of Career Development, 36,* 68–89.

Erikson, E. H. (1950). *Childhood and society.* New York: Norton.

Erikson, E. H. (1959). *Identity and the life cycle.* New York: Norton. (Reissued 1980.)

Erikson, E. H. (1982). *The life cycle completed.* New York: Norton.

Eriksson, P. S., Perfilieva, E., Bjork-Eriksson, T., et al. (1998). Neurogenesis in the adult hippocampus. *Nature Medicine, 4,* 1313–1317.

Ertel, K. A., Glymour, M. M., & Berkman, L. F. (2009). Social networks and health: A life course perspective integrating observational and experimental evidence. *Journal of Social and Personal Relationships, 26,* 73–92.

Eshbaugh, E., & Henninger, W. (2013). Potential mediators of the relationship between gender and death anxiety. *Individual Differences Research, 11,* 22–30.

Evans, R. I. (1969). *Dialogue with Erik Erikson.* New York: Dutton.

Eysenck, H. J. (1976). *Sex and personality.* Austin, TX: University of Texas Press.

Fabre, B., Grosman, H., Mazza, O., et al. (2013). Relationship between cortisol, life events, and metabolic syndrome in men. *Stress: The International Journal of the Biology of Stress, 16,* 16–23.

Facio, A., Resett, S., Micocci, F., et al. (2007). Emerging adulthood in Argentina: An age of diversity and possibilities. *Child Development Perspectives, 1,* 115–118.

Fahey, T., & Smyth, E. (2004). Do subjective indicators measure welfare? Evidence from 33 European countries. *European Societies, 6,* 5–27.

Fahlander, K., Wahlin, Å., Fastborn, J., et al. (2000). The relationship between signs of cardiovascular deficiency and cognitive performance in old age: A population-based study. *Journals of Gerontology: Psychological and Social Sciences, 55,* 259–265.

Family Caregiver Alliance. (2012). *Selected caregiver statistics.* Retrieved May 8, 2013, from http://www.caregiver.org/caregiver/jsp/content_node.jsp?nodeid=439

Federal Interagency Forum on Aging Related Statistics. (2012). *Older Americans 2012: Key indicators of well-being.* Retrieved March 23, 2013, from http://www.agingstats.gov/Main_Site/Data/2012_Documents/docs/EntireChartbook.pdf

Feeney, J., & Noller, P. (1996). *Adult attachment.* Thousand Oaks, CA: Sage.

Feifel, H. (1990). Psychology and death: Meaningful rediscovery. *American Psychologist, 45,* 537–543.

Feld, S., & George, L. K. (1994). Moderating effects of prior social resources on the hospitalizations of elders who become widowed. *Aging and Health, 6,* 275–295.

Feldman, H. (1971). The effects of children on the family. In A. Michel (Ed.), *Family issues of employed women in Europe and America.* Leiden, Germany: E. J. Brill.

Ferraro, K. F. (2001). Aging and role transitions. In R. H. Binstock & L. K. George (Eds.), *Handbook of aging and the social sciences* (5th ed., pp. 313–330). San Diego, CA: Academic Press.

Field, B. (2005). *Science hero: Dame Cicely Saunders.* Retrieved May 16, 2006, from http://myhero.com/myhero.asp?hero=Cicely_Saunders>06

Field, D., & Millsap, R. E. (1991). Personality in advanced old age: Continuity or change? *Journals of Gerontology: Psychological and Social Sciences, 46,* 299–308.

Field. D. (1999). Continuity and change in friendships in advanced old age: Findings from the Berkeley older generation study. *International Journal of Aging and Human Development, 48,* 325–346.

Finch C. E., & Crimmins, E. M. (2004). Inflammatory exposure and historical changes in human life-spans. *Science, 305,* 1736–1739.

Finch, C. E., & Austad, S. N. (2001). History and prospects: Symposium on organisms with slow aging. *Experimental Gerontology, 36,* 593–597.

Fingerman, K. L., Cheng, Y.-P., Birditt, K., et al. (2012). Only as happy as the least happy child: Multiple grown children's problems and successes and middle-aged parents' well-being. *Journals of Gerontology: Psychological and Social Sciences, 67*, 184–193.

Fingerman, K. L., Cheng, Y.-P., Tighe, L., et al. (2011). Parent–child relationships in young adulthood. In A. Booth, S. L. Brown, N. Landale, et al. (Eds.), *Early adulthood in a family context.* New York: Springer.

Fingerman, K. L., Miller, L. M., Birditt, K. S., et al. (2009). Giving to the good and the needy: Parental support of grown children. *Journal of Marriage and Family, 71*, 1220–1233.

Fingerman, K. L., Pillemer, K. A., Silverstein, M., et al. (2012). The Baby Boomers' intergenerational relationship. *The Gerontologist, 52*, 199–209.

Fingerman, K. L., VanderDrift, L. E., Dotterer, A., et al. (2011). Support of grown children and aging parents in Black and White families. *The Gerontologist, 51*, 441–452.

Finkel, E. J., Eastwick, P. W., Karney, B. R., et al. (2012). Online dating: A critical analysis from the perspective of psychological science. *Psychological Science in the Public Interest, 13*, 3–66.

Fisher, H. L. (2000). Lust, attraction, attachment: Biology and evolution of the three primary emotion systems for mating, reproduction, and parenting. *Journal of Sex Education and Therapy, 25*, 96–104.

Fisher, H. L. (2004). *Why we love: The nature and chemistry of romantic love.* New York: Henry Holt.

Fleeson, W. (2004). The quality of American life at the end of the century. In O. G. Brim, C. D. Ryff, & R. C. Kessler (Eds.), *How healthy are we? A national study of well-being at midlife* (pp. 252–272). Chicago: University of Chicago Press.

Flinn, M. V., Ward, C. V., & Noone, R. J. (2005). Hormones and the human family. In D. M. Buss (Ed.), *The handbook of evolutionary psychology* (pp. 552–580). New York: Wiley.

Florian, V., Mikulincer, M., & Taubman, O. (1995). Does hardiness contribute to mental health during a stressful real-life situation? The roles of appraisal and coping. *Journal of Personality and Social Psychology, 68*, 687–695.

Florido, R., Tchkonia, T., & Kirkland, J. L. (2011). Aging and adipose tissue. In E. J. Masoro & S. N. Austad (Eds.), *Handbook of the biology of aging* (7th ed., pp. 119–139). San Diego, CA: Academic Press.

Floyd, K., & Morman, M. T. (2005). Fathers' and sons' reports of fathers' affectionate communication: Implications of a naïve theory of affection. *Journal of Social and Personal Relationships, 22*, 99–109.

Flynn, J. R. (1987). Massive IQ gains in 14 nations: What IQ tests really measure. *Psychological Bulletin, 101*, 171–191.

Flynn, J. R. (2007). *What is intelligence? Beyond the Flynn effect.* New York: Cambridge University Press.

Folkman, S., & Moskowitz, J. T. (2004). Coping: Pitfalls and promises. *Annual Review of Psychology, 55*, 745–774.

Fontana, L., Colman, R. J., Holloszy, J. O., et al. (2011). Calorie restriction in nonhuman and human primates. In E. J. Masoro & S. N. Austad (Eds.), *Handbook of the biology of aging* (7th ed., pp. 447–462). San Diego, CA: Academic Press.

Foskett, N., Dyke, M., & Maringe, F. (2008). The influence of the school in the decision to participate in learning post-16. *British Educational Research Journal, 34*, 37–61.

Foster, A. C., & Kreisler, C. J. (2012). *Beyond the numbers: How parents use time and money.* U.S. Bureau of Labor Statistics. Retrieved March 19, 2013, from http://www.bls.gov/opub/btn/volume-1/how-parents-use-time-money.htm

Fouad, N. A., & Bynner, J. (2008). Work transitions. *American Psychologist, 63*, 241–251.

Fowler, J. (1981). *Stages of faith.* New York: Harper & Row.

Fowler, J. (1983). Stages of faith: PT conversation with James Fowler. *Psychology Today, 17*, 55–62.

Fowler, J. W. (2001). *Weaving the new creation: Stages of faith and the public church.* Eugene, OR: Wipf and Stock.

Fraley, R. C., & Shaver, P. R. (1999). Loss and bereavement: Attachment theory and recent controversies concerning "grief work" and the nature of detachment. In J. Cassidy & P. R. Shaver (Eds.), *Handbook of attachment: Theory, research, and clinical approaches* (pp. 239–260). New York: Guilford Press.

Fraley, R. C., Roisman, G. I., Booth-LaForce, C., et al. (2013). Interpersonal and genetic origins of adult attachment styles: A longitudinal study from infancy to early adulthood. *Journal of Personality and Social Psychology, 104*, 817–838.

Frankl, V. E. (1984). *Man's search for meaning* (3rd ed.). New York: Simon & Schuster.

Fraser, J., Maticka-Tyndale, E., & Smylie, L. (2004). Sexuality of Canadian women at midlife. *Canadian Journal of Human Sexuality, 13*, 171–187.

Freedman, V. A. (2011). Disability, functioning, and aging. In R. H. Binstock & L. K. George (Eds.), *Handbook of aging and the social sciences* (7th ed., pp. 57–71). San Diego, CA: Academic Press.

Friedman, B. X., Bleske, A. L., & Scheyd, G. L. (2000). Incompatible with evolutionary theorizing. *American Psychologist, 55*, 1059–1060.

Friedman, M. J. (2005). Introduction: Every crisis is an opportunity. *CNS Spectrum, 10*, 96–98.

Friedman, M., & Rosenman, R. H. (1959). Association of a specific overt behavior pattern with increases in blood cholesterol, blood clotting time, incidence of arcus senilis and clinical coronary artery disease. *Journal of the American Medical Association, 169*, 1286–1296.

Fromm, E. (1956). *The art of loving.* New York: Harper & Row.

Fukunaga, A., Uematsu, H., & Sugimoto, K. (2005). Influence of aging on taste perception and oral somatic sensation. *Journals of Gerontology: Biological and Medical Sciences, 60*, 109–113.

Fuller-Iglasias, H., Sellars, B., & Antonucci, T. C. (2008). Resilience in old age: Social relations as a protective factor. *Research in Human Development, 5*, 181–193.

Fung, H. H., & Carstensen, L. L. (2003). Sending memorable messages to the old: Age differences in preferences and memory for advertisements. *Journal of Personality and Social Psychology, 85*, 163–178.

Galambos, N. L., & Martinez, M. L. (2007). Poised for emerging adulthood in Latin America: A pleasure for the privileged. *Child Development Perspectives, 1*, 109–114.

Galambos, N. L., Barker, E. T., & Krahn, H. J. (2006). Depression, self-esteem, and anger in emerging adulthood: Seven-year trajectories. *Developmental Psychology, 42*, 350–365.

Gallagher, M. W., Lopez, S. J., & Pressman, S. D. (2013). Optimism is universal: Exploring the presence and benefits of optimism in a representative sample of the world. *Journal of Personality, 4*, 544–549.

Gana, K., Alaphilippe, D., & Bailey, N. (2004). Positive illusions and mental and physical health in later life. *Aging and Mental Health, 8*, 58–64.

Garcia, J. R., Reiber, C., Massey, S. G., et al. (2012). Sexual hookup culture: A review. *Review of General Psychology, 16*, 161–176.

Gates, G. J. (2011). *How many people are lesbian, gay, bisexual, and transgender?* Retrieved April 9, 2013, from http://williamsinstitute.law.ucla.edu/wp-content/uploads/Gates-How-Many-People-LGBT-Apr-2011.pdf

Gates, G. J. (2013). *Same-sex and different-sex couples in the American Community Survey: 2005–2011.* Retrieved April 9, 2013, from http://williamsinstitute.law.ucla.edu/wp-content/uploads/ACS-2013.pdf

Geary, D. C. (2005). Evolution of paternal investment. In D. M. Buss (Ed.), *The handbook of evolutionary psychology* (pp. 483–505). New York: Wiley.

George, L. G., Helson, R., & John, O. P. (2011). The "CEO" of women's work lives: How the Big Five Conscientiousness, Extraversion, and Openness predict 50 years of work experiences in a changing sociocultural context. *Journal of Personality and Social Psychology, 101*, 812–830.

George, L. K. (2006). Perceived quality of life. In R. H. Binstock & L. K. George (Eds.), *Handbook of aging and the social sciences* (pp. 320–336). San Diego, CA: Academic Press.

Geurts, T., van Tilburg, T. G., & Poortman, A.-R. (2012). The grandparent–grandchild relationship in childhood and into adulthood: A matter of continuation? *Personal Relationships, 19*, 267–278.

Gibbs, W. W. (2004). Untangling the roots of cancer. *Scientific American, 14*, 60–69.

Gidron, Y., Davidson, K., & Bata, I. (1999). The short-term effects of a hostility-reduction intervention on male coronary heart disease patients. *Health Psychology, 18*, 416–420.

Giele, J. Z. (1982). Women in adulthood: Unanswered questions. In J. Z. Giele (Ed.), *Women in the middle years* (pp. 1–36). New York: Wiley.

Gilligan, C. (1982). *In a different voice: Psychological theory and women's development*. Cambridge, MA: Harvard University Press.

Gluckman, P. D., & Hanson, M. A. (2004). Living with the past: Evolution, development, and pattern of disease. *Science, 305*, 1733–1739.

Glueck, S., & Glueck, E. (1950). *Unraveling juvenile delinquency*. New York: Commonwealth Fund.

Glueck, S., & Glueck, E. (1968). *Delinquents and nondelinquents in perspective*. Cambridge, MA: Harvard University Press.

Goel, M. S., McCarthy, E. P., Phillips, R. S., et al. (2004). Obesity among U.S. immigrant subgroups by duration of residence. *Journal of the American Medical Association, 292*, 2860–2867.

Goh, J. O., An, Y., & Resnick, S. M. (2012). Differential trajectories of age-related changes in components of executive and memory processes. *Psychology and Aging, 27*, 707–719.

Gohdes, D. M., Balamurugan, A., Larsen, B. A., et al. (2005). Age-related eye diseases: An emerging challenge for public health professionals. *Preventing Chronic Disease, 2*, 1–5.

Gold, D. T. (1996). Continuities and discontinuities in sibling relationships across the life span. In V. L. Bengtson (Ed.), *Adulthood and aging: Research on continuities and discontinuities*. New York: Springer.

Gold, J. M. (2012). Typologies of cohabitation: Implications for clinical practice and research. *The Family Journal, 20*, 315–321.

Goldberg, A. E., & Perry-Jenkins, M. (2007). The division of labor and perceptions of parental roles: Lesbian couples across the transition to parenthood. *Journal of Social and Personal Relationships, 24*, 297–318.

Goldberg, A. E., Smith, J. Z., & Perry-Jenkins, M. (2012). The division of labor in lesbian, gay, and heterosexual new adoptive parents. *Journal of Marriage and Family, 74*, 812–828.

Gómez-Pinilla, F. (2008). Brainfoods: The effect of nutrients on brain function. *Nature Reviews Neuroscience, 9*, 568–578.

Gonyea, J. G., & Hooyman, N. R. (2005). Reducing poverty among older women: Social security reform and gender equality. *Families in Society, 86*, 338–346.

Gorman, E. H. (2000). Marriage and money: The effect of marital status on attitudes toward pay and finance. *Work and Occupations, 27*, 64–88.

Gorman, J. M. (2005). In the wake of trauma. *CNS Spectrums, 10*, 81–85.

Gottfredson, L. S., & Deary, I. J. (2004). Intelligence predicts health and longevity, but why? *Current Directions in Psychological Science, 13*, 1–4.

Gottfried, A. E. (2005). Maternal and dual-earner employment and children's development: Redefining the research agenda. In D. Halpern & S. E. Murphy (Eds.), *From work-family balance to work-family interaction: Changing the metaphor* (pp. 197–217). Mahwah, NJ: Erlbaum.

Gottman, J. M. (2011). *The science of trust: Emotional attunement for couples*. New York: W. W. Norton.

Gottman, J. M., & Notarius, C. I. (2000). Marital research in the 20th century and a research agenda for the 21st century. *Family Process, 41*, 159–197.

Gough, H. G. (1957/1987). *Manual for the California Psychological Inventory*. Palo Alto, CA: Consulting Psychologists Press.

Gow, A. J., Johnson, W., Pattie, A., et al. (2011). Stability and change in intelligence from age 11 to ages 70, 79, and 87: The Lothian Birth Cohorts of 1921 and 1936. *Psychology and Aging, 26*, 232–240.

Goyer, A. (2010). *More grandparents raising grandchildren*. Retrieved March 21, 2013, from http://www.aarp.org/relationships/grandparenting/info-12-2010/more_grandparents_raising_grandchildren.html

Green, R. J. (2004). Risk and resilience in lesbian and gay couples: Comment on Solomon, Rothblum, & Balsam (2004). *Journal of Family Psychology, 18*, 290–292.

Greenberg, G., Halpern, C. T., Hood, K. E., et al. (2010). Developmental systems, nature-nurture, and the role of genes in behavior and development: On the legacy of Gilbert Gottlieb. In G. Greenberg, C. T. Halpern, K. E. Hood, et al. (Eds.), *Handbook of developmental systems, behavior and genetics*. Malden, MA: Wiley Blackwell.

Greendale, G. A., Kritz-Silverstein, D., Seeman, T., et al. (2000). Higher basal cortisol predicts verbal memory loss in postmenopausal women: Rancho Bernardo Study. *Journal of the American Geriatrics Society, 48*, 1655–1658.

Greenfield, E. A., & Marks, N. F. (2004). Formal volunteering as a protective factor or older adults' psychological well-being. *Journals of Gerontology: Psychological and Social Sciences, 59*, 258–264.

Greenwood, J. L. (2013). Parent-child relationships in the context of a mid- to late-life parental divorce. *Journal of Divorce and Remarriage, 53*, 1–17.

Greer, S. (1991). Psychological response to cancer and survival. *Psychological Medicine, 21*, 43–49.

Gregoire, J., & Van der Linden, M. (1997). Effects of age on forward and backward digit span. *Aging, Neuropsychology, and Cognition, 4*, 140–149.

Greve, W., & Bjorklund, D. F. (2009). The Nestor effect: Extending evolutionary psychology to a lifespan perspective. *Developmental Review, 29*, 163–179.

Gross, A. L., & Rebok, G. W. (2011). Memory training and strategy use in older adults: Results from the ACTIVE Study. *Psychology and Aging, 26*, 503–517.

Gruber-Baldini, A. L., Schaie, K. W., & Willis, S. L. (1995). Similarity in married couples: A longitudinal study of mental abilities and flexible-rigidity. *Journal of Personality and Social Psychology: Personality Processes and Individual Differences, 69*, 191–203.

Grunberg, L., Moore, S. Y., & Greenberg, E. (2001). Differences in psychological and physical health among layoff survivors: The effect of layoff contact. *Journal of Occupational Health Psychology, 6*, 15–25.

Gruntmanis, U. (2012). The roles of 5α-reductase inhibition in men receiving testosterone replacement therapy. *Journal of the American Medical Association, 307*, 968–970.

Gupta, S. (2006). The consequences of maternal employment during men's childhood for their adult housework performance. *Gender and Society, 20,* 60–86.

Guralnik, J. M., & Simonsick, E. M. (1993). Physical disability in older Americans [Special issue]. *Journals of Gerontology, 48,* 3–10.

Gurin, P., & Brim, O. G., Jr. (1984). Change in self in adulthood: The example of a sense of control. In P. B. Baltes & O. G. Brim, Jr. (Eds.), *Life-span development and behavior* (pp. 282–334). Orlando, FL: Academic Press.

Gutmann, D. (1975). Parenthood: A key to the comparative study of the life cycle. In N. Datan & L. H. Ginsberg (Eds.), *Life-span developmental psychology: Normative life crises* (pp. 167–184). New York: Academic Press.

Gutmann, D. (1987). *Reclaimed powers: Toward a new psychology of men and women in later life.* New York: Basic Books.

Haan, N. (1981). Common dimensions of personality development: Early adolescence to middle life. In D. H. Eichorn, J. A. Clausen, N. Haan, et al. (Eds.), *Present and past in middle life* (pp. 117–153). New York: Academic Press.

Hagestad, G. O., & Neugarten, B. L. (1985). Age and the life course. In R. H. Binstock & E. Shana (Eds.), *Handbook of aging and the social sciences* (2nd ed., pp. 35–61). New York: Van Nostrand Reinhold.

Haight, B. K. (1992). Long-term effects of a structured life review process. *Journals of Gerontology: Psychological and Social Sciences, 47,* 312–315.

Hale, S., Rose, N. S., Myerson, J., et al. (2011). The structure of working memory abilities across the adult life span. *Psychology and Aging, 26,* 92–110.

Halpern, D. F. (2005). Psychology at the intersection of work and family: Recommendations for employers, working families, and policymakers. *American Psychologist, 60,* 397–409.

Halter, J. B. (2011). Aging and insulin secretion. In E. J. Masoro & S. N. Austad (Eds.), *Handbook of the biology of aging* (pp. 373–384). San Diego, CA: Academic Press.

Hanson, R. F., Kilpatrick, D. G., Freedy, J. R., et al. (1995). Los Angeles County after the 1992 civil disturbance: Degree of exposure and impact on mental health. *Journal of Consulting and Clinical Psychology, 63,* 987–996.

Harding, S. R., Flannelly, K. J., Weaver, A. J., et al. (2005). The influence of religion on death anxiety and death acceptance. *Mental Health, Religion, & Culture, 8,* 253–261.

Hardy, D. J., & Parasuraman, R. (1997). Cognition and flight performance in older pilots. *Journal of Experimental Psychology: Applied, 3,* 313–348.

Hardy, M. A., & Shuey, K. (2000). Retirement. In E. F. Borgatta & M. L. Borgatta (Eds.), *Encyclopedia of sociology.* New York: Macmillan.

Hareven, T. K. (2001). Historical perspectives on aging and family relations. In R. H. Binstock & L. K. George (Eds.), *Handbook of aging and the social sciences* (5th ed., pp. 141–159). San Diego, CA: Academic Press.

Harman, J. J. (2011). How similar or different are homosexual and heterosexual relationships? In G. W. Lewandowski, Jr., T. J. Loving, B. Le, et al. *The science of relationships* (pp. 60–66). Dubuque, IA: Kendall Hunt.

Harmon, D. (1956). Aging: A theory based on free radical and radiation chemistry. *Journal of Gerontology, 11,* 298–300.

Harmon, K. (2012). How we all will live to be 100. *Scientific American, 307,* 54–57.

Harrington Myer, M., & Herd, P. (2007). *Market friendly or family friendly? The state and gender equality in old age.* New York: Russell Sage.

Harris Poll. (2005). *The religions and other beliefs of Americans 2005.* Retrieved May 16, 2006, from http://www.harrisinteractive.com/harris_poll/index.asp?PID=618

Harris Poll. (2007). *Belief in God.* Retrieved March 22, 2010, from http://www.galluppoll.com/

Harris Poll. (2011). *More than 9 out of 10 Americans continue to believe in God.* Retrieved June 25, 2013, from http://www.gallup.com/poll/147887/americans-continue-believe-god.aspx

Harrison, E. D., Strong, R., Sharp, Z. D., et al. (2009). Rapamycin fed late in life extends lifespan in genetically heterogeneous mice. *Nature, 460,* 392–395.

Hartung, P. J., & Niles, S. G. (2000). Using traditional career theories with college students. In D. Luzzo (Ed.), *Career development of college students: Translating theory and research into practice* (pp. 3–22). Washington, DC: American Psychological Association.

Hasher, L., & Zacks, R. T. (1988). Working memory, comprehension, and aging: A review and a new view. In G. H. Bower (Ed.), *The psychology of learning and motivation* (Vol. 2, pp. 193–225). San Diego, CA: Academic Press.

Hatfield, E. (1988). Passionate and compassionate love. In R. J. Sternberg & M. L. Barnes (Eds.), *The psychology of love* (pp. 191–217). New Haven, CT: Yale University Press.

Hawkes, K., O'Connell, J. F., & Blurton Jones, N. G. (1997). Hazda women's time allocation, offspring provisioning, and the evolution of long post-menopausal lifespans. *Current Anthropology, 38,* 551–577.

Hawkins, D. N., & Booth, A. (2005). Unhappily ever after: Effects of long-term, low quality marriages on well-being. *Social Forces, 84,* 451–471.

Hawkins, H. L., Kramer, A. F., & Capaldi, D. (1992). Aging, exercise, and attention. *Psychology and Aging, 7,* 643–653.

Hay, E. L., Fingerman, K. L., & Lefkowitz, E. S. (2007). The experience of worry in parent-adult child relationships. *Personal Relationships, 14,* 605–622.

Hayflick, L. (1977). The cellular basis for biological aging. In C. E. Finch & L. Hayflick (Eds.), *Handbook of the biology of aging* (pp. 159–186). New York: Van Nostrand Reinhold.

Hayflick, L. (1994). *How and why we age.* New York: Ballantine Books.

Hazan, C., & Shaver, P. (1987). Romantic love conceptualized as an attachment process. *Journal of Personality and Social Psychology, 52,* 511–524.

Hazan, C., & Shaver, P. (1990). Love and work: An attachment-theoretical perspective. *Journal of Personality and Social Psychology, 59,* 270–280.

Hazell, L. V. (1997). Cross-cultural funeral rites. *Director, 69,* 53–55.

He, W., & Muenchrath, M. N. (2011). *90+ in the United States: 2006–2008.* U.S. Census Bureau. Retrieved February 12, 2013, from www.census.gov/prod/2011pubs/acs-17.pdf

Heath, C. W. (1945). *What people are.* Cambridge, MA: Harvard University Press.

Heckhausen, J. (2001). Adaptation and resilience in midlife. In M. E. Lachman (Ed.), *Handbook of midlife development* (pp. 345–394). New York: Wiley.

Heggestad, E. D., & Andrew, A. M. (2012). Aging, personality, and work attitudes. In W. C. Borman & J. W. Hedge (Eds.), *The Oxford handbook of work and aging* (pp. 256–279). New York: Oxford University Press.

Helms, S. T. (1996). Some experimental tests of Holland's congruity hypothesis: The reactions of high school students to occupational simulations. *Journal of Career Assessment, 4,* 253–268.

Helson, R., & Kwan, V. S. Y. (2000). Personality development in adulthood: The broad picture and processes in one longitudinal sample. In S. Hampson (Ed.), *Advances in personality psychology* (Vol. 1, pp. 77–106). London, England: Routledge.

Helson, R., & Roberts, B. W. (1994). Ego development and personality change in adulthood. *Journal of Personality and Social Psychology, 66,* 911–920.

Helson, R., Kwan, V. S. Y., John, O. P., et al. (2002). The growing evidence for personality change in adulthood: Findings from research with personality inventories. *Journal of Research in Personality, 36,* 287–306.

Helson, R., Pals, J., & Solomon, M. (1997). Is there adult development distinctive to women? In R. Hogan, J. Johnson, & S. Briggs (Eds.), *Handbook of personality psychology* (pp. 291–314). San Diego, CA: Academic Press.

Henderson, C. E., Hayslip, B., Jr., Sanders, L. M., et al. (2009). Grandmother–grandchild relationship quality predicts psychological adjustment among youth from divorced families. *Journal of Family Issues, 30,* 1245–1264.

Henretta, J. C. (2001). Work and retirement. In R. Binstock & L. George (Eds.), *Handbook of aging and the social sciences* (pp. 255–271). San Diego, CA: Academic Press.

Henry, J. D., MacLeod, M. S., Phillips, L. H., et al. (2004). A meta-analytic review of prospective memory and aging. *Psychology and Aging, 19,* 27–39.

Heppner, M. J., & Heppner, P. P. (2009). On men and work: Taking the road less traveled. *Journal of Career Development, 36,* 49–67.

Hequembourg, A., & Brallier, S. (2005). Gendered stories of parental caregiving among siblings. *Journal of Aging Studies, 19,* 53–71.

Herd, P., Goesling, B., & House, J. S. (2007). Unpacking the relationship between socioeconomic position and health. *Journal of Health and Social Behavior, 48,* 223–238.

Herd, P., Robert, S. A., & House, J. S. (2011). Health disparities among older adults: Life course influences and policy solutions. In R. H. Binstock & L. K. George (Eds.), *Handbook of aging and the social sciences* (7th ed., pp. 121–134). San Diego, CA: Academic Press.

Heron, M., Hoyert, D. L., Murphy, S. L., et al. (2009). Deaths: Final data for 2006. *National Vital Statistics Reports, 57,* 1–134.

Hershey, D. A., & Wilson, J. A. (1997). Age differences in performance awareness on a complex financial decision-making task. *Experimental Aging Research, 23,* 257– 273.

Hess, T. M. (2005). Memory and aging in context. *Psychological Bulletin, 131,* 383–406.

Hess, T. M., Auman, C., Colcombe, S. J., et al. (2003). The impact of stereotype threat on age differences in memory performance. *Journals of Gerontology: Psychological and Social Sciences, 58,* 3–11.

Hess, T. M., Hinson, J. T., & Statham, J. A. (2004). Implicit and explicit stereotype activation effects on memory: Do age and awareness moderate the impact of priming? *Psychology and Aging, 19,* 495–505.

Heuveline, P., & Timberlake, J. M. (2004). The role of cohabitation in family formation: The U.S. in comparative perspective. *Journal of Marriage and Family, 66,* 1214–1230.

Hewitt, B., & de Vaus, D. (2009). Change in the association between premarital cohabitation and separation: Australia 1954–2000. *Journal of Marriage and Family, 71,* 353–361.

Hildreth, C. J., Burke, A. E., & Glass, R. M. (2009). Cataracts fact sheet. *Journal of the American Medical Association, 301,* 2060.

Hill, P. L., & Roberts, B. W. (2011). The role of adherence in the relationship between conscientiousness and perceived health. *Health Psychology, 30,* 797–804.

Hill, P. L., Turiano, N. A., Hurd, M. D., et al. (2011). Conscientiousness and longevity: An examination of possible mediators. *Health Psychology, 30,* 536–541.

Hill, R. D., Storandt, M., & Malley, M. (1993). The impact of long-term exercise training on psychological function in older adults. *Journals of Gerontology: Psychological and Social Sciences, 48,* 12–17.

Hoge, C. W., Castro, C. A., Messer, S. C., et al. (2004). Combat duty in Iraq and Afghanistan, mental health problems, and barriers to care. *New England Journal of Medicine, 351,* 13–22.

Holden, C. (2005). Sex and the suffering brain. *Science, 308,* 1574–1577.

Holland, J. L. (1958). A personality inventory employing occupational titles. *Journal of Applied Psychology, 42,* 336–342.

Holland, J. L. (1992). *Making vocational choice: A theory of personalities and work environments* (2nd ed.). Odessa, FL: Psychological Assessment Resources.

Holland, J. L. (1996). Integrating career theory and practice. In M. L. Savickas & W. B. Walsh (Eds.), *Handbook of career counseling theory and practice* (pp. 1–11). Palo Alto, CA: Davies-Black.

Holland, J. L. (1997). *Making vocational choice: A theory of personalities and work environments* (3rd ed.). Odessa, FL: Psychological Assessment Resources.

Holmes, T. H., & Rahe, R. H. (1967). The Social Readjustment Rating Scale. *Journal of Psychosomatic Research, 11,* 213–218.

Hope, C. W., McGurk, D., Thomas, J. L., et al. (2008). Mild traumatic brain injury in U.S. soldiers returning home from Iraq. *New England Journal of Medicine, 358,* 453–463.

Horn, J. L., & Cattell, R. B. (1966). Refinement and test of the theory of fluid and crystallized intelligence. *Journal of Educational Psychology, 57,* 253–270.

Horn, J. L., & Hofer, S. M. (1992). Major abilities and development in the adult period. In R. J. Sternberg & C. A. Berg (Eds.), *Intellectual development* (pp. 44–99). Cambridge, England: Cambridge University Press.

Hornsby, P. J. (2001). Cell proliferation in mammalian aging. In E. J. Masoro & S. N. Austad (Eds.), *Handbook of the biology of aging* (pp. 207–245). San Diego, CA: Academic Press.

Hoyer, W. J., & Verhaeghen, P. (2006). Memory and aging. In J. E. Birren & K. W. Schaie (Eds.), *Handbook of the psychology of aging* (6th ed., pp. 209–232). San Diego, CA: Academic Press.

Hoyert, D. L., & Xu, J. (2012). *National vital statistics reports, vol. 61(6).* Centers for Disease Control and Prevention. Retrieved November 17, 2012, from http://www.cdc.gov/nchs/data/nvsr/nvsr61/ nvsr61_06.pdf

Hrdy, S. B. (2011). *Mothers and others: The evolutionary origins of mutual understanding.* Cambridge, MA: Belknap.

Hughes, M. E., & Waite, L. J. (2009). Marital biography and health at midlife. *Journal of Health and Social Behavior, 50,* 344–358.

Hultsch, D. F., Hertzog, C., Dixon, R. A., et al. (1998). *Memory change in the aged.* Cambridge, MA: Cambridge University Press.

Hunte, H. E. R., & Williams, D. R. (2009). The association between perceived discrimination and obesity in a population-based multi-racial and multi-ethnic adult sample. *American Journal of Public Health, 99,* 1285–1292.

Hunter, S., & Sundel, M. (Eds.). (1989). *Midlife myths: Issues, findings, and practice implications.* Newbury Park, CA: Sage.

Huynh, J. Y., Xanthopoulou, D., & Winefield, A. H. (2013). Social support moderates the impact of demands on burnout and organizational connectedness: A two-wave study of volunteer firefighters. *Journal of Occupational Health Psychology, 18,* 9–15.

Hy, L. X., & Loevinger, J. (1996). *Measuring ego development.* Mahwah, NJ: Erlbaum.

Hyde, J. S., Essex, M. J., & Horton, F. (1993). Fathers and parental leave: Attitudes and experiences. *Journal of Family Issues, 14,* 616–638.

Idler, E. L. (2006). Religion and aging. In R. H. Binstock & L. K. George (Eds.), *Handbook of aging and the social sciences* (pp. 277–300). San Diego, CA: Academic Press.

Idler, E. L., Kasl, S. V., & Hays, J. C. (2001). Patterns of religious practice and belief in the last years of life. *Journals of Gerontology: Psychological and Social Sciences, 56,* 326–334.

Ihrke, D. K., & Faber, C. S. (2012). Geographic mobility: 2005 to 2010. Current Population Reports, P20-567. U.S. Census Bureau, Washington, DC.

Jacobs, S. (1993). *Pathologic grief: Maladaption to loss.* Washington, DC: American Psychiatric Press.

James, W. (1902/1958). *The varieties of religious experience.* New York: Mentor.

Jankowiak, W. R., & Fischer, E. F. (1992). A cross-cultural perspective on romantic love. *Ethnology, 31,* 149.

Jelenchick, L. A., Eickhoff, J. C., & Moreno, M. A. (2013). "Facebook depression?" Social networking site use and depression in older adolescents. *Journal of Adolescent Health, 52,* 128–130.

Jennings, J. M., Webster, L. M., Kleykamp, B. A., et al. (2005). Recollection training and transfer effects in older adults: Successful use of a repetition-lag procedure. *Aging, Neuropsychology, and Cognition, 12,* 278–298.

Jennings, P. A., Aldwin, C. M., Levenson, M. R., et al. (2006). Combat exposure, perceived benefits of military service, and wisdom in later life: Findings from the Normative Aging Study. *Research on Aging, 28,* 115–134.

Jensen, A. R. (1998). *The g factor: The science of mental ability.* Westport, CT: Praeger.

Johnson, M. K., Reeder, J. A., Raye, C. L., et al. (2002). Second thoughts versus second looks: An age-related deficit in reflectively refreshing just-active information. *Psychological Science, 13,* 63–66.

Johnson, M. L. (2009). Spirituality, finitude, and theories of the life span. In V. L. Bengtson, M. Silverstein, N. M. Putney, et al. (Eds.), *Handbook of theories of aging* (pp. 659–673). New York: Springer.

Johnson, M. M. S. (1993). Thinking about strategies during, before, and after making a decision. *Psychology and Aging, 8,* 231–141.

Johnson, N. J., Backlund, E., Sorlie, P. D., et al. (2000). Marital status and mortality. *Annals of Epidemiology, 10,* 224–238.

Johnson, R. W. (2004). Trends in job demands among older workers: 1992–2002. *Monthly Labor Review, 7,* 48–56.

Johnson, R. W., Kawachi, J., & Lewis, E. K. (2009). *Older workers on the move: Recareering in later life.* Washington, DC: AARP.

Johnson, S., & O'Connor, E. (2002). *The gay baby boom: The psychology of gay parenthood.* New York: New York University Press.

Johnston, K., Tanner, M., Lalia, N., et al. (2013). Social capital: The benefit of Facebook 'friends.' *Behaviour & Information Technology, 32,* 24–36.

Jones, C. J., & Meredith, W. (1996). Patterns of personality change across the life span. *Psychology and Aging, 11,* 57–65.

Jones, E. (1981). *The life and work of Sigmund Freud.* New York: Basic Books.

Jones, L. B., Rothbart, M. K., & Posner, M. I. (2003). Development of executive attention in preschool children. *Developmental Science, 6,* 498–504.

Jonsson, T., Atwal, J. K., Steinberg, S., et al. (2012). A mutation in APP protects against Alzheimer's disease and age-related cognitive decline. *Nature, 488,* 96–99.

Judge, T. A., Higgins, C. A., Thoreson, C. J., et al. (1999). The Big Five personality traits, general mental ability, and career success across the life span. *Personnel Psychology, 52,* 621–652.

Jung, C. G. (1917/1966). *Two essays on analytical psychology.* London, England: Routledge.

Jung, C. G. (1933). *Modern man in search of a soul.* New York: Harcourt, Brace, & World.

Jung, C. G. (1964). *Man and his symbols.* New York: Laurel.

Jung, C. G. (1971). *Psychological types* (Collected works of C. G. Jung, volume 6, Chapter X). Princeton, NJ: Princeton University Press

Kahn, R. L., & Antonucci, T. C. (1980). Convoys over the life course: Attachment, roles, and social support. In P. B. Baltes & O. Brim (Eds.), *Life-span development and behavior* (Vol. 3, pp. 253–268). New York: Academic Press.

Kahn, W. A. (1990). Psychological conditions of personal engagement and disengagement at work. *Academy of Management Journal, 33,* 692–724.

Kalish, R. A. (1985). The social context of death and dying. In R. H. Binstock & E. Shanas (Eds.), *Handbook of aging and the social sciences* (pp. 149–170). New York: Van NostrandReinhold.

Kanter, M., Afifi, T., & Robbins, S. (2012). The impact of parents "friending" their young adult child on Facebook on perceptions of parental privacy invasions and parent–child relationship quality. *Journal of Communications, 62,* 900–917.

Kapahi, P., & Kockel, L. (2011). TOR: A conserved nutrient-sensing pathway that determines life-span across species. In E. J. Masoro & S. N. Austad (Eds.), *Handbook of the biology of aging* (7th ed., pp. 203–214). San Diego, CA: Academic Press.

Kaptin, R., Thomese, F., van Tilburg, T. G., et al. (2010). Support for the cooperative breeding hypothesis in a contemporary Dutch population. *Human Nature, 21,* 393–405.

Karney, B. R., & Bradbury, T. N. (1995). The longitudinal course of marital quality and stability: A review of theory, method, and research. *Psychological Bulletin, 118,* 3–34.

Karpiak, C. P., & Baril, G. L. (2008). Moral reasoning and concern for the environment. *Journal of Environmental Psychology, 28,* 203–208.

Kasser, V. M., & Ryan, R. M. (1999). The relation of psychological needs for autonomy and relatedness to health, vitality, well-being, and mortality in a nursing home. *Journal of Applied Social Psychology, 29,* 935–954.

Katz-Wise, S. L., Priess, H. A., & Hyde, J. S. (2010). Gender-role attitudes and behavior across the transition to parenthood. *Developmental Psychology, 46,* 18–28.

Kaufman, G., & Uhlenberg, P. (2000). The influence of parenthood on the work effort of married men and women. *Social Forces, 78,* 931–949.

Keen, S. (1983). *The passionate life: Stages of loving.* New York: Harper & Row.

Kegan, R. (1980). There the dance is: Religious dimensions of developmental theory. In J. W. Fowler & A. Vergote (Eds.), *Toward moral and religious maturity* (pp. 403–440). Morristown, NJ: Silver Burdette.

Kegan, R. (1982). *The evolving self.* Cambridge, MA: Harvard University Press.

Kellehear, A., & Lewin, T. (1988–89). Farewells by the dying: A sociological study. *Omega, 19,* 275–292.

Kemp, C. L. (2005). Dimensions of grandparent–adult grandchild relationships: From family ties to intergenerational friendships. *Canadian Journal on Aging, 24,* 161–178.

Kersten, A. W., Earles, J. L., Curtayne, E. S., et al. (2008). Adult age differences in binding actors and actions in memory for events. *Memory and Cognition, 36,* 119–131.

Kessler, R. C., Berglund, P., Demler, O., et al. (2005). Lifetime prevalence and age-of-onset distributions of *DSM-IV* disorders in the National Comorbidity Survey Replication. *Archives of General Psychiatry, 62,* 593–602.

Kessler, R. C., Chiu, W. T., Demler, O., et al. (2005). Prevalence, severity, and comorbidity of 13-month *DSM-IV* disorders in the National Comorbidity Survey Replication. *Archives of General Psychiatry, 62,* 617–627.

Kessler, R. C., Mickelson K. D., Walters, E. E., et al. (2004). Age and depression in the MIDUS Survey. In O. G. Brim, C. D. Riff, & R. C. Kessler (Eds.), *How healthy are we? A national study of well-being at midlife* (pp. 227–251). Chicago: University of Chicago Press.

Kiecolt-Glaser, J. A., & Newton, T. L. (2001). Marriage and health: His and hers. *Psychological Bulletin, 127,* 472–503.

Kim, J. H., Knight, B. G., & Longmire, C. V. (2007). The role of familism in stress and coping processes among African American and white dementia caregivers: Effects on mental and physical health. *Health Psychology, 26,* 564–576.

Kim, S., Healey, M. K., Goldstein, D., et al. (2008). Age differences in choice satisfaction: A positivity effect in decision making. *Psychology and Aging, 23,* 33–38.

Kinderman, S. S., & Brown, G. G. (1997). Depression and memory in the elderly: A meta-analysis. *Journal of Clinical and Experimental Neuropsychology, 19,* 625–642.

Kira, I., Abou-Median, S., Ashby, J., et al. (2012). Post-traumatic Growth Inventory: Psychometric properties of the Arabic version in Palestinian adults. *The International Journal of Educational and Psychological Assessment, 11,* 120–137.

Kirby, S. E., Coleman, P. G., & Daley, D. (2004). Spirituality and well-being in frail and non-frail older adults. *Journals of Gerontology: Psychological and Social Sciences, 59,* 123–129.

Kirkcaldy, B., Furnham, A., & Siefen, G. (2004). The relationship between health efficacy, educational attainment, and well-being among 30 nations. *European Psychologist, 9,* 107–119.

Klein, R., Chou, C.-F., Klein, B. E. K., et al. (2011). Prevalence of age-related macular degeneration in the U.S. population. *Archives of Ophthalmology, 129,* 75.

Klempin, F., & Kempermann, G. (2007). Adult hippocampus neurogenesis and aging. *European Archives of Psychiatry and Clinical Neuroscience, 257,* 271–280.

Kleyman, E. (2000). From allies to adversaries? *American Psychologist, 55,* 1061–1062.

Kliegel, M., Mackinlay, R., & Jäger, T. (2008). Complex prospective memory: Development across the lifespan and the role of task interruption. *Developmental Psychology, 44,* 612–617.

Kliegl, R., Smith, J., & Baltes, P. B. (1990). On the locus and process of magnification of age differences during mnemonic training. *Developmental Psychology, 26,* 894–904.

Kline, G. H., Stanley, S. M., Markman, H. J., et al. (2004). Timing is everything: Pre-engagement cohabitation and increased risk for poor marital outcomes. *Journal of Family Psychology, 18,* 311–318.

Knudsen, K. (2012). European grandparents' solicitude: Why older men can be relatively good grandparents. *Acta Sociologica, 55,* 231–250.

Koenig, H. G. (2006). Religion, spirituality and aging. *Aging and Mental Health, 10,* 1–3.

Kohlberg, L. (1973). Continuities in childhood and adult moral development revisited. In P. B. Baltes & K. W. Schaie (Eds.), *Life-span developmental psychology: Personality and socialization* (pp. 180–204). New York: Academic Press.

Kohlberg, L. (1981). *Essays on moral development: Vol. 1. The philosophy of moral development.* New York: Harper & Row.

Kohlberg, L. (1984). *Essays on moral development: Vol. 2. The psychology of moral development.* San Francisco, CA: Harper &Row.

Kohlberg, L., Levine, C., & Hewer, A. (1983). *Moral stages: A current formulation and a response to critics.* New York: Karger.

Kolomer, S., & McCallion, P. (2005). Depression and caregiver mastery in grandfathers caring for their grandchildren. *International Journal of Aging and Human Development, 60,* 283–294.

Kozak, A., Kersten, M., Schillmöller, Z., et al. (2013). Psychosocial work-related predictors and consequences of personal burnout among staff working with people with intellectual disabilities. *Research in Developmental Disabilities, 34,* 102–115.

Kramer, A. F., & Willis, S. L. (2002). Enhancing the cognitive vitality of older adults. *Current Directions in Psychological Science, 11,* 173–177.

Krampe, R. T., & Ericsson, K. A. (1996). Maintaining excellence: Deliberate practice and elite performance in young and old pianists. *Journal of Experimental Psychology: General, 125,* 331–359.

Krause, N. (1993). Race differences in life satisfaction among aged men and women. *Journals of Gerontology: Psychological and Social Sciences, 48,* 235–244.

Krause, N. (2006). Social relationships in late life. In R. H. Binstock & L. K. George (Eds.), *Handbook of aging and the social sciences* (pp. 181–200). San Diego, CA: Academic Press.

Kreider, R. M. (2005). Number, timing, and duration of marriages and divorces: 2001. *Current Population Reports P70-97.* Washington, DC: U.S. Census Bureau.

Kreider, R. M., & Ellis, R. (2011). *Number, timing, and duration of marriages and divorces: 2009.* Retrieved March 27, 2013, from http://www.census.gov/prod/2011pubs/p70-125.pdf

Kremen, W. S., & Lyons, M. J. (2011). Behavior genetics of aging. In K. W. Schaie & S. L. Willis (Eds.), *Handbook of the psychology of aging* (7th ed., pp. 93–107). San Diego, CA: Academic Press.

Krettenauer, T., Ullrich, M., Hofmann, V., et al. (2003). Behavioral problems in childhood and adolescence as predictors of ego-level attainment in early adulthood. *Merrill-Palmer Quarterly, 49,* 125–153.

Kretzschmar, F., Pleimling, D., Hosemann, J., et al. (2013). Subjective impressions do not mirror online reading effort: Concurrent EEG-eyetracking evidence from the reading of books and digital media. *PLoS ONE, 8,* retrieved February 27, 2013, from http://www.plosone.org/article/info%3Adoi%2F10.1371%2Fjournal.pone.0056178

Kryla-Lighthall, N., & Mather, M. (2009). The role of cognitive control in older adults' emotional well-being. In V. Berngtson, D. Gans, N. Putney, et al. (Eds.), *Handbook of Theories of Aging* (pp. 323–344). New York: Springer.

Kübler-Ross, E. (1969). *On death and dying.* New York: Macmillan.

Kübler-Ross, E. (1974). *Questions and answers on death and dying.* New York: Macmillan.

Kuehn, B. M. (2005). Better osteoporosis management a priority: Impact predicted to soar with aging population. *Journal of the American Medical Association, 23,* 2453–2458.

Labouvie-Vief, G., & Diehl, M. (1998). The role of ego development in the adult self. In P. M. Westenberg, A. Blasi, & L. D. Cohn (Eds.), *Personality development: Theoretical, empirical, and clinical investigations of Loevinger's conception of ego development* (pp. 219–235). London, England: Erlbaum.

Labouvie-Vief, G., & Gonda, J. N. (1976). Cognitive strategy training and intellectual performance in the elderly. *Journals of Gerontology: Psychological and Social Sciences, 31,* 327–332.

Lachman, M. E. (2004). Development in midlife. *Annual Review of Psychology, 55,* 305–331.

Lamond, A. J., Depp, C. A., Allison, M., et al. (2008). Measurement and predictors of resilience among community-dwelling older women. *Journal of Psychiatric Research, 43,* 148–154.

Lampkin, C. L. (2012). *AARP: Insights and spending habits of modern grandparents.* Retrieved March 22, 2013, from http://www.aarp.org/content/dam/aarp/research/surveys_statistics/general/2012/Insights-and-Spending-Habits-of-Modern-Grandparents-AARP.pdf

Lane, C. J., & Zelinski, E. M. (2003). Longitudinal hierarchical linear models of the Memory Functioning Questionnaire. *Psychology and Aging, 18,* 38–53.

Laumann, E. O., Das, A., & Waite, L. J. (2008). Sexual dysfunction among older adults: Prevalence and risk factors from a nationally representative sample of men and women 57–85 years of age. *Journal of Sexual Medicine, 5,* 2300–2311.

Laursen, P. (1997). The impact of aging on cognitive function. *Acta Neurologica Scandinavica Supplementum, 96,* 7–86.

Lee, K. S., & Ono, H. (2012). Marriage, cohabitation and happiness: A cross-national analysis of 27 countries. *Journal of Marriage and Family, 74,* 953–972.

Lemasters, E. E. (1957). Parenthood as a crisis. *Marriage and Family Living, 19,* 352–355.

Leopold, T. (2012). The legacy of leaving home: Long-term effects of coresidence on parent–child relationships. *Journal of Marriage and Family, 74,* 399–412.

Lerman, R., & Sorensen, E. (2000). Father involvement with their nonmarital children: Patterns, determinants, and effects on their earnings. *Marriage and Family Review, 29,* 137–158.

Lerner, R. M. (2006). Developmental science, developmental systems, and contemporary theories of human development. In W. Damon & R. M. Lerner (Gen. Eds.), *Handbook of Child Psychology* (6th ed.), R. M. Lerner (Vol. Ed.), Vol. 1, *Theoretical models of human development* (pp. 1–17). New York: Wiley.

Levinson, D. J. (1978). *The seasons of a man's life.* New York: Knopf.

Levy, B. R., & Leifheit-Limson, E. (2009). The stereotype-matching effect: Greater influence on functioning when age stereotypes correspond to outcomes. *Psychology and Aging, 24,* 230.

Li, S.-C. (2012). Neuromodulation of behavioral and cognitive development across the lifespan. *Developmental Psychology, 48,* 810–814.

Lichtenstein, P., Hershberger, S. L., & Pedersen, N. L. (1995). Dimensions of occupations: Genetic and environmental influences. *Journal of Biosocial Science, 27,* 193–206.

Lieberman, M. (1996). *Doors close, doors open: Widows, grieving and growing.* New York: Putnam.

Lillberg, K., Verkasalo, P. K., Kaprio, J., et al. (2003). Stressful life events and risk of breast cancer in 10,808 women: A cohort study. *American Journal of Epidemiology, 157,* 415–423.

Lillis, J., Levin, M. E., & Hayes, S. C. (2011). Exploring the relationship between body mass index and health-related quality of life: A pilot study of the impact of weight self-stigma and experiential avoidance. *Journal of Health Psychology, 16,* 722–727.

Lindenberger, U., & Baltes, P. B. (1994). Sensory functioning and intelligence in old age: A strong connection. *Psychology and Aging, 9,* 339–355.

Lindenberger, U., & Baltes, P. B. (1997). Intellectual functioning in old and very old age: Cross-sectional results from the Berlin Aging Study. *Psychology and Aging, 12,* 410–432.

Lindwall, M., Larsman, P., & Hagger, M. S. (2011). The reciprocal relationship between physical activity and depression in older European adults: A prospective cross-lagged panel design using SHARE data. *Health Psychology, 30,* 453–462.

Liu, H., & Umberson, D. (2008). The times they are a changin': Marital status and health differentials from 1972 to 2003. *Journal of Health and Social Behavior, 49,* 239–253.

Liu, H., Bravata, D. M., Olkin, I., et al. (2007). Systematic review: The effects of growth hormone in the healthy elderly. *Annals of Internal Medicine, 146,* 104–115.

Liu, H., Bravata, D. M., Olkin, I., et al. (2008). Systematic review: The effects of growth hormone on athletic performance. *Annals of Internal Medicine, 148,* 747–758.

Liu, H., Reczek, C., & Brown, D. (2013). Same-sex cohabitors and health: The role of race-ethnicity, gender, and socioeconomic status. *Journal of Health and Social Behavior, 54,* 25–45.

Livingston, G., & Cohn, D. (2010). *Childlessness up among all women; Down among women with advanced degrees.* Retrieved April 1, 2013, from http://www.pewsocialtrends.org/2010/06/25/childlessness-up-among-all-women-down-among-women-with-advanced-degrees/

Livson, F. B. (1981). Paths to psychological health in the middle years: Sex differences. In D. H. Eichorn, J. A. Clausen, N. Haan, et al. (Eds.), *Present and past in middle life* (pp. 195–221). New York: Academic Press.

Livson, N., & Peskin, H. (1981). Psychological health at 40: Prediction from adolescent personality. In D. H. Eichorn, J. A. Clausen, N. Haan, et al. (Eds.), *Present and past in middle life* (pp. 184–194). New York: Academic Press.

Lobar, S. L. (2006). Cross-cultural beliefs, ceremonies, and rituals surrounding death of a loved one. *Pediatric Nursing, 32,* 44–50.

Löckenhoff, C. E., Duberstein, P. R., Friedman, B., et al. (2011). Five-factor personality traits and subjective health among caregivers: The role of caregiver strain and self-efficacy. *Psychology and Aging, 26,* 592–604.

Löckenhoff, C. E., Sutin, A. R., Ferrucci, L., et al. (2008). Personality traits and subjective health in the later years: The association between NEO-PI-R and SF-36 in advanced age is influenced by health status. *Journal of Research in Personality, 42,* 1334–1346.

Lockley, S. W., & Foster, R. G. (2012). *Sleep: A very short introduction.* New York: Oxford University Press.

Loevinger, J. (1976). *Ego development.* San Francisco, CA: Jossey-Bass.

Loevinger, J. (1997). Stages of personality development. In R. Hogan, J. Johnson, & S. Briggs (Eds.), *Handbook of personality psychology* (pp. 199–208). San Diego, CA: Academic Press.

Loew, B., Rhoades, G., Markman, H., et al. (2012). Internet delivery of PREP-based education for at-risk couples. *Journal of Couple & Relationship Therapy, 11,* 291–309.

Lofquist, D., Lugaila, T., O'Connell, M., et al. (2012). *Households and families, 2010: U.S. Census briefs.* Retrieved April 1, 2013, from http://www.census.gov/prod/cen2010/briefs/c2010br-14.pdf

Longino, C. F., Jr. (2001). Geographical distribution and migration. In R. H. Binstock & L. K. George (Eds.), *Handbook of aging and the social sciences* (5th ed., pp. 103–124). San Diego, CA: Academic Press.

Longino, C. F., Jr., & Bradley, D. E. (2006). Internal and international migration. In R. H. Binstock & L. K. George (Eds.), *Handbook of aging and the social sciences* (6th ed., pp. 76–93). San Diego, CA: Academic Press.

Lonky, E., Kaus, C. R., & Roodin, P. A. (1984). Life experience and mode of coping: Relation to moral judgment in adulthood. *Developmental Psychology, 20,* 1159–1167.

Looker, A. C., Borrud, L. G., Dawson-Hughes, B., et al. (2012). *Osteoporosis or low bone mass at the femur neck or lumbar spine in older adults: United States, 2005–2008.* National Center for Health Statistics Brief, No. 93.

Loving, T. J. (2011). Should I live with my partner before we get married? In G. W. Lewandowski, Jr., T. J. Loving, B. Le, et al. (Eds.), *The science of relationships* (pp. 80–83). Dubuque, IA: Kendall Hunt.

Lowe, S. R., Manove, E. E., & Rhodes, J. E. (2013). Post-traumatic stress and posttraumatic growth among low-income mothers who survived Hurricane Katrina. *Journal of Consulting and Clinical Psychology, 81,* 877–889.

Lucas, R. E., Clark, A. E., Georgellis, Y., et al. (2003). Re-examining adaptation and the set-point model of happiness: Reactions to changes in marital status. *Journal of Personality and Social Psychology, 84,* 527–539.

Lukaszewski, A. W., & Rooney, J. R. (2010). *The origins of extraversion: Joint effects of facultative calibration and genetic polymorphism.* Paper presented to the annual meeting of Human Behavior and Evolution Society, Eugene, OR.

Lund, O. C. H., Tamnes, C. K., Moestue, C., et al. (2007). Tactics of hierarchy negotiation. *Journal of Research in Personality, 41,* 25–44.

Lund, R., Rod, N. H., & Christensen, U. (2012). Are negative aspects of social relations predictive of angina pectoris? A 6-year follow-up study of middle-aged Danish women and men. *Journal of Epidemiology and Community Health, 66,* 359–365.

Lupien, S. J., de Leon, M., de Santi, S., et al. (1998). Cortisol levels during human aging predict hippocampal atrophy and memory deficits. *Nature Neuroscience, 1,* 69–73.

Lustgarten, M., Muller, F. L., & Van Remmen, H. (2011). An objective appraisal of the free radical theory of aging. In E. J. Masoro & S. N. Austad (Eds.), *Handbook of the biology of ging* (7th ed., pp. 177–202). San Diego, CA: Academic Press.

Lyles, C. R., Karter, A. J., Young, B. A., et al. (2011). Correlates of patient-reported racial/ethnic health care discrimination in the Diabetes Study of North Carolina (DISTANCE). *Journal of Healthcare for the Poor and Underserved, 22,* 211–225.

Lyons, N. P. (1983). Two perspectives: On self, relationships, and morality. *Harvard Educational Review, 53,* 125–145.

Maciosek, M. V., Coffield, A. B., Flottemesch, T. J., et al. (2010). Greater use of preventive services in U.S. health care could save lives at little or no cost. *Health Affairs, 29,* 1656–1660.

Madden, D. J. (2007). Aging and visual attention. *Current Directions in Psychological Science, 16,* 70–74.

Maddi, S. R. (2005). On hardiness and other pathways to resilience. *American Psychologist, 60,* 261–262.

Maestas, N. (2007). *Back to work: Expectations and realizations of work after retirement.* Santa Monica, CA: RAND.

Magdol, L., Moffitt, T. E., Caspi, A., et al. (1998). Developmental antecedents of partner abuse: A prospective-longitudinal study. *Journal of Abnormal Psychology, 107,* 375–389.

Mahieu, L., & Gastmans, C. (2012). Sexuality in institutionalized elderly persons: A systematic review of argument-based ethics literature. *International Psychogeriatrics, 24,* 346–357.

Maillot, P., Perrot, A., & Hartley, A. (2012). Effects of interactive physical-activity video-game training on physical and cognitive function in older adults. *Psychology and Aging, 27,* 589–600.

Manago, A. M. (2012). The new emerging adult in Chiapas, Mexico: Perceptions of traditional values change among first-generation Maya university students. *Journal of Adolescent Research, 27,* 663–713.

Manago, A. M., Taylor, T., & Greenfield, P. M. (2012). Me and my 400 friends: The anatomy of college students' Facebook networks, their communication patterns, and well-being. *Developmental Psychology, 48,* 369–380.

Mancini, A. D., & Bonanno, G. A. (2009). Predictors and parameters of resilience to loss: Toward an individual differences model. *Journal of Personality, 77,* 1805–1832.

Mancini, A. D., Robinaugh, D., Shear, K., et al. (2009). Does attachment avoidance help people cope with loss? The moderating effect of relationship quality. *Journal of Clinical Psychology, 65,* 1127–1136.

Manly, J. J., Jacobs, D. M., Sano, M., et al. (1999). Effect of literacy on neuropsychological test performance in nondemented, education-matched elders. *Journal of the International Neuropsychological Society, 5,* 191–202.

Mansson, D. H., & Booth-Butterfield, M. (2011). Grandparents' expressions of affection for their grandchildren: Examining grandchildren's relational attitudes and behaviors. *Southern Communication Journal, 76,* 424–442.

Marcia, J. E. (1966). Development and validation of ego-identity status. *Journal of Personality and Social Psychology, 3,* 551–558.

Marcia, J. E. (1980). Identity in adolescence. In J. Adelson (Ed.), *Handbook of adolescent psychology* (pp. 159–187). New York: Wiley.

Markman, H. J., & Rhoades, G. K. (2012). Relationship education research: Current status and future directions. *Journal of Marriage and Family Therapy, 38,* 169–200.

Markman, H. J., Rhoades, G. K., Stanley, S. M., et al. (2010). A randomized clinical trail of the effectiveness of premarital intervention: Moderators of divorce outcomes. *Journal of Family Psychology, 27,* 165–172.

Markman, H. J., Stanley, S. M., & Blumberg, S. L. (2010). *Fighting for your marriage* (3rd ed.). San Francisco, CA: Jossey-Bass.

Markman, H. J., Stanley, S. M., Blumberg, S. L., et al. (2004). *Twelve hours to a great marriage: A step-by-step guide for making love last.* San Francisco, CA: Jossey-Bass.

Marks, N. F. (1996). Social demographic diversity among American midlife parents. In C. D. Ryff & M. M. Seltzer (Eds.), *The parental experience in midlife* (pp. 29–75). Chicago: University of Chicago Press.

Marks, N. F., Bumpass, L. L., & Jun, H. (2004). Family roles and well-being during the middle life course. In O. G. Brim, C. D. Ryff, & R. C. Kessler (Eds.), *How healthy are we? A national study of well-being at midlife* (pp. 514–549), Chicago: University of Chicago Press.

Marshall, V. W., & Levy, J. A. (1990). Aging and dying. In R. H. Binstock & L. K. George (Eds.), *Handbook of aging and the social sciences* (pp. 245–260). San Diego, CA: Academic Press.

Martin, J. A., Hamilton, B. E., Ventura, S. J., et al. (2012). *Births: Final data for 2010. National Vital Statistics Report.* Centers for Disease Control and Prevention. Retrieved March 18, 2013, from http://www.cdc.gov/nchs/data/nvsr/nvsr61/nvsr61_01.pdf/#table01

Martire, L. M., & Schulz, R. (2001). Informal caregiving to older adults: Health effects of providing and receiving care. In A. Baum, T. A. Revenson, & J. E. Singer (Eds.), *Handbook of health psychology* (pp. 477–493). Mahwah, NJ: Erlbaum.

Martire, L.M., Keefe, F.J., Schulz, R., et al. (2006). Older spouses' perceptions of partners' chronic arthritis pain: Implications for spousal responses, support provision, and caregiving experiences. *Psychology and Aging, 21,* 222–230.

Martires, K. J., Fu, P., Polster, A. M., et al. (2009). Factors that affect skin aging: A cohort-based survey on twins. *Archives of Dermatology, 145,* 1375–1379.

Maslach, C., Schaufeli, W. B., & Leiter, M. P. (2001). Job burnout. *Annual Review of Psychology, 52,* 397–422.

Maslow, A. H. (1968/1998). *Toward a psychology of being* (3rd ed.). New York: Wiley.

Masoro, E. J. (2011). Terminal weight loss, frailty, and mortality. In E. J. Masoro & S. N. Austad (Eds.), *Handbook of the biology of aging* (7th ed., pp. 321–331). San Diego, CA: Academic Press.

Masters, K. S., & Hooker, S. A. (2012). Religiousness/spirituality, cardiovascular disease, and cancer: Cultural integration for health research and intervention. *Journal of Consulting and Clinical Psychology, 81,* 206–216.

Mastorci, F., Vicentini, M., Viltart, O., et al. (2009). Long-term effects of prenatal stress: Changes in adult cardiovascular regulation and sensitivity to stress. *Neuroscience and Biobehavioral Reviews, 33,* 191–203.

Mastracci, S. H. (2003). Employment and training alternatives for non-college women: Do redistributive policies really redistribute? *Policy Studies Journal, 31,* 585–601.

Masunaga, H., & Horn, J. (2001). Expertise and age-related changes in the components of intelligence. *Psychology and Aging, 16,* 293–311.

Mather, M., & Carstensen, L. L. (2003). Aging and attentional biases for emotional faces. *Psychological Science, 14,* 409–415.

Matthews, K. A., & Gump, B. B. (2002). Chronic work stress and marital dissolution increase risk of posttrial mortality in men from the Multiple Risk Factor Intervention trial. *Archives of Internal Medicine, 162,* 309–315.

Maylor, E. A. (1990). Age and prospective memory. *Quarterly Journal of Experimental Psychology, 42A,* 471–493.

Mayou, R. A., Ehlers, A., & Hobbs, M. (2000). Psychological debriefing for road traffic accident victims. *British Journal of Psychiatry, 176,* 589–593.

Mazerolle, M., Régner, I., Morisset, P., et al. (2012). Stereotype threat strengthens automatic recall and undermines controlled processes in older adults. *Psychological Science, 23,* 723–727.

McAdams, D. P. (2001). Generativity in midlife. In M. E. Lachman (Ed.), *Handbook of midlife development* (pp. 395–443). New York: Wiley.

McAdams, D. P. (2006). *The person: A new introduction to personality psychology* (4th ed.). Hoboken, NJ: Wiley.

McAdams, D. P., & de St. Aubin, E. (1992). A theory of generativity and its assessment through self-report, behavioral acts, and narrative themes in autobiography. *Journal of Personality and Social Psychology, 62,* 1003–1015.

McAdams, D. P., de St. Aubin, E., & Logan, R. L. (1993). Generativity among young, midlife, and older adults. *Psychology and Aging, 8,* 221–230.

McAdams, D. P., Hart, H. M., & Maruna, S. (1998). The anatomy of generativity. In D. P. McAdams & E. de St. Aubin (Eds.), *Generativity and adult development: How and why we care for the next generation* (pp. 7–43). Washington, DC: American Psychological Association.

McAndrew, F. T., & Jeong, H. S. (2012). Who does what on Facebook? Age, sex, and relationship status as predictors of Facebook use. *Computers in Human Behavior, 28,* 2359–2365.

McCay, C. M., Crowell, M. F., & Maynard, L. A. (1935). The effect of retarded growth upon the length of life span and upon the ultimate body size. *Journal of Nutrition, 10,* 63–79.

McClearn, G. E., & Heller, D. A. (2000). Genetics and aging. In S. B. Manuck, R. J. Jennings, B. S. Rabin, et al. (Eds.), *Behavior, health and aging* (pp. 1–14). Mahwah, NJ: Erlbaum.

McClearn, G. E., Johansson, B., Berg, S., et al. (1997). Substantial genetic influence on cognitive abilities in twins 80 or more years old. *Science, 276,* 1560–1563.

McClearn, G. E., Vogler, G. P., & Hofer, S. M. (2001). Environment-gene and gene-gene interactions. In E. J. Masoro & S. N. Austad (Eds.), *Handbook of the biology of aging* (pp. 423–444). San Diego, CA: Academic Press.

McConnell, A. R., Brown, C. M., Shoda, T. M., et al. (2011). Friends with benefits: On the positive consequences of pet ownership. *Journal of Personality and Social Psychology, 101,* 1239–1252.

McCrae, R. E., & Costa, P. T., Jr. (1987). Validation of the five-factor model of personality across instruments and observers. *Journal of Personality and Social Psychology, 52,* 81–90.

McCrae, R. R., & Costa, P. T., Jr. (1983). Psychological maturity and subjective well-being: Toward a new synthesis. *Developmental Psychology, 19,* 243–248.

McCrae, R. R., & Costa, P. T., Jr. (1984). *Emerging lives, enduring dispositions: Personality in adulthood.* Boston, MA: Little, Brown.

McCrae, R. R., & Costa, P. T., Jr. (1990). *Personality in adulthood.* New York: Guilford Press.

McCrae, R. R., & John, O. P. (1992). An introduction to the five-factor model and its applications. *Journal of Personality, 60,* 185–215.

McCrae, R. R., Costa, P. T., Jr., Pedroso de Lima, M., et al. (1999). Age differences in personality across the adult life span: Parallels in five cultures. *Developmental Psychology, 35,* 466–477.

McCrae, R. R., Terracciano, A., & 78 members of the Personality Profiles of Cultures Project. (2005). Universal features of personality traits from the observer's perspective: Data from 50 cultures. *Journal of Personality and Social Psychology, 88,* 547–561.

McCullough, M. E., Hoyt, W. T., Larson, D. B., et al. (2000). Religious involvement and mortality: A meta-analytic review. *Health Psychology, 19,* 211–222.

McDaniel, M. A., Pesta, B. J., & Banks, G. C. (2012). Job performance and the aging worker. In W. C. Borman & J. W. Hedge (Eds.), *The Oxford handbook of work and aging* (pp. 280–297). New York: Oxford University Press.

McFadden, S. H. (2000). Religion and meaning in late life. In G. T. Reker & K. Chamberlain (Eds.), *Exploring existential meaning: Optimizing human development across the life span* (pp. 171–183). Thousand Oaks, CA: Sage.

McGee, E., & Shevlin, M. (2009). Effect of humor on interpersonal attraction and mate selection. *Journal of Psychology: Interdisciplinary and Applied, 143,* 67–77.

McGowan, P. O., Sasaki, A., D'Alessio, A. C., et al. (2009). Epigenetic regulators of the glucocorticoid receptor in human brain associates with childhood abuse. *Nature Neuroscience, 12,* 342–348.

McGue, M., Bouchard, T. J., Iacono, W. G., et al. (1993). Behavioral genetics of cognitive ability: A life-span perspective. In R. Plomin & G. E. McClearn (Eds.), *Nature, nurture, and psychology* (pp. 59–76). Washington, DC: American Psychological Association.

McKee-Ryan, F. M., Song, A., Wanberg, C. R., et al. (2005). Psychological and physical well-being during unemployment: A meta-analytic study. *Journal of Applied Psychology, 90,* 53–76.

McLay, R. N., & Lyketsos, C. G. (2000). Veterans have less age-related cognitive decline. *Military Medicine, 165,* 622–625.

McMenamin, T. M. (2007). A time to work: Recent trends in shift work and flexible schedules. *Monthly Labor Review, 130,* 3–15.

Medina, J. J. (1996). *The clock of ages: Why we age, how we age, winding back the clock.* Cambridge, England: Cambridge University Press.

Menec, V. H. (2003). The relations between everyday activities and successful aging: A 6-year longitudinal study. *Journals of Gerontology: Psychological and Social Sciences, 58,* 74–82.

Meyer, B. J. F., Russo, C., & Talbot, A. (1995). Diverse comprehension and problem solving: Decisions about the treatment of breast cancer by women across the life span. *Psychology and Aging, 10,* 84–103.

Michelson, K. D., Kessler, R. C., & Shaver, P. R. (1997). Adult attachment in a nationally representative sample. *Journal of Personality and Social Psychology, 73,* 1092–1106.

Mikels, J. S., Larkin, G. R., Reuter-Lorenz, P. A., et al. (2005). Divergent trajectories in the aging mind: Changes in working memory for affective versus visual information with age. *Psychology and Aging, 20,* 542–553.

Mikulincer, M., & Shaver, P. R. (2009). An attachment and behavioral systems perspective on social support. *Journal of Social and Personal Relationships, 26,* 7–19.

Mikulincer, M., & Orbach, I. (1995). Attachment styles and repressive defensiveness: The accessibility and architecture of affective memories. *Journal of Personality and Social Psychology, 5,* 917–925.

Milevsky, A. (2005). Compensatory patterns of sibling support in emerging adulthood: Variations in loneliness, self-esteem, depression, and life satisfaction. *Journal of Social and Personal Relationships, 22,* 743–755.

Miller, A. S., & Stark, R. (2002). Gender and religiousness: Can socialization explanations be saved? *American Journal of Sociology, 197,* 1399–1423.

Miller, B. A., Chu, K. C., Hankey, B. F., et al. (2007). Cancer incidence and mortality patterns among specific Asian and Pacific Islander populations in the U.S. *Cancer Causes and Control, 19,* 227–256.

Miller, R. A., Harrison, D. E., Astle, C. M., et al. (2011). Rapamycin, but not resveratrol or simvastatin, extends lifespan of genetically heterogeneous mice. *Journals of Gerontology: Biological and Medical Sciences, 66*, 191–201.

Miller, T. Q., Smith, T. W., Turner, C. W., et al. (1996). A meta-analytic review of research on hostility and physical health. *Psychological Bulletin, 119*, 322–348.

Miyake, A., & Friedman, N. P. (2012). The nature and organization of individual differences in executive functions: Four general conclusions. *Current Directions in Psychological Sciences, 21*, 8–14.

Morgan, G. S., Wisneski, D. C., & Skitka, L. J. (2011). The expulsion from Disneyland: The social psychology impact of 9/11. *American Psychologist, 66*, 447–454.

Moskowitz, J. T., Folkman, S., & Acree, M. (2003). Do positive psychological states shed light on recovery from bereavement? Findings from a 3-year longitudinal study. *Death Studies, 27*, 471–500.

Mroczek, D. K., & Kolarz, C. M. (1998). The effect of age on positive and negative affect: A developmental perspective on happiness. *Journal of Personality and Social Psychology, 75*, 1333–1349.

Mroczek, D. K., & Spiro, A. (2003). Personality structure, process, variance between and within: Integration by means of a developmental framework. *Journals of Gerontology: Psychological and Social Sciences, 58*, 305–306.

Mroczek, D. K., & Spiro, A. (2005). Change in life satisfaction during adulthood: Findings from the Veterans Affairs Normative Aging Study. *Journal of Personality and Social Psychology, 88*, 189–202.

Murphy, M. L. M., Slavich, G. M., Rohleder, N., et al. (2013). Targeted rejection triggers differential pro- and anti-inflammatory gene expression in adolescents as a function of social status. *Clinical Psychological Science, 1*, 30–40.

Murray, C. E., & Kardatzke, K. N. (2009). Addressing the needs of adult children of divorce in premarital counseling: Research-based guidelines for practice. *The Family Journal, 17*, 126–133.

Musick, K., & Bumpass, L. (2012). Reexamining the case for marriage: Union formation and changes in well-being. *Journal of Marriage and the Family, 74*, 1–18.

Mustelin, L., Silventoinen, K., Pietilainen, K., et al. (2009). Physical activity reduces the influence of genetic effects on BMI and waist circumference: A study in young adult twins. *International Journal of Obesity, 33*, 29–36.

Nair, K. S., Rizza, R. A., O'Brien, P., et al. (2006). DHEA in elderly women and DHEA and testosterone in elderly men. *New England Journal of Medicine, 355*, 1647–1659.

National Alliance for Caregiving and AARP. (2009). *The economic downturn and its impact on family caregiving.* Retrieved January 22, 2010, from www.caregiving.org/data/EVC_Caregivers_Economy_ReportFINAL_4-28-09.pdf

National Alliance for Caregiving. (2009). *Caregiving in the U.S.* Retrieved March 22, 2013, from http://www.caregiving.org/pdf/research/CaregivingUSAllAgesExecSum.pdf

National Center for Health Statistics. (2011). *Health, United States: 2010.* Retrieved March 15, 2013, from http://www.cdc.gov/nchs/data/hus/hus10.pdf

National Center for Health Statistics. (2012). *Health, United States, 2011.* Centers for Disease Control and Prevention. Retrieved November 16, 2012, from http://www.cdc.gov/nchs/data/hus/hus11.pdf

National Eye Institute. (2012a). *Facts about cataracts.* Retrieved May 1, 2012, from http://www.nei.nih.gov/health/cataract/cataract_facts.asp

National Eye Institute. (2012b). *Glaucoma: What you should know.* Retrieved May 1, 2012, from http://www.nei.nih.gov/glaucoma/

National Heart Lung and Blood Institute. (2011). *What is coronary microvascular disease?* Retrieved November 26, 2012, from http://www.nhlbi.nih.gov/health/health-topicså/topics/cmd/

National Highway Traffic Safety Administration. (2009). *Identifying behaviors and situations associated with increased crash risk for older drivers.* Retrieved February 27, 2013, from http://www-nrd.nhtsa.dot.gov/Pubs/811093.pdf

National Highway Traffic Safety Administration. (2012). *Motor vehicle traffic crashes as a leading cause of death in the United States, 2008 and 2009.* Retrieved February 26, 2013, from http://www-nrd.nhtsa.dot.gov/Pubs/811620.pdf

National Hospice and Palliative Care Association. (2012). *Hospice care in America: 2012 Edition.* Retrieved August 8, 2013, from http://www.nhpco.org/sites/default/files/public/Statistics_Research/2012_Facts_Figures.pdf

National Institute on Aging. (2011). *NIH commissioned census report describes oldest Americans.* Retrieved November 17, 2012, from http://www.nia.nih.gov/newsroom/2011/11/nih-commissioned-census-bureau-report-describes-oldest-americans

National Institute on Aging (2013). Aging and your eyes. Retrieved August 18, 2013 from http://www.nia.nih.gov/health/publication/aging-and-your-eyes#.UnvA1BYlc1k

National Institutes of Health. (2008). *Research for a new age: Normal aging.* Retrieved October 29, 2012, from http://www.healthandage.com/html/min/nih/content/booklets/research_new_age/page3.htm\#start

National Institutes of Health. (2011). *Updated NIH sleep disorders research plan seeks to promote and protect sleep health.* Retrieved October 30, 2012, from http://www.nih.gov/news/health/nov2011/nhlbi-09.htm

National Institutes of Health. (2012). *Noise-induced hearing loss.* Retrieved May 1, 2012, from http://www.nidcd.nih.gov/health/hearing/pages/noise.aspx

National Senior Services Corps. (2012). *Fact sheet.* Retrieved April 29, 2013, from http://www.nationalservice.gov/pdf/factsheet_senior-corps.pdf

National Sleep Foundation. (2011). *Backgrounder: Later school-start times.* Retrieved August 27, 2012, from http://www.sleepfoundation.org/article/hot-topics/backgrounder-later-school-start-times

Neal, M. B., & Hammer, L. B. (2007). *Working couples caring for children and aging parents: Effects on work and well-being.* Mahwah, NJ: Erlbaum.

Neimeyer, R. A. (2000). Searching for the meaning of meaning: Grief therapy and the process of reconstruction. *Death Studies, 24*, 541–558.

Nelson, D. L., & Burke, R. J. (2002). *Gender, work stress, and health.* Washington, DC: American Psychological Association.

Nelson, D. L., Quick, J. C., & Simmons, B. L. (2001). Preventive management of work stress: Current themes and future challenges. In A. Baum, T. A. Revenson, & J. E. Singer (Eds.), *Handbook of health psychology* (pp. 349– 363). Mahwah, NJ: Erlbaum.

Nelson, L. J., & Chen, X. (2007). Emerging adulthood in China: The role of social and cultural factors. *Child Development Perspectives, 1*, 86–91.

Neria, Y., DiGrande, L., & Adams, B. (2011). Posttraumatic stress disorder following the September 11, 2001, terrorist attacks: A review of the literature among highly exposed populations. *American Psychologist, 66*, 429–446.

Neugarten, B. (1976). Adaptation and the life cycle. *Counseling Psychologist, 6*, 16–20.

Neugarten, B. L. (1970). Dynamics of transition of middle age to old age. *Journal of Geriatric Psychiatry, 4*, 71–87.

Neugarten, B. L. (1996). *The meanings of age: Selected papers of Bernice L. Neugarten.* Chicago: University of Chicago Press.

Neugarten, B. L., Moore, J. W., & Lowe, J. C. (1965). Age norms, age constraints, and adult socialization. *American Journal of Sociology, 70,* 710–717.

Newman, K. S. (2003). *A different shade of gray: Midlife and beyond in the inner city.* New York: New Press.

Newtson, R. L., & Keith, P. M. (1997). Single women in later life. In J. M. Coyle (Ed.), *Handbook on women and aging* (pp. 385–399). Westport, CT: Greenwood Press.

Neyer, F. J. (2002). Twin relationships in old age: A developmental perspective. *Journal of Social and Personality Relationships, 20,* 31–53.

Ng, T. W. H., & Feldman, D. C. (2008). The relationship of age to ten dimensions of job performance. *Journal of Applied Psychology, 93,* 392–423.

Ng, T. W. H., & Feldman, D. C. (2012). Evaluating six common stereotypes about older workers with meta-analytical data. *Personnel Psychology, 65,* 821–858.

Niemiec, C. P., Ryan, R. M., & Deci, E. L. (2009). The path taken: Consequences of attaining intrinsic and extrinsic aspirations in post-college life. *Journal of Research in Personality, 73,* 291–308.

Nisan, M., & Kohlberg, L. (1982). Universality and variation in moral judgment: A longitudinal and cross-sectional study in Turkey. *Child Development, 53,* 865–876.

Nisbett, R. E., Aronson, J., Blair, C., et al. (2012). Intelligence: New findings and theoretical directions. *American Psychologist, 67,* 130–156.

O'Donovan, A., Sun, B., Cole, A., et al. (2011). Transcriptional control of monocyte gene expression in post-traumatic stress disorder. *Disease Markers, 30,* 123–132.

Oertelt-Prigione, S., Parol, R., Krohn, S., et al. (2010). Analysis of sex and gender-specific research reveals a common increase in publications and marked differences between disciplines. *BMC Medicine, 8,* 70–80.

O'Leary, A. (1990). Stress, emotion, and human immune function. *Psychological Bulletin, 108,* 363–382.

O'Leary, K. D., Acevedo, B. P., Aron, A., et al. (2012). Is long-term love more than a rare phenomenon? If so, what are its correlates? *Social Psychological and Personality Science, 3,* 241–249.

Ogden, C. L., Carroll, M. D., Kit, B. K., et al. (2012). *Prevalence of obesity in the United States, 2009–2010.* NCHS Data Brief No. 82. Retrieved October 30, 2012, from http://www.cdc.gov/nchs/data/databriefs/db82.pdf

Old, S. R., & Naveh-Benjamin, M. (2008). Differential effects of age on item and associative measures of memory: A meta-analysis. *Psychology and Aging, 23,* 104.

Old, S. R., & Naveh-Benjamin, M. (2012). Age differences in memory for names: The effect of prelearned semantic associations. *Psychology and Aging, 27,* 462–473.

Olshansky, S. J. (2012). Aging, health, and longevity in the 21st century. *Public Policy and Aging Report, 20,* 3–13.

Olshansky, S. J., Antonucci, T., Berkman, L., et al. (2012). Differences in life expectancy due to race and educational differences are widening, and in many cases may not catch up. *Health Affairs, 31,* 1803–1813.

Omalu, B., Hammers, J. L., Bailes, J., et al. (2011). Chronic traumatic encephalopathy in an Iraqi war veteran with posttraumatic stress disorder who committed suicide. *Neurosurgical Focus, 31,* E3.

Orchard, A., & Solberg, K. (1999). Expectations of the stepmother's role. *Journal of Divorce and Remarriage, 31,* 107–123.

Oregon Department of Human Services. (2013). *Oregon Public Health Division: Death with dignity act.* Retrieved August 10, 2013, from http://public.health.oregon.gov/ProviderPartnerResources/EvaluationResearch/DeathwithDignityAct/Documents/year15.pdf

Organisation for Economic Cooperation and Development. (2011). *Doing better for families.* Retrieved April 1, 2013, from http://www.oecd.org/els/family/47701118.pdf

Organisation for Economic Cooperation and Development. (2013). *OECD Family Database: Mean age of mothers at first childbirth.* Retrieved March 19, 2013, from http://www.oecd.org/els/soc/SF2.3%20Mean%20age%20of%20mother%20at%20first%20childbirth%20-%20updated%20240212.pdf

Ornstein. P. A., & Light, L. L. (2010). Memory development across the life span. In R. M. Lerner (Series Ed.) & W. F. Overton (Vol. Ed.), *Handbook of life-span development: Vol. 1. Biology, cognition, and methods across the life span* (pp. 295–305). Hoboken, NJ: Wiley.

Ortega-Alonso, A., Sipilä, S., Kujala, U. M., et al. (2009). Genetic influences on change in BMI from middle to old age: A 29-year follow-up study of twin sisters. *Behavior Genetics, 39,* 154–164.

Orth-Gomér, K., Rosengren, A., Wedel, H., et al. (1993). Stressful life events, social support, and mortality in men born in 1933. *British Medical Journal, 307,* 1102–1105.

Papaharitou, S., Nakopoulou, E., Kirana, P., et al. (2008). Factors associated with sexuality in later life: An exploratory study in a group of Greek married older adults. *Archives of Gerontology and Geriatrics, 46,* 191–201.

Pargament, K. I., Koenig, H. G., Tarakeshwar, N., et al. (2001). Religious struggle as predictor of mortality among medically ill elderly patients. *Archives of Internal Medicine, 161,* 1881–1885.

Park, D. C., Lautenschlager, G., Hedden, T., et al. (2002). Models of visuospatial and verbal memory across the adult life span. *Psychology and Aging, 17,* 299–320.

Park, D. C., & McDonough, I. (2013). The dynamic aging mind: Revelations from functional neuroimaging research. *Perspectives in Psychological Science, 8,* 62–67.

Park, N. (2011). Military children and families: Strengths and challenges during peace and war. *American Psychologist, 66,* 65–72.

Passow, S., Westerhausen, R., Wartenburger, I., et al. (2012). Human aging compromises attentional control of auditory perception. *Psychology and Aging, 27,* 99–105.

Pearlin, L. I. (1980). Life strains and psychological distress among adults. In N. J. Smelser & E. H. Erikson (Eds.), *Themes of work and love in adulthood* (pp. 174–192). Cambridge, MA: Harvard University Press.

Pendergast, D. R., Fisher, N. M., & Calkins, E. (1993). Cardiovascular, neuromuscular, and metabolic alterations with age leading to frailty [Special issue]. *Journals of Gerontology, 48,* 61–67.

Perls, F. (1973). *The Gestalt approach and eye witness to therapy.* Palo Alto, CA: Science and Behavior Books.

Perls, T. T., Reisman, N. R., & Olshansky, S. J. (2005). Provision or distribution of growth hormone for "antiaging": Clinical and legal issues. *Journal of the American Medical Association, 294,* 2086–2090.

Peskin, H., & Livson, N. (1981). Uses of the past in adult psychological health. In D. H. Eichorn, J. A. Clausen, N. Haan, et al. (Eds.), *Present and past in middle life* (pp. 158–194). New York: Academic Press.

Peterson, C., Park, N., & Castro, C. A. (2011). Assessment for the U.S. Army Comprehensive Soldier Fitness Program. *American Psychologist, 66,* 10–18.

Pettingale, K. W., Morris, T., Greer, S., et al. (1985). Mental attitudes to cancer: An additional prognostic factor. *Lancet, 1,* 750.

Pew Research Center. (2009). *End-of-life decisions: How Americans cope.* Retrieved August 10, 2013, from http://www.pewsocialtrends.org/2009/08/20/end-of-life-decisions-how-americans-cope/

Pew Research Center. (2010). *Religion among the millennials.* Retrieved August 8, 2013, from http://www.pewforum.org/2010/02/17/religion-among-the-millennials/

Pew Research Center. (2013a). *Gay marriage: Key data points from Pew Research*. Retrieved April 9, 2013, from http://www.pewresearch.org/2013/03/21/gay-marriage-key-data-points-from-pew-research/

Pew Research Center. (2013b). *Modern parenthood: Roles of moms and dads converge as they balance work and family*. Retrieved May 18, 2013, from http://www.pewsocialtrends.org/files/2013/03/FINAL_modern_parenthood_03-2013.pdf

Phelan, K. (2005). Generativity and psychological well-being in middle-age adults. *Dissertation Abstracts International: Section B: The Sciences and Engineering, 65*, 4323.

Pierce, T., & Lydon, J. (2001). Global and specific relational models in the experience of social interactions. *Journal of Personality and Social Psychology, 80*, 613–631.

Pillemer, K., Suitor, J. J., Mock, S. E., et al. (2007). Capturing the complexity of intergenerational relations: Exploring ambivalence within later-life families. *Journal of Social Issues, 63*, 775–791.

Pinquart, M. (2003). Loneliness in married, widowed, divorced, and never-married adults. *Journal of Social and Personal Relationships, 20*, 31–53.

Pinquart, M., & Sörensen, S. (2000). Influences of socioeconomic status, social network, and competence on subjective well-being in later life: A meta-analysis. *Psychology and Aging, 15*, 187–224.

Pinquart, M., & Sörensen, S. (2001). Gender differences in self-concept and psychological well-being in old age: A meta-analysis. *Journals of Gerontology: Psychological and Social Sciences, 56*, 195–213.

Pinquart, M., & Sörnsen, S. (2003). Differences between caregivers and non-caregivers in psychological health and physical health: A meta-analysis. *Psychology and Aging, 18*, 250–267.

Pinquart, M., & Sörensen, S. (2005). Ethnic differences in stressors, resources, and psychological outcomes of family caregiving: A meta-analysis. *The Gerontologist, 45*, 90–106.

Pinquart, M., & Sörensen, S. (2007). Correlates of physical health of informal caregivers: A meta-analysis. *Journals of Gerontology: Psychological and Social Sciences, 62*, 126–137.

Plomin, R., & Nesselroade, J. R. (1997). Behavioral genetics and personality change. *Journal of Personality, 58*, 191–220.

Plomin, R., DeFries, J. C., Kropnik, V. S., et al. (2012). *Behavioral genetics* (6th ed.). New York: Worth.

Plomin, R., DeFries, J. C., McClearn, G. E., et al. (2008). *Behavioral genetics* (5th ed.). New York: Worth.

Polivy J., Herman, C. P., & Coelho, J. S. (2008). Caloric restriction in the presence of attractive food cues: External cues, eating, and weight. *Physiology & Behavior, 94*, 729–733.

Pollatsek, A., Romoser, M. R. E., & Fisher, D. L. (2012). Identifying and remediating failures of selective attention in older drivers. *Current Directions in Psychological Science, 21*, 3–7.

Ponds, R. W. H. M., van Boxtel, M. P. J., & Jolles, J. (2000). Age-related changes in subjective cognitive functioning. *Educational Gerontology, 26*, 67–81.

Poortman, A.-R., & van Tilburg, T. G. (2005). Past experiences and older adults' attitudes: A lifecourse perspective. *Ageing and Society, 25*, 19–30.

Porter, R. S. (2009). *Home health handbook*. Hoboken, NJ: Wiley.

Pratt, M. W., Golding, G., & Hunter, W. J. (1983). Aging as ripening: Character and consistency of moral judgment in young, mature, and older adults. *Human Development, 36*, 277–288.

Presser, H. B. (1995). Job, family, gender: Determinants of nonstandard work schedules among employed Americans in 1991. *Demography, 32*, 577–598.

Presser, H. B. (2000). Nonstandard work schedules and marital instability. *Journal of Marriage and the Family, 62*, 93–110.

Pruchno, R. (1999). Raising grandchildren: The experiences of black and white grandmothers. *The Gerontologist, 39*, 209–221.

Punnoose, A. R. (2012). Insomnia. *Journal of the American Medical Association, 307*, 2653.

Quick, H., & Moen, P. (1998). Gender, employment, and retirement quality: A life-course approach to the differential experiences of men and women. *Journal of Occupational Health Psychology, 3*, 44–64.

Quinton, D., Pickles, A., Maughan, B., et al. (1993). Partners, peers, & pathways: Assortative pairing and continuities in conduct disorder. *Development and Psychopathology, 5*, 763–783.

Radloff, L. S. (1977). The CES-D Scale: A self-report depression scale for research in the general population. *Applied Psychological Measurement, 1*, 385–401.

Rainie, L., Smith, A., & Duggan, M. (2013). *Coming and going on Facebook*. Pew Research Center Report. Retrieved April 22, 2013, from http://pewinternet.org/Reports/2013/Coming-and-going-on-facebook/Key-Findings.aspx

Rando, T. A. (1993). *Treatment of complicated mourning*. Champaign, IL: Research Press.

Rasmussen, C. H., & Johnson, M. E. (1994). Spirituality and religiosity: Relative relationships to death anxiety. *Omega: Journal of Death and Dying, 29*, 313–318.

Reed, D., & Yano, K. (1997). Cardiovascular disease among elderly Asian Americans. In L. G. Martin & B. J. Soldo (Eds.), *Racial and ethnic differences in the health of older Americans* (pp. 270–284). Washington, DC: National Academy Press.

Reed, G. M., Kemeny, M. E., Taylor, S. E., et al. (1994). Realistic acceptance as a predictor of decreased survival time in gay men with AIDS. *Health Psychology, 13*, 299–307.

Reeves, A., Stuckler, D., McKee, M., et al. (2012). Increase in state suicide rates in the USA during economic recession. *The Lancet, 380*, 1813–1814.

Reker, G. T. (1991). *Contextual and thematic analyses of sources of provisional meaning: A life-span perspective*. Paper presented at the biennial meeting of the International Society for the Study of Behavioral Development, Minneapolis, MN.

Resnick, H. S., Kilpatrick, D. G., Dansky, B. S., et al. (1993). Prevalence of civilian trauma and posttraumatic stress disorder in a representative national sample of women. *Journal of Consulting and Clinical Psychology, 61*, 984–991.

Rest, J. R., & Thoma, S. J. (1985). Relation of moral judgment development to formal education. *Developmental Psychology, 21*, 709–714.

Reuter-Lorenz, P. A. (2013). Aging and cognitive neuroimaging: A fertile union. *Perspectives on Psychological Science, 8*, 68–71.

Reuters. (2010). *Rising retirement ages in Europe compared*. Retrieved May 15, 2013, from http://www.thisismoney.co.uk/money/pensions/article-1696682/Rising-retirement-ages-in-Europe-compared.html

Rhoades, G. K., Stanley, S. M., & Markman, H. J. (2009). The pre-engagement cohabitation effect: A replication and extension of previous findings. *Journal of Family Psychology, 30*, 233–258.

Rhoden, E. L., & Morgentaler, A. (2004). Medical progress: Risks of testosterone replacement therapy and recommendations for monitoring. *New England Journal of Medicine, 350*, 482–492.

Richardson, J. L., Zarnegar, Z., Bisno, B., et al. (1990). Psychosocial status at initiation of cancer treatment and survival. *Journal of Psychosomatic Research, 34*, 189–201.

Riegel, K. (1973). Dialectic operations: The final period of cognitive development. *Human Development, 16*, 346–370.

Riemann, R., Angleitner, A., & Strelau, J. (1997). Genetic and environmental influences on personality: A study of twins reared together using the self- and peer-report NEO-FFI scales. *Journal of Personality, 65*, 449–475.

Riggio, H. R., & Desrochers, S. (2005). The influence of maternal employment on the work and family expectations of offspring. In D. F. Halpern & S. E. Murphy (Eds.), *From work-family balance to work-family interaction: Changing the metaphor* (pp. 177–196). Mahwah, NJ: Erlbaum.

Riley, K. P., Snowdon, D. A., Desrosiers, M. F., et al. (2005). Early life linguistic ability, late life cognitive function, and neuropathology: Findings from the Nun Study. *Neurobiology of Aging, 26,* 341–347.

Rix, S. E. (2011). Employment and aging. In R. H. Binstock & L. K. George (Eds.), *Handbook of aging and the social sciences* (7th ed., pp. 193–206). San Diego, CA: Academic Press.

Roberts B. W., & DelVecchio, W. F. (2000). The rank-order consistency of personality traits from childhood to old age: A quantitative review of longitudinal studies. *Psychological Bulletin, 126,* 3–25.

Roberts, A. H. (1969). *Brain damage in boxers: A study of the prevalence of traumatic encephalopathy among ex-professional boxers.* London, England: Pittman.

Roberts, B. W., & Mroczek, D. (2008). Personality trait change in adulthood. *Current Directions in Psychological Science, 17,* 31–35.

Roberts, B. W., Smith, J., Jackson, J. J., et al. (2009). Compensatory conscientiousness and health in older couples. *Psychological Science, 5,* 553–559.

Roberts, B. W., Walton, K. E., & Bogg, T. (2005). Conscientiousness and health across the life course. *Review of General Psychology, 9,* 156–168.

Roberts, B. W., Walton, K. E., & Viechtbauer, W. (2006). Patterns of mean-level change in personality traits across the life course: A meta-analysis of longitudinal studies. *Psychological Bulletin, 132,* 1–25.

Roberts, R. E., Deleger, S., Strawbridge, W. J., et al. (2004). Prospective association between obesity and depression: Evidence from the Alameda County Study. *International Journal of Obesity and Related Metabolic Disorders, 27,* 514–521.

Robinson, J. K., & Bigby, M. (2011). Prevention of melanoma with regular sunscreen use. *Journal of the American Medical Association, 306,* 302–303.

Robles, T. F., & Kiecolt-Glaser, J. K. (2003). The physiology of marriage: Pathways to health. *Physiology and Behavior, 79,* 409–416.

Rodrigue, K. M., Kennedy, K. M., & Raz, N. (2005). Aging and longitudinal change in perceptual-motor skill acquisition in healthy adults. *Journals of Gerontology: Psychological and Social Sciences, 60,* 174–181.

Roenker, D. L., Cissell, G. M., Ball, K. K., et al. (2003). Speed-of-processing and driving simulator training result in improved driving performance. *Human Factors: The Journal of the Human Factors and Ergonomics Society, 45,* 218–233.

Rogers, C. (1959). A theory of therapy, personality and interpersonal relationships as developed in the client-centered framework. In S. Koch (Ed.), *Psychology: A study of a science: Vol. 3. Formulations of the person and the social context.* New York: McGraw Hill.

Rogers, C. (1961/1995). *On becoming a person: A therapist's view of psychotherapy.* New York: Houghton Mifflin.

Rogers, R. L., Meyer, J. S., & Mortel, K. F. (1990). After reaching retirement age physical activity sustains cerebral perfusion and cognition. *Journal of the American Geriatric Society, 38,* 123–128.

Rönnlund, M., Nyberg, L., Bäckman, L., et al. (2005). Stability, growth, and decline in adult life span development of declarative memory: Cross-sectional and longitudinal data from a population-based study. *Psychology and Aging, 20,* 3–18.

Rosenberger, N. (2007). Rethinking emerging adulthood in Japan: Perspectives from long-term single women. *Child Development Perspectives, 1,* 92–95.

Rosenbloom, C., & Bahns, M. (2006). What can we learn about diet and physical activity from master athletes? *Nutrition Today, 40,* 267–272.

Rosenfeld, I. (2005). *Breakthrough health.* Emmaus, PA: Rodale Press.

Rosenkrantz Aronson, S., & Huston, A. C. (2004). The mother-infant relationship in single, cohabiting, and married families: A case for marriage? *Journal of Family Psychology, 18,* 5–18.

Rossi, A. S. (2004). The menopause transition and aging processes. In O. G. Brim, C. D. Ryff, & R. C. Kessler (Eds.), *How healthy are we? A national study of well-being at midlife* (pp. 153–201). University of Chicago Press.

Rowe, J. W., & Kahn, R. L. (1998). *Successful aging.* New York: Pantheon Books.

Ruby, M. B., Dunn, E. W., Perrino, A., et al. (2011). The invisible benefits of exercise. *Health Psychology, 30,* 67–74.

Ruiz, S. A., & Silverstein, M. (2007). Relationships with grandparents and the emotional well-being of late adolescent and young adult grandchildren. *Journal of Social Issues, 63,* 793–808.

Ruthig, J. C., & Allery, A. (2008). Native American elders' health congruence: The role of gender and corresponding functional well-being, hospital admissions, and social engagement. *Journal of Health Psychology, 13,* 1072–1091.

Ryan, R. M., & Deci, E. L. (2000). Self-determination theory and facilitation of intrinsic motivation, social development, and well-being. *American Psychologist, 55,* 68–78.

Ryan, R. M., & La Guardia, J. G. (2000). What is being optimized? Self-determination theory and basic psychological needs. In S. H. Qualls & N. Abeles (Eds.), *Psychology and the aging revolution: How we adapt to longer life* (pp. 145–172). Washington, DC: American Psychological Association.

Sabaté, E. (2003). *Adherence to long-term therapies: Evidence for action.* Geneva, Switzerland: World Health Organization.

Salkind, N. J. (2011). *Exploring research* (8th ed.). Upper Saddle River, NJ: Pearson.

Salthouse, T. A. (1984). Effects of age and skill in typing. *Journal of Experimental Psychology: General, 113,* 345–371.

Salthouse, T. A. (1991). *Theoretical perspectives on cognitive aging.* Hillsdale, NJ: Erlbaum.

Salthouse, T. A. (1996). The processing-speed theory of adult age differences in cognition. *Psychological Review, 103,* 401–428.

Salthouse, T. A. (2000). Aging and measures of processing speed. *Biological Psychology, 54,* 35–54.

Salthouse, T. A. (2004). What and when of cognitive aging. *Current Directions in Psychological Science, 13,* 140–144.

Salthouse, T. A. (2011). Neuroanatomical substrates of age-related cognitive deficits. *Psychological Bulletin, 137,* 753–784.

Salthouse, T. A., & Maurer, T. J. (1996). Aging, job performance, and career development. In J. E. Birren & K. W. Schaie (Eds.), *Handbook of the psychology of aging* (4th ed., pp. 353–364). San Diego, CA: Academic Press.

Salthouse, T. A., Babcock, R. L., Skovronek, E., et al. (1990). Age and experience effects in spatial visualization. *Developmental Psychology, 26,* 128–136.

Salthouse, T. A., Hancock, H. E., Meinz, E. J., et al. (1996). Interrelations of age, visual acuity, and cognitive functioning. *Journals of Gerontology: Psychological and Social Sciences, 51,* 317–330.

Sameroff, A. J. (Ed.) (2009). *The transactional model of development: How children and contexts shape each other.* Washington, DC: American Psychological Association.

Sanchez, L., & Thomson, E. (1997). Becoming mothers and fathers: Parenthood, gender, and the division of labor. *Gender and Society, 11,* 747–772.

Sands, R. G., & Goldberg-Glen, R. S. (2000). Grandparent caregivers' perception of the stress of surrogate parenting. *Journal of Social Services Research, 26,* 77–95.

Sanfey, A. C., & Hastie, R. (2000). Judgment and decision making across the adult life span: A tutorial review of psychological research. In D. Park & N. Schwarz (Eds.), *Cognitive aging: A primer.* Philadelphia, PA: Taylor & Francis.

Santillanes, G. (1997). Releasing the spirit: A lesson in Native American funeral rituals. *Director, 69,* 32–34.

Sayer, L. C. (2006). Economic aspects of divorce and relationship dissolution. In M. A. Fine & J. H. Harvey (Eds.), *Handbook of divorce and relationship dissolution* (pp. 385–406). Mahwah, NJ: Erlbaum.

Schacter, D. L. (1997). False recognition and the brain. *Current Directions in Psychological Science, 6,* 65–70.

Schaie, K. W. (1994). The course of adult intellectual development. *American Psychologist, 49,* 304–313.

Schaie, K. W. (1996). Intellectual development in adulthood. In J. E. Birren & K. W. Schaie (Eds.), *Handbook of the psychology of aging* (4th ed., pp. 265–286). San Diego, CA: Academic Press.

Schaie, K. W. (2006). Intelligence. In R. Schulz (Ed.), *Encyclopedia of aging* (4th ed., pp. 600–602). New York: Springer.

Schaie, K. W., & Willis, S. L. (1986). Can decline in adult intellectual functioning be reversed? *Developmental Psychology, 22,* 223–232.

Schaie, K. W., & Zanjani, F. (2006). Intellectual development across adulthood. In C. Hoare (Ed.), *Oxford handbook of adult development and learning* (pp. 99–122). New York: Oxford University Press.

Scharlach, A. E., & Fredrickson, K. I. (1993). Reactions to the death of a parent during midlife. *Omega, 27,* 307–319.

Schaufeli, W. B., & Bakker, A. B. (2004). Job demands, job resources and their relationship with burnout and engagement: A multisample study. *Journal of Organizational Behavior, 25,* 293–315.

Scheier, M. F., & Carver, C. S. (1993). On the power of positive thinking. *Current Directions in Psychological Science, 2,* 26–30.

Schiller, J. S., Lucas, J. W., Ward, B. W., et al. (2012). *Summary health statistics for U.S. adults: National Health Interview Survey, 2010.* Retrieved February 13, 2013, from http://www.cdc.gov/nchs/data/series/sr_10/sr10_252.pdf

Schlaghecken, F., Birak, K. S., & Maylor, E. A. (2011). Age-related deficits in low-level inhibitory motor control. *Psychology and Aging, 26,* 905–918.

Schneider-Graces, N. J., Gordon, B. A., Brumback-Peltz, C. R., et al. (2010). Span, CRUNCH, and beyond: Working memory capacity and the aging brain. *Journal of Cognitive Neuroscience, 22,* 655–669.

Schoenemann, P. T., Sheehan, M. J., & Glotzer, L. D. (2005). Prefrontal white matter volume is disproportionately larger in humans than in other primates. *Nature Neuroscience, 8,* 242–252.

Schoeni, R. F., Freedman, V. A., & Martin, L. G. (2008). Why is late-life disability declining? *The Milbank Quarterly, 86,* 47–89.

Schooler, C., Caplan, L., & Oates, G. (1998). Aging and work: An overview. In K. W. Schaie & C. Schooler (Eds.), *Impact of work on older adults* (pp. 1–10). New York: Springer.

Schover, L. R., Fouladi, R. T., Warneke, C. L., et al. (2004). The use of treatments for erectile dysfunction among survivors of prostate cancer carcinoma. *Cancer, 95,* 2397–2407.

Schryer, E., & Ross, M. (2012). Evaluating the valence of remembered events: The importance of age and self-relevance. *Psychology and Aging, 27,* 237–242.

Schulenberg, J. E., Sameroff, A. J., & Cicchetti, D. (2004). The transition to adulthood as a critical juncture in the course of psychopathology and mental health. *Development and Psychopathology, 16,* 799–806.

Schwartz, R. (1992). Is Holland's theory worthy of so much attention, or should vocational psychology move on? *Journal of Vocational Behavior, 40,* 170–187.

Scott, S. B., Poulin, M. J., & Silver, M. C. (2013). A lifespan perspective on terrorism: Age differences in trajectories of response to 9/11. *Developmental Psychology, 49,* 986–998.

Sebastiani, P., Solovieff, N., DeWan, A. T., et al. (2012). Genetic signatures of exceptional longevity in humans. *PLoS ONE, 7.* Retrieved October 23, 2012, from http://www.plosone.org/article/info%3Adoi%2F10.1371%2Fjournal.pone.0029848

Seeman, T. E., Bruce, M. L., & McAvay, G. J. (1996). Social network characteristics and onset of ADL disability: MacArthur studies of successful aging. *Journals of Gerontology: Psychological and Social Sciences, 51,* 191–200.

Seeman, T. E., Dubin, L., & Seeman, M. (2003). Religiosity/spirituality and health: A critical review of the evidence for biological pathways. *American Psychologist, 58,* 53–63.

Segerstrom, S. C., & Miller, G. E. (2004). Psychological stress and the human immune system: A meta-analytic study of 30 years of inquiry. *Psychological Bulletin, 130,* 601–630.

Seligman, M. E. P. (1991). *Learned optimism.* New York: Knopf.

Seligman, M. E. P., & Csikszentmihalyi, M. (2000). Positive psychology: An introduction. *American Psychologist, 55,* 5–14.

Selye, H. (1936). A syndrome produced by diverse nocuous agents. *Nature, 138,* 32.

Selye, H. (1982). History and present status of the stress concept. In L. Goldberger & S. Breznitz (Eds.), *Handbook of stress: Theoretical and clinical aspects* (pp. 7–20). New York: Free Press.

Semmer, N. (1996). Individual differences, work, stress, and health. In M. J. Schabracq, J. A. M. Winnubst, & C. L. Cooper (Eds.), *Handbook of work and health psychology* (pp. 51–86). Chichester, England: Wiley.

Shackelford, T. K., Schmitt, D. P., & Buss, D. M. (2005). Universal dimensions of human mate preferences. *Personality and Individual Differences, 39,* 447–458.

Shafto, M. A., Burke, D. M., Stamatakis, E. A., et al. (2007). On the tip-of-the-tongue: Neural correlates of increased word-finding failures in normal aging. *Journal of Cognitive Neuroscience, 19,* 2060–2070.

Shanahan, M. J. (2000). Pathways to adulthood in changing societies: Variability and mechanisms in life course perspective. *Annual Review of Sociology, 26,* 667–692.

Shapiro, A. F., Gottman, J. M., & Carrère, S. (2000). The baby and marriage: Identifying factors that buffer against decline in marital satisfaction after the first baby arrives. *Journal of Family Psychology, 14,* 59–70.

Shargorodsky, J., Curhan, S. G., Curhan, G. C., et al. (2010). Change in prevalence of hearing loss in U.S. adolescents. *Journal of the American Medical Association, 304,* 772–778.

Sharp, Z. D. (2011). Aging and TOR: Interwoven in the fabric of life. *Cellular and Molecular Life Sciences, 68,* 587–597.

Sheehy, G. (1976). *Passages.* New York: Dutton.

Sheehy, G. (2006). *Sex and the seasoned woman: Pursuing the passionate life.* New York: Random House.

Sheffield, K. M., & Peek, M. K. (2009). Neighborhood context and cognitive decline in older Mexican Americans: Results from the Hispanic established populations for epidemiologic studies of the elderly. *American Journal of Epidemiology, 169,* 1092–1101.

Sheldon, K. M., & Kasser, T. (2001). Getting older, getting better? Personal strivings and psychological maturity across the life span. *Developmental Psychology, 37,* 491–501.

Sheldon, P. (2012). Profiling the non-user: Examination of life-position indicators, sensation seeking, shyness, and loneliness among users and non-users of social network sites. *Computers in Human Behavior, 28,* 1960–1965.

Sherin, J. E., & Bartzokis, G. (2011). Human brain myelination trajectories across the life span: Implications for CNS function and dysfunction. In E. J. Masoro & S. N. Austad (Eds.), *Handbook of the biology of aging* (pp. 333–346). San Diego, CA: Academic Press.

Sherwood, P., Given, B., Given, C. W., et al. (2005). A cognitive behavioral intervention for symptom management in patients with advanced cancer: Results of a randomized clinical trial. *Oncology Nursing Forum, 32,* 1190–1198.

Shifren, J. L., & Hanfling, S. (2010). *Sexuality in midlife and beyond: Harvard Medical School Special Health Report.* Boston, MA: Harvard University Publications.

Shippee, T. P., Schafer, M. H., & Ferraro, K. F. (2012). Beyond the barriers: Racial discrimination and the use of complementary and alternative medicine among Black Americans. *Social Science and Medicine, 74,* 1155–1162.

Shively, S., Scher, A., Perl, D. P., et al. (2012). Dementia resulting from traumatic brain injury: What is the pathology? *Archives of Neurology, 69,* 1245–1251.

Shmotkin, D., Blumstein, T., & Modan, B. (2003). Beyond keeping active: Concomitants of being a volunteer in old age. *Psychology and Aging, 18,* 602–607.

Shneidman, E. S. (1989). The Indian summer of life: A preliminary study of septuagenarians. *American Psychologist, 44,* 684–694.

Siebenrock, K. A., Ferner, F., Noble, P. C., et al. (2011). The cam-type deformity of the proximal femur arises in childhood in response to vigorous sporting activity. *Clinical and Orthopedic Related Research, 469,* 3229–3240.

Siegler, I. C. (1994). Hostility and risk: Demographic and lifestyle variables. In A. W. Siegman & T. W. Smith (Eds.), *Anger, hostility, and the heart* (pp. 199–214), Hillsdale, NJ: Erlbaum.

Silverstein, M., & Marenco, A. (2001). How Americans enact the grandparent role over the life course. *Journal of Family Issues, 22,* 493–522.

Simpson, J. A., Collins, W. A., & Salvatore, J. E. (2011). Impact of early interpersonal experience on adult romantic relationship functioning: Recent findings from the Minnesota Longitudinal Study of Risk and Adaptation. *Current Directions in Psychological Science, 20,* 355–359.

Sims, R. V., McGwin, G., Jr., Allman, R. M., et al. (2000). Exploratory study of incident vehicle crashes among older drivers. *Journals of Gerontology: Biological and Medical Sciences, 55,* 22.

Sinnott, J. D. (1994). Development and yearning: Cognitive aspects of spiritual development. *Journal of Adult Development, 1,* 91–99.

Sinnott, J. D. (1996). The development of complex reasoning: Postformal thought. In F. Blanchard-Fields & T. Hess (Eds.), *Perspectives on cognitive change in adulthood and aging* (pp. 358–383). New York: McGraw-Hill.

Slavich, G. M., & Cole, S. W. (2013). The emerging field of human social genomics. *Clinical Psychological Science, 1,* 331–348.

Smetana, J. G., Killen, M., & Turiel, E. (1991). Children's reasoning about interpersonal and moral conflicts. *Child Development, 62,* 629–644.

Smith, B. J., Lightfoot, S. A., Lerner, M. R., et al. (2009). Induction of cardiovascular pathology in a novel model of low-grade chronic inflammation. *Cardiovascular Pathology, 18,* 1–10.

Smith, C. D., Walton, A., Loveland, A. D., et al. (2005). Memories that last in old age: Motor skill learning and memory preservation. *Neurobiology of Aging, 26,* 883–890.

Smith, J., & Baltes, P. B. (1999). Trends and profiles of psychological functioning in very old age. In P. B. Baltes & K. U. Mayer (Eds.), *The Berlin Aging Study: Aging from 70 to 100* (pp. 197–226). Cambridge, England: Cambridge University Press.

Smith, J., Staudinger, U. M., & Baltes, P. B. (1994). Occupational settings facilitating wisdom-related knowledge: The sample case of clinical psychologists. *Journal of Consulting and Clinical Psychology, 62,* 989–999.

Smith, S. K., & House, M. (2005, March 31–April 2). *Snowbirds, sunbirds, and stayers: Seasonal migration of the elderly in Florida.* Paper presented at the annual meeting of the Population Association of America, Philadelphia, PA.

Smith, T. W., & Gallo, L. C. (2001). Personality traits as risk factors for physical illness. In A. Baum, T. A. Revenson, & J. E. Singer (Eds.), *Handbook of health psychology* (pp. 139–173). Mahwah, NJ: Erlbaum.

Snarey, J. R. (1985). Cross-cultural universality of social-moral development: A critical review of the Kohlbergian research. *Psychological Bulletin, 97,* 202–232.

Snarey, J. R., Reimer, J., & Kohlberg, L. (1985). Development of social-moral reasoning among kibbutz adolescents: A longitudinal cross-sectional study. *Developmental Psychology, 21,* 3–17.

Snarey, J. R., Son, L., Kuehne, V. S., et al. (1987). The role of parenting in men's psychosocial development: A longitudinal study of early adulthood infertility and midlife generativity. *Developmental Psychology, 23,* 593–603.

Snowdon, D. (2001). *Aging with grace: What the Nun Study teaches us about leading longer, healthier, more meaningful lives.* New York: Bantam Books.

Solano, L., Costa, M., Salvati, S., et al. (1993). Psychosocial factors and clinical evolution in HIV-1 infection: A longitudinal study. *Journal of Psychosomatic Research, 37,* 39–51.

Soldz, S., & Vaillant, G. E. (1999). The big five personality traits and the life course: A 45-year longitudinal study. *Journal of Research in Personality, 33,* 208–232.

Somer, E., Maguen, S., Or-Chen, K., et al. (2009). Managing terror: Differences between Jews and Arabs in Israel. *International Journal of Psychology, 44,* 138–146.

Spearman, C. (1904). General intelligence, objectively determined and measured. *American Journal of Psychology, 15,* 201–203.

Spies, R. A., Carlson, J. F., & Geisinger, K. F. (2010). *The eighteenth mental measurements yearbook.* Lincoln, NE: University of Nebraska Buros Institute.

Spotts, E. L., Neiderhiser, J. M., Towers, H., et al. (2004). Genetic and environmental influences on marital relationships. *Journal of Family Psychology, 18,* 107–119.

Stanley, S. M., Rhoades, G. K., Amato, P. R., et al. (2010). The timing of cohabitation and engagement: Impact on first and second marriages. *Journal of Marriage and Family, 72,* 906–918.

Steindl-Rast, B. D. (1977). Learning to die. *Parabola, 2,* 22–31.

Stephens, M. A. P., Franks, M. M., & Townsend, A. L. (1994). Stress and rewards in women's multiple roles: The case of women in the middle. *Psychology and Aging, 9,* 45–52.

Stephenson-Abetz, J., & Holman, A. (2012). Home is where the heart is: Facebook and the negotiation of "old" and "new" during the transition to college. *Western Journal of Communication, 76,* 175–193.

Sternberg, R. J. (1986). A triangular theory of love. *Psychological Review, 93,* 119–135.

Stevens, J. (2010). *A CDC compendium of effective fall interventions: What works for community dwelling older adults* (2nd ed.). Atlanta, GA: Centers for Disease Control and Prevention.

Stigsdotter, A., & Bäckman, L. (1989). Comparison of different forms of memory training in old age. In M. A. Luszca & T. Nettelbeck (Eds.), *Psychological development: Perspectives across the life span.* Amsterdam, The Netherlands: Elsevier.

Stigsdotter, A., & Bäckman, L. (1993). Long-term maintenance of gains from memory training in older adults: Two 3-1/2 year follow-up studies. *Journals of Gerontology: Psychological and Social Sciences, 48,* 233–237.

Storandt, M. (2008). Cognitive deficits in the early stages of Alzheimer's disease. *Current Directions in Psychological Science, 17,* 198–202.

Su, R., Rounds, J., & Armstrong, P. I. (2009). Men and things, women and people: A meta-analysis of sex differences in interests. *Psychological Bulletin, 135,* 859–884.

Sugihara, Y., Sugisawa, H., & Harada, K. (2008). Productive roles, gender, and depressive symptoms: Evidence from a national longitudinal study of late-middle-aged Japanese. *Journals of Gerontology: Psychological and Social Sciences, 63,* 227–234.

Sugisawa, H., Liang, J., & Liu, X. (1994). Social networks, social support, and mortality among older people in Japan. *Journals of Gerontology: Psychological and Social Sciences, 49,* 3–13.

Super, D. E. (1957). *The psychology of careers.* New York: Harper & Row.

Super, D. E. (1990). A life-span/life-space approach to career development. In D. Brown & L. Brooks (Eds.), *Career choice and development: Applying contemporary theories to practice* (2nd ed., pp. 197–261). San Francisco, CA: Jossey-Bass.

Super, D. E., Savickas, M. L., & Super, C. M. (1996). The life-span, life-space approach to careers. In D. Brown & L. Brooks (Eds.), *Career choice and development: Applying contemporary theories to practice* (3rd ed., pp. 121–178). San Francisco, CA: Jossey-Bass.

Super, D. E., Starishevsky, R., Matlin, N., et al. (1963). *Career development: A self-concept theory.* New York: College Entrance Examination Board.

Sutker, P. B., Davis, J. M., Uddo, M., et al. (1995). War zone stress, personal resources, and PTSD in Persian Gulf War returnees. *Journal of Abnormal Psychology, 104,* 444–452.

Szinovacz, M. E., & DeViney, S. (2000). Marital characteristics and retirement decisions. *Research on Aging, 22,* 470–498.

Tan, J.-P., Buchanan, A., Flouri, E., et al. (2010). Filling the parenting gap: Grandparent involvement with U. K. adolescents. *Journal of Family Issues, 31,* 992–1015.

Tartaro, J., Luecken, L. J., & Gunn, H. E. (2005). Exploring heart and soul: Effects of religiosity/spirituality and gender on blood pressure and cortisol stress response. *Journal of Health Psychology, 10,* 753–766.

Taylor, S. E. (2002). *The tending instinct: How nurturing is essential to who we are and how we live.* New York: Holt.

Taylor, S. E., Klein, L. C., Lewis B. P., et al. (2000). Biobehavioral responses to stress in females: Tend-and-befriend, not fight-or-flight. *Psychological Review, 107,* 411–429.

Techner, D. (1997). The Jewish funeral—A celebration of life. *Director, 69,* 18–20.

Tennov, D. (1979). *Love and limerance.* New York: Stein & Day.

Teno, J. M., Clarridge, B. R., Casey, V., et al. (2004). Family perspectives on end-of-life care at the last place of care. *Journal of the American Medical Association, 291,* 88–93.

Teresa of Ávila, St. (1562/1960). *Interior castle.* Garden City, NJ: Image Books.

Terkel, S. (1995). *Coming of age: The story of our century by those who've lived it.* New York: St. Martin's Press.

Thoits, P. A. (2010). Stress and health: Major findings and policy implications. *Journal of Health and Social Behavior, 51,* S41–S53.

Thompson, S. H., & Lougheed, E. (2012). Frazzled by Facebook? An exploratory study of gender differences in social networking communication among undergraduate men and women. *College Student Journal, 46,* 88–98.

Thorson, J. A., & Powell, F. C. (1992). Meanings of death and intrinsic religiosity. *Journal of Clinical Psychology, 46,* 379–391.

Tomasetto, C., Alparone, F. R., & Cadinu, M. (2011). Girls' math performance under stereotype threat: The moderating role of mothers' gender stereotypes. *Developmental Psychology, 47,* 943–949.

Tomer, A., & Eliason, G. (2005). Life regrets and death attitudes in college students. *Omega: Journal of Death and Dying, 51,* 173–195.

Tomic, D., Gallicchio, L., Whiteman, M. K., et al. (2006). Factors associated with determinants of sexual functioning in midlife women. *Maturitas, 53,* 144–157.

Tooby, J., & Cosmides, L. (1990). On the universality of human nature and the uniqueness of the individual: The role of genetics and adaptation. *Journal of Personality, 58,* 17–68.

Toossi, M. (2012). Labor force projections to 2020: A more slowly growing workforce. Retrieved May 7, 2013, from http://www.bls.gov/opub/mlr/2012/01/art3full.pdf

Tornstam, L. (1996). Gerotranscendence—A theory about maturing into old age. *Journal of Aging and Identity, 1,* 37–50.

Torpy, J. M. (2004). Preventing cancer. *Journal of the American Medical Association, 291,* 2510.

Torpy, J. M., Burke, A., & Golub, R. M. (2012). Elements of hospice care. *Journal of the American Medical Association, 308,* 200.

Trivers, R. L. (1972). Parental investment and sexual selection. In B. Campbell (Ed.), *Sexual selection and the descent of man: 1871–1971* (pp. 136–179). Chicago: Aldine.

Truluck, J. E., & Courtenay, B. C. (2002). Ego development and the influence of gender, age, and educational levels among older adults. *Educational Gerontology, 28,* 325–336.

Tulving, E. (1985). How many memory systems are there? *American Psychologist, 40,* 385–398.

Tulving, E. (2005). Episodic memory and autonoesis: Uniquely human? In H. S. Terrace & J. Metcalfe (Eds.), *The missing link in cognition: Origins of self-reflective consciousness* (pp. 3–56). New York: Oxford University Press.

Tynkkynen, L., Tolvanen, A., & Salmela-Aro, K. (2012). Trajectories of educational expectations from adolescence to young adulthood in Finland. *Developmental Psychology, 48,* 1674–1685.

U.S. Bureau of Labor Statistics. (2009). *Women in the labor force: A data book.* Retrieved November 9, 2009, from http://www.bls.gov/cps/wlf-databook2009.htm

U.S. Bureau of Labor Statistics. (2012). *Number of jobs held, market activity, and earnings growth among the youngest baby boomers: Results from a longitudinal survey.* Retrieved April 28, 2013, from http://www.bls.gov/news.release/pdf/nlsoy.pdf

U.S. Bureau of Labor Statistics. (2013a). *Characteristics of minimum wage workers: 2012.* Retrieved April 28, 2013, from http://www.bls.gov/cps/minwage2012.pdf

U.S. Bureau of Labor Statistics. (2013b). *Economic news release: Families with own children: Table 4. Employment status of parents by age of youngest child and family type, 2011–2012 annual averages.* Retrieved May 7, 2013, from http://www.bls.gov/news.release/famee.t04.htm

U.S. Bureau of Labor Statistics. (2013c). *Employment status of the civilian population by sex and age.* Retrieved April 28, 2013, from http://www.bls.gov/news.release/empsit.t01.htm

U.S. Bureau of Labor Statistics. (2013d). *Household data annual averages: Table 24, Unemployed persons by marital status, race, Hispanic, or Latino ethnicity, age, and sex.* Retrieved May 1, 2013, from http://www.bls.gov/cps/cpsaat24.pdf

U.S. Bureau of Labor Statistics. (2013e). *Usual weekly earnings of wage and salary workers, first quarter 2013.* Retrieved April 28, 2013, from http://www.bls.gov/news.release/pdf/wkyeng.pdf

U. S. Bureau of Labor Statistics (2015). *Volunteering in the United States - 2014. Retrieved April 8, 2015 from* http://www.bls.gov/news.release/volun.htm

U.S. Census Bureau. (2011a). *Census bureau reports 55 percent have married one time.* Retrieved March 18, 2013, from http://www.census.gov/newsroom/releases/archives/marital_status_living_arrangements/cb11-90.html

U.S. Census Bureau. (2011b). *More young adults are living in their parents' home: Census Bureau Reports*. Retrieved March 12, 2013, from http://www.census.gov/newsroom/releases/archives/families_households/cb11-183.html

U.S. Census Bureau. (2012a). *College enrollment by sex, age, race, and Hispanic origin*. Retrieved April 29, 2013, from http://www.census.gov/compendia/statab/2012/tables/12s0281.pdf

U.S. Census Bureau. (2012b). *Statistical abstract of the United States*. Retrieved February 27, 2013, from http://www.census.gov/compendia/statab/2012/tables/12s1114.pdf

U.S. Census Bureau. (2012c). *U.S. Census Bureau projections show a slower growing, older, more diverse nation a half century from now*. Retrieved March 19, 2013, from http://www.census.gov/newsroom/releases/archives/population/cb12-243.html

U.S. Census Bureau. (2013). *Fertility: Historical time series tables, HF1*. Retrieved November 1, 2013, from http://www.census.gov/hhes/fertility/data/cps/historical.html

U.S. Department of Health and Human Services. (2004). *Statistics related to overweight and obesity*. Bethesda, MD: National Institutes of Health.

U.S. Department of Health and Human Services. (2013). *Federal poverty guideline: 2013*. Retrieved May 10, 2013, from http://aspe.hhs.gov/poverty/13poverty.cfm

U.S. Department of Labor. (2012). *Occupational noise exposure regulations*. Retrieved May 4, 2012, from http://www.osha.gov/pls/oshaweb/owadisp.show_document?p_table=standards&p_id=9735

U.S. General Accounting Office. (2004). *Defense of Marriage Act: Update*. Retrieved September 19, 2009, from http://www.gao.gov/new.items/d04353r.pdf

Uchino, B. N., Cacioppo, J. T., & Kiecolt-Glaser, J. K. (1996). The relationship between social support and physiological processes: A review with emphasis on underlying mechanisms and implications for health. *Psychological Bulletin, 119*, 488–531.

Underhill, E. (1911/1961). *Mysticism*. New York: Dutton.

United Nations Economic Commission for Europe. (2013). *Statistical database*. Retrieved May 8, 2013, from http://w3.unece.org/pxweb/dialog/Saveshow.asp?lang=1

United Nations Statistics Division. (2009). *Demographic and social statistics*. Retrieved January 22, 2010, from http://unstats.un.org/unsd/demographic/

University of Michigan Institute for Social Research. (2009). *Chore wars: Men, women, and housework*. Retrieved May 20, 2009, from http://www.nsf.gov/discoveries/disc_summ.jsp?cntn_id=111458

Unson, C., Trella, P., Chowdhury, S., et al. (2008). Strategies for living long and healthy lives: Perspectives of older African/Caribbean-American women. *Journal of Applied Communication Research, 36*, 459–478.

Usui, C. (1998). Gradual retirement: Japanese strategies for older workers. In K. W. Schaie & C. Schooler (Eds.), *Commentary: Impact of work on older adults* (pp. 45–84). New York: Springer.

Uttl, B., & Van Alstine, C. L. (2003). Rising verbal intelligence scores: Implications for research and clinical practice. *Psychology and Aging, 18*, 616–621.

Väänänen, A., Buunk, B. P., Kivimäki, M., et al. (2005). When it is better to give than to receive: Long-term health effects of perceived reciprocity in support exchange. *Journal of Personality and Social Psychology, 89*, 176–193.

Vaillant, G. E. (1974). Natural history of male psychological health, II: Some antecedents of healthy adult adjustment. *Archives of General Psychiatry, 31*, 15–22.

Vaillant, G. E. (1977). *Adaptation to life: How the best and brightest come of age*. Boston, MA: Little, Brown.

Vaillant, G. E. (1993). *Wisdom of the ego*. Cambridge, MA: Harvard University Press.

Vaillant, G. E. (2002). *Aging well: Surprising guideposts to a happier life from the landmark Harvard study*. Boston, MA: Little Brown.

Vaillant, G. E., & Vaillant, C. O. (1990). Natural history of male psychological health, XII: A 45-year study of predictors of successful aging at 65. *American Journal of Psychiatry, 147*, 31–37.

Valeo, T. (2012). The MP3 generation: At risk for hearing loss? *WebMD Home Health Guide*. Retrieved May 2, 2012, from http://children.webmd.com/guide/hearing-loss-mp3s

Van Alstine Makomenaw, M. (2012). Welcome to a new world: Experiences of American Indian tribal college and university transfer students at predominantly white institutions. *International Journal of Qualitative Studies in Education, 25*, 855–866.

van IJzendoorn, M. (1995). Adult attachment representations, parental responsiveness, and infant attachment: A meta-analysis on the predictive validity of the Adult Attachment Interview. *Psychological Bulletin, 117*, 387–403.

van Reekum, R., Binns, M., Clarke, D., et al. (2005). Is late life depression a predictor of Alzheimer's disease? Results from a historical cohort study. *International Journal of Psychiatry, 20*, 80–82.

Verma, J. (1999). Hinduism, Islam, and Buddhism: The source of Asian values. In K. Leung, U. Kim, S. Yamaguchi, et al. (Eds.), *Progress in Asian social psychologies* (pp. 23–36). Singapore: Wiley.

Vickers, A. J., Cronin, A. M., Maschino, A. C., et al. (2012). Acupuncture for chronic pain: Individual patient data meta-analysis. *Archives of Internal Medicine, 172*, 1–10.

Vogt, D. S., Pless, A. P., King, L. A., et al. (2005). Deployment stressors, gender, and mental health outcomes among Gulf War I veterans. *Journal of Traumatic Stress, 18*, 115–127.

Waddington, C. H. (1957). *The strategy of the genes*. London, England: Allen & Son.

Walaskay, M., Whitbourne, S. K., & Nehrke, M. F. (1983–84). Construction and validation of an ego-integrity status interview. *International Journal of Aging and Human Development, 18*, 61–72.

Waldstein, S. R., & Katzel, L. I. (2006). Interactive relations of central versus total obesity and blood pressure in cognitive function. *International Journal of Obesity (London), 30*, 201–207.

Walker, L. J. (1989). A longitudinal study of moral reasoning. *Child Development, 60*, 157–160.

Walsh, R. (2011). Lifestyle and mental health. *American Psychologist, 66*, 579–592.

Walton, G. M., & Cohen, G. L. (2007). A question of belonging: Race, fit, and achievement. *Journal of Personality and Social Psychology, 92*, 82–96.

Wang, P. S., Berglund, P., Olfson, M., et al. (2005). Failure and delay in initial treatment contact after first onset of mental disorder in the National Comorbidity Survey Replication. *Archives of General Psychiatry, 62*, 603–613.

Wang, P. S., Lane, M., Olfson, M., et al. (2005). Twelve-month use of mental health services in the United States. *Archives of General Psychiatry, 62*, 629–640.

Warr, P. (1994). Age and employment. In M. Dunnette, L. Hough, & J. Triandis (Eds.), *Handbook of industrial and organizational psychology* (Vol. 4, pp. 487–550). Palo Alto, CA: Consulting Psychologists Press.

Warr, P., Butcher, V., & Robertson, J. (2004). Activity and psychological well-being in older people. *Aging and Mental Health, 8*, 172–183.

Wasylyshyn, C., Verhaeghen, P., & Sliwinski, M. J. (2011). Aging and task switching: A meta-analysis. *Psychology and Aging, 26*, 15–20.

Waters, E., Merrick, S. K., Albersheim, L. J., et al. (1995). *Attachment security from infancy to early adulthood: A 20-year longitudinal study*. Poster presented at the biennial meeting of the Society for Research in Child Development, Indianapolis, IN.

Watson. P. J., Brymer, M. J., & Bonanno, G. A. (2011). Postdisaster psychological intervention since 9/11. *American Psychologist, 66*, 482–494.

Weatherbee, S. R., & Allaire, J. C. (2008). Everyday cognition and mortality: Performance differences and predictive utility of the Everyday Cognition Battery. *Psychology and Aging, 23*, 216–221.

Weaver, S. E., & Coleman, M. (2005). A mothering but not a mother role: A grounded theory study of the nonresidential stepmother role. *Journal of Social and Personal Relationships, 22*, 477–497.

Wechsler, D. (1939). *The measurement of adult intelligence.* Baltimore, MD: Williams & Wilkins.

Weiss, R. S. (1982). Attachment in adult life. In C. M. Parkes & J. Stevenson-Hinde (Eds.), *The place of attachment in human behavior* (pp. 171–184). New York: Basic Books.

Weiss, R. S. (1986). Continuities and transformation in social relationships from childhood to adulthood. In W. W. Hartup & Z. Rubin (Eds.), *On relationships and development* (pp. 95–110). Hillsdale, NJ: Erlbaum.

Wethington, E. (2000). Expecting stress: Americans and the "midlife crisis." *Motivation and Emotion, 24*, 85–103.

Whitbourne, S. K., Sneed, J. R., & Sayer, A. (2009). Psychosocial development from college through midlife: A 34-year sequential study. *Developmental Psychology, 45*, 1328–1340.

Whitbourne, S. K., Zuschlag, M. K., Elliot, L. B., et al. (1992). Psychosocial development in adulthood: A 22-year sequential study. *Journal of Personality and Social Psychology, 63*, 260–271.

Wiederhold, B. K. (2012). As parents invade Facebook, teens tweet more. *Cyberpsychology, Behavior, and Social Networking, 15*, 385.

Wilkinson, A. M., & Lynn, J. (2001). The end of life. In R. H. Binstock & L. K. George (Eds.), *Handbook of aging and the social sciences* (pp. 444–461). San Diego, CA: Academic Press.

Williams, A., & Nussbaum, J. E. (2001). *Intergenerational communication across the life span.* Mahwah, NJ: Erlbaum.

Williams, D. R. (1992). Social structure and the health behaviors of blacks. In K. W. Schaie, D. Blazer, & J. S. House (Eds.), *Aging, health behaviors, and health outcomes* (pp. 59–64). Hillsdale, NJ: Erlbaum.

Williams, G. C. (1957). Pleiotropy, natural selection, and the evolution of senescence. *Evolution, 11*, 398–411.

Williams, J. E., & Best, D. L. (1990). *Measuring sex stereotypes. A multination study* (Rev. ed.). Newbury Park, CA: Sage.

Williams, K., & Umberson, D. (2004). Marital status, marital transitions, and health: A gendered life course perspective. *Journal of Health and Social Behavior, 45*, 81–98.

Willis, L. M., Shukitt-Hale, B., & Joseph, J. A. (2009). Recent advances in berry supplementation and age-related cognitive decline. *Current Opinion in Clinical Nutrition & Metabolic Care, 12*, 91–94.

Willis, S. L., & Schaie, K. W. (1994). Cognitive training in the normal elderly. In F. Forette, Y. Christen, & F. Boller (Eds.), *Plasticité cérébrale et stimulation cognitive* (pp. 91–113). Paris, France: Foundational National de Gérontologie.

Willis, S. L., Tennstedt, S. L., Marsiske, M., et al. (2006). Long-term effects of cognitive training on everyday functional outcomes in older adults. *Journal of the American Medical Association, 296*, 2805–2814.

Wilson, R. S., Bennett D. A., & Swartzendruber, A. (1997). Age related change in cognitive function. In P. D. Nussbaum (Ed.), *Handbook of neuropsychology and aging* (pp. 7–14). New York: Plenum Press.

Wilson, R. S., Bennett, D. A., Beckett, L. A., et al. (1999). Cognitive activity in older persons from a geographically defined population. *Journals of Gerontology: Psychological and Social Sciences, 54*, 155–160.

Windsor, T. D., Anstey, K. J., & Rodgers, B. (2008). Volunteering and psychological well-being among young-old adults: How much is too much? *The Gerontologist, 48*, 59–70.

Wingfield, A., Tun, P. A., & McCoy, S. L. (2005). Hearing loss in older adulthood: What it is and how it interacts with cognitive performance. *Current Directions in Psychological Science, 14*, 144–148.

Wink, P., & Dillon, M. (2002). Spiritual development across the adult life course: Findings from a longitudinal study. *Journal of Adult Development, 9*, 79–94.

Wink, P., & Scott, J. (2005). Does religiousness buffer against the fear of death and dying in late adulthood? Findings from a longitudinal study. *Journals of Gerontology: Psychological and Social Sciences, 60*, 207–214.

Wood, W., & Eagly, A. H. (2002). A cross-cultural analysis of the behavior of women and men: Implications for the origins of sex differences. *Psychological Bulletin, 128*, 699–727.

Woodruff-Pak, D. S. (1997). *Neuropsychology of aging.* Malden, MA: Blackwell.

Woods, L. N., & Emery, R. E. (2002). The cohabitation effect on divorce: Causation or selection? *Journal of Divorce and Remarriage, 37*, 101–122.

World Health Organization. (2011a). *The top ten causes of death.* Retrieved November 27, 2012, from http://www.who.int/mediacentre/factsheets/fs310/en/index.html

World Health Organization. (2011b). *Visual impairment and blindness* (Fact Sheet No. 282). Retrieved April 27, 2012, from http://www.who.int/mediacentre/factsheets/fs282/en/

World Health Organization. (2012). *Ten leading causes of deaths in 2008: High-income and low- and middle-income countries.* Retrieved November 17, 2012, from http://gamapserver.who.int/gho/interactive_charts/mbd/cod_2008/graph.html

World Health Organization. (2013). *Gender and women's health: 2013.* Retrieved January 20, 2013, from http://www.who.int/mental_health/prevention/genderwomen/en/

Worthy, D. A., Gorlik, M. A., Pacheco, J. L., et al. (2011). With age comes wisdom: Decision making in younger and older adults. *Psychological Science, 22*, 1375–1380.

Wortman, C. B., & Silver, R. C. (1989). The myths of coping with loss. *Journal of Consulting and Clinical Psychology, 57*, 349–357.

Wrzus, C., Hänel, M., Wagner, J., et al. (2013). Social network changes and life events across the life span: A meta-analysis. *Psychological Bulletin, 139*, 53–80.

Wu, J.-R., Frazier, S. K., Rayens, M. K., et al. (2013). Medication adherence, social support, and event-free survival in patients with heart failure. *Health Psychology, 32*, 637–646.

Xiangkui, Z., Juan, G., & Lumei, T. (2005). Can self-esteem buffer death anxiety? The effect of self-esteem on death anxiety caused by mortality salience. *Psychological Science (China), 28*, 602–605.

Yamanski, K., Uchida, K., & Katsuma, R. (2009). An intervention study of the effects of the coping strategy of "finding positive meaning" on positive affect and health. *International Journal of Psychology, 44*, 249–259.

Yang, K.-S. (2006). Indigenous personality research: The Chinese case. In U. Kim, K.-S. Yang, & K.-K. Hwang (Eds.), *Indigenous and cultural psychology: Understanding people in context* (pp. 285–314). New York: Springer.

Yehuda, R. (2002). Current concepts: Post-traumatic stress disorder. *New England Journal of Medicine, 346*, 108–114.

Yesavage, J., Lapp, D., & Sheikh, J. A. (1989). Mnemonics as modified for use by the elderly. In L. W. Poon, D. Rubin, & B. Wilson (Eds.), *Everyday cognition in adulthood and late life.* Cambridge, MA: Cambridge University Press.

Yu, J. W., Adams, S. H., Burns, J., et al. (2008). Use of mental health counseling as adolescents become young adults. *Journal of Adolescent Health, 43*, 268–276.

Zhang, Z., & Hayward, M. D. (2001). Childlessness and the psychological well-being of older persons. *Journals of Gerontology: Psychological and Social Sciences, 56,* 311–320.

Zickuhr, K., & Madden, M. (2012). *Older adults and Internet use.* Pew Research Center. Retrieved February 27, 2013, from http://www.pewinternet.org/~/media//Files/Reports/2012/PIP_Older_adults_and_internet_use.pdf

Ziol-Guest, K. M., Duncan, G. J., & Kalil, A. (2009). Early childhood poverty and adult body mass index. *American Journal of Public Health, 99,* 527–532.

Zisook, S., Paulus, M., Shuchter, S. R., et al. (1997). The many faces of depression following spousal bereavement. *Journal of Affective Disorders, 45,* 85–94.

Zivotofsky, A. Z., & Koslowsky, M. (2005). Short communication: Gender differences in coping with the major external stress of the Washington, DC, sniper. *Stress and Health, 21,* 27–31.

Zogg, J. B., Woods, S. P., Sauceda, J. A., et al. (2012). The role of prospective memory in medication adherence: A review of an emerging literature. *Journal of Behavioral Medicine, 35,* 47–62.

Credits

Photographs

Cover Image My Good Images/Shutterstock

Chapter 1 Chapter Opener p. 1 AdShooter/Getty Images; p. 4 Barbara Bjorklund; p. 7 Sean Adair/Reuters/Corbis; p. 13 Peter Phipp/Alamy.

Chapter 2 Chapter Opener p. 31 JGI/Jamie Grill/Blend Images/Getty Images; p. 40 Goodluz/Shutterstock; p. 54 Andy Myatt/Alamy; p. 56 dov makabaw/Alamy.

Chapter 3 Chapter Opener p. 67 Monkey Business Images/Shutterstock; p. 80 janine wiedel/Alamy; p. 71 De Meester Johan/Arterra Picture Library/Alamy.

Chapter 4 Chapter Opener p. 97 Stockbroker/Alamy; p. 107 Blue Jean Images/Alamy; p. 120 Fuse/Thinkstock.

Chapter 5 Chapter Opener p. 129 Inti St Clair/Blend Images/Getty Images; p. 136 Johnny Greig/E+/Getty Images; p. 145 iofoto/Fotolia; p. 146 Sonderegger Christof/Alamy.

Chapter 6 Chapter Opener p. 163 Monashee Frantz/OJO Images/Getty Images; p. 168 Steve Prezant/Corbis.

Chapter 7 Chapter Opener p. 198 ACE STOCK LIMITED/Alamy; p. 205 image100/Alamy; p. 207 John Henley/Corbis; p. 216 Andersen Ross/Getty Images; p. 217 Steven Peters/Stone/Getty Images; p. 225 absolut/Shutterstock.

Chapter 8 Chapter Opener p. 233 Chicago Tribune/McClatchy-Tribune/Getty Images; p. 248 image100Businessx/Alamy.

Chapter 9 Chapter Opener p. 262 Comstock/Thinkstock; p. 265 Monkey Business/Thinkstock; p. 272 Corbis Premium RF/Alamy; p. 277 (left) Trikosko Marion S/Library of Congress Prints and Photographs Division Washington, D.C. 20540; p. 277 (right) World History Archive/Image Asset Management Ltd./Alamy; p. 287 Stephen Coburn/Shutterstock.

Chapter 10 Chapter Opener p. 291 Corbis Super RF/Alamy; p. 299 Alex Brandon/The Times-Picayune/Landov; p. 300 Monkey Business Images/Shutterstock; p. 306 Win McNamee/Getty Images News/Getty Images.

Chapter 11 Chapter Opener p. 319 Mykhaylo Palinchak/Shutterstock; p. 331 Charles Mistral/Alamy; p. 334 RubberBall Productions/the Agency Collection/Getty Images.

Chapter 12 Chapter Opener p. 343 Tetra Images/Getty Images; p. 348 Don Hammond/Corbis; p. 352 Ed Bock/CORBIS/Glow Images; p. 354 Laurence Monneret/Getty; p. 355 Mark Scott/Taxi/Getty.

Figures and Tables

Chapter 1 **Table 1-1** p. 8: Copyrighted by Pearson Education, Upper Saddle River, NJ; **Table 1-2** p. 14: From Baltes, P.B. (1987) "Theoretical propositions of life-span developmental psychology: On the dynamics between growth and decline" Developmental Psychology, 23, 611–626. Adapted with permission of the American Psychological Association; **Figure 1-1** p. 15: Based on Bronfenbrenner (1994). Ecological models of human development. In International Encyclopedia of Education (2nd Ed.) Vol. 3, pp. 1643–1647; **Figure 1-2** p. 17: How Healthy Are We? A National Study of Well-Being at Midlife Chapter 2 "Sex Differences in Health Over the Course of Midlife" by PD Cleary, LB Zaborski, and JZ

Ayanian, fig. 12, p. 55. Copyright © 2004 Reprinted by permission of the University of Chicago Press; **Figure 1-3** p. 18: From Galambos, N.L., Barker, E.T., and Krahn, H.J. (2006). Depression, self-esteem, and anger in emerging adulthood: Seven-year Trajectories. Developmental Psychology, 42, 350–365. Adapted with permission of the American Psychological Association; **Figure 1-4** p. 19: From Galambos, N.L., Barker, E.T., and Krahn, H.J. (2006). Depression, self-esteem, and anger in emerging adulthood: Seven-year Trajectories. Developmental Psychology, 42, 350–365. Adapted with permission of the American Psychological Association; **Figure 1-5** p. 20: From Whitbourne, S.K., Zuschlag, M.K. Elliot, L.B et al (1992) "Psychosocial development in adulthood: a 22-year sequential study" Journal of Personality and Social Psychology, 63, 260–271. Adapted with permission of the American Psychological Association; **Figure 1-6** p. 21: From Whitbourne, S. K., Zuschlag, M.K. Elliot, L.B et al (1992) "Psychosocial development in adulthood: a 22-year sequential study" Journal of Personality and Social Psychology, 63, 260–271. Adapted with permission of the American Psychological Association; **Figure 1-7** p. 25: From Spotts, E.L., Neiderhiser, J.M., Towers, H., et al (2004) Genetic and environmental influences on marital relationships. Journal of Family Psychology, 18, 107–119. Adapted by permission of the American Psychological Association; **Table 1-3** p. 27: SALKIND, NEIL, J., EXPLORING RESEARCH, 8th Ed., © 2012. Reprinted and Electronically reproduced by permission of Pearson Education Inc., Upper Saddle River, New Jersey; **Figure 1-8** p. 26: Data from Colcombe & Kramer, Psychological Science, 2003, 14, 125–130.

Chapter 2 **Figure 2-1** p. 36: How Healthy Are We? A National Study of Well-Being at Midlife, chapter 6, "The Menopausal Transition and Aging Processes" by AS Rossi; fig 2-2 Copyright (2004) Reprinted by permission of the University of Chicago Press; **Table 2-1** p. 38: U.S. Centers for Disease Control and Prevention, 2011; **Figure 2-2** p. 39: Ogden, C. L., Carroll, M. D., Kit, B. K., et al. (2012) Prevalence of obesity in the United States, 2009–2010. NCHS Data Brief No. 82. Retrieved on October 30, 2012 from http://www.cdc.gov/nchs/data/databriefs/db82.pdf; **Table 2-2** p. 40: Data from American Society of Plastic Surgeons (2012); **Figure 2-3** p. 41 Copyrighted by Pearson Education, Upper Saddle River, NJ; **Table 2-3** p. 42: Data from National Eye Institute, 2012; Hildreth, C.J., Burke, A.E., and Glass, R.M. (2009) Cataracts Fact Sheet. Journal of the American Medical Association 301, 2060; **Table 2-4** p. 44 US Department of Labor, 2012. Permissible noise exposure levels. (Table G-18); **Figure 2-4** p. 46: Data from Looker, A. C., Borrud, L. G., Dawson-Hughes, B., et al. (2012) Osteoporosis or low bone mass at the femur neck or lumbar spine in older adults: United States, 2005–2008. National Center for Health Statistics Brief, No. 93. Retrieved October 30, 2012 from http://www.cdc.gov/nchs/data/databriefs/db93.htm; **Table 2-5** p. 46: Adapted from National Institute on Aging (2013); CDC (2013); **Figure 2-5** p. 48: Based on data from American Heart Association (2012). High blood pressure: Statistical fact sheet. Retrieved November 6, 2012 from http://www.heart.org/idc/groups/heartpublic/@wcm/@sop/@smd/documents/downloadable/ucm_319587.pdf; **Figure 2-6** p. 54: Copyrighted by Pearson Education, Upper Saddle River, NJ; **Table 2-6** p. 57: Medina, J.J. (1996) The Clock of Ages: Why we age, how we age, winding back the clock. New York: Cambridge University Press; Shifren, J.L. and Hanfling, S. (2010) Sexuality in midlife and beyond: Harvard Medical School Special Health Report. Boston: Harvard University Publications; **Table 2-7** p. 64: Copyrighted by Pearson Education, Upper Saddle River, NJ.

Chapter 3 **Figure 3-1** p. 68: US Center for Disease Control and Prevention, 2012; **Table 3-1** p. 69 Data from National Center for Health Statistics, 2012; **Figure 3-2** p. 70: Data from Brault, M. (2012). Americans with Disabilities: 2010: Household economic studies. Retrieved on November 19, 2012 from: http://www.census.gov/prod/2012pubs/p70–131.pdf; **Table 3-2** p. 72: US Center for Disease Control and Prevention, 2012; **Table 3-3** p. 74: Based on Torpy (2004); U.S. Center for Disease Control and Prevention (2011); **Table 3-4** p. 75: Data from American Diabetes Association, 2012. http://www.diabetes.org/diabetes-basics/prevention/risk-factors/; **Table 3-5** p. 77: Alzheimer's Association, 2013. Reprinted with permission; **Table 3-6** p. 79: Data from Wong, Berglund, Olfson, et al. 2005; **Table 3-7** p. 82: Based on Radloff (1977); Andresen, Malmgren, Carter, et al. (1994); **Figure 3-3** p. 85: Barnes and Schoenborn (2012) Trends in adults receiving a recommendation for exercise or other physical activity from a physician or other health professional, Fig. 2, p. 2. Retrieved on February 18, 2013 from http://www.cdc.gov/nchs/data/databriefs/db86.pdf; **Figure 3-4** p. 87: US Center for Disease Control and Prevention, 2012; **Figure 3-5** p. 88: US Center for Disease Control and Prevention, 2012; **Figure 3-6** p. 93: From Gluckman, et al. (2004) Living with the past: Evolution, development, and pattern of disease. Science, 305, 1733–1739. Copyright © 2004. Reprinted with permission from AAAS; **Table 3-8** p. 94: Copyrighted by Pearson Education, Upper Saddle River, NJ.

Chapter 4 **Figure 4-1** p. 100: Data from Schaie (1983); **Figure 4-2** p. 102: Based on Salthouse (2004) What and when of cognitive aging. CURRENT DIRECTIONS IN PSYCHOLOGICAL sciences, 13, 140–144; **Figure 4-3** p. 105: Park, D. C., Lautenschlager, G., Hedden, T., et al. (2002), Models of visuospatial and verbal memory across the adult life span, Psychology and Aging, 17, 299–320. Copyright © 2002 by American Psychological Association. Reprinted by permission; **Figure 4-4** p. 108: Rönnlund, M., Nyberg, L., Bäckman, L., et al. (2005). Stability, growth, and decline in adult life span development of declarative memory: Cross-sectional and longitudinal data from a population-based study. Psychology and Aging, 20, 3–18. Copyright © 2005 by American Psychological Association. Reprinted with permission; **Figure 4-5** p. 112: Data from Mazerolle et al. (2012) Stereotype threat strengthens automatic recall and undermines controlled processes in older adults. PSYCHOLOGICAL SCIENCE, 23, 723–27; **Figure 4-6** p. 113: Copyrighted by Pearson Education, Upper Saddle River, NJ; **Figure 4-7** p. 114: From Fung, H.H. & Carstensen, L.L. (2003) "Sending memorable messages to the old: Age differences in preferences and memory for advertisements" JOURNAL OF PERSONALITY AND SOCIAL PSYCHOLOGY 85, 163-178. Adapted with permission of the American Psychological Association; **Figure 4-8** p. 118: From Charles, S.T., Mather, M. & Carstensen, L.L. (2003) "Aging and emotional memory: The forgettable nature of negative images for older adults" JOURNAL OF EXPERIMENTAL PSYCHOLOGY: General, 132, 310–324. Adapted by permission of The American Psychological Association; **Figure 4-9** p. 118: Data from McClearn, G.E. Johansson, B., Berg, S. et al (1997) Substantial genetic influence on cognitive abilities in twins 80 or more years old. SCIENCE, 5318, 1560–1563. Reprinted by permission of SCIENCE magazine; **Figure 4-10** p. 123: Zickuhr, K., & Madden, M. (2012). Older adults and internet use. Pew Research Center. http://www.pewinternet.org/~/media//Files/Reports/2012/PIP_Older_adults_and_internet_use.pdf. Copyright © 2012 by Pew Research Center. Reproduced by permission of Pew Research Center's Internet & American Life Project; **Figure 4-11** p. 125: Data from the National Highway Traffic Safety Administration (2009); **Table 4-1** p. 127: Copyrighted by Pearson Education, Upper Saddle River, NJ.

Chapter 5 **Table 5-1** p. 133: Based on Cejka, M.A. & Eagly, A.H. (1999) Gender-stereotypic images of occupations correspond to the sex segregation of employment. PERSONALITY AND SOCIAL PSYCHOLOGY BULLETIN, 25, 413–23 (Table 1, page 416); **Figure 5-1** p.136: Data from US Census Bureau (2011). More young adults are living in their parents' home: Census Bureau Reports. Retrieved

March 12, 2013 http;//www.census.gov/newsroom/releases/archives/families_households/cb11-183html; **Figure 5-2** p. 138: Data from Copen, C. E., Daniels, K., Vespa, J., et al. (2012). First marriages in the United States: Data from the 2006–2010 national survey of family growth. Retrieved on March 16, 2013 from http://www.cdc.gov/nchs/data/nhsr/nhsr049.pdf (Figure 1 page 5); **Figure 5-3** p. 139: Data from Lee, K.S. & Ono, H (2012). Marriage, cohabitation and happiness: A cross-national analysis of 27 countries. Journal of Marriage and Family, 74, 953–972; **Figure 5-4** p. 143: OECD (2012), OECD Family Database, OECD, Paris (www.oecd.org/social/family/database); **Figure 5-5** p. 150: Data from Marks, N.F., Bumpass, L.L. & Jun, H. (2004). Family roles and well-being during the middle life course. In O.G. Brim, C.D. Ryff, and E.C. Kessler (Eds.) How Healthy are we? A national study of well-being at midlife (pp. 514–549). The University of Chicago Press, 2004; **Figure 5-6** p. 152: Data from Federal Interagency Forum on Aging Related Statistics (2012) Older Americans 2012: Key indicators of well-being. http://www.againg.gov/Main_Site/Data/2012_Documents/docs/EntireChartbook.pdf (page 8); **Figure 5-7** p. 155: Based on data from Livingston, G., Cohn, D., et al (2010) Childlessness up among all women; down among women with advanced degrees. Retrieved on April 1, 2013 from http://www.pewsocialtrends.org/2010/06/25/childlessness-up-among-all-women-down-among-women-with-advanced-degrees/ (page 1); **Table 5-2** p. 159: Copyrighted by Pearson Education, Upper Saddle River, NJ.

Chapter 6 **Figure 6-1** p. 168: Based on Wrzus, C., Hänel, M., Wagner, J., et al. (2013). Social network changes and life events across the life span: A meta-analysis. Psychological Bulletin, 139, 53–80. (Figure 2, page 62); **Table 6-1** p. 173: Based on Hazan, C., & Shaver, P. (1990). Love and work: An attachment-theoretical perspective. Journal of Personality and Social Psychology, 59, 270–280; Bartholomew, K., & Horowitz, L.M. (1991) "Attachment styles among young adults: A test of four-category model" JOURNAL OF PERSONALITY AND SOCIAL PSYCHOLOGY, 61, 226–44; **Excerpt** on p. 175: J.M. Gottman. The Science of Trust: Emotional Attunement for Couples. Copyright © 2011 Reprinted by permission of W.W. Norton and Company; **Figure 6-2** p. 179: Gate, G.J. (2011) How many people are lesbian, gay, bisexual and transgender? © 2011 Reprinted by permission of the author; **Excerpt** on p. 181 Based on Parent/Child Relations. In D. Mangen & W. Peterson (eds) Research instruments in social gerontology (pp 114–128); **Figure 6-3** p. 187: Based on DeKay, W.T. (2000) "Evolutionary psychology" In W.C. Nichola, et al. (eds), Handbook of family, development and intervention (pp 23–40). New York: John Wiley & Sons, Inc.; **Figure 6-4** p. 189: Attar-Schwartz, S., Tan, J.P., Buchanan, A., et al (2009). Grandparent and adolescent adjustment in two-parent biological, lone parent, and step-families. JOURNAL OF FAMILY PSYCHOLOGY, 23, 67–75. © 2009. Adapted by permission of the American Psychological Association; **Figure 6-5** p. 191: Data from Milevsky, A. (2005). Compensatory patterns of sibling support in emerging adulthood: Variations in loneliness, self-esteem, depression, and life satisfaction. Journal of Social and Personal Relationships, 22, 743–755. (Table 1, page 748); **Figure 6-6** p. 194: Data from Brenner, J. (2013) Pew Internet: Social Networking. http://pewinternet.org/Commentary/2012/March/Pew-Internet-Social-Networking-full-detail.aspx; **Table 6-2** p. 195: Copyrighted by Pearson Education, Upper Saddle River, NJ.

Chapter 7 **Excerpt** on p. 199: Studs Terkel: Coming of Age: The Story of Our Century by those who lived here (1995) The New Press; **Table 7-1** p. 200: Based on Hartung & Niles (2000); "Using traditional career theories with college students." In D. Luzzo (ed) Career Development of college students: Translating theory and research into practice (pp 3–22); Super, D. E., Savickas, M. L., & Super, C. M. (1996). The life-span, life-space approach to careers. In D. Brown, L. Brooks, & Assoc. (Eds.), Career choice and development: Applying contemporary theories to practice (3rd ed., pp. 121–178) San Francisco: Jossey-Bass; **Figure 7-1** p. 201: Data from US Bureau of Labor Statistics (2013). Employment status of the civilian population by sex and age. http:www.bls.gov/news.releast/ empsit.t01.htm (Table A-1); **Figure 7-2** p. 203: Holland, J.L. (1992) Making vocational choice: A theory of personalities and work environments, 2/e. Copyright © 1992 by Psychological Assessment Resources. Reprinted by permission; **Table 7-2** p. 215: Data from U.S. Bureau of Labor Statistics, 2013; p. 225: Based on Pew Research Center (2013) Modern Parenthood: Roles of Moms and Dads converge as they balance work and Family. http://www.pewsocialtrends.org/ files/2013/03/FINAL_modern_parenthood_03-2013; **Figure 7-4** p. 221: Data from Toosi (2012) Labor force projections to 2020: A more slowly growing workforce. http://www.bls.gov/opub/mlr/2012/ art3full.pdf (Table 3, p. 50); **Figure 7-5** p. 222: Data from United Nations Economic Commission for Europe (2013). Statistical database. http://w3.unece.org/pxweb/dialog/Saveshow. asp?lang=1; **Figure 7-6** p. 224: Data from Federal Interagency Forum on Aging-Related Statistics. Older Americans 2012: Key indicators of well-being. http://www.agingstats.gov/Main_Site/Data/2012_ Documents/docs/EntireChartbook.pdf (p. 14); **Figure 7-7** p. 225: Data from Federal Interagency Forum on Aging-Related Statistics. Older Americans 2012: Key indicators of well-being. http://www. agingstats.gov/Main_Site/Data/2012_Documents/docs/ EntireChartbook.pdf (p. 12); **Table 7-3** p. 230: Copyrighted by Pearson Education, Upper Saddle River, NJ.

Chapter 8   **Table 8-1** p. 236: Data from McCrae, R.R. & John O.P. (1992) An introduction to the five-factor model and its applications. JOURNAL OF PERSONALITY, 60, 185–215, Table 1; **Figure 8-1** p. 237: Roberts, B.W. & DelVecchio, W.F. (2000). The rank-order consistency of personality traits from childhood to old age: A quantitative review of longitudinal studies. PSYCHOLOGICAL BULLETIN, 126, 3025, Figure 1, p. 15. Copyright © 2000 American Psychological Association. Adapted by permission of the American Psychological Association; **Figure 8-2** p. 239: Roberts, B. Q., Walton, K. E., & Viechtbauer, W. (2006). Patterns of mean-level change in personality traits across the life course: A meta-analysis of longitudinal studies. Psychological Bulletin, 132, 1–25. p. 15, Figure 2. Copyright © 2006 the American Psychological Association. Adapted by permission of the American Psychological Association; **Figure 8-3** p. 242: Roberts, B. W., Walton, K. E., & Bogg, T. (2005). Conscientiousness and health across the life course. Review of General Psychology, 9, 156–168. Figure 2, p. 161. Copyright (2005) the American Psychological Association. Adapted by permission of the American Psychological Association; **Figure 8-4** p. 244: Based on data from Riemann, R., Angleitner, A., & Strelau, J. (1997). Genetic and environmental influences on personality: A study of twins reared together using the self- and peer-report NEO-FFI scales. Journal of Personality, 65, 449–475. Table 2, p. 13; **Table 8-2** p. 247: Based on Erikson, 1950, 1959, 1982; **Figure 8-5** p. 249: Whitbourne, Zuschlag, Elliot, et al. (1992). "Psychosocial development in adulthood: A 22-year sequential study" Journal of Personality and Social Psychology p. 266, Figure 5. Copyright © 1992 the American Psychological Association. Adapted by permission of the American Psychological Association; **Table 8-3** p. 250: McAdams, D. P., & de St. Aubin, E. (1992). A theory of generativity and its assessment through self-report, behavioral acts, and narrative themes in autobiography. Journal of Personality and Social Psychology, 62, 1003–1015. Appendix, p. 1015. Copyright © 1992 the American Psychological Association. Adapted by permission of the American Psychological Association; **Figure 8-6** p. 251: McAdams, D.P. Hart, H.M. and Maruna, S. "The anatomy of generativity" In D.P. McAdams & E. de St. Aubin (Eds.) "Generativity and adult development: How and why we care for the next generation" American Psychological Association. pp. 260–271. Copyright © 1998 the American Psychological Association. Adapted by permission of the American Psychological Association; **Figure 8-7** p. 254: Based on data from Truluck and Courtenay, 2002. Truluck, J. E., & Courtenay, B. C. (2002) Ego development and the influence of gender, age, and educational levels among older adults. Educational Gerontology, 28, 325–336. Table 3, page 332; **Table 8-4** p. 255: Vaillant, George E.. Adaptive mental mechanisms: Their role in a positive psychology. American

Psychologist, Vol 55(1), Jan 2000, 89–98. Copyright © 2000 by the American Psychological Association. Adapted by permission of the American Psychological Association; **Figure 8-8** p. 258: Data from Maslow, A. H. (1968/1998). Toward a psychology of being (3rd ed.). New York: Wiley; **Excerpt** on p. 258: Seligman & Csikszentmihalyi (2000) "Positive Psychology: An Introduction" AMERICAN PSYCHOLOGIST, 55, page 5. Copyright © by the American Psychological Association. Adapted by permission.

Chapter 9   **Figure 9-1** p. 267: Copyrighted by Pearson Education, Upper Saddle River, NJ; **Figure 9-2** p. 268: Wink & Dillon (2002) Spiritual development across the adult life course: Findings from a longitudinal study JOURNAL OF ADULT DEVELOPMENT, 9, p. 87 Fig. 2. © 2002. Reprinted with kind permission from Springer Science+Business Media; **Figure 9-3** p. 269: Wink & Dillon (2002) Spiritual development across the adult life course: Findings from a longitudinal study JOURNAL OF ADULT DEVELOPMENT, 9, © 2002. Reprinted with kind permission from Springer Science+Business Media; **Table 9-1** p. 270: Based on Underwood, L.G. (1999) Daily spiritual experiences, Fetzer Institute/National Institute on Aging Working Group; **Figure 9-4** p. 271: Data from Tartaro, J., Leucken, L.J. & Gunn, H.E. (2005) Exploring heart and soul: Effects of religiosity/spirituality and gender on blood pressure and cortisol stress response. JOURNAL OF HEALTH PSYCHOLOGY, 10, pg 760 fig. 2; **Table 9-2** p. 275: Based on Kohlberg, Lawrence (1984). Essays on Moral Development, Vol. 2: The psychology of moral development. San Francisco, CA: Harper & Row; Kohlberg, L. (1976). Moral stages and moralization: The cognitive-developmental approach. In T. Likona (Ed.), Moral development and behavior: Theory, research, and social issues (pp. 31–53). New York: Holt; **Figure 9-5** p. 276: Data from Data from Colby, Kohlberg, Gibbs, et al. 1983; Nisan & Kohlberg, 1982; Snarey, Reimer, & Kohlberg, 1985; Colby, A., Kohlberg, L., Gibbs, J., et al. (1983). A longitudinal study of moral judgment. Monographs of the Society for Research in Child Development, 48 (1-2, Serial No. 200); Nisan, M., & Kohlberg, L. (1982). Universality and variation in moral judgment: A longitudinal and cross-sectional study in Turkey. Child Development, 53, 865–876; Snarey, J. R., Reimer, J., & Kohlberg, L. (1985). Development of social-moral reasoning among kibbutz adolescents: A longitudinal cross-sectional study. Developmental Psychology, 21, 3–17; **Excerpt** on p. 279 Fowler(1981)Stages of Faith, pages 171–172. HarperCollins Publishers, 1981; **Excerpt** on p. 280 R. Kegan(1980) There the dance is: Religious dimensions of development theory. In J. Fowler & A. Vergote. Toward Moral & Religious Maturity (pp 403–440) 1980 Silver Burdette. © 1980 Reprinted by permission of the author; **Excerpt** on p. 280: Fowler(1981)Stages of Faith, page 194. HarperCollins Publishers, 1981; **Table 9-3** p. 282: Copyrighted by Pearson Education, Upper Saddle River, NJ; **Excerpt** on p. 285: R. Kegan (1982) The Evolving Self. Cambridge, MA: Harvard University Press; **Table 9-4** p. 286: Copyrighted by Pearson Education, Upper Saddle River, NJ; **Excerpt** on p. 288: Sam Keen, The Passionate Life. (New York: HarperCollins Publishers) Copyright © 1983. Reprinted by permission of the author.

Chapter 10   **Figure 10-1** p. 295: Data from Almeida, D. M. (2005). Resilience and vulnerability to daily stressors assessed via diary methods. Current Directions in Psychological Sciences, 14, 64–68; **Figure 10-2** p. 296: Data from Almeida, D. M. (2005). Resilience and vulnerability to daily stressors assessed via diary methods. Current Directions in Psychological Sciences, 14, 64–68; **Figure 10-3** p. 297: Based on Lillberg, K., Verkasalo, P. K., Kaprio, J., et al. (2003). Stressful life events and risk of breast cancer in 10,808 women: A cohort study. American Journal of Epidemiology, 157, 415–423; **Figure 10-4** p. 301: Data from Yehuda, R., (2002). Current concepts: Post-traumatic stress disorder. New England Journal of Medicine, 346, 108–114; **Figure 10-5** p. 302: Based on Almeida, D. M., & Horn, M. C. (2004). Is daily life more stressful during middle adulthood? In O. G. Brim, C. D. Ryff, & R. C. Kessler (Eds.), How healthy are we? A national study of well-being at midlife (pp. 425–451). Chicago: University of Chicago Press; **Figure 10-6** p. 303: Scott, S. B., Poulin, M. J., & Silver,

M. C. (2013). A lifespan perspective on terrorism: Age differences in trajectories of response to 9/11. Developmental Psychology, 49, 986–998. © 2013 the American Psychological Association. Adapted with permission; **Figure 10-7** p. 303: Scott, S. B., Poulin, M. J., & Silver, M. C. (2013). A lifespan perspective on terrorism: Age differences in trajectories of response to 9/11. Developmental Psychology, 49, 986–998. © 2013 American Psychological Association. Adapted by permission; **Table 10-1** p. 315: Carver, C. S. (1997). You want to measure coping by your protocol's too long: Consider the brief COPE. International Journal of Behavioral Medicine, 4, 92–100; **Figure 10-8** p. 308: Data from Zivotofsky, A. Z., & Koslowsky, M. (2005). Short communication: Gender differences in coping with the major external stress of the Washington, DC sniper. Stress and Health, 21, 27–31; **Figure 10-9** p. 313: Based on Bonanno, G. A. (2005). Resilience in the face of potential trauma. Current Directions in Psychological Sciences, 14, 135–138; **Figure 10-10** p. 316: Peterson, C., Park, N., & Castro, C. A. (2011). Assessment for the U.S. Army Comprehensive Soldier Fitness Program. American Psychologist, 66, 10–18. © 2011 the American Psychological Association. Adapted by permission.

Chapter 11   **Excerpt** on p. 320: Written by Barbara Field for the MY HERO Project. Reprinted with permission from the MY HERO Project (myhero.com); **Excerpt** on p. 321: Neugarten, B. L. (1970). Dynamics of transition of middle age to old age. Journal of Geriatric Psychiatry, 4, 71–87; **Excerpt** on p. 325: Kübler-Ross, E. (1974). Questions and answers on death and dying. New York: Macmillan; **Figure 11-1** p. 330: Data from Teno, J. M., Clarridge, B. R., Casey, V., et al. (2004). Family perspectives on end-of-life care at the last place of care. Journal of the American Medical Association, 291, 88–93. American Medical Association, 2004; **Table 11-3** p. 332: Based on material from The American Cancer Society (2013); **Excerpt** on p. 333:

Wilkinson, A. M. & Lynn, J. (2001). The end of life. In R. H. Binstock & L. K. George (Eds.), Handbook of aging and the social sciences (pp. 441–461. San Diego, CA: Academic Press; **Excerpt** on p. 334: Victor W. Marshall and Judith A. Levy (1990) Aging and dying. In Handbook of Aging and the Social Sciences, 3rd Edition (invited but reviewed). Robert Binstock and Linda George (Eds.). San Francisco: Academic Press, pp. 245–260; **Table 11-4** p. 335 Data from Hazell, L. V. (1997) Cross-cultural funeral rites. Director, 69, 53–55; Lobar, S. L. (2006). Cross-cultural beliefs, ceremonies, and rituals surrounding the death of a loved one. Pediatric Nursing, 32, 44–50; Santillanes, G. (1997). Releasing the spirit: A lesson in Native American funeral rituals. Director, 69, 32–34; Techner, D. (1997). The Jewish funeral – A celebration of life. Director, 69, 18–20; **Excerpt** on p. 338: Feifel, H. (1990). Psychology and death: Meaningful rediscovery. American Psychologist, 45, 537–543. Copyright © 1990 the American Psychological Association. Reprinted with permission; **Figure 11-2** p. 340: Bonanno, G. A., Wortman, C. B., Lehman, D. R., et al. (2002). Resilience to loss and chronic grief: A prospective study from preloss to 18-months postloss. Journal of Personality and Social Psychology, 83, 1150–1164. Copyright © 2002. Reprinted by permission of the American Psychological Association.

Chapter 12   **Table 12-1** p. 345: Copyrighted by Pearson Education, Upper Saddle River, NJ; **Figure 12-1** p. 351: Copyrighted by Pearson Education, Upper Saddle River, NJ; **Figure 12-2** p. 364: Based on Waddington, C. H. (1957). The strategy of the genes. London: Allen & Sons; **Figure 12-3** p. 366: Copyrighted by Pearson Education, Upper Saddle River, NJ; **Excerpt** on p. 367: Janet Giele. Women in the Middle Years (John Wiley & Sons, 1982); **Excerpt** on p. 369: McCrae & Costa, 1983, Joint factors in self-reports and ratings: Neuroticism, Extraversion, and Openness to Experience. Personality and Individual Differences, 4, p. 245–255.

Author Index

A

AARP, 217–218
Abdel-Khalek, A. M., 322
Abou-Median, S., 307
Acevedo, B. P., 176
Achenbaum, W. A., 358
Ackerman, P. L., 101
Acree, M., 339
Adams, B., 314
Adams, C., 111
Adams, S. H., 83
Adelmann, P. K., 355
Adler, N., 87
Afifi, T., 194
Ai, A. L., 269
Ainsworth, M. D. S., 165
Aitken, R., 91
Ajrouch, K. J., 192, 380
Akiyama, H., 166, 192
Alaphilippe, D., 359
Albanesius, C., 44
Albersheim, L. J., 166
Aldwin, C. M., 305
Alea, N., 234
Alesina, A., 222
Allaire, J. C., 102
Allery, A., 91
Allison, M., 91
Allman, J., 86
Allman, R. M., 125
Almeida, D. M., 294–295, 300, 301, 302
Almeida, O. P., 51
Alparone, F. R., 207
Alterovitz, S. S.-R., 171
Alzheimer's Association, 76–78
Amato, P. R., 177, 184
American Academy of Orthopaedic Surgeons, 47
American Cancer Society, 332
American Diabetes Association, 75
American Hair Loss Association, 41
American Heart Association, 48
American Nutrition Association, 62
American Psychiatric Association, 79, 255, 298
American Society of Plastic Surgeons, 40–41
American Speech-Language-Hearing Association, 43
Amir, M., 324
Anderson, R. M., 34
Andresen, E. M., 81
Andrew, A. M., 211
Angleitner, A., 243, 244
Ano, G. G., 310
Anstey, K. J., 229
Antoni, M. H., 312
Antonovics, K., 214
Antonucci, T. C., 63, 166, 186, 192, 249, 311, 312, 380
Aquilino, W. S., 208
Ardelt, M., 322, 323, 359
Ardila, A., 119
Arevalo, J. M., 304
Aristotle, 260
Armstrong, P. I., 205
Arnett, J. J., 135, 204, 347

Aron, A., 169, 170, 171, 176
Aronson, J., 98
Aronson, S. R., 177
Arterburn, D. E., 75
Ash, I. K., 116
Ashby, J., 305
Aspinwall, L. G., 309
Astle, C. M., 35
Atchley, P., 125
Attar-Schwartz, S., 189
Atwal, J. K., 92
Ault-Brutus, A. A., 89
Auman, C., 111
Austad, S. N., 32, 86
Aviv, A., 34
Ayala, J., 191
Ayanian, J. Z., 17, 23, 86
Azaola, M. C., 137

B

Babcock, R. L., 119
Bachman, L. D., 119
Backlund, E., 141
Bäckman, L., 104, 107, 109, 117, 118
Baddeley, A. D., 104
Bahns, M., 61
Bailes, J., 78
Bailey, H., 105
Bailey, N., 359
Bainbridge, D., 382
Bakker, A. B., 212
Balamurugan, A., 42, 43
Baldwin, C. L., 116
Ball, K. K., 125
Ballard-Barbash, R., 74
Balsam, K. F., 180
Baltes, M. M., 356, 358
Baltes, P. B., 13, 14, 19, 29, 101, 107, 109, 116–117, 119, 126, 209, 356, 358
Banks, G. C., 210, 211
Barelds, D. P. H., 246
Barkan, S., 324
Barker, D. J., 92
Barker, E. T., 18, 19, 20
Barnes, P. M., 85
Bartholomew, K., 172
Barton, S. A., 187
Bartzokis, G., 49, 50
Bata, I., 92
Bates, J. S., 186
Batty, G. D., 102
Bauer, J., 253
Baum, A., 293
Baumeister, R. F., 167
Baun, M. M., 85
Bayard, K., 204
Beal, C. R., 207
Beauchaine, T. P., 180
Beaumont, J. G., 359
Becker, G., 143
Beckett, L. A., 119
Bedell, B. J., 77
Beers, M. H., 49

Bell, K. W., 382
Belsky, J., 144, 217
Bem, S. L., 132
Bengtson, V. L., 181
Bengtsson, T., 93
Benjamins, M. R., 267
Bennett, D. A., 103, 119
Berdasco, M., 73
Beresford, S. A. A., 121
Berg, C. A., 101, 104
Berg, S., 117
Berglund, P., 79–80, 89
Bering, J., 265
Berkman, L., 63, 167
Besser, A., 324
Best, D. L., 131
Biblarz, T. J., 178
Bielak, A. A. M., 117
Bigby, M., 61
Biggs, S., 186
Binns, M., 81
Biorck, J., 269
Birak, K. S., 106
Birditt, K. S., 182, 185, 192
Birkhill, W. R., 102
Birren, J. E., 323, 357
Bisno, B., 328
Bissig, D., 109
Bjerkeset, O., 81
Bjork-Eriksson, T., 49
Bjorklund, B., 4
Bjorklund, D. F., 190
Blackburn, E. H., 34
Blackwell, L., 240
Blair, C., 98, 101
Blanchard-Fields, F., 114
Blandon, A. Y., 192
Blehar, M., 165
Bleske, A. L., 132
Blieszner, R., 180
Bliwise, D. L., 56
Blom, V., 212
Bloom, B., 81
Bluck, S., 234
Blumberg, S. L., 174
Blumstein, T., 229
Blurton Jones, N. G., 190
Bogart, A., 75
Bogg, T., 242, 243
Bolles, D., 380
Bonanno, G. A., 299, 313, 314, 315, 339, 340
Bond, J. T., 217
Bonello, K., 179
Bookwala, J., 151
Booth, A., 141, 176
Booth-Butterfield, M., 186
Booth-LaForce, C., 173
Borrell, L. N., 304
Borrud, L. G., 45
Bouchard, T. J., 117
Bouchery, E. E., 83
Bowlby, J., 165, 166, 172, 182, 338, 340
Bradbury, T. N., 241
Bradley, D. E., 227
Brallier, S., 28
Brand, D., 119
Brault, M., 70
Bravata, D. M., 53
Brébion, G., 105
Brehmer, Y., 110

Brenner, J., 193, 194
Breslau, J., 84
Brim, O., 287
Brisette, I., 312
Brogaard, T., 329
Broman, C. L., 308
Bromberger, J. T., 51, 52
Brondolo, E., 90
Bronfenbrenner, U., 14, 15, 30
Brown, C. M., 193
Brown, D., 141
Brown, D. R., 269
Brown, G. G., 117
Brown, L. H., 186
Brown, M., 89
Brown, S. L., 184
Browning, E. B., 350
Brownley, K. A., 299
Bruce, M. L., 154
Brumback-Peltz, C. R., 106
Bryant, B., 314
Bryant, S., 355
Brymer, M. J., 299
Buchanan, A., 188, 189
Buchner, D. M., 121
Buman, M. P., 56
Bumpass, L. L., 141, 149, 150, 151
Burack, O., 110
Buring, J., 51
Burke, A., 331
Burke, A. E., 42
Burke, D. M., 107
Burke, R. J., 294
Burkhauser, R. V., 221, 222
Burns, J., 83
Buss, D. M., 167, 171, 245
Butcher, V., 359
Butler, R., 356
Buunk, B. P., 311
Bynner, J., 204
Byrd, M., 111

C
Cacioppo, J. T., 310
Cadinu, M., 207
Calder, N., 91
Calkins, E., 354
Calzo, J. P., 249
Campbell, J., 264, 280
Campbell, L. D., 169, 172, 192
Campbell, P., 151
Cannon, W. B., 381
Capaldi, D., 121
Caplan, L., 119
Caporeal, L. R., 167
Cappell, K. S., 106
Carlson, J. F., 23
Carmalt, J. H., 170
Carney, J. S., 269
Carr, D., 140
Carrère, S., 145
Carroll, M. D., 37, 39
Carskadon, M. A., 55
Carstensen, L. L., 114–115, 167
Carter, W. B., 81
Carver, C. S., 242, 306, 312
Casey, V., 329, 330
Caspi, A., 177, 237, 240, 241, 242, 245
Castro, C. A., 314, 315, 316
Cate, R. M., 164, 170

Catoni, C., 50
Cattell, R. B., 101, 236
Cavalli-Sforza, F., 304
Cavalli-Sforza, L. L., 304
Cave, S., 377
Cawley, J., 170
Cejka, M. A., 133
Centers for Disease Control and Prevention (CDC), 37, 46, 47, 55, 62, 68, 73, 74, 81, 85, 87, 89
Centofanti, M., 103
Cepeda, N. J., 109
Cerda-Flores, R. M., 187
Chan, D. K.-S., 213
Chang, E., 156
Charles, S. T., 115, 116, 298
Charness, N., 119
Chen, E., 305
Chen, X., 135
Cheng, G. H.-L., 213
Cheng, Y.-P., 182, 185
Cherkas, L. F., 34
Cherlin, A. J., 141
Cheung, F. M., 246
Cheung, S. F., 246
Chida, Y., 91, 269
Chin, L., 153
Chiou, W.-B., 62
Chiu, W. T., 80, 83
Chou, C.-F., 43
Chowdhury, S., 91
Christensen, K., 61
Christensen, U., 141
Chu, K. C., 88
Churchland, P. S., 381
Cicchetti, D., 135
Cicirelli, V. G., 182
Cissell, G. M., 125
Clancy, S. M., 209
Clark, A. E., 211, 359
Clark, C. M., 77
Clark, R., 304
Clark, R. L., 221, 222
Clarke, D., 81
Clarkson-Smith, L., 119
Clarridge, B. R., 329, 330
Clausell, E., 180
Cleary, P. D., 16, 23, 86
Clements, M. L., 174
Clunis, D. M., 60
Coall, D. A., 190
Coelho, J. S., 35
Coffield, A. B., 83
Cohen, G. L., 240
Cohen, P., 58
Cohen, S., 87
Cohn, D., 155, 156
Colby, A., 275, 277
Colcombe, S., 26, 102, 111, 120
Cole, A., 304
Cole, S. W., 304
Coleman, M., 157
Coleman, P. G., 359
Collins, W. A., 172, 173
Colman, R. J., 34, 35
Coltrane, S., 218
Compton, D. M., 119
Connerty, T. J., 305
Connidis, I. A., 192
Cooney, T. M., 184
Copen, C. E., 138

Coren, S., 85
Cornum, R., 315
Corr, C. A., 326
Cosmides, L., 246
Costa, M., 328
Costa, P. T., Jr., 234, 235, 238, 246, 353, 368
Costello, C. B., 204, 226
Courtenay, B. C., 253
Couzin, J., 92
Cowan, C. P., 144
Cowan, P. A., 144
Craig, J., 135
Craik, F. I. M., 105, 107
Crawford, D. W., 144
Crimmins, E. M., 93, 94
Cronin, A. M., 47
Cross, M. C., 179
Crowell, M. F., 34
Csikszentmihalyi, M., 258
Cullum, S., 119
Cumming, E., 131, 355
Curhan, G. C., 44
Curhan, S. G., 44
Curtayne, E. S., 107
Cutler, S. J., 229
Czaja, S. J., 209

D
Dalai Lama, 381
Dalby, P., 269
D'Alessio, A. C., 11
Daley, D., 359
Daniels, K., 138
Danner, D. D., 242
Dansky, B. S., 314
Das, A., 60
Davidson, K., 92
Davies, L., 192
Davis, J. M., 314
Davis, K. D., 215
Dawson-Hughes, B., 45
Deary, I. J., 102
Deci, E. L., 259–260
de Frias, C. M., 108
DeFries, J. C., 10, 117
DeKay, W. T., 187, 188
Dekel, S., 305
DeLamater, J., 57, 59, 60
DeLongis. A., 312
DelVecchio, W. F., 237
Demler, O., 79–80, 83, 89
Denollet, J., 327
Depp, C. A., 91
Der, G., 101
De Raad, B., 246
De Raedt, R., 321
Derby, R. W., 191
Desrichard, O., 111
Desrochers, S., 217
Desrosiers, M. F., 29
de St. Aubin, E., 250, 251
de Vaus, D., 177
DeViney, S., 223
de Waal, F., 167
DeWan, A. T., 63
Diehl, M., 234, 253
Diekman, A. B., 132
Diener, C., 360
Diener, E., 140, 359, 360
DiGrande, L., 314

Dillon, M., 263, 268–269
Ding, L., 74
Dixon, R. A., 105, 108, 126
Dormaszewska, K., 54
Dotterer, A., 182
Dougall, A. L., 293
Douglass, C. B., 135
Dressel, J., 125
Duberstein, P. R., 243
Dubin, L., 270
Duggan, M., 194
Duncan, G. J., 93
Dunlosky, J., 105
Dunn, E. W., 62
Duvall Antonacopoulos, N. M., 193
Dweck, C., 239–240
Dyke, M., 207
Dykiert, D., 101

E
Eagly, A. H., 132, 133, 204
Earles, J. L., 107
Eastwick, P. W., 171
Eber, H. W., 236
Edwards, B. K., 89
Eheman, C., 74
Ehlers, A., 314
Ehrensaft, M., 241
Ehrlich, M. F., 105
Eickhoff, J. C., 194
Ein-Dor, T., 305
Einstein, G. O., 109
Elder, G. H., Jr., 7, 135, 158, 353
Eliason, G., 323
Elliot, L. B., 20, 21, 249
Ellis, B. J., 132, 169, 172,
Ellis, L., 322
Ellis, M. J., 74
Ellis, R., 154
Emanuel, E. J., 333
Emanuel, L. L., 333
Emery, C. F., 117, 121
Emery, R. E., 177
Employee Benefit Research Institute, 220
Epel, E. S., 34
Epelbaum, E., 52
Ericksen, J. A., 206
Erickson, K. I., 120
Ericsson, K. A., 209
Erikson, E. H., 247–248, 261, 348
Eriksson, P. S., 49
Ertel, K. A., 167
Eshbaugh, E., 322
Essex, M. J., 215
Esteller, M., 73
Evans, R. I., 248
Eysenck, H. J., 245

F
Fabre, B., 298
Facio, A., 135
Fahey, T., 359
Fahlander, K., 117
Fairclough, D. L., 333
Family Caregiver Alliance, 223
Fastborn, J., 117
Federal Interagency Forum on Age-Related Statistics, 152, 224, 225

Feeney, J., 172
Feifel, H., 338
Feld, S., 310
Feldman, D. C., 210, 211
Feldman, H., 144
Feldman, L., 323, 357
Ferner, F., 47
Ferraro, K. F., 90, 131, 151
Ferrucci, L., 242
Field, B., 320
Field, D., 192, 238
Finch, C. E., 32, 93, 94
Fingerman, K. L., 150, 182, 183, 185
Finkel, D., 117
Finkel, E. J., 171
Fischer, E. F., 170
Fisher, D. L., 126
Fisher, H. L., 170
Fisher, N. M., 354
Flannelly, K. J., 322
Fleeson, W., 145
Flinn, M. V., 293
Florian, V., 315
Florido, R., 36
Flottemesch, T. J., 83
Flouri, E., 188
Floyd, K., 183
Flynn, J., 100
Folkman, S., 306, 309, 339
Fontana, L., 35
Forneris, C. A., 299
Foskett, N., 207
Foster, A. C., 144
Foster, H., 135
Foster, R. G., 55, 56
Fouad, N. A., 204
Fouladi, R. T., 58
Fowler, J., 265, 279–284, 288
Fraley, R. C., 173, 338
Frankl, V., 265
Franks, M. M., 311
Fraser, J., 57
Frazier, S. K., 329
Fredrickson, K. I., 305
Fredriksen-Goldsen, K. I., 60
Freedman, V. A., 70
Freedy, J. R., 314
Freeman, P. A., 60
Friedman, B., 243
Friedman, B. X., 132
Friedman, M., 90,
Friedman, M. J., 306
Friedman, N. P., 106
Friesen, W. V., 242
Fromm, E., 265
Fu, P., 61
Fukunaga, A., 45
Fuller-Iglasias, H., 311
Fung, H. H., 114
Furnham, A., 360

G
Galambos, N. L., 18–20, 135
Galinsky, E., 217
Gallagher, M. W., 91
Gallicchio, L., 59
Gallo, L. C., 90
Gana, K., 359
Gans, D., 33

Garcia, J. R., 59
Gartlehner, G., 299
Gastmans, C., 60
Gates, G. J., 178
Gatz, M., 121
Geary, D. C., 132
Geisinger, K. F., 23
George, L. G., 241
George, L. K., 310, 358, 359
Georgellis, Y., 359
Gerstorf, D., 117
Geurts, T., 186
Gibbs, J., 275
Gibbs, W. W., 73
Gidron, Y., 92
Giele, J., 367
Gilligan, C., 278, 290
Given, B., 151
Given, C. W., 151
Glaeser, E., 222
Glass, R. M., 42
Glotzer, L. D., 49
Gluckman, P. D., 92, 93
Glueck, E., 362
Glueck, S., 362
Glymour, M. M., 167
Gmeindl, L., 106
Goel, M. S., 89
Goesling, B., 88
Goh, J. O., 106
Gohdes, D. M., 42, 43
Gohm, C. L., 141, 359
Gold, D., 191, 267
Gold, J. M., 139
Goldberg, A. E., 144
Goldberg-Glen, R. S., 149
Golding, G., 276
Goldstein, D., 115
Golub, R. M., 331
Gómez-Pinilla, F., 85
Gonda, J. N., 102
Gonyea, J. G., 226
Gonzaga, G. C., 301
Gonzalez de Sather, J. C. M., 109
Goodman, W. B., 215
Goodsell, T. L., 186
Gordon, B. A., 106
Gorlik, M. A., 126
Gorman, E., 214
Gorman, J. M., 299
Gottfredson, L. S., 102
Gottfried, A. E., 217
Gottman, J. M., 145, 175, 241
Gough, H. G., 236
Gow, A. J., 100
Goyer, A., 149
Green, R. J., 180
Greenberg, E., 213
Greenberg, G., 11
Greenfield, E. A., 229
Greenfield, P. M., 193
Greenwood, J. L., 184
Greer, S., 327
Gregoire, J., 104
Greve, W., 190
Grosman, H., 298
Gross, A. L., 103, 109
Gruber-Baldini, A. L., 119
Grunberg, L., 213

Gruntmanis, U., 52
Gump, B. B., 298
Gunn, H. E., 269, 270, 271
Gupta, S., 217
Guralnik, J. M., 355
Gurin, P., 287
Gutmann, D., 147, 256, 261

H
Haan, N., 353
Hagestad, G. O., 137, 368
Hagger, M. S., 85
Haight, B. K., 357
Hale, S., 104
Halpern, C. T., 11
Halpern, D. F., 217
Halter, J. B., 50, 75
Hamer, M., 91
Hamilton, B. E., 142, 143
Hammer, L. B., 218
Hammers, J. L., 78
Hancock, H. E., 117
Hänel, M., 168
Hanfling, S., 57, 58, 59
Hankey, B. F., 88
Hanson, M. A., 92, 93
Hanson, R. F., 314
Harada, K., 229
Harding, S. R., 322
Hardy, D. J., 209
Hardy, M. A., 220
Hareven, T. K., 146
Harman, J. J., 179
Harmon, D., 33
Harmon, K., 63
Harrington Myer, M., 89
Harrison, D. E., 35
Harrison, E. D., 35
Harris Poll, 263, 321, 323
Hart, H. M., 250, 251
Hartley, A., 119, 124
Hartung, P. J., 200, 203
Harwood, H. J., 83
Hasher, L., 105
Hastie, R., 112
Hatfield, E., 170
Hausmann, L. R. M., 90
Hawkes, K., 190
Hawkins, D. N., 141, 176
Hawkins, H. L., 121
Hawkley, L. C., 304
Hay, E. L., 185
Hayes, S. C., 37
Hayflick, L., 33
Hays, J. C., 267
Hayslip, B., Jr., 189
Hayward, M. D., 156
Hazan, C., 172
Hazell, L. V., 337
He, W., 71
Healey, M. K., 115
Heath, C. W., 256
Heckhausen, J., 158
Hedden, T., 104
Heggestad, E. E., 211
Hekler, E. B., 56
Heller, D., 33
Hellerstein, J., 204
Helms, S. T., 203

Helson, R., 238, 241, 245, 256–257, 305
Henderson, C. E., 189
Hendricks, J., 229
Henley, S. J., 74
Henninger, W., 322
Henretta, J. C., 209
Henry, J. D., 109
Henry, W., 355
Henry, W. E., 131, 355
Heppner, M. J., 206
Heppner, P. P., 206
Hequembourg, A., 28
Herd, P., 88, 89
Herman, C. P., 35
Heron, M., 86
Hershberger, S. L., 208
Hershey, D. A., 113
Hertwig, R., 190
Hertzog, C., 105
Hess, T. M., 110, 111
Heuveline, P., 139
Hevey, D., 91
Hewer, A., 278
Hewitt, B., 177
Higgins, C. A., 241
Hildreth, C. J., 42
Hill, P. L., 242
Hill, R. D., 121
Hinson, J. T., 111
Hobbs, M., 314
Hofer, S. M., 61, 101
Hofmann, V., 253
Hoge, C. W., 314
Holden, C., 87
Holland, J. L., 202–203, 232
Holloszy, J. O., 35
Holman, A., 194
Holmes, T., 294, 311
Holtzman, S., 312
Hommel, B., 101
Hood, K. E., 11
Hooker, S. A., 270
Hooyman, N. R., 226
Hope, C. W., 78
Horgan, J. H., 91
Horn, J. L., 101, 119
Horn, M. C., 295, 302
Hornsby, P. J., 33
Horowitz, L. M., 172
Horton, F., 215
Hosemann, J., 124
House, J. S., 88, 89
House, M., 227
Hoyer, W. J., 107, 209
Hoyert, D. L., 72, 86
Hoyt, W. T., 270
Hrdy, S. B., 190
Huang, B., 269
Hughes, M. E., 140
Hultsch, D. F., 105
Hunkin, J. L., 34
Hunte, H. E. R., 304
Hunter, S., 352
Hunter, W. J., 276
Huppert, F. A., 119
Hurd, M. D., 242
Huston, A., 177
Huston, T. L., 144
Hutchinson, K., 184
Huynh, J. Y., 212

Hy, L. X., 253
Hyde, J. S., 143, 215

I
Iachina, M., 61
Iacono, W. G., 117
Idler, E. L., 267
Isaacowitz, D. M., 116

J
Jackson, J. J., 243
Jackson, J. S., 186
Jacobs, D. M., 119
Jacobs, S., 338
Jäger, T., 109
James, W., 266, 279, 285, 290
Jankowiak, W. R., 170
Jelenchick, L. A., 194
Jennings, J. M., 109
Jennings, P. A., 305
Jensen, A. R., 99
Jeong, H. S., 193
Jhalani, J., 90
Johansson, B., 117
Johnson, M. E., 323
Johnson, M. K., 106
Johnson, M. L., 323
Johnson, M. M. S., 113
Johnson, N. J., 141
Johnson, R. A., 85
Johnson, R. W., 223
Johnson, S., 178
Johnson, S. C., 35
Johnson, W., 100
Johnston, K., 193
Jolles, J., 121
Jones, C. J., 239
Jones, E., 170
Jones, L. B., 106
Jonsson, T., 92
Joyner, K., 170
Juan, G., 323
Judge, T. A., 241
Jun, H., 149, 150, 151
Jung, C. G., 147, 256, 265, 285, 290

K
Kahn, R. L., 166, 358
Kahn, W. A., 212
Kalil, A., 93
Kalish, R. A., 321
Kaltman, S., 314, 339
Kanter, M., 194
Kapahi, P., 35
Kaprio, J., 297
Kaptin, R., 190
Kardatzke, K. N., 184
Karney, B. R., 171, 241
Karter, A. J., 90
Kasl, S. V., 267
Kasper, J. D., 155
Kasser, T., 250
Kasser, V. M., 259
Kato, B. S., 34
Katsuma, R., 92
Katzel, L. I., 117
Katz-Wise, S. L., 143
Kaufman, G., 215
Kaus, C. R., 276, 278
Kawachi, J., 228

Keefe, F. J., 154
Keen, S., 288
Kegan, R., 280, 283, 285
Keith, P. M., 155
Kellehear, A., 326
Kelly, J., 144
Keltner, D., 313, 339
Kemeny, M. E., 328
Kemp, C. L., 186
Kempermann, G., 49
Kenealy, P. M., 359
Kennedy, K. M., 103
Kenrick, D. T., 167
Kersten, A. W., 107
Kersten, M., 212
Kessler, R. C., 79–80, 81, 83, 89, 172
Ketelaar, T., 132
Kiecolt-Glaser, J. K., 141, 142, 310
Kiely, K. M., 117
Killen, M., 278
Kilpatrick, D. G., 314
Kim, J. H., 151
Kim, S., 115
Kinderman, S. S., 117
King, L. A., 311
Kira, I., 305
Kirana, P., 59
Kirby, S. E., 359
Kirkcaldy, B., 360
Kirkland, J. L., 36
Kit, B. K., 37, 39
Kivimäki, M., 311
Klein, B. E. K., 43
Klein, L. C., 300–301
Klein, R., 43
Klempin, F., 49
Kleykamp, B. A., 109
Kleyman, E., 132
Kliegel, M., 109
Kline, G. H., 177
Knight, B. G., 151
Knott, V., 305
Knudsen, K., 186
Kobor, M. S., 305
Kockel, L., 35
Koenig, C., 323
Koenig, H. G., 310
Kohlberg, L., 271–272, 274, 275, 277, 286
Kolarz, C. M., 352
Kolomer, S., 149
Köpetz, C., 111
Koslowsky, M., 308, 309
Koster, E. H. W., 321
Kozak, A., 212
Krahn, H. J., 18, 19, 20
Kramer, A. F., 26, 102, 109, 120, 121
Krampe, R. T., 209
Krause, N., 311, 312, 359
Kravitz, H. M., 51, 52
Kreider, R. M., 154, 156
Kreisler, C. J., 144
Krettenauer, T., 253
Krohn, S., 51
Król-Zielinska, M., 54
Kropnik, V. S., 10, 117
Kryla-Lighthall, N., 167
Kübler-Ross, E., 324–326, 338, 340, 342
Kuehn, B. M., 46
Kuehne, V. S., 362
Kujala, U. M., 61

Kumar, R., 86
Kusy, K., 54
Kwan, V. S. Y., 238, 245

L
Labouvie-Vief, G., 102, 253
Lachman, M. E., 110, 147
LaGuardia, J. G., 259
Lalia, N., 193
Lamond, A. J., 91
Lampkin, C. L., 148
Lane, C. J., 103
Lane, M., 83, 84, 89
Lapp, D., 109
Larkin, G. R., 115
Larsen, B. A., 42, 43
Larsman, P., 85
Larson, D. B., 270
Larson, E. B., 121
Laumann, E. O., 60
Laursen, P., 119
Lautenschlager, G., 104
Leary, M. R., 167
Leather, D. M., 184
Lee, C. C., 209
Lee, K. S., 138, 177
Lee I.-M., 51
Lefkowitz, E. S., 185
Lehman, D. R., 314, 339
Leifheit-Limson, E., 111
Leiter, M. P., 212
Lemasters, E. E., 144
Leong, F. T. L., 246
Leopold, T., 137
Lerman, R., 216
Lerner, M. R., 72
Lerner, R. M., 14
Levenson, M. R., 305
Levert, E., 246
Levin, L. A., 164
Levin, M. E., 37
Levine, C., 278
Levinson, D. J., 283
Levy, B. R., 111
Levy, J., 334
Lewin, T., 326
Lewis, E. K., 228
Lewis B. P., 300
Li, S.-C., 101, 110, 117
Liang, J., 310
Lichtenstein, P., 208
Lieberman, M., 305
Light, L. L., 101, 107
Lightfoot, S. A., 72
Lillberg, K., 297
Lillis, J., 37
Lin, I.-F., 184
Lin, J., 34
Lindenberger, U., 101, 107, 116, 117, 119
Lindström, M., 93
Lindwall, M., 85
Lipsitt, L. P., 13
Liu, H., 53, 141
Liu, X., 310
Livingston, G., 155, 156
Livson, F. B., 367
Livson, N., 360, 361
Lloyd, S. A., 170
Lobar, S. L., 337
Löckenhoff, C. E., 242, 243

Lockley, S. W., 55, 56
Loevinger, J., 252–254, 259, 261
Loew, B., 176
Lofquist, D., 154, 178
Logan, R. L., 250
Longino, C. F., Jr., 227
Longmire, C. V., 151
Lonky, E., 276, 278
Looker, A. C., 45
Lopez, S. J., 91
Lougheed, E., 194
Loveland, A., 103
Loving, T. J., 177
Lowe, J. C., 158
Lowe, S. R., 305
Lucas, J. W., 71
Lucas, R. E., 359
Luecken, L. J., 269, 270, 271
Lugaila, T., 154
Lukaszewski, A. W., 246
Lumei, T., 323
Lund, O. C. H., 246
Lund, R., 141
Lustgarten, M., 33
Lustig, C., 109
Lydon, J., 173
Lyketsos, C. G., 118
Lyles, C. R., 90
Lynn, J., 330, 333
Lyons, M. J., 11
Lyons, N. P., 278

M
Maciosek, M. V., 83
Mackinlay, R., 109
MacLeod, M. S., 109
Madden, D. J., 106
Madden, M., 122–123
Maddi, S. R., 270, 315
Maestas, N., 228
Magdol, L., 177
Maguen, S., 304
Mahieu, L., 60
Maillot, P., 124
Maitland, S. B., 108
Malley, M., 121
Malmgren, J. A., 81
Manago, A. M., 135, 137, 193
Mancini, A. D., 313, 314, 315
Manly, J. J., 119
Manove, E. E., 305
Mansson, D. H., 186
Marcia, J. E., 204, 347
Marenco, A., 147
Maringe, F., 207
Markman, H. J., 174, 176, 177
Marks, N. F., 149, 150, 151, 155, 229
Marshall, V., 334
Marsiske, M., 102
Martens, E. J., 327
Martin, J. A., 143
Martin, L. G., 71
Martinez, M. L., 135
Martire, L. M., 151, 154
Martires, K. J., 61
Marty-Gonzales, L. F., 187
Maruna, S., 250, 251
Maschino, A. C., 47
Mashek, D., 169, 170
Maslach, C., 212

Maslow, A., 257–258, 259, 261, 282
Masoro, E. J., 36
Massey, S. G., 59
Masters, K. S., 270
Mastorci, F., 93
Mastracci, S. H., 204
Masunaga, H., 119
Mather, M., 114, 115, 167
Maticka-Tyndale, E., 57
Matlin, N., 200
Matthews, M. D., 315
Maughan, B., 368
Maurer, T., 209
Mayer, K. U., 19
Maylor, E. A., 106, 107
Maynard, L., 34
Mayou, R. A., 314
Mays, V. M., 249
Mazerolle, M., 111
Mazza, O., 298
McAdams, D. P., 158, 250–251, 253
McAndrew, F. T., 193
McAvay, G. J., 154
McCallion, P., 149
McCarthy, E. P., 89
McCay, C., 34
McClearn, G. E., 33, 61, 117
McConnell, A. R., 193
McCoy, S. L., 116
McCrae, R. R., 234, 235, 238, 246, 260, 353, 369
McCullough, M. E., 270
McDaniel, M. A., 109, 210, 211
McDonough, I., 98
McFadden, S. H., 322
McGee, E., 170
McGee, H. M., 91
McGee, M., 119
McGowan, P. O., 11
McGue, M., 117
McGurk, D., 78
McGwin, G., Jr., 125
McKee, M., 213
McKee-Ryan, F. M., 213
McLay, R. N., 118
McMenamin, T. M., 214
Medina, J. J., 57
Meinz, E. J., 117
Mendelsohn, G. A., 171
Menec, V. H., 359
Meredith, W., 239
Merrick, S. K., 166
Messer, S. C., 314
Meyer, B. J. F., 113
Meyer, J. S., 120
Michelson, K. D., 172
Mickels, J. A., 114, 115, 167
Mickelson K. D., 81
Micocci, F., 135
Mienaltowski, A., 114
Mikels, J. S., 114
Mikulincer, M., 165, 172, 315
Milevsky, A., 190, 191
Miller, A. S., 267
Miller, B. A., 88
Miller, G. E., 293, 305
Miller, L. M., 182
Miller, R. A., 35
Miller, T. Q., 242
Millsap, R. E., 238

Miyake, A., 106
Mladinic, A., 132
Mock, S. E., 185
Modan, B., 229
Moen, P., 229
Moestue, C., 246
Moffitt, T. E., 177, 241
Mogle, J., 298
Moon, M., 221, 222
Moore, J. W., 158
Moore, S. Y., 213
Moorman, S., 57
Moreno, M. A., 194
Morgan, G. S., 305
Morgentaler, A., 51
Morisset, P., 111, 112
Morman, M. T., 183
Morris, P. A., 14
Morris, T., 327
Mortel, K. F., 120
Moskowitz, J. T., 306, 309, 339
Mroczek, D. K., 239, 352, 358
Muenchrath, M. N., 71
Muller, F. L., 33
Müller, V., 110
Murphy, M. L. M., 305
Murphy, S. L., 86
Murray, C. E., 184
Musick, K., 141
Musick, M. A., 267
Mustelin, L., 61
Myerson, J., 104
Mykletun, A., 81

N
Nair, K. S., 53
Nakopoulou, E., 59
National Alliance for Caregiving and AARP, 217, 218
National Center for Health Statistics, 69
National Eye Institute, 42
National Heart Lung and Blood Institute, 73
National Highway Traffic Safety Administration, 124
National Hospice and Palliative Care Association, 331
National Institute on Aging, 46, 71
National Institutes of Health, 32, 43, 55
National Senior Services Corps, 228
National Sleep Foundation, 55
Naveh-Benjamin, M., 107
Neal, M. B., 218
Neergaard, M. A., 329
Nehrke, M. F., 249
Neiderhiser, J. M., 25
Neimeyer, R. A., 314
Nelson, D. L., 213, 294
Nelson, L. J., 135
Neria, Y., 314
Nesselroade, J. R., 244
Neugarten, B. L., 9, 131, 137, 158, 321, 368
Neumark, D., 204
Newman, K. S., 147
Newton, T. L., 142
Newtson, R. L., 155
Neyer, F. J., 191
Ng, T. W. H., 210, 211
Niemiec, C. P., 260
Niles, S. G., 200, 203
Nilsson, L. G., 107
Nisan, M., 275, 276
Nisbett, R. E., 98
Noble, P. C., 47

Noller, P., 172
Noone, R. J., 293
Nordahl, H. M., 81
Notarius, C. I., 175
Nussbaum, J. E., 181
Nyberg, L., 107, 108
Nyklicek, I., 327

O
Oates, G., 119
O'Brien, P., 53
O'Connell, J. F., 190
O'Connell, M., 154, 178
O'Connor, E., 178
Oertelt-Prigione, S., 51
Ogden, C. L., 37, 39
Old, S. R., 107
O'Leary, A., 328
O'Leary, K. D., 176
Olfson, M., 80, 83, 89
Olkin, I., 53
Olshansky, S. J., 53, 63
Omalu, B., 78
O'Neill, G., 229
Ono, H., 138, 139, 177
Orbach, I., 172
Orchard, A., 157
Or-Chen, K., 304
Oregon Department of Human Services, 332
Organisation for Economic Cooperation and Development, 142, 143, 156
Ornstein. P. A., 101, 107
Ortega-Alonso, A., 61
Orth-Gomér, K., 310
Osmond, C., 92
Ostrosky-Solis, F., 119
Oswald, A. J., 211
Oyebode, J., 151

P
Pacheco, J. L., 126
Pals, J., 256
Papa, A., 339
Papaharitou, S., 59
Parasuraman, R., 209
Pargament, K. I., 310
Park, D. C., 98, 105
Park, N., 315, 316
Parol, R., 51
Parrish, M. S., 269
Passow, S., 106
Pasupathi, M., 111
Pattie, A., 100, 102
Paulus, M., 339
Pearlin, L., 294
Pedersen, N. L., 117, 208
Pedroso de Lima, M., 238
Peek, M. K., 88
Pendergast, D. R., 354
Perfilieva, E., 49
Perl, D. P., 77
Perls, F., 287
Perls, T. T., 53
Perretti, A. E., 215
Perrino, A., 62
Perrot, A., 124
Perry-Jenkins, M., 144
Peskin, H., 360, 361
Pesta, B. J., 210, 211
Peters, A., 50

Peterson, C., 315, 316
Pettingale, K. W., 327
Pew Research Center, 178, 219, 267, 321, 324
Phelan, K., 153
Phillips, L. H., 109
Phillips, R. S., 89
Piaget, J., 272, 290
Piazza, J. R., 295, 298, 301
Pickles, A., 368
Pierce, T., 173
Pietilainen, K., 61
Pillemer, K., 182, 185
Pillemer, K. A., 150, 185
Pinquart, M., 71, 151, 155, 358, 359
Pleimling, D., 124
Pless, A. P., 311
Plomin, R., 10, 117, 244
Polivy J., 35
Pollatsek, A., 126
Polster, A. M., 61
Ponds, R. W. H. M., 121
Poortman, A.-R., 183, 186
Porter, R. S., 39, 41, 42, 50
Posner, M. I., 106
Poulin, M. J., 302, 303
Powell, F. C., 321
Powell, L. H., 270
Pratt, M. W., 276
Presser, H. B., 214, 215
Pressman, S. D., 91
Priess, H. A., 143
Pruchno, R., 186
Punnoose, A. R., 56
Putney, N. M., 33
Pychyl, T. A., 193

Q
Quick, H., 229
Quick, J. C., 213
Quine, S., 153
Quinton, D., 368

R
Radloff, L. S., 23, 81
Rahe, R., 294, 311
Rainie, L., 194
Rakowski, W., 355
Rando, T. A., 338
Rasmussen, C. H., 323
Ratnasingan, M., 322
Raye, C. L., 106
Rayens, M. K., 329
Raz, N., 103, 120
Rebok, G. W., 103, 109
Reczek, C., 141
Reed, D., 89
Reed, G. M., 328
Reeder, J. A., 106
Reese, H. W., 13
Reeves, A., 213
Régner, I., 111, 112
Reiber, C., 59
Reimer, J., 275
Reisman, N. R., 53
Reker, G. T., 281–282
Resett, S., 135
Resnick, H. S., 314
Resnick, S. M., 106
Rest, J. R., 276, 286
Reuter-Lorenz, P. A., 106, 115

Reuters, 222
Rexbye, H., 61
Rhoades, G. K., 174, 176
Rhoden, E. L., 51
Rhodes, J. E., 305
Richardson, J. L., 328
Richmond, L. S., 164
Riegel, K., 265
Riemann, R., 243–244
Riggio, H. R., 217
Riley, K. P., 29
Rix, S. E., 202, 223, 227, 228
Rizza, R. A., 53
Robbins, S., 194
Robert, S. A., 88, 89
Roberts, A. H., 77
Roberts, B. W., 237, 238, 239, 240, 241, 242, 243, 245, 305
Robertson, J., 359
Robinaugh, D., 313
Robinson, J. K., 61
Robles, T. F., 141
Rod, N. H., 141
Rodgers, B., 229
Rodrigue, K. M., 103
Roenker, D. L., 125
Rogers, C., 258, 287
Rogers, R. L., 120
Rohleder, N., 305
Roisman, G. I., 173, 180
Romoser, M. R. E., 126
Rönnlund, M., 107, 108
Roodin, P. A., 186, 276, 278
Rooney, J. R., 246
Rose, N. S., 104
Rosenberger, N., 135
Rosenbloom, C., 61
Rosenfeld, I., 39, 45
Rosengren, A., 310
Rosenman, R., 90
Rosin, A., 86
Ross, M., 115
Rosselli, M., 119
Rossi, A. S., 36, 146
Rothbart, M. K., 106
Rothblum, E. D., 180
Rounds, J., 205
Rovine, M., 144
Rowe, J. W., 358
Ruby, M. B., 62
Ruiz, S. A., 189
Russo, C., 113
Ruthig, J. C., 91
Ryan, R. M., 259–260
Ryckewaert, R., 321

S
Sabaté, E., 122
Sacerdote, B., 222
Sacks, J., 83
St. Teresa of Ávila, 284–285
Salkind, N. J., 27
Salmela-Aro, K., 135
Salthouse, T. A., 49, 101, 102, 105, 107, 117, 119, 209
Salvati, S., 328
Salvatore, J. E., 172, 173
Sameroff, A. J., 14, 135
Sampson, N., 84
Sanchez, L., 143
Sanders, L. M., 189
Sands, R. G., 149

Sanfey, A. C., 112
Sano, M., 119
Santillanes, G., 337
Sasaki, A., 11
Sauceda, J. A., 122
Savci, E., 178
Savickas, M. L., 200
Sayer, A., 250
Sayer, L. C., 157
Schacter, D. L., 109
Schaefer, H. M., 50
Schafer, M. H., 90
Schaie, K. W., 99, 100, 102, 103, 119, 126
Scharlach, A. E., 305
Schaufeli, W. B., 212
Scheier, M. F., 242, 312
Scher, A., 77
Scheyd, G. L., 132
Schiller, J. S., 71
Schillmöller, Z., 212
Schlaghecken, F., 106
Schmitt, D. P., 171
Schneider, J. A., 77
Schoenborn, C. A., 85
Schoenemann, P. T., 49
Schoeni, R. F., 71
Schooler, C., 119
Schott, L. L., 51, 52
Schover, L. R., 58
Schrader, S. S., 181
Schryer, E., 115
Schulenberg, J. E., 135
Schultheiss, D. E. P., 206
Schulz, R., 151, 154
Schwartz, R., 203
Scott, J., 322
Scott, S. B., 302, 303
Seay, R. B., 114
Sebastiani, P., 63
Seeman, M., 270
Seeman, T. E., 154, 270
Segerstrom, S. C., 293
Seligman, M. E. P., 91, 258, 315
Sellars, B., 311
Selye, H., 293–294, 317
Semmer, N., 212
Shackelford, T., 171, 187, 188
Shafto, M. A., 107
Shanahan, M. J., 134
Shapiro, A. F., 145
Shargorodsky, J., 44
Sharp, Z. D., 35
Shaver, P. R., 165, 168, 172, 173, 338
Shear, K., 313
Sheehan, M. J., 49
Sheehy, G., 146, 352
Sheffield, K. M., 88
Sheikh, J. A., 109
Sheldon, K. M., 250
Sheldon, P., 194
Shen, D., 74
Sherin, J. E., 49, 50
Sherwood, N. E., 75
Sherwood, P., 151
Shevlin, M., 170
Shifren, J. L., 57, 58, 59
Shiner, R. L., 237, 240, 241, 242
Shippee, T. P., 90
Shively, S., 77
Shmotkin, D., 229

Shneidman, E., 355
Shoda, T. M., 193
Shuchter, S. R., 339
Shuey, K., 220
Siebenrock, K. A., 47
Siefen, G., 360
Silventoinen, K., 61
Silver, M. C., 302, 303
Silver, R. C., 341
Silverstein, M., 147, 150, 156, 182, 183, 189
Simmons, B. L., 213
Simonsick, E. M., 355
Simpson, J. A., 172, 173
Sims, R. V., 125
Sinnott, J. D., 126, 265
Sipilä, S., 61
Skitka, L. J., 305
Skovronek, E., 119
Slavich, G. M., 304, 305
Sliwinski, M. J., 106
Small, B. J., 104, 117, 118
Smetana, J. G., 278
Smith, A., 194
Smith, B. J., 72
Smith, C. D., 103
Smith, J., 109, 119, 209, 242, 243
Smith, J. Z., 144
Smith, M. C., 111
Smith, M. J., 105
Smith, R. G., 312
Smith, S. K., 227
Smith, T. W., 90,
Smylie, L., 57
Smyth, E., 359
Snarey, J. R., 275, 276, 278, 362
Sneed, J. R., 250
Snowdon, D., 28–29, 242
Sokolowski, T., 329
Solano, L., 328
Solberg, K., 157
Soldz, S., 256
Solomon, M., 256
Solomon, Z., 305
Solovieff, N., 63
Somer, E., 304
Son, L., 362
Song, A., 213
Sorensen, E., 216
Sörensen, S., 71, 151, 358, 359
Sorlie, P. D., 141
Spanier, G. B., 144
Spearman, C., 99
Spector, T. D., 34
Spies, R. A., 23
Spiro, A., 239, 358
Spotts, E. L., 25
Springer, K. W., 140
Spry, N., 51
Stamatakis, E. A., 107
Stanley, S. M., 174, 177
Starishevsky, R., 200
Stark, R., 267
Starr, J. M., 101
Statham, J. A., 111
Staudinger, U. M., 126, 209
Stawski, R. S., 295, 301
Steinberg, S., 92
Steindl-Rast, B. D., 341
Stephens, M. A. P., 311
Stephenson-Abetz, J., 194

Steptoe, A., 269, 270
Sternberg, R. J., 101, 104, 170
Stevens, J., 55
Stewart, J., 87
Stigsdotter, A., 109
Stone, A. J., 204, 226
Storandt, M., 77, 121
Strauch, B., 134
Strelau, J., 243, 244
Strong, R., 35
Stuckler, D., 213
Su, R., 205
Sugihara, Y., 229
Sugimoto, K., 45
Sugisawa, H., 229, 310
Suh, E., 141, 359, 360
Suitor, J. J., 185
Sun, B., 305
Sundel, M., 352
Super, C. M., 200–201
Super, D. E., 200–201, 231
Sutin, A. R., 242
Sutker, P. B., 314
Swartzendruber, A., 103
Szinovacz, M. E., 223

T
Takahashi, K., 166
Talbot, A., 113
Tamnes, C. K., 246
Tan, J.-P., 188, 189
Tanner, M., 193
Tarakeshwar, N., 310
Tartaro, J., 269, 270, 271
Tatsuoka, M. M., 236
Taubman, O., 315
Taylor, A. C., 186
Taylor, S. E., 301, 309, 328
Taylor, T., 193
Tchkonia, T., 36
Techner (1997), 337
Tennov (1979), 170
Tennstedt, S. L., 102
Teno, J. M., 329, 330
Terkel, S., 199
Terracciano, A., 246
Thoits, P. A., 90
Thoma, S. J., 276, 286
Thomas, J. L., 78
Thomese, F., 190
Thompson, C., 217
Thompson, S. H., 194
Thomson, E., 143
Thoreson, C. J., 241
Thorson, J. A., 321
Tighe, L., 182
Timberlake, J. M., 139
Tolvanen, A., 135
Tomasetto, C., 207
Tomer, A., 323
Tomic, D., 59
Tooby, J., 246
Toossi, M., 221
Tornstam, L., 265
Torpy, J. M., 74, 331
Towers, H., 25
Town, R., 214
Townsend, A. L., 311
Trella, P., 91
Trivers, R. L., 143

Truluck, J. E., 253, 254
Trzesniewski, K., 240
Tulving, E., 106, 108
Tun, P. A., 116
Turiano, N. A., 242
Turiel, E., 278
Turner, C. W., 242
Tynkkynen, L., 135

U
Uchida, K., 92
Uchino, B. N., 310
Uddo, M., 314
Uematsu, H., 45
Uhlenberg, P., 215
Ullrich, M., 253
Umberson, D., 141
Underhill, E., 266, 284–285, 290
United Nations Economic Commission for Europe, 221, 222
United Nations Statistics Division, 217
U.S. Bureau of Labor Statistics, 201–202, 204, 210, 212, 214, 215, 228
U.S. Census Bureau, 124, 135, 136, 138, 140, 148, 155, 178, 210, 215, 227
U.S. Department of Health and Human Services, 225
U.S. Department of Labor, 43, 44
U.S. General Accounting Office, 178
University of Michigan Institute for Social Research, 140
Unson, C., 91
Usui, C., 229
Uttl, B., 100

V
Väänänen, A., 311
Vaillant, C. O., 361
Vaillant, G. E., 254–256, 261, 353, 361, 362, 364, 368
Valeo, T., 44
Valliant, G. E., 10
Van Alstine, C. L., 100
Van Alstine Makomenaw, M., 135, 137
van Boxtel, M. P. J., 121
VanderDrift, L. E., 182
Van der Linden, M., 104
van de Vijver, F. J. R., 246
van IJzendoorn, M., 166
van Reekum, R., 81
Van Remmen, H., 33
van Tilburg, T. G., 183, 186
Vasconcelles, E. B., 310
Ventura, S. J., 142, 143
Verhaeghen, P., 106, 107
Verkasalo, P. K., 297
Verma, J., 246
Vespa, J., 138
Vicentini, M., 93
Vickers, A. J., 47
Viechtbauer, W., 238, 239, 245
Viltart, O., 93
Vogler, G. P., 61
Vogt, D. S., 311

W
Waddington, C. H., 363–364
Wagner, J., 168
Wahab, E. A., 322
Wahlin, Å., 104, 117, 118
Waite, L. J., 60, 140
Walaskay, M., 249
Waldstein, S. R., 117
Walker, L. J., 276
Walsh, R., 85

Walters, E. E., 81
Walton, A., 103
Walton, G. M., 240
Walton, K. E., 238, 239, 242, 243, 245
Wan, C.-S., 62
Wanberg, C. R., 213
Wang, P. S., 80, 83, 89
Ward, B. W., 71
Ward, C. V., 293
Warneke, C. L., 58
Warr, P., 209, 211, 359
Wartenburger, I., 106
Wasylyshyn, C., 106
Waterreus, A., 51
Waters, E., 165, 166
Watson. P. J., 299
Weatherbee, S. R., 102
Weaver, A. J., 322
Weaver, S. E., 157
Webster, L. M., 109
Wechsler, D, 99
Wedel, H., 310
Weiss, R. S., 165, 182
Westerhausen, R., 106
Wethington, E., 353
Whitbourne, S. K., 20–21, 249, 250
Whiteman, M. K., 59
Wiederhold, B. K., 194
Wight, V. R., 204, 226
Wilbur, K. H., 156
Wilkinson, A. M., 330, 333
Williams, A., 181
Williams, D. R., 304, 329
Williams, G. C., 86
Williams, J. E., 131
Willis, S. L., 102–103, 119
Wilson, J. A., 113
Wilson, R. S., 103, 119
Windsor, T. D., 229
Winefield, A. H., 212
Wingfield, A., 116
Wingo, P. A., 89
Wink, P., 263, 268–269, 322

Winter, P. D., 92
Wisneski, D. C., 305
Wolf, J. L., 155
Wood, W., 132, 204
Woodruff-Pak, D. S., 49
Woods, L. N., 177
Woods, S. P., 122
World Health Organization, 43, 72, 75, 81
Worthy, D. A., 126
Wortman, C. B., 314, 339, 340
Wright, J., 151
Wrzus, C., 168
Wu, J.-R., 329

X
Xanthopoulou, D., 212
Xiangkui, Z., 323
Xu, J., 72

Y
Yang, C.-C., 62
Yang, K.-S., 246
Yano, K., 89
Yehuda, R., 299, 301
Yesavage, J., 109
Young, B. A., 90
Yu, J. W., 83

Z
Zaborski, L. B., 17, 23, 86
Zacks, R. T., 105
Zanjani, F., 99
Zarit, S., 185
Zarnegar, Z., 328
Zelinski, E. M., 103
Zhang, J. X., 246
Zhang, Z., 156
Zickuhr, K., 122–123
Ziol-Guest, K. M., 93
Zisook, S., 339
Zivotofsky, A. Z., 308, 309
Zogg, J. B., 122
Zuschlag, M. K., 20–21, 249

Subject Index

A

Ability/expertise trade-off, 209
Acceptance, as reaction to death, 323–324
Accommodate, lens and, 42
Achievement
  in career identity, 204
  personality traits and, 241–242
Activities, quality of life and, 359
Acute conditions, 69
Adaptive/maladaptive outcomes *vs.* happiness, 369
Adaptive nature of cognition, 110–111
ADLs (activities of daily living), 70
Adult Career Concerns Inventory
    (ACCI), 200
Adult development. *See also* Model of adult growth and
    development
  age and, 11–12
  bioecological model of development, 14–15
  change, sources of, 5–9
  concepts in, 3–5
  defined, 3
  developmental research, 15–29
  introduction to, 1–30
  life-span developmental psychology approach, 13, 14
  perspectives on, guiding, 13–15
  stability, sources of, 9–11
Adult development, themes of, 344–357
  emerging adulthood (age 18–24), 346–348
  late adulthood (age 75 and older), 354–357
  middle adulthood (age 40–64), 350–353
  older adulthood (age 65–74), 353–354
  review of, 345–346 (*See also* Adult functioning, changes in
    domains of)
  young adulthood (age 25–39), 348–350
Adult development, variations in successful, 357–369
Adult functioning, changes in domains of, 345–346
  cognitive change, 345
  family and gender roles, 345
  major tasks, 346
  meaning, 346
  personality, 346
  physical change, 345
  relationships, 345
  work roles, 346
Affectional solidarity, 181
Affection in family relationships, 181
African Americans. *See also* Racial and ethnic groups
  discrimination and, health-related effects of, 304
  grandparent-grandchild relationships, 186
  life expectancy of, 89
  racial discrimination in health care, 89–90
Age
  biological, 12
  chronological, 11–12
  death anxiety and, 321–322
  functional, 12
  posttraumatic stress disorder and, 311
  psychological, 12
  quality of life and, 359
  social, 12
  stress-related disorders and, 301–302

Ageism, 5
Age trends in work experience, 209–211
  job performance, 209–210
  job satisfaction, 211
  job training and retraining, 210–211
Aging parents, caring for, 151–154
Agreeableness, 234–243
AIDS, 76, 328
Alarm reaction, 293
Alaskan Natives, health of, 89. *See also* Racial and ethnic
    groups
Alcohol, coping and, 308
Aldosterone, 50
Alternative to being single, 140
Alternative to marriage, 139
Alzheimer's disease, 76–78
Ambivalence, 185
Amenity move, 227
American Indians, health of, 89. *See also* Racial and ethnic
    groups
Analyses in developmental research, 23–26
  comparison of means, 23
  correlational analysis, 23–25
  meta-analysis, 26
Anger, as reaction to death, 328
Anthropomorphizing, 193
Antibodies, 50
Antioxidants, 33
Anxiety disorders, 80
Anxious preoccupation, as response to imminent death, 327
APOE E4 gene, 76
APP gene, 76
Asian Americans, health of, 88
Asset income, 224
Assistance animals, 84–85
Assistive technology, 84
Associated solidarity, 181
Asymmetrical changes, 132
Atherosclerosis, 72
Athletic abilities, changes in, 53–54
Attachment
  concept of, 165
  in intimate partnerships, 172–173
Attachment behaviors, 165
Attachment orientation, 165–166
Attachment theory, 165–166
Attention-deficit/hyperactivity disorder (ADHD), 82–83
Attraction, 170–172
Attraction system, 170
Attrition, 20
Atypical families, social roles in, 154–157
  childless, 155–156
  divorced (and remarried) adults, 156–157
  lifelong singles, 154–155
Atypical stages of life, 4
Auditory acuity, 116
Autonomy
  in ego development, 253
  in self-determination theory, 259
Avoidant-denial strategy, 114
Awakening stage of mystical experience, 284

B

Balance, changes in, 54
Bargaining, as reaction to death, 325
B cells, 50
Behavior genetics, 10
Behavior patterns
  individual differences in health, 90–92
Being motives, 257
Bereavement. *See* Death and bereavement
Berlin Study of Aging, 19–20, 107, 109, 116
"Big Five Model," 234–243
Bioecological model of development, 14–15
Biological age, 12
Biological clock, 5, 131, 350–351
Biology, 5
Biosocial perspective, 132
Body composition, changes in, 37–39
Body mass index (BMI), 37, 38
Bone mass density (BMD), 45
Bones, changes in, 45–47
  osteoarthritis, 47
  osteoporosis, 45–46
  patient adherence to treatment for bone loss, 46
Botox, 40
Brain, changes in, 49
Brain aging, 117
Breast cancer
  individual variations/adaptations to dying, 327
  stress and, 297, 305, 312
Bridge job, 228
Brief COPE Inventory, 307
Brief Multidimensional Measure of Religiousness/Spirituality
    (BMMRS), 270
Buffering effect, 310–311

C

California Psychological Inventory (CPI), 236
Caloric restriction (CR), 34–35
Cancer, 73–75. *See also* Breast cancer
  cervical, HPV vaccine and, 74
  death from, 74
  individual adaptations to dying, 326, 327, 329, 331, 332
  survival rates, 327
Cardiovascular disease, 71–73
Cardiovascular system, changes in, 48
Career
  commitment, retirement and, 223–224
  defined, 199–200
  development, Super's theory of, 200–201
  patterns, gender differences in, 201–202
Career consolidation, 254
Career Development Inventory (CDI), 200
Career recycling, 210
Career selection, 202–209
  changes over adulthood, review of, 230–231
  family influences, 206–208
  gender and, 204–206
  genetics, 208
  theories of, 202–204
Caregiver burden, 151
Caregiving
  for adult family members, work and, 217–218
  gender and, 149–151
  impact of, 151
Caregiving orientation, 166
Care receiver, becoming, 153–154
Cataracts, 42
Center for Epidemiologic Studies Short Depression Scale
    (CES-D 10), 81, 82

CES-D 10. *See* Center for Epidemiologic Studies Short Depression
    Scale (CES-D 10)
Change
  defined, 3–4
  inner, 4–5
  internal change processes, 6
  outer, 4
Change, sources of, 5–9
  nonnormative life events, 9
  normative age-graded influences, 5–6
  normative history-graded influences, 6–8
Chemical peels, 39
Childless families, 155–156
Children. *See also* Grandparents; Parent-child relationships
    in adulthood
  cohabitation and, 177
  departure of (empty nest), 146–147
  gender roles in couples with, 143–144
  problem, in adulthood, 185
Choice board, 113
Chronic conditions, 69
  individual differences in cognitive change, 117
Chronic life strains, stress and, 294
Chronic traumatic encephalopathy (CTE), 77
Chronological age, 12
Chronosystem, 14, 15
Cialis, 58
Climacteric
  in men, 51
  in women, 51–52
Cochlea, 43
Cognitive assistance, 122–126
  driving, 124–126
  electronic games, 123–124
  e-readers, 123–124
  medication adherence, 122
  social networking, 122–123
Cognitive change, 97–128
  cognitive assistance, 122–126
  decision making and problem solving,
    112–116
  individual differences in, 116–121
  intelligence, 99–101
  memory, 103–112
  review of, 126–127
Cognitive change, review of, 345
Cohabitation, 138–139, 176–178
  children and, 178
  cultural acceptance of, 177
  marriages and, 177–178
  selection effect, 177
Cohort, 7–8
Collectivism, 282
Commitment stage to career identity, 204
Commonalities, 3
Common-cause hypothesis, 116
Communal qualities, 131, 147
Community dwelling, 71
Comorbid, 80
Comparison of means, 23
Competence, in self-determination theory, 259
Complementary and alternative medicine
    providers, 83
Conformist stage of ego development, 252
Conjunctive faith, 280–281
Conscientiousness, 235–243
Conscientious stage of ego development, 252
Consensual solidarity, 183
Contextual perspective, 110–112

Continuity of change
  differential, 237, 240
  environmental influences, 244–245
  evolutionary influences, 245–246
  explanations of, 243–246
  genetics, 243–244
Continuous stretches of life, 4
Conventional level of Kohlberg's stages of moral reasoning,
    275, 278
Convoy, 166
Convoy model, 166–167
Coping
  behaviors, 306–310
  Brief COPE Inventory, 306, 307
  defined, 293
  drugs and alcohol as coping mechanism, 308
  effectiveness of, 309
  emotion-focused, 308
  meaning-focused, 309
  personality traits and, 312
  proactive coping, 309–310
  problem-focused coping, 308
  religious coping, 310
  social coping, 309
  social support and, 310–312
Coping flexibility, 309
Correlational analysis, 24
Cortisol levels, 270, 271
Crossover of gender roles, 147
Cross-sectional study, 16–17
Crystallized intelligence, 101
Cuckold rate, 187
Cultural differences in quality of life, 359–360
Cultures, 6
Cyclic GMP, 58

D
Daily stressors, 294
Dark adaptation, 42
Dark night of the soul stage of mystical experience, 285
Death
  from cancer, 73
  from cardiovascular disease, 72
  rates, 69
Death, meanings of, 321
  as an organizer of time, 321
  as loss, 321
  as punishment, 321
  as transition, 321
Death and bereavement, 319–341
  adaptations to dying, individual, 326–329
  after death occurs, 333–341
  choosing when to die, 332–333
  choosing where to die, 329–332
  farewells, importance of, 326
  finitude, 323
  a good death, importance of, 330
  grieving process, 338–341
  process of, 324–333
  reactions to death, stages of, 324–326
  ritual mourning (funerals and ceremonies),
      333–337
  understanding of, achieving, 320–324
Death anxiety, 321–323
  age and, 321–322
  defined, 321
  gender and, 322
  personality traits and, 322–323
  religiosity and, 322
Decentering, 275

Decision making and problem solving, 112–116
  avoidant-denial strategy, 114
  choice board, 113
  positivity bias, 115
  problem-focused approach, 114
  socioemotional selectivity theory, 115–116
Declarative memory, 106–108
Defense mechanism, 254
Defensiveness, 174
Deficiency motives, 257
Dementia, 76, 77
Demographics, 118–119
Denial, as reaction to death, 325
Departure of children (empty nest), 146–147
Depression, as reaction to death, 325
Depressive symptoms, 81
Descriptive research, 27–28
Designs in developmental research, 26–29
  descriptive research, 27–28
  experimental, 27
  qualitative research, 28–29
  quantitative research, 28
  questions in, 16–17
Desire, sexual, 59
Despair, ego integrity *vs.*, 248, 356
Detribalization, 283, 350
Developmental-origins hypothesis, 92
Developmental patterns, asynchrony of, 366
Developmental psychology, 2
Developmental research, 15–29
  analyses, 23–26
  designs, 26–29
  measures, 22–23
  questions, 15–16
Developmental research methods, 16–22
  attrition, 20
  cross-sectional study, 16–18
  longitudinal study, 18–20
  sequential study, 20
Dexterity, changes in, 54
DHEA (dehydroepiandrosterone), 52
Diabetes, 75
Diagnostic and Statistical Manual (DSM)
    3rd edition *(DSM-III)*, 79
Differential continuity, 237–238, 240
Diffusion stage to career identity, 204
Digit-span task, 104
Disability, 69–71
Discrimination
  posttraumatic stress disorder and, 304
  stress-related disorders and, 304
Diseases, 71–79
  Alzheimer's disease, 76–78
  cancer, 73–75
  cardiovascular disease, 71–73
  diabetes, 75
  people living with, 78–79
Disengagement, 355–356
Disequilibrium, 365–369
  adaptive/maladaptive outcomes *vs.* happiness, 369
  asynchrony of developmental patterns, 366
  cumulative effects of, 368–369
  flowchart of, 366
  major life changes, 367
  outcome of, 366–369
  periods of, 365–367
  personality and role requirements, poor match between, 366–367
  personality or spiritual development, 367
  role transitions, 366
  stability and age, 365

Distal causes, 132
Distal predictors, 358
Distress, 293. *See also* Stress
Divorced (and remarried) adults
  late-life, 184–185
  social roles, 156–157
Dizygotic twins, 10, 24–25, 208
DNA methylation, 11
Domestic migration, 227
Dopamine, 170
Downregulate (or silence), 73
Driving, 124–126
Drugs, coping and, 308
DXA scan, 45

E
Earnings
  retirement and, 224–226
  of women, 204, 218
Economic exchange theory, 143
Egalitarian roles, 140
Ego development, 252–254
  autonomous stage of, 253
  conformist stage of, 252
  conscientious stage of, 252–253
  impulsive stage of, 252
  individualistic stage of, 253
  integrated stage of, 253
  integrative themes in, 253
  self-aware stage of, 252
  self-protective stage of, 252
Ego integrity, 248
  vs. despair, 248, 356
Electronic games, 123–124
Emerging adulthood, 135
Emerging adulthood (age 18–24), 346–348
  review of, 345–346
Emotion-focused coping, 308
Empty nest (departure of children), 146–147
Engaged cohabitation, 177
Environment, stability and, 10–11
Epigenetic inheritance, 11, 73
Episodic memory, 106–107
E-readers, 123
Erectile dysfunction (ED), 58, 60
Erikson's stages of psychosocial development, 247–252
Erotic dreams, 60
Estrogen, 51, 52
Ethical principles of moral reasoning, 278
Ethnicity. *See* Racial and ethnic groups
Eudaimonia, 259
Evocative transactions, 245
Evolutionary psychology, 132, 167–169
Evolutionary truce, 283
Exchange theory, 170
Executive function, 106
Exhaustion in general adaptation syndrome, 293
Exosystem, 14, 15
Expansion of gender roles, 147
Experimental design, 27
Expertise, 119
Explicit memory, 106–108
Extended families, 181
Extraversion, 237–246
Eye, 42–43. *See also* Vision, changes in

F
Facebook friends, 193–194
Face-to-face meeting, 171, 194
Factor analysis, 235, 236, 246

Faith, 278–281
  defined, 278
  stages of, 278–281 (*See also* Fowler's stages of faith development)
Family
  career selection and, influences on, 206–208
  interaction, patterns of, 181–182
  retirement and, 223
Family members, social relationships with, 180–192
  family interaction, patterns of, 181–182
  grandparent-grandchild relationships, 186–190
  intergenerational solidarity theory, 181
  parent-child relationships in adulthood, 182–185
  siblings, 190–192
Family roles, review of changes in, 345
Fantasies, sexual, 60
Farewells, importance of, 326
Fatalism (stoic acceptance), as response to imminent death, 328
Fathers in workforce, 215–216
Feeling in-between, 347
Feminization of poverty, 226
Fighting spirit, as response to imminent death, 328–329
Fight or flight responds, 293
Filter theory, 170
Finances, retirement and, 222–230
Finitude, 323
Five-Factor Model (FFM), 234–243
Fluid intelligence, 101
Flynn effect, 100
Food deserts, 62
Foreclosure stage to career identity, 204
Foster Grandparents Program, 228
Fowler's stages of faith development, 279–282
  conjunctive faith, 280–281
  individuative-reflective faith, 279
  points about, 281–282
  research findings, 281–282
  synthetic-conventional faith, 279
  universalizing faith, 281
Free radicals, 33
Friendship
  in adulthood, 192–196
  defined, 192
  Facebook friends, 193–194
  networks, 192–193
  pets as friends, 193
Functional age, 12
Functional solidarity, 183
Funerals and ceremonies, 333–337

G
G, 99
Gay partnerships, 178–180
Gender
  career patterns and, 201–202
  career selection and, 204–206
  death anxiety and, 322
  grandparent-grandchild relationships, 186
  individual differences in health, 86–87
  posttraumatic stress disorder and, 300–301
  quality of life and, 358–359
  stress-related disorders and, 300–301
Gender crossover, 256–257
Gender roles
  asymmetrical changes, 132
  caregiving and, 149–150
  in couples with children, 143–144
  crossover of, 147
  defined, 131
  in early partnerships, 140
  expansion of, 147

Gender roles (*continued*)
  at midlife, 147
  review of changes in, 345
  stereotypes compared to, 131–132
  symmetrical changes, 132
Gender stereotypes, 131–132
General adaptation syndrome, 293
Generation, 7. *See also* Cohort
Generativity, 248–252
  defined, 248
  fatherhood's impact on, 251
  Loyola Generativity Scale for measuring, 250–251
  vs. self-absorption, 247, 248
  vs. stagnation, 247, 250
Genetic limits, 33–34
Genetics
  career selection and, 208
  cognitive change and, individual differences in, 121
  continuity of change and, explanations of, 243–244
  health and, individual differences in, 92
  primary aging and, 61
  stability and, 10
Genotype, 92
Gerotranscendence, 265
GH (growth hormone), 52
Glaucoma, 42
Good-boy or good-girl orientation, 282
Good death, 330
Goodness of fit, 309
Gradual retirement, 228
Grandfamilies, 148
Grandmother effect, 190
Grandparent-grandchild relationships, 186–190
  gender and, 187
  grandmother effect, 190
  informal care, 188
  in racial/ethnic groups, 186–187
  in time of family crisis, 188–190
Grandparents
  becoming, 147–149
  raising grandchildren, 148–149
Grant Study of Harvard Men, 10
Gray matter, 49
Great Depression, 7
Grief work, 314
Grieving process, 338–341
Guilt, initiative *vs.*, 247

H
Hair, changes in, 41
Happiness *vs.* adaptive/maladaptive outcomes, 369
Hardiness, resilience and, 270, 315
"Having a choice over challenges" strategy, 259
Hayflick limit, 33
Health, individual differences in cognitive change, 116–117
  chronic disease, 117
  hearing, 116–117
  medication, 117
  vision, 116–117
Health and health disorders, 67–94. *See also* Diseases
  common, 69
  disability, 69–71
  individual differences in health, 85–95
  intelligence used to predict, 102
  marital status and, 140–142
  mental disorders, 79–84
  morbidity rates, 69–71
  mortality rates and causes of death, 68–69
  nonmedical solutions, 84–85
  personality traits and, 242–243

quality of life and, 358
quest for meaning and, 269–271
retirement and, 223
review of, 93
self-ratings of, 71
Hearing, changes in, 43–44
  individual differences in cognitive changes, 116–117
Hearing aids, 44
Heart disease, stress and, 297–298
Hedonia, 259
Helplessness/hopelessness, as response to imminent death, 327
Heritability of cognitive abilities, 117
Heritability scores, 117
Hierarchy of needs, Maslow's, 258–259
Hippocampus, 120
Hispanic Americans. *See also* Racial and ethnic groups
  discrimination and, health-related effects of, 304
  as grandparents, 186
  health risks of, 89
  racial discrimination in health care, 89–90
HIV, 89
Holland's theory of vocational interests, 203
Hookups, 59
Hormonal system, changes in, 50–53
  climacteric in men, 51
  climacteric in women, 51–52
  DHEA (dehydroepiandrosterone), 52–53
  estrogen, 51, 52
  GH (growth hormone), 52–53
  menopause and, 51
  progesterone, 51, 52
Hormone replacement, 52–53
  DHEA replacement, 53
  growth hormone replacement, 53
  hormone replacement therapy, 52
  for menopause, 52
  testosterone replacement therapy, 52
Hormone replacement therapy, 52
Hospice approach, 331
Hospice care, 331–332
Hostility, 91–92
Hot flash, 52
Household labor, 218–219
Human papillomavirus (HPV) vaccine, 74
Human social genomics, 304
Hyaluranic acid, 47

I
IADLs (instrumental activities of daily living), 70
Identity, 248
  vs. role confusion, 248, 249, 250, 254
Identity exploration, 347
Illumination stage of mystical experience, 285
Imaging techniques, 77
Immune cells, 328
Immune response to stress, 293
Immune system
  changes in, 50
  response to imminent death and, 328
Improvised explosive devices (IEDs), 78
Impulse control disorders, 82–83
Impulsive stage of ego development, 252
Income, retirement and, 224–226
Individual differences, defined, 3
Individual differences, in cognitive change, 116–121
  decline, subjective evaluation of, 121
  demographics and sociobiographical history, 118–119
  genetics, 117–118
  health, 116–117

intellectual activity, 119–120
physical exercise, 120–121
schooling, 119
Individual differences, in health, 85–94
developmental origins, 92–94
gender, 86–87
genetics, 92
lifestyle, 85–86
personality and behavior patterns, 90–92
racial and ethnic groups, 988–989
racial discrimination in health care, 89–90
review of, 94
socioeconomic status, 87–88
Individual differences, in primary aging, 60–63
genetics, 61
lifestyle, 61–62
race and ethnicity, 62–63
socioeconomic factors, 62–63
Individual differences, in quality of life, 358–360
activities, 359
age, 358
cultural differences, 359–360
gender, 358–359
health and socioeconomic status, 358
marital status, 359
psychosocial factors, 359
race and ethnicity, 359
social comparisons, 359
social integration, 359
Individual differences, in resilience, 314–315
hardiness, 315
positive emotion, 315
self-identity, 315
Individual differences, in stress-related disorders, 300–305
age, 301–303
discrimination, 304
environment-gene interactions and, 304–305
gender, 300–301
Individualism, 281
Individualistic stage of ego development, 253
Individual principles of conscience orientation, 284
Individuative-reflective faith, 279
Industry vs. inferiority, 247
Inferiority, industry vs., 247
Initiative vs. guilt, 247
Inner changes, 4–5
Insomnia, 56
Instability, positive, 347
Institute for Human Development longitudinal study, 268
Institutional move, 227
Instrumental qualities, 131
Integrated stage of ego development, 253
Integrative themes in ego development, 253
Intellectual activity, 119–120
Intelligence, 98–103
age changes in overall intelligence, 99–101
components of, 101–102
crystallized, 101
defined, 98
expertise, 119
fluid, 101–102
Flynn effect, 100
health and longevity predicted by, 102
psychometrics, 99
reversing declines in, 102–103
Interactionist view, 11
Intergenerational effects, 93
Intergenerational family structure, 181
Intergenerational solidarity theory, 181–182
Internal change processes, 6

Internal working model, 165, 264
Internet, 122
Intimacy, 248
vs. isolation, 247, 248
Intimate relationships, 169–180
attachment, 172–173
attraction, 170–172
cohabitation and marriage, 176–178
establishing, 169–173
exchange theory, 170
filter theory, 170
libido, 169
lust, 169–170
mate selection, 169
personality traits and, 241
same-sex partnerships, 178–180
successful marriages, 174–176
Intra-individual variability, 239–240
Inventory of Psychosocial Development (IPD), 249
IQ (intelligence quotient), 99–101. See also Intelligence
measures, 22
scores, 99–101, 117, 127
tests, 99, 101
Isolation, intimacy vs., 247, 248

J
Job burnout, 212
Job expertise, 209
Job insecurity, 213–214
Job loss, 213
Job performance, 209–210
Job satisfaction, 211
Job training and retraining, 210–211

K
Kinship move, 227
Kohlberg's stages of moral reasoning, 273–278
conventional level, 273, 274
data, 275–277
decentering, 275
ethical principles, 277, 278
evaluation and comment, 278
good-boy or good-girl orientation, 273
individual principles of conscience orientation, 274, 275
naive hedonism orientation, 273
postconventional level, 274
preconventional level, 273
punishment-and-obedience orientation, 273
social contract orientation, 274
social order maintaining orientation, 273
unity orientation, 277

L
Labor force, 221–222
Late adulthood (age 75 and older), 354–357
disengagement in, 355–356
life review in, 356–357
review of, 356
selective optimization with compensation in, 356
Late adulthood, social roles in, 151–154
care receiver, becoming, 153–154
living alone, 152–153
Laughter, resilience and, 315
Learning-schema theory, 132
Leaving (and returning) home, 135–137
Leisure-time interests, retirement
and, 224
Lens, 41–42
Lesbian, gay, bisexual, and transgendered (LGBT) people,
178–180

Levitra, 58
LGBT people. *See* Lesbian, gay, bisexual, and transgendered (LGBT) people
Libido, 169
Life-change events, 294
Lifelong singles, 154–155
Life review, 356
Life-span developmental psychology approach, 13–14
Life-span/life-space theory, 200
Lifestyle
  individual differences in health, 85–86
  primary aging and, 61–62
Limerance, 170–172
Living alone, in late adulthood, 152–153
Living will, 323–324
Longevity
  caloric restriction, 34–35
  genetics, 33, 63
  intelligence used to predict, 102
Longitudinal study, 18–20
Long-term store, 104
Loudness scale, 43
Loyola Generativity Scale (LGS), 250–251
Lust, 139
Lust system, 140

M
MacArthur Foundation, 87
Macrosystem, 14, 15
Macular degeneration, 43
Major depression, 81
Major life changes, disequilibrium in, 367
Major life events, stress and, 294, 297
Major tasks, review of changes in, 346
Manipulative transactions, 245
Marcia's theory of career selection, 204
Marital crisis effect, 141
Marital friendship, 145
Marital happiness
  health and, 142
  marital stability compared to, 141
  parenthood and, 144–145
Marital resources effect, 141
Marital selection effect, 141
Marital stability, 141
Marital status
  quality of life and, 359
Marital status and health, 140–142
Marriage
  cohabitation and, 176–177
  negative patterns in, 175–176
  successful, intimate partnerships and, 174–176
  tests of satisfaction, interaction, and problem solving, 173–175
  unhappy, risk factors for, 174
  work and, 214–215
Maslow's hierarchy of needs, 258–259
Masturbation, 57
Mate selection, 169
Mature adaptation, 254–256
Meaning
  quest for (*See* Quest for meaning)
  review of changes in, 346
Meaning-focused coping, 309
Meaning systems, study of age-related changes in, 265–271
  approaches to, 265–266
  quest for meaning, changes in, 266–269
  religion, spirituality, and health, 269–271
Mean-level change, 238–239, 240

Measures in developmental research, 22–23
  personal interview, 22
  standardized tests, 22
  survey questionnaire, 22
Medication
  adherence, 122
  individual differences in cognitive change, 117
Memory, 103–112
  adaptive nature of cognition, 110–111
  contextual perspective, 110–112
  declarative memory, 106–108
  declines in, slowing, 109–110
  defined, 103
  digit-span task, 104
  episodic, 106–107
  executive function, 106
  long-term store, 104
  name-retrieval failures, 107
  nondeclarative (procedural) memory, 108–109
  prospective, 109
  semantic, 107–108
  sensory store, 104
  short-term (primary), 104–106
  short-term store, 104
  stereotype threat, 111–112
  stores, 104
  tip-of-the-tongue phenomenon, 107
  word-finding failures, 107
  working, 104–106
Menopause, 51
Mental disorders, 79–84
  anxiety disorders, 80
  impulse control disorders, 82–83
  mood disorders, 81–82
  substance abuse disorders, 83
  treatment of, 83–84
Mental health disorders, 298–299
Mental Measures Yearbook (Spies and Plake), 23
Mesosystem, 14, 15
Meta-analysis, 26
Microdermabrasion, 39
Microsystem, 14
Microvascular disease (MVD), 73
Middle adulthood (age 40–64), 350–353
  biological clock in, 350–351
  marriage and, 351–352
  midlife crisis and, 352–353
  review of, 345–346
  social clock in, 350
  work and, 351–352
Middle adulthood, social roles in, 145–151
  aging parents, caring for, 149–151
  departure of children (empty nest), 146–147
  gender roles, 147
  grandparent, becoming, 147–149
Midlife crisis, 352–353
Midlife in the United States (MIDUS) National Survey, 17
Mild cognitive impairment (MCI), 77
Minnesota Multiphasic Personality Inventory (MMPI), 236
Mistrust, trust *vs.*, 247
MMPI, 22, 236
Model of adult growth and development, 363–369
  adaptive/maladaptive outcomes *vs.* happiness, 369
  age-linked shared, physical and psychological developments, 363
  episodes of stable life structure and disequilibrium, 364–367
  influences on adult development, 363–364
  outcome of disequilibrium, 367–369
  stable periods and age, relationship of, 365
  transitions, cumulative effects of, 368–369
  turning points, 365–367 (*See also* Disequilibrium)

Modern Maturity Sexuality Survey, 57
Monozygotic twins, 10, 24–25, 208
Mood disorders, 81–82
Moral reasoning, 272–278. *See also* Kohlberg's stages of moral reasoning
    data, 275–277
    defined, 271
    evaluation and comment, 278
    measurement of, 272
Moratorium stage to career identity, 204
Morbidity rate, 69
Mortality rates and causes of death, 69
Mothers in workforce, 216–217
Mouth, taste and, 45
Muscles, changes in, 47–48
Myelin, 49
Myers-Briggs Type Indicator, 22
Mystical experience, 284–285
    awakening stage of, 284
    dark night of the soul stage of, 285
    illumination stage of, 285
    purification stage of, 284–285
    unity stage of, 285
Mysticism, 284
Mysticism (Underhill), 266

N

Naive hedonism orientation, 273
Name-retrieval failures, 107
National Alliance of Caregivers, 218
National Comorbidity Survey, 79, 80, 81
National Health and Nutrition Examination Survey, 87
National Longitudinal Mortality Study, 141
National Longitudinal Survey of Youth, 216
National Senior Services Corps, 228
National Study of Daily Experiences (NSDE), 295
National Study of Gay and Lesbian Parents, 178
National Survey of Sexual Health and Behavior, 60
Native Americans, health and, 89. *See also* Racial and ethnic groups
Natural immunity, 293
NEO Personality Inventory, 235, 236, 246
Nervous system, changes in, 49–50
Networks, friendship, 192–193
Neurofibrillary tangles, 76
Neurogenesis, 49–50
Neurons, 49
Neuroticism, 238–245, 256, 368
Neurotransmitters, 170
NK cells, 328
Noise exposure, 44
Nondeclarative (procedural) memory, 108–109
Nonmedical solutions, 84–85
    assistance animals, 84
    assistive technology, 84–85
Nonnormative life events, 9
Nontraditional student, 210
Norepinephrine, 170
Normative age-graded influences, 5–6
    biology, 5
    defined, 5
    internal change processes, 6
    shared experiences, 5–6
Normative history-graded influences, 6–8
Normative life events, 9
Normative solidarity, 181
Nose, taste/smell and, 44–45
Nuclear families, 181
Nun Study of the School Sisters of Notre Dame, 28
Nutritional supplements, 50

O

Obesity
    Alzheimer's disease and, 77
    body mass index, 37, 38, 39
    cancer risk and, 75
    cardiovascular disease and, 73
    defined, 37
    developmental origins hypothesis and, 93
    diabetes and, 75, 76
    lifestyle and, 85, 86
    in older adults, proportion of, 39
    in racial and ethnic groups, 89
    risk factors for, 39, 41
    telomere length and, 34
Obsessive-compulsive disorder, 80
Obsessive love, 170–172
Occupational gender segregation, 204, 205–206
Odor receptors, 45
Older adulthood (age 65–74), 353–354
    review of, 345–346
Olfactory membrane, 44–45
On Death and Dying (Kübler-Ross), 324
Onset, 80
Open ended personal interview, 22
Openness, 235–245
Optimism, 91
Organ transplant donor, 324
Osteoarthritis, 46–47
Osteoporosis, 45–46
Outer changes, 4
Outward appearance, changes in, 36–41
    body composition, 37–39
    skin, 39–41
    weight, 37
Oxidative damage, 33

P

Pacific Islanders, health of, 88–89
Palliative care, 331
Parental imperative, 143
Parental investment theory, 143
Parent-child relationships in adulthood, 182–185
    intergenerational solidarity theory, 182–184
    late-life divorce, effects of, 184–185
    problem children in adulthood, 185
Parents
    aging parents, caring for, 149–151
    becoming, 142–145
    departure of children (empty nest), 146–147
    gender roles in couples with children, 143–144
    marital happiness and, 144–145
    surrogate, 149
    work and, 215–217
    in young adulthood, 142–145
Partners. *See also* Intimate relationships
    becoming, 142–145
    gender roles in early partnerships, 140
    marital status and health, 140–142
    sexual, 59
Passages (Sheehy), 352
Passion, 170–172
Passionate love, 170–172
Patient adherence to treatment for bone loss, 46
Peak experiences, 258
Pensions, 224
Perimenopause, 51
Personal computers, 122
Personal interview, 22

Personality, 233–260
  continuity of change, explanations of, 243–246
  defined, 234
  development, disequilibrium in, 367
  individual differences in health, 90–92
  measures (*See* Measures in developmental research)
  quest for meaning and, integrating, 282–285
  review of changes in, 346
  role requirements and, poor match between, 366–367
  structures (*See* Personality traits)
Personality development, theories of, 247–260
  ego development, 252–254
  gender crossover, 256–257
  mature adaptation, 254–256
  positive well-being, 257–260
  psychosocial development, 247–252
Personality factors, 235
Personality states, 235
Personality structures. *See* Personality traits
Personality traits, 234–243
  achievement and, 241–242
  coping with stress, 320
  death anxiety and, 332
  defined, 235
  differential continuity, 237–238
  factors and, 234–236
  Five-Factor Model (FFM) of personality and, 236
  functions of, 240–243
  health and, 242–243
  intra-individual variability, 239–240
  mean-level change, 238–239
  relationships and, 241
Personal life and work, 211–219
  caregiving for adult family members, 217–218
  household labor, 218–219
  the individual, 212–214
  marriage, 214–215
  parenthood, 215–217
Person-environment transactions, 245
Pets as friends, 193
Phased retirement, 229
Phobias, 80
Physical behavior, changes in, 53–60
  athletic abilities, 53–54
  balance, 54
  dexterity, 54
  sexual activity, 56–60
  sleep, 55–56
  stamina, 54–55
Physical change, review of, 345
Physical changes during adulthood, 31–64. *See also* Physical
  behavior, changes in; Primary aging
  bones, 45–47
  brain, 49–50
  cardiovascular system, 48–49
  hormonal system, 50–53
  immune system, 50
  muscles, 47–48
  nervous system, 49–50
  outward appearance, 36–41
  overview of, 63–64
  respiratory system, 48–49
  senses, 41–45
Physical disease, stress-related, 297–298
Physical exercise, 120–121
Physician-assisted suicide, 332
Plaques, 72
Plasticity, 49
Plastic surgery, 40
Positive avoidance (denial), as response to imminent death, 327

Positive emotion, resilience and, 315
Positive psychology, 258
Positive well-being, 257–260
Positivity bias, 115
Possibilities, imagining, 347
Postconventional level of Kohlberg's stages of moral
  reasoning, 275
Postformal stages, 265
Positive instability, 347
Postmenopause, 51
Postparental stage, 146. *See also* Middle adulthood, social roles in
Posttraumatic stress disorder (PTSD)
  age differences in, 301–303
  defined, 298
  discrimination and, 304
  gender differences in, 300–301
  resilience and, 313–314
Posttraumatic stress syndrome (PTSD), 78
Poverty, feminization of, 226
Preconventional level of Kohlberg's stages of moral
  reasoning, 275
Preengaged cohabitation, 177
Prelude to marriage, 140
Premenopause, 51
Presbyopia, 42
Prevalence, 80
Primary aging
  defined, 32
  individual differences in, 60–63
  reversing, 63
Primary aging, theories of, 32–35
  caloric restriction (CR), 34–35
  genetic limits, 33–34
  oxidative damage, 33
Primary memory, 104–106
Privacy, in sexual activity, 59–60
Private beliefs and practices, changes in, 267–268
Proactive coping, 309–310
Proactive transactions, 245
Problem-focused approach, 114
Problem-focused coping, 308
Problem solving. *See* Decision making and problem solving
Procedural (nondeclarative) memory, 108–109
Progesterone, 51, 52
Propecia, 41
Prospective memory, 109, 122
Proximal causes, 132
Proximal predictors, 358
Pruning, 49
PSEN1 gene, 76
PSEN2 gene, 76
Psychological age, 12
Psychological health, 360–361
Psychometrics, 99
Psychosocial adjustment, 361
Psychosocial development, 247–252
  Erikson's stages of, 247–252
Psychosocial factors in quality of life, 359
Punishment-and-obedience orientation, 273
Pupils, 41, 42
Purification stage of mystical experience, 284

Q
Qualitative research, 28–29
Quality of life, individual differences in. *See* individual differences,
  in quality of life
Quantitative research, 28–29
Quest for meaning, 263–289
  commentary and conclusions, 287–289
  defined, 263

importance of, 264–265
   meaning systems, study of age-related changes in, 265–271
   personality and, integrating, 282–285
   spiritual development, theories of, 271–282
   transition, process of, 285–287
Questions, in developmental research, 16

R

Racial and ethnic groups
   grandparent-grandchild relationships, 186
   individual differences in health, 88–89
   primary aging and, 62–63
   quality of life and, 359
Racial discrimination in health care, 89–90
Random mutations explanation, 73
Rapamycin, 35
Reactive heritability, 246
Reactive transactions, 245
Relatedness, in self-determination theory, 259
Relationships, review of changes in, 345
Reliability of standardized tests, 23
Religion, quest for meaning and, 269–271
Religiosity
   death anxiety and, 322
   defined, 265, 322
   meaning systems and, 265
Religious coping, 310
Reminiscence, 323
Replicative senescence, 33
Research. *See* Developmental research
Research methods. *See* Developmental research methods
Residence, retirement and, 226–227
Resilience, 312–316. *See also* individual differences, in resilience
   defined, 312
   as grief reaction, 338, 339
   posttraumatic stress disorder and, 313–315
   trauma and, reactions to, 313–314
Resistance, 293
Resistance resources, 306
Resistance training, 48
Respiratory system, 48–49
Response-oriented viewpoint, 294
Restylane, 40
Resveratrol, 35
Retinas, 41
Retired and Senior Volunteer Program (RSVP), 228
Retirement, 219–229
   alternatives to, 227–229
   career commitment and, 223–224
   defined, 219
   effects of, 224–227
   family and, 223
   gradual, 228
   health and, 223
   leisure-time interests, 224
   phased, 229
   preparation for, 220
   reasons for, 222–224
   returning to the workforce, 228
   shunning, 227–228
   timing of, 220–222
   volunteer work, 228–229
Retirement-related value, 223
Returning (and leaving) home, 137
Reversing primary aging, 63
Revised NEO Personality Inventory, 235, 236
Ritual mourning, 333–337
Rogaine, 41
Role confusion, identity *vs.*, 247, 248, 249, 253
Role requirements, personality and, 366–367

Role salience, 201
Role transitions, 131
   disequilibrium in, 366
Romantic love, 170–172

S

Saliva, 45
Same-sex couples, sexual activity in, 60
Same-sex partnerships, 178–180
Schooling, 119
Seasonal migration, 227
Seattle Longitudinal Study, 99, 119
Secondary aging, 32, 69. *See also* Health and health disorders
Selection effect, 177
Selective optimization with compensation, 356
Self, focusing on, 347
Self-absorption, generativity *vs.*, 247, 248
Self-actualization, 257, 259–260, 282
Self-aware stage of ego development, 252
Self-determination theory, 259–260
Self-identity, resilience and, 315
Self-preoccupation, 281
Self-protective stage of ego development, 252
Self-ratings of health and health disorders, 71
Self-transcendence, 264, 282
Semantic memory, 106–107
Senile plaque, 76
Senior Companion Program, 228
Sense of purpose in life, 323
Senses, changes in, 41–45
   hearing, 43–44
   smell, 44–45
   taste, 44–45
   vision, 41–43
Sensorineural hearing loss, 43
Sensory store, 104
Sequential study, 20–21
Serotonin, 170
Sexual activity, changes in, 56–60
   cyclic GMP, 58
   erotic dreams, 60
   masturbation, 60
   physical ability, 57–58
   privacy, 59–60
   response in older adults *vs.* younger adults, 57–58
   same-sex couples, 60
   sexual desire, 59
   sexual fantasies, 63
   sexual partner, 59
Sexual problems
   erectile dysfunction (ED), 58, 60
   treatment for, 60
   vaginal dryness, 58
Shift work, 214
Short-term life events, stress and, 294
Short-term memory, 104–106
Short-term store, 104
Sibling relationships, 190
SIREAC types of vocational interests, 203
Sixteen Personality Factor Questionnaire (16PF), 236
Skin, changes in, 39–41
Sleep, changes in, 55–56
Sleep apnea, 55
Smell, changes in, 44–45
Social age, 12
Social clock, 5, 131
   in emerging adulthood (age 18–24), 348
   in middle adulthood (age 40–64), 350
   in older adulthood (age 65–74), 353
   in young adulthood (age 25–39), 350

Social comparisons, quality of life and, 359
Social contract orientation, 274
Social coping, 309
Social integration, quality of life and, 359
Social networks
    cognitive assistance and, 122–123
    convoy model and, 166
    Facebook friends and, 194
    negative effects of, 311–312
    theories of social relationships and, 166, 168
Social order maintaining orientation, 273
Social relationships, 163–196
    defined, 164
    friendships in adulthood, 192–194
    intimate partnerships, 169–180
    with other family members, 180–192
    review of changes in, 195–196
Social relationship theories, 164–169
    attachment theory, 165–166
    convoy model, 166–167
    evolutionary psychology, 167
    similarities in, 168–169
    socioemotional selectivity theory, 167
Social roles, 129–160
    in atypical families, 154–157
    defined, 130
    gender roles and gender stereotypes, 131–134
    in late adulthood, 151–154
    in middle adulthood, 145–151
    review of, 159–160
    social timing, 158–160
    transitions and, 130–131
    in young adulthood, 134–145
Social role theory, 132
Social Security benefits, 219, 222–223
Social support, 310–312
    buffering effect of, 310–311
    coping and, 311
    defined, 310
    in social networks, 311–312
Social timing, 158–159
Sociobiographical history, 119
Socioeconomic status (SES)
    defined, 87
    factors in primary aging, 62–63
    individual differences in health, 87–88
    quality of life and, 358
Socioemotional selectivity theory, 115, 167
Specific immunity, 293
Spiritual development, theories of, 271–282. *See also* Quest for meaning
    faith, development of, 278–281
    moral reasoning, development of, 272–278
Spirituality
    changes in, 269–271
    defined, 267
    development, disequilibrium in, 367
Spouse, becoming, 137–142
Stability, defined, 3
Stability, sources of, 9–11
    environment, 10–11
    genetics, 10
    interactionist view, 11
Stages
    defined, 4
    typical and atypical, 4
Stagnation, generativity *vs.*, 247, 248, 250
Stamina, changes in, 54–55
Standardized tests, 22

Stem cells, 49
Stepfathers, 157
Stepmothers, 157
Stereotype threat, 111–112
Stimulus-oriented viewpoint, 294
Stoic acceptance (fatalism), as response to imminent death, 328
Stress, 292–312
    coping with, 306–312 (*See also* Coping)
    defined, 292
    general adaptation syndrome, 293
    immune response to, 293
    resilience, 312–316
    response-oriented viewpoint, 294
    stimulus-oriented viewpoint, 294
    types of, 294–296
Stress, effects of, 296–306. *See also* individual differences, in stress-related disorders
    mental health disorders, 298–299
    physical disease, 297–298
    stress-related growth and, 305–306
Stressors, 292
Stress-related growth, 305–306
Stretching, 48
Structured personal interview, 22
Subjective well-being, 358 *See also* individual differences, in quality of life
Substance abuse disorders, 83
Successful adult development, variations in, 360–363
    psychological health, 360–361
    psychosocial adjustment, 361
    quality of life, 358–360
Successful aging, 358–360. *See also* individual differences, in quality of life
Super's theory of career development, 200–201
Surrogate parenting, 149
Survey questionnaire, 22
Swedish socioeconomic scale, 208
Swedish Twin Registry, 208
Swedish Twin Study database, 10, 25
Symmetrical changes, 132
Synthesizing model, 283–284
Synthetic-conventional faith, 279

T
Taste, changes in, 44–45
Taste buds, 45
T cells, 50, 328
Telomeres, 33, 34
Terrorist attack of September 11, 2001, 7
Testosterone, 51
Testosterone replacement therapy, 52, 59
Throat, taste and, 45
Tip-of-the-tongue phenomenon, 107
Tongue, taste and, 45
TOR, 35
Transition
    to adulthood, 134
    social roles and, 130–131
Transition, process of, 285–287
Trauma, reactions to, 313–314. *See also* Posttraumatic stress disorder (PTSD)
    grief work, 314
Traumatic brain injury (TBI), 77
Tribalization, 349, 350
Trust *vs.* mistrust, 247
Twin studies, 10
Type A behavior pattern, 90
Type B behavior pattern, 90
Typical stages of life, 4

U

Unemployment, 212
U.S. National Health Interview Survey, 71
Unity orientation, 277
Unity stage of mystical experience, 285
Universalizing faith, 281
Useful field of view (UFOV), 125

V

Vaginal dryness, 52, 58
Validity of standardized tests, 22
Variability, intra-individual, 239–240
The Varieties of Religious Experience (James), 266
Viagra, 58
Victoria Longitudinal Study, 105
Vision, changes in, 41–43
    cataracts, 42
    dark adaptation, 42
    eyes, parts of, 41
    glaucoma, 42
    individual differences in cognitive change, 116–117
    macular degeneration, 43
    presbyopia, 42
    risk factors for age-related visual conditions, 42
Visual acuity, 41–42
Vocational interests, 203
Volunteer work, 228–229

W

Waddington's image of epigenetic landscape, 363
Wechsler Adult Intelligence Scale (WAIS-IV), 99

Wechsler Scales, 22
Weight, changes in, 37–39
Well-being, positive, 257–260
White matter, 49
Women
    cardiovascular disease and, death from, 72
    climacteric in, 51–52
    earnings of, 204, 218
Women's Health Study (WHS), 51, 52
Word-finding failures, 107
Work, 199–219. *See also* Retirement
    age trends in work experience, 209–211
    careers, selecting (*See* Career selection)
    changes in careers over adulthood, review of, 230–231
    importance of, in adulthood, 199–202
    personal life and, 211–219
Work engagement, 212
Working memory, 104–106
Work-related value, 222–223
Work roles, review of changes in, 346
Work strain, 294
Work stress, 294
Work Values Inventory (WVI), 206

Y

Young adulthood (age 25–39), 348–350
    review of, 345–346
Young adulthood, social roles in, 134–145
    becoming a parent, 142–145
    leaving (and returning) home, 135–137
    spouse or partner, becoming, 137–142